MW01115788

Psychic Awakening

A Guide to Mediumship Abilities, Telepathy for Beginners, Numerology, Astral Projection, and Highly Sensitive People

Free Bonus from Silvia Hill available for limited time

Hi Spirituality Lovers!

My name is Silvia Hill, and first off, I want to THANK YOU for reading my book.

Now you have a chance to join my exclusive spirituality email list so you can get the ebooks below for free as well as the potential to get more spirituality ebooks for free! Simply click the link below to join.

P.S. Remember that it's 100% free to join the list.

~~$27~~ FREE BONUSES

- 9 Types of Spirit Guides and How to Connect to Them
- How to Develop Your Intuition: 7 Secrets for Psychic Development and Tarot Reading
- Tarot Reading Secrets for Love, Career, and General Messages

Access your free bonuses here
https://livetolearn.lpages.co/psychic-awakening-paperback/

Table of Contents

Part 1: Psychic Abilities

Unlocking Your Inner Medium and Ability for Divination, Telepathy, Astral Projection, Connecting with Spirit Guides, and Clairvoyance

Introduction

While the existence of psychic abilities is still a much-debated topic, there are countless examples of people being able to hear, see, sense, or perceive information no one else can. So, one of the first steps toward unlocking your potential psychic skills is dissociating the spiritual concept from how mediumship is portrayed through mainstream channels. Working on your psychic abilities is a highly spiritual practice. While doing this, you'll rely on your intuition to set you on the right path. The journey toward discovering one's inherent spiritual gift is different for everyone, as each psychic has a unique combination of cultural and religious background and personality traits.

Psychics experience extrasensory stimuli on different spiritual, mental, and physical levels. For that reason, there is a broad spectrum of extrasensory abilities that people can experience. This book will introduce you to the clairs - the four fundamental powers physics often relies on. They include skills such as seeing, hearing, and feeling the messages one receives or simply knowing it in their mind without realizing how it got there. These abilities allow psychics to peek into the future and learn to elevate themselves spiritually.

Divination can be done with or without any specific tool. However, the latter helps psychics communicate with spirits and guide them when they need information or insights about the future. You'll also learn about telepathy and astral projection - two skills linked to the *aura*. Auras are a unique form of energy that people with extrasensory gifts can only perceive.

When it comes to spiritual communication in general, this practice must be approached carefully and with great precaution. Apart from benevolent spirits and guides, you may rely on for helpful information, you'll also encounter some not-so-friendly spirits. This book offers plenty of practical advice on protecting yourself against them and cleaning yourself or anything else they might have tainted with their influence. If this doesn't work and these forces still manage to get their hold on you or someone else, you can also resort to the psychic healing techniques you'll learn about in this book. These will also work to spruce you up when psychic work drains your mental and physical energy.

Although many psychics develop their abilities during childhood, these often become buried under a mountain of conditioned beliefs. Being told that sensitivity to stimuli no one else experiences isn't a good thing can make anyone feel disconnected from their psychic gifts. Not to mention the stress and expectations of daily life. Fortunately, this doesn't have to mean that you'll lose your abilities. And even if you haven't felt them beforehand, they might still be there, lying dormant and waiting for you to awaken them.

Through the numerous examples of how others have discovered their powers and user-friendly techniques you can use to find your own, this book will guide you through this challenging yet incredibly rewarding journey. Now, to unlock your inner medium, you'll need to arm yourself with patience. Your powers will not appear magically overnight, nor will they start to develop when you finally reveal them. To elevate them to the highest level, you'll need to continuously practice and keep honing your intuition. So, if you're prepared to embark on this journey, by all means, let's delve right into it!

Chapter 1: Are You Ready for Psychic Abilities?

Perception is a very powerful thing. Imagine this: You're sitting with your friends, and one of them leans into you and says, "something is wrong with Shelly; she isn't acting like herself." You take a look at Shelly, but she's acting normal. Not long after, Shelly's facial expressions change, and she breaks down in tears, saying, "I am not okay, and I can't hold it in any longer." You look at your friend in disbelief and wonder whether she's a psychic or if she's just more perceptive than you.

Being a psychic is generally described as having the ability to perceive all types of sensory data spiritually, physically, and emotionally.
https://www.pexels.com/photo/white-moon-on-hands-3278643/

This opening chapter will help you grasp the fundamentals of psychic abilities, what they are and feel like, and the beliefs and science behind them. Thanks to a quick and self-informative quiz, you'll also find out whether you're a psychic yourself.

Understanding Psychic Abilities

Being a psychic is generally described as having the ability to perceive all types of sensory data spiritually, physically, and emotionally. In most cases, this ability starts in early childhood. A parent or grandparent may have passed down this gift to you, or you may have grown up in an environment that enabled you to develop and nurture this ability.

Not everyone with psychic abilities is aware that they possess this gift. Like in the previous example, they may think they are just perceptive – or empaths. Some people try to force their intuition to see whether they are indeed psychics. However, this is something you can't force; in most cases, your abilities will come out naturally. For instance, you're relaxing with a glass of wine or taking a shower. Suddenly, you find the solution to a problem you've been struggling with or figure out something about someone you haven't noticed before. This may be a sign that you are a psychic, which you may not immediately be ready to accept, blaming your spur of enlightenment on the booze instead. That said, this information came to you somewhere – it could very well be your psychic abilities unveiling themselves to you.

Psychic abilities allow you to see and feel things about others that most people can't. Psychics often experience synesthesia, where two of your senses overlap due to external stimuli. For instance, you may see shapes when listening to music or hear a specific sound when smelling something, or in the case of a psychic, you begin associating a color or shape with a person. You may think something is wrong with you if you see a color around someone, but what you see is their aura.

People with psychic abilities can sense something isn't right, unable to explain why or how they have this feeling. For instance, your friend invites you to dinner at a well-known restaurant, but you suggest another one instead because, deep down, you feel uneasy about that particular venue. Later that evening, you learn that a fire broke out at that restaurant on the same night you were supposed to have dinner there. You probably think this was just a coincidence, but chances are it was your gut feeling warning you. While most people have a gut feeling, a psychic's intuition is more powerful than anyone else's and can even save their life.

If you possess psychic abilities, your dreams can even help guide you toward something or send you a specific message. Some dreams can be vivid or seem like visions that are so powerful that you can't ignore them. For instance, your deceased brother comes to you in a dream to tell you to call his wife. You call her and find out she's going through something and could use your help. Similarly, your psychic ability may also show in the form of a daydream. For instance, you are taking a shower and see an image of money. Upon arriving at work, your boss informs you that everyone will get a bonus this quarter as a thank-you for the team's hard work. You may also think of someone from high school and then run into them later that day or read a message from them the following day.

Everyone experiences a wide range of emotions daily. However, psychics tend to experience strong ones without an apparent, rational explanation. For instance, you may have the urge to cry for no reason, then later receive news from your sister that your cousin has just passed away. None of these are coincidences, especially if they are recurring incidences. While it's easy to dismiss these as pure fantasies, opening your eyes and being willing to accept your "extraordinary" abilities can enable you to tap into your psychic potential.

There is a common element in all these examples and situations: feeling or seeing something before it happens. Most people attribute this to having a sixth sense – it can help you pick up on supernatural signals and perceive things that other people aren't aware of.

Psychic Abilities and Extrasensory Perception

People naturally depend on their five senses to perceive and understand everything going on around them. However, everyone has a sixth sense that they rarely pay attention to Extrasensory perception (ESP). Many people consider it to be the same thing as intuition is a gift that can only be developed through the use of your sixth sense. Your sixth sense will allow you to perceive things beyond your five senses, hence the extrasensory name perception.

Extrasensory perception often manifests as a strange, uneasy feeling you experience before something bad happens. Because your body is made up of energy, the sixth sense is the perfect tool to respond to other people's energy. For instance, you arrive at the office only to feel inexplicably uncomfortable, as if something just went down. You discover that one of your co-workers was just laid off. You haven't seen your co-worker, heard gossip, or even whispers. You have simply picked up on the energy in the room using your sixth sense.

The sixth sense is the inner voice that makes you aware of things that can't be perceived with your other senses. It's this feeling inside of you that just "knows something," such as if someone is trustworthy or not at first glance. You can experience the sixth sense in various ways, like feeling something in your body, hearing a voice, seeing a vision, smelling something, tasting something bad in your mouth, or simply knowing.

Using your psychic ability implies tapping into your sixth sense or ESP to see, hear, or feel things that may not be obvious to your other senses. So, to develop psychic abilities, you must be attuned to your sixth sense and understand that what your gut feeling is telling you isn't a coincidence or something that you should dismiss. You can't be a psychic if you don't fully utilize and rely on your sixth sense.

People with Psychic Abilities

The word "psychic" has been thrown around a lot lately. Some people dismiss it because they can't comprehend that such power truly exists, whereas others can attest to these abilities as they have experienced them firsthand. Certain people are reluctant to believe in these abilities because history hasn't been kind to psychics, to say the least. According to a psychic medium and author, Bernadette Gold, who grew up in the 1960s, it was a hard time for psychics as people struggled to understand or embrace those with this unique gift. As a result, it took her decades to realize that she was an empath and had psychic abilities.

Nowadays, people have grown more tolerant and accepting, and more and more people are encouraged to be their truest selves. If you suspect you have this unique ability, you should embrace it. You probably wonder how you can tell whether you have this gift. The examples mentioned above may give you a clue. However, reading about people who experience psychic abilities firsthand can give you a better idea of what this gift feels like.

There is a story about a woman who saw a vision of her mother's friend's house ravaged by a storm. The vision was so vivid that she even saw the faces of everyone who lived under that roof. The very next day, a hurricane hit the area where her mother's friend lived. While the woman didn't think there was anything to her vision, she admits that she usually experiences an odd feeling before something bad happens.

A woman and her husband wanted to have a child. The woman was depressed for years because they weren't able to conceive. One day, she went on a hike and saw a clear image of a little boy. She saw every detail of his face, what he was wearing, the color of his eyes and hair. It was as if he was truly there. Two years later, she gave birth to a boy who was the spitting image of the kid she was in her vision.

Another person tells a story about driving his friend to the airport. As he was getting in his car, something inside told him not to leave the airport. So, he decided to stay in his car for half an hour in case his friend missed his plane. He claims he just couldn't bring himself to leave. A few minutes later, a powerful earthquake hit. Cars were shaking, and people were frantically fleeing the airport. His distraught friend called him, asking if he could come and pick him up. He told him that, luckily, he was still there. He admitted to having experienced this feeling on various occasions before, with his gut telling him to do or not do something.

People with this ability say it's easy for them to pick up on things in their surroundings that most people don't notice. They also often get premonitions about themselves or their families; sometimes, a sudden vision or voice can serve as a lifesaving warning. They are highly sensitive to what goes on around them. They are also empathetic individuals who can sense other people's emotions even when they attempt to mask their feelings. Some say they can learn personal information about others by getting visuals when they are around them. People with this ability also say it comes naturally to them, just like using their other senses. After all, no one thinks before they hear or smell something – the same applies to using your sixth sense.

The Science behind Psychic Abilities

You may be surprised to learn that the U.S. government has conducted various research and experiments on the topic of psychic abilities. These experiments aimed to learn about psychic spying and prove that people can have paranormal abilities. Academic experts have reviewed this secret government research and concluded that having paranormal abilities isn't a farce, contrary to what many people have been claiming. According to California University professor Jessica Utts, it has been scientifically proven that having psychic abilities is possible. She added that since we now know these abilities are real, there is no need for further research. It's best to use these resources to understand how these abilities work. Oregon University psychology professor Ray Hyman agrees with Utts that things now seem more hopeful than ever regarding the topic of psychic abilities.

Psychologist William McDougall and founder of parapsychology J. B. Rhine also conducted their own experiments to prove that people can have psychic abilities. They used cards with specific symbols and asked participants to guess the card being held. Chance also played a role in this experiment, as some people simply guessed instead of knowing which card it was. However, researchers are still using this experiment and letting statistics be the main determinant. This experiment typically involves 25 distinct cards. If someone guesses five cards, they may be just lucky. However, if they guess 15 or 20 cards, this can reduce the likelihood of chance as a primary factor, showing that these individuals may use their psychic abilities. Researchers use statistics to determine whether the participants are using their psychic abilities or simply guessing.

The Rhine also improved his research by using dice instead of cards. The results showed that some people could use their psychic abilities to guess the dice correctly, and the results were very positive. Participants could use their abilities when the experiments were conducted in a controlled environment.

Despite persisting doubts and general defiance toward anything out of the ordinary, scientific research has shown that people can indeed possess psychic abilities.

Can Anyone Have Psychic Abilities?

Yes, anyone can nurture this skill and develop psychic abilities. We all possess a sixth sense, even if we don't use it or aren't even aware that we have it. Since having psychic abilities mainly depends on using your sixth sense, anyone can have this gift - tapping into your sixth sense and using it can help you unlock this special gift. You must start believing in yourself and paying attention to your intuition and what it's trying to tell you. Don't ignore or dismiss the things you see, feel, or hear. Your sixth sense is here for a reason, often to guide or protect you; it's the gateway to unlocking and sharpening your psychic abilities.

Quiz

Now that you've learned about psychic abilities, you probably wonder if you possess this gift. You may already have psychic abilities but aren't aware of them. This simple "true" or "false" quiz will answer the question you have been pondering: Do I already have latent psychic abilities?

Check "True" to the statements that apply to you and "False" to the ones that don't.

1. Your gut feeling often warns you about things that later turn out to be true.

    • True

    • False

2. You often experience déjà vu.

    • True

    • False

3. You often see lights or colors around living things.

    • True

    • False

4. You have visions or flashes of certain events before they occur.

    • True

    • False

5. You have vivid dreams that provide guidance, a warning, or reveal certain information.

    • True

    • False

6. You experience strong emotions like grief, joy, fear, or excitement inexplicably, only for an incident to happen later and explain these emotions.

    • True

    • False

7. You can tell when someone is deceiving you or lying to you.

    • True

    • False

8. You often get a positive or negative feeling from a particular place.
   - True
   - False
9. You have family members who have psychic abilities.
   - True
   - False
10. External stimuli can easily overwhelm you.
    - True
    - False
11. You sometimes simply know things with no rational reason for how you got this information.
    - True
    - False

If your answers are overwhelmingly true, there's a chance that you are a psychic. However, if you answer mostly false, there is no need to fret. You may simply need to figure out how to tap into your abilities and unlock your gift, which you will learn more about later in the book.

Explanation

To help clarify things, let's explain the prompts in this quiz and what each one aims to check.

Gut Feeling

A gut feeling strongly resembles intuition. However, the main difference is that you can also experience a sensation in your body, which generally doesn't happen with intuition. It's usually a feeling that you know something. For instance, you get goosebumps when you enter a particular place or feel strangely uneasy when you meet a certain person. This is your gut feeling telling you that something isn't right.

Déjà Vu

Déjà vu is a French term that means "already seen." It's a feeling you get during an event or situation that something is very familiar or that you've experienced it before – when *you know that you haven't.* For instance, you go to a restaurant for the first time, and as you take a seat, you get this feeling that you've been there before. While you know this is the first time you have visited this restaurant, or it has just opened, you still can't shake this feeling.

Lights or Colors

The light and colors you see around people are called *auras*. An aura is an invisible energy field that radiates from all living things; its energy is often spiritual, and only a person with psychic abilities can see or feel it. The color of a person's aura can reveal a great deal about them and their emotions. An aura is similar to a "vibe," so when you react to someone's vibe, whether positively or negatively, you are most likely feeling their aura.

Visions or Flashes

This statement checks whether you've ever experienced premonitions.

Vivid Dreams

Some people struggle to learn the difference between a vivid dream and a regular one. In short, vivid dreams feel more "real" than regular dreams. They're so intense that you won't be able to forget or ignore them. If you wake up and your dream feels like something that happened in your real life and lingers in your memory, then this dream is trying to tell you something.

Strong Emotions

This statement checks whether you're able to feel something before it occurs.

Spotting Liars

This statement aims to see how perceptive you are when spotting liars.

A Place's Vibe

Sometimes, a place has a strange vibe or is filled with negative people, making you feel uneasy.

Family Members

Relatives often pass down psychic abilities. If one of your parents or grandparents has this gift, you may also have it.

External Stimuli

Psychics tend to be more sensitive to external stimuli than most people.

Knowing

When your sixth sense makes you aware of something, you just know that this information is true, even if you don't have evidence to support it.

Ultimately, anyone can be a psychic. Every person is born with a sixth sense, but as they grow up, they rely on the logical part of their brains and often neglect this gift they have. In parallel, others nurture and develop this sense, opening the door to a world of possibilities and things you never knew were there. Your sixth sense is waiting for you to tap into it so you can explore the psychic world and everything it has to offer. Regardless of your personality type or spiritual goals, becoming a psychic is a process that requires patience and dedication. Now that we've covered the basics, it's time to delve deeper into the realm of psychic powers.

Chapter 2: The Clairs I. Supernatural Seeing and Hearing

Have you ever walked through the woods and sensed something was about to happen? Maybe you heard a twig snap or a bird fly away just before something started creeping toward you. That sixth sense, —or Clairvoyance, is your ability to sense and understand things beyond what your five senses can detect. The idea of having a "sixth sense" has fascinated people for centuries. The ability to perceive things beyond our basic senses would be a truly remarkable and useful skill, especially in this digital age when we are constantly bombarded with information. Culturally, we seem to be moving away from focusing on our sensory experiences and more toward virtual experiences in the form of virtual reality, video games, apps, etc. In response, many people are developing Clair abilities as a way to reconnect with something that has been lost in modern society: sensing the world through physical sensation rather than digital devices.

Clairvoyance is your ability to sense and understand things beyond what your five senses can detect.
https://www.pexels.com/photo/healthy-man-people-woman-6943955/

While most people don't inherently have this sixth sense, anyone can develop it with practice and dedication. This chapter will help you understand the Clairvoyant inside you by igniting your ability to see things beyond what your natural senses can detect.

What Are the Clair Senses?

The Clair senses are a set of supernormal abilities mentioned in multiple cultures and societies since time immemorial. Generally speaking, these involve the ability to see, hear, smell, or feel things that would normally be undetectable by human senses alone. They give us access to information about spirits, energy, and auras around us. Some claim that these senses let people see ghosts or spirits and communicate with them.

These senses were first brought to light by Rudolf Steiner in the early 20th century as part of his philosophical anthroposophy movement, which combined aspects of various other schools of thought, including Christianity, Hinduism, and Buddhism.

Many people today regard Clairvoyance (seeing), Clairsentience (feeling), Clairaudience (hearing), and Claircognizance (knowing) as esoteric or occult concepts. Whichever way you look at it, some people can perceive things more clearly than others. For most of us, this remains a mystery to gain knowledge on, but for some, it's a gift they were born with.

The Clair senses are psychic abilities you can develop with practice and patience. These include Clairvoyance and Clairaudience. People who develop these senses are known as Clairs. Although some people have stronger abilities than others, anyone can learn to strengthen their abilities through consistent practice. People with acute Clairvoyant skills tend to be more sensitive, perceptive, and more in tune with spiritual things around them.

Clairvoyance and Clairaudience are two types of psychic abilities. Both involve tapping into your sixth sense to know things without having to experience them firsthand. Clairvoyance is the ability to know what's going on in someone's life by visualizing it, while Clairaudience is the ability to hear what someone is thinking without them saying a word. If you want to develop these abilities, you can do so by clearing your mind and tuning out distractions so you can focus more clearly. Practicing gratitude to open yourself up to better things in your life will also be a great tool in your spiritual arsenal.

Clairvoyance (Seeing)

Since the dawn of time, humans have been fascinated by the idea of seeing beyond the visible, tangible world. From Merlin and his apprentice in "The Sword in the Stone" to Harry Potter and his schoolmates at Hogwarts, fictional characters who possess special abilities beyond what most people can see have captured our imagination. Now, as it turns out, these fictional stories are based on reality! You may be right if you've ever felt there was more to this world than what meets the eye. The concept of Clairvoyance originates from the French *Clair* (clear) and *voyance* (vision).

Thanks to Clairvoyance, you can intuitively understand what is going on in another person's life, either in the present or the future. It gives insight into other people's feelings, thoughts, and intentions, all with little information on their part. For example, if your best friend is feeling down but hasn't told you why, you might see it through Clairvoyance. Clairvoyant abilities typically involve clear visual images and feelings. You may see a vivid image of what's troubling your friend or feel like you're actually there. You may also see images of what hasn't happened yet but is likely to. Of course, the level of clarity varies from person to person. Some people experience their images as clearly as if they were watching a movie.

In contrast, others witness them as if they were watching them through a foggy window. As a Clairvoyant, you also can perceive things beyond the normal range of human perception. It can be defined as the ability to perceive information that cannot be obtained through the five ordinary senses. This includes seeing things that are not physically present and perceiving events in the past or future – independently and with other sensory information.

Signs That You Are Clairvoyant

Now that we've defined Clairvoyance, it's time to see if you have this special ability. Clairvoyant people often have an "open mind" and are aware of their surroundings. They tend to be keen observers and can pick up on details, often unconsciously. Clairvoyant people often have a higher-than-average IQ and can see things from a distance or in a non-sensory way. They may also be more creative and intuitive. They also excel at organizing things, especially when visualizing a situation to plan ahead. They also tend to be good at reading people and understanding what they want from them. Lastly, they have strong intuition, which can help them comprehend things better than others.

There are many ways to tell if you might have a gift of Clairvoyance. You might:

- Have dreams or visions that have come true
- Feel the presence of spirits
- See visions in your mind or on paper
- Learn things by intuition or feel other people's feelings
- Sense voices or images in your head.

In addition, you should consider your past experiences and how you were able to look into the future or know about something before it happened.

Developing Clairvoyant Abilities

You've probably heard about Clairvoyant abilities before, such as being "gifted" or "born with it." While there's no way to know whether you were born with Clairvoyant abilities, everyone can develop them. These include seeing things happening right now or in the future, and seeing what someone else is thinking or feeling. Some people have a natural ability for Clairvoyance and can see things almost immediately, whereas others take longer to develop them.

Here are a few useful tips for developing Clairvoyant abilities:

- Mind your surroundings. The more you pay attention to what is happening around you, the more likely you'll see things others miss.
- Think about what you want to see and visualize it clearly in your mind. This helps merge your Clairvoyance with your conscious thoughts and create a clearer vision of what is happening around you.
- Train yourself not to be afraid of what might be revealed; instead, embrace it as a gift from above.
- Incorporate meditation and relaxation techniques into your daily routine.
- Look for signs in your surroundings that suggest something is about to happen. Pay attention to things like unusual behavior in children or house pets or changes in the weather.

- Register for a reputable online course that will help you develop Clairvoyant abilities.

- Dream journaling is a superb way to bring your thoughts and feelings to the surface so you can explore them in greater depth. While you write, focus on whatever thoughts and feelings are on your mind.

- Researching Clairvoyance and other psychic abilities can help you better understand your own skills and learn how to hone them.

- Solicit an expert or Clairvoyant to see if they can help you develop your abilities.

In short, Clairvoyance is the ability to see through the mind's eye. The first step to accessing your mind's eye is to learn how to relax. Deep breathing and progressive muscle relaxation are two effective ways to alleviate stress and increase concentration. You can also use meditation techniques to open your mind's eyes. Sitting quietly, closing your eyes, and focusing on your breathing is the simplest yet most effective technique for opening your mind's eye. Other techniques you can use include visualizing yourself in a place you love to open up your heart or picturing yourself doing something you want to do to bolster your creative mind. Whatever works best for you - the goal is to practice opening your mind's eye so you can see what is happening around you.

Clairaudience (Hearing)

A person with clairaudience has the capacity to hear with exceptional clarity beyond the range of normal human hearing. This skill slightly differs from Clairvoyance, which is the ability to see beyond normal human sight. A person with this ability can hear subtle energies in the form of sounds that are inaudible to most people. Some call this ability "spiritual hearing," as they can hear spirits communicating with them through auditory tones. It's also closely related to Clairvoyance. Some people have the natural ability to hear and see things that other people cannot. Some may not even know about their hidden abilities until an unfortunate event triggers them. That said, there is no need to be afraid because these special powers can help you in many ways, whether at home, during a job interview, or even during a test at school. Let us take a closer look at Clairaudience and how it can help you in your everyday life.

Clairaudience is the ability to intuitively understand what is said and is happening around you, either in the present or the future. Like Clairvoyance, Clairaudience can sometimes be symbolic, like hearing an alarm clock ringing, but there's no alarm clock in the room. It can also be used to hear distant sounds, such as a bird singing in a tree or a train passing – or receive information about another person. You could also describe it as hearing something without anyone speaking. For example, if your friend is upset and doesn't tell you why you might tap into Clairaudience to know what's troubling them. Like Clairvoyance, Clairaudience can be visual or auditory. If you're upset and want to know what others think about you, Clairaudience can help with that, too. As useful as this ability is, external factors such as loud noises can be a disturbance, which can prevent you from perceiving any deeper sound.

Signs That You Are Clairaudient

If you possess Clairaudient abilities, you may be able to hear energy without any physical sound. It's an extrasensory perception that allows people to hear inner voices, sounds, and images. Clairaudience can manifest in many ways – from hearing your name called in public to catching the sounds of birds chirping or wind blowing. Although it isn't always clear whether the sounds are real or imagined, some people with Clairaudience feel a strong connection between their minds and the world around them. Clairaudients may also feel compelled to move objects with their mind and talk to themselves out loud. They may also suffer from sleep paralysis and experience vivid dreams. Some people with Clairaudience may have a family history of hearing voices or have experienced auditory hallucinations as a child. Some people describe it as a feeling of pressure in their ears that goes away after taking a deep breath. Others say they can hear colors or even taste them. Still, others report being able to hear things that are way out of their line of sight.

There are many ways to tell if you might have a gift of Clairaudience. You might:

- Be able to sense the emotions, health state, and other conditions of a person far from you
- Be able to communicate with someone who isn't physically present
- Retrieve lost objects or people

- Hear colors when perceiving the aura of other people. One way to describe this ability is "hearing from within." It may be part of the gift of empathy, otherwise known as empathic intuition.

- See the image of what's making someone angry or upset, or hearing them speaking to you although they never said a word

- See and hear something happening in another location or hear someone's thoughts or feelings.

Developing Clairaudient Abilities

Clairaudient abilities entail hearing sounds that others cannot hear. This can include all kinds of noises, from an electrical appliance's hum to an upset baby's cry. Some people may be born with this ability, but it can also be developed through training. Training for Clairaudience often involves listening to recorded sounds and identifying the source of each one. Learning to recognize and distinguish different sounds is essential to developing Clairaudience skills. Once you've learned how to recognize different noises, you can begin to hone your abilities, so you can reliably distinguish them.

There are many ways to develop Clairaudient abilities. Some people elect to use earplugs, while others wear headphones. Others wear special headbands or contact lenses to help tune out distracting noises. Whatever method you choose, practice regularly to build your skills and confidence.

Here are a few useful tips for developing Clairaudient abilities:

- Stay calm. This can help you quieten your thoughts so you can tune into the subtle energies or sounds around you.

- Be patient. Developing Clairaudience takes time and lots of patience to strengthen your ability.

- Practicing is the only way to develop your Clairaudience ability.

- Talk to yourself. This might sound strange, but it works. Doing so clears your mind of other thoughts and emotions so you can make room for new ones. This helps you tap into your intuition.

- You're more likely to tap into your intuition by focusing on one thing at a time and tuning out other distractions.

Meditation is great for quieting your mind and helping you focus. When you meditate, you clear your mind of other thoughts and emotions to pick up subtle energies and sounds around you. Try meditating on the sound of plants or even your own chakras.

- Try to record different sounds that you hear. This can help you identify the different sounds and frequencies.
- Identifying emotions can help you recognize the different emotions that you hear.
- Consulting various resources on developing Clairaudience can help you learn more about the ability.
- Working with a Clairaudient healer or Clairaudient reader can help you in your journey to develop Clairaudience.
- Since both are closely related, you can use Clairvoyance as a way to strengthen your Clairaudience ability.

How to Develop Your Clair Skills?

With consistent practice, you can improve your ability to access images and sounds that are beyond your senses. To improve your Clairvoyance and Clairaudience, start by getting into a state of meditation:

1. Calm your body and mind so you can focus on receiving information. You can do this by sitting in a quiet and dark room or by walking outside and taking slow, deep breaths while tuning everything else out.

2. Remain calm. You might find that you're more relaxed when you do these exercises if you find a quiet spot where you can sit and relax without being distracted by noise or other people.

3. Next, focus your attention on what is happening around you. Close your eyes, take a deep breath, and tell yourself that you're about to receive information and images about specific people or things.

4. Open your eyes and focus on one person or object you want to receive information about. If it's a person, you can try tuning into their emotions and thoughts or focusing your attention on a specific object they're holding.

5. After you've received an image or a piece of information, write it down or speak it out loud so that you don't forget it. Try to meditate for at least 10 minutes every day, and make it a habit to try and receive information about people and things around you.

Remember that everyone has these abilities. Naturally, it's normal to feel a little anxious at first when attempting to access your Clairvoyant or Clairaudient abilities. These skills are part of your identity and can be developed with practice. This can be done by dedicating time to daily meditation and focusing on receiving information. You can also try to visualize the images and words you're receiving as you meditate. Once you've become more comfortable with these abilities, it should become easier to sharpen them.

5 Ways the Clairs Can Help You

Clairvoyance and Clairaudience are just two examples of what are known as secondary senses. These senses can be developed with practice and patience. There's no magic or witchcraft involved here – anyone willing to invest time in developing them can do so successfully.

1. **Identifying different energies:** With the help of the Clairs, you can easily identify different energies around you. This can enable you to stay away from harmful energies.

2. **Improve your relationships:** The Clairs can help you better understand your partner, friends, and relatives. It can help you bring out the best in your relationships.

3. **Healing:** The Clairs can also help you in healing. Whether you're a trained healer or an enthusiast, you can use your Clairaudience to heal yourself or the people around you.

4. **In your job:** The Clairs can help you identify subtle sounds and sense things around your workplace. You'll be able to perform better at work and connect with others as a result.

5. **Studying:** The Clairs can help you study better. You can focus better on your lessons, boost your focus, and be more receptive to new knowledge from professors and peers.

A Word of Caution

Psychic powers are the ability to sense, see and communicate with other realms or dimensions. However, these powers can result from several factors, including genetics, trauma, stress, and even physical illness. Psychics and their clients often report feeling uncomfortable, confused, and anxious after a session. This could be because they may not understand what is happening during their session or because they're unsure about the legitimacy of the psychic's abilities. Moreover, some psychics may use their abilities to exploit vulnerable people; using psychic powers is not always positive. It's important to remember that only you know what your body is capable of doing and what you can handle.

Note: You may be hearing voices or seeing things not only due to the Clairs but also *mental illnesses.* Consult a licensed professional if you feel confused, insecure, or anxious about your mental health. All Clair senses, including telepathy, are subject to this disclaimer.

A lot can be said about developing your Clairvoyance and Clairaudience abilities. Ultimately, Clairvoyance doesn't come easy to most people. It takes patience, perseverance and practice to develop and use this special skill in your everyday life. The ability to see beyond what is normally perceived opens up a whole new world of possibilities. It can allow you to see what others cannot hear and understand what others cannot understand. It's an amazing gift to work with, whether you can see into the future or not.

Chapter 3: The Clairs II. Psychic Knowing and Feeling

Did you know that your mind is a virtual warehouse of untapped potential? You can unlock clairvoyant abilities known as Claircognizance and Clairsentience using hidden parts of your mind. These Clairs are another set of intuitive senses that describe specific manifestations of intuition, specifically knowing and feeling.

You can unlock clairvoyant abilities known as Claircognizance and Clairsentience using hidden parts of your mind.

https://www.pexels.com/photo/city-landscape-fashion-man-6669855/

If you're reading this, it's probably because you've experienced some kind of odd premonition or sensed something with your sixth sense. Chances are you're not alone. These experiences are common for people who have discovered their hidden psychic abilities or "Clairs." In this chapter, we'll further explore the world of the Clairs and how they can help boost your intuition and inner knowing.

What Makes Us Want to Know and Feel?

We live in a time of rekindled interest in the paranormal, spirituality, and other "taboo" topics that have typically been ignored or dismissed as nonsense. This is especially true for phenomena that most people find inherently uninteresting or unbelievable. Few things fall under this category more than the sixth sense, which is the ability to perceive the world beyond our natural senses. However, with almost every corner of the internet exploding with videos about aliens, ghosts, or spirits, it's no wonder that interest in these Clair senses has skyrocketed as of late. Practitioners claim that they can read energy and pick up on the thoughts and emotions of others – whether human or non-human entities.

Today, people are seeking new ways to unplug and find peace. We're witnessing the rise of meditation apps, yoga studios, and mindfulness practices. In this new age of spirituality, we also see increasing interest in knowing what truly matters. This is because people want more than just a guided meditation, where a stranger tells them what to think about for 20 minutes. They want something that's tailor-made for their needs and interests. That's why people are looking for Clair techniques and exercises that go beyond reading books, listening to lectures, or watching videos on the topic. With the help of the Clairs, you can expand your mind's horizons and reach new levels of perception that you didn't know were possible.

Claircognizance (Knowing)

Chances are you've been curious about your Claircognizant abilities. If you have an interest in the paranormal and all things mysterious, wonderful, and strange, then Claircognizance is the perfect ability for you. The term "Claircognizance" means having a heightened intuition combined with knowledge from an outside source. This may sound like something from Harry Potter or even The Twilight Zone – after all, most of us don't know much about Clairvoyance or Clairsentience. However, they both describe what many people might simply refer to as that "sixth sense."

Claircognizance is a mode of consciousness best described as clear or inner knowing. It's something we all have inside us – you just have to know how to access it. This psychic ability is often referred to as a "hunch," an "intuitive hit," or a "gut feeling." While some people rely on Clairvoyance to receive information, Claircognizant people rely on their ability to "know" information. Claircognizance occurs when you receive a strong insight or impression about something. For example, if you're trying to decide between two jobs or two college classes, and you just know that you need to take one over the other, that is Claircognizance at work.

Signs That You Are Claircognizant

Being Claircognizant means having "mindsight," in other words, the ability to see in your mind what other people are seeing and feeling. Claircognizant people are aware of their surroundings. They notice details, such as whether someone looks uncomfortable or where the nearest restroom is located. They also know when something feels unusual and can name the cause. If you are Claircognizant, you know what's going on around you. You're present and aware and can understand what other people don't see. This means that your senses are working to their best and that you're processing everything you experience healthily. If you feel your senses aren't working at optimal capacity, your diet is one of the first things to (re)consider. In fact, eating a carbohydrate-rich diet can lead to a decrease in blood glucose levels, which can make it harder for your brain to function properly. You also need to ensure you're getting enough sleep so that your body can recover and re-energize itself for the next day.

As established, Claircognizance is an intuition, so the signs will vary from person to person. The best way to figure out if you have this psychic ability is to pay attention to your feelings, dreams, and overall gut instinct.

There are many ways to tell if you might have a gift of Claircognizance. Ask yourself:

- Do you have a constant gut instinct?
- Are you always feeling like something is right or wrong?
- Do you just "know" that something will happen?

- Do you often have strong emotional reactions to certain situations?

If you find that you constantly rely on your gut or instinct, it could be your Claircognizance at work. While many Clairvoyants experience prophetic dreams, Claircognizants often receive different types of messages in their sleep. Suppose you often dream about future events or different people, places, and situations with which you have no connection. In that case, this could be your Claircognizance manifesting itself. Have you ever been in a situation where you knew exactly what to do, even if you had never been in that situation before? Did it feel like you knew the outcome before you even took action? If yes, this could be your Claircognizance kicking in.

Developing Claircognizance Abilities

You must first unblock your energy to develop Claircognizance and become more in tune with your inner voice. Many people subconsciously block their Clairvoyance due to past experiences or emotions. However, it's crucial to unblock your energy so your abilities can blossom fully. Otherwise, your psychic gifts will be inhibited. Now that you know what Claircognizance is and understand its signs, it's time to unblock your energy and allow your Claircognizance to thrive.

Here are some helpful tips for unblocking your Claircognizance:

- **Exercise:** Physical exercise releases endorphins and gets your blood flowing. By engaging in physical activity regularly, you'll increase your serotonin levels, which are key in unblocking your energy.

- **Meditate:** Meditation grounds you and gets in touch with your innermost thoughts and emotions. It helps you become mindful of how you're feeling and what you're thinking.

- **Dream journaling:** Journaling is an effective way to get in touch with your emotions. By writing down your thoughts and feelings, you can better understand yourself.

- **Talking to a therapist:** Seeing a therapist is a great way to work through past experiences that are negatively affecting you. This can be helpful for gaining clarity about the blockages in your life and how to overcome them and move forward.

Clairsentience (Feeling)

If you've ever experienced sudden intuition about someone or something, you're likely a Clairsentient soul – a soul who can sense and intuit information through their sixth sense. They can sense things that most people cannot detect with their regular senses. In fact, they know things mostly based on intuition rather than direct observation. Since this is such an uncommon ability, it's helpful to understand what makes someone a Clairsentient individual. Let's take a closer look at how Clairsentience works, who can possess it, and why some people may not even know they have the ability until it's triggered.

Clairsentience is the ability to sense and feel the emotions of people, animals, plants, and even inanimate objects. Clairsentient individuals are referred to as "sensitive" or "highly sensitive" people because they're more likely to be aware of subtler stimuli than most. Since the sensitivity of Clairsentients is so unique, it's also important to understand what makes them different from other people. Like many things about these individuals, their heightened intuition can be attributed to their inherent nature and experiences.

How Does Clairsentience Work?

Aside from being an extrasensory perception, Clairsentience is an ability to perceive information about the outside world without using the five traditional senses. Just like there are different types of sensory receptors in our eyes, ears, nose, etc., there are also different receptors inside our bodies. These receptors send and receive information from the environment and our surroundings. The theory is that Clairsentients have a heightened sensitivity to these receptors. This allows them to perceive and feel subtle energies others cannot perceive or notice. The brain then interprets these signals as feelings or emotions. Although it's not certain how Clairsentience works, many believe that people with these heightened abilities have a lower threshold for stimulation than average.

Signs That You Are a Clairsentient

Clairsentients can experience the world in a radically different way. Typically, they can describe the emotions of others, smell or taste negative vibes, and even receive information from inanimate objects like maps or books that others have handled. The human energy field is made up of various kinds of subtle energy. Clairsentience is the ability to feel energy or "vibes" from a person, place, or object. People with Clairsentience abilities can feel vibrations in the air and detect the emotions, thoughts, and intent of the people around them. Moreover, some Clairsentient people can hear voices and sounds from other dimensions. They can also sense when a loved one is nearby and know what they're feeling simply by sensing the emotion in their surroundings.

There are many ways to tell if you might have the gift of Clairsentience, including:

- You are intuitive
- You have a deep connection with nature and animals
- You feel emotions such as sadness or anger more intensely than others
- You feel anxious when in a highly stimulating environment
- You prefer quiet, undistracted environments
- You are empathetic toward others
- You are highly creative and artistic
- You have a strong imagination
- You are sensitive to light, sound, smells, and taste
- You are sensitive to touch
- You have low blood pressure or a strong pulse
- You feel a constant need to cleanse yourself and your surroundings

Developing Clairsentience Abilities

You can develop Clairsentience by performing mindfulness exercises, meditation, or aromatherapy to raise your chakra levels. You can also work with crystals and gemstones to enhance your psychic abilities. Some Clairaudient people may even use tarot cards to gain insight into a particular situation. Clairsentience can be developed in several ways, including practicing and learning how to use these abilities. This may include seeking out other people with the same abilities as you, reading books and articles about Clairsentient abilities, and developing the skills necessary to use them. There are no real rules on how much practice is needed, as it depends on each individual's needs. Like any new skill, however, the more you do it, the better you'll get at it. So, be patient, and keep practicing.

Here are some helpful tips on how to unblock your Clairaudience:

- Pray or meditate to open your mind and sense all the energies around you.
- Picture yourself surrounded by white light and visualize any negative vibes being cleansed away.
- Get in touch with your feelings and be mindful of how you feel.
- Be creative. Visual and creative activities stimulate the right side of the brain, which is associated with clairaudience.
- Be empathetic. Shift your focus from yourself and toward others.
- Be aware of your surroundings. Take note of any odd feelings or vibes you might be getting from a certain place.
- Stay positive and surround yourself with positive folks. Because negativity can shut down your psychic abilities, avoid hanging out with people who always complain and drain your energy.
- Keep an open mind. Try not to dismiss your intuitions or gut feelings as silly or ridiculous, as things that don't make sense can often become clairvoyant visions.
- Be patient. Developing these abilities takes time, so don't get frustrated if you don't see immediate results.

If you think you can sense and feel emotions, but you aren't sure, start paying more attention to your surroundings and the people around you. If you're in a crowded environment, try to focus on just their energies and emotions. Pick one person and imagine what they might be feeling. From there, move on to the next person. As you do this, visualize the emotions as colors. This will help you lock in on what you're feeling with better accuracy. Another way you can practice this skill is by focusing on your own feelings. What emotions do you feel if you're in a calm and happy place? Do you feel happy or excited? By practicing this on yourself, you can train yourself to feel the emotions of others around you.

More Possible Clair Senses That You Might Have

A Clairvoyant person is often depicted as an old mystic with a snowy beard and long, unkempt hair. However, this image doesn't reflect the truth about Clairvoyants. There are many Clair abilities any regular person can have. It's like a light that can be switched on in your third eye or sixth sense. Let's find out exactly what some of the other Clair abilities are and if you can recognize them in yourself.

Clairalience

Clairalience is the ability to feel heightened awareness that can be described as "being in the moment." It occurs when you can perceive and respond to your surroundings with greater, more accurate perception. This can result from various factors, including ambient noise levels, distractions, overstimulation, or any combination of these. Clairalience is an umbrella term to describe any enhanced awareness that can lead to positive outcomes. It can be triggered by the environment we live in or by our interactions with other people. For some, it can even be triggered by certain emotions or situations. It's important to note that there is no one-size-fits-all definition for Clairalience since everyone will experience it in different ways. The key is to be aware when you're experiencing heightened perception and take advantage of whatever opportunities arise from this state.

Clairalience commonly describes sensations of well-being or euphoria. In fact, it's distinct from and often confused with euphoria. Euphoria is an emotional state characterized by feelings of happiness and excitement. Because it's an emotional experience, it can be difficult to distinguish between euphoria and Clairalience. However, the difference is that, while euphoria is short-lived, Clairalience can feel like a more sustained high. Many things, including exercise, meditation, and walks in nature, can induce Clairalience. While it's often associated with positive emotions, it can also be experienced in response to negative experiences, such as trauma or stress.

In addition, Clairalience doesn't necessarily have to be experienced consciously. For example, a dog who has just played fetch might be experiencing Clairalience without knowing it. A common misconception about Clairalience is that it always means you feel happy or blissful. While feelings of happiness often accompany feelings of well-being, they can also be associated with other internal states, like anxiety and sadness.

How to Practice Clairalience

Be present *in the moment*, fully engaged in what you're doing, and observe your surroundings. The more aware you are of your surroundings and the emotions of those around you, the better you will understand their feelings and empathize with them.

Pay attention to the sensations you feel in your body and your surroundings. For example, if someone is upset in the office, notice how their body feels as they walk by you.

- Are they tensed or shaky?
- How do their shoulders look?
- Do they look tired or stressed?
- Are there any physical signs that might reveal whether or not their stress level is high?

Next, try to empathize with others' emotions by imagining how they feel when they are experiencing different situations. This can help you put yourself in their shoes and better understand why they might feel the way they do.

Clairtangency

Clairtangency is the ability to sense or "feel" the presence of another person, which can be perceived through various senses, such as vibrations or smells. Clairtangency is often described as an "open line" with someone's spirit or soul. It can lead to a deep connection between two people, whether a friendship or a romantic relationship. This sense is often described as a feeling of comfort, serenity, and safety near another person. It can be felt both physically and mentally. The physical sensation of being close to another person may include warmth, tingling sensations, or even rumbling sounds if they touch the skin. Clairtangency is sometimes called "feeling energy" because it is not always easy to put into words.

Many people with this ability claim to "feel" the flow of time in their own bodies. While anyone can experience it, some describe it as being able to feel time flowing through their hands or feet. It's a form of Clairvoyance where a person can sense the texture of an object and understand its origins, such as when someone has handled the object and left their energy behind. This phenomenon usually occurs when a person is under extreme emotional stress. Because there are no concrete scientific explanations for how this ability works, it has been compared to other unexplained phenomena, such as ESP and other psychic abilities.

How to Practice Clairtangency

You can decode the messages being sent by people and objects around you by paying attention to your surroundings and picking up on subtle energy signals.

Tuning into your own energy body is the next step. This is where you'll find your chakras and other energetic centers. It is possible to detect subtle changes in your energy by tuning into these areas of your body. You might experience these changes when you feel anxious, tired, or disrupted by the energy field around you.

Once you've mastered this area, practice on a meaningful object in your life; with a little time, you will begin to see a shift in the surrounding energy field when holding this object. You can then apply your new awareness to unfamiliar objects from the past. If you have Clairtangency, they will speak to you.

Clairgustance

Clairgustance is the ability to taste and smell a flavor that isn't present in the environment. This can be related to the past, present, or future. It combines your sense of smell and the ability to perceive scents from other people. You can experience it if you have ever smelled someone else's perfume or cologne or if you have been close enough to someone else to smell their body odor or sweat. Clairgustance is a form of extrasensory perception (ESP). It can be experienced as a tingling sensation in the back of the throat or an overwhelming sense that something amazing is nearby. Clairgustance may also point to something else, such as an impending disaster. For example, if you were standing near a spot and suddenly smelled smoke, indicating a potential fire, you would have Clairgustance. That said, it's not always easy to tell what is going on when you encounter this kind of feeling. It can be a little scary if you don't know how to interpret it.

Clairgustance is not just about smelling something in someone else's presence, like their perfume – it also includes detecting smells from far away. In addition, if you can detect the smells of food cooking at home on a very early morning before anyone has had breakfast, you may have Clairgustance. This heightened Clair can be due to genetics and lifestyle choices, such as consuming certain foods or beverages, past-life memories, and stress levels and hormones.

How to Practice Clairgustance

There is much more to tasting and smelling than many people realize. By training yourself to discern flavors, you're training your mind to become more discerning in all other areas of your life. Sharpening your sense of smell can also allow you to pick up on subtle emotions, which can be helpful for those who work with the dead or tend to be psychically sensitive.

So, where do you start? First, relax your mind and body, then take a deep breath and try to focus on your sense of smell. What do you smell? Start by noticing the strongest scents in the air, and then work your way down your nose to the tip of your tongue. Focus on whether you get a negative or positive feeling associated with the smell.

There are a few general rules you should follow when practicing taste and smell:

- Try not to eat or drink anything while trying to train your senses.
- Start a scent journal to track your experiences with different scents over time.
- Practice in a clean environment, as concentrating on several smells can confuse your senses.

Lastly, remember that it takes time to get used to being able to detect these things, typically anywhere between a few hours and a few days.

The ability to know and feel subtle energies is a unique gift that not everyone inherently possesses. Fortunately, this chapter and the previous one will have given you a better understanding of these special abilities and how to develop them. When they're present, they can be an incredibly enriching and rewarding experience for both the individual and those around them. While it can sometimes be difficult to identify these special individuals, once you know what to look for, it's easy to spot them in any crowd. If you feel what we've discussed resonates with you, don't hesitate to explore these special abilities and discover what they can teach you about yourself and your purpose.

Chapter 4: Psychic Protection and Shielding

Being a psychic or medium often means engaging in an extended exercise in vulnerability while also working hard to protect yourself from said vulnerability. The capacity for such openness and a willingness to connect with others is a unique gift, but it must be nurtured and protected. Using your psychic capabilities means working with your energies more than you normally would, so it's important to *proceed with caution.* If you're not careful, you may end up soaking up everyone's thoughts and negative vibes, which will inevitably impact your life in unpleasant ways. The key to being a successful medium is learning to balance your own needs as an individual with the needs of others you'll be helping. This dedicated chapter will guide you and provide some useful pointers to help you protect yourself from unwanted influences.

If you're not careful, you may end up soaking up everyone's thoughts and negative vibes.
https://www.pexels.com/photo/woman-in-white-shirt-holding-orange-and-white-lollipop-6943953/

Barring "Invasions"

Looking at matters through a metaphysical lens, the world is made up of energies – it's the way things come into being and how everyone communicates. As biological creatures, clueing into this pool of energy is essential to how we evolve and connect with other beings in the world. The downside of this is that our processes are malleable, easily influenced, and can cause us to go down a million divergent paths. It's really a "choose your own adventure" sort of game, which is why one must be careful as a psychic.

At the same time, no one can invade your energy source unless you let them, so rest assured that you have some control over the matter. Each individual is ultimately the gatekeeper of their energy field, so you won't easily get roped into anything if you don't want to. Luckily, no alien being will come rushing into your body, taking over without your consent. Part of the work you will need to master is preventing your open nature from becoming too open and figuring out the best pace for you. However, all of that work begins with a clear sense of your own powers and the fact that you are in control, not the other way around. Without a clear understanding of these power dynamics, you won't be able to master these techniques and may run the risk of letting the universe wreak more havoc on your life than you bargained for. Harmful spirits or entities with bad intentions may feel free to use you as their vessel, and your energies will deplete quickly.

For that reason, getting the hang of psychic protection and shielding is an absolute must-have skill for any psychic to possess, whether or not they're new to the practice. Fortunately, a plethora of cleansing, protection, shielding, and banishing rituals exist, not only for yourself but for the people you're trying to help. There's also a multitude of smudging rituals, prayers, and chants you can fill the home with if your main interest is to protect a physical space like the home. Some of these techniques have a long history and are so popular that you may have noticed smudge sticks, crystals, and the like being sold on the market, sometimes for a hefty price tag. In reality, some of these practices are simpler than you'd think.

Smudge Sticks

Let's begin with one of the simpler techniques to guarantee you and your space protection: smudge sticks. These are bunches of herbs bound together by twine. Certain herbs are selected for their specific properties, with some of the most popular being rosemary, white sage, or Yerba Santa. Depending on your specific needs at any given moment, you can combine different herbs or simply stick to one bunch of the same. Then, when you're ready, you burn the herbs and wave the smoke in the direction of the person or space you'd like to offer the protection. The act of burning the smudge stick is known as smudging, hence the name.

Various cultures and peoples have practiced this ancient ritual in many places. Native Americans, in particular, used smudge sticks to clear out low vibrations or any energies that felt stuck in a particular place. They believed that the act of smudging helped create positive energy and allowed people to lift their spirits. If you're looking to protect yourself, you can point the smoke toward your own body and then wave the burning stick in different directions throughout the home to ensure that your living space is similarly full of positive energy and is well protected from any negative vibes.

Banishment Rituals

This is a more involved form of shielding yourself from being too open and safeguarding your psychic abilities. Banishment rituals are complicated but important to master and perform from time to time, depending on the context. To perform this, you will need the following:

- **An altar:** In the center of your ritual space, regardless of where you choose to set it up, is your altar, as well as the instruments representing the four classical elements. Classical elements are what we know as earth, water, air, and fire. Modern occultists have also introduced aether, also known as the fifth element of quintessence. This material fills the area of the universe just beyond the terrestrial sphere. This element serves to explain different kinds of natural phenomena, such as the traveling of light and gravity, whose nature isn't necessarily represented within the other four elements.

The next two elements are optional and ultimately boil down to your own beliefs:

- Those practicing magic typically wore ceremonial robes or ritual garb.
- A ritual sword or athame. This is used to gesture toward different points of the cross and to help draw pentagrams if you so choose.

First and foremost, create the astral cross in your body by pointing to the areas that correspond with the understanding of the Tree of Life, repairing the words forehead, feet, right shoulder, left shoulder, and heart, respectively. Extra points if you can say these words in Hebrew to follow the Kabbalah tradition.

Next, formulate the pentagrams, beginning in the East, saying the names of the negative energies you need to banish. You can visualize these in blue light or light a candle as you work and focus on the burning flame. This part of the ritual is meant to invoke the elements as you simultaneously banish whatever is causing you trouble. The four pentagrams are connected by a circle, which is also drawn in the air. You would typically start from the North point to the East point.

The third step can be adjusted according to what you're looking for and your own set of beliefs. However, they tend to follow the Kabbalah version by invoking the archangels, a part of the ceremony that entails the psychic standing in front of the cross at the altar and declaring that the archangels Raphael, Gabriel, Michael, and Uriel are all present, visualizing them as the four cardinal points.

Finally, this is repeated another time to ensure that the spirits are banished and that your aura and home are cleansed accordingly.

Safeguarding Packets and Tools

We discussed smudge sticks earlier, which are a simple yet essential tool in any psychic's arsenal. Another bundle that is good to keep on hand is a patch of palo santo and selenite. Together, the herb and the powerful crystal will help keep you safe – the palo santo is great for clearing away any lingering negativity in your home, while selenite can help prevent bad vibes from making their way in. It is advisable to keep this little bundle near your front door as an effective safety precaution.

Do you need extra protection when you're outside the home? Carry around some crystals to help protect you from any unwanted forces and their influences. One protective stone that can help you safeguard your aura and prevent you from being too open is black tourmaline. They're shiny, rough, and jagged. Still, these modest-looking specimens are excellent for protection and are easy to carry in your back pocket. You can also keep them at your office desk or at your home library if these are spaces you feel may be *porous* and tend to attract bad energy. Keeping these crystals around will help you feel secure and strong.

Sachets are another excellent way to keep you protected. These little packets not only smell lovely, but they help to safeguard you against unwanted forces. They're generally made up of basil, rosemary, star anise, juniper berries, and other herbs and essential oils like lavender rose or orange. You can look up different mixes and choose the relevant herbs according to your needs. Sachets are excellent for your home, office, and even your car. If you carry a bag with you everywhere you go, you can also put a little sachet in there. All you have to do is create your blend and scoop them into a little pouch, hanging them wherever you like.

If you like to keep things simple, go with the classic solution of using salt to banish bad vibes and protect yourself from unwanted emotions or energies. Throw salt over your shoulder the old-fashioned way, or get into the habit of salting the corners of your room and the doorway to your home. Obviously, this often gets messy, so you can keep a small bowl of salt near the areas in question to help eliminate negative energy.

Aligning the Chakras

One excellent way of ensuring you're protecting yourself and your energy reserves as you pursue psychic work is to ensure that your chakras are aligned. You can engage in different exercises to help you with this. For one, the popular auric egg exercise is a good step toward meditation that allows you to breathe in and visualize warm light making its way to different chakra centers in your body.

For starters, sit down with your back straight while maintaining a relaxed position. Then, visualize yourself within an oval-shaped field (like an egg, hence the name) that extends toward the center of your body and stretches three feet in every direction. Mentally trace the egg shape from the highest point you can imagine from your head, focusing on a pure white color-led light leading the way. While you can perform the exercise using different colors, white light is the most effective way to imagine a peaceful aura surrounding you, working to keep you safe from bad energies.

The next step involves anchoring this bright white light in the center of your body while taking deep breaths, feeling the beat of your heart, and allowing it to resonate throughout your body. These steadying breaths are key to helping you feel calm and at peace. Then, on one breath, imagine light entering your body and as you exhale, allow the light to expand and fill your head, then your arms, back, torso, and feet. You should be able to feel the light moving in every direction to ignite your chakras and allow you to feel comforted. Continue to breathe and visualize the light moving around you, thereby banishing anything that doesn't serve you while centering your body.

Meditate for at least five to ten minutes until your body feels calmer and more relaxed. Doing this daily ensures that you maintain your energy source, making it more difficult for other energies to enter without your consent. It's a way of "future-proofing" your mind and body so that you're not allowing different thoughts or vibes to enter as you use your psychic abilities. Meditating for a few minutes a week should help you meet your goals without trouble.

Cultivating Awareness

As mentioned, meditation is one way of cultivating an awareness of your body and thoughts. Being empathetic is a wonderful and essential trait any good psychic should have. However, it can also be taxing, especially if you're not taking the appropriate steps to protect yourself.

Daily affirmations are like incantations you can use to help you stay attuned to your body and needs. There isn't one that you need to follow in a textbook fashion – you can draft whichever version you like. For example, you can write or say to yourself something along the lines of: "My energy can rise to high levels and has the capacity to rid my home and other places of evil. A bright light follows me, and I can help the people I love and care for." You can incorporate this affirmation into any daily ritual you've devised for yourself – it can end a meditation session, a yoga workout, candle burning ritual, or you use a smudge stick throughout the home.

You can also write it down daily, first thing in the morning. While journaling may be an odd thing to mention in the context of psychic protection and shielding, it definitely has a place in your bid to become more aware of your "self" and the different energies coursing throughout your body and the universe. For example, you can start your day by noting which areas in your life seem to deplete your energy the most. Alternatively, pinpoint places that you'd like to make stronger and bring more focus to in your daily life. Once you have a list in hand, you can zero in on it and begin to whittle down the things that have been upsetting to you or the relationships you recognize need more work. Then, focus your powers on solving them one by one.

You can also get into the habit of writing down different things you've noticed throughout the day. Take notice of the things around you or the different places in your practice that may need to be refined. Commit yourself to one to two pages a day. This is a simple way of cleansing your aura and clearing your mind, making you a more powerful and steady psychic medium over time.

Practicing psychic work isn't a walk in the park. It requires constant practice and attunement to different areas in life you hope to focus on. While there are many elaborate rituals you can pursue or crystals you can buy, a lot of this work falls to you. It's imperative to recognize that you must listen to your inner self and maintain your energy levels accordingly. As a psychic, focusing on the past is actually not a great idea – working hard to make yourself stronger mentally and emotionally in the future is the best way to protect your unique gifts and hone them.

Chapter 5: Divination Tools for Psychics

Divination practices are often employed to predict future events by seeking guidance from the unknown. Each technique uses different tools to perform the reading. Interpreting these readings is also an essential part, which is where the psychics come in. Psychics have an enhanced sensory perception that allows them to use certain tools to perform divination. Throughout history, there have been many methods of divination. While some of these divination techniques have faded over time, many are still frequently used for psychic readings.

Divination practices are often employed to predict future events by seeking guidance from the unknown.
https://www.pexels.com/photo/healthy-wood-man-love-6944906/

Psychics have employed countless divination tools to make predictions and interpretations for centuries. Using these tools is not mandatory for a psychic, as they can do well without them. However, using divination tools for psychic readings only enhances the quality and accuracy of the readings. Today, the most commonly used divination tools include pendulums, tarot cards, astrology, scrying, dowsing, runes, i-ching coins, and many more. This chapter will dive deeply into the world of divination tools and equip you with all the knowledge you need regarding these tools.

Pendulums

Pendulum magic is one of the most popular divination techniques that provide insightful results. A pendulum is basically a crystal, rock, or metal hanging at the end of a chain. Traditionally, this technique is used to locate hidden water or other valuable materials. People also use it to seek answers and guidance regarding their problems. The principle of pendulum magic is based on energy manifestation. Essentially, everything in this world has unique energy or vibration – in this case, the crystal of the pendulum manifests its energy and draws upon the energy of the space to provide answers.

Today, pendulums are used in all kinds of rituals and psychic readings. A common method is to hover the pendulum over a paper with "yes" and "no" written. You're supposed to concentrate on the question you wish to answer and set your intention. The pendulum does the rest. Getting a pendulum board with multiple answers to your questions is also common practice. This will help you understand the reading better and assist with the interpretation.

Pendulums are pretty simple instruments, so they can be easily personalized if you want to create your own unique pendulum. You can select a crystal that has personal significance to you or is proven to help your task. Each crystal has a specific kind of energy and is therefore used for specific purposes.

Crystal Balls

The use of crystal balls is overwhelmingly popular among psychics, according to popular culture. In contrast, the technique of using a crystal ball to envision shapes and visions of the future is a meticulous and highly challenging process. Mastering this technique only comes with tremendous practice and patience, which only a few can achieve. The technique itself is called scrying, which helps the seeker gain insight into the future. It's the process of gazing into a reflective surface, in this case, a crystal ball, and using your intuition and psychic abilities to attract any messages from the universe in the form of shapes, visions, and images.

These images can then be interpreted with regard to the circumstances or background information to form a deeper understanding of the issue. While most are made of clear quartz, you can use any type of crystal for making a crystal ball. Generally, amethyst, calcite, and even obsidian crystals are used to design crystal balls for scrying and divination.

Crystals

Crystals hold a unique place in the world of psychics. They're used in many divination tools and even separately for divination purposes. As explained before, crystals have a unique energy signature that helps connect psychics to their inner wisdom and intuition. When using crystals, trusting one's gut feeling or sixth sense is the most crucial part. If you can't trust your intuition, no divination tool will be able to help you. In that regard, crystals assist with connecting with your intuition as they're able to build a bridge between the spiritual world and your own. Each type of crystal specializes in the clearance of a specific chakra. For instance, amazonite is said to enhance emotional intelligence, whereas amethyst helps clear the crown chakra.

Tarot Cards

Another well-known divination tool, tarot cards, is frequently used by psychics to receive guidance about past, present, and future scenarios. The deck of tarot cards consists of 78 cards, with 56 Minor Arcana and 22 Major Arcana. Each card is unique in its own way, featuring an illustration that can be interpreted in different ways. The position of the card also matters when interpreting the reading. For instance, if the illustration is upside down or upright, it will have a different meaning. Moreover, the sequence of the cards will also change the outcome of the reading.

To practice this technique, you simply need to lay out a few cards after setting the intention of the reading. Next, depending on the position of each card, you'll need to interpret them based on the seeker's background. You should preferably use a tarot card guide at first to understand what each illustration means and how to interpret the positions. After a while, you'll start to get the hang of it and make more accurate readings.

It is said that the Major Arcana are connected with the life lessons that must be completed throughout one's lifetime. On the other hand, the Minor Arcana cards are associated with the day-to-day experiences and ordeals one has to face. Each deck of tarot cards also contains 16 Court cards. These cards symbolize the personality traits of the seeker. Another category in the tarot deck includes the Suits, representing the four elements of nature.

Contrary to popular belief, tarot card readings are more concerned with intuition and guidance rather than fortune-telling. The knowledge gained from these readings helps strengthen one's intuition and sense of perception. Aside from being simple to understand and learn, tarot cards are great tools for psychic development. While this technique doesn't necessarily provide direct answers, you'll be free to interpret the readings as you see fit.

Ouija Board

Here's another divination technique whose popularity mainly owes to the entertainment industry. Almost everyone is familiar with the Ouija board and how it's used. However, unlike the popular idea that they're only used for contacting spirits, Ouija boards can be employed for various divination purposes. These boards are engraved with numbers 1 to 9 and all the alphabet. A "yes" and "no" are also available on the board for easy communication.

To practice this divination method, carefully put your fingers on top of the triangular piece of the Ouija board. Then, you need to concentrate on the question you need to be answered. The spirit or universal guides will move the planchette toward the answer it wants to give. While performing this practice, you must be cautious as it can open up a pathway for negative spirits and risk possession.

Dowsing Rods

Dowsing is another popular divination method traditionally used to detect hidden objects and water sources. This method is a little different compared to other typical divination methods, considering it isn't used to predict future circumstances but instead for seeking guidance and finding hidden information from universal guides. Today, psychics employ this method to identify when they come across a spirit. You'll likely encounter a spirit or guide present to help you during the practice. When you do, the dowsing rods you're holding will make a cross or X shape. When you observe this, ask your questions.

To practice this technique, hold the dowsing rods lightly from the ends. You'll witness the rods automatically moving upward or downward when you find what you're looking for, whether it's hidden minerals, precious ore, water, or a spirit. You must continually practice using the dowsing rods to familiarize yourself with the technique before you use them for a serious matter.

Oracle Cards

Oracle cards, often confused with tarot cards, can serve as a daily form of spiritual guidance. They're often combined with tarot cards to get a detailed reading but can also be used separately for a standard reading. These cards come with special messages and don't have a specific number of cards. You could get an oracle card deck of about 30 cards or maybe one with just 12 cards. Besides the illustrations and symbols on these cards, they're equipped with poetic statements that provide deep insight into one's life situation. Many oracle cards have Celtic themes, while others relate to astrology.

Considering the non-traditional nature of these cards, many practitioners don't get the hang of them. Therefore, don't be surprised if it takes a while to figure out the themes and concepts behind these cards. You may even feel frustrated at times, but don't give up. Usually, oracle cards are used to make one-card-a-day readings, but some psychics even make three-card readings for reflection.

Scrying Mirrors

Like crystal ball reading techniques, scrying mirrors predict future events using a reflective surface. The practitioner will get visions or images when gazing deeply into the reflective surface, which will be relevant to the questions asked. Usually, this method is carried out using a crystal ball or plain mirrors, but if you don't have access to these, you can always opt for a bowl of clear water. Scrying requires a reflective surface, so mirrors aren't a prerequisite for this method. Although this is a very effective method of divination, people seldom get close to mastering this art. It takes both time and practice to master the technique of scrying. The practitioner will have to be in complete sync with their intuition and spirituality. In the event of an inability to master this process, the practitioner will get hard to decipher results and thus face difficulty.

I-Ching Coins

The use of I-Ching coins is another traditional divination method, dating as far back as 2700 BC. This method manifests the yin and yang energy to find meaning and make predictions. In older versions of this divination tool, the coins used to be engraved with yin and yang symbols, but today, they've become vastly modified and contain many variations of engravings. Start by assigning each symbol to the two sides of a coin. Once you've done this, toss the coin and write down the results. Repeat these five more times, and you'll get a pattern of results or code that will translate as a hexagram number. Use a guidebook to interpret this number, and you'll get your results.

Runes

Runes are ancient symbols used to communicate between the Scandinavian people, which is where this method originates. In time, these runes became a means of divination and were printed on small stones or wooden blocks. You can carve your own runes into wood chips or purchase a premade set from the market. To practice this technique, all you need to do is place the rune stones or blocks into a pouch and set the intention of the ritual. Once you've asked your question mindfully and attentively, pour out the rune stones and let them scatter. You will get a series of stones or blocks with runes. This can be interpreted with aid from a detailed guidebook, not only to understand the meanings of the runes but also what the position of each one means. Only then will you be able to completely interpret what the universe is trying to tell you through this divination method.

Angel Cards

Although angel cards are often confused with tarot cards or oracle cards, they're separate from both concepts. Angel cards are meant to draw on the energy of our angel guides to seek guidance from them. This type of divination tool is mainly used to find out more about one's future, finances, love life, and family matters. There are different variations of angel cards, so select the ones that draw you close to them the most.

While tarot cards focus on the metaphysical meanings of life, angel cards approach angelic concepts and provide a different interpretation.

Start your practice by setting the intention for the process and bringing the deck of angel cards close to your body, placed near your heart. This will allow you to connect with your angel guides or spirits. When you're ready, draw a few cards and lay them out on the table. Examine the illustration and position of each of these cards to make an interpretation of the reading. Use a guidebook until you get the hang of each of the cards' meanings.

Astrology

An eminent divination technique, astrology has regained massive popularity over the past few years. Essentially, astrology relies on the position of the stars at a given moment and connects it with our specific persona. We can tune into nature and the universe through astrology to discover more about ourselves. The cosmos is constantly in motion, which can help connect our present state with the star's positions.

We can define astrology as the study of the relationship between celestial activity and events taking place on earth. Earthly events can include your career, relationships, finances, fortune, and wellness insights. Astrology uses the specific birth charts of each person to get a specific reading for them. This can then be interpreted more deeply to get guidance about all aspects of life. In parallel, birth charts tell a lot about a person, their past, and their probable future. Personal compatibility can also be determined using this method.

Numerology

Numerology is concerned with numbers, their combinations, and various mathematical symbols. This divination practice can help you tap into the underlying patterns of the universe and identify who you are deep within. One important aspect in the practice of numerology is your life-path number. This number is usually calculated using your date of birth and represents your present personality. This number highlights the specific traits and characteristics that are a big part of your life and will remain influential throughout your existence.

This divination technique ultimately looks at numbers to find the hidden meaning. Often, certain numbers present themselves to us again and again. These are not simply coincidences but, in fact, a pattern that the universe is asking us to identify. Another important aspect of numerology is our life number, which is associated with our birth date and intentions. Natal charts are also commonly used in numerology practices.

Tea Leaves

A less common divination tool used among psychics is tasseomancy, or the use of tea leaves to predict the near or far future. This technique requires specially made tea cups to help interpret the marks left behind from tea leaves.

To practice this method, first, brew fresh tea and drink it, but not completely. Make sure you leave a few drops behind. Move the cup in a circular motion and slowly drain the remaining liquid. However, ensure you don't drain the tea leaves with the liquid. Once you've done this, you'll begin to observe a pattern or shape forming inside the cup. Roughly sketch these images in your journal and interpret them with regard to the question at hand.

Divination tools are a great way to better connect with your spiritual energy and manifest the universe's energies to help guide you. However, we should always be mindful of how we use these tools. Understanding and learning different divination techniques allows you to comprehend how your spirit guides want to communicate with you. From there, you can further clear the communication path between yourself and the universal guides.

Nowadays, tarot cards are the most popularly used divination tool. This is followed by pendulum magic and the use of crystals. Each of these divination tools has multiple purposes, and as a psychic, you have both the skill and the ability to master these techniques and enhance your spiritual connection. Psychic practitioners also use other techniques like incense, essential oils, palmistry, and crystals to clear their chakras, enhance their vibrations, and strengthen their intuition. Ultimately, only you will determine which practice or practices resonate with you the most and help you achieve your goals as a psychic.

Chapter 6: Types of Spirits and Guides

Until now, you've had a chance to unlock and sharpen your psychic skills and learn what tools to use and how to protect yourself during psychic work. After this, you've probably become increasingly curious about spiritual communication and finding allies in the spiritual world. This chapter will introduce you to the spirits and guides you can ally yourself with. Some of these friendly beings will contact you on their own, while others need to be called on. The former can appear periodically or just once, depending on how and when you need them. Other spirits and guides may accompany you through your entire life. Either way, knowing who they are, how they can help you, and how they manifest themselves will help you establish a meaningful connection with them.

The one guide you'll always be able to count on is none other than your higher self.
https://www.pexels.com/photo/crop-female-future-teller-with-tarot-cards-on-table-4337135/

Ancestors

The most commonly appearing spirits and guides are the ancestors. These are the souls of people with whom you had a blood relationship, which makes contacting them easier. In most cases, you've never met them, although you might have heard about them from living relatives. Whether they lived twenty years before you or two hundred, the ancestral spirits have ascended to a higher plane from where they watch over you. Some may be waiting for reincarnation to acquire more spiritual wisdom and become more enlightened, while others remain in the abyss to help the younger generations. Since they're related to you, they might reach out to you if they feel you could use their help. However, in most cases, you'll need to contact them if you require their wisdom. Ancestors are known to send subtle yet clear messages, appearing in your dreams in their spiritual form. Or you may unexpectedly see or hear their name in certain situations. You can heed their wisdom for divination, spiritual healing, and any time you feel stuck in your life.

Departed Loved Ones

Like the ancient ancestors, recently departed loved ones may also become your spiritual guides. However, they might remain for a short period until you need them – or, in most cases, until they need you. These are people you knew personally, so more often than not, they'll need your help to move on or accept their role in the spiritual plane. That isn't to say that they can't help you in return. In fact, because you know them personally and vice versa, they'll be able to assist you more quickly and efficiently than ancestral spirits. For example, suppose you need guidance choosing the right career path. In that case, a recently departed soul may be more attuned to what you actually desire to fulfill your professional dreams. They can appear in dreams and visions, or you may hear their voice giving you the advice you need. They can also send you small signals, such as their favorite song, on the radio. You may also suddenly encounter or think about their favorite color, food, flower, or a personal object they once held dear.

Role Models

Even if you've had no close relationship or blood kinship with a person, they can still become your spiritual guide. Any person who influenced you in life can continue to do so after passing. This can be a role model, a person you admire for their qualities, someone with whom you share your life philosophy, or anyone else. Even famous people who inspire you can become spiritual guides. They may not appear to you personally, but they can send you small messages and advice if and when needed. You'll most likely need to contact them to gain their assistance, but if they're willing to help you, they'll make sure you receive their messages.

Ascended Masters

When someone reaches the highest spiritual level in their former life, they may remain in the spiritual plane to assist the living. These are the ascended masters, offering help to anyone who needs it, regardless of their cultural or religious background. They lived their lives gathering spiritual knowledge, which earned them a unique place in the spiritual world. While some of these souls may also be awaiting future reincarnation, most linger as supporting spirits, as they have much wisdom to share with the next generations. Being in an ascended form, they can access even more knowledge from the higher planes. A group of ascended masters can communicate amongst themselves, often working together to help multiple people simultaneously.

While you may encounter souls who were known to be famous spiritual masters during their lives, you may also meet one without realizing who they are at first. However, when they decide to share their knowledge, you'll be surprised to see how much they can teach you. Some masters choose their students and only work with mediums they feel they can trust to use their knowledge as they would. Others can be contacted for various purposes. Ascended masters can appear in their human form or as spiritual beings with auras. There is also a chance they might not materialize at all. Rather, they leave along signs that you'll pick up with your extrasensory gifts. They also have their unique energy, which is more empowering than the influence of other spiritual guides. Feel free to tap into it and use it as an anchor as you embark on the experiences they guide you toward.

The Higher Self

The one guide you'll always be able to count on is none other than your higher self. This is the being you're destined to become, and because of this, it will do everything it can to aid and advance your spiritual growth. They'll provide a gateway to information hidden in your unconscious mind. The best part about communicating with your higher self is that you won't even have to reach deep into the spiritual world to do it. You're not looking for a spirit version of yourself outside your body – instead, you're looking for a part that's inside you. If you want to reach out to your higher self, intuition is the only tool you need. They can help you separate the rational thoughts from the spiritual messages buried deep inside your soul. This can come in handy during divination, healing, and many other practices. There are numerous ways your higher self can manifest. For example, it may come as a sudden thought nudging you to look beyond the surface regarding a specific area of life. It may also be a gut feeling about a person or job you're considering applying for or a need to surround yourself with people who can provide you with wisdom and love.

Animals and Other Natural Guides

Most psychic beliefs hold that the entire living world is enveloped in the spirit, and all living beings have an essence. Therefore, it isn't surprising that when you venture into the spiritual world, you'll encounter several animal spirits ready to help you. Animal spirits and guides can be just as powerful as their human counterparts – they only communicate differently. Most often, they'll leave you subtle signs. You may see an animal appearing in your dreams a couple of times, in which case, they're trying to communicate with you because they have important news for you. There are different types of animal guides and spirits. Some will appear only for a short period when they're needed, and others will accompany you during a difficult stage in your life. Others will only show you how to encounter your permanent guide.

Some believe that plants may also have the ability to forward spiritual messages. Psychics who love connecting with nature or work in spiritual healing may get signals from herbs and other plants. Like animals, plants may also try to communicate by appearing around you or appearing as visions and in your dreams. They can also be called upon and asked to show specific ways for their uses.

Spirit Animals

Unlike animal guides that appear and disappear when their mission of helping you with a particular task is done, spirit animals are more loyal creatures. These are often the spiritual versions of a pet you've recently lost. They remain beside you to help you heal and allow you to move on. If they see that you still need their guidance after that, they may accompany you for the rest of your life. Spirit animals may also appear to people who haven't had any connection to them in life. An animal may appear to a child to teach them a lesson and remain by their side as the child grows into an adult. They can teach you valuable life lessons far more than any other human spirit can. Animals are driven by their instincts and are willing to listen to them - something people often forget how to do. Their advice can come in handy when you can't make a decision or have trouble discerning the true scope of a challenging situation. They can appear in pictures, movies, music, your dreams, or in the park if it's their natural habitat.

Deities

Depending on your religious beliefs, you may also have deities as spiritual guides. Some believe deities are the primordial spiritual ancestors, the source of all human souls. Other religions say that deities were once people themselves: like ascended masters, they've reached a level of spirituality in which they've gained divine status. After their final reincarnation, they've become spiritual guides ready to help people whenever needed. They typically appear in forms of energy, which is how you'll perceive them with your extrasensory gifts. If you feel a sudden burst of energy after praying to a deity, they let you know they're ready to guide you. They can aid you in your spiritual journey – especially if your goal is to reach a higher plane one day. They may also assist you during divination or when you have trouble discerning whether you're making the right decision or not.

Angels

Despite popular beliefs, angels don't only guide people with certain religious ideologies; they can assist anyone who needs their help. Also, you'll encounter different types of angels on your spiritual journeys as a medium. Angels typically send messages on their own and don't need to be contacted. However, you'll have to pay extra careful attention to your surroundings – even more so if you haven't worked with them before. You can receive messages in many forms, and while some signs will be loud and clear, others will be so subtle that if you aren't careful, you might overlook them. Fortunately, angels always carry meaningful messages. If you miss their signals at first, they'll likely try to reach you again and again until you start paying attention.

Guardian Angels

Like spirit animals, guardian angels are only linked to one person. As their names suggest, they are your personal guardians. However, you may have more than one angel guarding you throughout your life. While these beings devote their lives to helping one person, they know that not all of them can assist in everything. Just like humans, they have their own personalities and interests. As your personality grows and your interests change, you'll need help from angels more attuned to you during each particular phase. Whichever guardian angel you have by your side at any moment in time, if you need their help, they'll come to your aid. While most angels emerge without being called, guardian angels can also be summoned. Like deities, angels aren't likely to appear in their true form. Instead, they'll send signals through your dreams, visions, words, people, situations, or opportunities. They can be a source of wisdom for spiritual growth and divination. They'll also provide support and unconditional love when you need spiritual healing.

Archangels

Archangels are the most powerful figures in the angelic world. They've gathered wisdom in certain aspects of life, which makes them "experts" in these areas. Due to their status, they are less likely to appear without being summoned. When called, they'll leave their specific energy at your disposal. They can lend you great power, and you'll definitely feel the energy shift when they appear. Archangels can help many people at once, so they only appear in their energetic form. That said, they'll only appear if they feel that their energy is what you truly need. Otherwise, you may get another angel who'll only help you discover what you need. For example, if you need an angel with healing powers, you need to summon the strength of Archangel Raphael. If you want to reveal the truth or find a way to protect yourself from lies, Archangel Michael will be the angel to turn to.

Helper Angels

There are "lesser" angels who don't have a specific task yet, nor do they have immense power like archangels. Instead, they're looking out for all of humankind. These helper angels roam the divide between the worlds, waiting to see if anyone needs their assistance. Chances are, if it's the first time you're sending messages to the angelic world, it will reach one of these free-roaming angels first. When they receive a call for help, they'll see if they can be of aid or if they need to refer you to another guide. Helper angels can be most helpful in specific situations when you need a boost of spiritual assistance in your psychic work. For example, they'll provide that help when you want to find a way to befriend your colleagues at your new workplace. If they can't help, the helper angel will pass on your message to an archangel.

Light Beings

Spiritual guides can come from far beyond the worlds in our galaxy. They can also come from other galaxies and even be ancestral spirits. According to certain beliefs, the inhabitants of all galaxies are related to each other. They can also communicate in spiritual form. Just as souls can reincarnate in this world or any other galaxy, they can also be reborn in other galaxies. Souls you encounter from another universe are called *light beings*. Even if they live light-years away, they can share the wisdom of their ancestors and become unique guides. Because they aren't familiar with our world, they can offer a different perspective. It is often helpful when you want to see things with better clarity.

They may appear in the form of energy, a spark, a flicker of a star in the sky, a name of a new star written in the newspaper, or any other astrological or astronomical phenomenon. While not every medium is sensitive to their messages, if you receive them, feel free to take advantage of their knowledge.

Transitional Species

Depending on your religious and cultural background, you may also encounter spirits that belong to transitional species. Typically, these beings are part human and part animal or another creature. The most common guides among transitional beings are fairy-like creatures, mermaids, and centaurs. However, other magical beings like harpies, fauns, or sphinxes can also become spiritual guides. Some of these creatures live in the spiritual world, whereas others have a realm of their own. While not all of these are friendly, plenty of them can become your ally in times of need. Their human part helps you form a connection with them far more quickly than you would do with some animal guides. You will have an easier time communicating with them because they'll understand you better. However, and for the same reason, they'll often expect your help in return for theirs. They can protect you when you're in the spiritual world (or theirs) and prevent malicious transitional beings and spirits from crossing into our world. They can assist with spiritual healing. Most transitional species will appear in their true form – whether in your dreams, visions, or in pictures and symbols linked to them – and which you keep seeing all around you.

Universal Spiritual Energy

Some psychics don't hear, see, or sense signals from a particular spirit. This may be a transitional period, or you may never be able to rely on one guide. However, you may be able to tap into the universal spiritual energy. It doesn't matter whether you feel this energy emerging from nature or the universe itself. If you can tune into its frequency, you'll be able to sense how it permeates your senses and surrounds everything around you. It ties you to every other part of itself. This means it helps you access information without relying on a particular being. You'll always have access to this energy – you'll just have to reach for it. This is similar to how you connect to your higher self. Except, here, the wisdom comes from the outside. If you can't find your spiritual guide and can't access the spiritual wisdom you need through your subconscious either, the universal spiritual energy may be the best source to turn to. You may gain access to your guide through this energy, or you may continue relying on it if you still don't feel connected to a guide in the future. Even if you form a connection with a specific spirit, the universal spiritual energy can help deepen your bond.

Chapter 7: Methods of Spirit Communication

Continuing with the topic of spirits and guides, this chapter discusses the practical side of spiritual communication. In the following pages, you'll learn plenty of user-friendly methods and rituals for getting in touch with spirits and guides, from meditation to divination to journaling. You'll also receive valuable tips for honing your intuition and training yourself to become better at spiritual communication. Spiritual energy is on higher planes, so it may take some time and practice to achieve the desired results. That being said, when you start enjoying the fruits of your labor, all your efforts will be worth it.

Spiritual energy is on higher planes, so it may take some time and practice to achieve the desired results.
https://www.pexels.com/photo/assorted-tarot-cards-on-table-3088369/

Start Asking the Spirits

The best way to begin developing an ability for spiritual communication is to start asking the spirits. If you're at the dawn of your spiritual journey, your daily tasks may distract you from knowing that you have higher powers to rely on. By getting into the habit of asking, you're reminding yourself that you always have access to guidance – whether it comes from within you, your spiritual guide, a deity, or the universe itself. Besides, the more times you ask them for any form of assistance, the more gifts they'll bestow upon you.

To help you get started, consider how spirits and guides can help you achieve your goals. Make a list of 3-5 issues you need help with, and choose a being whom you want to ask for assistance. Ask one question at a time and wait for the answering message. When you get your answer, take your time to ponder it so you can resolve your issue successfully. After this, you can move on to asking the next question. Beginners should start with blood ancestors or recently passed loved ones, as they're typically the easiest to contact due to your shared relationship. If you've already established a relationship with a particular spiritual guide, you can ask them, too. Whether you prefer to ask the spirits after focusing on your question for a few minutes or do it within the scope of an elaborate ritual, make sure you're being polite and respectful. Present the issue as an offering, invite the spirit or guide to help, and express your gratitude for the assistance you might receive in advance. Making this a daily habit will enable you to establish a clear line of communication with your spiritual allies.

Ask for Specific Guides

Asking for specific guides will make it much easier to reach them. It will also help you avoid encountering unhelpful or malicious spirits and creatures. Consider what kind of guidance you need and who may help you with it. Be specific and think about who will offer the highest truth on that particular occasion, as this is the spirit you want to align yourself with. Don't overthink it – most of the time, you'll know who to call on instinctively. And if you truly need their help, they'll come. Once you've established who to call, you can send a message anytime. Generally speaking, it's best not to wait until the problem escalates. Instead, tackle it while you only need a little help. As a beginner, you may have trouble focusing on maintaining a connection for an extended period. This is only exacerbated by stress, so try to avoid it by seeking spiritual assistance as soon as you detect a problem. Better yet, don't wait for it to arise at all. Talk to all your guides regularly, and when they notice you have a problem, the one you need will reach out to you.

Look Out for Signs

Sometimes, spirits and guides will contact you on their own – especially if they have meaningful information to share with you or want to warn you about something or someone. Make sure to keep all your senses open for their signs. The same applies to situations where you're reaching out to them. While you wait for their response, you'll need to be vigilant and pay special attention to your environment. The simplest way to do this is to stop whatever you were doing for a few minutes from time to time and become more present. Empty your mind and explore what your senses tell you about your environment. This grounding helps slow your vibrations to align with the energetic signals the spirits send you, allowing you to notice them. Whether you'll hear, see, sense, or simply know you've received the wisdom depends on the scope of your abilities. Remember, it can appear everywhere around you, but it can also come from within you.

Align Your Energies with Mediation and Prayer

Whether you have trouble defining your problem or focusing on your intention, it can hinder your ability to reach out to your spiritual allies. A short meditation session can help you regain focus and discover what you need help with. It will also allow you to align your spiritual energy with the energy of the spirits and guides. Start by finding a tranquil space where you won't be distracted. Turn your focus away from your conscious thoughts so your mind isn't occupied with worries and to-do lists. Then, start focusing on your breath. Take a few deep breaths and feel how the air travels through your body. When you feel relaxed, visualize a warm, golden light enveloping you from all sides. Picture the guide you want to call on, and feel their energy meeting you through the light around you. Be positive and grateful for the energy that will now allow you to ask anything you want. Then, proceed to ask your question or seek assistance. Repeat this process for 5-20 minutes every day or whenever you feel disconnected from the spiritual energies.

Alternatively, you can say a prayer, with or without meditation. You can recite one before or after meditative exercises, or simply when sitting at your altar, or anywhere you get the chance to reflect on spiritual communication. Although it doesn't have to be a long prayer, don't forget to give thanks. You can say something like this:

"Thank you, my guide, for illuminating my path and showing me what to do regarding my health/work/relationship. I ask you to keep leading me in the right direction, and thank you for whatever blessing you may give, for I know I will need it for sure."

Build an Altar

While altars are traditionally associated with religious practice, you don't have to follow a specific belief system to build a dedicated sacred space. Altars are also ideal for spiritual practices because they allow you to focus your energy and intention on what you're doing. Even building a simple altar and decorating it with a few meaningful items can take your mind off other stressful tasks. An altar can be any flat surface you want to dedicate to your practice. How you set it up depends on its purpose. If you work with deities, you'll need to represent them by their symbols, favorite offerings, and color correspondences. If the purpose of the altar is to honor your ancestors, you can decorate it with their favorite items, food, drink, colors, photograph, or personal possession. To adorn an altar for spiritual guides and animal spirits, you'll have to get to know them first. That way, you can use items they cherish and find inviting enough to come to your side. You can use your altar to seek help, express your gratitude, meditate, journal, or engage in any other spiritual practice that allows you to reach higher planes.

Use Divination

As we've explored in a previous chapter, you can use several divination tools for spiritual communication. Tarot cards, Oracle cards, and Norse runes are just some of the most popular methods. Each offers a simple way to contact your guide and ask for an answer, assistance, alignment, or whatever you need to attain your future goals. The tools you use will serve as conductors for the messages flowing back and forth between you and your guides. If you've never used divination tools, you may want to try several of them to see which ones fit you best. You can make your inquiry as simple or as complex as you want. For starters, ask a simple question by holding one object in your hand (one card, rune, or another tool). After closing your eyes, shift your focus to the energy surrounding the object in your hands. Take a few deep breaths in the meantime to help you relax and ground yourself. Then, ask your guides or spirits for their assistance, and open your mind to the answers you'll receive.

Try Journaling

Writing to your spirit guides is another way to contact them. While you can simply write on a piece of paper, you may want to turn this into a regular habit. If so, get a journal for penning your thoughts and wishes regarding spiritual help. This practice will allow you to revisit them in the future and track your progress in sharpening your psychic abilities. If you want to use the journal to get in touch with your guides, you may want to start with an invitation and expression of gratitude, such as follows:

"Thank you, my guide, for revealing the wisdom you wanted me to have. I welcome you to come to me in these lines."

Then, take a deep breath and let your thoughts flow. Write them as they come, whether they're random ideas, visions, short or long stories, or anything you haven't thought of before. They may all contain a message your guide wants you to have. So don't second guess anything, and instead, just record them. Your guides may also choose to speak directly to you while you're in the process of writing. You should generally write in the first person; if you've suddenly switched to the second person, your guide may be writing these lines. Or your handwriting may change when they take over. After you're done, read over what you've written and try to interpret their message.

Another way to communicate with spirits through writing is dream journaling. Instead of writing down your thoughts during waking hours, you're recording your dreams. Recite a quick prayer of gratitude before going to bed and ask your question. Place your journal and a pen on your nightstand. That way, you can record the messages you've received in your dreams as soon as you wake up before they disappear from your conscious mind.

Hold Silent Gatherings

One of the best ways to honor a spiritual ally is to hold a silent gathering, usually dinner, for them. In some traditions, this is done as a family gathering to honor past ancestors. However, you can also do this to reach out to any spirit or guide by yourself. Choose a sacred space you've cleansed beforehand to ensure only positive energy surrounds you. Prepare the spirit's favorite meals and drinks and leave the place at the head of the table empty for them. Serve the meal to all participants (including the soul you've invited) and sit opposite them. When you've finished your meal, offer a thought to the spirit. This could be a few lines expressing gratitude, a question, or anything you may want to say to them at that moment. Do this silently, and leave the room in the same way.

Appreciate Your Guides

As we've seen, from time to time, you'll want to show appreciation for your guides and spirits. This will help you keep your relationship strong. Apart from thanking them for the blessings they send your way, you'll also want to give thanks for any opportunities and assignments that helped your spiritual development. You may find these challenging at times, but it's critical to let the spirits know you're grateful for them – and that they're welcome to send more wisdom your way.

Make an Offering

Whether you do it at your altar, during a gathering, or any other way, making an offering is a superb way to show appreciation toward a particular spirit or guide. Remember that the offering doesn't even have to be a physical item. Surrendering a piece of information about your problem works just as well. Your spiritual allies won't mind even if you do it to vent or give yourself a break. It's like getting to know a friend. They want to know how to help you, and you are giving them a tool to do so by offering something about yourself. They'll also be grateful because they know that your offering is a show of trust.

Ask the Spirits and Guides for Their Names

If you're working with your ancestors or the soul of a departed loved one, pet, or anyone you knew by name, you probably won't have trouble finding a connection with them. Names have an incredibly powerful effect on forging bonds between souls. Like you would when meeting a new person in the physical world, learning each other's names is often enough to break the ice and get the conversation going. However, if you don't know the name of the spirit or guide you're trying to call (or who is trying to reach you), everything becomes more challenging. If this happens, feel free to ask their names and offer yours in return. They may already know yours, but saying it will make it more likely that they reveal theirs, too. Focus on your intention, and ask for their names in your thoughts. The first name that comes to you is the name of the spirit who answered your query.

Additional Tips

Trusting your psychic ability is perhaps the most challenging task you'll ever face as a new medium. You'll need to fully believe that your gift will allow you to call on your guide and interpret their messages. So, if you have trouble with spiritual communication, you should look into yourself to see why. Do you trust your instincts, your gateway to your psychic gifts? If not, practice honing them through simple exercises until you become confident in your abilities. The more you practice this, the more frequently you'll be able to receive spiritual messages and allow them to guide you through the journey of life. Your gifts and the wisdom you receive can be helpful to others as well.

You'll also learn to trust your spiritual guide. While many psychics go above and beyond to make their guides trust them, they still have trouble returning the sentiment. If you doubt their ability to guide you, your bond will never be strong enough. Remember, spirits and guides possess a higher knowledge. They're aware of plans and fates you have no knowledge of, and the ones willing to become your allies are there to protect, guide, and love you. Don't try to control the situation by focusing on the outcome you think you want them to lead you toward. Let them decide, and you won't regret it.

Another tip to facilitate your spiritual communication session is to ground yourself afterward. Spiritual energy is empowering, but the energy shift you feel when receiving a message can be unsettling. It can prevent you from interpreting the information correctly and make you fearful of the next session. To avoid this, perform a quick grounding exercise after each session. You can do this by taking off your shoes and feeling the found with the soles of your feet, sitting on a rock in the park, or simply finding a patch of nature and taking in its stillness. Do anything that works as a reminder of your presence in this world and your human experiences.

Chapter 8: Journey into the Astral World

In this dedicated chapter, you'll learn everything you need to know about astral projection. You'll understand what the astral body and plane are and find out more about the idea behind astral projection. You'll discover various benefits of this practice, as well as some other ways in which you can achieve out-of-body experiences. Finally, you'll find a step-by-step guide on how to perform astral projection.

Everything that happens beyond our normal level of consciousness, including our dreams and out-of-body experiences, occurs in the astral body.
https://www.pexels.com/photo/man-love-people-woman-6014742/

What Is an Astral Body?

Yogic philosophers believe that we have three bodies (the physical, astral, and causal) that operate as the instruments of the soul. For starters, the astral body is considered the physical body's equivalent in the spiritual plane and isn't as prominent as the physical body.

Our **astral body** is subtler than the physical body and contains the "astral tubes" or "nadis," energy channels that carry the universal life force known as the prana. A person's mind and senses also lie in the astral body.

The **causal body** is the subtlest and can be found within the physical and astral bodies. It's the body that carries a person from their current life to their following reincarnation. This body also includes a record of a yogi's actions, experiences, and mental imprints in all plights of existence.

Our emotions and imagination are all channeled into the physical body from the astral body. The astral body is believed to detach from the physical one whenever we lose consciousness, sleep, or take any type of drugs or pain-relieving medications. That way, we don't feel any emotions or pain. The idea of the astral body entails that practitioners believe in the existence of the afterlife. This is because it is believed that our physical bodies are carried into the other realms via this vehicle after we die.

Everything that happens beyond our normal level of consciousness – including our dreams and out-of-body experiences – occurs in the astral body. This is why you must increase your awareness of this medium by meditating, partaking in Shamanic practices, or practicing any other method that can help you enter a trance state. Some yogis suggest that the astral body can appear as an aura floating around the physical body. Even though the astral body keeps changing colors, it's comparable to ether and is believed to be tied to the physical body's navel by a silver string.

What Is the Astral Plane?

Plato was the first to come up with the philosophy of the astral plane. He posited that planetary heavens exist in this realm and is home to the astral body. By the 19th century, the term astral plane was used by Theosophists and neo-Rosicrucians.

The concept of the astral plane was expanded upon by oriental, medieval, esoteric, and classical philosophies, as well as other religions and belief systems. This plane is thought to be traversed by human souls before they're born and after they die. Angels, spirits, and other divine beings reside in this realm. Some people believe that the astral plane is where the spirits live permanently after they die. They believe it's where the soul reunites with God and associates it with heaven.

What Is Astral Projection?

Many ancient cultures have conducted this esoteric practice known as astral projection. Nowadays, yogis and other spiritualists believe it can help them enrich their spiritual practices. They also use it as a self-help tool. In reality, astral projection sounds a lot more complicated than it is. While some aspects of transcending your body are bound to be challenging, you can master the process thanks to dedication and practice.

Astral projection is an *intentional* out-of-body experience. These unique occurrences are mostly associated with lucid dreaming. Simply put, out-of-body experiences alter the brain's perception of your physical body. Your brain may be convinced that a part of your being is exiting your body. However, this is only because your brain's body schema at that moment is foreign – you, therefore, get the feeling that your consciousness is separated from your physical body for the duration of the experience.

Yogis who practice astral projection believe that the soul detaches from the body during an out-of-body experience. As such, it takes off to another realm of consciousness, which is essentially the astral plane. While science has not yet agreed that a person's soul can exist separately from the physical body, not all spiritual phenomena can be explained or supported by tangible facts. Many people think that out-of-body experiences are a way of proving that a soul exists. However, this level of consciousness is simply an alternative means for brain function.

You can expect to be in a dreamlike state when practicing astral projection; the only difference is that you'd still be conscious, lucid, and in full control of your actions and decisions. You can also achieve this level of consciousness through self-hypnosis or meditation. Once you access this state, you can use your mind to transcend your astral body to other planes, allowing you to explore your mental renditions of all dimensions, time, and space.

What You Can Do with Astral Projection

- **Experience Spiritual Growth.** You can expand your consciousness by practicing astral projection. It gives you the opportunity to visit the plane of the afterlife before death, offering validation for what comes after you die. It allows you to experience the continuous nature of our consciousness and souls.

- **Work On Personal Growth.** Out-of-body experiences can help you visualize your goals as they unfold. They also promote creative thinking in problem-solving. These experiences can help you in your professional life, too. Fiction writers can benefit from visualizing the plot and action in their stories. Astral projection requires you to train your imagination, which can benefit artists, designers, and performers. You can use these experiences to get clearer divination answers.

- **Enrich Your Learning Experiences.** Astral projection serves as an opportunity to grasp a deeper understanding of the world and embark on higher learning journeys. It's an opportunity to start observing the world with an inner vision so you can understand the mystery behind hidden realities. Out-of-body experiences can help you deeply explore the relationship between your physical body and other levels of consciousness and energetic fields. It also helps you understand the relationship between other planes and the physical world and that of our levels of consciousness and the surrounding energies. Astral projections can also help you discern the role of a person's emotions in any given interaction.

- **Understand Spiritual Immortality.** You can fully grasp the concept of spiritual continuity by insulating your consciousness and astral body from your physical body. You can also find out what it's like to experience numerous aspects of the physical world through an astral lens. You can use this experience to gather deeper insight into shamanic practice, divination methods, and other forms of magic. Many people seek out-of-body experiences because they allow them to experience several emotions and activities like romance, intimacy, sex, and love from astral perspectives.

- **Try Time Travel.** Astral projection allows you to remember or even engage in first-time experiences of the past. You can read the Akashic records, which are a collection of all thoughts, feelings, words, actions, emotions, events, and intentions that have happened in the past, are happening right now and will happen in the future. You can seek answers to any questions you have from the Akashic records. Out-of-body experiences enable you to explore history as it was and discover your relationships in the previous reincarnation. You can embark on as many astral adventures as you want.

- **Learn to Help In the Inner Planes.** Those types of experiences teach you to spread goodwill, positivity, and peace in the inner planes. It also allows you to help and heal those who are ill, people who are dying, and souls who have just died. Practicing astral projection can teach you to diagnose health conditions and work with healing energies on psychological and physical levels. Out-of-body experiences supplement your physical vision with an astral point of view.

- **Contact Divine Beings.** Through astral projection, you can spiritually communicate with spirits, angels, spirit guides, souls that passed, and other divine entities. This practice increases your psychokinetic and clairvoyant abilities and allows you to determine where lost people, pets, documents, or belongings are located. You can see your chakras and certain thought forms, which is the process of manifesting your desires.

- **Experience Astral Travel.** Astral projection allows you to travel without moving your physical location through Earth and the world beyond. Whether you wish to see your friends or explore remote places, you can do it all via out-of-body experience. You can venture into the past and explore the future. You can see past your past and future reincarnations or selves. You can travel through space to see the planets, the moon, and even the astral plane. Astral projection can take you to places you'd otherwise never be able to access, such as the inside of an active volcano, the Earth's core, or the ocean's depths.

Our consciousness is far more extensive than we think. We don't always realize that a part of ourselves is constantly encouraging us to channel conscious things out of ones that are currently unconscious to make more of ourselves. Now, what does it mean to be able to make something conscious out of what's already unconscious? How do we get in touch with this inner calling? We simply have to truly believe that we really are more than how we perceive ourselves – so we can consciously go beyond the limitations of who we are.

This way of thinking is the essence of the workings of astral projection and how you can use it to your benefit. All humans are a lot more than just physical entities. Our being is a lot more intricate and deeply layered than just a physical body, a soul, and a mind.

Other Out-of-Body Experiences

You can explore the power of consciousness over the physical world through self-hypnosis, hypnosis, and other types of meditation. Those practices are meant to induce certain physical sensations that can help us enter a higher level of trance. A trance state or altered level of consciousness is a dreamlike, semi-conscious state. Lucid dreaming is considered a form of astral projection because lucid dreamers are conscious during their sleep and have some control over their dreams.

There are five different altered levels of consciousness, ranging from very light trance to very deep trance. The first is a state that causes you to become more aware of your physical sensations, thoughts, and emotions, and can be achieved through mindful meditation. A very deep trance is characterized by the total loss of one's consciousness (like being in a coma or experiencing dreamless sleep). When conducting any type of spiritual work, such as astral projection, it's best to operate those two extremes. The second (light trance), third (medium trance), and fourth (deep trance) are generally the best-altered levels of consciousness to work with, as they yield the best results depending on your intentions.

Besides entering a trance state, you can use hypnosis to give rise to complex response patterns. By doing so, you can learn to control your pain, strengthen your immune system, or decrease tension in your body. This is how powerful your consciousness is – you can use it to induce any biological effect. Meditation, biofeedback, and hypnosis can all be used to encourage your physical body to alter some of its functions and even start new ones.

You can also change your brain function by detaching it from your physical being so it can operate independently. Our being is not limited to our physical body. Biology is merely a tool that facilitates spiritual growth and allows you to explore the physical realm.

How to Perform Astral Projection

Step One: Prepare Yourself

Experienced practitioners may be able to induce astral projection just by clearing their minds and lying in bed before visualizing their astral body exiting their physical being. If you're just starting, you can search for a guided online meditation to help you *ground yourself.* For this to work, you must be in a very calm state and release any expectations or attachments to a certain result. Don't attach yourself to the idea of having to project astrally, as this can create unnecessary tension and anxiety. Instead, you should feel relaxed and look forward to experiencing new sensations throughout the process.

Invariably, everyone's experience with astral projection will be different. You may come to realize unique things or discover that you feel comfortable using one method of astral projection over the other after a period of experimentation. That said, the basics of getting in touch with your astral body so you can access the astral plane are pretty much the same.

You can't do astral projection on-demand – there are specific steps you must follow first. Think of this as a prepping phase that allows you to tap into astral aspects of your consciousness.

It's always best to start by making meditation a regular part of your routine. It can be as simple as taking a couple of minutes at the start and end of your day for mental solitude if you don't already have a regular meditation routine. If you struggle to achieve mental clarity and peace on your own, you can experiment with guided meditation, crystals, incense, or meditation apps.

You can access a deeper trance state through self-hypnosis to connect with your astral body. Here's a brief guide on how to conduct self-hypnosis:

1. Change into comfortable clothing and find a quiet spot where you won't be interrupted.

2. Set your intention. In that case, your goal is astral projection.

3. Fixate your gaze on a focus point. You can light a candle and focus on its flame as a reference.

4. Draw your eyes shut and bring your awareness to your breathing. Shift your awareness to your breath every time your mind gets distracted. Notice any tension in your body and visualize it drifting away with your exhalations.

5. Visualize your idea of a happy place and remain there for a while.

6. Repeat a mantra that helps you ground yourself and feel calm.

7. Once you're completely calm, visualize your goal vividly. Imagine everything down to the smallest detail and engage all your senses.

8. Affirm your intention or goal.

9. When you're ready, prepare to exit your hypnotic state by picturing yourself inhaling energy from your surroundings and sending it back with each exhale. You feel lighter each time until your body returns to its normal state.

10. Count down from 10 and tell yourself that you'll open your eyes and feel energized once you reach 1.

Note: Some people prefer to use lucid dreaming as a tool to access an altered level of consciousness instead. This would be a good option if you already practice dream work.

Step Two: Get in Touch with Your Astral Body and the Astral Plane

As you're meditating, visualize your projecting self (imagine a nearly transparent version of you) leaving your physical body. You may not achieve the desired outcome the first few times, which is entirely normal. However, you'll eventually get there with thorough practice.

Step Three: Begin Astral Traveling

You're only ready to start astral traveling if you're confident in your ability to separate both your astral and physical bodies. You can test if you're all set by trying to observe your physical body from an etheric point of view.

Once you're prepared, you should think of a destination you want to visit or a goal you want to accomplish by being in the astral plane. You shouldn't allow yourself to meander around this plane with no clear intention.

Slowly bring yourself back to the present moment whenever you're ready. You should always cleanse your space after you're done astral projecting. Be careful not to leave any undesirable energies lingering around.

Now that you've read this chapter, you can use astral projection for spiritual growth, introspection, healing, and more. You'll be able to access the astral plane a lot more easily once you familiarize yourself with the process. Many seasoned yogis can connect with their astral selves and journey into the astral world by simply practicing meditation. Don't lose hope if you don't get there right away – and ... *trust the process.*

Chapter 9: Telepathy - Communicating without Words

This chapter explores the concept of telepathy in depth. Here, you'll come across a few real stories of how telepathic connections were used to save lives. You'll also find a step-by-step guide on sharpening your telepathic abilities and establishing a connection to send and receive messages.

We all have innate telepathic powers that we can channel.
https://www.pexels.com/photo/wood-man-love-people-6014745/

What Is Telepathy?

Face-to-face or phone call conversations, letters, e-mails, and text messages are among the first few things that come to mind when we think about communication. No one ever thinks about mental communication. If you're new to the world of spirituality and have never explored the concept of telepathy before, then images of magic tricks and superheroes probably cross your mind upon hearing the word "telepathy."

Believe it or not, you don't need a wand and a bunny in a hat to communicate with others mentally. No need to be a seasoned psychic, either. We all have innate telepathic powers that we can channel. While some people's telepathic gifts are quite prominent, others need to spend more time and energy to foster and manifest them more effectively. Our ability to connect with other people's consciousness is a generational ability passed down from our ancestors.

So, what is telepathy, really? Telepathy is often depicted as the ability to have a full-on, back-and-forth conversation with someone else. However, it involves sending or receiving emotions and thoughts to or from another person. It is one of the forms of ESP or extrasensory perception.

As you can infer, telepathy takes place from a distance. The two people don't have to be in the same place, and it doesn't require the involvement of other senses like touch, sight, or hearing. Telepathic activities can be broken down into numerous types. However, the following four are the most popular:

- **Communication:** Telepathic communication is a direct form of interaction with another person without having to speak to them.

- **Control:** This is the ability to control or influence a person's behaviors, actions, or thoughts.

- **Reading:** Telepathic reading is the power to sense or hear a person's thoughts.

- **Impressing:** This is the ability to ingrain a certain thought, image, or word into someone else's mind.

Telepathy is a power that extends beyond our basic level of consciousness. To fully understand this ability, you must get to know the inner workings of humans on a more profound level and be able to connect deeply with other people's consciousness.

This can be done if you think of everything inside your body as vibrating energies. Our bodies generate frequencies that can tune into the consciousness grids of others. If both energies align, a telepathic connection can be established. Once you get the hang of it, you'll find that this energetic alignment is as direct as any of the physical senses we use to communicate on a daily basis.

Twin Telepathy

Twin telepathy is a phenomenon we've seen on TV numerous times. There's a popular belief that twins can communicate without saying a word. Perhaps you've seen a set of twins always complete each other's sentences, or who can tell what the other is going to say or do next? Sometimes, this connection is so strong that an individual can tell whenever their twin is wounded, unwell, or sad. Much research has been conducted to explore the validity of twin telepathy.

A very popular story about a set of twins prevailed back in 2009. Gemma Houghton, who was 15 at the time, had saved her twin after she was sent a telepathic message telling her that her sister was in need of help. Houghton described the experience as a sixth sense. She was on her home's ground floor when she felt a sudden burst of anxiety. For some reason, she took this as a sign to go upstairs to check on her sister, somehow sensing that she was unwell. When she did, she found that Leanne, her twin, had lost consciousness. Gemma was able to pull her out of the bathtub, which was filled with water, and saved her with CPR. When she was taken to the hospital, the doctors said Leanne had suffered a seizure.

One of the several reasons why twins are thought to have natural telepathic connections is that they have identical energetic frequencies and grids of consciousness.

They were created, nurtured, born, and raised under the same conditions, which is why they have almost identical vibrational levels. They don't need to align themselves to each other's frequencies to connect – the step that requires the most effort already comes naturally to them.

Telepathic communication is still possible for those who don't have twins (or wish to connect with someone other than their twin). However, we'll need to work harder to tune into the targeted person's frequency.

While the process can sound incredibly complex, you may be surprised to find that you already exhibit some signs of telepathic powers.

Signs You Have Telepathic Abilities

If you're mature enough to read and understand this book, you've likely undergone many life experiences. What you don't know is that many of these experiences are telepathic. You may think you know so little about telepathy – you've never tried to fine-tune this ability before. However, upon reading this section, you'll find yourself recalling numerous experiences, some going as far back as your childhood, flooding through your mind.

Your Intuition and Telepathic Abilities Are Always in Play

One experience I vividly remember from my childhood involved a woman (who I believe had ill intentions). When I was around 10, the school bus used to drop me off at a stop that was 5 minutes away from my home on foot. Although the walk sometimes felt exhausting after a long day at school, I mostly enjoyed it. It was the most peaceful time of my day, away from annoying schoolmates and my loud baby brother.

The night before a particularly long and tiring day, I dreamt that a woman in a red coat wanted to kidnap me. I used to have nightmares every now and then as a child. However, this dream felt strangely intense. It came with such vivid emotions that I couldn't shake them off the following morning.

I had forgotten about it by the time the bus dropped me off. I was feeling so sleepy that the walk home was rather burdensome. I remember tripping over right when I thought I couldn't wait to get home. Now, guess who suddenly appeared right over me? A lady in a red coat. She held her hand out to help me up and said, "Do you need a ride? Poor kid. You look very tired." I jumped up on my feet and sprinted home as fast as I could.

You're probably wondering what this has to do with telepathy. The answer can be broken down into two portions:

1. I was a child. Children give in to their instincts more easily and naturally than adults do. We think over and over before we act, even when we feel an inexplicable pull toward a certain path. We're all familiar with the "should I follow my heart or my head?" dilemma. This is why children welcome their telepathic powers as they are. They don't spend much time thinking things

over. Trusting our instincts allows us to align with the frequencies of others more easily. When we let loose, we can gain insight into what a person has in store for us.

2. It was a dream. Telepathy usually happens during our dreams. This is because when we are asleep, we enter a very deep trance state, which makes our brain waves vibrate at a frequency that makes them responsive to a large amount of information. Since all human events are recorded in the Akashic records, the dream I had about the lady in the red coat was already happening in real-time.

Other Signs You Have Telepathic Powers

Your Third-Eye Is Trying to Tell You Something

Do you usually get headaches around the center of your forehead? Perhaps you feel tension or tingling sensations around that area. If you do, then this is a sign that you may have telepathic powers. Sensations in the center of your forehead mean one of two things: either you're receiving telepathic energy, or your third-eye chakra is expanding. In any case, you shouldn't worry at all. Work on sharpening your telepathic abilities and opening your third eye; these odd sensations will decline over time.

You're Highly Empathetic

Empathy and telepathy are very closely related. While telepathy is the ability to read or influence other people's thoughts, empathy is the tendency to pick up on other people's feelings and deeply relate to them. Empaths mostly receive waves of energy and emotions rather than give them off. Telepathic individuals, however, can send and receive energies and messages. Honing your empathic abilities can allow you to develop them into telepathic ones.

You Feel Oddly Close to the Spiritual Realm

If you're reading this book, this is likely a sign that you may be telepathic. Not everyone feels compelled to explore the world of spirituality. That said, those who do are likely in possession of gifts. Your consciousness already knows everything that you are. It realizes that you have gifts that you need to foster, even if you haven't fully realized so yourself. You should explore your telepathic abilities if you've always felt the inexplicable need to connect with your spirit guides or access the Akashic records. People who are truly aligned with the natural world are also typically gifted.

You're Quick to Tell When Someone Is Lying

Can you easily tell whenever someone is not being truthful or is only giving you half of the story? Telepathic individuals have a claircognizant aspect to their powers, namely, the ability to sense when someone is presenting inaccurate information.

You Receive Other People's Direct Thoughts

If you're clairaudient, you may also be unknowingly telepathic if you hear other people's thoughts or have a feeling that you just know what they're thinking; your chances of possessing telepathic powers are high. This sign, however, is mainly relevant to those who've worked on developing and refining their gift.

You Can Transmit Messages to Other People

Telepathy is two-way communication. Besides being able to hear what others are thinking, you should be able to transmit messages to them, influence their thoughts, or ingrain a particular word or thought in their minds. This ability is also relevant to experienced individuals.

Why Use Telepathy?

Possessing telepathic abilities sounds rather "cool." However, this gift is also incredibly beneficial. Often, we find ourselves at a loss for words. Do you ever feel like you want to say something but don't know how to say it? Perhaps you can't say it at all.

How often have you wished you could call your ex-partner and tell them everything in your heart? Whether you want to scream at them for hurting you or wish to tell them that you still love them deeply, it's not the right thing to do. Telepathy, in cases like these, can be a very handy tool.

Honing your telepathic skills can allow your higher self to deliver messages you can't express in the material world. This can pave the way for closure, forgiveness, and even deeper connections.

You may feel silly or anxious at first. Be that as it may, it helps to think of your telepathic abilities as a sixth sense that you're still getting the hang of. Say you were raised as a bilingual child, but for some reason, you stopped using your second language ever since you turned 5. Twenty years later, you won't be able to speak the language, but it won't sound completely foreign to you. You just need to familiarize yourself with it and slowly start remembering it.

Telepathy is a vehicle that can get you in touch with other people, animals, celestial bodies, and nature. The more you embrace your gifts, the more you'll pick up on the messages conveyed by your ancestors and spirit guides.

How to Hone Your Telepathic Powers

Like other psychic practices, establishing a telepathic link with another person is a skill that requires plenty of work and practice. You must approach the process with a systematic plan, which is why doing it on your own can be quite overwhelming. Fortunately, the following guide is a great starting point:

Practice Meditation Techniques

Practicing meditation can help you enter a light trance state to prepare yourself for telepathic endeavors. If you have a meditation practice that you feel comfortable doing, make sure to incorporate it into your daily routine. If not, you can experiment with various techniques until you find those that don't feel forced. Worrying about whether you're doing it right defies the whole purpose of meditation – clearing your mind. You can also look up guided meditation videos or podcasts if you wish. Aside from clearing your mind, meditation teaches you how to intentionally focus your mind. It also trains you to redirect your thoughts whenever unwanted ideas enter your brain.

Imagine that you're working on an important project. Whenever an idea comes to mind, someone barges into your office to ask you a question. You start to formulate an idea, but someone enters again, asking you to sign off on a document. Essentially, this is exactly what your experience with attempting a telepathic practice would be like if you fail to clear your mind beforehand.

Pinpoint Your Strength

Like every other endeavor, some people are more skilled in a certain area. When it comes to telepathy, some practitioners are stronger senders, while others are better receivers. Keep in mind that neither strength trumps the other. It depends on what you naturally gravitate toward, and you'll work with both skills either way. However, it helps to start working with what you're more skilled at. Once you master that skill, you can start working on the other one.

If you're wondering whether you're a stronger sender or receiver, ask yourself which of the following situations you are most likely to find yourself in:

1. You call a friend that you haven't contacted in a while just to hear them say, "I was just going to call you," or "you've been on my mind lately."

2. A person comes to mind just a few moments before they call you out of the blue.

If the first situation sounds more relevant, you're likely a receiver. You're more skilled at sending messages if it's the latter.

Try Receiving Messages

Each time you talk to someone, make a conscious effort to tune into their thoughts. Do your best to identify their thoughts, regardless of what they say. This will likely be received as a feeling – you may "just know" that this is what they're thinking about. If you wish, you can practice with someone you trust first. Ask them to think of any topic, so you can try to figure it out. Avoid working with someone who's doubtful about this entire process, as they may cause a vibrational block.

Try Sending Messages

Always remember that you can't decode a message unless you're consciously making an effort to receive one. You can strengthen this ability by practicing the "hello-goodbye" method each time you walk into any room. After you say hello to everyone the way you usually do, say "goodbye" rather than "hello" in your mind. Pay close attention to their facial reaction. Are they taken aback or surprised? If they appear to be confused, then they likely received your message.

Research Telepathic Exercises and Practice Them

Luckily, there are numerous telepathic exercises available online. Find a few and test them out. You can start with this exercise:

1. Find a trusted someone to practice with. Use any deck of cards that you wish to work with.

2. Ask the other person to stay in a different room. Make sure that neither of you can see the other.

3. Draw four random cards and arrange them in front of you. Keep them facing down so you can't read them.

4. Flip any card over and draw in deep breaths. Relax and focus on the image on the card and consciously send this mental image to your practice partner.

5. As the receiver, they should open themselves to the message and accept it. Once they identify it, they should send it back to the practice.

6. Switch roles so you can practice the receiver's role as well.

When performing this exercise, make sure to lean into your intuition. Don't second-guess yourself, and proceed as your instinct tells you.

Telepathy in Love

Establishing a telepathic connection with your partner is similar to establishing one with your twin. Those who fall in love and build profound connections with each other typically have similar vibrational frequencies.

In the winter of 2012, a middle-aged woman called Tracy Granger was driving on frozen roads. Tragically, her car crashed into a block of ice, which caused it to fall down a humungous mountain. She was left with severe fractures in numerous areas of her body, including her ribs and neck. Granger was unable to seek help and knew that no one would be able to find her.

As a last resort, she communicated telepathically with her husband, who immediately felt her need for help. A few hours later, Granger was found lying in the snow at the site of the accident. Even though she was severely injured, she recovered fully.

Now that you know everything about telepathy, you're ready to explore your abilities and start honing your skills. Remember that you already have all the tools you need to get in touch with consciousness to transmit and receive telepathic messages.

Chapter 10: Psychic Healing and Self-Care

As multi-dimensional beings, humans possess psychic abilities. These supernatural abilities come from the spirit that inhabits your body. Think about it – you are a physical being and have physical abilities and needs. You're also a spiritual being, so you have spiritual capabilities and needs. These abilities differ from one person to another. No matter how different these are, they still have the same form: energy. When you exercise these psychic abilities, you also extract energy. Naturally, the more fuel you use, the less you have.

As multi-dimensional beings, humans possess psychic abilities.
https://www.pexels.com/photo/healthy-man-people-woman-6944691/

If you've spent a lot of time using your psychic abilities, you may have felt a bit tired afterward. Not taking a break or some time out to feed your spirit will eventually drain you out. If you've felt like your energy has dimmed, then you may be interested in knowing when and how to self-care so you can avoid a spiritual burn-out. This final chapter suggests various ways you can practice self-care and psychically heal yourself and others.

Psychic Healing

In essence, spiritual healing is comparable to visiting a therapist or going to the dentist. It's simply a healing session where you or your healer will replace the negative with the positive. There are different reasons one should be spiritually healed; perhaps just a regular session where you nourish your soul or for protection if you feel spiritually attacked or drained. Although endless factors lead to a healing session, the reasons are not as important as the *symptoms.*

Recognizing the symptoms will lead you to the root of the issue – besides, the faster you point out the symptoms, the faster you will heal. If you're psychically drained, you'll most likely experience fluctuations in your intuition. Struggling with listening to your intuition is another telling sign. You may also feel like your empathy has been negatively affected. This can manifest as ambivalence about people, animals, plants, or anything you care about. Losing focus in meditation is also another sign that you're psychically drained. If you were spiritually attacked, your root and sacral chakra would be affected the most. That is to say, you'll most likely suffer from unexplainable fatigue and may struggle with feeling safe in your body or out in the world.

Now that you know what to look out for, it's time to explore different methods to help you overcome this psychic mishap. In this dedicated section, you'll learn about herbs, breathwork, and various methods that can help you overcome this hurdle.

Herbs

Herbs are versatile ingredients you can use to heal and protect yourself and others. Their incredible properties can be used in various ways. For example, you can start with simple exercises like saging your house. Since sage has cleansing properties, it can clear the negative energy that's occupying a place or shrouding a person's aura.

First and foremost, open your windows. It's vital to aerate the space so that the negative energy can exit it. Get a sage bundle or sage leaves and safely set it afire to sage your house, especially your bedroom. Make sure you leave the burning sage in the space where you spend the most time. If you're healing someone, then draw a circle around them with sage smoke. Envision the smoke ridding the negative energy and ask the person you're healing to do the same. Rosemary also has remarkable cleansing properties, so you can burn it next to the sage for a more potent effect. Here are other herbs with cleansing properties:

- Parsley
- Cilantro
- Peppermint
- Holy basil

Sometimes, the negative energies in our lives can manifest as disturbing dreams or nightmares. Luckily, some herbs ensure a good night's sleep and keep your bad dreams at bay. These notably include:

- Thyme
- Lavender
- Chamomile
- Bay laurel
- Juniper

These herbs can be used in a variety of ways. You can burn them and ask them to clear the negative energy that's been haunting you and protect you during your sleep. If you don't wish to burn them, place the herb of choice in a small bag and slide it underneath your pillow. Set your intentions with the herbs, then go to sleep as usual. You can apply these methods with a friend who's also been struggling with a similar issue. Simply hand them an herb bag and give them clear instructions on how to use it.

Aromatherapy

The practice of aromatherapy can help you heal while experiencing joyful and relaxing states of consciousness. You can use aromatherapy while meditating, sleeping, dancing, visualizing, or relaxing after a long day.

You can use a candle diffuser or an electric diffuser. If you don't have either of them, then create a simple makeshift diffuser. Boil water in a pot and put your essential oils in. Take the pot to your room of choice and enjoy the aromatic experience.

Below, you'll find several essential oils recipes for your inner and psychic healing. To ensure a successful outcome, repeat words of affirmation as you inhale the aromatic scents. Draft positive affirmations that align with your healing experience.

For example, suppose your goal is psychic healing. In that case, you can repeat phrases such as: "As I breathe in this air, I am spiritually healing" or "My spirit is healing from all that is negative; my spirit has regained its positive energy." Use these statements as inspiration to draft your own for optimal, personalized results.

Healing Essential Oils

Recipe 1:

- 180 ml water
- 2 drops of Peppermint
- 3 drops of Eucalyptus
- 3 drops of Lavender
- 3 drops of Lemon

Recipe 2:

- Empty spray bottle
- 20 drops of Orange
- 40 drops of Lavender
- 40 drops of Frankincense
- ⅓ cup of Honey
- ⅓ cup of Avocado oil
- ⅓ Castile soap

Recipe 3:

- 180 ml water
- 1 drop of German Chamomile
- 4 drops of Lavender

- 4 drops of Orange

Recipe 4:
- 180 ml water
- 2 drops of German Chamomile
- 4 drops of Cedarwood
- 4 drops of Lavender

Breathwork

Breathwork is a broad term that refers to mindful breathing exercises. It's so powerful that it can alter the mind, body, and soul states. According to recent scientific research, sustained breathwork can heal the nervous system and effectively decrease anxiety, anger, and depression while promoting relaxation and alertness in the body (Zaccaro et al., 2018).

Various types of breathwork have healing properties. Go over the list below and check in with yourself to see which ones you'd like to try first. That said, it's important to note that breathwork can be dangerous for people with heart issues and pregnant women, so use this method mindfully and carefully.

Mindful Breathing

Mindful breathing is effective technique spiritualists use all the time. It's also known as the breath focus technique. This type of breathwork revolves around words of affirmation and visualization. The images you'll see in your mind's eye, accompanied by affirmations and breathwork, can psychically heal you.

Instructions:
1. Lie down or sit in a meditative pose.
2. Observe your breathing rhythm.
3. Do not change it, simply go on with it.
4. Place your palms on your abdomen and take a deep breath (your abdomen should be moving with your breath).
5. Now, switch between your regular and deep breathing a few times.
6. Notice how both of them differ from the other.
7. Take two shallow breaths.
8. Now, take two deep ones.

9. Place your palms below your stomach and let your stomach relax.

10. Witness how it inflates and deflates with your breathing.

11. Now, sigh every time you exhale.

12. Begin your visualization journey. Picture yourself healing from the inside out, imagine yourself feeling content and relaxed, or whatever image brings you joy.

13. You can also start reciting your words of affirmation. For example: *"I am psychically healing. I am spiritually healed."*

14. As you inhale deeply, picture yourself inhaling healing air that cures your insides.

15. As you exhale, picture the negativity exiting your body.

16. When you're done, reflect on how you're feeling in the moment.

Belly Breathing

This method is known as diaphragmatic breathing. It's commonly used to treat **PTSD**, trauma, and insomnia. Traumatic experiences greatly affect you mentally, emotionally, spiritually, and physically. Trauma gets stored in the body, which affects your chakras and causes an imbalance in your spiritual well-being. Diaphragmatic breathing helps you release trauma from the body and gradually heal from it.

Instructions:

1. Sit on comfortable pillows or lie down on a soft surface, like a yoga mat.

2. Feel the tension in your shoulders and relax them.

3. Place the palm of your dominant hand on your chest.

4. Put the other palm on your stomach.

5. Inhale slowly through your nostrils and feel the air entering your body all the way down to your stomach.

6. Feel the air moving the hand on your stomach.

7. Contract your abdominal muscles.

8. Exhale through the mouth.

9. Apply pressure on your stomach and notice how it falls as you exhale.

10. As you inhale and exhale, try to keep the chest still.

11. The only organ that should be moving is your stomach.

12. Repeat this cycle as many times as needed for the best results.

Pranayama Breathwork: Alternate Nose Breathing

Pranayama breathwork is a yoga breathing exercise. Yogis use this method to cleanse the body of unwanted energies and refill it with new, refreshing ones. Alternate nose breathing is one of the exercises used in Pranayama breathwork. It also has healing powers and rids the body of anxiety and stress. Make sure you follow the method correctly for effective results.

Instructions:

1. Sit in a comfortable position.
2. Cross your legs.
3. Place your right hand on your nose and your left palm on your left knee.
4. Exhale.
5. Apply pressure with your right thumb on your right nostril.
6. Inhale through your right nostril.
7. Close your left nostril with your fingers.
8. Remove your thumb from the right nostril.
9. Inhale and exhale through the right nostril.
10. Apply pressure on your right nostril again.
11. Remove fingers from the left nostril.
12. Exhale.
13. The pattern is complete. You can do this as many times as you like.

Crystals

Crystals are an effective tool people use to heal themselves and others. Every stone has its distinct energy and frequencies, which vibrate with different parts of the human body.

As you may know, there are hundreds of chakras in the body. Think of them as little energetic portals that give out and store energy. There are seven main chakras among the other ones. These chakras form a vertical line from your pelvic bone to the center of your skull. This line is vital and governs your spiritual, physical, emotional, and mental well-being. For that reason, these chakras must be maintained and unblocked so that you can fully enjoy yourself.

Every chakra responds to certain crystals because they vibrate at identical frequencies. If you're looking to heal yourself using crystals. Identifying the problem is the first step. For instance, if you've been stuttering more than usual or if you find it difficult to speak your mind, it may be that your throat chakra is blocked. Once the problem is identified, you'll need to pick a throat chakra crystal that you feel connected to.

Building on the previous example, let's say that you picked sodalite. Start by cleansing your crystal with incense or soil. Charge it with energy from the sunlight or moonlight. Now, set your intentions. Speak to the stone and ask it what you need it to do for you. Finally, place the stone on your throat and feel its energy replenishing your throat chakra. Imagine that the crystal is replacing the negative energy with positive energy. Give a dull color to the energy you do not want and a more pigmented color to the energy you wish to bring in.

Here, you'll find a collection of stones that have the power to unblock the seven main chakras. You'll also learn how blocked chakras show up as different symptoms that you may have previously experienced.

Root Chakra

Symptoms of a blocked root chakra: feeling lost, feeling empty, and disconnected from yourself and others, heightened anxiety, feeding your insecurities with material things, and fear of the future and change.

- Bloodstone
- Hematite
- Tiger's Eye
- Red Jasper
- Garnet
- Black Obsidian
- Smoky Quartz
- Carnelian

Sacral Chakra

Symptoms of a blocked sacral chakra: disconnection from your sensual and sexual self, low libido, difficulty experiencing joy and pleasure, and lacking desire and motivation.

- Amber
- Orange Sapphire
- Orange Calcite
- Vanadinite
- Bumblebee Jasper
- Sunstone
- Fire Agate
- Imperial Topaz

Solar Plexus Chakra

Symptoms of a blocked solar plexus chakra: irritability, trust issues, adopting the victim mentality, irresponsible behavior, and low self-esteem.

- Pyrite
- Yellow Tourmaline
- Moonstone
- Lemon Quartz
- Golden Quartz
- Mookaite
- Fire Opal
- Yellow Smithsonite

Heart Chakra

Symptoms of a blocked heart chakra: difficulty letting go of the past, low empathy, poor boundaries, entertaining toxic relationships, paranoia, and anger issues.

- Malachite
- Aquamarine
- Fluorite
- Rose Quartz

- Green Calcite
- Amazonite
- Turquoise

Throat Chakra

Symptoms of a blocked throat chakra: social anxiety, struggling to speak your mind, poor communication, dishonesty, indecisiveness, and insensitivity.

- Sodalite
- Angelite
- Lapis Lazuli
- Azurite
- Danburite
- Blue Lace Agate
- Blue Chalcedony
- Kyanite

Third Eye Chakra

Symptoms of a blocked third eye chakra: entertaining judgmental thoughts, disconnection from dreams, spirits, and nature, poor intuition and gut feelings, and inactive imagination.

- Apophyllite
- Chiastolite
- Azeztulite
- Lepidolite
- Purple Fluorite
- Sugilite
- Chrysocolla
- Opal

Crown Chakra

Symptoms of a blocked crown chakra: lack of direction, inability to commit to goals, disconnection from spirituality, and inability to connect with self and others.

- Pearl
- Celestite
- Selenite
- Amethyst
- Labradorite
- Cacoxenite
- Seraphinite
- Dumortierite

Protection

Protecting yourself spiritually involves healing yourself psychically and caring for your spiritual self. If you've been spiritually attacked or if certain people or places lower your vibrations or darken your aura, you clearly need to protect yourself before stepping out of the house. Fortunately, there are many ways to spiritually protect yourself.

First and foremost, guard your house. When cleaning your house, add salt or sea salt to your water and soap to mop the floor. Salt is a powerful cleansing tool. Secondly, block your mirrors. Mirrors act like gateways or portals. Someone might be sending you malevolent energies through them. Clean your mirrors with a mixture of salt, water, and soap. Then, blow sage smoke toward the mirror. Draw a pentagram on the mirror with the smoke or with the salt water. Pentagrams will block negative energies from ever reaching you and polluting your space.

You can also set protective crystals around the house, such as black obsidian, selenite, or black tourmaline. These stones will shield you from negative energies. Alternatively, you can wear these stones as necklaces or pendants to protect yourself when meeting new people.

Lastly, envision a protective circle of light shielding you and protecting your aura from any unwanted energies. You can do this when you're at work, in the company of others, or when you feel uncomfortable around certain people or in unfamiliar environments.

Seek Guidance

Seeking spiritual guidance should be part of your self-care routine. While there are multiple ways to receive guidance from the spirit world, it's always best to receive it in a way that's most comfortable for you. For instance, if you're a tarot reader, then you may prefer seeking guidance through the cards.

Spiritually speaking, every being has been assigned a team of spirit guides before they entered the earth realm. This spirit team loves you unconditionally and assists you throughout your life. Naturally, people have sought guidance from this spirit team since time immemorial. If you wish to establish contact with them, then simply speak to them (you can refer to the chapter on spirit communication). Express your genuine gratitude for their existence in your life and ask them about anything that's occupying your mind. Ask them to give you signs so that your questions are answered.

There are also other ways to receive answers from your protectors. You can create a yes or no board and use a pendulum to understand what your spirits are asking you to do. You can also invite your spirit guides to a tarot session where they draw the cards that answer your questions.

Ultimately, healing is an essential process that elevates one's spiritual status and enhances their earthly experience. It's an ongoing process that never ends. In other words, you'll need to go through healing journeys as long as you're alive. The type of healing you need will differ from others because it is unique to you. This means checking in with yourself and seeing what your body, mind, and spirit need from you. Don't be tempted to compare your well-being to others, nor should you compare your healing journey with others' healing process. Everyone is different and will require various kinds of healing methods.

Whether you're a self-healer or you heal others, you must show empathy for yourself and others. In that regard, empathy is key to successful healing. This is why it's essential that you unblock your chakras and maintain their overall balance. You can do this by using crystals and these stones when healing others. Breathwork is yet another powerful tool that will help you heal yourself or others if you're a breathwork instructor.

Don't forget to have a spiritual self-care routine. This can take the form of house protection rituals and shielding yourself from unwanted energies. Seeking guidance is also another way you can spiritually take care of yourself. It can be done through contacting your spirit guides, conducting a tarot session, or any other psychic method that will offer you meaningful guidance.

Conclusion

As you've learned from this insightful book, psychic abilities rely on using one's extrasensory perception (ESP), also called sixth sense. This sense is tied closely to intuition, meaning a person with highly developed psychic skills has an intrinsic ability to pick up supernatural signals. Tapping into your intuition is another key step for awakening any latent psychic ability you may possess. The tips included in the opening chapter can teach you which signs you should pay attention to when trying to discover your skills. However, the only sure way to know you're on the right track is by listening to your gut feelings.

Among the most common psychic abilities one might discover in themselves are the clairs. These skills provide the pillars for psychic powers, and each clair has a unique contribution to their host medium on their own. Clairvoyance allows you to receive messages in visions, while clairaudience is the ability to hear spiritual messages. Likewise, clairsentience enables the medium to receive information through different sensations in their body, whereas claircognizance is a unique ability that comes with sudden knowledge without the receiver being aware of where or what form the message has come from.

While some of the messages may only confirm the knowledge you already possess in your subconscious, revealing them comes through your psychic abilities. To receive them, you must reach into the abyss, for which you'll need protection. Whether you're a beginner or an experienced medium, you'll never know what kind of unwanted or harmful forces you may find yourself against when trying to communicate through spiritual messages. Fortunately, there are effective ways to protect yourself against them and cleanse yourself, your space, and others from their negative influences. As it happens, the same applies to divinatory practices. While physics rarely uses tools for gazing into the future, they're helpful if you need future-related information from the spiritual world. Make sure these tools are properly cleansed and maintained as well.

Once you've discovered and begun to sharpen your psychic power and learned which tools can enhance it, you can move on to explore the different types of spirits and guides. Not all spirits you encounter during spirit communication will be friendly. Others may not be interested in working with you. For that reason, knowing how to distinguish between the spirits will allow you to choose your allies more carefully and establish a secure line of communication with them. There are several ways to communicate with spirits and guides; the one you should use depends on your intentions and skills. Certain guides or spirits may also have distinct preferences toward a form of communication, and you'll need to respect these.

Another psychic skill we've explored in this book is astral projection. This ability allows practitioners to use their astral body for journeying to the astral world. Practitioners may use several methods to have an out-of-body experience and step onto the astral plane, where it's easier for them to communicate. Telepaths, on the other hand, can communicate with living people using only their minds.

Last but not least, you've learned that using your powers can take a toll on your health. Other times, you'll be affected by negative energies despite your best efforts to prevent this. Either way, you'll need to be ready to heal yourself if and whenever needed. Implementing simple psychic self-care techniques into your daily routine will help you keep your mental and physical health in check and enable you to grow into an accomplished medium.

Part 2: Telepathy for Beginners

The Psychic Development Guide to Telepathic Abilities

Introduction

Telepathy is the ability to receive and deliver thoughts and feelings to and from another person, regardless of the distance between you. This process is done without involving any of the five senses of smell, sight, touch, hearing, or taste. Telepathic communications can only occur between people operating on similar levels of consciousness. This means that the closer the person you have in mind is to you, the more successful your efforts will be.

You may be surprised to learn that we are all blessed with the gift of telepathy. We just have to know how to nurture and develop it correctly to establish telepathic connections with others. So many people are unaware of this possibility because they're usually highly skeptical or even ignorant. One sure way to block off all psychic tendencies is by doubting this power or your ability to perform telepathy effectively, which is definitely not a good start. Telepathy only works if you trust that it's possible and have faith in your ability to send and receive messages in this way.

Learning to tap into another person's consciousness can significantly improve all your relationships. It helps you to understand and relate to people better, and it becomes easier to deal with others when you can read them like an open book.

You can also extend your telepathic connection to other living beings, such as animals. Imagine being able to intuitively feel your pet's wants and needs at all times. Since animals are more sensitive to potentially dangerous situations, you can pick up on their anxiety in good time to protect them and yourself from imminent hazards.

When reading this book, you'll learn everything you need about telepathic communication. It is the ultimate psychic development guide to awaken your psychic abilities. It is perfect for those who are entirely new to the subject and individuals who have some knowledge about psychic development but are looking to develop telepathy in particular.

This guide is a comprehensive and interesting journey into the art of telepathy. It is easy to read and comes with hands-on methods and instructions on nurturing skills like mind-reading and sending mental messages to others. Here, you will find out how to establish a telepathic bond with anyone you have in mind. You'll learn how to be open and receptive to other people's telepathic messages and recognize signs that someone is already trying to mentally communicate with you. You'll come across exercises that will help you improve your focus and concentration skills, which will help you throughout your telepathic endeavors.

This book will also teach you how to use telepathy to send positive and healing energies to others. You'll find numerous exercises and meditation techniques to help you channel and direct healing energy toward a specific person. Finally, you'll learn how to identify when someone is sending or attempting to send you negative energy or even feeding off your energy. The last chapter provides detailed instructions on effectively protecting yourself against these energetic attacks.

Chapter 1: Is Telepathy Real?

In the X-men movies, Professor X's superpower is reading people's minds even over a great distance. He also can project his thoughts into the minds of other mutants and people's minds. As you have seen from the movies, he can communicate telepathically even with those who don't share his gift. He can also control others, which makes him powerful and, at times, dangerous. People watch these movies and wonder if this superpower is real or just the product of the writer's imagination. Movies tend to exaggerate and amplify simple gifts, turning them into superpowers for dramatic effect. Although superpowers aren't real, skills are, and you can develop any skill you want with the right training and hard work.

Telepathy isn't just a beautiful and unique gift. It can also be very helpful.
John C. Osborn, CC0, via Wikimedia Commons:
https://commons.wikimedia.org/wiki/File:Telepathy_(26882)_-_The_Noun_Project.svg

Unfortunately, there are various misconceptions about telepathy; we will dispel these a little later. In real life, telepathy is different from how it is portrayed in movies. To start off with, it isn't a superpower, nor is it dangerous. It also doesn't let you control other people. This is a good thing because you don't need the burden of a superpower and end up being chased by bad guys all the time. Real telepathy allows you to communicate with others using thoughts rather than words.

In this chapter, you will learn about telepathy, its history, and the scientific research that backs it up.

What Is Telepathy and How Does It Work?

Movies like Star Wars and X-men may have given you an idea of what telepathy is like. However, it is best to forget everything you have learned about telepathy from the media and look at the topic from a fresh perspective. Telepathy is the ability people can develop to communicate with each other using their thoughts. Instead of the mouth, with telepathy, the mind does the talking. In other words, telepathy is a non-verbal and non-physical form of communication. You don't need to use any of the five senses; it is simply a direct communication between minds. People can send thoughts to one another even when they aren't in the same room. For instance, you may think of one of your high school friends and then receive a phone call from them the next day. When you were thinking of your friend, they picked up this thought and acted on it by calling you. Have you ever called a friend or a family member and they tell you, "I was just thinking about you. This is crazy..."? Well, it isn't crazy; in some cases, it is no coincidence. This could be telepathy at work.

So, to answer the main question here, yes, telepathy is real. There is a type of ability called extrasensory perception or ESP that is usually exchanged and perceived without using the five senses. Psychics, clairvoyants, and telepaths all use ESP. There are still people who regard telepathy as a farce or something that Hollywood has invented. However, the science behind telepathy has proven these people wrong. In fact, it isn't just human beings that can use telepathy but animals, like monkeys, use it too.

It is best described as the activity of the brain's nerves, which emit electrical signals transmitted as messages, allowing people to communicate with each other. Scientists have discovered that they can read these signals using advanced electronic devices. They placed electrodes on top of the heads of a group of volunteers to record the brain's electrical activity. However, these signals pass through the brain membranes, the skull, and the skin. This may have impacted the accuracy of the results, but this is one of the few methods scientists use to understand how telepathy works.

So now that they had witnessed these signals, the next step was to decode them. This can be tricky because brains have their own language, which is "thought." Scientists got their volunteers to produce electroencephalography activity. For instance, the same type of electrical brain activity is released when you think of moving your arms. With further study, the scientists could recognize a few patterns in the thought process. So, volunteers were asked to focus on specific thoughts.

The next step was to transmit these thoughts to another person's head, which is the act of telepathy. Scientists transmitted the thoughts through electrodes. Other methods don't require using wires. They used certain devices to create a magnetic field to facilitate the transmission of thoughts. A volunteer focused on a specific thought that the researchers read as electroencephalography activity, which was transmitted through a magnetic field created by a TMS (Transcranial Magnetic Stimulation wand). This stimulated the brain of another volunteer, and they began seeing flashes of light.

This experiment was conducted at the University of Barcelona. As complicated as it sounds, it helped scientists to see that thoughts could be transmitted from one person to another, thus proving telepathy is real. Despite the science, did we really need experiments to prove that? If you watch your day-to-day life closely, you will notice that you have been communicating your whole life telepathically. People use their brains to send messages to each other all the time.

Telepathy can be viewed as mentally influencing another person's mind. Simply put, a person can think of a specific thought to make another person think the same. The first person is aware that their thought is a message meant to influence someone else. This isn't meant to exert control over someone. On the contrary, it could be used to help them or even ask for help. For instance, you broke down in the middle of nowhere, and your phone battery died. You can telepathically bring someone to where you are by using telepathy and influencing their thoughts. This is a type of telepathy called MOBIA, which stands for "mental or behavioral influence of an agent."

In other cases, the receiver is the one who is aware of the telepathy instead of the one sending the thought. For instance, when someone is waiting to get news or certain information, they can meditate or focus on the news they are expecting, so when they get a thought or image in their mind, they are aware that this is the message they were waiting for.

Telepathy isn't just a beautiful and unique gift. It can also be very helpful. You may find yourself in a situation where you want to say something but find yourself unable to put your thoughts into words. Or maybe you want to reach out to someone, but you don't know how to take the first step or what you'll say to them. In this case, you can communicate your thoughts by allowing your higher self to take charge and deliver the message you are struggling with. In fact, there are emotions so deep and raw that they are better expressed telepathically rather than during a conversation. A good example of this is getting closure after a breakup or forgiving someone. This type of message can have a deeper meaning when sent telepathically.

Nervousness can sometimes take over, and many wish they had a skill to help them during these situations. Telepathy, properly developed, can become the trait you rely on when you are in need. If you are new to telepathy, it will help you think of it as a sixth sense or a second language you can use. For example, you speak French, and you meet a French person who doesn't speak a word of English. In this case, you will speak to them using your second language instead of French because this is the only way you can communicate with them. The same applies to telepathy, as it is a language that you can use when there is no other way to communicate, and unlike French, telepathy is a universal language.

Types of Telepathy

There are different types of telepathy that you need to know about before you start to tap into your telepathic gift.

Mental Telepathy

Mental telepathy, also referred to as "thought transference," is a type of telepathy where two people communicate with each other using their minds. In other words, it is about transferring thoughts between two individuals. Concentration is key with this type of telepathy. The two people involved must be focused and conscious of the telepathic process.

In the eighth century, there was a Buddhist master called Padmasambhava. He studied various Buddhist practices and brought them to his home in Tibet. He wanted future generations to benefit from his teaching; He decided to employ mental telepathy to transmit his teachings to other Buddhist masters. This way, he could guarantee that his teachings wouldn't be lost, and each generation of masters would pass them down to the next.

Author Alice Ann Bailey, who worked closely with Tibetan masters, believes that in a couple of hundred years, most people will communicate using mental telepathy. This is a sentiment that Facebook founder Mark Zuckerberg also echoed.

Instinctual Telepathy

Instinctual telepathy isn't as strong as mental telepathy. In fact, it is considered one of the weakest forms. Animals and humans use this type of telepathy, and some cultures still use it. Instinctual telepathy allows a person to pick up on someone else's needs or feelings. The person doesn't have to be nearby to signal these needs. This type of telepathy works at a distance, and for it to be effective, one must employ their solar plexus chakra, which is located in the stomach area and is responsible for emotions and instinct. According to Hawaiian priests, people can communicate telepathically through their solar plexus. They believe the subtle body of a person, the invisible energetic field that surrounds every person, sends an invisible thread to another person's solar plexus, connecting both people. They then can communicate telepathically using these threads.

A person doesn't receive the telepathic message right away. You first receive the message instantly, and then, the instinct transfers it to the rational part of you, which then delivers it to the mind, which processes it like a memory. The more two people communicate telepathically using this "thread," the stronger their connection becomes. The threads of both people braid with each other to create an unbreakable bond. You can easily send out threads to others just by shaking hands or looking at each other.

In Africa, people use a different method of instinctual telepathy. In the Kalahari Desert in South Africa, people believe that there is a stream of energy, often silver, that connects all living beings with each other. The solar plexus also plays a role here since the stream of energy stretches out from the belly button. Think of these streams as phones with each person on a line and communicating with one another.

In Australia, some cultures believe in the "Miwi," which allows them to see and hear things from a distance. "Miwi" is located in the solar plexus chakra, which means instinct or soul. People get this gift from their parents, and they pass it down from one generation to the next. There are also cultures in Japan that use the solar plexus to communicate instinctively.

The west also has a term for it, and that's a "gut feeling." People call it the inexplicable feeling they get in their gut about a situation or person. You have probably experienced this feeling on more than one occasion. You may have felt that someone couldn't be trusted based on a gut feeling or decided that your gut swayed you toward it. In their day-to-day life, everyone makes decisions based on their instinct, and even detectives will follow a lead based on a hunch or a gut feeling.

In 2004, Parapsychologists Marilyn Schlitz and Dean Radin conducted experiments to prove that people can communicate telepathically using their gut feeling. The test subjects were all couples, and each couple was separated into different rooms. In one room, Radin and Schlitz showed one person different pictures that evoked emotions. The other person was placed in a different room with electrodes and was monitored. They found that the person in the second room responded to strong emotions evoked by the first person, which proved that the gut feeling has its own brain and perceptions.

Spiritual Telepathy

Just as the name suggests, spiritual telepathy involves communicating from one soul to another. It is the highest form of telepathy, requiring the soul, brain, and mind to be aligned. This will allow you to mediate between the spiritual and physical worlds. It allows you to reach enlightenment and access information provided by the divine. This information can help you solve problems in the physical world and help others as well. In fact, one of the greatest artists of all time, Leonardo da Vinci, believed that a painter's mind is inspired by the divine and that if the spirit wasn't involved, he would not be able to produce art. Michelangelo also believed that the divine was the source of his creativity. This belief was illustrated in his painting "The Creation of Adam." In the painting, God is depicted in what looks like the human brain and extends his hand to a man who represents divine inspiration.

The History of Telepathy

The concept of telepathy is nothing new. Ancient cultures like the Greeks and Egyptians believed in telepathy. The ancient Greeks believed that they could communicate with others through dreams. The ancient Egyptians also shared the same thoughts about dreams. They believed that spirits are able to communicate and send each other messages in dreams. This is probably why ancient cultures took their dreams so seriously because they believed they meant something.

Psychologist, F.W. Myers, was the one who coined the term "telepathy" in 1882. Myers was one of the people who helped form the Society of Psychical Research. During that time, significant research was carried out on the topic of physical sciences. Great advances in this field paved the way for scientists to dig deeper into the topic of mental phenomena. They were hoping to make sense of certain paranormal phenomena. As a result, the term "telepathy" came into being, with Myers working to prove that telepathy is real.

Zener Cards Experiment

Throughout history, scientists have always been curious about telepathy and have worked to find proof that this intriguing concept is real. J. B. Rhine, the founder of parapsychology, came up with an experiment to test for telepathy. This experiment was called "the Zener cards experiment." Rhine used five cards, each with a different shape: a cross, a square, a star, three wavy lines, and a circle. However, this experiment wasn't Rhine's first attempt to navigate the world of telepathy. He first used to play cards with volunteers, who were mostly students. The volunteers would try to guess which card the researchers were holding. However, the results of this experiment weren't accurate, as people weren't really guessing but were suggesting their favorite cards instead. Rhine wanted to get more precise results, so he came up with the Zener cards. The idea was to choose shapes the volunteers weren't connected to or associated with. The experiment was named Zener after the involvement of Rhine's friend, psychologist Dr. Karl Zener. It was Zener who came up with the five shapes because he believed that most people wouldn't be biased toward any of them. Naturally, chance played a role here, but a person wouldn't guess the right cards five or ten times by chance. This meant that there was a possibility that a person doing this was a psychic.

Rhine then decided to use the same method to test for telepathy. Two people were placed in different rooms, and one of them would look at each of the cards. This person would then try to send an image of each card to the person in the next room using telepathy. The person in the other room would try to guess the image communicated to them. The more a person was able to guess the card, the clearer it was that they were gifted. For instance, if someone guessed right 15 or 20 times, they were no longer guessing. They were, in fact, using telepathy to communicate with one another.

The Ganzfeld Experiment

Parapsychologists conducted this experiment to further prove that telepathy is more fact than fiction. Volunteers were asked to wear a paper mask with the edges taped. A red light was turned on and filled the room, ensuring it *didn't* flicker. This was intended to cause sensory deprivation. No noise was allowed in the room except for white noise. One person was placed in this room, while the other was placed in a different one. The person in the normal room was asked to focus on a picture. Meanwhile, the other person would describe the hallucinations they experienced in the red light room. If their experience was the same as the picture the other person was focusing on, then both people were communicating telepathically, and this experiment was a success.

CIA Investigation

In the '70s, the CIA investigated the concept of telepathy to spy on the Soviet Union. In 2017, classified information came to light that showed the CIA had a program that was called "Project Star Gate." The CIA was looking for people who had special gifts like telepathy or psychokinesis. They sought the help of the famous psychic Uri Geller. They hoped to take advantage of his telepathic powers and learn how to read other people's minds. The analysis of the results of this experiment was very hopeful in proving that individuals can indeed have paranormal abilities.

Telepathy and Quantum Physics

There is a theory that suggests that telepathy and quantum physics are connected. The theory postulates that the brain can receive and influence "quantum fluctuations" from other people's brains. According to Albert Einstein, all humans are connected to this universe, and the idea that we are separated from one another is an illusion. As a result, people can communicate with each other using telepathy. This theory also echoed how many cultures believe people can connect with each other using a stream of energy or an invisible thread.

Can Anyone Be a Telepath?

Telepathy is a skill, and just like any other skill, you can learn it and develop it with time. Anyone can be a telepath, but this isn't something that will happen overnight, nor will it give you the same powers as Professor X. With time, learning, and training, many may be able to send and receive messages using their minds.

FAQs

Is telepathy dangerous?

No, telepathy isn't dangerous. It is simply a form of non-verbal communication that can influence thoughts to allow you to communicate with someone or ask for help.

Can anyone practice telepathy?

Yes, anyone can practice telepathy. It is a skill that you can develop over time if you train and work hard.

Is everyone born telepathic?

Yes, everyone is born telepathic. However, it can become rusty when you ignore your gift or stop paying attention to it.

Will I become a telepath once I start training?

Not right away, but you will get better with time and practice.

Is good health associated with telepathy?

Yes, being healthy is necessary to be able to communicate using your mind. When you are sick, your body, mind, and soul weaken, which can influence your telepathic abilities.

How do I know that my message has been sent?

You will know in your gut that your message has been sent. It's a feeling you'll get inside that your thoughts have reached the other person's attention. You can then stop communicating and wait for the reply.

How do I know someone is communicating with me telepathically?

You will think, feel, imagine, or have certain desires toward something. Don't ignore these feelings, as they may mean someone is telepathically trying to communicate with you.

How will telepathy help me?

Connecting with others on a higher level allows you to better understand and relate to them and their struggles. This can improve your relationships and help you establish strong bonds.

We are all connected, and no man is an island. You may be getting telepathic messages, but maybe you aren't aware. As a result of skepticism and the stereotypes surrounding telepathy, most people see the messages as coincidences or think they imagined things. Open your heart and mind to the universe and give yourself a chance to be at one with it and all its beings.

Chapter 2: Learn to Meditate First

Suppose you want to learn how to develop your telepathic abilities. In that case, the first step is *believing* it is possible. Telepathy, also known as "mind reading," is the ability to communicate with others without using words or any other physical means. It is a natural ability that we all possess, but most of us are unaware of it – or do not know how to use it.

A crucial step in your training to develop your telepathic ability is to learn how to meditate.
https://www.pexels.com/photo/woman-meditating-in-bedroom-3772612/

The good news is that telepathy is a skill that can be learned and developed with practice. This chapter will cover the basics of telepathy and how you can start using it in your everyday life.

Believe in Yourself

The first and most important step in learning telepathy is to believe in yourself. We all have the ability to communicate telepathically, but many of us block it out because we don't believe it is possible. Ask yourself why you want to learn telepathy. What are your motivations? Focusing your energies and developing your abilities will be easier when you have a clear purpose.

Start with baby steps. Do not try to force a telepathic connection but just let it happen naturally. The more you practice, the stronger your abilities will become.

Be Open-Minded

To be a good telepath, you need to be open-minded. This means being receptive to the thoughts and feelings of others. It also means being willing to share your own thoughts and feelings with others. When you are open-minded, you will find it easier to establish a telepathic connection with someone.

Be with Someone You Trust

When starting out, it is best to practice with someone you trust. This could be a family member, friend, or even a pet. Choose someone open-minded and receptive to the idea of telepathy. Once you have established a connection with this person, you can start practicing with others.

Create a Relaxing Environment

To be successful, create a relaxing environment. This means being in a quiet place where you will not be interrupted. Make sure that you are comfortable and not feeling rushed. Focusing your energies and establishing a connection will be easier when you are relaxed.

Focus on Your Intentions

When you are trying to establish a connection with someone, focus on your intentions. This means having a clear purpose for why you want to connect with this person. It will also clear your mind so you can open up the channels.

Let Go of Your Ego

To be successful in telepathy, you need to let go of your ego. Stop trying to control the situation or the other person and open yourself up to the idea that you might not always be successful. When you let go of your ego, you will find it easier to establish a connection.

Practice Visualization

One of the best ways to develop your telepathic abilities is to practice visualization. This means picturing yourself sending and receiving messages to and receiving them from another person. Visualize the other person clearly, and see yourself communicating with them.

You can also try to send a specific message to the other person. For example, you could focus on sending the word "Hello" to them. See the word clearly in your mind, and then let it go. Trust that the other person will receive the message.

Telepathy is a skill that takes time and practice to develop. Do not get discouraged if you do not see results immediately. Remember to believe in yourself and be open-minded; you will eventually start seeing results.

Meditation and Telepathy

A crucial step in your training to develop your telepathic ability is to learn how to meditate. Meditation will help clear your mind and focus your thoughts, two essential components of successful telepathy. If you've never meditated before, don't worry - it's not as difficult as it seems. This chapter will teach you the basics of meditation and explain how to get started.

What Is Meditation?

Mediation is an ancient practice used throughout history to help people achieve complete mental and physical well-being. In its simplest form, meditation is a way of clearing your mind and focusing your thoughts. When you meditate, you allow yourself to become fully present in the moment and let go of all distractions. This helps you relax or de-stress and improves your focus and concentration.

Different types of meditation all share the same basic goal: to make peace with the mind and allow you to focus on the present moment. Some common types of meditation include mindfulness, transcendental, mantra, focused, and guided meditation.

Hinduism and Meditation

Meditation is central to Hinduism, one of the world's oldest religions. Hindus believe it can help you connect with the divine and lead to inner peace and enlightenment.

All types of meditation involve focusing the mind on a single object or thought. This can be done by sitting quietly and focusing on your breath or by repeating a mantra (a sacred word or phrase).

Pranayama in Hinduism

Pranayama is a type of breathing exercise often used in meditation. It helps to calm the mind and control the breath, two important components of successful meditation.

Pranayama is usually done by sitting comfortably and focusing on the breath. The breath is then slowly exhaled through the nostrils, and the process is repeated.

To do pranayama, sit with your spine straight and close your eyes. Place your hands on your stomach, and inhale deeply through your nose. As you inhale, feel your stomach rise. Then exhale slowly through your mouth. Repeat this process for several minutes.

Yoga and Meditation

Yoga is also an ancient Indian practice that combines physical exercises, breathing techniques, and meditation. Yoga can help to improve your flexibility, strength, and balance, as well as calm the mind and relax the body.

Yoga is often used as a tool for meditation. The physical postures and breathing exercises help to focus the mind and prepare the body for meditation.

To get started with yoga, find a class or video suitable for your fitness level. There are many different types of yoga, so you can choose a class that is right for you.

Start by doing a few minutes each day, and gradually increase the amount of time you spend practicing. Yoga is a great way to prepare your body and mind for meditation.

Guided Meditation

Guided meditation involves someone else guiding you through the process. This can be done in person or by listening to a recording. Guided meditation is a great way to learn how to meditate if you are a beginner.

There are many different types of guided meditation, but they all have one thing in common. They help you to focus and direct your attention. This is helpful, particularly if you have difficulty meditating on your own. Guided meditation can also be used to explore specific topics or areas of focus, such as relaxation, stress relief, or self-compassion.

If you are interested in trying guided meditation, many resources are available. You can find guided meditation recordings online or at your local library. You can also take a class or workshop or participate in a meditation group.

Hinduism teaches that the goal of meditation is to still the mind and experience the true nature of reality. This process is known as nirvana, which is said to be the ultimate goal of life.

Meditation is not easy, but it is worth the effort. The benefits include improving your mental and physical health, having more peace of mind, and experiencing a deeper connection with the divine.

If you're interested in trying meditation, many resources are available to help you. You can find books, classes, and retreats that will teach you how to meditate.

It is essential to find a method that works for you and stick with it. Meditation is a journey, not a destination. There is no one right way to meditate, so find a method that feels comfortable and that you can continue for as long as you want to meditate.

How to Meditate

Now that you know a little about meditation, it's time to learn how to do it. The good news is that anyone can learn to meditate, regardless of experience or ability. Just follow these simple steps:

1. **Find a relaxing place to meditate.** You can meditate indoors or outdoors, in a quiet room, or in the midst of chaos. The only requirement is to find a spot where you can comfortably relax without being disturbed.

2. **Gently close your eyes and take deep breaths.** Relax your whole body and clear your mind of all thoughts. As you inhale, focus on filling your lungs with fresh air. When you exhale, let all the tension and stress of the day disappear.

3. **Begin to focus on your breathing.** Pay attention to the sensation of your breath as it enters and exits your body. Notice the rise and fall of your chest or stomach as you breathe.

If you can't focus for extended periods, that's okay. Meditation is not about clearing your mind completely - it's about learning to focus despite the presence of distractions.

Continue focusing on your breath for as long as you like. When ready to wind it up, take a couple of deep breaths and get up.

Meditation Tips for Beginners

Here are a few tips to help you get the most out of your meditation practice:

Don't Expect Miracles

Meditation is a tool, not a magic wand. It will take time and practice to see the benefits. Start with just a few minutes a day. You can gradually increase the time you meditate as you get used to it.

Be Patient

Meditation is a journey, not a destination. There is no need to rush. Meditation is not a race, so there's no need to try and clear your mind completely in one sitting. Just start with a few minutes a day and work your way up from there.

Practice Daily

Meditation takes practice, so don't get discouraged if it's difficult at first. It takes time to learn how to keep peace of mind, but you will eventually be successful with patience and persistence.

Find a Comfortable Position

You don't have to sit in a lotus position or anything like that - just find a position that you can comfortably maintain for the duration of your meditation.

Set a Timer

Set a timer when you meditate, so you don't have to worry about how long you've been sitting there. Just choose a comfortable length of time (5-10 minutes is a good starting point) and let the timer do the rest.

Stay Consistent

The more you meditate, the better your results will be. So, find a time you can guarantee you can stick to and set it aside as an unbreakable appointment with yourself. Even a few minutes of meditation daily can make a big difference.

With these tips in mind, you're ready to start meditating! Just remember to be patient and go at your own pace. Meditation is a journey, not a destination - so enjoy the ride.

Benefits of Meditation

Meditation has a host of benefits for both the mind and body. Here are just a few of the ways that meditation can improve your life:

Reduces Stress

Meditation has been shown to be an effective way to reduce stress. It can help to calm the mind and body and promote relaxation. In Hinduism and Buddhism, meditation is used to help people achieve enlightenment. With regular practice, it can help to improve your mental and emotional well-being.

Improve Focus and Concentration

Meditation can also help to improve focus and concentration. One study found that those who meditated were better able to focus on a task and had improved memory recall. In addition, meditation has been shown to increase activity in the parts of the brain responsible for attention and focus.

Improved Sleep

Meditation can also help to improve your quality of sleep. Meditating for 20 minutes before bedtime improved the quality of sleep and speed of falling asleep compared to people who did not meditate. In addition, they were less likely to wake up during the night.

Mental and Physical Health

Meditation has also been shown to improve mental and physical health. People who meditated had lower levels of anxiety, depression, and stress. They also had a better immune function and improved cardiovascular health. Meditation has also been shown to reduce pain perception.

Increased Creativity

Meditation can also help to increase creativity. This is because when you meditate, you are training your mind to be more open and flexible. This means that you will be better able to come up with new ideas and solutions to problems. Also, because meditation can help to increase focus and concentration, it can help you to execute your ideas better.

So, meditation is a great way to do it if you want to increase your creativity!

Enhanced Self-Awareness

Meditation can also help to enhance self-awareness. This is because it lets you quiet the chatter of your mind and focus on your thoughts and feelings. This can help you to better understand yourself and your needs. In addition, self-awareness can help you to make better choices in your life.

Improved Emotional Health

Meditation can also help to improve emotional health. This is because it helps to reduce stress and anxiety. In addition, it increases positive emotions such as happiness, love, and compassion. Meditation can also help you to deal with difficult emotions such as anger, sadness, and fear.

Expanded Consciousness

You will find your consciousness is expanded, and you can tap into o a higher state of awareness when you meditate regularly. You will be more connected to your inner thoughts and feelings in this state. You will also be more aware of the world around you. This can help you to better understand yourself and your place in the world.

Stepping Stone for Telepathy

Not only does meditation have all of these great benefits, but it can also help to improve your telepathic abilities. This is because meditation hones your focus and concentration. With regular practice, meditation will help you to develop your telepathic abilities.

How Meditation Improves Telepathic Ability

Regarding meditation and psychic abilities, there is a common misconception that to develop psychic ability, one must have been born with some sort of supernatural gift. This could not be further from the truth! In fact, meditation is one of the most effective ways to improve your telepathic ability.

How Does Meditation Work to Improve Telepathy?

When you meditate, you train your mind to focus and be more aware. With regular practice, you will find that it becomes easier and easier to focus your mind on a single thought or object. As your ability to focus improves, so does your ability to tune into the thoughts and feelings of others.

Telepathy is all about energy and vibration. Everything in the universe vibrates at a certain frequency, and our thoughts and feelings are also made up of energy. When you focus your mind during meditation, you are raising your own vibration and becoming more attuned to the vibrations of others. This makes it easier to tune into their thoughts and feelings and communicate with them deeper.

As well as improving focus, meditation helps to still the mind and to quieten the mental chatter, which is essential for clear communication. It also helps to open up your third eye chakra, which is responsible for psychic abilities. A calm mind is a more receptive mind, and a more receptive mind is better able to receive telepathic messages.

Another way meditation works to improve telepathic ability is by expanding consciousness. As your consciousness expands, you will become more aware of the world around you. This includes the thoughts and feelings of others. With regular practice, you will find that it becomes easier and easier to tune into the thoughts and feelings of others.

When you are physically and mentally healthy, your telepathic abilities will also be stronger and more reliable. That's why it's so important to take care of your body and mind - and to meditate regularly. Meditation will clear your mind and reduce stress and anxiety. It will also help you to connect with your higher self and to access your intuition and inner wisdom.

Finally, meditation helps to increase your overall energy and vibration. The higher your vibration, the easier it is to connect with others on a psychic level. When you meditate regularly, you will find that your vibration gradually begins to rise, making it easier for you to connect with others telepathically.

You will be able to send and receive messages more clearly, and your abilities will continue to develop as you meditate more. So, if you want to improve your telepathic ability, add meditation to your daily routine! The more you meditate, the stronger your telepathic abilities will become. Just like any other skill, it takes practice and patience. But with regular meditation, you will find that your ability to communicate telepathically will improve greatly.

Meditation is a powerful tool that can be used to improve telepathic ability. By training the mind to focus and be more aware, you can tune into the thoughts and feelings of others more easily. Meditation also helps to still the mind and to open up the third eye chakra.

In addition, it helps to expand consciousness and to increase your overall energy and vibration. The more you meditate, the stronger your telepathic abilities will become.

Chapter 3: Raise Your Vibration

High vibrational frequency can help you easily send and receive messages via telepathy. In this chapter, we'll explore vibrational energy and why raising your vibration is necessary to communicate successfully. You'll understand the link between vibration and telepathy and recognize signs that show you whether you have a high or low vibration. Finally, you'll find tips on raising your vibrational frequency.

High vibrational frequency can help you easily send and receive messages via telepathy.
https://www.pexels.com/photo/silhouette-of-man-at-daytime-1051838/

What Is Vibrational Energy?

Everything in the world is composed of energy. Even our bodies are made of vibrating particles that generate energy. You may be surprised to learn that some healthcare approaches, like vibrational medicine, use the vibrational energy that the patient's body creates for healing.

Vibrations are rhythmic. Some of these rhythms, like the changing seasons, take place on a large scale. Others occur within our bodies. The breath we take, circadian rhythms, and heartbeats are just a few examples of rhythms you can measure. However, there are also countless other minuscule vibrations happening inside our bodies. For instance, the molecules within each of our cells are constantly vibrating. Some vibrations are smaller than 0.001 of the diameter of just one of your hairs.

Together, these vibrations create waves of electromagnetic energy, impacting how your body functions and triggering changes inside your cells. Not all molecules vibrate at the same rate. They can be either slower or faster, depending on the body temperature and other internal and external conditions.

Our behaviors, thoughts, and feelings can influence the rhythms and vibrations in our bodies. For instance, negative emotions, like anxiety, trigger the release of cortisol, a stress hormone. This hormone may cause the heart rate to speed up. Music also generates vibrational frequencies. These will interact with our energetic fields and induce changes in the body. This is why listening to calming music can help you get your heart rate to slow down. The vibrations emitted by external sources impact our emotions, thoughts, and body function.

Vibrations generated by our thoughts and behaviors can also change the smaller rhythms in our bodies. You can change the vibrational speeds of the atoms in your body by changing your environment, taking control of your emotions, managing your thoughts, and being mindful of your actions. Since electromagnetic energy travels in waves, influencing changes in your body's nano vibrations can ripple further, creating changes in your overall mental and physical well-being.

Why Is It Important to Raise Your Vibration?

Raising your vibration is among the best ways to nurture your spiritual, mental, emotional, and physical health. The process of raising your vibration is a lot easier than you think it is. However, before we get into that, let's explore why you would want to raise your vibrations.

Eliminates Negative Energy

It works to get rid of negative energy. It helps you create a space for yourself where thoughts, objects, attachments, imprints, and people with low vibrations and low densities can't function. Having low vibrational energy makes you vulnerable to the negativity of others. Other people's words and behavior can easily influence your mood and emotions. Having low vibrational energies can even put you at risk of being susceptible to spells and curses. However, take charge of your energy and always maintain a high vibrational frequency. You will be untouchable to undesirable vibrations. We only interact and resonate with vibrations that match our own, meaning that anything beneath your energy will not be considered a part of your reality.

Helps You Manifest Abundance

This also means you'll be able to manifest abundance into your life easily. You're already vibrating on the same energetic frequency of everything you want. Being more focused and aligned with your desires can help you make them a part of your reality.

Gives You a Sense of Direction

Maintaining high vibrational frequencies can give you a sense of direction and control in your life. Instead of being subject to the dynamics of the world around you and letting yourself be affected by undesired situations, thoughts, and feelings, you can control what your energy interacts with. Being able to bring your desires into reality changes you from a secondary character in the world to the narrator of your own story.

Increases Your Spiritual Awareness

Eliminating lower vibrational frequencies from your life can also help you with your spiritual endeavors. Since higher vibrational frequencies mean fewer intrusive thoughts and blockages, you can focus your attention on becoming more spiritually aware. You'll learn how to optimize your thoughts and feelings to be more balanced internally and with the world around you.

Helps You Foster Deeper and More Energetic Connections

Raising your vibration expands your aura and makes your energy more powerful. It increases the energetic space you take up in the world, making it easier to cultivate deep connections with everything around you. This makes you more grounded and aligned with nature and the universe around you. It teaches you to stay in the present moment, reminds you to express your gratitude toward Mother Earth, and gets rid of unwanted thoughts. Raising your vibration is the hardest part. Maintaining your effort, however, is relatively easy because your vibrational energy is a self-filling cup. Gratitude, a positive mindset, and being grounded can help you further elevate your vibrational frequency.

Enhances Your Spiritual Gifts

Since a higher vibrational frequency means stronger energetic connections and fewer internal blockages, you can expect your spiritual gifts to be improved. You can enhance your four clairs of intuition (which include clairaudience, clairsentience, claircognizance, and clairvoyance) by raising your vibrations, which enhances your telepathic effort. You may even discover that you possess new spiritual gifts that you knew nothing about before you raised your vibration.

Allows You to Feel Empowered

Feeling empowered is one of the best feelings in life. Nothing has the same effect as knowing exactly what you want in life and understanding what you're capable of. Think of what our brains and energies can do; we are very powerful beings. Raising your vibrations can help you realize this, meditate on how connected you are to the universe, and learn your role in the world. Being spiritually aligned and fostering a positive state of mind can help you to achieve your personal development goals.

Makes You More Compassionate

With higher vibrations, you'll find you feel generally happier, which makes you become more compassionate. You start giving out more love and positive energy to everyone around you. Sending love out to the world is one of the most healing gifts you can give to those around you.

Boosts Your Overall Well-Being

Low and negative energy makes you feel depleted and flat. Diminishing these emotions makes you feel more energized and increases your vitality. Maintaining high vibrational energies makes you more driven and attentive and increases your vitality. It elevates your overall well-being and sense of self.

Vibration and Telepathy

Raising your vibrations is essential when it comes to telepathic communications. Increasing your vibrational awareness automatically makes you more intuitive, which, in turn, enhances your psychic powers. Being highly intuitive improves your claircognizant (clear knowing), clairsentient (clear feeling), clairvoyant (clear seeing), and clairaudient (clear hearing) senses, which allows you to communicate more effectively using telepathy. We will explore the clairs in more depth throughout the following chapter.

A higher vibrational frequency also allows you to tap into other people's energies more effectively. You can communicate telepathically with someone only when you have a similar vibrational frequency. You can't tune into a person's consciousness if they have a higher vibration than yours.

Keeping your vibrational energy high also protects you from unwanted intrusions by negative energy. You're vulnerable to their fears, ideas, and thoughts whenever you tap into someone's consciousness. Maintaining high frequencies allows you to release everything that isn't yours.

Do I Have a Low or High Vibration?

The higher your vibrations, the more you experience positive feelings and qualities. People with high vibrational energies are generally more peaceful, loving, compassionate, and forgiving. In retrospect, suffering from low vibrational energies leaves you with a plethora of negative and unwanted feelings and emotions like hatred, regret, greed, and fear. Those with low vibrational energies are prone to develop conditions like depression, anxiety, and other physical ailments.

High vibrations make you more attuned to your higher self, consciousness, and universe.

Take a moment to think about who you truly are. What are you without your interests, knowledge, belongings, passions, personality, feelings, and thoughts? Would you cease to exist if all your memories and experiences were stripped away from you? No. You'd still have your consciousness. Raising your vibration can help you connect with this elemental aspect of yourself or your true nature.

The lower your vibration, the more you lose touch with who you are and your highest self. This makes your life experiences more challenging.

Before we explore the signs that you have a high or low vibration, there are a few things to keep in mind. There is no black or white regarding who or what you are. You can't have 100% low or high vibrations. You'll always fall somewhere on a spectrum, whether that is 20% low and 80% high, 65% low and 35% high, and so on. This is why you should always avoid labeling yourself as one or the other.

You should also remember that understanding your vibrational frequency is meant to be good for you and not give you an excuse to label others. Unfortunately, many people tend to segregate others with low vibrations once they understand what energy is. It's good to protect yourself from energy vampires and negative individuals. However, instead of cutting these people off and advising others to stay away from them, you can maintain your own vibrational frequency by practicing meditation and gratitude and keeping a positive mindset.

Signs You Have a Low Vibration

- You feel stuck in life
- You don't have a clear sense of direction
- You're not empathetic toward yourself or others
- You're emotionally disconnected
- You have quick and intense emotional reactions
- You always feel tired and lethargic
- You have ego-centric tendencies
- You've been told that you think the world revolves around you
- You find it impossible to leave old or unhealthy habits behind
- You never feel fulfilled
- You have a pronounced shadow self
- You argue with others a lot
- You struggle with poor life choices
- You always feel guilty about something. Even if you aren't, you find yourself searching for something to feel guilty about.
- You complain frequently
- You find forgiveness challenging, whether it's toward yourself or others
- You can't see the beauty in life
- You're in constant despair
- You don't know what you want in your life

- You have self-sabotaging tendencies
- You're often very skeptical
- You usually feel jealous or resentful
- You eat a lot of processed and unhealthy foods
- You eat an unbalanced diet
- You find it hard to feel gratitude
- You're physically unhealthy
- You've been told you're needy
- You demand a lot from others
- You consume a lot of violent media content (music, video games, movies, books, etc.)
- You always focus on the negative things in life
- You always feel like a victim
- Your relationships always bring you pain
- You struggle to make progress in any area of your life

Signs You Have a High Vibration

- You have high self-awareness. You are conscious of your actions, words, feelings, and behaviors and realize their impact on others.
- You're emotionally balanced. Your emotional reactions don't blow out of proportion.
- You know when to take yourself seriously and when to let loose
- You often nurture yourself and others
- You're attuned to your body and its needs
- You're generally empathetic. You are sensitive to the needs of others and try to see things from their perspective.
- You feel connected to something greater than yourself
- You find it easy to experience joy and happiness
- You approach life with ease and a sense of humor
- You're self-disciplined

- You realize that you don't need something or someone else to be happy
- You generally feel strong, energetic, and healthy
- You don't struggle with patience
- People find it easy to open up to you
- You live in the present and don't spend too much time dwelling on the past or worrying about the future
- You don't feel the need to start arguments or get the last word in
- You're confident in yourself and your capabilities
- Forgiveness toward yourself and others comes easily to you
- It feels like you know what you want to do in life. You've found your calling.
- You have a strong intuition
- You are often the adviser, teacher, or peacemaker in your friend group, and all your relationships
- You usually experience synchronicities
- You often feel or express gratitude for all that you have
- You're able to delay gratification and pleasure when you know it's not in your best interest
- You try to lead a clutter-free life
- You are open to new experiences, people, ideas, and beliefs
- You're very creative and inspired
- You eat a balanced diet
- You eat raw and unprocessed food
- New opportunities come to you easily
- You don't experience much disappointment in your life. This is because you don't attach yourself to relationships and habits that don't serve you.
- You understand that "passing things," like people and material items, are temporary, which is why you don't cling to them
- You like to consume inspirational and relaxing content (music, TV shows, movies, books, etc.)

How to Raise Your Vibration

Raising your vibration is not a difficult endeavor like many assume, but it requires time, effort, and patience.

You often have to change your lifestyle to raise your vibrational energy. The extent of these alterations depends on your current habits. If you smoke and eat takeout daily, you'll have to put in more work than those who don't.

Letting go of your unhealthy habits and getting used to the changes in your life is perhaps the hardest thing about raising your vibration. However, once you get the hang of it, you'll realize that it's the best decision you've ever made. You'll elevate many aspects of your life in the process.

Before starting this journey, you need to understand that raising your vibration is not a one-time process. If you don't keep up your effort, your energetic frequency will fall again.

Here are some things you can do to raise your vibration:

Practice Gratitude

This is the simplest thing you can do to raise your vibrational energy. Negativity is your worst enemy - it is detrimental to your physical, mental, emotional, and spiritual health. Make it a habit to name three things that you're thankful for as soon as you wake up in the morning and before you go back to sleep. Think about all the great things that you receive in your day and take them for granted.

Try to change your perspective about your life's "negative" aspects. For instance, if you wish to find a less tiring job, try to change your thinking instead of resenting it. Be thankful that you have a job that allows you to pay your bills. This isn't an invitation for toxic positivity or guilt-tripping yourself. The aim is to recognize your life's blessings and express gratitude toward them, no matter how big or small.

Meditate

Incorporating meditation into your daily routine can be a great way to start your day or blow off some steam before you go to bed. Meditating helps you let go of intrusive thoughts and relieve anxiety symptoms. It helps you connect with yourself and the world around you. Practicing meditation regularly trains your mind to think positively and is a great way to lift your mood and vibrational frequency.

Surround Yourself with Nature

Break away from the hustle and bustle of life and go for a long walk in nature. You can also consider keeping a few plants at home and caring for them. Nature has a calming effect on the mind and body. It can ease symptoms of depression and anxiety and reduce cortisol levels in the blood.

Practice Positive Thinking

Negative thought patterns are habitual, and habits are hard to break. However, you should take small steps toward adopting a positive attitude. Remind yourself that everything in life happens for a reason, and trust that the universe is always working in your favor, as this can help you respond to undesirable situations more easily.

Be Around People Who Make You Feel Good

As mentioned above, working toward raising your vibrational frequency is not an excuse to segregate those with lower vibrations. However, you should take precautions whenever you're around negative-minded individuals. Consciously take control of your emotions and thoughts, and be careful not to absorb any energies which aren't yours. You should also aim to spend time with people who make you feel good. Spending time with individuals with higher vibrations can help you raise your own.

Try to Be Generous and Forgiving

You will struggle to adopt positive characteristics like forgiveness and generosity if you have a very low vibrational frequency. The rewards, however, are worth your effort.

Eat a Healthy and Balanced Diet

The food you consume also influences your vibrational frequency. Lower your meat, processed food, fried food, and alcohol intake as they have low vibrational frequencies. Making healthier food choices elevates your energy.

Raising your vibrational frequency has numerous benefits for the mind, heart, soul, and body. It empowers you, gives you a sense of direction in life, makes you more thankful and compassionate, and, most importantly, enhances your spiritual gifts. Becoming more intuitive can help you communicate telepathically more effectively. It also ensures that you don't accidentally absorb thoughts, feelings, and behaviors that aren't yours in the process.

Chapter 4: Nurture Your Clairs

As you've probably gathered from what you've read so far, intuition plays an essential role in telepathy. So, what better way to develop this skill than trusting the intuitive guidance coming from your senses? Telepaths rely on their ability to use their extrasensory gifts - known as the clairs. The four clairs are the fundamental pillars of your psychic powers, and honing them is an enormous step forward toward becoming a successful telepath. This chapter will introduce you to the clairs and offer valuable advice on developing the two most prominent ones - clairvoyance and clairaudience. These two reveal themselves in pictures or spoken worlds, both of which can send powerful messages to a telepath.

Intuition plays an essential role in telepathy.

The Clairs

If you use Tarot cards, runes, or other forms of intuitive practices, you may have already had a chance to use the clairs. For example, you may have had instances when you just knew the meaning of the card, rune, or any other tool as soon as you picked it up. You may not have even started thinking about it, but you already know what they're telling you at that moment. Or, even if you don't practice any of these, you may have been pondering about an issue that had you worried, and suddenly, you understood and have an answer to the situation. You sensed, heard, saw, or knew something that helped calm you down and found a solution to your issue. If yes, you've received intuitive guidance through one or more clairs.

The four clairs are clairvoyance, clairaudience, clarcognition and clairsentience. Most people are born with at least one of these senses, but not everyone is aware of them. Yet anyone can develop and tap into them, which is great news for telepaths. However, only a few people have an instinctive ability to tap into these senses. Most people have to actively work on sharpening them. The first step in connecting with your clairs is acknowledging them. This allows you to let your guard down and let them guide you intuitively toward changes or whatever path you've chosen for yourself. If this path is being a telepath, all the more reason to take the time to understand how your clairs can empower your physic abilities. The clairs can teach you how to be empathetic with your intuition. And by showing how your intuitive decisions can benefit you, they'll encourage you to trust it enough to let you make decisions.

Not only that, but through the clairs, you can pick up messages, understand the guidance and recognize other forms of wisdom you may telepathically receive. Whether you want to consult with spirits and other enlightened beings or communicate through your telepathic abilities, the clairs will be the perfect tool for it. The spirits and other beings may prefer communication in a particular way, and a heightened intuition will pick this up. The clearer your Clair senses are, the more likely you'll be able to receive and decipher these messages correctly. Understanding and nurturing your clairs will help you to uncover your values and establish your identity as a telepath. They'll teach you what works for you in your psychic practices and what you can do to elevate them to a higher level.

Clairvoyance

Despite being the most common of the clairs, clairvoyance is probably the most misunderstood. While most people know that clairvoyants can see things others are unaware of, it goes far beyond this. Clairvoyance is essentially a psychic's third eye - and this is even truer for telepaths. Whether you receive a subtle visual message like a flash of color, experience vivid premonitions, or detailed visions depends on many factors. Psychic seeing is different for each person experiencing it because everyone has ingrained patterns which contribute to how they perceive information. Some mediums can even visualize messages from the past, depending on how they receive messages. Others describe the information they receive popping up as (for them well-known) symbols. In modern times, people have also referred to clairvoyance as seeing messages in a window, just as one would on a widescreen TV, computer, or mobile phone. You may also get clear visions of someone trying to warn you about something that is coming in the future. Or a person with a distinct trait appears and serves as a reminder of something you need to do in the present. The messages you receive through this clair are metaphors. For example, if you see someone carrying a large backpack, this may indicate that you're bearing a heavy burden. Whereas, if you see the earth moving beneath you, this may mean you feel that your life is unstable and you're standing on shaky ground.

Clairaudience

The other form of information telepaths rely on is auditory messages. These are spoken words you get through clairaudience. The words that come through are intuitive messages that sound similar to your voice - especially if you hear them in your head. It's also possible to sense them with your outer (normal) hearing, in which case they often sound like a different person's voice. Whether you know this person or not, you'll be able to clearly distinguish their voice. Besides thoughts, clairaudients can also hear music - not to mention sounds that may sound like they're coming from this world and some that come from the spiritual realm. With sufficient practice, you can make the acoustic messages louder and clearer. Just like their visual counterparts, the auditory signals also vary in clarity. Sometimes, they can be as clear as your own voice, coming through as a short and straightforward message. For instance, you may hear a voice telling you that you should wait until you receive a promotion before purchasing a car. At other times, they'll come through unfiltered and require a little patience before you understand their point.

For example, you can hear someone telling you very loudly that you must stop controlling your life. In this case, you'll need to examine in which area of your life you need to loosen control.

Clairsentience

Clairsentience is the sense that relies on tactical stimuli. In most cases, the message will take the form of a physical reaction to something you do or experience. For example, you're viewing a picture of a frozen landscape, and you suddenly start feeling cold. Or you touch someone's hand and suddenly feel they are about to experience something unusual. These sensory experiences are all characteristic of clairsentients. While they rarely impact telepaths directly, these tactile messages represent the perfect way to sharpen your intuition. They teach you how listening to intuition can lead to extraordinary information. Sometimes, instead of pointing out something you were aware of in your gut, clairsentience will tell you that something isn't as it is supposed to be. This is another form of intuitive insight, a visceral sensation that if you don't change your currency course of action, you can expect trouble in the future. The messages can come off as positive or negative emotions, symptoms of illnesses, and even physical injuries. Sometimes the source will be clear, whereas, at other times, you'll have to put in more effort to find out where the message comes from. For example, you may experience pain, fear, and other uncharacteristic emotions related to a place, a situation, or an event. Or you'll feel the energy shift inside your body - and you'll have to figure out why it happened. You may also be able to read the emotions of others. This may come even easier than understanding your feelings - especially your gut feeling.

Claircognizance

Sometimes a medium doesn't even have to see, hear or feel a message. They'll know something is true or needs to be done. It just appears in their mind as intuitive wisdom without being backed up by rational thoughts. This is called claircognizance or psychic knowing, another indirect factor that may affect telepaths. Sometimes, the message will be a strong awareness that something is wrong or an insight you need to focus on in your psychic power. Either way, you'll know the information you've received to be accurate simply because your intuition tells you it is. You won't know how or why your gut urges on it, but you won't question it either - which you'll probably do at the start of your journey until you decide to use the wisdom you receive to guide you.

Telepaths may also use claircognizance to develop their telepathic abilities further. Simply having your gut feelings to back you up can make you more accurate during your psychic work. It's also worth mentioning that it's one of the most efficient channels you can use for communication. After all, you won't have to focus on hearing, seeing, or sensing anything. You just have to listen to your intuition, and you can have the information in your mind in a matter of seconds. Let's say you have a complex relationship with someone. Because of this, you can't decide how you feel about them. You can tap into your gut feelings and discover you have a bad feeling about this person.

Developing Your Psychic Senses

Most mediums have a preferred way of receiving psychic messages. They may be sensitive to all forms, but one of them will always be more influential. After some practice, you may be able to tune into several clairs. However, at the beginning of your journey, you should focus on only one form of extra sensory stimuli. Telepaths will typically need to nurture clairvoyance (physical seeing) or clairaudience (psychic hearing). Tuning into these can increase your awareness of your higher self. It'll also give you a different perspective for observing your intuition and allow you to practice and sharpen your telepathic abilities.

Developing Clairvoyance

Developing clairvoyance may sound easy, but it's probably the hardest one to master. You need to be attuned to potential visual messages, which is only possible if you tap into your intuition. Once you've conquered that, your clairvoyance skills will become more powerful, and the messages will become clearer.

Non-Verbal Communication with Your Intuition

Everyone is born with intuition. However, most people stop relying on it because of different societal rules, expectations, professional pursuits, or the stressful nature of day-to-day life. If this is the case with you, working with your intuition will be just as strange and awkward as seeing a friend you haven't seen in years. Your subconscious will have memories of your working together. However, the dynamic of your relationship has changed over the years. And although you are both the same people as you were before (literally), you and your intuition may as well be complete strangers. To work together again, you'll need to renew your relationship. To do this, stop from time to time and devote a couple of minutes to getting to know your intuition, as you would with a childhood friend. Ask questions frequently to learn how you can work together in the future. These don't have to be overly reflective questions but simple inquiries about your inner feelings. A great exercise for this is color-coding your emotions and asking your intuition to help identify them. For example, think about a recent experience - maybe a frustrating conversation you've had with a friend. Let's say you've assigned the color yellow to frustration. When asking your intuition, it will pick it up easily because you already have this information in your conscious mind. Over time, the color will be linked to the emotion subconsciously, which will come in handy next time you need to identify the feeling. Let's say you had a similar experience with someone else and aren't sure about the feeling it caused you. When tapping into your intuition, you need to ask it to show you the color of your emotion. If you suddenly see the flash of yellow, you'll instantly know you're frustrated.

Surveying and Predicting Your Environment

Scanning your environment is another great way to cultivate clairvoyance. To do this, sit or stand in the middle of a room or larger space. If you're standing, start moving around and look for potential signs in your environment. You can also do a quick survey with your eyes if you're sitting. Pay attention to all the sights. Is there any particular one you feel drawn to? Perhaps something you find appalling? Make sure to look into every corner and piece of furniture you can see from your position. As awkward as this exercise sounds, you've probably done this many times before when you were in an unfamiliar setting, waiting in line, or wanted to avoid an uncomfortable conversation. You just weren't aware of doing it. Practicing it consciously will help you familiarize yourself with your surroundings, so you can pick up subtle visual signs. Eventually, you'll be able to use these skills to explore settings you don't know well. This is the next step in learning to use clairvoyance. Once you can confidently use the clair to explore familiar settings, you can consider visiting a place you haven't visited before. Close your eyes and set an intention of seeing the place in question. This will prompt your mind to visualize it. Memorize how you've imagined the place to look (you can also draw or describe it in a few lines to help you retain the memories). Go there physically, and compare your vision to reality. See how many shapes and positions you recognize. If you find a few that look very familiar, you are on the way to developing sharp clairvoyance skills.

Dream Analysis

Yet another way to access psychic seeing is by exploring your subconscious through dreams. When you're awake, your mind may limit how many visual signals you can receive. This is because absorbing more would threaten your ability to live a balanced and functional life. However, the information you haven't been able to store in your consciousness may still reach you but get tucked away in your subconscious instead. Dreams often symbolize an alternate reality - one in which you can see and experience more. They allow you to move more freely - and explore your environment and access the full potential of your extrasensory gifts. To do this exercise, before going to bed, set an intention of what you want to explore in your dreams. Place a pen and paper on your nightstand and go to sleep. Falling asleep, you'll tune into your fluid subconscious. When you wake up, think about everything you've seen in your dreams, and draw or write down any sight you feel is relevant.

Developing Clairaudience

Clairaudience is much easier to develop than clairvoyance, yet people often aren't aware of having this ability. However, if you prefer learning through auditory signals, love listening to music, talking to yourself, and giving advice to people after listening to them, you may already have the innate ability of clairaudience. Here are a few ways to link your intuition to this skill and sharpen them both.

Listen to Your Environment

The easiest way to reveal your psychic hearing skills is to practice listening to the sounds in your environment. This will make your physical hearing more sensitive and allow you to pick up auditory messages subconsciously. To do this, you'll only need to close your eyes and start paying attention to sounds you don't usually focus on. If you're outside, this may be the sound of leaves rustling under your feet or people talking around you. Tune in to the different sounds and focus on them for a short time. The more you practice this, the wider your hearing range (both physical and psychic) will be.

Ask for Messages

Once you've learned to pick up simple sounds, you can start asking for specific auditory messages. Consider a question that has been occupying your mind lately. Ask this question or anything else you may want to learn from a spiritual guide or simply from your gut. Keep your ear open for the response. It can come in any form - a song on the radio, a word you hear during a conversation – or even a random sound you hear on the street.

Meditation

Meditating with your intuition is another highly recommended way to nurture clairs. And meditating with specific auditory signals is particularly good for sharpening your psychic hearing skills. For example, you can listen to guided meditation, relaxing music, or any other soothing sound that widens your range of auditory experiences. You may also simply choose to listen to the sound of your own breathing. You'll need a tranquil spot, comfortable clothes, and a quiet and peaceful environment. Turn off your electronics and ensure you won't be disturbed by other sounds from your surroundings. Close your eyes and listen to the air traveling through your body. Note any particular sounds you hear and when you hear them next time, compare the two sounds and the respective emotions they evoke.

Disclaimer

Having the ability to use your extrasensory senses can be wonderful. At the same time, they can represent a challenge, especially for beginners. Hearing voices and seeing things can be scary because these senses are also associated with mental illnesses. In the beginning, you may start hearing or seeing things when you least expect them, not to mention how distracting it can be to work on these gifts in today's world when noise and visual pollution is all around us. If you aren't prepared for a message, you may think you're experiencing a symptom of mental illness. However, when you hear or see things due to a mental illness, you're not experiencing reality. You're experiencing a signal your subconscious conjured as an alternate level of understanding. Receiving messages through the clairs is different. These messages come from your own intuitive awareness. They are real - and you should feel better after accepting them. Once you fully acknowledge your gifts, you'll see how much value they can add to your life. When you elevate your awareness of your senses, you'll be prompted to listen to your intuition more and more. With enough practice, you'll be able to look forward to the following messages and explore how you can use your gifts in telepathy. However, if you keep experiencing confusion, insecurity, anxiety, or another symptom that can make you question your mental health, consult a licensed professional about them. Don't practice clairvoyance or clairaudience until you've worked through these issues and have ensured that you'll be able to keep your mental well-being in check.

Chapter 5: Establish a Telepathic Bond

A telepathic bond is a connection you develop with another person, often someone in your circle, like a family member, friend, or energetically close to you. To communicate with someone telepathically, you need to establish a connection or a telepathic bond between the two of you. As a beginner, having this bond will facilitate easy telepathic exchanges. Telepathy is about exchanging thoughts, so this process will naturally require you to focus on your thoughts. This connection is established on a higher level as it doesn't require verbal communication. As mentioned in a previous chapter, some cultures believe you can create a telepathic bond with someone just by shaking hands or exchanging glances.

A telepathic bond is a connection you develop with another person, often someone in your circle.
https://www.pexels.com/photo/adult-affection-beads-blur-371285/

There are various ways to help you establish a telepathic bond with someone. Meditation is often a very effective technique. You can sit in a quiet place, take deep breaths with your eyes closed, focus on your breathing, and visualize this person. You can also write their name on a piece of paper and meditate while holding this paper. Having an accurate image of the person in your head is essential while visualizing. Seeing that instinct is significant in telepathic abilities, you can rely on it and your gut feeling to guide you through this process. You will feel it in your gut when the connection is created.

Carefully choose who you bond with for this to work. As a beginner, you can't just establish a bond with a complete stranger. It's better to bond with people you are already familiar with - like your partner, parents, siblings, close friends, or anyone with whom you feel an energy connection. Look for people who you feel comfortable around. They are the ones who have positive vibes that lift everyone's spirits. You may also find yourself connecting with them on a higher vibrational level. You will experience emotions like excitement, joy, and gratitude. Find people who make you feel good about yourself and love yourself more when you are around them.

Competition can threaten your relationships and weaken your bonds with people. Choose people you don't constantly compare yourself to, and do not choose those with whom you feel ashamed or insecure around. Bond with people with whom you feel free to be yourself. Anxiety has become the disease of the age, and most people are concerned either with worries about the future or regrets from the past. However, there are always people who make you feel at peace when you are around them and who silence all your doubts - even the critical voice in your head. Connect with these people, the ones who keep you calm, the ones who make you happy and only focus on the present moment. You don't have to talk or do anything to have fun; you can sit quietly with them without saying a word and still feel comfortable and at ease. There are no awkward silences.

Sometimes you put your guard up and build walls around you either to protect yourself or because you cherish your privacy. However, some people make you take these walls down and let you become your truest and most vulnerable self when you are around them. You open up to them and can share feelings and secrets you haven't shared with anyone before. They make you feel heard and create a safe space for you to be yourself and share all your secrets, as you know that they will never judge you. These are the people you want to create a telepathic bond with.

You connect with these people on every level and trust them because you know they have your best interests at heart. They keep you balanced, and you feel your vibe with them on every level. Deep down, you know the people you want to bond with. It's an instinct that makes you feel connected with them on some level, whether it's spiritually or energetically. When choosing someone to bond with telepathically, ensure that they only bring positive vibes and feelings to your life.

Don't bond with negative people who want to cause you harm. Many energy vampires are out there and will only bring negativity to you. A telepathic bond involves exchanging thoughts, and you don't want negative thoughts in your head or in your life. Listen to your gut. It will tell you if you go off course and choose the wrong person.

Twins Telepathy

You have probably seen it in movies or heard real-life stories about twins sharing a telepathic connection. Twins' telepathy is when one twin knows what the other is thinking or feeling, even when they aren't in the same place. Twins already have a unique relationship with each other. They shared a womb and have the same genes, and, in the case of identical twins, they share the exact same features. Twins also share similar brain patterns, which scientists believe is the reason behind their telepathic bond. Both fraternal and identical twins share this bond. They have a natural understanding of each other's emotions and feelings. For instance, when a twin is in trouble, the other twin will feel in their gut that something bad has happened. It isn't just their emotional connection that is strong, but their physical connection as well. Some twins have also reported that they often feel a physical sensation when their twin is in pain or suffering from emotional distress. For instance, one twin can feel pain in their chest at the same moment their sibling is having a heart attack, or a twin can feel pain in their abdomen while their twin sister is giving birth.

Twins may also act in the same way even when they aren't together. For example, they may call or text each other at the same time, cook the same food, and buy the same clothes. This proves that twins are attuned to each other's thoughts and emotions and that they may know what the other person is going to say or even finish each other's sentences. In fact, even twins who weren't raised together still share some similarities that go beyond their physical appearance, which shows that twins don't have to be raised in the same home or environment to share a telepathic bond. Researchers believe that twins who aren't raised together may share an even more powerful telepathic bond than those who are raised together. They have also explained that some twins who are raised together may try to fight this bond. Each twin may want to find their own identity away from the other and express their own individualism. As a result, they may do things or act in a certain way just to be different.

The concept of twins' telepathy has been around for centuries and has fascinated people all over the world. French author Alexandre Dumas was inspired by this idea, and it was the theme of his novella "The Corsican Brothers." The novella was about twins who weren't raised together yet shared a telepathic bond. Dumas described this bond as if they both shared the same body. When one felt physical or mental pain, the other felt it as well. Dumas's wording is very interesting as this is how twin telepathic bonds often seem - like two souls sharing the same body and brain.

Twins grow up bonded, so it doesn't feel strange or abnormal to them. For this reason, they use it without thinking. They don't need to meditate or even try to establish a bond because it is already there and active.

Many real-life stories of twins' telepathic bonds go beyond eating the same dish at a restaurant. It can even save their lives. Gemma Houghton, a young girl who lives in Britain, shared her telepathic story with her twin. She has a fraternal twin sister, and one night as she was relaxing at home, she had a feeling that her sister was in trouble. Her sister was taking a bath, so Gemma went up to the bathroom to check on her. She knocked at the door and called her sister, but there was no answer. Gemma opened the door to find her sister unconscious underwater in the bathtub. Gemma's sister almost drowned as she suffered a seizure and passed out. Luckily, Gemma sensed her sister needed help, came to her rescue, and saved her life. The twins' telepathic bond saved Gemma's sister's life.

Another example is of twins who were referred to as the Jim Twins. Their story was so popular that it was covered in various publications and websites. Interestingly, the Jim Twins, who were male, weren't raised together and didn't know about each other. However, both men married two women who shared the same name, both adopted dogs, gave them the same names, and even named their children the same names. Skeptics may claim that this is nothing more than pure coincidence. However, there are things that are just too strange to be coincidences, and this story is one of them. It wasn't a single similarity; it included wives, pets, and children's names. This means that even though they weren't aware of it, these twins were telepathically bonded and attuned to each other's thoughts.

There was another story of a girl whose ankle suddenly started swelling for no reason, only to find out later that her twin sister had broken the same ankle. There was also a story of a man who said he experienced excruciating pain in his chest at the same time his twin brother had a heart attack. There is yet another story of twin brothers who were working in a woodshop when one of the twins heard his brother saying that he wanted sandpaper, so he handed it to him. Interestingly, the brother never said out loud that he wanted the sandpaper. He only thought about it, but the other twin could hear his brother's thoughts because of their strong telepathic connection.

There were other twin brothers who we'll call Twin A and Twin B. Twin A was on his honeymoon, and Twin B was with his wife in his home. There was a break-in, and Twin B was robbed. At the same time, Twin A told his wife to pack her bags as they had to go back now because he sensed something terrible had happened to his brother. Another story is of teen twins. One of them was working while the other was having fun with his friends. The second twin and his friends had an accident in the middle of nowhere with no cellphone reception. When they managed to get service, he found that his brother had called him, so he called him back to tell him about the crazy accident. The other twin answered the phone, freaking out and asking his brother if everything was okay. He told him that he strongly felt something was wrong, so he called his twin to check on him.

Another twin said that his brother was on vacation with his wife. When the twin on vacation experienced sunburn, the other one felt hot and extreme pain in his skin. A young woman said that one day she was at work and fainted for a few seconds for no reason. When she recovered, she received a phone call to go to the hospital. She found out later that her twin sister had passed away at the same time as she had fainted. There is also the story of a girl who went to get a blood test while her twin was at school. The one at school noticed a broken blood vessel in her arm. She found out later it was the exact spot her sister had had the blood test.

Twin telepathic bond isn't something that they establish with age. It has always been there. This was clear from the story of these toddler twins. Toddler 1 and Toddler 2 were two years old at the time. Toddler 1 was playing calmly at her aunt and uncle's home while her twin, Toddler 2, was with their parents. Toddler 2 got her finger stuck in the door and required stitches. Toddler 1, who was still at her uncle's home, began crying and screaming frantically. Her aunt and uncle tried to do everything to calm her, but she was hysterical and shaking. All of a sudden, she calmed down and stopped crying. When her parents arrived with her injured twin sister, the aunt and uncle told them of Toddler 1 crying and shaking. The parents were shocked because, at the same time, Toddler 2 was getting her stitches. However, this story is even stranger because Toddler 2 was calm and didn't cry or flinch. Even the doctors thought that this was strange. The parents, aunt, and uncle believe that Toddler 2 transferred her pain telepathically to Toddler 1.

Thousands of stories about twins experiencing a telepathic bond prove Dumas had a point. It can sometimes feel as if they share the same body and mind.

Meditation Techniques

As much as meditation is an effective technique to strengthen telepathic abilities, it can also help strengthen your telepathic bond with the people in your life. Practice these techniques with your partner, sibling, friend, or anyone with whom you want to establish a telepathic connection. Even if you don't have a telepathic bond yet, these techniques will help you create one. For these techniques to work, sit in a quiet room without any distractions.

Meditation Exercise 1

1. Sit in a comfortable position.
2. Bring a string of mala beads to meditate on and hold them while you also hold hands.
3. Chant OM at the same time.
4. Each of you should move a bead with every OM sound.
5. Repeat the OM while breathing 25 times. Focus on your voice and breathing.

6. Next, focus on your partner's voice and breathing as they also chant 25 times.

7. Now, chant OM together.

8. Keep chanting until you finish the beads.

9. After you finish, chant OM one more time and feel the connection and bond between you and your partner.

Meditation Exercise 2

1. Sit in a comfortable position opposite each other.

2. Stare into each other's eyes.

3. Take slow and deep breaths while focusing on your breathing.

4. Feel the air as it comes in and out of your chest.

5. Keep focused on your breath, breathe slowly, and don't force it.

6. Keep doing this for a couple of minutes.

7. Next, you can begin the breathing exercise.

8. You or your partner can be the one who sets the pace for your breathing.

9. Take a deep breath and count to five.

10. Hold your breath and also count to five.

11. Breathe out while counting to seven.

12. Your partner should be following your breathing.

13. You both focus on each other's breathing.

14. Repeat the breathing exercise with your partner for five minutes.

15. Now, allow your partner to set the breathing pace.

16. Repeat the breathing exercise again for five minutes.

17. While breathing, make sure you take deep breaths, focus on your breathing, and keep staring at your partner.

Meditation Exercise 3

1. Sit in a comfortable position across from each other.

2. Close your eyes.

3. Breathe in and out deeply and feel your body relaxing.

4. Next, as you have relaxed your mind and body, open your eyes.

5. Stare into each other's eyes and focus on each other's breathing.

6. Now, as you look into their eyes, you will be able to see yourself in them.

7. You are no longer two individuals but two souls in one body.

Meditation Exercise 4

1. Burn scented candles around the room.

2. Sit opposite each other in a comfortable position.

3. Set intentions for what you hope to achieve from this meditation exercise - which is establishing a telepathic bond with your partner.

4. Close your eyes and set your intention. You can either repeat it to yourself or visualize it.

5. Now, create a telepathic connection with your partner. This connection can also be an emotional one. You can establish an emotional connection with them since this person is someone you trust and who is close to you.

6. Once you feel a connection is established, breathe in and out slowly.

7. Now, visualize there is a chord made of light flowing through you and them and connecting you together.

In a way, we are all connected, but some connections are stronger than others, while some bonds take time to establish. Creating a telepathic bond is possible with the people you love and care about because you already share an emotional connection. Believe that you can establish this connection, and let meditation guide you. If you are a twin, you are one of the lucky few with a telepathic bond with someone without even trying.

Chapter 6: Listen to Other's Messages

Telepathy is a two-way street. To communicate effectively with someone, you must be able to send and receive messages. In this chapter, we focus on the latter component of telepathy. You'll find out how to receive telepathic messages and read minds effectively. You'll also learn to recognize signs that someone is sending you telepathic messages and learn several mind-reading methods.

To communicate effectively with someone, you must be able to send and receive messages.
https://www.pexels.com/photo/silhouette-photography-of-people-2627060/

Reading Minds

Receiving telepathic messages requires you to hone your mind-reading skills. Believe it or not, we unconsciously try to read people's minds all the time. We spend a lot of time wondering why a person is acting a certain way, overthinking the reasoning behind their words, trying to understand their emotions, and wondering what goes inside this person's mind. The conclusions we reach are often based on our own intuition, which is powered by the depth of our connection with that person, and what we already know about them. We are always intuiting and observing other people's body language to find out whether they're engaged, bored, lying, tired, active, etc. We also try to anticipate their reactions to certain situations or news.

While reading minds from a psychic perspective requires more effort and consideration, you can benefit greatly from the type of mind-reading you do every day. This is why you should involve your consciousness and actively lean into your intuition in the process.

The following steps can guide you toward developing your mind-reading abilities:

How to Read Minds

Mind-reading requires a lot of time, effort, and practice, like every other skill. Your focus should be on practicing mindful thinking. Observing and reflecting on your environment and those around you can help you read minds more easily.

Step 1: Enter an Open and Receptive Mental State

The first thing you need to do is learn to let go of all your judgments. As scary as it may sound, you need to open yourself up to other people's energies and allow them to engulf you. Reading minds won't be possible if you can't accept and respond to others. Whether you're sending or receiving a message, you must realize that telepathic communications are mostly about the other person rather than yourself. This is the mindset and energy you need to approach this endeavor.

By keeping your mind and energy open, you'll be able to connect with other people's energy more effectively. It also increases your awareness and keeps you present in the moment. You can achieve this state of mind by practicing mindfulness, meditation, or breath-work techniques. Doing yoga is also a great way to ground yourself.

Step 2: Choose a Person

Psychic work always works best when you're focused on a specific intention. Selecting one person to work with will help you yield the best results. Once you choose a person, focus entirely on them. Visualize their face and imagine their features down to the last detail. Think of their posture, how they walk or stand, how they sound and talk, and their overall behavior and body language. Capture a mental image of the essence of that person.

Afterward, you need to separate the person in your mind from their surroundings. This can be hard to do at first, as you'll probably start replacing their actual environment with one of your own imagination. The key here is to eliminate any distractions in the background and focus only on them.

Step 3: Focus Harder

Now that you've separated the person from their surroundings, you need to move your attention to their face. Keep eye contact with them for 10 seconds. Holding your gaze for longer than that can make them uncomfortable, and anything shorter than 10 seconds won't let you connect effectively.

Break eye contact and start feeling the energy that you've drawn from them. Explore their thoughts, feelings, and emotions. You'll find that these things are already rushing into your mind.

Step 4: Deepen the Connection

After you get a sense of that person's energy, you need to work on deepening their connection. You're going to get a sense of what you wish to ask them after you gain insight into their thoughts. Allow this experience to guide the entire conversation. Keep in mind that these thoughts may be fun and nice or extremely dark and deep. Whatever they are, you have to maintain openness and receptiveness. Embrace these thoughts and discuss them with the person you're connected with.

Mind-Reading Tips

The greatest thing about learning to receive mental messages is that it requires you to boost your energetic flow, which you can do just by sharpening some of the skills that you already use daily. Mind-reading is significantly easier to develop than other psychic skills.

Here are some activities you can do to enhance your energetic flow and develop mind-reading skills:

Increase Your Emotional Intelligence

Being able to read a person's mind depends largely on your ability to read their emotions accurately. You can only do this if you have high emotional intelligence.

People who have high emotional intelligence:

- Read other people's body language
- Actively listen and reflect on other's words
- Listen to the person's tone and notice the way they speak

A person's tone of voice, body language, and attitude can tell you a lot about their feelings and what they truly mean. For instance, you can only tell if a person is being sarcastic or genuine through their voice and physical expressions.

Become a Better Listener

Many people don't realize that listening is a communication skill. It is actually the cornerstone of communication. If you think about it, you'll find that you often listen to other people to respond to them rather than to understand them.

Being understood is among most people's deepest desires. We all respond negatively when we feel overlooked. It makes sense that the other person will become closed off and non-receptive if you don't make an effort to understand their perspective.

Stay present and keep your mind from wandering whenever you're talking to someone. Listen to what they're saying and reflect on it. If listening is a vital life skill, it is the core of mind-reading.

Seek out Emotional Connection

While some people have very little empathy, we are all empathetic beings. Unfortunately, technological advancements have gone a long way toward diminished in-person communications, making it very easy to lose touch with our empathetic emotions. You should actively tune into your empathy by exploring your feelings. Once you're ready, try to focus on other people's feelings and consider how they understand and react to their own emotions.

Don't Jump to Conclusions

We always attempt to make sense of the world around us by making up stories - it's a human instinct. What do you do when someone sees your text and doesn't reply right away? Your brain probably comes up with a dozen different scenarios explaining why they left you without responding. You start wondering if you said something wrong, so you read your text over and over again at least a hundred times. To ease your anxiety, you tell yourself that perhaps they got into another fight with their family, which is why they didn't get the chance to reply. This made-up scenario, however, makes you worry even more. Then, you remind yourself of how busy their schedule is and how they probably forgot to get back to you.

Regardless of what the situation is and how reasonable you believe your assumptions are, you need to remember that you don't have enough information to form an opinion or conclusion. You don't know anything about their situation and intention, which means that your imagination has actually filled in most of what you think you know. The next time you make assumptions, remember to collect enough information before overreacting to other people's actions.

Signs Someone Is Sending You Telepathic Messages

Here are some signs that someone is trying to send you telepathic messages:

You Can Communicate Via Eye Contact

If someone is sending you telepathic messages, it can feel as if you're having a conversation with them whenever your eyes meet. This is because your eyes are used to communicating with each other. As explained in the exercise at the beginning of the chapter, you can subconsciously communicate your mood to a person. Experienced practitioners of telepathy can also guide a person's actions via eye contact.

You Receive a Psychic's Confirmation

If you suspect someone is trying to communicate with you telepathically, you can always get more clarity by consulting a professional psychic. Keep in mind that many "psychics," especially many of those who can be found online, are scammers. Use this as an opportunity to lean into your intuition. You probably shouldn't book another session with that psychic if something feels off.

Your Mood Swings Are Intense

Is your mood extremely unstable these days? Do you often alternate between periods of joy and sudden intense sadness? This may be your body's way of trying to deal with telepathic messages. For instance, if you're receiving a negative message, your body may translate it as sadness. The energies that these messages carry can affect your mood. Do you recall feeling disoriented and overwhelmed? This is likely a result of the information you're receiving.

They Interact with You in Your Dreams

Telepathic communications can also take place during sleep. If one of your friends appears in your dreams after a period of no contact, then they could be sending you telepathic messages. Recall as many details as you can, including how you felt during the dream. Think about how you felt when you woke up. The only way to determine whether this was an innocent dream or a communication attempt is to find out whether it is relevant to real life. If possible, talk to that person to find out whether your dream really carried a message. If you woke up feeling unsettled, then your friend may be telling you that they need your help. If it was a happy dream, then they may be excited to share joyful news with you.

Your Thoughts Are Attuned

If you feel that your thoughts are attuned to someone else's thoughts, it may be because you're telepathically communicating. For instance, your friend may sing a part of a song that was just stuck in your head, or they may say that they were craving pasta when you were just thinking the same. If you're communicating telepathically with someone, you can influence each other's thoughts.

They Are an Open Book

If you can easily tell what a person is thinking and how they're feeling, then you probably have an established telepathic connection. This is especially the case if this easy-to-read person isn't very close to you. You don't need to know much about a person's motivations, reactions, moods, and body language to be able to know what they're thinking and feeling if they're sending you telepathic messages.

Mind-Reading Exercises

If you're still not ready to tap into anyone's mind and read their thoughts, you can start by practicing with someone you trust. Incorporating mind-reading exercises into your routine can help you strengthen your intuition and will facilitate openness and reception. Keep in mind that you may not get the result you want straight away, so keep practicing. However, don't be discouraged. It takes time to be able to connect deeply with someone and completely trust your intuition to guide you throughout your interaction. The more you practice, the easier and more natural it will get.

These four simple exercises can train your mind to receive telepathic messages from others:

Have Your Partner or a Close Friend Ask You to Get Something for Them

Tell your close friend or partner that you'll pass by the grocery store after work. Ask them to clear their mind and relax. You can also ask them to do a simple meditation if they're willing. Once they're ready, they should mentally ask you to pick a specific item up from the store. They can visualize you doing it while repeating the statement to themselves multiple times before letting it go completely. When you go to the store, let your intuition guide you toward the item they requested. Try again if you don't get it right.

Ask Them to Send You a Mental Image

Sit quietly with your friend or partner. Focus on each other and assume that you're connecting with each other's minds. Your friend should imagine a certain image, such as a teddy bear. They shouldn't give you any hints about what they're thinking. Tap into the mental image that they're sending and try to intuit what it is. Get all your senses involved in the process. You don't necessarily have to see a teddy bear in mind, but you can sense things like comfort or softness.

Ask Them for Permission

Sit in front of your partner or friend. Touch your knees and hands together and maintain eye contact. Once you're settled, ask them for permission to read their mind. When they grant it to you, tell them something that you suspect about them. For example, you can say, "I suspect you haven't told me you received a new job offer." You must involve your intuition in the process because it will help you determine a suspicion that you believe is true.

Your partner or friend should repeat the statement back to you in a way that acknowledges it. For example, they can say, "I understand that you think I never told you I received a new job offer." They shouldn't confirm or deny the statement or add anything to it. You should be able to sense whether the statement is correct after hearing it from them. Ask them if your suspicion is correct. They should offer an answer and the needed clarification. Thank each other for your willingness to explore assumptions, and understand and listen to each other.

Guess Who's Calling You

Don't rush to see who's calling you each time your phone rings. Instead, take the time to tap into whoever is calling you. See if you already know who it is. You'll not get it right each time. However, the more you practice, the better the results you'll yield. Asking for confirmation from the person calling you can help you verify your guesses.

Mind-reading is not a special psychic ability that only the gifted can develop. Anyone can learn to read minds and receive telepathic messages from others. You can easily read other people's minds once you nurture your emotional intelligence, lean into your intuition, and work on your active listening skills. Chances are that someone is wittingly or unwittingly trying to communicate with you telepathically already. You can know for sure by watching out for the signs we mentioned above.

Chapter 7: Send Messages to Others

Now that you know how to be receptive to telepathic messages, we'll explore the other component of telepathy: sending messages to others. In this chapter, you'll learn how to communicate mentally with anyone, no matter how far away they are. You'll also learn to recognize a few signs that your messages have been successfully delivered to the person in mind.

Being able to send telepathic messages to others is a great tool, especially when you have something to say but don't know to do it.

https://www.pexels.com/photo/silhouette-of-man-sitting-on-grass-field-at-daytime-775417/

Sending Telepathic Messages

Sending telepathic messages to others is a great tool, especially when you have something to say but don't know how to do it. Sending mental messages also comes in handy when you want to talk about your thoughts and feelings, or reach out to an ex, even when it isn't the right thing to do.

Unfortunately, the dynamics of life, relationships, and communication aren't always easy - there will be times when you can't speak what is in your heart. This is why learning to work with your higher self to deliver these messages via telepathy can be of great advantage. Telepathic communications can help you get closure and forgiveness and deepen connections.

You may struggle to work out if you're communicating correctly at first. It's normal to feel anxious and even silly, as well. However, it helps to think about telepathy as a sixth sense that you're trying to rediscover. Developing your telepathic skills is similar to remembering an old instinct you have. Say you're a talented artist who hasn't drawn in years. You won't be able to draw portraits as perfectly as you once did the first few times around. You may not get the proportions right at all. With practice, however, you'll become more dexterous, and everything will eventually start coming back to you.

Telepathy is an instrument that connects you to the world around you. The best thing about this skill is that it can be nurtured and developed by everyone. We all have the ability to send mental messages, images, and ideas to others, but few people are aware of this possibility.

It's best to practice telepathy with someone that you already are strongly connected to, such as a close friend, family member, or partner. As you recall from the previous chapters, telepathic communication only takes place when you're vibrating on another person's energetic frequency. This means that you're likely telepathically communicating with them on some level, even if you don't realize it. A good place to start would be by paying attention to the mental interactions that are already taking place between you two.

Here is how you can master the art of sending telepathic messages:

Start in a Meditative State

Find an empty and quiet place to sit down. Get yourself comfortable and feel the tension leaving your body. Relax your limbs, jaw, and face muscles. Allow your shoulders to drop down. Empty your brain and visualize all intrusive thoughts flowing out of your brain. Once you enter a light trance state, start visualizing the person you wish to connect with. Envision them sitting or standing right in front of you as you send them feelings of gratitude or love. Imagine that these emotions are a form of energy that you can pass on to them.

Send Small Messages to a Loved One

You enter a deep trance state when you fall asleep, which is why it's possible to establish dream telepathic connections. To do that, ask your higher self for permission to access your highest consciousness to send someone a message before you go to bed. Use your thoughts to send a loved one a small message. Ask them, telepathically, to send their response to the message if they received it.

Be Open to Responses

If you do this correctly, the other person will likely call or text you the next day. They may mention that they've been thinking about you a lot recently or just felt the need to contact you or check on you today. If it's someone that you're no longer in contact with, they may reach out more subtly or passively. For instance, they may communicate with you on social media. Don't be discouraged if you don't receive a response. Sending telepathic messages can take a lot of time and practice to master. You should also keep in mind that you didn't necessarily fail if you didn't hear back from anyone. For instance, if you're dealing with an ex, they'll probably fight back the instinct to contact you.

Patience Is Key

Psychic endeavors require great levels of patience. Like everything in life, you can't be an expert overnight. You have to trust that you'll improve at your own pace. Telepathy also requires a lot of repetition, especially if you're new to the craft. You also need to understand that some people are better at sending messages than receiving them, and vice versa. Even though sending and receiving are both vital parts of telepathy, they require relatively different skill sets. It's okay to be naturally inclined toward one more than the other. You just need to identify which of them is your stronger suit so you can spend more time nurturing the other.

Reach out to a Mentor

Very few people realize the importance of maintaining good spiritual hygiene. Taking care of your spiritual wellness is crucial if you're working toward psychic development. Reach out to psychic mentors, book reiki healing sessions, and explore other holistic healing methods to cleanse your energy. You have to be very careful with telepathic communications because you're vulnerable to fears, thoughts, emotions, and ideas that aren't yours.

Sending Telepathic Messages from a Distance

Many people still don't fully understand the concept of telepathy and don't accept it as a valid means of communication. You'll come across many skeptics throughout your psychic and spiritual development journey. Many people will openly look down on you and speak negatively of your beliefs and practices. We're bringing this up because you can't let these voices get to you. If you doubt, for a second, that telepathy doesn't work, your efforts will be in vain. If you're vulnerable to criticism, it's best to keep your practices to yourself or talk about them only with people you trust until you're fully confident about your abilities. With that in mind, let's explore how to send telepathic messages to anyone, regardless of the distance.

Believe in the Power of Telepathy

The first and most critical step in successfully sending telepathic messages to others is to fully believe in the power of telepathy and trust in your ability to practice it effectively. You don't shop online unless you're sure you'll receive your order. You don't keep worrying if you'll get scammed as long as you're shopping from a trusted vendor. You should approach telepathy with the same mindset. Place your order and let it go.

Telepathy and other psychic undertakings are already beyond our basic human comprehension. Spirituality is much greater than us, so it makes sense that your mind won't get the job done if you're tentative about the whole process. Having doubts, whether you affirm them or not, slows down your ability to deliver a telepathic message to someone. To avoid any disappointment, you should make sure that you're 100% positive about telepathy and have faith in your power to send mental messages.

Keep a Calm Mind and Body

When practicing telepathy, your mind and body should be calm as they would be if you're practicing mindfulness or meditation. You have to be as relaxed and peaceful as you can be. You don't need to take a trip to the mountains or a secluded beach to be able to communicate with someone telepathically. Just choose a time and place where you usually feel safe and comfortable. Make sure you won't be disturbed for the duration of your practice. Some people like to mentally connect with others right before they go to bed. Make sure that your room is at the perfect temperature - not too hot that you feel uncomfortable or too cold that you feel bothered. It should be chilly enough that it feels nice to curl up in your blanket. Keep the room pitch-black to avoid any distractions and find comfort in the silence. This way, you'll be able to get in tune with your higher consciousness and focus solely on the telepathic process.

This may not necessarily work for you. Some people feel uneasy when it's too dark or feel sleepy as soon as they lie down on the bed. Explore your own likes and dislikes and experiment until you find your ideal setting and environment, whether it is a local beach, forest, or even a spot that gives you the perfect view of the cityscape.

Use the Power of Visualization

To send your message, visualize the person you wish to communicate with down to the tiniest detail. Picture them vividly and feel their presence with your senses. Engage all your senses in the process. Imagine their eyes and how it feels to look right into them. Inhale their scent and listen to their voice. Visualize them right in front of you. Look at them and tell them what you wish to say.

Imagine the process as if it were real. Feel yourself saying your message, whether it's an expression of love or just something that you wish to communicate. You can also ask them to call, text, or do anything else. Telepathic messages should also be sent with good and loving intentions. Avoid using it to send negative energy to a person.

Once you feel like you've told them everything you wish to say, draw a deep breath and smile slightly. Open your eyes when you're ready. Even though it will take you a bit of practice, telepathic communications should feel natural and come as easily as in-person interactions.

Basic Telepathy Exercise

Find a trusted partner to practice this telepathy exercise with, and follow these steps:

Step 1: Sit across from your partner around 1.5 to 2 feet apart. This distance should be intimate yet not too uncomfortable. Since you shouldn't cross your legs, your partner will not be right in front of you. Their legs should lie next to each other on the floor. Keep your hands locked together or folded to your chest.

Step 2: Look directly into each other's eyes without straining your vision. So instead of looking at them diagonally, keep your vision straight and just look at their right or left eye, depending on the side they're on.

Step 3: Now that you're focused on each other's eyes, you should both slowly expand your scopes of vision until you encompass each other's full faces. In a minute or two, the image of the other person's face will start changing. You'll experience increased blurriness. When this happens, tell your partner of this change. Don't go into any details. Just mention the intensity of this occurrence. Even though it seldom takes more than a couple of minutes, you should be open to the idea of spending 10 minutes doing this exercise if needed. This is because the human brain is trained to ignore any inconsistencies in its perception. The hardest thing about this exercise is finding the right words to communicate the changes in your vision as they undergo several levels of intensity.

Step 4: Each time you notice and communicate a change, verify that your partner is experiencing them at the same time and level of intensity. The stronger the changes, the more intense the visual alterations will be, so expect to feel overwhelmed and unsettled. You may need to take a break in order to regather your mental strength.

This exercise aims to train your mind to focus entirely on a certain action rather than your thoughts. Thoughts are highly subjective, so this activity aims to duplicate a similar level of subjectivity through an experience. Your mind will be too busy trying to see your partner's face clearly while staying focused on just one of their eyes. If you do this exercise correctly, you'll be too engaged to think.

Once you go past the stage of simple blurriness, the rest of the changes are hallucinatory. Your mind will be so surprised by the image you're seeing that it captures your full attention, generating even more intense hallucinations. If you start feeling uncomfortable, change your attention to something else or blink a few times.

"Eyes are the windows of the soul." Focusing on each other's eyes with this level of intensity gives you access to each other's consciousness. This means that when one of you is experiencing a hallucination, the other person is likely to experience it too. With practice, you'll be able to tell if what you're experiencing is a product of the other person's perception. When you notice that your partner is hallucinating, you'll naturally withdraw your visual concentration and will no longer duplicate your perception. Moving your attention from them will also cut off their hallucination.

The more you practice, the easier it will become for you to tune into other people's consciousness. All you'll need to do is focus on a person so you can duplicate their experiences.

Signs Your Telepathic Messages Are Received

Influence and Observe

If you're not willing to ask your partner or friend if they feel the urge to do something you want them to do, you can just watch their actions. Influence their thoughts by focusing on something that you want them to do.

Keep it simple. For instance, you can start thinking about your friend asking you to hang out. If they text you to ask if you're free without prior discussion of any plans, then they've received your message. Experiment often to make sure that it wasn't just a coincidence.

Your Friends Check on You

If you're facing a problem and start wondering if you should call them and ask for help, you may find them already calling you if you're telepathically connected. Your thoughts will travel to the right place, allowing you to receive help before you even ask for it. This can only happen with people you're very close and energetically attuned to.

They Dream About You

While this requires a higher level of telepathic skills, you can try to influence a person to dream about you. If you succeed, they'll probably tell you that they dreamt about you.

You Have Growing Similarities

If you're working on sending your thoughts to someone, you'll notice that you're both growing interested in similar things. If your friend mentions a place you want to go to or hums the melody of a song stuck in your brain, then your messages are being delivered.

Now that you've read this chapter, you can easily communicate with others telepathically. All you need to do is trust in the power of telepathy and your ability to do it successfully. With practice, you'll be able to send messages to people just by focusing your attention on them.

Chapter 8: Exercise Your Telepathic Muscles

Mind reading and telepathy only work if you fully control your will and can concentrate completely on something. Otherwise, your brain waves will be interrupted by many outside influences in the way, and you'll find it difficult to communicate telepathically. On that note, one should be well-versed in communication techniques as well as understanding other people's emotions and expressions. Only then can you be a successful telepath. Otherwise, you'll end up failing this task.

Mind reading and telepathy only works if you're in full control of your will and can concentrate completely on something.

https://www.pexels.com/photo/man-wearing-black-cap-with-eyes-closed-under-cloudy-sky-810775/

Now that you've learned both aspects of telepathic communication, you can finally put what you've learned into practice to send and receive telepathic messages. However, you can't expect to be a master mind reader just because you know the theory or techniques of developing telepathy skills. This unique skill requires a lot of practice, without which you'll just be another amateur mind reader who can't get it right. Although your effort may seem fruitless at the beginning, with consistent practice and concentration, you'll be able to accomplish wonders.

You've already gone through some basic techniques and scenarios to develop your mind-reading skills, but you won't become a master with a few techniques overnight. So, to help you further on this journey, this chapter is full of exercises and scenarios where you'll get to develop your telepathic skills with the help of some friends. Go through each exercise and apply it in real-life scenarios. Even if you aren't successful at first, after a while of practicing, you'll notice a marked improvement.

Before you start, create a harmonious energy or rapport between yourself and the person whose mind you're trying to reach. You can do this by meditation or rhythmic breathing, which you've already learned about in a previous chapter. Many people overlook this process step and end up making little to no progress in their telepathic journey.

It is important that you form a connection with the person you're trying to read so that a mental bridge can connect your mind. This is the best way to avoid any interference from other people's minds and only get through to the person you're communicating to telepathically. The stronger your rapport, the better you'll be able to communicate.

Finding Locations

To successfully carry out this practice, you'll need to guide your friend, let's call them the transmitter, to concentrate their will or thoughts while sending them toward your mind. It will then be your task to catch the signals being sent to you. Start this exercise by standing, blindfolded, in the middle of the room together with your transmitter. Ask the transmitter to mentally select one corner of the room without telling you which they have chosen.

They must then project their will into your mind by concentrating really hard. At this point, you must also have a completely passive and receptive state of mind. There shouldn't be thoughts clouding your brain lest they clutter your mind. After a moment has passed, you will feel yourself wanting to move in a particular direction; even though you have no sense of direction, your mind will work automatically toward moving to that location. You may not get this right the first few times, but practicing will make your intuition better and your brain sharper.

Finding Large Objects

The next exercise is to find large objects like furniture items in the room. Don't get impatient if these tasks don't seem too interesting at the moment, as they are just preparing you for future tasks you'll need to accomplish. Ask the transmitter to focus on a piece of furniture or any large object in the room and mentally guide you toward it. While doing this, they will also be responsible for guiding you away from bumping into obstacles as you'll be blindfolded. For instance, if the transmitter is mentally directing you toward a chair, it should send psychic signals for you to receive. Continue practicing this exercise until you can find every piece of furniture in the room. Repeat the same exercise to find small objects if you'd like a more demanding challenge.

Finding Hidden Objects

Once you've mastered how to find objects in a room, it's time to learn how to find hidden objects that only the transmitter knows about. Ask your friend to hide a small object like a key, watch or phone in a cabinet, under a book, or in some hidden space while you stay out of the room. Once they've hidden the object, you can come inside the room and be mentally directed toward the hidden object. For this practice, you don't need to be blindfolded, considering the object is not in your sight. The transmitter will need to guide you toward the object by giving mental instructions like "up," "down," "left," "right," etc. you'll need to let your mind become completely receptive toward their signals.

Finding a Person

This exercise should be done with more than one person, a minimum of three people other than you. Start by asking them to select the person they'll need to locate. Everyone except you should know who has been chosen. After this, start by finding the person's general location by letting your mind guide you. You should be getting telepathic signals from the others' thoughts regarding the location you need to be at. Once you've found the general location of the person you're supposed to find, you'll have an intuitive feeling about whether you're in the right or wrong place. Then, start moving according to the urges you get. After a few attempts of this exercise, this feeling will get stronger, and you'll be able to recognize it better.

Finding a Book

Ask your friend to select a book from a bookcase and then put it back, either in the same place or somewhere else. Then, use your telepathic skills to find out which book was selected. This process will be very similar to the finding small objects exercise, but people will be a lot more surprised at this feat. Make sure you keep your mind open to mental guidance from your friend's mind or try to reach into their mind to get guidance or information. Move along the bookcase while letting your intuition and telepathic abilities guide you, and you'll automatically know which book was selected.

The Floral Tribute

This practice, again, requires more than one person and a bouquet of flowers. Ask one of the people to choose a flower from the bouquet and pick another person they want to give the flower to. Let them discuss the name of the person who's getting the flowers while you stay out of the room, unaware of their discussion. Once they've decided, pick up the separated flower, and take the hand of the transmitter, i.e., the person who picked out the flower for someone else. By doing this, you'll be able to read their mind through contact telepathy and find out the person for whom the flowers are intended.

The Hidden Jewelry

Again, you'll need more than one person for this exercise. Ask them to hide a small piece of jewelry on the person of someone without letting you know. For this exercise, you will need to combine what you've learned from the previous exercises to find a person and then the object. First, let your telepathy guide you toward the person's general location and then toward where they've hidden the piece of jewelry.

The Reunited Couple

This practice requires more than four people to be present for better practice. The audience should select two people to be married and one person to officiate their wedding. They should stand in the middle of the room as if they were about to be married, with the parson standing between them while you stay out of the room. Once they've done this and get back to their places or seats, you will need to find each person and arrange them in the positions they took without you knowing. For instance, the bride should be in her place, and the groom and parson should be in their respective places. While this may sound difficult, once you practice this technique, you'll realize that it's simply a variation of the exercise where you had to locate a person.

Replacing the Pin

This practice is another jaw-dropping feat of telepathy. For this exercise, your friend should insert a pin somewhere on the wall. The place should be accessible and not out of sight. Once they've made an indentation or mark, they should remove the pin and hide it somewhere in the room. Now, you have to let your intuition guide your sense of direction, and first, find the pin and then the general location of the indent. Keep in mind that finding the pin will be similar to you finding a small object. Finding the indentation's location is the same as finding a specific location in the transmitter's mind. Once you've narrowed down the general location of the indentation, use your hands to feel around for the indent.

The Reconstructed Tableau

This practice also requires a number of people to participate. Ask them to form a tableau and take specific positions in the group. Once they've finished, they should go back to their original positions, and you can come back into the room. While this may seem difficult, it's nothing you can't accomplish with a little practice. You will be required to reconstruct the tableau and arrange everyone according to their spots in the tableau. If you're having trouble reading someone's thoughts, specify a single person as the transmitter and focus on their thoughts so you're not confused.

The Theft

This exercise requires someone to act as a thief and steal someone (the victim) else's piece of jewelry or cash. The thief should then hide the stolen goods somewhere around the room and return to their original position. Your task will be to identify the thief, find the object, and finally identify the victim, and then return their belongings to them. This exercise is yet another combination of the exercises you've previously learned.

The Murder and the Detective

This is a spectacularly impressive feat if you can achieve it. Ask your friends to designate the roles of murderer and victim among themselves. They should also select an object, such as a dagger or a murder weapon. The scenario will be something along the lines of a murder carried out by someone using a dagger, which is then hidden in the room by the murderer. The murderer also dumps the victim's body (sitting in a chair, standing). Finally, the murderer themselves will get into position somewhere in the room. Now, once you enter the room, locate in sequence: the dagger, the victim, and finally, the murderer.

The Mental Image

This exercise will help you send someone a mental image through telepathic communication. For this, you will need to connect your mind with your friend's or partner's mind. Once you've done this, try imagining a specific image, but don't tell them about it. This could be anything, but don't be too specific on your first try. For instance, don't send them an image of a TV show scene but instead stick with a simple image like that of a teddy bear. Then, ask your partner to open their minds to your thoughts and ask what they see. It is very possible that this practice will not be successful for a while because your partner may not be used to telepathic communication, but you may start to get real results after a while.

Mind reading is something many people don't believe is possible, but if we open our minds to the possibility of this concept, anything is possible. The most important part of mastering telepathy is the development of a strong mental connection and control over your thoughts. This can only be done with lots and lots of practice, which you will hopefully find interesting to do. You may get stuck while practicing some of these exercises, but don't get frustrated or lose hope because practice does make perfect.

Chapter 9: Heal through Telepathy

While telepathy is commonly known as a mind-to-mind communication tool, it can also be used for much more noble purposes. Sending restorative energy to others (psychic or telepathic healing) is a popular way of using telepathic gifts. A common bond between two people allows telepathy to exchange energy between the sender's and recipient's minds - which is how psychic healing is conducted. Empowered by a surge of positive energy, the recipient's thoughts will influence their body and mind to restore themselves to a healthy and balanced state. Telepathic healing can be used as a distant healing approach or in-person when the recipient prefers an energetic healing method that doesn't require a manual application. This chapter delves into the meaning and practices of telepathic healing, including different techniques, meditation exercises, and more. You'll learn how to direct healing energy towards those in need - especially if the person is already telepathically bonded to you.

The Reiki distance healing method is one of the most common telepathic healing approaches.
https://www.pexels.com/photo/smiling-crop-woman-with-crossed-hands-5340278/

Telepathic Healing Exercises

The number of telepathic healing exercises is vast - and you may need to try a few before finding what works best for you and the people you're trying to heal. Here are some helpful telepathic healing exercises you can try.

Reiki Distant Healing

The Reiki distance healing method is one of the most common telepathic healing approaches. Developed by Master Usui, the founder of Reiki, distance healing is a specific and convenient technique for pain relief and the eradication of other symptoms. It can be applied anywhere, anytime - regardless of the physical location of the sender and the recipient. The patient doesn't have to do anything but be ready to receive the healing energy at the time indicated by the healer. They may be asked to relax their body and mind when they expect a burst of energy to come through and provide feedback about their state after receiving the power. The rest is up to the healer, who prepares their own body and mind for the session.

To perform Reiki distant healing, you should have a basic understanding of Reiki energy. This is essentially the same as psychic energy. It's the power that lies within you, allowing you to live a healthy and balanced life. You can manipulate it and channel it to where it's needed most to rebalance an energy point (chakra) or system in someone's body. This requires using Reiki symbols - written characters with a unique power of their own. One of the characters you'll need for distance healing is the Reiki Distant Healing symbol (Hon-Sha-Ze-Sho-Nen). This is often used combined with one or more empowering signs like Cho Ku Rei and Sei-He Ki.

Cho Ku Rei, the power symbol, is often used in distance healing in a traditional sequence called the Reiki Sandwich. While the arrangement in question can be used for other purposes, in this case, it consists of two empowering symbols and the distance healing symbol between them. Here is how to heal through this method:

- Write the recipient's name and the purpose of the energy transfer on a piece of paper. Fold and keep this paper in your hands, palms facing each other.

- Close your eyes and let your body and mind calm by focusing on your breath.

- Repeat the intention written on the paper, visualize Cho Ku Rei, and connect your psychic power to the energy of the symbol.

- Switch your focus to visualizing the distant healing symbol and picture it on top of or just beside Cho Ku Rei.

- Next, visualize another Cho Ku Rei symbol appearing on top or on the other side of Hon-Sha-Ze-Sho-Nen.

- Now that the Hon-Sha-Ze-Sho-Nen is backed up on both sides, you'll be able to send it to empower the recipient's energetic system.

- Focusing on your telepathic connection, you can start transferring the distant healing sequence into the recipient's mind, along with a boost of positive energy.

- Don't try to channel the energy toward a specific area. Telepathic healing is about sending the receiver positive and encouraging messages, so they can deal with their own issues.

- Visualize the healing energy enveloping your client and soak in every detail of your experience. You will want to share it with them in the future and compare it with their experience during the session.

After the energy transfer has been completed, let the client digest the new sensation for a few minutes or hours before inquiring about their experience and current state. If they describe feeling more relaxed than before, the positive energy has begun to take effect in their body or mind. Some clients may experience visions of certain activities, objects, events, or emotions. If they had something like this, see whether these were similar to what you've received. This will help you develop your telepathic abilities even more. If the recipients need any additional help in the future, you will already have a bond with them. This will make it easier to connect to them for healing purposes.

Healing through Telepathic Meditation

Whether you need to apply distance healing or not, meditation can be a great way to transfer positive energy. If someone calls you for telepathic healing, you can do a quick meditation exercise to help relieve their symptoms. Here is how to perform a psychic healing session through this method:

- Find a quiet space and get into a comfortable position. If the recipient is participating in a live healing session, you must ensure they are comfortable too.

- Ask them to take a few deep, relaxing breaths and do the same. If they aren't in the same room as you are, you'll need to consult with them first about the timing of the session. Tell them when you'll do it and how to relax as described above.

- When you're ready, close your eyes and focus on your telepathic connection with the person.

- Once you've ensured that the bond is strong enough, start concentrating on the problematic areas. For example, if they've complained about back pain, you start focusing on visualizing their back.

- Work on actively visualizing the positive energy reaching the person's mind and channeling it toward the affected area for 10-15 minutes.

- After that, take another deep breath, and disconnect from the recipient's energy. Slowly open your eyes as your mind returns to its own thoughts.

- Ask the recipient about their experience. Do they still feel the symptoms the same way? Has a new sign appeared?

- If they feel more energized, but some of their symptoms are still present, you should repeat the session as often as necessary.

- If a new symptom appears, you shouldn't continue healing the recipient, as this could be the sign that you're about to aggravate their condition.

Energizing the Upper Chakras

The chakra system is the primary recipient of healing energy. Each of the seven main chakras (also called energy points) requires a specific energy balance. However, the two upper chakras are the most sensitive to receiving positive energy. The crown and the third eye chakras are the recipients of the telepathic gift. They are responsible for distributing it toward the rest of the person's energetic system. They aid spiritual growth (both the healers and the recipients) - and can help the body and mind fend off diseases and heal from certain conditions. By energizing the crown and the third eye chakras regularly, you can create an effective energetic defense mechanism for the recipient. By establishing the communication between your upper chakras and the recipients, you'll be able to tap into their needs more efficiently. This will help you send clearer, more intuitive messages and share visions and other sensory signals that balance the chakras in question.

Here is how to balance the crown chakra:

- For this chakra, you'll need to meditate while visualizing or otherwise sensing the universal life entering your mind. You can do this before the session or anytime during the day when you need to sharpen your telepathic abilities.
- You can prepare for meditation with breathing exercises or yoga poses that affect the top of your head.
- If you are doing the meditation just before a healing session, the entire work should be performed at night. Preferably when the moon and the stars are visible in the sky.
- You can make this meditation part last as long as you need to feel your crown chakra re-aligned and ready to engage in psychic energy transfer.

Here is how to balance the third eye chakra:

- The third eye chakra is highly spiritual. To balance it, you'll need to focus on your spiritual needs.
- Before your healing session, do a quick deep breathing exercise and follow up with a pose that increases blood flow circulation to the brain. You can find several yoga poses that fit this description. Or you can lie on the ground and put your legs up against the wall.
- Sit up, and begin your session by focusing on your third eye. Try to open it by visualizing or manifesting through any of the other clair senses.
- Listen to what your intuition tells you about healing the recipient in front of you. Let it help you manifest the best way to send positive energy.

Crystal Healing

Like Reiki symbols, crystals also have their own unique energy. As parts of nature, their power comes from nature's universal life force, which makes them a great tool in telepathic healing. If needed, crystals can also be charged with additional energy - whether it's yours or it comes from other natural elements, like the sun, the moon, or the spirits. Crystals can be combined with other psychic healing methods, such as telepathic meditation, affirmations, or any technique you prefer. The stones can be used one by one or set up in a crystal grid, which joins and concentrates their natural energy, making them even more powerful.

Depending on the level of healing required, crystals can provide the additional reinforcement you need to get the telepathic healing message across. Apophyllite, for example, is known to enhance psychic abilities. To use it during healing, follow these steps:

- Before your session, ensure you and the recipient are comfortable, relaxed, and undisturbed during the energy transfer.

- Take the crystal into your hands or wear it on your body as a charm during the session.

- Take a deep breath and start gazing into the reflective surface of the stone. It will be the perfect tool for self-reflection - allowing you to see how powerful your psychic energy is.

- Let your mind relax and lose focus of your everyday preoccupations, and drift intuitively onto any thoughts or stimuli it wants to.

- Focus on the most positive thoughts or any thoughts that can tell you how to help the recipient through telepathy. You may receive guidance for healing and boosting your mental telepathy skills.

- Meditate or do a deep breathing exercise while keeping your connection with the crystal. Then, slowly start channeling the wisdom you collected toward the recipient, along with plenty of positive energy.

Past Life Regression Exercise

Past life regression is another healing approach that has gained popularity. And telepaths can make great use of it. It takes the patient beyond the experiences in their current life - and taps into the spiritual wisdom they've accumulated during their past lives. It involves getting a person into an altered state of consciousness (commonly known as a trance), during which they can access memories and experiences from other lifetimes. This helps the person understand themselves better. It also provides an opportunity to explore the recipient's personality traits, behavior patterns, potential health issues, and symptoms. All this can come in handy when trying to perform telepathic healing. Knowing how a person's soul has related to their environment in the past can give you a clue on how to channel the positive energy toward them so that they receive it as intended. Each past life is a surface on a person's multifaceted soul. You can obtain spiritual and personal growth and energetic healing by gaining awareness of each of them. Here is how to do a past life regression session:

- Start by getting both yourself and the recipient into a comfortable position. Get rid of all distractions, such as sounds and lights.

- Ask the recipient to close their eyes and relax their body. Prepare to send encouraging messages and positive energy through the sessions.

- Guide the person into a trance by asking them to calm their mind and focus on their breathing. They should take deep breaths until they feel their thoughts drifting away from everyday preoccupations.

- Advise them that they'll see a picture appearing - almost like a window opening in front of their eyes.

- Ask them to focus on light sources they can see appearing in their vision, as this will help them to see things more clearly.

- The picture should continue to widen and sharpen until they can make out individual details.

- Tell them to start moving in the space they see in their vision. Encourage them to open any doors or windows if they have these in front of them.

- Tell them to focus on what they can see when looking through the doors or windows they've opened. Are there any people in front of them? If yes, can they identify themselves with one of them?

- This will prompt them to discover their past soul selves and start exploring what that person did, thought, and felt.

- When they feel ready, they should slowly walk back to the initial point they saw when entering the trance and slowly start returning to the present.

- They may not find out much on the first attempt, but with enough practice, you can help them discover a lot about their soul.

Healing through Prayer and Affirmation

Prayers are well known for their healing effects. If the telepath and the recipient share similar beliefs, they can participate in prayer together. Or you can encourage the recipient to recite prayers by sending them positive energy. The prayers will elevate their spirit, and they'll be even more receptive to the healing energy. While prayers are often used as psychic healing tools for larger groups and communities, an affirmation can have the same effect on individual recipients. Both are great for distance healing because you aren't relying solely on your psychic power - but the power of their own mind to heal its energy. Positive affirmations are often used as a confidence booster and not necessarily a healing agent. However, a telepath can amplify the power of these positive messages. You can send them short affirmations through your telepathic gift and encourage them to repeat these daily. By prompting the recipients to recite positive affirmations frequently, you're creating an internal consistency within their minds that allows them to heal.

Tips for Telepathic Healing

As with any other telepathic practice, healing through telepathic energy requires at least two participants: you (the energy sender) and one or more recipients. While anyone can receive restorative powers, directing it toward them and ensuring it takes effect is sometimes a lot more challenging than it sounds. Apart from having a strong ability to tap into divine wisdom (which lies within you) and sending its power through time and space, you'll also need to be connected to the recipient. Just like people of many religions form a connection with the deities they follow and receive blessings and healing, you will need a strong bond between you and the recipient. Successful telepathy-receipt relationships are built on trust. So, as the first step, you'll need to reassure the recipient that you can tap into the source of divine energy and channel it to restore their energetic balance. Working in small steps and sending energy in small increments will allow you to show them you can contribute to their recovery. You can also form a connection that has nothing to do with healing, but it will give you more leverage. And when faith is established, their ability to receive the healing energy will improve even more, and their recovery will accelerate.

A telepath's subconscious can connect to the recipient's subconscious mind and heal their energetic system. However, permanent relief can only be obtained if the recipient's subconscious learns how to intuitively tap into its own healing energy. To do this, you'll need to form a powerful connection and send positive energy in a specific way by paying attention to the different channels. This takes plenty of time and practice to master - but it can be a life changer for people suffering from chronic conditions who need frequent relief and energy rebalancing.

Emotional bonds, while not always necessary, certainly help transmit healing messages. Because you are closer to your loved ones emotionally, you'll heal their energy through telepathy more quickly. The strongest bonds are between parents and children, siblings, and spouses - but even people in close romantic relationships or friendships can effectively heal each other. You'll also be more likely to feel their need for energetic healing, even without them telling you about it. While you should ensure you have their consent, getting permission to heal from a person you have a close relationship with will rarely be an issue. They'll already trust you. So, if you want to practice telepathic healing, the best way to start is with your loved ones. Tap into the energy of their mind and see if they need some help. If yes, send them a short burst of energy by focusing on the area they signaled they have issues with. Ask for their feedback. That way, you can see whether your techniques have worked or if you need to change something the next time you try helping someone through your psychic powers.

Disclaimers

The transfer of vicarious experiences can have an incredibly powerful effect on the recipient of the telepathic energy. Using your energy, you can balance out another person's spiritual energy, re-energizing them and helping them face their health challenges. That said, telepathic energy can't cure disease or injury. If the person who is seeking out telepathic healing suspects they have any physical or mental condition, they should consult a healthcare specialist regarding treatment. Once their doctor has established a diagnosis and conventional treatment plan, the patient can revisit the possibility of telepathic sessions as an additional therapy for their condition. If the person has already been diagnosed when they start considering telepathic healing, they should still consult their doctor regarding the combination of treatments. Their doctor should determine whether telepathy can be used in conjunction with conventional Western therapy. This is particularly true if the person suffers from a mental health condition. Undergoing telepathic healing can be an overwhelming experience, even for healthy minds. The messages can be confusing, and the energy can be too powerful. And if someone's mental well-being is not at its best, the session can do more harm than good. Other contraindications for receiving psychic therapy exist in patients suffering from seizures and certain heart conditions such as arrhythmia. Needless to say, you shouldn't perform telepathic healing if you aren't feeling well, either. This can affect the efficacy of your work - not to mention aggravating your own condition.

Make sure you always have the consent of the person you are trying to heal before you begin your session. Otherwise, they won't be receptive to positive energy. And by sending it, you could upset their energetic system even more. To avoid this, explain to the recipient what you're going to do and what they can expect from a telepathic healing session. Do this regardless of your chosen method and who you will be healing. This is a crucial step - and you shouldn't skip it even if the person is someone very close to you. Ask for consent before each session, even if they're already familiar with the procedure. If you're doing distant healing, call or text the person to ask for their permission before sending the energy. This will also allow you to ensure they'll be prepared to receive it.

Chapter 10: Raise Your Telepathic Protections

Regardless of what walk of life you come from, it's likely that at some point, you will encounter someone who just seems to drain all the energy out of you. These people are often called "energy vampires" because they seem to live off the positive energy of others. Energy or psychic vampires can be found anywhere, from the office to your own family. They come in all shapes and sizes and can equally be men or women.

What's more, energy vampires don't just suck your energy; they can also influence your emotions and thoughts. If you're not careful, they can even control you. So, how do you know if someone is an energy vampire? And what can you do to protect yourself from them? This chapter will explore those questions and provide you with some tips for dealing with negative energy.

Energy Vampires

At first glance, an energy vampire might seem like just another annoying or uncomfortable person. But, in reality, this term refers to someone who actively leeches away your energy, leaving you feeling exhausted and depleted. These individuals tend to be negative, manipulative, and self-centered, always focused on their own needs, and never willing to put effort into building genuine connections with others. If you find yourself repeatedly feeling drained after interacting with certain people, you may be dealing with an energy vampire.

While it can be difficult to deal with them, there are strategies you can use to protect yourself from their toxic influence. You may need to limit your time with them or simply set clear boundaries around what's acceptable and what isn't. Ultimately, having a strong sense of who you are and knowing when to say no is one of the best ways to keep yourself from being engulfed by an energy vampire.

Identifying Negative Energy

When dealing with negative energy, knowing where to start can often be difficult. Many people struggle with feelings of pessimism and negativity, but they may not be sure how to get out of that frame of mind. However, you can use a few simple strategies to identify and eliminate negative energy from your life. By staying alert to negativity and actively working to replace harmful thought patterns with more positive ones, it is possible to identify and counteract negative energy in your life.

1. Notice Mood Changes

When you notice changes in your mood or energy levels, examine the possible causes. For example, if you find yourself feeling more irritable than usual or experiencing a lack of motivation and your productivity is low, there could be something else at work besides just having a bad day or an illness. Negative energy can manifest itself in many different ways, and it is vital to recognize these changes so that you can take action as needed.

Whether it's avoiding certain people or places, seeking counseling, or simply pulling back from responsibilities for a while, noticing mood changes is an essential step toward treating whatever underlying issue may be the cause. Identifying negative energy allows you to take control of your life and pursue your true potential.

2. Check for Physical Symptoms

Recognizing negative energy can be difficult, especially when it is influencing your emotions or thoughts. However, some physical symptoms may also indicate the presence of this type of energy. For example, you may feel a general sense of heaviness or sluggishness while around someone with negative energy. Or you may notice that your mood suddenly takes a turn for the worse when interacting with this person. You could also start feeling unwell physically, experiencing headaches or stomachaches that seem to come out of nowhere.

By being aware of these physical symptoms and paying attention to them, you'll be better able to identify when negative energy is affecting your life and figure out ways to protect yourself from it. In the end, cultivating good energetic hygiene is essential to maintain mental and emotional well-being. And by becoming attuned to physical symptoms like those described above, you can stay alert and empowered in your efforts to guard against negativity.

3. Determine If There's a Pattern

When it comes to the presence of negative energy in your life, there can often be no clear indication. You may feel uncomfortable or uneasy without knowing why, or something that you once thought was positive may suddenly seem negative. However, some signs can indicate the presence of unwanted negative energy. For example, recurring bad luck or a general feeling of unease or pessimism can be signs that something is amiss.

Regularly experiencing physical manifestations (such as skin rashes or headaches) could also be manifestations of distress caused by negative energy. Ultimately, identifying and eliminating harmful negative energy from our lives is an essential step toward living happier and healthier. With awareness and intention, we can free ourselves from the negativity surrounding us and begin creating positive change in our lives.

4. Listen to Your Instincts

Whether you realize it or not, everyone is affected by negative energy. This can come in many forms, from toxic relationships and stressful work environments to bad habits and unhealthy lifestyle choices. Perhaps this is why so many people have learned to listen to their instincts, tuning in to their gut feelings as a way to identify and avoid negative energy.

Of course, this can be easier said than done. One of the keys to identifying negative energy is learning how to truly hear what your instincts are telling you. That means resisting the urge to dismiss or override those warning signs with logic and reason. Instead, try to be mindful of your emotions at all times, paying attention to cues like anxiety, stress, anger, or sadness as clues that something may not feel right. Additionally, take note of your physical reactions, ailments like headaches or stomachaches that crop up when you're around certain people or in certain situations.

If you notice any red flags, then it's time to take action and remove yourself from whatever situation is causing that negativity. Whether it's a toxic relationship that brings out the worst in you or a job that leaves you constantly exhausted and stressed out, responding proactively by listening to your intuition will help protect you from negative energy and keep you feeling balanced and happy. Ultimately, your instincts do know best!

5. Consider the Person's Actions

When we encounter people who seem to spread negative energy, it is natural to feel uneasy or anxious. This can be particularly true in larger groups or situations where it is difficult to avoid these individuals. But what does it mean when we talk about negative energy? In essence, this concept refers to how mean, spiteful, or harmful actions affect us physically, emotionally, and spiritually. While many people may dismiss such actions as mere "bad vibes," the truth is that negative energy produces very real effects. It can cause stress, depression, anger, and even physical illness.

So how do you identify the presence of this type of energy and manage its effects? One way is simply to consider a person's actions. If they seem motivated by selfishness or cruelty toward others, negative energy may be at play. By recognizing these behaviors and seeking support from loved ones and professionals when needed, you can break free from this toxic influence and live a happier life.

6. Get a Second Opinion

When it comes to identifying and dealing with negative energy, there is no better source than a second opinion. After all, often, another person has had the same experience and has the insight needed to spot anything that may be off or out of alignment. Whether you're trying to get clear in your situation or simply looking for someone else to bounce ideas off, getting a second opinion is a smart way to go. Not only will you get validation, and you'll gain greater clarity on any unsettling feelings, but you'll also benefit from the insights of an objective outsider who can explain what they and others are seeing from the outside. So don't hesitate to ask for help when it comes to dealing with negative energy. Get a second opinion and take control of your situation.

7. Look at the Big Picture

At first glance, it can seem as if negative energy is all around us. Whether we are dealing with toxic coworkers, stressful family situations, or overwhelming financial burdens, it can sometimes feel like there's no escape from the constant barrage of negative feelings and emotions. However, if we take a step back and look at the big picture, we can start to see that these negative experiences are just a small part of our lives. Likewise, we can begin to recognize that our ability to cope with these situations ultimately comes down to our attitudes and responses. We can learn to deal with it more effectively by cultivating resilience, positivity, and mindfulness in the face of negativity. At the end of the day, this may be one of the most vital skills that we have as humans; learning how to persevere through difficult times to come out stronger on the other side.

8. Identify Your Own Emotions

When it comes to emotions, it can be difficult to identify exactly what we are feeling. This is especially true when our feelings are negative or difficult to express. However, paying attention to our emotions and understanding why we are feeling a certain way is crucial. One of the best ways to do this is by observing the energy around us. Negative energy can manifest itself in many ways, from feelings of anxiety or depression to physical symptoms like headaches or difficulty concentrating.

By becoming aware of these signals, we can identify our negative emotions and take steps to address them. Whether that means changing our habits or seeking professional counseling, identifying our own issues is an essential first step toward managing our mental and emotional well-being. Start paying attention today. You never know what valuable insights may be lying just beneath the surface.

9. Educate Yourself about Gaslighting, Gossiping, and Fear-Mongering

If you're looking to improve your mental and emotional well-being, one of the best things you can do is learn about the different types of negative energy that exist in the world. This includes everything from gaslighting and gossiping to fear-mongering, all of which are designed to feed off our fears and vulnerabilities to lower our self-esteem and leave us feeling helpless and powerless.

The first step toward dealing with these negative forces is identifying them, as many people don't even realize this negativity is manipulating them. Next, once you see that a particular person or situation is working out in a toxic way toward you, it's crucial not to give them any further power or fuel through your thoughts and actions. Whether it's breaking free from an abusive relationship or maintaining strong boundaries with difficult people at work or in your personal life, remember that you always have the right to take care of yourself first by refusing to let others treat you with disrespect or abuse. Ultimately, this is the key to finding happiness, peace of mind, and success in all areas of life.

10. Pay Attention to the Language

As the saying goes, "Think before you speak." One of the vital skills that we need to develop as communicators is to pay attention to the language that we use when interacting with others. Whether we are having a face-to-face conversation or sending an email or text message, we must consider the energy and impact of our words. This means avoiding negative language and focusing our statements on positive and supportive messages. For example, instead of saying things like "You're always late" or "Everything you do is wrong," it's better to express your concerns in terms such as "I would appreciate it if you could be more punctual." By being mindful of our language, we can create more positive and uplifting energy that is good for everyone involved.

Dealing with Negativity

When dealing with negativity, get and stay grounded and keep a positive attitude. This can be difficult when faced with criticism or pushback, especially if the naysayers are loud or influential. However, remember that not everyone's opinion matters and that their negativity only reflects their insecurities or biases. With this mindset in place, you can confidently approach these challenging situations, focusing on your goals and priorities rather than worrying about what other people may think. By staying focused on the bigger picture and remaining true to your values, you can achieve success and rise above the negativity around you. In the end, that's what truly matters. Here are some more tips:

1. Raise Your Vibration

Raising your vibration is a big first step toward dealing with negativity. This can be challenging, especially when stressful situations or negative people surround us. However, you can control your state of mind no matter what is happening around you. One effective way to do this is through mindfulness exercises like meditation or deep breathing. These practices help calm the mind and bring your attention to the present moment, shifting your focus away from any negative thoughts or energies that may drag you down. By consciously cultivating positive energy within yourself, you can stay grounded and maintain a higher state of vibration, even in the face of negativity.

2. Create Healthy Boundaries

When it comes to creating healthy boundaries, one should know how to deal with negativity and hostility. Whether this comes from coworkers, family members, or even strangers, it's essential to have strategies to deal with negative energy in a calm, confident manner. Some key tools include staying grounded during challenging interactions, focusing on maintaining a positive attitude even if it feels forced, and knowing your limits and when you need to walk away.

By developing these skills and staying true to your values and priorities, you can create healthy boundaries around negativity that will allow you to flourish both personally and professionally. And remember that while others may try to pull you down, it's up to you whether they succeed or not. So always stand strong, stay positive, and create healthy boundaries.

3. Avoid Energy Vampires

If you want to lead a happier and more fulfilling life, avoid energy vampires, people, or situations that drain your positive energy and bring you down. These can be difficult to identify at first, as they often come in the form of seemingly innocent comments or activities. For example, a rude coworker may make snide remarks behind your back, sabotaging your professional reputation or the news may focus on all of the bad things happening in the world, making you feel overwhelmed and hopeless about your collective future.

Ideally, you want to distance yourself from these energy vampires to reclaim your power and stay focused on what is most important to you. One way to do this is simply by recognizing when negativity is swirling around you and being aware of how it may be affecting your emotions and daily activities. Ultimately, it's up to you to take back control of your life and resist falling into the trap of negativity. With a little patience and determination, you can easily conquer those energy vampires that stand between you and blissful happiness.

4. Be Proactive

As we go through life, it's inevitable that we'll encounter negativity from time to time. Negative attitudes can be deeply troubling and discouraging, whether it comes from our colleagues at work, our friends and family, or even strangers on the street. So how do we deal with negativity proactively and positively? The key is to approach these situations with care and kindness. Try to understand where the negativity is coming from, and take steps to defuse any tension or conflict before it has a chance to build up. You might also consider ways to shift your mindset so that you see negativity as an opportunity for growth rather than a source of frustration and anger. Being proactive in dealing with negativity can help you maintain your mental well-being while also keeping others happy and at ease.

5. Practice Forgiveness

To achieve peace and happiness in our lives, we must learn to practice forgiveness. Whether forgiving ourselves or others, letting go of negative emotions and feelings can be a crucial part of moving forward. Unfortunately, this can sometimes be easier said than done, especially when the negativity comes from difficult people or challenging situations. However, with time and patience, it is possible to learn how to deal with these situations in a way that feels authentic.

This may involve seeking out support from loved ones or practicing techniques like mindfulness or self-compassion. Ultimately, perseverance is key when learning to practice forgiveness. But when we eventually stumble upon success, the resulting feelings of relief and lightness will make all of the effort worthwhile. So, whatever your situation may be, remember that the benefits of forgiveness are always well worth the struggle.

6. Cut Energetic Ties

There are many options for cutting energetic ties and banishing bad vibes. Some people choose to burn sage or Champaka incense, which have cleansing properties that help purify the air and eliminate negativity. Others may prefer to use affirmations, repeating positive statements out loud until they sink in and take root in their minds. Still, others might find crystals helpful for absorbing and transmuting negative energies such as selenite or black obsidian. The key to banishing negativity is to align your thoughts with positive intentions and release any doubts or fears that might be holding you back. With a little practice, you can become a powerhouse of positivity and easily cut energetic ties with any unwanted negative energy.

7. Surround Yourself with Positive People

Living a happy, healthy life means surrounding yourself with positive people. This is because we are always influenced to some degree by those around us. If you are hanging around with folks who tend to focus on the negative aspects of any situation, you will find yourself doing the same. On the other hand, people who always seem to see the silver lining in any cloud can be an invaluable source of support and inspiration.

If you find that you are constantly surrounded by negativity and pessimism, there are certain steps that you can take to deal with this. First, try to understand why these individuals repeatedly bring you down. Are they going through difficult times in their own lives? Do they feel insecure or inadequate themselves? You will develop effective coping strategies by gaining a better understanding of what underlies this negativity.

We all need people in our lives who will challenge us and help us grow. So, if one or two members of your social circle routinely drive you crazy with their negative attitude, don't let this stop you from cultivating meaningful relationships with others. Instead, maintain balance and surround yourself with people who make you feel good about being alive. After all, what's the point of hanging out with other people if it isn't making your life better? The choice is yours. Choose happiness by surrounding yourself with positive people who believe in your abilities and celebrate your successes.

8. Visualize Happiness

Happiness is something that we all seek, and yet it can be surprisingly hard to find. This is especially true in today's fast-paced, often stressful world, where we are constantly bombarded with all sorts of issues, including negativity and difficulties. So how can we learn to visualize happiness amid the chaos of daily life? One key is to practice accepting everything that comes our way, both good and bad. This means seeing the bright side of things and understanding that setbacks and struggles are simply part of the human experience. By opening ourselves up to all aspects of life, both positive and negative, we can learn to appreciate every moment as a gift and stay focused on what truly matters most. And by doing so, we will start to visualize happiness every day.

To be a successful telepath, it is essential to raise your protective shields. This involves clearing your mind of distractions, focusing your thoughts on the task at hand, and building a strong mental barrier that can deflect any unwanted influences. There are many effective strategies for boosting your defenses, including meditation, visualization exercises, and affirmations. You may also want to incorporate other techniques, such as grounding and shielding crystals, into your routine to help reinforce your protective shields. With time and practice, you will successfully keep all outside forces at bay and ensure that only beneficial energies make their way into your mind. So, raise those shields, focus your mind, and hone your telepathic abilities today.

Conclusion

At first glance, the idea of telepathy may seem like something out of a science fiction novel or a magic trick. After all, how can mere thoughts or ideas be transmitted from one person to another, seemingly at will? In reality, telepathy is a scientifically proven phenomenon, and it has been the subject of numerous groundbreaking experiments in the 20th century. For example, researchers have found that certain individuals can regulate brain waves and send signals directly into the brains of others via stored mental images. They have also discovered that these signals can be amplified by transmitters and receivers and even used to convey messages – sometimes cross-country!

Though our understanding of this unique ability is still limited, it's clear that telepathy is not just something out of a science fiction story – it's real and waiting to be harnessed for all sorts of potential uses. Its potential is only limited by our imagination. Some people believe that telepathy may even be the key to unlocking other abilities, like precognition or clairvoyance. This easy-to-follow guide has informed you about everything you need to know about this fascinating ability, including how to develop your telepathic skills.

In this book, you learned about the history of telepathy and some of the groundbreaking experiments that have been conducted on this phenomenon. We also explored how meditation can help improve your telepathic abilities and some of the different ways you can use telepathy in your everyday life. You learned how to use telepathy to communicate with others, share messages and even heal yourself and others.

Raising your vibration and establishing a telepathic bond with others are essential steps in harnessing this ability, and we explored how to do both of these things. From there, we delved into the nitty-gritty of how to send and receive telepathic messages. Through practice and repetition, you can hone your skills and become a master of this ability. And finally, we looked at how you can use telepathy to heal yourself and others. The final chapter contains some essential tips on how to protect yourself from negative energies when using this ability.

Telepathy is a fascinating phenomenon that has long captured the imagination of scientists, artists, and everyday people alike. Despite centuries of skepticism and ridicule from those who don't believe in its existence, there is significant scientific evidence to support the claim that telepathy is real and scientifically proven. Even more impressive, this power can be developed and honed to infinite potential through repeated practice, yielding powerful results both for individuals and for society as a whole.

Just look at some of the incredible examples in recent history. Neuroscientists have used telepathic techniques to successfully treat post-traumatic stress disorder in veterans. Athletes have harnessed these abilities to improve their performance on the field, and ordinary people have used telepathy to connect with friends and loved ones across great distances. This ability holds tremendous potential for improving our lives and expanding our horizons.

Now that you've completed this book, you should have a good understanding of what telepathy is and how it works. You should also be well on your way toward developing your telepathic abilities. Whether it is clairvoyance, clairsentience, or any other form of extrasensory perception, remember to always use your abilities for good purposes. Telepathy is a powerful tool that can be used for both positive and negative purposes. It's up to you to decide how you will use it. So, what are you waiting for? Start practicing today and see what amazing things you can do!

Part 3: Numerology for Beginners

An Essential Guide to Numbers and Their Meanings, Divination, and Astrology

Introduction

A Latin saying goes, *"omnis in numeris sita sunt."* What it means is that everything is hidden in numbers. This is further bolstered by the words of Madame Helena Petrovna Blavatsky, the most famous occult medium of the 19th century, who said, *"Number underlies form and guides sound."* It lies at the root of the manifested universe. This shows how powerful numbers are.

There is nothing in existence that does not possess shape, size, or dimension, all rooted in numbers. For this reason, numbers possess personal energy signatures or vibrations. Sound, for instance, is produced by vibrations that are audible at the rate of 20 to 20,000 vibrations per second. Above this benchmark is ultrasonic sound, and below it is subsonic.

Light, heat, speed, music, and friction are all dependent on vibration, hence numbers. Even color is composed of vibrations in a different octave. All the colors we see correspond to the wavelength of oscillation reflected. This is why, beyond the vibration of the color violet, the human eye cannot pick up additional colors; the vibration rate beyond violet is so minute that the human eye cannot capture it.

In this book, you'll learn the importance of numbers and begin to understand how they shape every aspect of your life. Unlike other books out there, this book is easy to understand, takes you by the hand, and shows you everything you need to know. You're about to have a much richer, fuller, more rewarding life than you ever thought possible, and you're going to do it using numbers. If you've never really liked numbers or if you hate math, your relationship with these powerful figures is about to do a 180-degree turn so fast it will make your head spin! Life is a numbers game, you see, and once you master it, it's like having all the cheat codes – you may feel invincible. So, if you're ready to begin, let's explore the wonderful world of numerology.

Chapter 1: What Is Numerology?

Humans have had an ambivalent relationship with numbers since time immemorial. Scratch marks on bones and cave walls from 30,000 years ago have been found to represent the lunar phase, which helped in the fields of agriculture and weather prediction. Ancient Babylonians used numbers to foretell eclipses and other phenomena.

Ancient Egyptian priests and priestesses – called hem netjer and hemet netjer – used numbers to foretell the flooding of the Nile. They did this using a nilometer, a vertical column submerged into the river that bears marks or intervals that indicate the river's depth. One of the historically important nilometers is on the elephantine island of Aswan, on the south border of Egypt.

Arithmancy, or arithomancy, originates from the Greek words *"arithmos"* (number) and *"manteia"* (divination), making it a science that studies divination using numbers. It was practiced by Hebrews, Chaldeans, and ancient Greeks – and has been succeeded by numerology today.

Despite their differences of opinion on certain subjects, Numerologists all agree that numbers have a mystical significance. In arithmancy and other forms of number mysticism, alphabets are assigned numbers using a set of rules. Words can be converted to numbers when their individual letters are added together. For this reason, people's names bear a specific significance. They also believe that everything in the world contains vibrations that can be traced back to the mystical properties of numbers. New age or modern numerologists incorporate powerful items like crystals, essential oils, gemstones, colors, and energy points (chakras) into their practice.

Disease has a specific vibration. This was proven by Dr. Abrams, an American physician who invented an instrument that measured the human body's reactions to determine the numerical value to be assigned to each disease. According to Abram, once numerical values are assigned to a disease or condition, their respective cures can be determined using numbers. Later, in 1985, Karin Lee Abraham published a book called "Healing through Numerology" in which she stated that every ailment had a specific vibrational rate. She constructed an illness chart and provided the best medication for the sick using her knowledge of numbers and vibrational frequencies.

As the theory stated, each number has an inherent unique vibration that gives it its specific characteristics. These characteristics may explain a person's behavior or determine the level of compatibility between two lovers. Numerology can help determine the lucky day or number of a person. Recurring numbers may give pointers that outline how the world works or the importance of certain events or people. To the average numerologist, nothing happens by chance. It is all predestined, and the answers lie in numbers.

The Origin of Numerology

The roots of numerology are incomplete without the Hebrew alphabet, the esoteric teachings of the Kabbalah, ancient teachings, and Pythagoras. This is because numerology is a science intricately woven with philosophies, myths, and mysticism.

Pythagoras is fondly called the "Father" of numbers. He was a Greek philosopher born in the year 569 B.C. At the age of 56, in the year 536 BC, he journeyed south of Italy, and in the Greek-speaking region called Crotona, he established the first university in history. There, he taught a combination of science and religion. Along with esoteric teachings, he taught the secrets of numbers and their vibrations to a select few. These discourses were so secret that they were never recorded in writing. Those who did so, intentionally or unintentionally, suffered the death penalty.

Many of his original works were lost after his death. Those who wrote about him did so hundreds of years after his demise. Writers who divulged the teachings later did so carefully by infusing lessons with a barrage of confusing information that would cause the attention of all but the true seeker to stray. Many historians have reason to believe that many of the discoveries and personality traits ascribed to him were the work of his devotees.

That notwithstanding, there are still a few manuscripts that have been preserved. Information about the university states that students abided by very stringent rules. They never had any in-person contact with Pythagoras until they had passed several initiations and were at a higher level of study. Even when contact was initiated, Pythagoras wore a robe that shielded him from prying eyes, so no one was really able to get an accurate description of him.

The father of numbers readily accepted children or initiates with a life path number of 7 into the school because, according to him, they were meant to learn the secret teachings. Other interested candidates who had a different path number had to pass a series of tests, such as being given a symbol like a triangle to meditate on.

Pythagoras opined that numbers lay at the heart of all creation. He claimed that understanding divinity could be achieved by understanding numbers. Suffice it to say that Pythagoras's science of numbers was founded on Kabbalistic teachings.

According to Underwood Dudley in his book "Numerology: or what Pythagoras wrought," the philosopher and his disciples were of the strong opinion that *all is number.*" Their study of number mysticism discovered that adding up a series of odd numbers starting with the number one always resulted in a square number.

This further enforced their principle that everything in the world can be described and measured in terms of proportions, dimensions, and numbers. In the same way, everything in this world, animate or inanimate, can be reduced to a number or set of numbers. This is a belief held by both scientists and mathematicians alike.

Modern numerologists ascribe intangible qualities to numbers and to individuals using their names. This may seem strange, but it is believed that the numbers one through to nine have special properties resulting from their inherent vibrational frequencies. Some of these qualities come from Pythagorean teachings. In contrast, others may result from how different cultures worldwide perceive and use numbers.

Numerologists typically use the name written on the birth certificate for a reading. According to them, unborn babies choose their names themselves and psychically communicate them to their parents to ensure they suit them and yield the correct numbers. The birth name holds more power over any nicknames, changed names, or names adopted post-matrimony.

To determine a person's number, the numerologist singles out each letter of their name and their corresponding numbers on a chart. The numbers are added together, and if the result is a two-digit number, both digits are added together to reveal a single digit, which becomes the personal number of that particular client.

Many practitioners enlist charts and diagrams to analyze numbers, letters in names, and their relationships with one another. The diagrams and charts are rooted in astrology and serve to add a deeper layer of information or meaning to the numerological reading. The charts used will be discussed later in the book. Regardless of the charts or methods employed to obtain a reading, the results sound similar to a horoscope.

You can use numerology to help you figure out the best career path suited to an individual's numerological makeup, lucky numbers, colors or days, positive behavioral attributes, negative tendencies. You can also learn a lot about their possible health issues (if birthdate is provided) and their desirable traits in a romantic partner.

Misconceptions about Numerology

Numerology is affected by the name change - Numerology is a science rooted in spirituality. Most people who understand what numerology is, describe it as applied mysticism. Therefore, it is wrong to see it as a simple numbers game that one can alter for personal gain.

If your name is changed at some point in your life, the numerologist will read both the birth name and the new name. However, the new name is a façade and will be treated as a subset of the original or given name.

Numbers attributed to the facade will not bear the same significance as the numbers attached to your original name and thus will be noted as a supplemental reading. Your free will and the decisions you make are the factors that can greatly influence your life and future. All numbers do is aid in self-interpretation so that your flaws are known, and you change your numerical vibration to influence public perception concerning you. Your fate and destiny are still yours to shape. Understanding this is the key to creating a truly balanced and fulfilled life.

When you have established a person's numbers, you can delve into their weaknesses, strengths, karmic debts, career, and relationship options, as well as help to gently align their thoughts and goals with reality, a form of manifestation if you will. This way, the individual is better equipped to face life's challenges with power and knowledge of what exists and which is to come.

Numerology readings are based on analyzing the numbers most significant in your life. They only provide an idea, a guide, or a precautionary measure concerning the past, present, and future. They are not designed to operate magically overnight, and neither do they guarantee a lack of well-being. No number completely answers life's questions or accurately predicts the future because reality, as we know it, is always changing.

Numerology is time-based - this is false. This is where numerology differs from astrology. In numerology, the exact time of birth or place of birth is not required for a reading, whereas in astrology, the birthplace and time of birth are pertinent pieces of information, without which readings cannot be conducted.

Numerology can help ascertain the perfect romantic partner - If this were true, wouldn't we all value our birth charts above our passports or social security numbers? Yes, it is possible to determine your personal number from a reading. This number may reveal certain aspects of your life (hidden or not), including what to expect in the perfect partner. Potential partners also have personal numbers. Hence, compatibility can be determined if a seasoned numerologist looks at both numbers.

After this, predictions will be offered concerning your future as a couple and whether the relationship is worth pursuing. Numerology has its gains, but is it something you should believe blindly over the free will exercised in choosing a mate? Should your choice of a partner depend first and foremost on matching numbers and gaining a favorable prediction?

Success is guaranteed with a name change - A true numerologist will never deceive you into believing that changing your name will guarantee a change of fortune, destiny, or fate. A new name changes your number vibrations so that people perceive you differently. It may also guide you toward seeing a better path, one that helps you achieve your goals and attract abundance.

Numerology readings are only associated with determining and reading the birth number - This assertion is one of the funniest and probably the most annoying to many practitioners. It's like saying milk is the only nutrition a cow can offer. (No offense intended to vegans and vegetarian readers.)

The belief that only birth numbers are of importance in a numerology reading is another false assertion and one that will be proven in future chapters of this book. Besides the "popular" birth number, many other numbers are significant during numerology readings. Personality numbers, life path numbers, balance numbers, karmic debt numbers, and others are numbers that can be interpreted in a typical numerology reading.

The myth of a lucky number or numbers - Not to rain on your parade, but a number, an object, or a person is lucky because of their belief and nothing else. All numbers are special, with unique vibrations and meanings.

According to numerology myths, the lucky numbers are 5, 6, and 8. People with the number 5 have earned their wealth through smart business dealings, strategic knowledge, wise investments, and hard work. Those with the number 6 gained wealth through marriage or inheritance, while those with the number 8 earned wealth through sheer luck. This is not always the case; anyone can lose money or gain money without necessarily having a lucky number in their corner.

If you are convinced that numerology will help you at the gambling tables or help you win the lottery, you should probably seek better financial advice, unless you enjoy having a hut at the end of Queer Street (a British colloquialism meaning to be in financial instability or embarrassment). Think long and hard before tattooing the numbers 3, 5, 6, or 8 on your wrist just because rumors say they are a sure-fire way to boundless wealth.

Numerology gives a certain level of significance to destiny numbers as they set the bar for your dreams and aspirations. Since numerology is not always an exact science and your life is not a 10th-grade chemistry project or a melt and pour soap masterclass, it is always advisable to refrain from giving too much relevance to destiny numbers (or numbers at all) over the trajectory of your life. The numbers are a guide. Deciding whether they directly affect your future is another kettle of fish entirely.

Karmic debt numbers are a bad omen - The obsession people have with these numbers always leads to misconceptions. Karmic numbers DO NOT represent the punishment or nemesis one will experience in this reality. Instead, they point toward behavioral patterns that should be avoided, such as abuse of power, abuse of freedom, or the presence of ego and negativity in previous lifetimes.

The concept of false firsts - In the hope of a stronger bond, most couples choose an auspicious marriage date to gain good fortune, have a longer-lasting marriage, and so on. They fail to realize that the day they met is more important in numerology than the date they pick to get married.

Only a small number of individuals are old souls - A famous delusion in numerology is the old soul myth, which is linked to only individuals with master numbers such as 11, 22, 33, etc. There are single-digit numbers such as 7 and 9, which are lonely spiritual numbers, and individuals with these numbers are seen as old souls as well.

Also, karmically challenged digits like 2 and 4 are additions of the master numbers 11 and 22. People with the number 2 are old souls existing to iron out past life connections, while the number 4 is an old soul balancing karmic debt in this life by suffering through health challenges.

A full chart must be created to understand your full numerological impression. This simply means an expert in numbers must interpret all of your numbers, including destiny, karmic debt, and expression numbers, to paint a full picture of your personality. When creating or referring to your numerology chart, you must understand that the numbers describe more than they predict, so it is wise not to limit yourself to whatever is told to you during a reading.

Numerology, as we have mentioned before, is a guide. It provides you with the incentive needed to make a decision at a time when you are confused about what step to take. Since numerology points out your strengths and weaknesses, you can make better-informed decisions and avoid pitfalls or situations that highlight your weaknesses or leave you feeling incompetent. Of course, there is always the option to convert your known weaknesses into strengths.

It is also superstitious to believe that you can be limited by numbers. For example, just because your life path number is 4 (which is usually an ominous number for most people) does not ultimately brand you as an unlucky person or indicate that fulfillment, fame, and love will elude you. It may help if you get several readings to obtain a clearer idea of your potential and limitations in life. Once you get rid of the misconceptions concerning numerology, the following chapters explain a few ways they can benefit you in your everyday life.

Chapter 2: Types of Numerologies

In earlier times, mathematics played a key role in the inception of numerology. Thousands of years ago, the practice of numbers was understood in a myriad of ways depending on the predominant culture, belief, and period during which it prevailed. True, it may not have gained scientific approval, but it did have a major effect on civilization in general.

Every type of numerology in existence has its own unique way of interpreting numbers and analyzing results. Clear-cut and distinct information is obtained no matter which system is used, which, in turn, guides a person in gaining knowledge of themselves. There are five main types of numerology, namely:

- Chaldean
- Kabbalah
- Tamil or Vedic
- Chinese
- Western or Pythagoras

Chaldean Numerology

Chaldean, or mystical, numerology is one of the most ancient numerology systems in the world. It originated from the Chaldeans, who walked the Earth in the 10th century BCE and briefly reigned over ancient Babylon (modern-day Iraq). The Chaldeans were famed for their superior intelligence and analytical skills. Besides numerology, they also contributed greatly to astrology and mathematics. They were also ardent students of the stars and planetary alignments - born scholars who sought to understand the mystical secrets of the universe.

Chaldean numerology is said to be the foundation of numerology, but historical records have shown the Vedic system existed a long time before the Chaldean system. Although this system is complex to master compared to others, it is the most accurate yet least popular method in use today.

This system is deeply rooted in the calculations of vibrations emitted by numbers, which lend them special or mystical characteristics. The vibrations of the numbers were said to have been written on ancient tablets by the gods dating back 2,500 years ago. Numbers go from one through to eight and are interpreted to yield meanings represented by various numbers (mostly one through to fifty-two). The number nine is considered sacred and is thus avoided during readings. In Chaldean numerology, the numbers assigned to each letter are not established by virtue of alphabetical order but by the innate vibrations possessed by each of the letters.

In other numerology methods, the approximated or reduced single digit is analyzed to study information about a person. If the sum arrived at is a nine, the value is retained. The Chaldean system uses both single and double-digit numbers, which are evaluated to yield calculations of vibrations and sounds. While the single digits describe the outer influences, the double digits offer information about the inner personality profile of the individual.

This way, it shows a complete and clear schematic of your life, including your likes, desires, dislikes, personality, and your path in life. Chaldean numerology is so precise that it even tracks energy fluctuations that surround you when another person calls your name. This is possible because calling out a name sends energy waves and frequencies to you and to those around you at that time.

Pandit Sethuraman is a famous Indian numerologist who did extensive research on both the Chaldean and Kabbalah numerology systems. He concluded that the ancient Chaldean system was the most authentic and precise system in existence. In Chaldean numerology, the name analyzed isn't your birth name but the name you are commonly known by. Hence, if your name is Katherine Herman, but you are commonly called Katie Herman, the Chaldean school of numerology will analyze the latter name instead of the former. Here are the numerical values for the letters of the alphabet in Chaldean numerology:

- A, I, J, Q, and Y have a value of 1
- B, K, and R have a value of 2
- C, G, L, and S have a value of 3
- D, M, T, have a value of 4
- E, H, N, and X have a value of 5
- U, V, and W have a value of 6
- O, and Z has a value of 7
- F and P have a value of 8

Kabbalah Numerology: The Origins

The Kabbalah doctrine is one with ancient origins in mystic Judaism. The Kabbalah is a primordial method used in divination and finding esoteric interpretations in Judaism and religious texts. *Kabbalah* itself translates to "tradition" in Hebrew and reflects on esoteric knowledge and principles that foster communion and a relationship between humans and the divine. Kabbalah places greater emphasis on human nature rather than on the body and everything else. The Kabbalistic practitioners of the early 10th century developed their own method of arcane interpretations of old Jewish texts. Today, this belief system serves as a reference through which followers of Judaism decipher deeper meanings in the Tanakh (Jewish Scripture).

Gematria: The Door to Kabbalistic Numerology

Gematria is the key numerological system showing the correspondence of Hebrew letters with numbers. It is the backbone of Kabbalah, and its correlation with Kabbalah forms the unique system that is Kabbalah numerology. The first Kabbalists created the Gematria to help understand and transcribe ancient Jewish texts. In the Gematria, every Hebrew script letter is given a specific number, right down to the final letter, which is assigned the number 900.

Understanding Kabbalah Numerology

The Kabbalah system of numbers is one of the more popular forms of numerology. It has received recognition and praise from celebrities like Britney Spears, Ashton Kutcher, Demi Moore, and Madonna. Its popularity steadily increases as more and more celebrities delve into Jewish esoteric wisdom, judging by the red strings on their wrists.

The significance of using your name to find your number can be attributed to the belief that names hold great significance when it comes to an individual's soul, destiny, and existence. The idea behind this system is the belief that one can gain a greater understanding of themselves from their personal numbers. It differs from other numerology systems in that it uses the individual's full name and not a significant number or a birth date.

In this system, names are given greater prominence than numbers. The script used originated from the Hebrew alphabet and is further analyzed by taking note of the birth name, which is useful in predictions.

This should not be confused with a newer form of Kabbalah numerology that adapts Roman letters.

There are ten main energies used in Kabbalah for calculations and predictions. They are:

- Malkut "Sovereignty"
- Yesod "Foundation"
- Hod "Majesty"
- Netzach "Victory"
- Tiferet "Glory"
- Gevurah "Strength"
- Chesed "Mercy"
- Binah "Understanding"
- Chokhmah "Wisdom"
- Keter "Crown"

These energies contain 22 vibrations in a range of 1–400. Significance is placed on the wisdom derived from the soul and mind rather than that from flesh and blood. This is because the mind lacks physical existence while the flesh is material. Pure enlightenment requires a level of understanding beyond corporeal limitations in order to truly know oneself. In this system, each letter is assigned a specific value which is used for calculations and analyses.

Kabbalah numerology aims to foster honesty and a deeper understanding based on your number. This is because each name corresponds to a number, and the numbers are significant to you as a person and others who bear the same name or have the same number as you do.

Finding Your Kabbalah Number

The Kabbalah system, as mentioned above, is based on the Hebrew script, in which every letter corresponds with a particular number. The Kabbalah system may have its roots in the Hebrew alphabet, but the correlation of letters with numbers differs. These are the numerical values of the alphabet according to Kabbalah numerology:

- Letters A to I are numbered from 1 to 9, respectively.
- Letters J to R are also numbered 1 to 9, respectively.

• Letters S to Z are numbered 1 to 8, respectively.

Finding your Kabbalah number works by taking the numerical value of each letter in your given name; first name, middle name (where applicable), and surname, then adding them up to give a total value. If the total value is a double-digit or triple-digit number, simply add all the values to give a single-digit figure. It is common to see triple-digit figures in names with letters of high numerical value. After the summation, divide the figure by 9. If there is a remainder after the division, add one to the remainder to get your Kabbalah number.

For instance, if the sum of the letters in your name is 27, divide 27 by 9 to get 3, then add 1, and your Kabbalah number is given as 4. There are some cases where the sum may yield a number like 81. In this case, since it's a double-digit number, add 8 + 1 to give 9. Then as the rules go, divide the sum by 9, the resulting figure is 1, add 1, and the Kabbalah number becomes 2. Finding your Kabbalah number is pretty easy as long as the formula is followed.

The Significance Behind the Numbers in Kabbalah System

Like in all other systems, each number has an energy or vibration associated with it. The significance behind the numbers from 1 through to 9 is shown below.

1. Emergence and progress.

2. Balance, care, and expansion.

3. Love, innovation, optimism, and originality.

4. Misfortune, adversity, and practicality.

5. Change, formation, creation, free spirit.

6. Accomplishment, fulfillment, result, nurturing.

7. Spirituality and enlightenment.

8. Inspiration, abundance, impulse, and success.

9. Serendipity, luck, selflessness, and accomplishment.

Each number has multiple meanings and energetic signatures, so just because your number is the ominous 4 and not as serendipitous as the numbers 2 or 9, there is no need to worry. The numbers are only a guide and not a prediction of a lack of success or happiness in your walk through life. The numbers merely warn you of the challenges ahead. But who in life does not have challenges? They are inevitable for even those assigned the luckier Kabbalah numbers. Kabbalah numbers intend to advise you on the best course of action to take regardless of whatever bumps in the road lie ahead.

What Makes Kabbalah Numerology Special?

What makes the Kabbalah system unique is the fact that it bridges the gap between the finite and infinite, the physical and metaphysical realms, helping us understand the connection between the finite and material world and the infinite Godhead, or Ein Sol. The key difference between the Chaldean and Kabbalah systems of numerology is the respective values of certain letters which differ between these systems.

The letter "A" has the value of 1 in both methods, whereas the letter "V" has the value of 6 in Chaldean numerology while it corresponds to the number 4 in Kabbalah. This is the case because the range of numbers in the Kabbalah system is greater than in other systems—approximately 400 life paths that accrue to 22 letters or vibrations.

Secondly, other Western and Chaldean numerology methods will evaluate birth dates and assign a number known as the life path number based on them. The Kabbalah only analyzes the given name as it appears on the birth certificate. For this reason, practitioners believe this system to be less accurate when compared to other numerology methods.

Tamil Numerology

Tamil numerology is also called Vedic or South Indian numerology. It is named after Tamil Nadu, a state in south India. In the past, it was studied by Indian sages and is one of the oldest forms of numerology still in existence. Like in the Kabbalah system, the numbers range from one through to nine. Each number possesses a specific vibration or characteristic that increases self-awareness and knowledge.

This system posits that every soul chooses to reveal themselves using a birthday and a vibration that allows for further evolution of their consciousness on this plane. The numbers ascribed to each individual stand for their ego, psychological wellbeing, and the karmic remnants they possess throughout their lifetime. This helps to identify strengths and weaknesses they were born with so they can learn from their experience in this lifetime. This numerology method makes use of Vedic squares, a variant of the 9 by 9 multiplication table found in traditional Islamic art, motifs, and Hindu geometrical configurations.

The Vedic tables in Tamil numerology show the spiritual link between an event and a number that helps in its prediction. The tables can also be used to analyze the vibrational qualities of baby names, comprehend the harmonic patterns and alignments of planets in astrology, foretell the future to a great extent, and discover personality traits. On the other hand, name-number calculation can be a bit taxing since it requires complex measurements depending on the sound frequency produced by each number.

In Tamil numerology, three numbers are associated with every individual: The *destiny number, the psychic number*, and the *name number.* The psychic number is determined by the individual's birth date. For instance, if the birth date is March 20th, the psychic number will be 2+0=2. The psychic number is 2. The psychic number gives an idea of the individual's perception of themselves, their core beliefs, and the personality attributes they exhibit. It hints at how the individual treats or deals with those around them and gives insight into their karma or their actions in a past life.

The destiny number tells how the world sees you and is calculated by adding the numbers in your birth date together. Destiny numbers signify how the world perceives you. This is calculated by summing up the numbers in your birth date and birth year to a single digit. So, on March 20th, 2015, it would be 3+2+0+2+0+1+5=13 and, furthermore, 1+3=4. Hence, the person would have a destiny number of 4.

The name number tells us of the individual's relationship with others. It is calculated using a mathematical formula based on the sound frequencies that accrue to a certain number.

For instance, in Tamil numerology, the number 4, which is deemed unlucky in the Kabbalah system, is ruled by Uranus. Individuals who are pragmatic, humble, practical, and bubbly are number four. They are adventure seekers who are quite invested in life's physical and material aspects. They are also famous for being reliable, trustworthy, and great confidants. Their practicality and discipline make them suitable for managerial and organizational positions. In fact, the best jobs for number four individuals involve finance and taxes.

On the other hand, numbers representing accomplishment and success in Kabbalah numerology actually indicate failure with money in Tamil numerology due to their overly generous nature and need for worldly comforts. How ironic is that?

Tamil Letter-Number Correspondence

Planet	Number	Alphabet
Sun	1	A, I, J, Q, Y
Moon	2	B,K,R
Jupiter	3	C,G,L,S
Rahu/Uranus	4	D,M,T
Mercury	5	E, H, N, X
Venus	6	U,V,W
Ketu/Neptune	7	O,Z
Saturn	8	P,F
Mars	9	-

Chinese Numerology

The Chinese system of numerology has been in use for over 4,000 years. It is founded on mysticism and the ancient knowledge of the I-Ching. The popular assumption behind this system is that numbers could be auspicious or inauspicious based on the Chinese word that the number is homophonous with or similar to in pronunciation.

The practice of assigning good or bad luck to numbers is not unique to the Chinese. Other East Asian nations with a history of similar beliefs and Han characters adopt this practice. This is because luck in East Asian culture is related to the concept of destiny, so if someone is deemed lucky, their destiny is believed to have been blessed by the gods. For instance, the Chinese word for "one" is homophonous with the Mandarin word for "honor." Here, one is neither lucky nor unlucky, but this may symbolize loneliness or single status. The number 8 is homophonous with the Mandarin word for prosperity and is termed an auspicious number. The number 9 signifies power/eternity, while the number 4 is similar in pronunciation to the Chinese word for death or misfortune. Hence, it is avoided by the Chinese.

Following this analogy, number combinations are valued for their reference to luck and prosperity, such as 28, 39, 26, etc. Along with their belief in fate and luck, the Chinese study mystical number combinations and associated relationships in nature. For instance, they believe that there are 12 vessels that circulate air and blood throughout the body. These vessels coincide with the 12 rivers flowing through the central kingdom. Also, the 365 days in the year are connected mystically to the 365 body parts used to locate acupuncture points in Chinese unorthodox medicine.

The simplest method of Chinese numerology is the Lo Shu Square. This square is based on the story of a tortoise that possessed nine perfect squares on its shell, as noted by the Emperor seated on the Luo River's banks.

The early Lo Shu square was called the magic square because it had three rows and columns of numbers, which added up to 15, regardless of whether the numbers were taken horizontally, vertically, or diagonally. Another peculiar feature of the square is that even numbers are arranged at the corners while the odd numbers form a cross or T-shape in the middle. The arrangement of numbers in the square looks something like this:

4	9	2
3	5	7
8	1	6

In recent times, the Chinese have developed a modern version of the magic square called the "hidden cross" to teach Chinese numerology to westerners. The hidden cross does not use the lunar year and has simpler arithmetic calculations. The numbers in the hidden cross are arranged thus:

3	6	9
2	5	8
1	4	7

Interpreting the outcomes of either the magic square or the hidden cross requires an in-depth knowledge of what the squares and the numbers symbolize. The top row in the square stands for mental capabilities, e.g., analytical ability; the bottom row signifies practical or the rational mind, strength, physical strength, or athleticism, while the middle row represents emotions, intuition, and feelings. According to the Chinese system, the number 1, for instance, is an indicator of interpersonal relationships. If, according to the readings, you have:

- **One 1:** This shows you have difficulty expressing your thoughts to others.

- **Two 1s:** You have an easy time communicating with and understanding others.

- **Three 1s:** You can communicate with others but are prone to occasional mood swings.

- **Four 1s:** Your caring and sensitive nature is admirable, but you find it hard to verbalize.

- **Five or More 1s:** You find social situations uncomfortable. You adopt unhealthy coping mechanisms such as over-drinking or overeating.

It is easy for skeptics to dismiss the beliefs of East Asians as superstitious and over the top, but their belief in the power of numbers permeates every aspect of their daily lives. In 1988, for instance, many pregnant Chinese women trooped to the hospital in droves to ask for a cesarean section to have their babies born as "dragon children" with double prosperity destinies. Chinese entrepreneurs also employ numerology when naming their businesses in the hope that this will attract good fortune and a large customer base.

The Chinese government often auctions cars with inauspicious license plates; individuals pay a pretty penny to have customized automobile license plates, up to \$60,000 or higher! Also, in Chinese numerology, the numbers are linked to an element:

- Water — 1
- Earth — 2, 5, and 8
- Wood — 3 and 4
- Metal — 6 and 7
- Fire — 9

The Asians are not the only people who are superstitious about numbers. Many westerners, for instance, are afraid of the number 13, particularly when it falls on a Friday. Skeptics fathom the fear of 13, which stems from the fact that Judas Iscariot was the 13th person to arrive at the venue of the last supper. Although historians believe that the inauspicious 13 and the fear of it began much earlier, Airlines do not have a 13th row. Hotels omit 13th floors from their buildings. Formula 1 race cars are numbered 12, then 14, skipping the number 13. The fear of number 13 even has a name which is *triskaidekaphobia.*

In China, instead of the number 13, the number 4 is considered ominous because it has the same pronunciation as the Chinese word for death. In Japan, the ominous number is 9 because it has the same pronunciation as the Japanese term for suffering or torture. Italians are wary of the number 17 because, in roman numerals, it is interpreted as XVII, which could be rearranged to VIXI, meaning "my life is over." I could go on and on about the love-hate relationship humans have with numbers, but that isn't the purpose of this book.

Western or Pythagorean Numerology

This form of numerology will be the main focus of this book. The Chaldean system had an immense influence on the ancient Greeks, and hence the Pythagorean system developed. It was during the era of Greek imperialism and when taking control of Babylon that the Greeks discovered the Chaldean numerology scripts, and from these, the western system was born.

Western or Pythagorean numerology is a system developed by the Greek philosopher and mathematician Pythagoras. He invented this system because he believed everything in nature could be reduced to numbers or mathematical calculations. This is a more modern system and that which this book will focus primarily on, although ideas will be imported from other forms of numerology.

Pythagoras believed that a lot could be learned about a person from their name and core number. He also proposed that every number had both a positive and negative quality.

Inspired by the Chaldean script, he formulated a logical method of numbers. His addition of mathematical knowledge and logic lent some credence to the system. The Pythagorean system has a linear progression in the affinity between letters and numbers. The numbers range from one to nine and hold specific vibrations like all other systems. He assigned the numbers 1 through to 9 in the following sequence: A = 1, B = 2, until I = 9.

There is also the existence of master numbers like 11, 22, and 33. These numbers are usually rounded to a single digit. The numbers allow one to draw a complete chart linked to the planets and astrology that describes all the attributes of the individual requesting a reading as well as maps out a clear-cut trajectory/pattern of life. This system is commonly used by western nations and is easily the most popular form of numerology out there.

The Pythagorean chart looks something like this:

1	2	3	4	5	6	7	8	9
A	B	C	D	E	F	G	H	I
J	K	L	M	N	O	P	Q	R
S	T	U	V	W	X	Y	Z	

The Spread of Pythagorean Numerology

After his death, Pythagorean numerology achieved fame and acceptance throughout the mathematical community, and several Greek philosophers and mathematicians adopted his theories. Plato, in particular, in his book called *Timaeus*, written in the 4th century B.C., borrows Pythagorean numerology in describing cosmology as a product of the divine ruled by numerical and mathematical truths.

Even today, western numerology is continuously evolving and has formed the foundations of major arcane societies such as Freemasons, Rosicrucians, and the Theosophical Society.

The person to credit for the spread of numerology in the past century is William John Warner (Count Louis Harmon to some people) or Cheiro. This Irish astrologer and master of the occult coined his moniker from the word "Cheiromancy"—the art of palm reading. Cheiro was a self-acclaimed clairvoyant who used his talent for numbers and the mystic sciences to predict events and conduct readings for popular figures such as Mark Twain, Thomas Edison, and the Prince of Wales.

Numbers in the Pythagorean System

Pythagorean numerology analyzes five main numbers:

1. Life path number
2. Birthday number
3. Personality number
4. Heart's desire number
5. Expression number

Each number reveals a different facet of an individual's persona. When combined, they give detailed insight into a person's character, the challenges they face, and the talents they might have. The numbers will be discussed in detail in later chapters.

Every numerology system is different. Each bears an identity and pattern of calculation unique to them. No system is better than the other, as different countries and people tend to favor systems closer to home. Each will give varying results based on belief and honesty. However, these days, the Pythagorean system of numbers has become more mainstream because modern practitioners laud it as the most accurate and easy-to-use system in existence.

With advancements in technology and the advent of the internet, many numerology calculations are done online. Popular numerology practitioners advertise their art and the form of numerology they practice, so you can choose what works best for you when faced with the different forms of numerology calculators on the internet.

Chapter 3: Seeing Single Digits?

The numbers one through to nine form the backbone of numerology since all multiple digits can be reduced to a single digit. For example, 25 can be reduced to 7, 18 to 9, and so on. For example, certain double-digit figures have unique meanings, such as 13, 14, 16, and 19, which are karmic debt numbers, and 11, 22, 33, and so on, which are master numbers. This chapter will cover the single digits 1 through to 9. You will learn how each number affects you, your health, career, love life, etc., and what it means for you if you see them repeatedly.

One: The Proactive and Primal Force

One is the number of creativity, efficiency, leadership, and autonomy. Seeing this number repeatedly could symbolize the start of something fresh and original in your life. The number 1 represents an individual who is creative and empowered to bring their desires into reality.

You are likely to come across this number many times on your spiritual journey. You may find that you usually have many questions before seeing the number 1. You could be searching for answers in your love life or career. The number 1 signifies that you are close to the breakthrough you have been waiting for. When this happens, be mindful of what you focus on since the positive focus is an integral part of the manifestation process.

In terms of love and your love life, people with life path number 1 are very demanding and emotionally difficult to handle. If you and someone with the number 1 are in a relationship, it signifies a deepening of the bond between you and your partner. If you are single, then you won't be single for long because someone amazing is about to come and sweep you off your feet - someone who will change the course of your life forever! Just listen to your heart and let it guide you to your intended destination.

Number 1 is a reminder to count your blessings. The divine wants to remind you of the fact that the highest expression of yourself is seen in the value and love you bring to the lives of others. It reiterates the love you have from family and friends. You have so much that you take for granted, and this number reminds you that it's these little things that make your life truly beautiful. Recognize the blessings you do have so that the universe sends more your way.

Two: The Wise Diplomat

The number 2 is the first prime number and is called the "odd" prime. It is a number that signifies balance, harmony, and partnership. On the flip side, it symbolizes conflict and resistance. In Asia, 2 is known as the number of good luck. A popular Chinese adage goes thus, *"Hao shi cheng shuang,"* which means good things come in pairs. It is quite common to see Asians carve a symbol in pairs on products, brand names, etc., to signify twice the value and twice the happiness. In the lunar year, the Chinese people exchange sweet oranges in multiples of two.

The vibrational signature of the number 2 is that of service, receptivity, and cooperation. Seeing the number 2 is a sign that the universe knows you are a hard worker and seeks to encourage you. However, you must be open to compromises and peaceful conflict resolutions, especially with people you loathe being around. The number 2 is also a sign that you will achieve the security and stability you deeply crave. The key is to stay alert and receptive both to your needs and that of others.

This number signifies that you ought to stop being pushy and allow the universe to work in your favor. It also reminds you that everyone you meet in your life is an avenue through which you can grow as a human being. In terms of progress and achievement, the number 2 symbolizes that you will soon be rewarded for your hard work and that the universe will rejoice with you in your achievements. All that is left for you to do is close that chapter of your life and remember the lessons you have gained from your experience since every step you take brings you closer to your divine mission.

In love and relationships, the number two is a symbol of fidelity and trust. These two virtues will come in handy in nurturing the present relationship you have with your partner. Communication and empathy are always key to a harmonious relationship. Your ego has no place here.

Three: The Creative Spark

Three is a number representative of the divine trinity, a symbol of the unity of mind, soul, and body. As such, it symbolizes guidance, protection, and support from the divine realm.

The number 3 in spirituality is considered the number of concordance and wisdom. It embodies the energy of joy, hope, advancement, creativity, communication, inner guidance, and materialization. The number 3 may appear in our experience at any time of day, either in work-related files, addresses, or phone numbers. You may also find yourself doing things in threes, going to a particular place, or getting the same item three times.

Constantly seeing the number 3 is a sign of good things to come. It also means you should have more faith in your abilities, be more self-assured, and remain positive in thought and deed. Seeing this number means you are in alignment with your spiritual guides and guardian angel. It reminds you to live life fully by doing the things you love. Learning that skill you have been putting off or engaging in the hobby you have always wanted to do may always seem daunting with number 3, but it is always in your best interest. Failure to tap into your creative well of energy or spontaneity will lead you to the brink of depression and anxiety.

In love, 3 urges you to be more confident, express yourself and listen to your heart. It may signify the right time to begin something new with a potential love interest if you are single. With the number 3, your intuition is strong, and you should learn to believe in yourself more.

In terms of social connection, 3 reminds you of how much you have relegated your social life to the back burner, even though you are an affable person. Your guardian angel is encouraging you to surround yourself with like-minded people who share your vision and passion. This way, they will fuel your energy and motivation. This will, in turn, broaden your horizons and give you a better perspective regarding the next steps to take in life.

Four: The Practical

The number 4 is symbolic of the four winds in the cardinal points - north, east, west, and south - which are also the four sacred directions. Also, the main elements in existence are water, air, earth, and fire.

The number 4 is more concerned with earthly and practical matters. A number 4 persona is well organized, methodical, practical, and honest in their dealings. A born leader, the number four person is mature and balanced. However, some of their vices like impatience, obstinacy, and intolerance may creep in. The number 4 could also be a reminder to make your usually rigid mindset more flexible; only this way will you be on the right path to awakening the dormant talents you have embedded within.

Constantly seeing the number 4 is a message from the guardian angels telling you the steps needed to achieve your goals. They are advising diligence, organization, discipline, and dedication in all endeavors while they look out for you and work on your behalf.

This number also symbolizes additional motivation and determination you need to cross the finish line in whatever challenges you are facing at the moment. The process of transformation, though tough, will make you a better person. Open your heart and eyes to new possibilities and let positive energies flow inward.

In love, the number indicates a need to bring stability into your relationship to strengthen the bond between you and your partner.

Five: The Dynamo

From all indications, 5 symbolizes several important things, from good luck to future predictions and necromancy. To a lot of people, the number five represents good luck.

The number 5 indicates positive change, so seeing this number is a sign that more of them are about to flood your life, and everything will turn out to be in your favor. Number 5 is linked to individualism, independence, intelligence, curiosity, liberty, and adventure. Number 5 people, according to numerology, are known for always being on the move, never staying in a place, or sticking to one thing for too long.

5 tells you to slow down, be more responsible and consider the future as much as you enjoy living in the present. Since the number 5 is concerned with sensual experience (which is ever-changing), the universe urges you through this number to embrace the sphere of existence that remains constant throughout life—the spirit.

In terms of health, the number 5 indicates a necessity to make lifestyle changes to improve mental and physical health and vitality. You may be seeing this number because you have taken on some sensual habits that are detrimental to your health and spirit. It simply means you need to step back from the path you have taken and re-evaluate because you are not living up to your full potential. Learn from your life experiences and quit burying your head in the sand. It is time to take charge of your life and create your own destiny because nothing is a coincidence.

Six: The Caregiver

In esoteric teachings, 6 is represented by the hexagon, which, when dissected, is composed of two overlapping triangles, much like the number six is formed by the summation of two number threes. The hexagon is seen in the seal of Solomon and the Star of David. According to esoteric teachings, it connotes the integration of the conscious mind (as seen by the upward-facing triangle) and the unconscious mind (the downward-facing triangle). This union of two opposites—the conscious and unconscious mind—represents harmony and balance.

6 teaches us the importance of finding balance in our lives. A lot of times, humans are carried away by the goings-on in the external world. A 6 represents an obsession with things like academic qualifications, finances, careers, and fitness goals. The number 6 appears to remind you not to allow these outward achievements to overshadow your spiritual well-being.

When this number frequently appears in your life, it serves as a reminder to find a way to balance your emotions and time, as well as being careful in your career and domestic life. Refuse to burden yourself with more responsibilities than you can handle, despite your loving and giving nature.

The number 6 is also a wake-up call for you to discover your triggers or those things that make you emotionally restless or drawn to self-sabotage and destructive behaviors. Strive for contentment instead of material things.

The number 6 urges you to be more aware of the energy you transmute and take time to develop the hidden qualities in your subconscious. Allow repressed memories to surface and, dare I say it, be selfish. It is time for you to put yourself first for a change. Practice self-love while finding time in between to show love to others.

Seven: The Seeker

The number 7 is a blend of the diligent 4 and the mystical 3. As a result of this, 7 embodies the perfect blend of practical and metaphysical attributes. It is a number associated with spiritual awakening, inner wisdom, intuition, self-awareness, and mysticism.

7 has an extremely high frequency and vibration, so this is not the time to doubt your choices and decisions. Put less faith in the opinions of others and more faith in your own instincts because the universe is completely behind you.

7 is also known as a herald of good luck, happiness, and material wealth. When it appears before you constantly, it is a powerful embodiment of the patience, persistence, and inner will you possess. It is a reminder that you can do whatever you set your mind to, as long as you believe in your abilities.

In love, 7 may mean that you are not totally open to your significant other. Hiding or suppressing your emotions or refusing to discuss them to avoid conflict can negatively impact you and your relationship in the long run. Also, 7 cautions you when meeting new people.

Eight: The Wealthy

8 is a sign that abundance will soon be coming your way. 8 symbolizes the flow of energy and infinite perfection. In numerology, a person with a life path or birth number 8 is usually associated with success, enormous

miracles, power, and abundance. 8 is the number of rewards, justice, and balancing the scales. For this reason, it is one of the karmic numbers in numerology.

As a karmic number, 8 apprises you of how you will get whatever you put out into the universe. Show kindness and love, and it will be returned to you tenfold. The opposite will also come back to you, so be careful of your actions and approach to life.

In esoteric teachings, 8 is the union of two squares (connoting earthly order) and the octagon, which represents the start of the transformation of the square into a circle (connoting eternal order).

Seeing this number constantly is a reminder to you to have more faith in yourself and step out of your comfort zone. 8 is linked to self-esteem, harmony, and confidence, so do not be afraid to trust your gut and take bold steps. The number 8 may indicate that you will manage to achieve balance in life after a long period of strife and discomfort. As a result of your hard work, prosperity and abundance are on the horizon for you. With the number 8, expect a financial boom in the near future.

In love, 8 points to your relationship problems being resolved. If you are single, it means that your search for true love may be over, and the partner you deserve will come into your life faster than you expected.

Nine: The Renewer

Numerologists and esoteric scholars regard 9 as the number of completion or culmination of a cycle after which numbers revert to zero, as seen in the Gematria. In esoteric teachings, 9 represents the last dimension where celestial energy manifests itself in the material world.

From a spiritual standpoint, the number nine represents intellect, influence, humanitarianism, compassion, enlightenment, and innovation. The goal of those on life path 9 is to understand the gifts they possess and teach them to others.

It signifies your guardian angel is trying to convey a message. Seeing 9 constantly might mean that someone you care about is in need of your assistance. So, find ways to help those around you with the little that you do have. Your ability to show empathy to others may be amplified at this time, so take measures to positively influence those around you. By doing this, you will reap the rewards of joy and happiness.

If you are thinking of pursuing a new career or changing jobs and you see the number 9, it represents a clarion call for you to consider a vocation that is more humanitarian – since it will be more fulfilling in the long run.

In love, 9 urges you to look inward and evaluate your path together with your significant other to see if you are both on the right path. It may mean it's time to spice things up in the bedroom to increase your bond.

Chapter 4: Master and Power Numbers

The master numbers consist of the numbers 11, 22, and 33. These numbers come with special traits and higher vibrations compared to single-digit numbers. On a karmic level, individuals with master numbers have learned all the lessons that accrue to the single digits 1–9 before their birth and are on this plane to improve humanity.

Having a master number as part of your core numbers could be a source of strength, but I won't pretend it does not pose its own set of challenges. Finding ways to cope and take control of the curveballs and downsides associated with master numbers is the best way to live a happy and prosperous life.

As 11, 22, and 33 comprise 1, 2, and 3, respectively, they are considered the ONLY master numbers because they possess elevated insight and form the triangle of the enlightenment - a triangle of revelation, manifestation, growth, and a higher perspective. In the triangle, 11 is the creator and visionary, 22 is the builder of visions who fine-tunes the dreams brought forth by 11, and 33 represents the creative who shares the finished vision with the rest of the world.

Having a master number does not guarantee success because the freedom of choice trumps all predictions. It is possible for you to have more than one master number in your chart. The potential and power are present, but since success won't drop in your lap, you will require focus, effort, and opportunity to showcase your talents to the world.

Master number guidance is only applied when discovered in your numerology chart as core numbers (derived from your birthday or life path number), soul urge numbers, destiny numbers, or personality numbers. Those numbers will be discussed in detail in further chapters. Also, Pythagorean numerology is the only system of numerology used in master number determination. Because of the power in these numbers, it is advised that you become familiar and in tune with all the numbers that appear on your chart to decipher whether master numbers are hidden within your chart.

11 — The Master Visionary

This number is made of double ones and symbolizes the height of both masculine energy (1) and feminine energy (2) derived when the master number is reduced to a single digit. For this reason, this master number combines the intuition and confidence of 1 with the sensitive intuition of the number 2. The expression of 11 may be confident intuition, but it constantly walks a tightrope between greatness and self-destruction. As the first of the master numbers, it has the spiritual quality of *"as above, so below."*

In many readings, 11 is reduced to 2, but where 2 is a passive and quiet follower, 11 is fiercely independent, a loner, and a leader. Having double the qualities of the artistically inspiring and spiritual number 1, number 11 is called the psychic master since such persons are interested in exploring beyond the barriers of the non-physical dimension while combining it with empathy, sensitivity, and intuition.

An 11 individual is spiritual, cooperative, and sensitive. This enables them to sense subtle auras and energies – and possess a *psychic knowing*.

It's almost like they can hear your thoughts out loud and sense your fears. This strong sense of awareness is, to them, both a blessing and a curse. The high-spirited 11 places more emphasis on belief, faith, and credence. They rely more on their inner spiritual voice instead of their logical brain. Hence, they are not the most rational thinkers in the group.

Those with this number are regarded as old souls, able to handle stressful situations in a calm and diplomatic manner. 11 is a number linked to faith and the future. As such, individuals with this number may have some qualities of clairvoyance, prophecy, or other psychic abilities. The downside for people having this number is that when their energies are not focused on a particular endeavor, they tend to be restless, fearful, and even anxious. This may lead to panic attacks and the development of phobias. They also suffer from vulnerability to stress, impracticality, self-conflict, and a lack of self-confidence.

The number 11 reminds you of the limitless opportunities that await exploration. Do not be afraid to act on anything that gives you a sense of joy and purpose. Embrace new beginnings and make small changes to the circle of people you surround yourself with.

22 — The Master Builder

This is one of the most successful of the master numbers. 22 is brimming with energy and potential, which is why such individuals must work to achieve success in causes larger than themselves. They are born to serve humanity as a whole. Positive traits associated with this number include practicality, discipline, ambition, idealism, great accomplishments, self-confidence, and dynamism. Negative traits include arrogance, aloofness, aimlessness, and a propensity to micromanage and manipulate others.

22 has a lot of esoteric significance. The original Hebrew alphabet consists of 22 letters, symbolic of everything from creation to eternity.

This master number has all the inspirational qualities of 11 and the down-to-earth nature of 4. As long as these individuals work towards humanitarian causes instead of personal ambition, they have the capacity to make every dream of theirs come true. This actualization of dreams is a trait of 4, which 22 is reduced to. If you have a life path of 22, you will find that you are able to unite many to achieve a single goal. You are a visionary who possesses not only the ability to see potential in a certain idea, but also one who can bring that idea to life. Somehow, you already know what will work and what won't. This is probably the reason why you are geared towards controlling or manipulating others instead of surrendering your will to the greater cause.

If your energies are not devoted to practical affairs, you will lose your ambition and potential. This leads to you being as tightly wound as an analog clock in your youth. The trick here is to have enough work to avoid being idle and balance work with a conduit to expel negative energy, for instance, comedy or a hobby. In love, you find it difficult to face your shortcomings. Your intense focus on your goals could lead to mood swings and frigidity, which affect your love life.

33 — The Master Teacher

This is the most spiritually evolved and enlightened of the master numbers. 33 possesses a higher vibration than 6. What makes this master number special is its extremely sincere devotion. It is the most influential of the three master numbers since it has the attributes of both 11 and 22. They are simply expressed to a greater degree.

A fully evolved 33 is extremely rare. It has a blend of the powers of creativity and expression (3) and the caregiver/teacher extraordinaire vibe (6). It is no surprise that it is the rarest among the master numbers. Even if you have a 66 in your core number, mastering the traits that go with it is not for the faint of heart.

Numerous instances exist that speak to the divine status of the number 33. The human spine, for instance, has 33 segments. The tree of life in the Jewish Kabbalah has 22 paths, 10 globes, and an invisible death, making it a total of 33 steps to enlightenment. The first temple of Solomon stood for 33 years. Jesus lived 33 years, and King David reigned for 33 years.

Seeing this number constantly is a sign from the angels that you need to quit being a wallflower and express your opinions more. It is a number that usually appears to those feeling lost and forlorn. Hence, it is an assurance that a series of events that will cause personal growth are incoming. However, you need to meditate on your past actions so that you can become a better version of yourself. Forgive yourself for your past and be grateful for how far you have come and how strong you have become.

In love and relationships, 33 is a sign for you to rid yourself of toxic friendships and people and focus your energy on those who love you the way you deserve to be loved. Stop thinking about what used to be or what once was and shift your mental energy to what is and what is to come.

Power Numbers

These are also called "goal," "reality, "maturity, or "realization" numbers. Like master numbers, power numbers are double digits with identical numbers, making them possess double the traits of their component numbers. Power numbers are derived by summing up the destiny numbers and the life path number. Think of master and power numbers as twins with similar attributes working together. Their potential for success is greatly amplified.

Your power numbers contain the energy available to accomplish your life goals and enhance your chosen career. It is an indication of how you can make a difference in the world and the lives of those around you on your path toward finding happiness in life. The power numbers are 44, 55, 66, 77, 88, and 99.

The impact of power energy does not come into full force immediately after awakening. It takes a few years. Around middle age (40-45), its resonance becomes clearer, and your perspective on the world shifts. How dramatic this shift is will depend on whether you have a power number with single dissimilar digits or double yet similar digits. If the former is the case, your power number obtains a new resonance. In the case of the latter, the resonance is amplified.

Here, we will calculate the power number of the famous South African entrepreneur, Elon Reeve Musk, using the Pythagorean chart.

The destiny number from his name would look like this:

- E+L+O+N= 5+3+6+5= 19. Reduced to a single digit, 1+9= 10. Further reduced, 1+0=1
- R+E+E+V+E= 9+5+5+4+5= 28; 2+8=10; 1+0=1
- M+U+S+K= 4+3+1+2=10; 1+0=1
- Destiny number - 1+1+1= 3

Life path number from his birthday (28th June 1971):

- 2+8=10; 1+0= 1
- 0+6=6
- 1+9+7+1= 18; 1+8=9
- Life path number is 1+6+9= 16 (reduced to 7)

From these calculations, Elon's power number will be life path + destiny number, which is 7+3=10 (reduced to 1).

Not everyone has a double-digit power number. No matter what your power number is, you are special.

44 — The Master Healer

This power number combines and amplifies the vibrations of 8 and 4. It is a rare number in numerology and is fondly referred to as the master healer. If you fall into this group, you need time, balance, and a stable foundation to hone your innate talents and realize your true potential. 4 is the most detail-oriented power number in numerology, and 44 guarantees twice the detail, all geared towards success. You have prudence and extreme drive, which makes them fashion well-thought-out game plans for success in realizing their goals. You practice big picture visualization and have a good understanding of plans that lead to long-term success. You have a fondness for hierarchy and structure, coupled with a penchant for discipline and dedication. There are a number of magical powers of manifestation. Since this number reduces to the auspicious number 8, you are extremely lucky in life or anything to do with material wealth. You possess the Midas touch and attract abundance.

Sometimes you're susceptible to greed, especially when your focus on creating wealth supersedes other aspects of your life. Your family and love life are always in jeopardy. You might also be plagued by perfectionism paralysis because your intense desire to get your ducks in a row may just mean you never get to do much or take any steps.

All in all, this power number is the perfect blend of pragmatism, efficiency (4), balance, abundance, and realism (8). Seeing this number constantly is a sign from the divine that you should rid yourself of doubts concerning your future because you are already tuned to the frequency of abundance. It also signifies that you pay attention to the people around you since they may be channels for new opportunities.

55 — The Unconventional Leader

55 is the one that thinks outside the box, the mad scientist, so to speak. 55 is the fun and freedom-loving 5 paired with the independent and confident 1. This master number is the force that breaks new grounds, reaches new heights, and is a whirlwind to be reckoned with in terms of

disciplined, structured, and persistent energy of 44. Despite all of this, there is much more to 88 than material abundance.

As an 88 person, you are more focused and driven compared to 44, and even though both 88 and 44 appreciate solid plans in place, 88, as a more amplified version of 44, does not get caught up in materialism that 44 is bound to since it reduces to the spiritual number 7.

In matters of love, where 44 is clingy and dependent, 88 is more trusting and gives their significant other a lot of freedom. An 88 individual is the most objective person you will ever meet. The 88 is also a great judge of character and can see both sides of an argument clearly if compared with other power numbers.

Constantly seeing this power number is never a coincidence. It is a sign from the angels stating that all you wish for in life (not necessarily material in nature) is about to come your way. The only question now is how well equipped you are to handle this abundance. Seeing 88 is a gentle reminder to you to help people in need with the barrage of blessings coming your way. In the area of relationships, it advises that you show more love to your partner and initiate intimacy more than you are presently doing.

99 — The Master Humanitarian

This signifies humanitarianism, global awareness, consciousness, and tolerance. 99 reduces to 18, which in turn reduces to the single digit 9. 18 is a combination of the fiercely driven leader in 1 and the pragmatic visionary in 8, making this power number one you can depend on to make this world a better place.

Since 99 is the amplified version of the single digit 9, it means both the good and ugly traits of the number 9 are expressed in their most extreme forms. What is peculiar about this power number is the fact that it reduces back to itself, 9, which is not the same case with the other power numbers. As a result of this, individuals with 99 as their core number are more likely to focus on the energies of 9 in this lifetime.

99 symbolizes maturity, understanding, and the completion of a cycle. This number is similar to the introspective and internally-oriented 77 but possesses a high level of independence. 99 goes beyond the self-love expected from 1, the need for material wealth (2), the need to protect relationships and the home front (3, 4, 5), the need for a successful career (6), a love life (7), or the search for spirituality (8). 9 is concerned

with universal love, encompassing all the elements important to all the numbers before it.

If you are a 99 individual, your main focus is on charitable acts since you are naturally giving of your time and energy. On the flip side, you can be more idealistic than the 44 and 66. Your Pollyanna-tinged lenses could also be laced with bitter cynicism, which makes you doubt yourself when you engage in charitable acts and question others' intentions when they act kindly toward you.

In love, 99 signals the end of loneliness. Love is in your near future. If you are in a relationship, this power number foretells a longer period of love and happiness. Your significant other will do anything to ensure you are loved and cared for. As number 9 signals finality, it also implies that people doing all they can to keep their relationship afloat will finally have the courage to break things off, move on, and start anew.

Chapter 5: Numerology and Astrology

Astrology is derived from the Latin root words "astro," meaning "star" and "logia," meaning "study of." This is an ancient science used to forecast human events and terrestrial affairs according to the placement or position of celestial bodies in the sky. Simply put, it is a science that studies the effects the cosmos has on human lives. Astrology has been in existence since the 2nd millennium BC. It was once considered a scholarly tradition by Greeks and Southeast Asians and is closely related to alchemy, medicine, astronomy, and metrology.

Astrology is often used interchangeably with astronomy. Both have common roots but are different from each other. While astrology is regarded as a pseudoscience, astronomy is the scientific study of the earth and every celestial body existing outside the earth's atmosphere and influence. Astrology studies the origins of these celestial bodies, their movements, and how they relate to or influence one another. According to popular poet and philosopher Ralph Waldo Emerson, astrology is astronomy brought down to earth and applied in the affairs of men."

The Link between Astrology and Numerology

Pythagoras discovered the relationship between both sciences in the 6th century BC – and both were used to make predictions. It is safe to say the Greek mathematician was the first person to find the connection between the stars, planets, and numbers after decades of intensive research.

Astrology is useless without numerical data concerning the person or event being investigated. This is because precise mathematical calculations need to be made to determine the position, angles, and heavenly bodies. In Vedic astrology, for instance, Siddhanta, a branch of Vedic astrology, uses numbers and arithmetic calculations to determine planetary positions, retrogressions, solar or lunar eclipses, etc.

Numerology charts study numbers in relation to planets, other celestial bodies, and horoscopes. All numbers are governed by certain planets, which allow these numbers (and people born under the influence of those numbers) to have certain personality traits. In Vedic astrology, the Vedic square is used to analyze the precise angles and positions of the planets and stars at the time of an individual's birth. The positions are then noted, vibrations of numbers written down, and these are then compared to present positions for predictive purposes or personality assessments.

Numerology and astrological readings reinforce each other in such a way that a higher meaning is deduced when both readings are combined. The fusion of astrology and numerology is called "astro-numerology" and is used in creating birth charts and horoscopes to help people find their meaning in life.

Numbers and planets are grouped based on the type of energy they possess, namely masculine and feminine (refer to the Tamil numerology chart in chapter two). The planets have numbers ascribed to them, and these numbers have specific vibrations and characteristics. These numbers are, in turn, linked to the zodiac signs to determine personality traits.

For instance, the sun is given the number 1. The sun is the king of the solar system and 1, the creator of all other numbers. Individuals with this number in their chart are assertive, independent, and rule the roost. The moon is linked to the number 2, which represents feminine energy, a pair, and the interdependence of two individuals. Number two individuals are peaceful, romantic, and sentimental. The fusion of numerology and astrology is used by many to name babies, pets, business ventures, and so on.

Pure scientists may dismiss numerology and astrology as groundless ramblings, but many scientists believed in the power of numbers, the planets, and the stars.

Hippocrates, the father of medicine, was a firm believer in the fact that a patient's astrological sign gave hints about their medical history and the diseases they were most predisposed to. Johannes Kepler, a German philosopher, mathematician extraordinaire, and pupil of the Danish astronomer, Tycho Brahe, believed strongly in the influence of celestial bodies on people and the Earth.

He went ahead to change the world by applying numbers in the formulation of the three laws of planetary motion, successfully applying mathematics, geometry, and physics to the study of the stars. Albert Einstein provided mathematical theories and descriptions concerning universal order and the machinations of the human psyche based on astrology and the vibrations given off by numbers.

From these explanations, it is clear to see how both metaphysical sciences influence, depend on, and complement one another. No astrologer worth their salt can properly plan or read a birth chart with a shoddy grasp of the meaning and symbols of numbers. Numerologists may not need to have an absolute understanding of astrology, but some basic knowledge of planetary influence will supplement their art.

1 — Ruled by the Sun (Zodiac Alter-Ego: Leo)

The sun is the ruling celestial body for individuals born on the 1st, 10th, 19th, or 28th of any given month. The sun is the king of the solar system, around which all other planets revolve. Any planet that gets too close to the sun deteriorates. According to Hindu scriptures, the sun obeys cosmic law, is home to our ancestors, and is the first in a line of the Vasus (dwelling places of consciousness). The sun is exalted in Aries, the first of the zodiac signs.

Like the lion, 1's are vivacious, authoritative, opinionated, and clear in their expressions. They enjoy the attention they get and have a difficult time changing their mindset or purpose. They love their freedom and march to the beat of their own drum. They care a great deal for others, make friends easily, and have no difficulty getting favors from people in positions of authority. They are blessed with good fortune, influence, courage, strong bodies, and more vitality than the average person.

A major defining characteristic is their love for luxury. They spend extravagantly on themselves and others and are notorious showoffs. A typical Leo has the latest and boldest fashion items the minute they hit the shelves. They also dislike criticism, so think long and hard before you fact-check or criticize a number 1. Try buttering them up with compliments before you drop your critique. Don't worry. They will listen because, deep down, the truth matters more to them than their own personal opinions. Like the sun, the number one is a source of illumination to others and is disciplined, practical, straightforward, and committed to serving humanity.

Budgeting and saving are two precautions to take. These are not entirely alien concepts, but they tend to avoid each other.

2—Ruled by the Moon
(Zodiac Alter-Ego: Cancer)

The moon is the ruling celestial body of individuals born on the 2nd, 4th, 11th, 20th, and 29th of any given month. Those born on the 29th are the luckiest. The sun may be the chief celestial body, but the moon is essential for the survival of the earth and all its inhabitants. The moon reflects the sun's light via an alchemical process involving special gems on the moon's surface called "moon crystals" (chandra mukhi mani). The moon crystals have a medicinal effect on the planet, which is why healing plants and herbs thrive more at night under the light of the moon.

Though only 15% as strong as the sun, the moon has rays that effectively penetrate the soil, affecting plant life, moisture content, and growth from germination through to harvest. Science has also proven that plants fare better with rhythmic exposure to moonlight and are more robust when harvested in the last week of the lunar cycle. I guess Wiccans have been onto something their whole lives! This is the reason why an alternative name for the moon is "soma," or nectar.

The moon is a giant ball of feminine, nurturing, creative energy, much like the number 2, which is governed by it. People with psychic number two are sensitive and emotional, sensuous, romantic, and appreciative of art and beauty, traits which the zodiac sign of Cancer is known for. The moon governs cancer and is exalted in Taurus.

The moon's constant waxing and waning phases make people prone to mood swings and emotional instability. They go from happy and hopeful to moody and depressed in moments. Psychic number 2 enjoys solitude, but those born on the 11th take extra measures to self-isolate. Number 2 individuals have a mucus-dominated disposition. The moon influences the left nostril, the left eye, the left-hand channels of the body, and the brain's right hemisphere.

Evolved number 2s always see through to the end whatever project they set their mind to. They are reserved by nature, but friendships are sacred. In case 2, you have a friend for life. Their docile nature is a magnet for narcissists and people who wish to take advantage of them. They are warriors fond of making the same mistakes over and over. Although they are very attractive, they have a huge amount of self-doubt and, as a result, fall prey to a little flattery.

3 — Ruled by Jupiter
(Zodiac Alter-Ego: Sagittarius, Pisces)

Jupiter is the ruling celestial body for people born on the 3rd, 12th, 21st, or 30th of any given month and those with the destiny number 3. Those born on the 12th are the most fortunate. Those born on the 30th are usually the least fortunate.

Jupiter is a gigantic self-illuminating body that gives off more energy than it receives from the sun. It is the largest of all the planets in the solar system, and its size earned it the name "Guru" in Sanskrit, which means "remover of darkness" or "heavy." According to the Vedic scriptures, Jupiter is a planet representative of knowledge, hard work, righteousness, courage, boldness, and speech. Jupiter is exalted in cancer and associated with the Rigvedic deity Vachaspati, the god of eloquence.

Jupiter reigns over Pisces and Sagittarius and is exalted in Cancer. Jupiter rules over the ninth house of the birth chart (the house of fate) and is co-ruler of the 12th house (the house of the unconscious). As ruler of the house of fate, its position in the birth chart is of the utmost significance as it determines education, marriage, and childbirth. A female's birth chart can determine the lifespan, behavior, status, and character of her life partner. When Jupiter is positioned in opposition to the sun, Saturn, or Uranus, marriage is delayed or ends in divorce.

Number 3 individuals are popular, hard-working, dependable, ambitious, and self-confident. They are very future-oriented individuals who dislike working as subordinates; thus, they create opportunities for entrepreneurship. Like the Sagittarius star sign, 3s love to travel and are eager to meet as many people as they can within their lifespan. They have a strong sense of observation and logic, and their hard-working nature ensures that they are always busy with one thing or the other. They try to rest but usually can't switch their brains off. Like number 1, they value compliments and being appreciated for anything they do.

3s are blessed with the gift of the gab, even though their sense of humor might be offensive to many. Their short temper and assertive nature make them a lot of enemies, and as a result, they keep a small circle of friends. Not to worry, they are great friends since they are helpful and keep their promises.

4 — Ruled by Uranus
(Zodiac Alter-Ego: Aquarius)

Uranus is the ruling celestial body of individuals born on the 4th, 13th, 22nd, or 31st of any month. In Scorpio, Uranus is exalted. The characteristics mentioned below also apply to people who have a destiny or name number of 4, although these qualities are more pronounced in individuals with a soul number of 4. 4 is the number associated with cosmic static integrity and is an ideally stable number. There are four seasons and four cardinal points. For example, many objects of esoteric significance have four sides or angles, for example, the mandala, the crucifix, and the square.

Individuals under its influence are illogical, dull, and lazy, with short attention spans. They often become detectives, spies, conspirators, or revolutionaries because of their aversion to work and their unconventionally genius ideas. Uranus causes fear, doubt, hostility, ignorance, and big plans that take an eternity to fulfill. This makes individuals under its influence work harder than most and, in the end, stack up bad karma that isn't good for them.

An evolved 4 is creative with artistic talents and is blessed with physical attractiveness, boldness, intelligence, and a highly secretive nature. Most of the time, in their endeavors, they side with the opposition or the underdog, which can create enemies. This is because they possess a specific viewpoint that enables them to see the truth inherent in all things. When Uranus is allied with Jupiter or Venus, individuals gain access to psychic sciences like tantra.

The unfavorable part of Uranus makes individuals selfish, arrogant, aggressive, and pessimistic. This, in turn, causes them opposition, humiliation, and other difficulties not easily diagnosed by medical means. In the worst cases, the individuals develop suicidal tendencies. Uranus is the day ruler of Aquarius and the 11th house (the house of friendship) on the birth chart. Friends of Aquarius include Virgo, Pisces, Gemini, and Sagittarius. Its enemies are Leo and Cancer.

Astrologers compare Uranus with smoke; it is amorphous but permeates every surface and crevice. It has the element of air. Because number 4 individuals are sensitized to the difference between good and evil, they have strong powers of judgment and are very doubtful and critical of others. They are also extremists; there is no middle ground for them. They either fiercely love or fiercely hate, but on the flip side, they are reliable, patient, and steadfast friends with large hearts. They are not interested in accumulating riches but give abundantly to the community and the needy.

5 — Ruled by Mercury
(Zodiac Alter-Ego: Gemini, Virgo)

Mercury is the ruling celestial body of individuals born on the 5th, 14th, and 23rd of any month or whose name or destiny number adds up to 5. Those born on the 23rd are the luckiest, while the least fortunate are those born on the 14th. Mercury, the smallest planet in the solar system, is fondly called Kumar (youthful in Sanskrit) because of its evergreen nature. It is also called "Buddha" (intellect in Sanskrit).

Mercury is a gender-neutral celestial body associated with the element of earth. It influences the nervous and respiratory systems and intelligence, education, and eloquence. Mercury is a planet of extremes. They can be quite money-minded and materialistic on the one hand or disinterested in wealth accumulation and drawn to austere living on the other. This planet may be auspicious and benevolent, but its influence on individuals could make them cunning, deceitful, serious, and manipulative. However, 5s, just like the planet governing them, are forces of nature, attractive, fond of travel or adventure, eloquent, soft-spoken, and lovers of the arts.

4s have a quick wit and are broad-minded scholars. Their brains are never at rest. They are constantly trying to fill it with new information. They are jovial, impulsive, and very dedicated to consuming a lot of their energy to create a jolly atmosphere and make people happy. This usually backfires because no one is capable of pleasing everyone. Their impulsivity does not allow for long-term planning or lifelong friendships, even though they make friends very easily.

Their merchant nature predisposes them to take big risks, and some of them acquire wealth in this way. They are intuitive, adaptable, and have a clarity of expression that is envied by other signs. They are spendthrifts by nature and do not believe in only one source of income. Add this to their speculative nature and willingness to take risks, and you have a sign that's never in need of money.

Number 5 is always in a hurry. They value their time more than anything else. The best advice for 5 is to relax more. This helps them get over their intense and broody natures. They should also, under no circumstance, lose their jovial nature and sense of humor.

6—Ruled by Venus
(Zodiac Alter-Ego: Taurus, Libra)

Venus is the ruling celestial body of individuals born on the 6th, 15th, and 24th of any given month. The 24th is the most fortunate of the 6. This also applies to people with destiny or name number of 6. 6s are romantic, active, sensual, and passionate as a result. Venus influences the reproductive organs, eyes, throat, chin, and kidneys. Venus-dominated individuals have doe eyes, beautifully proportioned bodies, and a lively yet graceful persona.

Venus governs men in a different way than it does women. The 6s have a mesmerizing magnetic personality. They are lovers of refined tastes and hobbies. Members of the opposite sex are easily drawn to them, and their social nature makes it easy for them to engage with a variety of people. They dislike sloppiness, disorder, and dirt.

It is easy for a 6 to learn the deeply guarded secrets of others, but their secretive nature makes them confidants you can trust. Trust them to enforce their will without coercion and to hide their anger under a deceptive smile. They love and desire companionship and despise solitude.

It is best to avoid planning revenge and stewing over past wrongs. This affects their nervous systems adversely. They are advised to avoid spicy foods, fats, oils, and sweet dishes. Weak periods are in April, October, and November when Venus is retrograde. Peak periods include April 20th through May 18th and September 21st through October 19th.

7—Ruled by Neptune
(Zodiac Alter-Ego: Pisces)

Neptune is the ruling celestial body for individuals born on the 7th, 16th, and 25th of any given month. This also applies to people with a destiny or name number of 7. The qualities of Neptune are predominant in people with the psychic number 7. Neptune is exalted in Leo. It is gender-neutral, although many astrologers consider it feminine. Neptune is a deeply spiritual planet that bestows upon a 7 wisdom, non-attachment to worldly cares, lack of ambition, and a high dose of sensitivity.

Neptune is more powerful at night and, when in a favorable position in the birth chart, gives seven psychic abilities such as healing through herbs, reiki, witchcraft, food, and occult sciences. 7s, like their zodiac counterparts Pisces, live in an imaginary world of their own making. They are quite intelligent, love debates, and have their own brand of logic. They are usually shabby or cosmopolitan in appearance. Their body chemistry is dominated by the element of air, and because of this, they are restless.

Neptune's allies are Mercury, Saturn, Venus, and Uranus. Jupiter is neutral, while the sun, moon, and Mars are their enemies. The negative influence of Neptune makes the 7 indecisive, moody, restless, and destructive. They make many mistakes and encounter a lot of failures in life. This failure is usually utilized as a steppingstone to their success.

With a Piscean, uncertainty is their stock in trade, but don't be fooled. There is a method to their madness and an order to their chaos. Many individuals become poets, arbitrators, writers, artists, scientists, and numerologists. The key is well-structured guidance to make their mark on the world. Individuals in this category are romantic, noble, kindhearted, and authentic. They live their lives unapologetically and without a care in the world. Space and freedom are deeply important to them, and this makes them advocates of social justice.

8—Ruled by Saturn
(Zodiac Alter-Ego: Capricorn)

Saturn is the ruling celestial body of individuals born on the 8th, 17th, or 26th of any given month, as well as those with the name or destiny number 8. Saturn is the furthest planet in the solar system and is exalted in Libra.

When Saturn is in an unfavorable position in a birth chart, the individual under its influence becomes gloomy, greedy, and macabre. Saturn is the most destructive and disadvantageous of all the malefic planets. As the planet of darkness, it reigns supreme over the dark side of human nature and the awareness of right and wrong (the human conscience). If this planet is positively positioned in a natal chart, it will bring to its beneficiary wisdom, a sharp sense of right and wrong, sincerity, honesty, a long life, leadership, organizational abilities, a sense of authority, and leadership qualities.

Because Saturn rules over old age (like Mercury rules over youth), the Saturn subjects behave like older individuals and are more mature in appearance compared to their actual age. Saturn influences the hair, nails, teeth, skin, bones, skeleton, and nervous system. Saturn has allies in Neptune, Mercury, and Saturn. Jupiter is neutral, while the sun, moon, and Mars are their enemies.

8 is a number of determination and tenacity. They are hard-working people who accept the toughest challenges and surmount them. They prefer solitude, but when they decide to engage in social situations, communities, or other groups, they are sincere in their dealings. Even with their honest intentions, they are the most misunderstood by everyone, family and friends included. Their distinctive personas give them a very strong presence. It is easy to tell when an 8 (or a *Saturnine*) walks into a room because they subsume all other auras.

8 is unpredictable, lacks humor, and will never get your joke (so don't bother!) They feel very lonely at heart, and though their outward appearance looks menacing, in their hearts, they are fuzzy teddies who will jump through hoops and the fires of the underworld for their friends and loved ones.

9—Ruled by Mars
(Zodiac Alter-Ego: Aries, Scorpio)

Mars is the ruling celestial body of individuals born on the 9th, 18th, or 27th of any given month. It also applies to people with a name or destiny number of 9. Those born on the 9th are tougher, rougher around the edges, but most fortunate. People born on the 27th are much gentler and more critical, while those born on the 18th have inner turmoil, selfishness and will become very quarrelsome in the future. Mars rules over Aries and Scorpio. It is exalted in Capricorn.

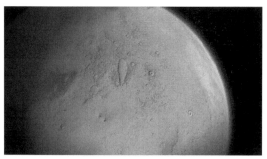

Mars is personified in Vedic texts as a strong figure with masculine energy. Mars is regarded as the commander in chief of all the planets in the solar system. The English word "martial" is derived from the qualities possessed by this planet. Duty, bravery, a sense of purpose, self-confidence, order, discipline, and courage.

Astrologers consider Mars to be a destructive planet because individuals under its influence are selfish and egotistical, putting their desires above others'. Its influence makes people headstrong, argumentative, fiery-tempered, lovers of dangerous weapons, cruel, restless, and violent. Mars also creates instability in romance and marital life when it dominates the 1st, 4th, 7th, or 10th house of their birth chart.

Martians and the number 9 are lovers of martial arts (no surprise there), politics, public speaking, hunting, sports, contests, and debates. They achieve the zenith of their power from 27 to 40 years of age. The Sun, Moon, and Jupiter are allies of Mars. Mercury is an enemy, while Venus, Saturn, Pluto, and Uranus are neutral.

Chapter 6: The Karmic Debt Numbers

The earliest mention of the word "karma" is found in the Rig Veda, an ancient compendium of Vedic Sanskrit hymns. Karma is derived from the Sanskrit word "karman," which literally translates to action, fate, or effect.

Karma is a concept in Hinduism and Buddhism that teaches how the sum of a person's deeds in previous and present lifetimes creates a system of actions and reactions that either impact or determine their fate in future lifetimes. This sum of a person's actions (beneficial or harmful) throughout a soul's reincarnated existence creates the cycle of birth-rebirth (samsara). In Vedic texts, the lord of Karma is the planet Saturn.

Karma is divided into three types:

1. **Sanchita**: Sanchita means "heaped together." Thus, this is the sum or collection of past karmas ready to be experienced after reincarnation.

2. **Prarabdha:** Karma is experienced by the body and forms a small part of Sanchita Karma.

3. **Agami**: Karma is formed from our actions here and now.

This universal law of karma is called the principle of cause and effect, and it governs all consciousness. It is important to know two facts. The first is that karma is different from fate. We all possess free will and are in charge of fashioning our destinies. The second is that not all karma is experienced in one lifetime. Some could accumulate to return in later incarnations. Humans are said to produce karma in four ways:

1. Words.
2. Thought.
3. Deeds performed personally.
4. Acts that others carry out as a result of our direction, instigation, or instruction.

Karma can only be repaid while we are alive. Death robs us of our power to act (Kriya Shakti) and our power to do (Kriya Mana). Hence, we can only wait until we are incarnated in another body to resolve our karma. Judging by this analogy, animals and infants are unable to create new karma since they are unable to distinguish between right and wrong.

Karma in Numerology

The question now is: what does karma have to do with numbers? The idea behind karma in numerology is that the soul carries both wisdom and challenges from events we faced or mistakes we made in previous lifetimes. These karmic conditions are revealed to us through the science of numbers.

Karmic Debt vs. Karmic Lessons

Both concepts are interwoven since they both concern karma from previous lifetimes. A karmic debt is an event or transgression that occurred in a past life that you are atoning for. On the other hand, a karmic lesson is a collection of situations, experiences, and themes from previous lifetimes that we didn't learn any lessons from. These situations keep repeating themselves until you learn something from them.

Karmic debts speak to the present challenges you face, while karmic lessons point to the tools missing in your life that could aid you in your quest to evolve. This follows the basic assumption that we are all souls, born to evolve towards higher states of enlightenment. In numerology, karmic debts are calculated differently from karmic lessons.

Karmic lessons are discovered by looking at the full letters of your given name as stated on your birth certificate and finding out which numbers are missing. To calculate the karmic lesson number for Clarence John Smith, these are the numerical values of the name according to Pythagorean numerology:

- C – L – A – R – E – N – C – E = 3 – 3 – 1 – 9 – 5 – 5 – 3 – 5
- J – O – H – N = 1 – 6 – 8 – 5
- S – M – I – T – H = 1 – 4 – 9 – 2 – 8

From the example, it is clear that some numbers appear more than once. The only number missing is the number 7. So, for Clarence, his karmic lesson is 7.

Signs You Have Karmic Debt

1. You find yourself catering to or caring for certain kinds of people. This may be karma's influence on you as a form of payback for misdeeds or selfishness in a past life.

2. You are always facing or struggling with problematic patterns or cycles. It could be anything from abusive relationships to financial debt. This would point toward a past life of excessive indulgence in either sex or material gain.

3. You experience patterns of behavior you can't explain. There is a saying that goes, "*That which cannot be explained in this lifetime is certainly rooted in a past life.*" This is often the only way to make sense of irrational phobias we may have or patterns of behavior we are sure were not picked up from our present existence. It may all stem from a previous life, whether it is a fear of fire, an aversion to happiness, or certain foods.

4. There are unlimited opportunities for mastery in this lifetime. You may try to skirt around or ignore the karmic issues you face. Failure to address these debts keeps them in your life until you settle the score and gain mastery of the lesson your karma is trying to teach you. Like any vicious cycle, unfulfilled karmic debts feel like a trap and can transform into dangerous habits if you fail to develop self-awareness. Instead of addressing your debts, you just keep piling on more with time.

5. You have at least one karmic relationship in this life. A karmic relationship is one that is undeniably strong and fulfilling on the one hand but emotionally draining, unpleasant, and toxic on the other. This points to a debt you owe the person from a previous lifetime.

6. Karmic numbers are present in your birth chart. These are the most obvious, and a full explanation will be given below.

What Numbers Carry Karmic Debt?

The karmic debt numbers are 13, 14, 16, and 19. They are considered only when they appear in any of your core numbers, namely:

- **Life Path Number:** Calculated from the date of birth. Life path numbers that add up to any of the karmic digits or include numbers 1, 4, 5, and 7 since they are the single-digit reductions of the double-digit karmic numbers.

- **Soul Urge Number:** Calculated from the addition of consonants in your name.

- **Personality Numbers**: From the numbers in your birthday and month.

- **Expression Number:** From the sum of digits that make up your name.

Another method of calculating your karmic number is by adding together your name number and life path number. Note that the name used must be your birth name as it is written on your birth certificate. Do not use pet names or any adopted names. Once you accept and begin to understand the debts you must atone for in this lifetime, you have the rare opportunity to break the cycle and quit repeating the same mistakes again and again. This will finally set your soul free. Some people do not have a karmic debt number, but this is very rare.

The absence of a karmic number simply means your soul journey has a different meaning, one not tied to the concept of repaying past life debts. But if you do have one, it's not a curse or anything to be afraid of. Whether you have a karmic debt number or not, the fact remains that we are all fighting our personal battles or struggling with one pattern or the other. Below is a list of karmic debt numbers and how you can use them as a steppingstone for personal growth. Each of these karmic debt numbers has a specific significance, outlines a specific level of hardship in this lifetime, and teaches a particular type of lesson. An individual can have more than one karmic debt number, and I will address each of these numbers and explain their lessons.

Karmic Debt Number 13/4

A karmic debt of 13 or a life path of 4 implies abuse of morals for personal gain in a past life. This karmic debt signifies that you were probably lazy and self-indulgent in a previous life or that you had no self-control.

Laziness comes naturally to most humans, but this is especially true for those with this karmic number. Your aversion to work in a previous life prevented you from completing or attempting tasks. Staving off a lazy attitude is the most prominent life lesson associated with this number.

This is why people with 13 usually encounter numerous roadblocks and have to put in more effort than most to achieve success. How then does one work off this debt? Accountability. Yes, you will need to hold yourself responsible for your actions. Your purpose is to learn that there is no substitute for hard work.

When it comes to self-indulgence, the appearance of this karmic debt number is a result of the fact that you achieved most or all of your success using the sweat or effort of others in your previous life. You were a pro at avoiding responsibilities and found joy in taking credit for their effort rather than your own.

Karmic number 13/4 demands that you set your sights on aspects of life unrelated to pleasure. This karmic debt number may also point to an addiction of some kind in a past life for the sake of personal gain. If the same habit rings true in this lifetime, then you need to desist immediately.

Now let's talk about lacking self-control. Because of self-indulgence, you naturally have no control whatsoever over your impulses, be they your temperament, emotions, sexual desires, or love for intoxicants. In the past, you indulged in the basest urges of your mind without a care for how they affected your health, state of mind, or how they affected others around you. This debt number urges you to develop healthier habits (which help you live better in the long run) and improve your self-control because that will help you achieve your dreams in this life.

While maintaining discipline and order in your life, understand that there is always room to let new and creative ideas flow in from any source. Learn to be vulnerable around others. Don't be so set in your ways that you gloss over a fantastic idea simply because of your idealistic tendencies or lack of willingness to put in any effort.

Karmic Debt Number 14/5

A karmic debt number of 14 or a life path of 5 implies abuse of freedom in a past life or a problem with you relinquishing control or power to others, sometimes to the detriment of your wellbeing. This karmic debt number concerns independence, personal power, and self-direction. The main messages contained in the number 14 are fear and hope.

Individuals in this category of karmic debt suffer from escapism and wanderlust. As a result, focus does not come easily to them, and this is rooted in the number 5 (the reduced number 14) in their numerology chart. 5 has an adventurous spirit and has the habit of dumping people they know in favor of someone new and interesting. Your mission in this lifetime? Work through and get rid of the shiny-new-toy syndrome you have. Cultivate and invest in yourself, your health, finances, and present relationships because quality trumps quantity at any given time.

Rein in your fear. On the flip side of escapism and adventure is paralyzing fear. 5s and 14s may be courageous in the face of adventure, but beneath all that bravado is undiluted fear. This is because escapism presents its own unique brand of challenges that manifest in various forms, like the fear of escapism itself and the knowledge that excessive indulgence may bring you harm. There's also the fear of the unknown, drawn from the fact that you find commitment unappealing. You are constantly afraid of being so poor or helpless that you are at the mercy of others. The solution to this is to find a way to confront those fears head-on. Worrying won't solve your problems.

Karmic Number 16/7

A karmic debt number of 16 or a life path number of 7 implies a vain nature and an inflated ego that connects all of your previous lives to the present one. This means that, in the past, your arrogant nature caused a great deal of torment to those around you. A quote by Benjamin Franklin says, *"A man wrapped up in himself makes a very tiny bundle."* With the number 16/7, your past life was probably riddled with events where your sense of self-importance was used for non-constructive purposes, which is why your debt seeks to deflate your ego and keep you in touch with your inner self. This group needs to learn humility and how to drop bad habits to have a fresh, great beginning.

Humility is one karmic debt of ego that is one of the most difficult to overcome because it requires an endless cycle of deaths and rebirths (samsara) to gain humility and prove yourself worthy with each incarnation. Like the phoenix rising from the ashes, you must let go of old and harmful patterns to give way to a newer and more reformed version of yourself.

16/7 also implies transgressions regarding love and relationships in a previous lifetime. This can occur as a repetitive string of relationships where you either break others' hearts or get your heart broken. To address this karmic cycle, there is a need for you to remain mindful in your day-to-day activities and commit to connecting with others. When you start to become more thoughtful and self-aware, you think more about how your words might affect others and, as such, put more thought into them.

You have to let go of your bad habits to allow new and better energy to flow in. Humans naturally have an ego. It's a given. It is hard for many to admit the battles they fight in this lifetime. Why do you think therapy is pricey? With ego problems that have transcended lifetimes, handling the situation is even direr. You probably have a grand plan laid out for your life by a particular age, only for life to toss a monkey wrench and make a caricature of all your grand schemes. The lesson taught by this karmic number is flexibility and adaptability when faced with life's challenges.

It is difficult, if not downright impossible, for you to cultivate meaningful relationships with others. You find it hard to be vulnerable toward other people. Your pride never lets you ask for company either – and for this reason, you come across as pompous and self-absorbed. Because of a lack of social skills and an absence of close relationships, you are often misunderstood by people. Those with the typical number 7 (reduced to 16) are often thought to be unapproachable. Your body language is closed off, and your smiles come as often as it takes a comet to appear in the sky. You do a great job of showing others that you do not care about their opinion of you, so you make rash decisions that sabotage relationships you already have and new ones that are in the formation stages.

Do things differently in this lifetime. Instead of burning bridges like you usually would, expand your intuition and open yourself up to new paths, influences, ideas, and people. Practice listening to others and nurturing your relationships. You will find yourself surrounded by people who genuinely love and care for you with time.

Karmic Debt Number 19/1

A karmic number of 19, or a life path of 1, points to you having lived a narcissistic, manipulative, and selfish nature in a past life. You cared more about your assets, talents, and outward appearance. You also looked down on others, using them only to help you get ahead. You may have also been a cruel slave driver, punishing your subordinates and others of a lower social class than you

Debt number 19 is heavily linked to the abuse of power in a previous life. This selfish attitude has carried over to this lifetime, making you still turn down your nose at others. The lesson taught by 19 is the importance of focusing your attention outward and towards others instead of inwards and towards yourself. Refusal to acknowledge this debt can quickly turn your life into a self-imposed prison sentence until you recognize the importance of independence and the value of interdependence. With 19/1, you quickly realize that no man is an island. We all need each other to survive.

The superficial tendencies in the past that led to this debt amount teach three main lessons. One lesson is about shedding your pride. Like number 1 (reduced to 19), individuals in this category are very self-reliant and a bit of a know-it-all. They enjoy their own company, resolve all their issues alone, and do not accept or appreciate advice from anyone but themselves. Their self-realized ideals may be great, but they are bound to make a lot of mistakes that they find hard to forgive themselves for. The sooner they shed their pride, one-man-army mentality, and self-imposed independence, accepting that true balance comes from letting others in, the quicker they achieve success.

If you have a karmic debt of 19/1, do not be afraid or ashamed of what people will think when you ask for help. What's the worst that could happen? They refuse, right? But not everyone will refuse you, so there is nothing to worry about. Keep in mind that it is easier to stand on your own two feet while holding onto the hand of another for support and friendship.

Another lesson is being of service to others. It's possible that you were blessed with wealth and a variety of talents in a previous life, which you used to enrich and advance yourself. 19 comprises 1-signaling the genesis

Calculating Your Birthday Number

This is the easiest core number to calculate. Your day of birth is all you need. For instance, if Jessica was born on the 11th of March, her birthday number is 11.

For double-digit birthday numbers, certain numerologists analyze their single-digit values (post-reduction). For instance, someone born on the 17th will definitely have 17 as their birthday number, but the numerologist will take the reduced digit 8 (1+7) into consideration. It is, however, important to understand that while numbers like 17 and 26, for instance, may have the same reduced single-digit value, the expression of traits will certainly differ.

17, for instance, combines the assertive, confident, and obstinate number 1 with the intellectual, insightful, yet solitary number 7. While 26 combines the gentle, sensitive, diplomatic 2 with the creative, nurturing, and self-sacrificing 6. Knowledge of this number helps you understand your positive traits and helps you work towards minimizing or totally eliminating the negative ones.

Below is a list of all the birth numbers and their dominant personality traits, from numbers 1 through 31.

- **(1)**

You are a pioneer, an initiator with an energetic and creative personality. A natural leader of the pack, you play by your own rules because you have what it takes to carry out your plans. You have excellent business instincts, and you play to win. You are a master at using knowledge for a specific purpose. You are also a key source of influence and motivation for others.

Weaknesses

- You have an iron will. Your strong sense of what you like and dislike does not win you many friends.

- Your extreme need for independence and your domineering attitude make you a difficult person to work with or for. It's not like you mind anyway, since you dislike the restrictions that come with working with others.

- Anger and frustration come to the fore when things do not go the way you like them. Your favorite words are "I," "Yes," and "Now," in no particular order.

Ideal Professions

1 can succeed anywhere, but for them to truly shine like the alphas they are, they must be placed in work environments where routine and monotony do not exist. Their quick wit and flexible minds demand situations that will involve making spur-of-the-moment decisions and challenge their ingenuity to find ways to work around impossible situations.

1 is pleased to create reliable irrigation in the Sahara, design an automobile, create an impossibly catchy advert, or persuade a frugal businessman to buy a multimillion-dollar house. They would never thrive with jobs that involve, say, a cashier in a mall with fixed prices for goods, a toll booth collector, or even worse, a frozen pea tester.

Famous 1's: Dr. Phil, Justin Bieber, Penn Badgley, Missy Elliot

• (2)

As a diplomat and peacemaker, you are everything I am not. That is what makes you the Robin to their Batman. You are emotional, sensitive, intuitive, and in tune with your environment. Nothing escapes your attention, even if you don't talk about it. You are highly adaptable, affectionate, and warm and demand the same measure of affection from your loved ones.

Your family is very important to you. You thrive in a harmonious environment and love being made to feel safe and secure. You excel at continuing a project rather than starting it and work best with partnerships. Unlike someone who enjoys being on stage, you are content being the power behind the throne. You may not get all the accolades that are due to you, but that does not change the fact that you are indispensable in any endeavor.

Weaknesses

• Your extreme attention to detail and your environment can sometimes leave you stressed and high-spirited.

• Your emotional nature makes you prone to manipulation and leaves you vulnerable to people who tend to take you for granted.

• You suffer from a lack of self-confidence and are prone to bouts of depression.

Ideal Professions

Your talents are best concentrated in any field of endeavor that highlights your diplomatic skills. Human relations, business communication, legislation in private companies, and political ambassadorship. You will also fare well in the fields of medicine, art, civil service, and education.

Famous 2's: Ina Garten, Bon Jovi, Donatella Versace, and Dwayne "The Rock" Johnson.

• **(3)**

An enthusiastic and creative soul with the gift of garb. A 3 will talk their way out of a fight and take their opponents to lunch soon after. These smooth operators are the most charming and witty individuals you will ever meet. There is never a dull moment with them. They are highly imaginative individuals who have no problem attracting romantic interest. They always have a full social calendar that leaves others wondering how they never get burned out. They are also magnets for luck and abundance.

Weaknesses

• Your sense of imagination keeps you perpetually in your own little world. You are far from being realistic.

• You have a serious case of leaky pockets. Your spending abilities leave a lot to be desired.

• Your eternal optimism and childish innocence make you vulnerable to manipulators and narcissists.

• Your creative mind is eternally chaotic – you never finish anything you start.

Ideal Professions

Any area of creativity will work. 3 will do well as an artist, writer, poet, or actor. Sports or science will suit them too.

Famous 3's: Mel Gibson, Martha Stewart, Kendall Jenner, Tiffany Haddish

• (4)

4s are the salt of the earth. Diligent, loyal, conservative, and precise, the typical 4 is relied upon to manage and organize. They are not given to hurried or pie in the sky solutions; rather, they are ambush predators. With patience second to none, they will sit and wait, persevering until they "pounce," achieving their goals. 4s are always indispensable and in demand because they can fit into any endeavor and would not hesitate to tread where others have failed and come out successful.

Weaknesses

- Rigidity or inflexibility of thought makes you lose out on opportunities.

- Conservative beliefs and an emphasis on routine could make these individuals boring to be around.

Ideal professions

All professions in the world need a 4. They are required in areas where patience, responsibility, attention to detail, and organization are required. 4s do not merely work for monetary gain but truly enjoy their jobs.

Famous 4's: Audrey Hepburn, Heath Ledger, Barack Obama, Megan Markle.

• (5)

The only thing more important than freedom to a 5 is money, which, ironically, is one of the requirements to enjoy freedom. Lovers of adventure, change, and travel, they are thrill-seekers and adrenaline junkies who are always on a quest of some sort. They are highly adaptable individuals, gifted communicators, and creatives who come up with last-minute solutions to problems.

Weaknesses

- Your wanderlust makes you irresponsible and averse to discipline.

- You can be overconfident and obstinate, especially when you feel there are too many restrictions imposed on you.

- Impatient, impulsive, and prone to overindulgence in sex, food, and intoxicants.

Ideal Professions

Any job that requires you to be on the go or has flexible hours is ideal. Digital nomad jobs like website development, drop-shipping, blogging, digital marketing, freelance jobs, photography, etc. Sales is also a good option for you due to your sound communication skills.

Famous 5's: Christiano Ronaldo, Pharrell Williams, Tilda Swinton, Neymar

- **(6)**

This kind, compassionate, self-sacrificing caretaker is the mayor of the middle ground. They know how to strike a compromise and settle disputes effectively like no other. They are family-oriented and have a considerable measure of artistic flair. Their sense of responsibility and devotion keeps them focused in the area of relationships.

Weaknesses

- Being everyone's shoulder to cry on could leave you burnt out emotionally and physically.

- Your self-esteem problems leave you vulnerable to praise and flattery, which could lead you to make awful decisions to please others.

- Prone to extremes in sentimentality and sensitivity. You are either bawling your eyes out or laughing at the top of your lungs.

Ideal Professions

6's are the best caregivers you will find. Jobs that are suited to caring for people make them gravitate towards fields like alternative healing, health and mental therapy, social service, medicine, nursing, teaching, etc.

- **(7)**

These seekers of truth and wisdom have a mind as sharp as a samurai sword and as flexible as graphene. They are not given to emotional outbursts and have a balanced view of life. They are also unafraid of unforeseen circumstances, not because they are prepared, but because they will readily adapt and come out on top. 7 has excellent intuition and a strong interest in the metaphysical, scientific, and technical. You work methodically and finish whatever you start.

Weaknesses

- Emotions are uncharted territory for you. You are sensitive and feel deeply but find it hard to express yourself to others.

- 7s do not hesitate to use the word "no" freely. This is as a result of their cold, self-centered and analytical minds, which makes them very cynical.

Ideal Professions

They are more improvisers than solo performers or team players. 7 is best suited for jobs that require rhythmic activity and require rapid-fire decision making and big picture visualization, such as law enforcement, financial management, law enforcement, etc. Your ability to control your emotions also makes you suited for emergency medicine, surgery, professional coaching, athletes, etc.

Famous 7's: Paul Rand, Anna Kournikova, Charles Dickens, Jackie Chan.

• (8)

Born leaders, efficient managers with a knack for business and a penchant for making money, 8 is daring, original, competitive, ambitious, and goal-oriented. 8 can be compared to a pit bull. They are high-energy, self-confident people who will challenge you (and themselves) every step of the way, but when they sink their teeth into a project, they play to win. 8s have a presence so powerful it can be intimidating to others.

Weaknesses

- Greed that stems from over-ambition.

- A domineering attitude. 8 does not take kindly to signs of weakness from themselves or others.

- Heavy spending and a tendency to be show-offs.

Ideal Professions

8s are fashioned to create gold from silt. They can work anywhere but are suited to managerial roles, independent contractors, or entrepreneurs. They can also be found in business, industry, science, and entertainment.

Famous 8's: John D Rockefeller, Mauricio Macri, John Grisham, Gordon Ramsey

- **(9)**

The perfect combination of pragmatism and romantic idealism, 9 can dream of a life of luxury or the manna from heaven while flipping burgers at a diner to make ends meet. They are firm believers in doing what they can today while waiting for a brighter tomorrow. They have broad-minded thinking, are effective communicators, and can relate well with others. Their humanitarian streak ensures that they constantly strive to make the world a better place. They always attract money from unlikely sources and are known to have a stroke of luck.

Weaknesses

- A penchant for melodrama when expressing your feelings.

- Revenge-driven and has a difficult time forgiving or letting go of past wrongs.

Ideal Professions

Their calm, adaptable, and helpful nature makes them suitable for jobs with stability and consistency, such as librarians, recreational therapists, caretakers, teachers, and psychologists.

Famous 9's: Natalie Portman, Adam Sandler, Catherine (Duchess of Cambridge).

- **(10)**

Highly ambitious, independent, and intuitive, you have the uncanny ability to reinvent yourself no matter how many trials you face. You are also optimistic, creative, and authentic, with a passion for inspiring others. You are a loyal and devoted partner and friend.

Weaknesses

- Like number 1, you dislike details, so you tend to begin projects but leave them to others to finish them.

- You enjoy the thrill of the hunt and tend to suffer intense waves of jealousy over the success of others.

- Routines are the quickest way to frustrate you. You become dull and even fall ill when exposed to drudgery.

Ideal Professions

Team leaders in any field, jobs that require constant risk, speed, and heroics (formula 1 racer, fireman, stunt double, test pilot, police officer).

Famous 10's: Nikola Tesla, Judy Garland, Karl Lagerfield, Sofia Vergara

- **(11)**

Idealistic, with intuition so keen they are called the anatomists of the human soul, 11s understand people so well they can understand words unsaid and guess hidden intentions. You have a gift for sensitizing people toward certain pursuits, usually philosophical or idealistic. You are drawn to nature and are a lover of animals, great and small. You require a balanced lifestyle because, though you have the capacity for leadership, you prefer either to point the way to discovery or become an example others can emulate.

Weaknesses

- Your emotional and sensitive nature makes you easily hurt by the criticism of others.

- You are more intuitive and rational, which gives you a flair for the dramatic.

- You tend to live your life according to the wishes of others instead of your own because you care too much about what others think.

Ideal Professions

Jobs that require intuition and include the role of advisor are best suited for you. So, you will fare well in guidance counseling, academia, scientific research, statistics, health/nutrition advice, etc.

Famous 11's: Jennifer Aniston, Amitabh Bachchan, Thomas Edison, Didier Drogba

- **(12)**

Brimming with talent, originality, and vitality, 12 is the life and soul of any gathering and the very personification of a good time.

You are a child at heart who is blessed with an impressive vocabulary and a wide knowledge of various subjects. Your amiable personality brings you friends from all walks of life.

Weaknesses

- The tendency to focus energy on trivial matters and people.

- You may be talented in making lemonade from lemons, but you are prone to moodiness and self-pity.

- Your varied interests may imply that sometimes you spread yourself too thin: a jack of all trades and master of none.

Ideal Professions

12 has talents suited to a variety of professions, but it is important for them to choose their vocations in the same way one would choose a spouse. They need to work in a field they are passionate about in order to give it all their energy. Money is not their inspiration to work.

Famous 12's: Jeff Bezos, Swami Vivekananda, Charles Darwin, Abraham Lincoln.

- **(13)**

Solid and practical, 13 is a lover of family, tradition, and community. You have an eye for detail and possess clarity of thought. You have a lot of creative ideas seeking an avenue for expression. You appreciate nature, design, beauty, and animals. You are an energetic, hard worker who is not afraid to share your opinions. You have a finely tuned sixth sense which either annoys or amazes people you come into contact with.

Weaknesses

- Your ability to apply yourself to long hours of work can leave you burnt out. On the flip side, you may feel you have not found the work you are meant to do, so you tend to wander from job to job, relationship to relationship, unable to apply yourself to any.

- You have an established routine and, as such, refuse to give way to newer creative ideas, even when it's obvious your method takes forever to get things done.

Ideal Professions

You are not predisposed to a particular line of work. You tend to do whatever it is that interests you and excel at it.

Famous 13's: Robbie Williams, Liam Hemsworth, Alfred Hitchcock, Tyler Perry

• (14)

An adventurer with a magnetic personality, a rebellious streak, and a dislike for conventions, 14 always has a bag packed and ready to go. You are easily bored and need to be stimulated constantly to feel alive. You are famous for your spur-of-the-moment decisions. You are good with words, popular in social circles, and a wonderful catch as a romantic partner (if the person gets your attention and holds it long enough).

Weaknesses

- Your restless nature ensures that you never stick to one thing, be it a profession, relationship, or dwelling.

- Beneath your love for change and excitement is insecurity, such that manifests in your life as mood swings and rash decision making.

- You tend to overindulge in sex, drugs, food, or alcohol as a means of escape.

Ideal Professions

14 is extremely talented and versatile. They display competence in any field or endeavor they set their minds to. But they are best suited to jobs involving excitement and change. The more daring they are, the better. They will do well as SWAT team members, bomb explosion experts, aerospace engineers, war correspondents, adventure filmmakers, etc.

Famous 14's: Albert Einstein, Mark Zuckerberg, Earvin "Magic" Johnson, Condoleezza Rice.

• (15)

Highly creative, with a gift for languages and a strong inclination towards the visual arts, 15 is independent, very sensitive, and sympathetic to the plight of others. They are devoted to friends and family and can be very self-sacrificing, even to the point of self-harm. However, their multi-talented nature includes sharp business and financial acumen, which ensures their success in life.

Weaknesses

- You do not react well to criticism and get hurt easily because of your sensitive nature.

- People tend to take advantage of your help and presence for their selfish gain because of your trusting nature.

Ideal Professions

You are drawn towards fields where support and care for others are essential. However, since you are always seeking validation from others, you will do well in the fields of healthcare, social service, sports as a coach or personal trainer, physical therapist, or home health aide.

Famous 15's: Martin Luther King Jr., Agatha Christie, Emma Watson, Prince Harry (Duke of Sussex).

- **(16)**

The perceptive, intuitive, inquisitive, and extremely analytical 16 can spot a phony from two miles away. They can tell lies from truth faster than you can flip a pancake. They dislike surprises, large crowds, noisy atmospheres, and loose ends. Their analytical mind and unparalleled levels of concentration allow them to gain depths of knowledge in various fields. You are drawn to the metaphysical and philosophical. Although when you put yourself out there, you are great company and easy to relate with.

Weaknesses

- You have two mood ranges; impractical and dreamy or moody and bitter. This makes you feel alone at heart, pessimistic and depressed.

- Your introverted and inflexible nature keeps you from adapting easily to change.

Ideal Professions

16s work hard to become perfectionists in their chosen field, but they are attracted to extremes. You either find them in something as profound as spirituality or metaphysical pursuits or in something as tedious and mundane as computer programming, coding, tax law, accounting, etc.

Famous 16's: Madonna, Abel Makkonen, Tesfaye alias "The Weekend," Pope Benedict XVI, Geronimo.

- **(17)**

The highly independent, ambitious 17 is blessed with sound judgment that makes them a whiz at business and finance. Like the 8, which is a reduced form of the 17, they are efficient managers and organizers, skilled at seeing the big picture. Your capabilities are greater than those of the average person, and you know this all too well. Do NOT attempt to deceive a 17. They have the memory of an elephant. They are also not given to gossip and hearsay. As far as the typical 17 is concerned, if there is no supporting evidence, something does not exist.

Weaknesses

- Your over-inflated ego and high expectations of yourself tend to cloud your judgment. This prevents you from handing over authority and delegating to others. You constantly micromanage others and feel no one can do a better job than you do.

- Your love for status and the lavish life encourage abysmally poor saving habits.

- You have a hard time handling failure. It always feels like a blow to your ego.

Ideal Professions

17, like 8, was born to make money. They can make it out of thin air. They fare well in positions that give them some form of authority over others, regardless of the field. Often, they are managers, team leaders, coordinators, and administrators.

Famous 17s: Michelle Obama, Al Capone, Victoria Beckham, Venus Williams

- **(18)**

The broad-minded 18s are pioneers in their field, admired by many with a knack for organizing and inspiring people. They are drawn towards the arts. It is little wonder that many artists are found in this category. You have a sharp mind with the ability to assimilate vast amounts of information, like a memory card, only you have no limits. Despite your calm, aristocratic appearance, your deepest satisfaction lies in getting your hands dirty in service to humanity.

Weaknesses

- Your luck with money makes you an impulsive spender. Also, people tend to borrow large sums of money from you with the intention of paying it back.

- You are usually prone to extremes in behavior. It's either you are extremely wealthy or extremely envious of another's success; highly intuitive or insanely oblivious of your surroundings.

- Violent temper tantrums alienate you from friends or loved ones and cause difficulty in forgiving others.

- They feel a high level of insecurity despite their dedication to work and their notable intelligence.

Ideal Professions

18 is a late bloomer who tends to have a finger in every pie before settling on one. Usually, they try out a lot of professions but are ideally suited to the fields of religion, law, public and social work, and politics.

Famous 18s: Jada Pinkett Smith, Sia, Steven Spielberg, Pep Guardiola, Pope John Paul II

- **(19)**

The highly independent, self-sufficient maverick is personified by 19. They have high levels of endurance and responsibility, but their need for self-sustainability is so extreme it trumps every other need they may have. They are hard workers and indispensable in every field or endeavor. People are attracted to them because of the efficiency with which they perform their duties. You are highly idealistic, sensitive, and find yourself smack-dab in the middle of dramatic situations, though you have no issues keeping your cool.

Weaknesses

- Failure makes you bitter and negative.

- You have problems controlling your temper, but the good part is that you don't stay mad for too long.

- You tend to be nervous when faced with difficult situations.

- You have bad spending habits.

Ideal Professions

You have what it takes to be a star in virtually any field since you are able to work both alone and as a team player. You are, however, more attracted to jobs that offer the opportunity for self-development. Industry conferences, mentorship programs, academic pursuits, internships, and skill advancement qualifications are best suited for you.

Famous 19s: Bill Clinton, Maria Sharapova, Benedict Cumberbatch, Gabrielle Bonheur "Coco" Chanel

- **(20)**

A typical 20 possesses self-awareness, tact, diplomacy, and is able to sense the feelings of others while effectively maintaining their center. Like birthday number 2, the 20s operate best as advisors and the power behind the throne. They are moved by harmony, beauty, and love. They are quite affectionate and desire lots of physical shows of affection, such as hugs, cuddles, etc. These individuals will give a southern belle a run for her money with their polite speech, impeccable manners, and regard for the time of others. But be careful; that same sugary tongue will deal out its special dose of poison when hurt.

Weaknesses

- There is a constant need for love, support, and encouragement, and failure to get this from a support system could lead to depression or a lack of determination.

- They are prone to extreme mood swings and a lack of self-esteem. They can be pleasant one minute and inconsolably sad the next.

Ideal Professions

They are suited to jobs where they act as advisors, ambassadors, or diplomats. They also shine in areas like medicine since they have the ability to deliver sensitive news with tact.

Famous 20s: Rihanna, Trevor Noah, Cindy Crawford, Ruby Rose

- **(21)**

The highly creative and imaginative 21 is a delight to be around. They have a strong desire to succeed, and for them, no mountain is too high. These social butterflies are highly influential and have a social calendar booked well in advance. They add an artistic flair to everything they do. They are always on the receiving end of affection and have opportunities to succeed thrown at them from every corner.

Weaknesses

- They have everything handed to them on a platter. As such, they can be quite materialistic and refuse to develop their talents, relying solely on charm and wit to get them through life.

- They are always a bundle of nervous energy due to their habit of overcommitting. Learning to say no will do them some good.

Ideal Professions

The ability to influence should not be wasted on small talk. It is necessary to channel focus towards jobs that require them to put ideas into words and charm the socks off people. Examples include sales, advertising, marketing, politics, writing, law, or philanthropy.

Famous 21s: Queen Elizabeth, Ernest Hemingway, Stephen King, Samuel L. Jackson.

- **(22)**

A great builder, organizer, and manager capable of materializing any dream they set their heart to, 22 is a picture-perfect example of patience, discipline, order, and more than an ample serving of intuition. Your pragmatism finds you front and center of large projects and at the helm of affairs. You are a walking paradox. You have tall and lofty dreams on the one hand, and on the other, you fear the height of your ambitions. This war between idealism and pragmatism is your defining characteristic.

Weaknesses

- They have a difficult time trusting anyone. As a result, they find it hard to delegate or be in a stable relationship.

- They spend a lot of time with friends who take advantage of them and have nothing to offer in return.

- An intense fear of failure that sometimes stops them from dreaming big.

Ideal Professions

It is easy for them to excel in any field they choose. Their blend of intuition, practicality, and diligence makes them adaptable to any job, from a hairstylist to a member of parliament.

Famous 22's: Naomi Campbell, Maggie Q, Meryl Streep, Arsène Wenger, Andrea Bocelli

- **(23)**

For a 23, life is an adventure, and because of this, they live every day as if it's their last. They are the chameleons of the group. A part of them craves change, while the other is flexible enough to adapt to whatever life throws at them. They are versatile, sociable, creative, sensitive, and, most of all, freedom-loving. Punishing a 23 is easy: just keep them cooped up in one spot for a considerable length of time. They are like smoke; their restless nerves will fray until they find a means to escape.

Weaknesses

- They have a penchant for thinking they are always right.

- They have a tendency to get bored and restless when they lack a positive outlet for their nervous energy.

- They like to overindulge in food, drugs, alcohol, and sex, quite possibly because of a fear of missing out on life.

Ideal Professions

Their discomfort with a routine makes them suitable for jobs with flexible hours that allow them to try new things. Pilots/flight attendants, travel bloggers, and even scientific researchers and inventors are good examples.

Famous 23s: Miley Cyrus, Ludovico Einaudi, Kangana Ragnaut, Alan Turing

- **(24)**

The self-sacrificing, sensible 24 is a hard worker who expects everyone to put in as much effort as they do. You have a gift for restoring peace and harmony to those around you, but your availability as a shoulder to cry on puts you in more trouble than you can handle. Your systematic approach to issues makes you easy to reason with but difficult to control. You are financially fortunate.

Weaknesses

- Overly emotional with a flair for melodrama, 24 tends to magnify issues concerning them. They have the woe-is-me act down to a science.

- People take advantage of your sensitive nature to ask for help; many times, you lose yourself in a bid to satisfy others.

- Their intuitive nature makes them impractical, and as such, they need constant advice from rational people.

Ideal Professions

It is essential for 24s to pursue a career not for financial benefit but for the purpose of self-realization and inner peace. They are attracted to teaching, art, medicine, social work.

Famous 24s: Steve Jobs, Floyd Mayweather, Jean-Paul Gaultier, Bob Dylan

- **(25)**

The 25s have a sound rational mind with the ability to think intellectually and analytically. They believe in the motto, "for every problem, there is a solution." You are able to investigate and thoroughly research subjects to discover information. You require solitude and tranquility to recharge your batteries.

Weaknesses

- Prone to mood swings and addictions,

- Most of them usually have backgrounds with bitter childhood memories. As a result, they are cynical and mistrustful of the intentions of others.

Ideal Professions

Their ability to investigate and research makes them suitable for jobs in law and law enforcement, healthcare, academia, history, etc.

Famous 25s: Virginia Woolf, Ralph Waldo Emerson, George Orwell, Aretha Franklin, Pablo Picasso.

• (26)

26 is great with money and talented in the business. No one under 26 is ashamed to accept responsibility. They are proud of their accomplishments. They are realists who see the bigger picture but neglect the fine print. It is a challenge for them to balance their love of materialism with their need to help others. They love being surrounded by harmonious company but have trouble making friends as they find it hard to relate to people their age.

Weaknesses

- A dog-eat-dog attitude in business makes you inconsiderate towards others.

- Difficulty in accepting mistakes and failure in life turns you into a pessimist.

- Having an ostentatious attitude, your need for social status and acceptance makes you spend a little too lavishly.

Ideal Professions

You thrive in vocations where you are given the opportunity to be proud of your accomplishments, or else you might lose interest. Business, sports, finance, and commerce. Your tendency to lead a team makes you an excellent team leader or manager.

Famous 26s: Jose Mourinho, Ellen DeGeneres, Melania Trump, DJ Khaled.

- (27)

Guiding others comes naturally to you because of your gift of insight and understanding. While others think within certain conventions, you don't just think outside the box; to you, there is no box! For this reason, you are tolerant of the viewpoints of others and value the right to express yourself freely. You have an aristocratic bearing and are a true humanitarian whose satisfaction comes from the act of helping others. The influence of 2 and 7 makes you fiercely independent, with a desire for a spiritual connection.

Weaknesses

- They are late bloomers. They need a lot of time to choose their path.

- Impatience and impulsiveness expose them to self-destructive behavior.

Ideal Professions

Any field that is in line with art and creativity is fine. They are also excellent leaders, managers, and executives in the fields of religion, politics, and law.

Famous 27s: Wolfgang Amadeus Mozart, Henry Kissinger, Quentin Tarantino, Ulysses Grant

- (28)

Your gift for leadership is best expressed through teamwork. Unlike many who are given to loud and brash displays of power, you apply rationality and gentle coercion. Your ambition and independence mean you are always jumping headfirst into taking risks, which usually pay off handsomely. You are unapologetically yourself and do not mind standing out in a crowd.

Weaknesses

- Fond of their own thought process and deeply averse to change.

- They can be temperamental, jealous, and competitive when they are not successful, complimented for their efforts, or not the center of attention.

- They make money easily and spend it the same way.

- They may appear aloof because they have a hard time trusting anyone.

Ideal Professions

You are so versatile and have a variety of career options. Since it is rare for you to run out of ideas, you will thrive in jobs in commerce, tourism, politics, consumer goods, advertising, entertainment, and event management.

Famous 28s: Lady Gaga, Elon Musk, Jacqueline Kennedy Onassis, Bill Gates.

• (29)

The highly intuitive mind of 29 thinks in Technicolor. You pull ideas from the sky like magicians pull bunnies from a hat. You feel a connection to all things spiritual and have a strong dependence on your environment. As a leader, you are idealistic and philosophical, though, like Luna Lovegood, your detachment from the world does not mean you are incapable of conducting yourself in social situations. If patience were a currency, you would be the richest of all the numbers.

Weaknesses

- You are a late bloomer, which is why, in your youth, you are given to bouts of mood swings, unnecessary drama, and fights.

- They are very unpredictable and can be extremely jealous of others.

Ideal Professions

Your idealism makes you slightly unsuitable for the cutthroat world of business, but it is possible to find a person who thrives in the oddest of professions since they generally go for professions that emulate their natural talents.

Famous 29s: Oprah Winfrey, Michael Jackson, Chadwick Boseman, John F. Kennedy

• (30)

Your high level of creativity makes you an artist at heart. It is advisable that if you do not have an artistic career, you should consider taking it up as something to pass the time. Your quick wit, charismatic nature, and communication skills attract people to you in droves. People forgive you for things they would never pardon anyone else for. In return, you bless them with your presence and your special brand of feel-good energy.

Weaknesses

- They have people around them all the time but find it hard to create and maintain meaningful relationships.

- Their childlike innocence and naiveté can be frustrating. For those they are in a relationship with, it's like dating Peter Pan.

Ideal Professions

Any field with creative and artistic endeavors will suit them like a glove. They can write, paint, perform on strange occasions, do voice acting, and a myriad of other things.

Famous 30's: Tiger Woods, Piers Morgan, Cameron Diaz, Vincent Van Gogh.

- **(31)**

A lover of traditional values, community, and family, you favor practicality and perform your duties with precision and diligence. You are a nature lover, brimming with creativity and artistic talent that seeks ways of concrete expression. All in all, you are a harmonious blend of function, form, and aesthetics.

Organization and leadership come naturally to you. Your well-honed senses miss nothing. This is why you are the fine-tooth comb in any field you apply yourself to. You are ten times more prepared than others for surprise eventualities. You do not suffer foolery well, but your magnetism seems to attract it. People rely on you at work, but you still feel you have not found your calling in life.

Weaknesses

- Set in their traditional ways, they are hardly receptive to new ideas.

- The tendency to overwork – leading to frustration.

- They have difficulty trusting people.

Ideal Professions

Your talents are versatile, and you are suited to any profession. However, since you are an excellent leader and a skilled diplomat, you shine in fields requiring that you act in a managerial or leadership capacity.

Famous 31s: Baba Vanga, Justin Timberlake, J.K. Rowling, Al Gore.

Chapter 8: Life Path Number

The life path number is one of your numerology chart's most important core numbers. Alternative names for life path numbers include your birth force number, ruling number, or birth path number. Your life path number is the first number any numerologist will analyze as it reveals:

- Your Personality (who you are).
- Your Life's Mission (the reason behind your existence on Earth and lessons you will master while accomplishing your mission).

The life path number not only outlines your inherent strengths and weaknesses as a person but foretells the kind of experiences that may come your way as you fulfill your purpose on Earth.

Calculating Life Path Numbers

The life path number is calculated using the date of birth. It is calculated in three ways:

- Reducing down
- Adding across
- Adding down

Of the three methods of calculation, numerologists deem the first two to be the most accurate. Neither method is "better" than the other. They are used by practitioners as a simple matter of personal preference or for ease of calculation. Feel free to use whichever method appeals to you. The general guideline, regardless of which method you choose, is to reduce double-digit numbers to a single-digit number unless the total figure falls into the master number category (11, 22, or 33).

The Reducing-Down Method

Step 1: Add up the numbers in the day, month, and year of your birth date individually.

Step 2: Reduce double digits in any of the summations (if any) to single-digit numbers.

Step 3: add all the derived numbers and reduce them to a single digit. If the total yields a master number, leave it as it is.

Note that some numerologists are of the opinion that master numbers should be further reduced to single digits in life path calculations while others object to it. The choice of calculation is up to you. For numerologists in the latter category, this method is the most accurate to determine master numbers. Let's find the life path for the birth date of January 3, 1906.

Month = 1

Day= 3

Year = 1906

1+9+0+6=16; 1+6= 7

Total: 1+3+7= 11

The life path number for the above date of birth is 11/2, a master number.

The Adding-Across Method

This is the second and simplest method of all.

Step 1: Add a plus sign after each individual number in your birthdate and add each digit across the board. Ensure you write down the full birth year as it appears on your birth certificate. For instance, if you were born in the year 1960, calculate it as 1960, not 60.

Step 2: Sum up all double-digit numbers where applicable and reduce the digits until you derive a single-digit number. The exceptions to this case are totals like 11, which becomes 11/2, 22 becomes 22/4, and 33 becomes 33/6

Let's calculate the life path number for the date January 3, 1906

Month + Day + Year

$1 + 3 + 1 + 9 + 0 + 6 = 20;$

(Further reduction) $2+0 = 2$

As you can see from the example above, steps are taken to further reduce the double-digit result to get a single-digit life path number.

When looking at compound totals, it pays to take note of the number 0 in totals like 10, 20, 30, and so on before reducing them down. This is because the number 0 is not just a placeholder or a null digit. It represents spirit, wholeness, inclusivity, and the infinite possibilities offered by the universe. In numerology, 0 is thought to embody the power of God, which is why it acts like a chameleon, amplifying the vibration of the number that exists beside it.

So, if we apply this logic in calculating the life path number for January 3, 1906= 20; 2+0= 1 (life path number 2 amplified by 0).

In some cases, you may end up with a single-digit life path number that needs no further reduction. Here's an example:

March 2, 2001: $3+2+2+0+0+1= 8$

Chaldean numerology places great importance on the value known as the compound total. The benefit of using the second method over the first, apart from the ease of calculation, is that the double-digit total (compound number) post summation provides extra knowledge about the type of life path number it is.

For instance, a 14/5 life path number will differ from that of a 23/5. This is because the former contains the number vibrations 1 and 4 while the latter has 2 and 3. They may have similar reduced single digits, but their expressions will differ slightly. Thus, an insight into the compound total helps you understand better your life path expression.

From the two methods of calculation described above, you have observed that one calculation favors the revelation of a master number over the other.

Adding-Down Method

This is the third and least commonly used method of calculating life path numbers.

Step 1: Sum up the Month, Day, and Year in a single column. So, for October 13, 1969:

10

+ 13

1969

————

Total 1992

You could decide to reduce the year of birth down to two digits, so for instance, 1969 becomes (1+9+6+9=25). In this example, I am choosing to leave the year of birth as is.

Step 2: Sum up the digits in the total and reduce them to a single digit for the life path number. Remember, the exceptions are the master numbers 11/2, 22/4, and 33/6. So, the life path number for the birth date in our previous example is worked out like this:

10

+ 13

1969

————

Total 1992

$1 + 9 + 9 + 2 = 21$

$2 + 1 = 3$

The life path number is 3.

Now, let's repeat the adding down method for the date January 3, 1906

1

+ 3

1906

_____

Total 1910

$1 + 9 + 1 + 0 = 11$

From the three different methods discussed, it is obvious to see the reducing down and adding down method gave a master number for the same date while the adding across method gave a single-digit figure amplified by 0. Which calculation is accurate? That's the conundrum! Since neither method is accurate or inaccurate, just different, the method you use depends on your personal taste, and the methods will likely affect the answers you obtain.

Numerology is not a one size fits all jumper. Note, however, that only the master number calculations produce this challenge. This difference in answers could occur anytime you end up with either a 2, 4, or 6. For this reason, many numerologists use all three methods and go with the majority rule figure for their answer. The best option is understanding the traits of the master numbers and comparing them to their corresponding single numbers to determine which of them is the best fit.

Descriptions of Each Life Path Number

Life Path Number 1 — The Individualistic Leader

Life path 1 individuals are pioneers who created a cut above the rest to continually break away from the mold and walk by their own rules. Your courage, creativity, positive nature, and tenacity are your greatest strengths. Your uniqueness sometimes makes you feel different and alienated from the rest of the crowd. Don't be disheartened. Your DNA is fashioned to stand out, not fit in.

Your individuality is your gift to the universe, so use it to your advantage and, instead of trying to let societal rules and norms get to you, take steps to improve the quality of your own life. Dare to believe in yourself but be careful not to let your ambitious nature get the better of you because there is no such thing as competition on this plane in the grand scheme of things.

When you begin to understand and accept the interconnectedness of all things, only then will you reach your full potential. Surround yourself with individuals who believe in your dream because your life purpose is only fulfilled when you guide others lovingly toward causes that benefit humanity.

Affirmation: *"I choose to walk a path that helps me embrace my independence, strength, and individuality."*

Life Path Number 2 — The Collaborator and Peacemaker

A sense of harmony and unity is a major requirement for people with life path 2. Tuning in to their emotions and that of others comes naturally to them. You are honest to a fault, a terrific listener and counselor with the uncanny ability to get people to tell you their deepest darkest fears and secrets.

You possess the gift of both energetic and verbal healing. You cannot tolerate disagreements, and you always leave good impressions on the people you meet. You are dedicated to nurturing relationships and give the shirt off your back to help someone in need.

Live by your personal values even when it means you may be criticized and underappreciated. Never forget to stand up for yourself when it counts and ask for help when the pressure from helping others makes you feel like you might crack. It is okay to accept help too. You are fulfilling your life purpose when you care for, heal and nurture others as long as you do not sacrifice your needs and independence in the process.

Affirmation: *"My sensitivity is my gift to the world. I love, heal and care for myself and others."*

Life Path Number 3 — The Expressive Creative

A life path 3 individual is magnetic, creative, and expressive. Their communicative abilities shine, whether it is among friends, colleagues, or anyone else. Eternally optimistic, they radiate boundless positivity, imagination, and humor that help them in their quest to succeed. Putting their talents to good use helps improve their well-being emotionally, physically, and mentally.

Though one of their weaknesses is commitment (to things, tasks, and people), they speak honestly from their hearts and are always willing to lift or inspire people. People envy their personality, intelligence, and how easy their life seems on the outside, but life path 3 struggles within to balance their lofty ideals with realism. Their ability to express has a darker side seen in the act of gossiping, criticizing, exaggerating, and complaining. Once they understand the power in their words, they will realize how they sabotage themselves with negative speech.

Affirmation: *"I am a center for love, joy, and positive energy. I express my thoughts to create a happy life."*

Life Path Number 4 — The Diligent Worker

Practicality, reliability, logic, a keen mind, and strong will are some of the traits ascribed to individuals with life path 4. They know exactly what they want and are not afraid to work long and hard to achieve it. They have organized balanced lives and are the pillars of any community or endeavor they find themselves in. Their tenacity and discipline get the work done, but their greatest struggle is doing away with their fixed mindset and opinions about certain things.

If 4 had a quote, it would definitely be, *"If it ain't broke, don't fix it."* Dynamism and thinking on their feet are not their forte, which is why they miss out on a lot of opportunities since they waste a lot of precious time thinking about it. But, when they apply themselves to an idea, no matter how new it is, they always excel.

As a life path 4 person, you fulfill your life's mission when you uplift others by using practical step-by-step solutions to their problems. Do this in such a way that you do not demand perfection from yourself and others. Find time to relax and let your hair down.

Affirmation: *"I let go of my need to control; I seek to promote order that makes the world a better place."*

Life Path Number 5 — The Free-Spirited Adventurer

Individuals with a life path number of 5 are the most prejudice-free people on the planet. They are always ready with out-of-the-box thinking and solutions to problems. The motto "You Only Live Once" is more than a cool saying; for them, it is a way of life. For this reason, they seem unbothered about what the future may bring, not because they are unafraid, but because they have what it takes to adapt.

Their self-indulgence and focus on the present lead them to make some very damaging decisions financially, romantically, and otherwise. But they bounce back quickly. They have a variety of talents but are advised to use both their talents and freedom wisely. Their life purpose is fulfilled when they teach others what they have learned through experience.

Affirmation: *"I embrace myself for who, and what I represent. I am willing to explore every life experience to become a better version of myself."*

Life Path Number 6 – The Responsible Caretaker

Ever heard Immanuel Kant saying, "veni, vidi, amavi?" It is an Italian saying outlining rules for happiness as "something to do, someone to love and something to hope for." This is the golden rule adhered to by life path 6.

Blessed with enough compassion to feed a small community, the 6s spread light, love, and generosity wherever they go. They are happiest when in close contact with others, nurturing and caring for them. They dream of having their own family or a domestic setting because being responsible for others brings them joy.

Their need to cater to others and put themselves in the shoes of anyone else but their own ensures they are burdened with a myriad of responsibilities which they juggle really well. There is a dark side to caring for others. It can be draining, and there are many occasions where your love is neither appreciated nor reciprocated. And while you are blessed with a lot of "love reserve," you must seek a balance between caring for yourself and others. As a 6, you are fulfilling your purpose by tapping into your selflessness and providing unconditional love to all and sundry, without ignoring your own needs in the process.

Affirmation: *"I am compassionate with others and myself; I am grateful for my life and its lessons."*

Life Path Number 7 – The Contemplative Truth Seeker

Life path 7 individuals radiate peace, love, and serene energy. These deep thinkers question the reason behind everything and seek to understand the mysteries of the universe. 7s as seekers of knowledge are drawn to spirituality, and even if they are not spiritual, life always throws them an experience that forces them to open their minds.

These individuals are usually introverted, aloof, withdrawn, and feel lonely or left out at times despite their intense need to relate well with others. The only exceptions to this pattern of social ineptitude are for those with an "outgoing" astrology chart (containing core numbers of either 1, 3, or 5) or those with a life path of 24/7.

6 has the potential to succeed in any career because of their love for research and the extrapolation of information; however, they may gravitate towards careers in history, spirituality, or metaphysics. 7s are fulfilling their purpose when they uncover the truth and discover the hidden meaning behind life and existence.

Affirmation: *"I am deeply connected to my higher self. I am blessed with the gifts to discover spirituality that benefits humanity."*

Life Path Number 8 — The Business Minded Executive

With life path number 8, rest assured that the universe has granted you wealth, prosperity, and power. These confident, practical, and gifted leaders live by their own principles and exude an air of abundance. Blessed with the ability of manifestation, their powerful minds choose to focus on their hopes and dreams rather than on their fears or uncertainties.

They are great judges of character with excellence in business and politics, but their workaholic tendencies and propensity to focus on materialism over everything else are two of their greatest weaknesses. Success to you is directly proportional to status, achievement, and money. This belief puts other aspects of your life, such as your romantic life, family, and social life, in jeopardy. Your life path is fulfilled when you are empowered, have a healthier relationship with money, and are generous to the people around you.

Affirmation: *"I am a success magnet, I attract abundance, and I am in control of my destiny."*

Life Path Number 9 — The Empathetic Humanitarian

Philanthropy and the spirit of compassion are first and foremost in the heart and minds of individuals with life paths 9. Regardless of their fields of endeavor (which are many), they know they exist to make the world a better place for others to live in.

Their challenge, however, is their judgment and bias towards others and a failure to accept their own imperfections. Facing this challenge is the first step to making a change in an already imperfect world. Their creative and artistic side is drawn to art, nature, beauty, harmony, design, public speaking, or any other field, which gives their imagination and creativity an outlet to shine.

9s, like the 7s, are attracted to mysticism and spirituality. Some even have extrasensory perception. Many 9s have either had a hard time growing up or have been subject to family drama over the years. Being able to see a silver lining in negativity and being able to forgive yourself and others are two of the ways that you can remain selfless enough to fulfill your purpose of spreading kindness and love to humanity.

Affirmation: *"I release the hurt from the past to embrace the present; I care for others and receive care in return."*

Life Path Number 11 – The Inspiring Teacher

Life path 11 is one of the master numbers in numerology. As a result, individuals with this life path are blessed with an increased level of intuition, insight, and spiritual awareness. This life path is always a bit of a challenge because of the opposing forces of 1 and 2. This implies that the independent, take-charge attitude of 1 could be influenced by the emotional sensitivity of 2.

Your purpose in life is to discover your truth and achieve self-mastery. It is also essential to let go of your ego so that you can truly love and believe in yourself. Your ability to feel intensely and uplift others must be balanced by the ability to set clear boundaries and knowing when to say no, serving humanity without letting yourself go in the process. Once you step into your power and surrender to a cause greater than yourself, there will be no limit to what you can do, be or achieve. Your purpose as an 11/2 life path is to work for the greater good to make a real impact in the world.

Affirmation: *"I inspire, enable and empower others to conceive an extraordinary life."*

Life Path Number 22 – The Master Builder

Numerologists claim that this is the most powerful yet most challenging life path number of all. As a 22, you are a powerhouse of optimism and positivity who has the ability to manifest dreams into reality through practical methods. Your rational and methodical approach makes you a gifted manager, organizer, and all-around "people-person." You are a visionary with the ability to see the bigger picture without missing the tiny details. You sometimes suffer an inferiority complex, refusing help due to fear of criticism or shame.

You have mastered appearing controlled on the surface, but like the proverbial duck, you are flapping around, overflowing with emotions beneath. An overbearing attitude and constant self-censure are maladaptive behaviors that can stop you from reaching the heights you desire for yourself.

It is your responsibility to evolve so that you transform your archetype into one that is grounded and centered at all times. Once you can achieve this, the universe will constantly have your back as long as it is for a cause that benefits humanity. Your life purpose is fulfilled when you create, expand, and promote causes greater than your personal interests.

Affirmation: *"I exist to serve humanity with everything I possess in a way that improves my own life in turn."*

Life Path Number 33 — The Cosmic Guardian

A life path number 33/6 means you exist to bring happiness and joy to the world and to others through your powers of compassion, creativity, and talent for healing. Your nurturing abilities make you gifted with people, especially children. The zesty vibrations of the fun-loving 3 are manifested in your child-like innocence and how you see the world as something of perpetual wonder.

Do not forget that no one can draw from an empty well. While giving love to others, do not hesitate to keep some for yourself. Do not force care on others to the extent that you interfere with their free will. Allow people to take charge of their own lives and heal sometimes. This is where you apply logic to ensure control of your emotions. You are fulfilling your purpose when you apply yourself to healing the world through compassion, creative expression, teaching, or healing.

Affirmation: *"I fully embrace my divine calling to heal, love, and teach humanity."*

Chapter 9: Your Growth Number

What Are Growth Numbers?

The growth number is also called the *key number,* and it is a number based on the summation value of the vibrations inherent in the individual letters of your first (documented) birth name. The sum is reduced to a single digit or a master number. The growth number describes the energy which enlightens your life experience. It permits you to have a clearer understanding of the lessons you are here on earth to learn. This is why, even though the growth number is not a core number, it is considered a sub-lesson to the life path number, which is a core number in numerology.

The growth number points to inherent latent traits you (or your little one) can encourage or develop. Even though the growth number is not a core number, it is connected to each of the core numbers in a special way. For instance, since the growth number is derived from the given first name, it is included in the calculation of the soul urge and destiny numbers. This means that whatever name you choose for yourself (or your child) has a 50 percent effect on the core numbers.

Karmic lessons are derived from the summation of the first name (growth number), middle, and last name. The maturity number is derived from the addition of the destiny and life path numbers. Hence, the growth number is 50 percent of your destiny number, seeing as it is calculated from your documented first name. This shows that even more than what you eat, you *are* what name you are known as. It is not an overstatement to say that the name you choose determines a lot of things about your existence.

Calculating Growth Numbers

Growth numbers are calculated using the Pythagorean chart. For instance, let's calculate the growing number of the name Cedric Adams White.

C – 3

E – 5

D – 4

R – 9

I – 9

C – 3

$3 + 5 + 4 + 9 + 9 + 3 = 33$ (No further reduction is needed since it is a master number).

Some names could have a single-digit growth number, like the name Jane.

J – 1

A – 1

N – 5

E – 5

$1 + 1 + 5 + 5 = 12$

$1 + 2 = 3$

Some Facts to Note about Growth Numbers

Growth numbers are general and not specific in the description. The extent and manner in which your growth number affects you are dependent on many variables, namely your core numbers, interests, etc.

Subtle differences in the spelling of the name can affect the growth number. For instance, the name Anne has a growing number of 16 (1+6) = 7. Note the karmic debt number 16, which revolves around issues concerning trust. Another variant of the same name, ANN, is 1+5+5=11/2. Note the master number present.

Master numbers are never reduced to growing numbers. This is because it is necessary to acknowledge the intense vibrations they contain. Think of your growth number as a bonus gift. Because it is the only aspect of the numerology chart that exclusively yields the positive expression of a number, it can redress the balance of debts, potential weaknesses, conflicts, and so on in other areas of the chart.

For instance, if you were born on a day that gives the 4 (13) life path number, meaning it carries the karmic debt of selfishness, neglect, and laziness in a past life, taking on a name with the growing number of 1 will help smooth out the potential hardships specific to the 1 energy. The extra 1 gives an added vibrational boost that helps you combat laziness. This aspect of balance and counterbalance should be handled by an expert numerologist during a consultation so that a list of suitable names can be drawn out, and the one that gives you the most benefit can be chosen.

It is worth bearing in mind that each growth number has both positive and negative aspects. For this reason, there is a need to cultivate the positive habits of our numbers so that you encounter less resistance in your existence on earth.

1 — Love, Light, Creator, Leader

Balanced: An extremely creative soul with the power to manifest their dreams into reality. You are independent, confident, original, and a goal-getter. They crave perfection and excellence in all their endeavors. All in all, this vibration is a recipe for entrepreneurs, innovators, and pioneers. And the law of attraction surrounds you in all its glory.

Unbalanced: Aggressive, unfocused, little or no power of manifestation, tyrannical, and overconfident. They over-analyze the present, past, and future and lack manifesting abilities. As a result, relationships, projects, and other endeavors fall apart for no apparent reason. Your social circle is lacking because of your negative and domineering attitude.

Note: This growth number will be thoroughly amplified or influenced by other names on the chart.

2 — Diplomat, Harmony Bringer

Balanced: Diplomacy runs in their blood. They are successful mediators and peacekeepers. They work best with a team because group settings and harmonious cooperation are their forte. They are sensitive, intuitive, and empathize with others seamlessly. They are adaptable, flexible, and comfortable in the shadows; their qualities are more mental than physical as they are not as physically strong as 1s.

Unbalanced: Issues with self-confidence, fear, indecision, being submissive to a fault, fears of being alone, extremely sensitive, and prone to depression or mood swings. They can be pessimistic when things do not go according to plan.

3 — Creative, Vibrant, Expressive

Balanced: 3 has a way with words, and their skills as master communicators allow them to express themselves creatively (particularly with oration or writing). For them, it's always glass half full. They have an unending zest for life and living. They make the best salespeople, comedians, motivational speakers, and entertainers.

Unbalanced: Irresponsibility, overconfidence, indifference to the plight of others but themselves, exaggeration, penchant for melodrama (most of which they are responsible for starting), liars, the deep-seated fear of failure concerning their talents. They are often unable to sustain long-term relationships (romantic or not), oversensitivity to criticism, and immaturity.

4 — Reliable, Stable, Practical

Balanced: Principled, foundation builder, innovator, closet rebel. Their genius births a lot of ideas that need a creative outlet to be made manifest. They are aware of their duties and what it takes to achieve them. These perfectionists are at the top of the chain when it comes to organizational abilities and getting things done in the most practical way. Consistency, diligence, routine, and structure are their watchwords. They have hidden (sometimes dormant) abilities for spiritual healing and light work. They are family-oriented and function better when the home front is at peace.

Unbalanced: Stickler for routine, which leads to a rigid mindset, miserly nature, pessimism about life, obsession with details to the point of perfectionism. They often harbor distrust in what the future holds. They exhibit fear of missing out (FOMO) and, ironically, are also afraid of what tomorrow may bring.

5 — Ingenious, Adventurous, Optimistic

Balanced: Artful, enthusiastic, imaginative, and adaptable to change with the times, 5 has a magnetism that they wear like a second skin. They are outgoing, exuberant, and "explorers" in numerology. They have versatile talents and find they excel at almost anything they try. Great at all forms of communication, 5 is a charmer, a social butterfly, and an all-around entertainer. 5 is unable to sit still. Their gifts, when channeled positively, could do wonders for their careers and finances.

Unbalanced: Fickle-minded and extremely unreliable, they can either be passionate and driven or be nonchalant and dependent on others. They are always in a financial pickle because of their bad investments and spending habits, temperamental, easily and endlessly distracted, and prone to addiction and overindulgence.

6 — Nurturing, Loving, Loyal

Balanced: Because of their relationship to the planet Venus, number 6 is primarily focused on domestic life and relationships. They are magnetic, artistic, and devoted to their friends and loved ones. They are level-headed and adaptable and have an innate desire to bring peace and harmony to everyone in their environment. For this reason, they tend to nurture people at the expense of their own happiness and comfort, attracting endless responsibilities they really don't need. Many express a secret love for mystic sciences such as tantra, witchcraft, the occult, etc.

Unbalanced: Irritatingly self-righteous, narrow-minded with traditional beliefs, hypocritical, prone to envy, burnout, melancholy, and temper flare-ups.

7 — Spiritual, Wise, Analytical

Balanced: According to Pythagoras, the father of numerology, the number 7 is shaped like a shepherd's hook, and it symbolizes the path of kundalini energy from the base of the spine to the third eye (tisra til/tenth gate) on our forehead between our eyebrows. As a highly spiritual number, individuals with a growing number of 7 are innovators and visionaries. They are resilient, strong, with sharp minds, especially in matters relating to spirit and spirituality. They are always researching and constantly try to decipher information. Reclusive, private, introverted, and indifferent to the mundane, they are driven to understand the hidden mysteries of the human mind and cosmos. They have problems with social connections, friends, and relationships.

Unbalanced: Emotionally distant, fearing failure, domineering attitude, inability to empathize, difficulty in expressing emotions, suffering from crippling anxiety, temperamental pessimism, over-critical of themselves and others, prone to depression and loneliness.

8 — Logical, Ambitious, Tenacious

Balanced: Their sound and rational judgment makes them fantastic leaders and executives. They are goal-oriented, assertive, resourceful, and highly focused. For this reason, they tend to gravitate toward positions of authority in their chosen field to become self-established business owners. Their charisma and tenacity often influence them to take on challenges that seem greater than they are. Often, in their bid to "make their mark" on the world, they concentrate on financial and material pursuits at the expense of their family and relationships. This is why they have problems balancing their professional and personal lives.

Unbalanced: Materialistic, self-serving, a desire to control people or situations, domineering, temperamental, mistrustful of others, tactless, obsessive, anti-social

9 — Mystic, Humanitarian, Teacher

Balanced: The number 9 is a firm believer in the adage "kindness costs nothing." The true humanitarians of the numerology chart thrive on change, transformation, and goodwill. They see the bigger picture in all things.

Their nature demands that they "fix" the world's imperfections, which is totally impossible. Their need for harmony is balanced out by their desire to delve into spirituality and the unknown. 9. They could either be in touch with their instinct and elemental magnetism, or they could be oblivious to their instinctual power so that it becomes stagnant. The typical response of a 9 to painful situations is denial or an attempt to live in a false construct of bliss and peace. The greatest challenge a 9 has is the need to overcome their indecisiveness and negative thoughts.

Unbalanced: Disconnected from reality, unforgiving, fault-finding, chronic worriers, conceited, difficulty in trusting others, frustrated with mundane events.

11 — Goal-getter, Spiritual, Philanthropist

Balanced: Rational, adaptable, and creative enough to make a difference in the world, the number 11 is a master number that has similar traits to the number 2. They are empathetic individuals who really mean it when they say they know how others feel. They are charismatic with extensive knowledge of hidden truths. 11 has an underlying sense of justice and fairness, and their methods are unconventional.

Unbalanced: Caring about the opinions of others, obstinate, egotistic, prone to temper tantrums and mood swings.

22 — Ambitious, Cooperative, Humanitarian

Balanced: Capable of manifestation through cooperation and relationships. They are dedicated to connecting with others towards a common goal. Their purpose in life is to be of service to others and to humanity. 22 has a knack for integrating their knowledge of metaphysics into day-to-day living. They have no patience for fools or pretenders. Their life experience is riddled with hardships that point them in the direction of self-fulfillment in service. Many 22s have chosen to reincarnate for the purpose of helping humanity (case in point, the Dalai Lama). They are drawn to the universal language of music.

Unbalanced: Moody, aimless, angry, aloof, impractical, big talkers.

33 — Broad-minded, Selfless, Motivators/Guardians

Balanced: Knowledgeable, zealous, with a powerful need to help others even when they do not feel at their best, 33 has mastered the art of selfless service. 33s are usually slow bloomers and do not awaken their talents until maturity or middle age. Sensitive, responsible, and cautious, 33 is known as the master guardian or teacher.

Their purpose in life is to teach and provide guidance to others using their life experiences. They are specialists in motivating people and raising their vibrations. This is why they end up leaving a legacy of positive footprints in the world. Mastering the vibrations of this number is quite challenging, and to see one who has embraced in totality their gifts as a master teacher is indeed rare.

Unbalanced: Perfectionists, self-righteous, controlling, compulsive liars (because they fear hurting the feelings of others), careless, burdened by the gift of extreme insight, low self-esteem.

General Questions Concerning Growth and Name Number Calculators

Q: Is it compulsory to calculate the name numbers for documented names I seldom or never use in real life?

A: Absolutely. Your documented or legal name has vibrations influencing every sphere of your life. Even in situations where you use a shortened version of your first name, your middle name, or even an alias, the influence of your given name cannot be ignored or denied. The only way to get an accurate numerology reading is to use your full name as it appears on your birth certificate, whether you frequently use it or not.

Q: What about instances where names have changed following matrimony, anglicization, or divorce?

A: Your documented name is still the major name you are influenced by regardless of whatever life experiences you may have had that warranted a compulsory name change or amendment.

Q: What about a case where a name has certain letters or accents that are not in the Pythagorean chart?

A: If your given name has letters or accents like å, â, é, è, ç, ï, ñ or ø, it is advised that you use the numeric value of the letter as it appears in the Pythagorean chart without the accent. For compound letters like the "æ" commonly found in the Scandinavian, Norwegian, or Icelandic alphabet, you have to split the letters "into individual constituents "a" and "e." In which case, a = 1, and e = 5, the summation of which has the numerical value of 6.

Q: Is it possible to change my name vibration by choosing a new name for myself?

A: The answer is a big no. The systems that keep track of name vibrations on this plane are replicated in the etheric plane, where the akashic records are kept. These records contain an energetic signature of everything that has transpired on this earthly plane and to mankind in all times, whether past, present, or future. The akashic records can only be accessed, read, and their contents cleared or changed by an experienced numerologist or practitioner. Employing the help of an expert numerologist for a name change remains the only way to rewrite a name in these records, which inadvertently changes the experience you attract on a physical and spiritual level.

Chapter 10: Your Destiny Number

The Meaning and Importance of Destiny Numbers

In Pythagorean or Western numerology, the destiny number is the second most important number in an individual's numerology chart. Alternative names for the destiny number include name number, expression number, and complete name number. Chaldean numerologists refer to the destiny number as the purpose number.

    The name might differ between both systems, but the common theme is the fact that both systems acknowledge the destiny number, which reveals your life's mission and the feats you are destined to accomplish on earth. Many practitioners believe that destiny numbers should be considered along with the life path number when making career choices. This is because the destiny number reveals tasks or jobs you will be successful in handling as well as the aspects of your life (personality traits, goals, stumbling blocks) that must be refined to help you reach your full potential.

The destiny number is calculated from your original, documented name, as it is written on your birth certificate. Whether or not you use or like those names, they reveal the predetermined destiny you were born to fulfill. This applies to circumstances where you have changed your name for one reason or another or taken on an extra name following marriage, adoption, or religious rites. No matter what the circumstance, the energy from your given name remains with you for the rest of your mortal existence.

If the circumstances were such that your parents couldn't decide on a name for you for a while and the name "baby" was written on your birth certificate for a time period as brief as one hour, then the name "baby" must be considered during the numerological reading. If you were adopted and are unaware of your birth name, then your adopted name may be read instead, always bearing in mind that an essential piece of information will be lacking from your reading.

Western numerologists are of the opinion that a name change or an alias based on your birth name yields a new destiny number, but this new number does not in any way, shape or form affect your original destiny number vibration. Instead, it works alongside it, boosting its power and adding that extra oomph to your life in the form of additional lessons, life experiences, abilities, and talents.

The destiny number shows how you react to situations you encounter in life. Are you someone that prefers the spotlight, or are you content with a supportive role? Do you wade through life as an active or passive participant? This number also shows how well you work and relate to others. This number is a melting pot of both your inner persona and the persona you want the rest of the world to see.

What Name to Use in Destiny Number Calculation

To get the most accurate figure for your destiny or expression number, it is advised that you use your name as it appears on your birth registration, birth certificate, or whichever legally recognized document records the name you received at the time of your birth, even if you rarely use it, or are not well known by those names.

This also means that if your name is misspelled or your mother's maiden name is on record, it will be included with a hyphen after your surname. Alternately, if you were given the name "baby girl" or "baby boy," these names must be taken into consideration. There are other special circumstances that may arise, such as:

- **The addition of an extra name post-birth:** Some cultures and religious rites insist on an additional name. For instance, the Catholic rites of baptism and confirmation require the adoption of the name of a saint. Or maybe Uncle Giles' condition for inheriting his estate was that you took his name. As much as you may want that inheritance, your new moniker isn't the name you would use when calculating your destiny number. You are advised to revert to your birth name.

- **Missing or lost birth certificate:** It is possible that your birth certificate may have been missing, or lost due to a fire incident, flood, or a lazy midwife who neglected to report your fabulous arrival into the world. There is an easy fix for this problem. You could order your birth certificates from the registrar in the state or county of your birth, the chief of vital statistics in the United States, or similar offices in developed nations. Simply search the internet for a suitable office and voila! Problem solved. If none of the solutions work, you could use the name that was listed on your school documents as an infant.

- **Adoption:** It is normal practice to have adoption records sealed in many countries. This makes it difficult for adopted children to obtain their original birth certificates. If this is the case for you, you could search the internet for organizations that specialize in the research of adoption records. If this is impossible, then, and only then, can you use the name given by your adoptive parents. The fun fact about adoptive names is that when adoptees are finally able to retrieve their original birth certificate, they discover that the destiny numbers derived from their given names are similar to those calculated from their adoptive names.

- **Birth in foreign countries:** If your parents were living in a country like North Korea, Japan, or the middle east, you may discover that in place of your birth name is hangul, kanji, or Arabic calligraphy, then do not fret. Use the name your parents intended for you to have or your full name as a child.

- **Suffixes like I, II-IV, or Junior:** If there is a generational suffix such as a roman numeral or "Junior" attached to your name, numerologists advise that you use your given name without the additional bells and whistles in order to arrive at the most accurate calculation of your destiny number. This is because the suffixes are not an essential part of your name but are merely add-on references.

- **Name change following marriage or a legal procedure**: Some people may have had to change their names after marriage or as part of a witness protection program. Numerologists believe that the exact name you were given at birth, even if there is an error in spelling, is the name vibration you carry with you through your whole life. So, regardless of the personal or professional reasons surrounding your name change, only your given name should be used to calculate name-related core numbers in numerology because, to be honest, your new name is not the name you were given at birth, and it, therefore, has no power over your destiny.

Calculate Your Destiny Number

Calculating your destiny number only requires one piece of vital information; your exact and full name, as it was written on your birth certificate, or if you happen to fall into any of the special categories mentioned above, your name as it appeared on your school documents as a child. Here is a step-by-step way to calculate your destiny number:

1. Write down the letters in your name, making sure to leave ample space between your first, middle name(s), and last name/family name. This is important so that you are able to add up the

number in small chunks.

2. Underneath each letter for every name, pen down the number vibrations that coincide with the letters written down. Refer to the Pythagorean chart in chapter 9 for further clarification. Remember that suffixes and generational references are not to be included, and extra letters similar to but not part of the English alphabet should be calculated as the letters closest to it in the chart. So, ö should be read as O, ä as A, and æ as A and E, respectively.

3. Sum up the number vibrations in your first name and reduce the number down to a single digit. Do the same for your middle and last names.

4. To get your destiny number, add up the numerical values of the reduced digits from your first, middle, and last names and reduce the resulting figure to a single digit.

For instance, let's calculate the destiny number of an imaginary person called Mary-Anne Clark.

Mary: $4 + 1 + 9 + 7 = 21; 2 + 1 = 3$

Anne: $1 + 5 + 5 + 5 = 16; 1 + 6 = 7$

Clark: $3 + 3 + 1 + 9 + 2 = 18; 1 + 8 = 9$

What is the destiny number of the 44th president of the United States, Barack Hussein Obama?

Barack: $2 + 1 + 9 + 1 + 3 + 2 = 18; 1 + 8 = 9$

Hussein: $8 + 3 + 1 + 1 + 5 + 9 + 5 = 32; 3 + 2 = 5$

Obama: $6 + 2 + 1 + 4 + 1 = 14; 1 + 4 = 5$

Barack Obama has a destiny number of 1. From his chart, you can see the number 1 appears multiple times, indicating leadership, innovation, and a pioneering attitude. The number 5 also appears multiple times, showing that he is the type of person who loves to be active, creative, and busy. Do the numbers not fit his personality profile?

Destiny numbers are fun things to calculate. Bear in mind that they don't just affect humans. Destiny numbers can tell or affect the personality profile of pets too. That sassy cat of yours who wants its dinner at a particular time and will go to any length to get your attention, such as blocking your view while you watch a rerun of your favorite show or meowing while staring at the clock, may be number one.

The Meanings of Different Destiny Numbers

(1)

Determined, independent, and self-sufficient, you rule the roost. You have a competitive spirit and will do whatever it takes to succeed. Your authenticity and "take-no-prisoners" approach toward fulfilling your potential make people see you as the dictatorial sort. They are not wrong because you tend to like your own ideas better than anyone else's.

You enjoy the outdoors and freedom and dislike it when people put restrictions on you or keep tabs on you. You are unafraid of standing out from the crowd, whether it's through fashion, speech, or your unique approach to doing things. You love being the center of attention, and for you, compliments always go a long way towards buttering you up.

It is imperative for you to remember that the opinions of others matter. You might even learn a thing or two from others. Curb your tyrannical tendencies. Life isn't a ship where you have to bark out commands to get things done. Gentle persuasion may be far from your usual approach, but it wouldn't hurt to try it once in a while.

(2)

Insightful, cultured, intuitive, refined, and sensitive, you are the kind that has tact down pat. You could sashay into any space and effectively read the room. This is not just handy for organizing seating arrangements at weddings. Your intuition and sensitivity allow you to constructively use your words so as not to hurt someone else. You are a wonderful listener. Everyone finds themselves spilling their guts at your feet while you heal them using your words and empathy.

You enjoy being the steady force backstage, influencing others to be the best version of themselves, as opposed to the number one who wants to be at the front and center of every parade. You can be trusted to juggle multiple tasks at once and still be on time for that appointment without breaking a sweat. You thrive when working in partnership with others.

You are not troublesome by nature, but you can't stand it when people take advantage of you or others, and you have no qualms about shutting perpetrators out. You are a student of life. People can depend on you to know the weirdest facts as you are constantly collecting and curating knowledge.

During your service to others, remember to set firm boundaries for your own personal and mental health needs. Don't say yes when you mean no. Also, control your tendency to sulk when offended. After all, people make mistakes, and a lot of people will step on your tender feet (and heart).

(3)

Optimism, enthusiasm, friendship, self-expression, and happiness are the backbone of anyone with a destiny number of 3. You love life and are not afraid to show it. Your zest for life, just like your aura and laughter, is contagious. You can raise the energy of any room you walk into, and as a result, the party does not start until you have walked in.

You have the gift of the robe and are aware that persuasion is more effective than force in getting you what you want. As a result, you improve your argument rather than raising your voice. You can sell ice to an Eskimo.

Your eternal youthfulness and child-like nature could make you petulant at times. For instance, you could play pranks but not like them as much when the favor is returned.

You enjoy attention from others and play up your appearance to get it. Because you enjoy being everyone's friend, you may find yourself juggling more responsibilities than you think you are able to handle.

Try as much as you can to keep your engagements and commitments to a minimum. Do not take on more than you are able to handle effectively. Time management, concentrating your energies, and being more responsible are in your best interests. Enthusiasm is nice, but you need to learn practicality.

(4)

If there was ever a number that could be likened to a mountain, this would be it. You are steady, reliable, structured, dependable, and practical. Patience, diligence, and perseverance are your mantras. You can be trusted to complete every task laid out for you, even if it takes you some time to finish. The elephant has nothing on you when it comes to recall. You can remember even the most insignificant things. It is both your blessing and your curse.

As a detail-oriented person, you work best when there is a timetable, list, method, or routine for you to follow. This is sometimes a bad thing because routines (and consequently you) are not very amenable to change. The slightest change in a process you are used to can throw you off your game, so you are not the most adaptable fellow on the planet.

Your honest, sincere, and down-to-earth nature makes you one of the best friends anyone can have, as they can be sure to stick by you through thick and thin. You are very conscious of your time and finances. This quality of yours makes you a super saver, but on the flip side, your frugal nature stops you from experiencing the best life has to offer. It's fun to partake in something frivolous once in a while. There! I said it. Wipe the look of horror from your face and whip out that bucket list you have tossed to the bottom of the drawer.

(5)

Like the pentagram that points in five directions at the same time, you are the king or queen of multitasking. You can talk on the phone, watch TV, cook dinner, and read a book all at the same time. This quality of yours is possibly due to your dislike of routine (how odd that it follows the number 4) and monotony. You are always full of restless and pent-up energy. Even in bed, your mind is never asleep.

In contrast to the rigid lists needed by 4, you require change and variety to function well. You are not only multitalented – but also multifaceted. Your inquisitive nature causes you to question everything. The irony, however, is the fact that you dislike people questioning you. You are impulsive, creative, spontaneous, and will leave a venue or a person that is dull to you before anyone can say, Jack. You may be a walking, breathing party waiting to happen at a moment's notice, but my advice to you is to slow down, take the time to smell the roses, and think of all the wonderful experiences you have missed because you are always in a hurry. Sometimes a night at home does more good than a party at the club.

(6)

Affectionate, nurturing, and loving, a 6 will always leave you better than they found you. Your mantra is, "Let peace reign on earth, and may it start with me." You are responsible, reliable, and enjoy catering to others. Your hospitality and integrity know no bounds, even when it comes to people you've just met and barely know.

You have an amiable and even-tempered personality, you do not shy away from volunteering, and you're always happy to take on more than your share of the responsibility. You are attracted to music, art, and nature. You also have a keen eye for color and design. You love the good life and are not afraid to shell out the big bucks for your comfort.

While caring for others is ideal, practice self-love because you also need attention and care. Don't be in a hurry to give out unsolicited advice. Sometimes people just want to work things out for themselves. Your need for materialistic comforts should not overshadow your logic. I am sure you can wait for a sale on that cashmere sweater or strike a bargain for your favorite bottle of bubbly.

(7)

A typical 7 reminds me of Spencer Reid from the show Criminal Minds. Remember the smart dude who saw patterns in everything and always had his nose buried in a file, book, or board? You're intelligent, analytical, and able to retain large amounts of information. Your skeptical nature ensures that you never believe anything at face value or via hearsay, which is just as well because you dislike gossip and gossipmongers. You will always require proof. You won't even believe someone died until you see the body.

You are a loner who uses solitude to recharge your batteries. You always appear cold and aloof, but you feel things deeply and are one of the best and most loyal friends one could have. I have met 7s who appear frigid but are loving and caring dog or cat dads. Your aristocratic bearing and refined tastes complement your desire for perfection in all you do. You are an old soul attracted to the unknown and the spiritual.

You believe in the law of karma and, because of this, strive to walk on the straight and narrow even when no one is watching. It might be painful to hear this as a 7, but you need to widen your social circle. This will only happen when you learn the art of small talk and understand that it's alright to approach people for conversation first. Stay away from antidepressants, intoxicants, and stimulants. Your mental constitution is usually more affected than others by these substances since you are almost always melancholy.

(8)

8 is an ambitious, money-driven business tycoon who has a lot of goals and little or no patience for dreams. You are a skilled manager and organizer who works well under pressure and keeps a level head in times of emergency. You are capable of handling any task, but you become irate when you are micromanaged. Instead, you love to be the one marshaling out orders instead.

You are quite conscious of your diet, physical health, and fitness, and you monitor them daily. That, and the fact that a polished appearance screams wealth and status. As an 8, if the letters Z, H, or Q do not appear in your given name, you have a tendency to rapidly gain or lose weight under stress.

Tact is necessary even at work. When you give others a chance to express their opinions, you are more likely to command the respect due to you. Also, find time to balance your life. As a workaholic, your nose is always on the grindstone, and as such, you have little or no time for extracurricular activities or romance. Go out there and have fun; the world can wait!

(9)

A visionary and a humanitarian, you have a deep appreciation for art, music, culture, beauty, and nature. You have the ability to influence and tolerate others, which is why you don't understand why everyone else can't get along. You are either widely traveled or a geography buff with knowledge of diverse people, cultures, and food. You are caring, generous, and kind-hearted, always willing to help others or give freely of yourself to whoever asks.

You are extremely loyal in partnerships – but forming one-on-one relationships can be a bit of a hassle. The wisdom you are blessed with is a result of having weathered a lot of difficulties and bad experiences in life. Learn to forgive others who offend you or who are not as thoughtful or as generous as you are. People are wired differently, and as a number 9, the most precious gift you can give to the world is total acceptance and selfless service.

(11)

11 is a master number, which means it has a higher and stronger vibration than destiny number 2. Spiritual, idealistic, and highly imaginative, you have immense capability to influence people and events. The energy of 1 means you enjoy being in the spotlight, leading, and managing people.

You are highly intelligent and a great listener with superior powers of communication. As a highly imaginative and curious person, you are here to learn everything the world has to teach you. You spend more time daydreaming than achieving any set goals. Your enhanced levels of intuition and extrasensory perception enable you to align yourself with a higher purpose, one that makes a difference in this world.

Your ability to weave stories predisposes you to the habit of compulsive lying, embellishment, and exaggeration. Also, you tend to be self-righteous and critical of others, forgetting that your path is to shine a light, not to point fingers.

(22)

The dedicated, inspirational, focused, and charismatic master number 22 is a forward-thinking visionary who, in their quest for mastery, constantly converts dreams into solid reality to reach a higher level of consciousness. 22s are practical loners that combine the creativity and intuition of 1 with the compassion and sensitivity of 2 with the tenacity and determination of 4 to make dreams a reality.

As long as you do not let your crippling fear of failure sneak up on you, the world is your oyster. Your workaholic tendencies will burn you out before you have a chance to achieve whatever it is that you desire. Like number 4, you are extremely self-righteous and high-strung. Be more accommodating of others as you put your many talents to good use.

(33)

This master number is a higher vibration or octave of the number 6. The evolved 33s are on this plane to raise the awareness and consciousness of everyone through their experiences and acts of selfless service.

The perfectionist nature of the 6 combined with the double dose of carefree attitude and sensitivity from the 3 results in the 33 being a high achiever who, unfortunately, seeks the validation of others. A fully evolved 33 is one who has completely embraced their imperfections and detaches from their personal feelings to create a positive change in the world. It is safe to say that evolved 33s are very rare as it is quite easy to fall prey to negative means of self-expression such as gossiping, complaining, and criticizing.

Chapter 11: The Soul Urge Number

The soul number (also called the soul urge, soul desire, or heart's desire number) is one of your numerology chart's most important core numbers. The soul number is the reduced sum of the digits represented by the vowels in your birth name. Unlike your destiny or personality number, the soul urge number is a mirror to your soul and a direct reflection of your given name. Embracing and tapping into this energy is important because it is an echo of the deepest desires of your subconscious mind. This number discloses your innermost desires, thoughts, habits, and baseline responses to stimuli. Only the soul number reflects the core of your soul, what you care about or crave the most in this world to feel content. It is a number indicative of your hopes, wishes, and dreams – and represents your personality in relationships.

How to Calculate the Soul Urge Number

Calculating your soul urge number requires that you extract the vowels present in your given name. The values of the vowels as they appear in the Pythagorean chart are:

- A = 1
- E = 5
- I = 9
- O = 6
- U = 3
- Y = 7

A harmony between your life path number and your soul urge number helps you to easily make decisions. Any discordance between the two means that you will be conflicted in many of the choices you have to make because of the ongoing war between your head and your heart. On the rare occasions where both numbers are the same, living your most authentic life becomes a piece of cake.

The rat race called life can dull the calling of your soul, making it difficult to understand what it is your soul truly longs for. This is why certain practices such as yoga, qigong, conscious meditation, and quiet alone time are essential. These activities not only feed the soul, but they also allow it to make its needs known to you via your intuition. All you have to do is open your heart and really listen.

The soul urge number is calculated using the vowels in your name as it appears on the birth certificate. When calculating soul numbers in numerology, consider the system used in the calculation. For instance, in Chaldean numerology, Y is considered a vowel, while in the western system, it is a consonant sometimes and a vowel at other times. In Western numerology, Y is considered a vowel when there is a lack of vowels in that particular syllable or if the letter Y is sandwiched between or next to two consonants, as seen in names like Yvette, Wynn, or Lacy. In names like these, the Y sound is pronounced as "ee." Other numerologists consider Y a vowel when it comes before another vowel in a name or syllable so that both Y and the said vowel together provide the vowel sound. This is seen in names like Doyle, Tracey, Emily, etc.

To confuse you even further, certain practitioners consider the letter W to be a vowel when it is followed by another vowel in a name or syllable so that together they provide the vowel sound, or in a case where W appears sandwiched in between two vowels. These conflicting theories make for a dizzy head, so my advice is that you go with whatever feels right to you.

Reducing-Down Method

- **Step 1:** Extract the vowels from your birth certificate's name and attach the numerical values for each of the vowels.

- **Step 2:** Sum up the numerical values from the extracted vowels, adding the vowels in each name separately, so they form individual totals.

- **Step 3:** Add up the double-digit totals for each name (unless they add up to a master number) and reduce them to a single digit. You could also decide, in this method, to add the double-digit compound number (total) and then reduce it to a single digit.

Example: A B R A H A M L I N C O L N

1 1 1 9 6

(1+1+1=3) (9+6=15; 1+5=6)

3 + 6= 9

Abraham Lincoln's soul urge number is 9.

Also, remember that it is totally your choice to reduce master numbers 11, 22, or 33 down to 2, 4, and 6, respectively. Some practitioners leave master numbers as is wherever they appear in a numerology chart, while others reduce them further down.

The Adding-Across Method

The adding across method is the most widely used. It involves you adding up the sum total of the numerical values of the vowels in your name and adding them across. After this, you reduce it to a single digit (with the exception of master numbers). Both methods of calculation reveal the same answer.

Example: A B R A H A M L I N C O L N 1+1+1+9+6= 18 (1+8) = 9

1 1 1 9 6

Your soul number represents the aspects of you that the rest of the world rarely gets to see. It could indicate the traits and talents you possess, whether or not they are developed, exhibited, or dormant, as well as your feelings or attitude towards others, love, and relationships. Understanding your soul urge number is the key to realizing the hidden aspects of you and the different levels of your inner nature, some of which you fear others finding out about as it may cause you some level of embarrassment or ridicule.

Knowing the soul numbers of your loved ones will enhance family and personal relationships as you will relate better with them, knowing why they do what they do and what feeds the desires of their soul. For instance, that tough and buff friend of yours with a soul number of 2 may not want others to find out that he bawls his eyes out during sappy scenes in movies. In the same way, your boss with a soul number of 6 may not want it made public that he has a soft spot for children, older people, and cute animals. This is why this number is a core number in the chart. It helps you know what drives people and enables you to relate to them in ways they can understand.

When calculating your soul urge number, use all the names on your birth chart. Yes, even if you have two or more middle names separated by a hyphen. If you are calculating by hand, turn your sheet of paper horizontally (landscape instead of portrait) so it contains more letters in this situation.

Soul Urge Number 1

Strong Leadership Skills: This number implies charisma, individuality, self-sufficiency, and independence. A number 1 is confident in their abilities and unbothered by the fact that they have to make tough calls from time to time. A soul urge of 1 means your deepest desire is to lead, not follow. Your strong leadership tendencies, ability to thrive in fast-paced environments, and creative spark mean that you can wield vibrations that manifest anything you set your mind to.

For this reason, people look up to you. Some may even envy you. But while your deepest desire may be leadership, you must take note of the influence of other numbers on your chart and their interaction with your soul urge number. This is because your chart may show your heart wants one thing and your head wants another. The key is to find harmony and work in alignment with your wisdom while referring to the numbers on the chart. Do this, and success will naturally gravitate towards you.

Charisma: Whether you want it or not, everyone wants a piece of you. For this reason, you are often the center of attention regardless of how you act or attempt to be a wallflower. This is because the energy of one has two major traits; leadership and the ability to influence others. As a leader, being thoughtful and caring towards your team or tribe is as natural to you as breathing. Your compelling and authentic personality is magnetic and commands respect.

Enthusiasm: Your level of intelligence means you put in the work to research topics that people often gloss over. As a result, it is difficult to get you excited about anything. However, when you have your hopes up about something, you have a way of winning people over, infecting everyone with a healthy level of motivation and excitement. It is possible that you may have eccentric or controversial views, but you always have a way to push your unique perspective onto people, convincing anyone that a healthy dose of controversy is essential to success.

Feeling Indispensable: That is when confidence has crossed the line over to arrogance. You almost never let anyone try their hand at something you want because you feel no one can do a better job than you can. This may work for you sometimes, but the greatest leaders need loyal followers, and no one is going to be loyal for too long to someone with a domineering personality.

Soul Urge Number 2

Sensitive: Is your heart allergic to the news? Do you cry at the sad scenes in movies? Are you the first to kiss and make up after an argument? If you have done the calculations and ended up with soul urge number 2, then you are an intuitive and sensitive soul. Your innermost desire is to love and be loved in return. You may dislike your emotional nature, but it is your greatest asset. Because without emotional sensitivity, there can be no intuition. And intuition gets you out of tough situations before they even occur. Embrace your heart and trust your gut because it is always spot-on.

You are the loyal and faithful sidekick, the yin to number 1's yang. You represent everything that number one isn't, and that is not a bad thing. Whereas number 1 is individualistic and a trailblazer, number 2 is sensitive and interested in harmony and balance. You don't have to be the center of attention. The spotlight could be behind the scenes too. You feel under-appreciated, but there is no 1 without a 2. All leaders need someone steady, stable, and reliable whom they trust.

The Need for Harmony: As a born peacemaker, you have an innate need for peace and harmony in life. You're the one always resolving conflicts and smoothing out ruffled feathers. Never allow your need for balance to stop you from expressing your opinions, especially when the occasion calls for you to speak your mind or defend yourself. Regardless of what others think, people will listen to you and like you even when they disagree with your point of view.

Strong Level of Intuition: many times, you wish you could feel less than you do. Never regard your strong intuition as a burden, but rather as a means of guiding those you care about. Let go of your self-doubt, connect with your intuition, and trust the process. Many people will flock to you for your wise counsel.

Soul Urge Number 3

Charisma: The French phrase "joie de vivre" is personified as soul urge number 3. These charismatic, witty individuals come with an inbuilt desire to entertain others and express themselves. They are popular in all the circles they find themselves in, and they leave an unforgettable impression on others. Like the butterfly, you are always perching from flower to flower, receiving compliments, and basking in as much attention as you can. As much as you love the trappings of luxury, you are quite adaptable to the constant surprises life brings. You live not in the moment but in *the second*, never worrying about what tomorrow may bring. Your deepest desire is to develop and express your brand of magic.

Born Entertainers: Put a soul urge 3 in a small gathering and give it a few minutes - they will convert that gathering into a sizable crowd. Their magnetism is infectious. Their happy, chatty, slightly eccentric, and outgoing nature ensures that people keep coming back for more. However, your tendency to chat may also lead you to overshare when you are anxious or tell lies for no reason whatsoever. Resist the temptation to always be the performer in every social situation you find yourself in. Slowing down does not mean you have lost your touch.

Innate Creativity: soul urge 3s can't help the creative streak they are born with. For them, self-expression and artistic flair come naturally. This is why they are easily bored by menial or routine jobs; their nature strongly forbids it, gravitating instead towards careers that allow them to utilize whatever unique talents they have. They may love money, but it is certainly not their motivation in choosing a career. Their charm and wit help them make all the right connections for success.

Soul Urge Number 4

Hard Work and Discipline: The main traits of soul urge 4 are stability, reliability, punctuality, and productivity. The typical foursome is a stickler for routines that scream practicality. To them, hard work is the backbone of success, and they are willing to invest copious amounts of time and effort to achieve their goals.

The need for structure: You thrive well in environments or setups that have a known organizational hierarchy. People depend heavily on you because you always get the job done. You are always on time, and you have no qualms about picking up the slack for others or assuming extra responsibilities. You take care of your body, your loved ones, your living quarters, and your mind. The play-by-play keeps you anchored somewhat. The only problem with your methods is that the slightest change to your routines can leave you destabilized and unhinged.

Working toward a Goal: You are always working towards something. There is no time for recreation or leisure. Although this is awesome for achieving goals, your social life suffers. You may not be a trailblazer like 1 or as creative as 3, but you notice every last detail and fine-tune any plan to perfection. You are happy to blend into your surroundings and are not interested in the spotlight, but if anyone tries to disorganize your carefully crafted image or process, they automatically become a threat, and you won't let go without a fight.

Soul Urge Number 5

Talented and creative, Soul Urge 5 is multitalented, intelligent, and has varied interests. They are the very definition of thinking outside the box. Their unconventional thoughts help them grasp even the most complex concepts quickly, while their eccentric ways and zest for life ensure they are never short of company. Their innermost desire is to travel, explore, and learn as much as they can.

Spontaneous: Only a 5 would change course halfway to their destination and have their agents on speed dial while at it. Your restless energy craves freedom at all costs, and you take risks with everything. Life is always a roller coaster for you. Many perceive you as highly unreliable because of the way you change your mind on a whim. You have so much reserved energy and passion that it is difficult to find an outlet for it all. You change careers and relationships at the drop of a hat, possibly because the thrill of the chase is more interesting to you than the end result.

The Need for Freedom: Your need for freedom is paramount. It's not something you hide from anyone who gets close to you. You dislike being under any restrictions, and commitments don't come easily to you. You never finish what you start. You are tolerant of others. You are a riot, but life is never boring for or with you.

Soul Urge Number 6

All about Others: Soul urge number 6: immersing themselves in the needs of others, so they lose sight of what they want too. Their trusting and caring nature sometimes makes them oblivious to the world around them. In the end, they put their trust in the wrong people.

Nurturing: 6 spends a lot of time nurturing others. Relationships and love affairs with other people are usually very tedious, time-consuming, and complicated for them. Unconditional love is something that they understand. This is why they can keep their promises of fidelity and loyalty to the people they care about. Letting go does not come easily for them. Ending a relationship may feel like the foundations of the relationship have been thrown out of whack. But sometimes, it has to happen to make sure that the people in their lives are worth the time and effort.

Traditional Values: You love tradition, family values, nature, and pets. You are a peacemaker who strives for harmonious relationships and cooperation. Wealth may not be foremost in your mind, but you treasure financial and emotional stability. You are big on commitments, and your word is your bond.

Soul Urge Number 7

Organizing: 7 is the soul-urge number of the controller. You have a very strong will and a deep faith in your competence. All you need is enough confidence in yourself to overcome obstacles and achieve success. For this reason, you are usually an excellent organizer and planner. You are also not afraid to be openly critical of others. This comes with incredible persuasion abilities. You can easily convince people if you want it badly enough.

Perfection: Born leaders or people who take the lead around the world, their influence will spread far and wide if they can make it happen by their efforts alone. This is a very ambitious person with a hunger for power and control. He/she may be domineering, overbearing, and aggressive. They may make such a lasting impression on people that they leave them little opportunity to react or breathe.

Integrity: Integrity is of the utmost importance to you. You are likely to have absolute faith in your beliefs and principles. You can also be brutally honest, even if it hurts the person receiving your criticism. Yours is probably not the best personality type for teamwork because you like to take charge, and you do not want anyone second-guessing your decisions.

Soul Urge Number 8

Giving: 8 is the soul-urge number of the giver. This is a person who has a sense of belonging that they find in people. Their love for others is unconditional and open-minded. They are warm and caring, with a true sense of community and humanity. 8 gives to others without expecting anything in return. They feel better when they have given—a drive in this direction towards selfless love is something that no one can deny or resist.

You Are Very Much in Touch with Your Emotions: Idealistic and passionate, you follow your heart into love affairs even if they do not go where you expect or wish they would. You are the type of person that you would not care to have as a friend or love interest. You can be very fickle and often act on instinct rather than logic. If you feel it is right to do so, you make decisions based on what feels good at the time, not necessarily what is right.

You're Non-Materialistic: you have a very open mind and are not interested in material things like money or status. You will take on many causes throughout your lifetime, even if they prove to be difficult or thankless tasks. Your desire to give your all for others is always present and remains until the end of your days. You are a true humanitarian, and your heart is always in the right place. You have no interest in owning many things or having a lot of wealth, regardless of how much money you make. This is something that you have in common with people who have the same soul urge number and who feel as if they have enough material goods to last them for their lifetime or for multiple lifetimes. But that does not mean you are not interested in helping others out. In fact, you are more than willing to give selflessly to those around you once you get the chance.

You Live Life by Your Own Rules and Beliefs: Yours is a personality full of energy, determination, purpose, and initiative. You have the drive and determination to achieve whatever you set your mind to.

Soul Urge Number 9

A visionary and dreamer, 9 is the soul-urge number of the visionary. They are dreamers of big dreams and have a natural ability to see into the hearts of people and situations. 9 has an instinct that tells them when things may be changing for the better or worse in their lives. Their intuition about people can be seen through their unerring sense of knowing who they can trust and who they cannot. They are willing to take risks in life by giving themselves over to others and going to places where they may not otherwise go. Traveling and learning new things are also part of their soul urge.

Busy Body: 9s are hyperactive souls who seem to never be at rest, even when they are sleeping. They always have something going on in their minds and in their lives. You may find them running from one project to the next without being able to sit still long enough to really take a deep breath.

Social Butterfly: The majority of 9s love being around other people and thrive on interaction with others without having a need for solitude or quiet time on the side. They have a capacity for leadership but can also be very comfortable following another's instructions if necessary.

The overall lesson of number nine is based on giving (9 + 1 = 10, 1 + 0 = 1), learning to say no, doing things that scare you, overcoming self-imposed limitations, and letting go of the past. For some people, the journey to learning these life lessons will be long and hard, but those who do will gain tremendous wisdom from the experience that can be applied for the rest of their lives.

The Universal Law of Karma: You're here to learn fulfillment. This universal law is based on the more basic principle of cause and effect. Whatever we think, say, or do has causes that affect our lives in some way. These can be seen as good effects or bad effects depending on how we see ourselves, the world, and all of life around us.

Chapter 12: Your Personality Number

In Numerology, the personality number is among the five fundamental numbers.

It's probably safe to say that the personality number is the least known of the two primary numbers sourced from the destiny, or expression number (also known as the "Total Name number"). The other is the Soul Urge Number - and, whereas the Soul Urge Number is calculated solely on the basis of the vowels in your full name in childhood, the Personality Number is determined solely on the basis of consonants.

The Personality Number: What Does It Mean?

That this is the most important number is fairly self-explanatory—it describes the persona. When interacting with other people around the world, your distinguishing characteristics and qualities help to define who you are. As a result, it frequently and uncannily describes the individual's individual style and favorite attire.

It's interesting to note that some modern numerologists refer to this number as the "Quiet Self." They do not use it as a predictor of outward behavior but rather as a marker of what an individual hopes to accomplish in the outside world.

When it comes to an understanding of oneself and also being able to master affirmation, self-compassion, and self-love, the number zero must be taken into account.

In addition, learning more about this tiny section of your numerology chart can provide you with helpful hints on how to improve, grow, and mature in certain areas of your life.

Calculating Your Personality Number

There are two ways to do this. First, you can subtract your soul urge number from your destiny number using Pythagorean numerology. When you use this method, you're not going to get numbers 11 or 22 unless you make use of the subtotals.

The other method is to add all the numerological values of your name's consonants and continue to sum them up till you reduce them to a master number or a single digit. Keep in mind that you can't get this number using your married name or your nickname. You have to use the full name on your birth certificate, including your middle name. Even if your name is misspelled, you must use it as it is. For your convenience, here are the consonants and their values:

- A – 1
- B – 2
- C – 3
- F – 6
- G – 7
- H – 8

- J – 1
- K – 2
- L – 3
- M – 4
- N – 5
- P – 7
- Q – 8
- R – 9
- S – 1
- T – 2
- V – 4
- W – 5
- X – 6
- Z – 8

As for the letter Y, sometimes it's a consonant, sometimes it's a vowel. It all depends on the word it is in and how it sounds. For instance, Y is a consonant when it takes the place of a hard consonant sound, like Yolanda, Toyota, and so on. Y can also follow a vowel, in which case it's not a consonant, as is the case in words like Maya, Gray, and Kaysha.

Personality Numbers and Meanings

Personality Number 1 is a person who stands out from the crowd.

This numerology number is a good choice for a leader. They are honorable and lovable because they are number one. In general, they possess outstanding characteristics.

A number 1 is a fearless leader who possesses exceptional levels of resilience and stamina. They are extremely effective and are always at the vanguard of all they do. They have been endowed with the capacity to manage people and see endeavors through to completion.

Personality Number 2 is a gregarious and outgoing individual.

The central message of this number is that of friendship and companionship. Number 2s are aesthetically pleasing, gentle, and meticulous in their attention to detail. It is the function of number 2 to act as a mediator. They are dependable and reasonable. Since they are calm, gentle, and credible, people in the number 2 position make excellent mediators. Also noteworthy is the fact that this numerology is remarkably down-to-earth, pleasant, and attentive. Their sensitive personalities allow them to be extremely patient.

Personality number 3 is a character with a distinct personality.

This number has a remarkable ability to communicate thoughts and feelings. They are friendly and chatty – and amazingly talented in the arts. People who fall into the third category are eternal optimists, which makes them a delightful and enjoyable presence. With this numerology, it is simple to express love and affection. They are excellent conversationalists who exude enthusiasm and enthusiasm for their work. Additionally, they are excellent listeners.

Personality Number 4 is a character with a unique personality.

The number 4 represents someone who is hardworking, serious, and practical. These individuals have a high level of dependability, reliability, and credibility. They have a strong attachment to their families and to their community. Many people believe that the number 4 represents a highly dedicated person. People with this numerology possess a strong desire to learn – and are respectful and dedicated to the core. The number 4 personality is characterized by its inner strength and determination.

Personality number 5 is the freedom-loving, adaptable, and adventurous type.

The number 5s are a unique breed. Originality, quick-fire wit, and a dash of nervous energy characterize this individual's presence, making them unforgettable. Interactions with this number are exhilarating and elicit deep thought from the participants. When they share their ideas, they are bursting with enthusiasm, and their limitless energy serves as an inspiration to those around them.

Personality number 6 has sympathy and compassion as the overarching themes that run through it.

The roles of defender and caregiver bring great satisfaction to this individual. When it comes to number 6, you can lean heavily on them for help because of their loving disposition; they have a high level of responsibility, are generous, and make excellent counselors. The number 6 exudes calmness and patience and can bring people together in a group setting. People turn to them for comfort when things are going wrong.

Personality number 7 has the appearance of being an outsider or a loner.

They are sociable once you get to know them, despite their outward appearance. This person is extremely perceptive, and they are interested in how things work. They are people who are interested in learning new things. People who fall into the seventh category are driven by a desire to learn and to ask difficult questions. Because they are highly philosophical, they may come across as incomprehensible. People pay attention to them because of their inherent wisdom, despite appearing to be secretive and sometimes difficult to understand. The words of people who are assigned the number 7 are frequently profound.

Personality number 8 is an interesting one. When it comes to taking on executive positions of influence, this number makes a strong impression on others.

They have a global perspective, are friendly, and are optimistic. Number 8s have a strong sense of authority and influence. They have a commanding presence as well as an infectious enthusiasm that makes them stand out. Number 8 is a capable and hardworking individual who will gladly complete any task assigned to him. They are capable of taking on and managing large-scale projects with outstanding success.

Personality number 9 will frequently appear to be younger than their actual age.

You get the impression that they are friendly and generous. The number 9 represents dependability, selflessness, understanding, compassion, and a desire to be of service. Others can rely on this individual because they exude spiritual energy. People come to them for guidance and wisdom. They are extremely tolerant of others and have compassionate hearts.

Personality number 11 is a person with unique traits.

The master number 11 is always interested in spiritual developments. This number is extremely dedicated to spiritual matters, possessing superior intuition when compared to the average person. These individuals possess tremendous healing potential. It is possible that they will become engaged in the health and wellness industry if they aren't already.

Because of their gentle and patient nature, they make excellent friends or romantic partners. 11s exude warmth and kindness everywhere they go, enticing others to approach and become closer to them. The spirituality of the number 11 is also an important aspect of their overall personality.

Personality number 22 is a master who gets their hands dirty. Number 22 possesses both a strong intuitive side as well as a centered, practical side to them. Fashions that are both practical and long-lasting are favorites of this group. These individuals are excellent communicators who also have a strong understanding of delegation. They are usually accompanied by a large group of people who are all eager to lend a hand with whatever major project they are working on.

22s want to profoundly impact the world in which they live. They are brought into the world with untapped potential and inexhaustible inner strength. They are constantly trying to figure out what they can do to make a positive difference in other people's lives, whether it is through a business venture, a governmental policy, or a new philosophical approach.

Their primary objective in life is to contribute to the improvement of the world. In the meantime, they will continue to experiment until they discover their true calling, which will enable them to bring about the positive change they wish to see in the world.

Personality Number 33 indicates that the person who possesses that number is extremely friendly.

Such people care about other people and animals, and this is immediately evident to everyone. It may be explained by a strong sense of empathy and compassion for other people and animals. They are always willing to stand up for the underdogs and, on occasion, even play the part of martyr. People born under the number 33 have the ability to be positive role models for others because they want to bring harmony to all people and are motivated by this goal. Number 33s are known for their strong nurturing abilities. They develop into excellent counselors who are deeply committed to those near and dear to them. They take love very seriously, and they prefer long-term marriage and a warm, stable home life. Because of their compassionate nature, they are also capable of curing the wounds of others. For such people, every situation is an opportunity to learn something new, which is why they can appear to be excellent teachers at times. When they enter into an honest and warm union, they become content and are able to offer their nurturing abilities.

Chapter 13: Your Attitude Number

Your attitude number is the most important piece of your numerology chart. It is an expression of where you come from, your basic characteristics and traits, and the general outlook you have on life. It reveals what makes you who you are and gives an insight into why we do what we do.

It can also help facilitate goal setting for both personal development and general progress in life, as well as determining whether or not it's time for a change in your life. This number indicates what makes you a unique individual and how you see the world around you. It reveals how much of your personality is due to your background or situation in life and what aspects of yourself are created from your current circumstances.

How to Determine Your Attitude Number

To calculate your attitude number, all you have to do is add the numbers in your birth month and day together. You won't need your birth year for this one. As usual, you'll have to reduce the numbers down to a single digit. For instance, say you were born on December 25. Your attitude number would be:

December has 12 days.

1 plus 2 equals 3

Day: 25

2 + 5 equals 7.

7 + 3 = 10.

Reduce 10 to a single digit, and you have 1. Therefore, your attitude number is 1. In the words of one of the deepest philosophers of our time, that's "quick math."

Attitude Number 1: You're Driven

They're outgoing, social people who are all about action. They get things done and are willing to take the lead whenever necessary. They have high expectations and can be demanding at times. They're usually self-reliant, confident, ambitious, and self-assured, as well as strong-willed people who know when to follow their gut instinct instead of letting someone else lead the way. Deeply spiritual, creative, and intuitive with a strong sense of direction in life, they rarely make plans and prefer to go with the flow. They procrastinate as little as possible before going with their gut instincts rather than making plans ahead of time.

If this is your attitude number, you're the sort of person who doesn't like to seek help from others. When people think of you, terms like "driven" and "aggressive" come to mind. Sometimes people may think that you're a bit standoffish. However, this is only because you're very used to handling your own business, and you tend to be influential and a leader naturally.

Your Challenges: you're likely to be depressed, unable, or cynical if you refuse to act from a place of authenticity. If you are not currently an independent person in any aspect of your life, you must channel all of your energy towards setting yourself free, or else you will find your creativity and zest for life stifled.

Attitude Number 2: You're Persevering

People with this attitude tend to be obliging, benevolent, and pretty touchy-feely. If this is you, you're a very nice person. You're very in touch with your instincts, and you love everything mystical and otherworldly. More than anyone else, you are very aware of the vibrations and feelings that everyone around you exudes. More often than not, this means that you are influenced by the ideas and feelings of those that are physically closest to you.

Since you are very instinctual and mystical, you appear as quite an interesting individual. You have a very deep sense of empathy for people, and you are truly interested in how their lives are going. Usually, this is because you think your own life is boring, even though other people would beg to differ.

Your Challenges: You tend to take things a little too personally, and sometimes your emotions get the best of you because you are very sensitive. Try to understand that not everybody has the depth of emotional understanding that you do and that sometimes people aren't necessarily trying to hurt you but are simply ignorant.

Attitude Number 3: You're Dynamic

You're dynamic, alluring, clever, social, and savvy if you have this attitude number. You also have a wonderful sense of humor and an appreciation for the comical. More often than not, you're the life of the party. As long as you're part of a gathering, everyone's energy is positive and excited. The downside of this superpower is that everyone else feels the same way when you're in a bad mood. You never wallow in negative emotions. You're very quick to bounce back, and you often have a great time performing for people around you. This performance is not about being inauthentic but is rooted in a genuine desire to see people happy.

Your Challenges: Because you have a deep-seated fear of criticism, you might find yourself constantly keeping your dreams on the back burner. You may also do this because you have emotional baggage that weighs you down. Try to understand that no matter what you do, there will always be people who do not approve, and that is completely fine and is not a statement as to your worth. Also, it's fine to feel terrible and still take action on the things that matter to you. Usually, action will bring you out of that deep, dark well and spur you on to greatness.

Attitude Number 4: You're Sensitive

Those who have this attitude are dependable, reliable, dedicated, always faithful, and legit in all they do. You are a very grounded person, and so you're not a big fan of taking risks or surprises. For this reason, people think of you as being a little too inflexible and often assume that you don't enjoy life as much as you should. The reality of the situation is that you're simply concerned about other people and how they are doing. You are especially concerned about the people that are near and dear to your heart, and you don't want them to get wrecked by a reckless decision.

Your Challenges: Sometimes, you allow your inflexible nature to get in the way of your success. As much as stability and financial security matter to you, you can sometimes cut yourself off from avenues to success when you refuse to step outside your lane. You dare to do the unfamiliar sometimes. That is when the magic happens.

Attitude Number 5: You're Creative

When people meet you, they see someone who is brave, lively, and always bright. You have an uncanny understanding of change, and you're willing to accept it. You are very fun to be around and can be quite the coquette. You're the sort of person who enjoys being the center of attention, even if you don't necessarily struggle for it.

A brave soul is in touch with their sensitive side. You are the sort of person who's always on the lookout for new things. If something seems to be out of the ordinary, you are very drawn to it because you want to know a lot more. For this reason, you love to travel because you believe that there is a lot to experience in the world and you want to enjoy everything you can. You're probably the sort of person who says, "Try everything once."

Your Challenges: Your propensity to swing from one extreme to another can be rather disruptive if you're not careful. You tend to create unfavorable circumstances in life because you're trying to define what personal freedom means to you. The irony is that you will often create restrictions in your own life in your quest for personal freedom. To fix this problem, simply understand that you were always free. Keep your cheerful disposition and remain adventurous, even when you feel fearful. In fact, you should allow the fear to inspire you to take action anyway, and when things don't go your way, don't try to keep such a tight leash on everyone and everything.

Attitude Number 6: The Analyst

If this is you, you place friends, family, and lovers above everything else in life. You also have a deeply profound appreciation for your colleagues at work, especially when they help to make things easier for you. You have lovely healing energy around you that you can tap into if you want to. As a deeply analytical person, you tend to want to take control of all that you can, and you do this because you are particular about having perfect results. Something about you just draws many people to you.

Your Challenge: You have to learn to find balance when it comes to your sense of responsibility, especially when it comes to yourself versus other people. Because you have a tendency to be a perfectionist in all that you do, you may find that this perfectionist trait has a tendency to reduce your happiness and willingness to accept yourself or other people. Understand that you don't always have to get it right. Being flawed and making mistakes is part of the human experience.

Attitude Number 7: You're Harmonious

When people are around you, they get the sense that if they ever met Albert Einstein, he would probably be just like you. You come off as really thoughtful and scholarly, even scientific. You are very clever, and it's very obvious. You are a mystery in the flesh. The fact that you're a bit of an introvert just amplifies the mysterious aspects of you. You are usually one of the first people to notice when things are different, and you have the uncanny ability to analyze details that most people never think of.

Your Challenge: you have a tongue so sharp it can slice a molecule into a billion pieces. You can also be pretty sarcastic, often as a guide for your anger, expressing it in ways that you often playoff as a joke. However, you know, you're not kidding. You also have a tendency to be superficial about life. Try to temper your words with kindness and see things from other people's perspectives. When you feel upset, make a point of communicating that clearly and respectfully to the offending party. Also, stop being afraid of having things that matter to you in life. You can still dive deep into life experiences while maintaining an air of playfulness.

Attitude Number 8: You're Secretive

You are the one who can give the person with attitude number 1 a run for their money when it comes to leadership. There is iron in your veins, and you were very dedicated and passionate about finishing what others had begun and quit. You don't understand the meaning of the word "quit." This is why people often turn to you to lead them in major projects and situations in life, especially when it comes to politics, business, and entrepreneurial affairs. You are the ultimate provider, and you are excellent with finances. When it comes to making sure the people you love are cared for, you leave no stone unturned. If it's something that's going to make you money to be able to take care of your family, you can bet that you're interested in it because it's a little too hard for you to hold on to money for a long time. You know you have this tendency, and so you mitigate that risk by being proactive with your finances. When it comes to the way you relate to people, no one ever has to second guess what you say or wonder if you meant what you meant. This is because you're particular about being clear in your communications and leaving no room for doubt or questioning.

Your Challenge: you're not very good with authority. You're also not quite adept at letting go of hurtful and difficult things from the past. This is usually because you've had to deal with some horrific and challenging experiences from childhood, and so you continue to allow those past experiences to color your present and future. It's okay not to be the one in charge every now and then. In fact, by allowing others to shine every now and then, you show your generous and magnanimous side, and people appreciate that and will gladly let you lead, too. Also, realize that past results do not predict future outcomes and that at any moment right now, you can take charge of your life and choose something different and better.

Attitude Number 9: Prudence Personified

You are an extraordinarily gentle person who is very aware of other people's needs. If people had to describe you, they would say that you were the ultimate saint, the quintessential martyr. You're always more concerned about how everyone else is doing than yourself, and this is not from some need to be thought of as important or appreciated just because it feels good. You're a true bleeding heart in a good way, often concerned with making the world a much better place for one and all.

Because of your humanitarian ideals, charisma, and social pull, you are able to bring people together and get them moving on things that will be good for the world. This makes you a very powerful leader in a different way from attitude number 8 or 1 person.

Your Challenge: because you are so in touch with people's needs and how they can live much better lives, you sometimes find yourself going through hardship. Realize that as much as you want to save the world, you can't save those who don't want to save themselves. Also, recognize which burdens are yours and which aren't and which you'll need to enlist some help for. This salvation business is not something you can do on your own, and you're going to need all the help you can get. Another problem comes you're your tendency to often fight for other people, and you tend to easily get frustrated and exhausted as a result. Every now and then, you need someone in your corner too. Let someone else take the lead. It doesn't make you a terrible person to step back and feed your soul. Remember, you can't give what you don't have.

Chapter 14: Your Heredity Number

Your hereditary number is inherited from your parents. Usually, the father's name is the more prominent one, unless your parents decided to give you your mother's last name or join their last names to give you instead. This number gives you your backstory. It allows you to understand your roots and how they can affect you for the better or for worse. They also show you the way you interact with others socially. Think of this number as the entirety of your family tree's socio-cultural heritage. It helps you understand your family's vibrational set point. To be clear, this number may not have many far-reaching implications for your own personal life, so you shouldn't beat yourself up for not having the "right family" if you're not fond of the meaning of your number. Just think of it as a number with some extra information that you can use if you want to.

How to Calculate Your Hereditary Number

This number is calculated by summing all the letters in your mother's last (maiden) name and your father's last name. Let's assume your mother's last name is Jetson and your father's last name is Hall. We're going to work with our usual letter-number correspondence.

J + E + T + S + O + N

= 1 + 5 + 2 + 1 + 6 + 5

= 20

=2

H + A + L + L

= 8 + 1 + 3 + 3

= 15

=6

2 + 6 = 8

Your hereditary number would be 8. Now, let's check out the meanings of each one.

Hereditary Number 1

This number bestows you with a lot of confidence. You can be bold about going after your dreams because you have self-assurance. This is why you are very likely to be found at the top of the food chain no matter what aspect of life you are involved in. You're probably a loner, and because of this, you need to foster a sense of independence. Your desire for independence could be touched by a bit of egotism. Despite this, the fact that you can have a lot of time to yourself means you have endless opportunities to express the boundless creativity within you. Freedom and independence allow you the room you need for self-improvement.

When it comes to working, you're a natural-born leader, and everyone thinks of you as qualified and capable. This is why whenever you decide to give guidance or instructions to others, they quickly accept them. In other words, you are a master organizer.

You're also likely to be great in business, making huge strides where others fail. You have courage that lasts centuries and an iron that will never bend, no matter what obstacles challenge it. The energy of number one means you're likely to have major success in your professional life because you have deep ambition and are desirous of climbing the social ladder. You can also be pretty prideful and sometimes even a little too domineering. Every now and then, your nerves overwhelm you.

Hereditary Number 2

Your social skills are very impressive. There's nothing you love more than being in contact with other humans. You have excellent manners in your family and outside, which means that you are a great mediator and diplomat. You understand the importance of balance and moderation in all that you do. You're also very loved by your dear ones. You're the kind of person who many people flock to, seeking your company. And it's not just because you're a very kind person. You make an excellent colleague and partner. You are trustworthy, and you have common sense in spades.

You exude kindness and harmony. You know how to take your natural, peaceful nature and use it for the greater good, and there is nothing more that you appreciate than when two people can work harmoniously together or when two enemies become friends again. You value tradition and all things that are durable and solid. Your lifestyle is luxurious and sociable for the most part. However, that does not stop you from being patient and persevering when you have to achieve your goals. You're all about the finer things in life and feeling comfortable. For this reason, you will stop at nothing to make sure that you achieve your desires. Because of how kind you are, you have to be very careful about allowing others to mistake your kindness for weakness.

Hereditary Number 3

If this is your hereditary number, you have an uncanny ability to adapt, regardless of the situation you're facing. You're also incredible at assimilation. Because of these two traits, you never have issues with being misunderstood right out of the gate. Being absolutely clear is a talent for you. While not everyone in your family may be the world's greatest orator, chances are it's easy for you to talk because you have the gift of gab. This number is all about expressing yourself skillfully, and no one can argue that you are exceptionally sociable. In fact, some might even say that you're a bit of a chatterbox.

Number three is also all about creativity. So, when it comes to your job, you have a lot of options about what you'd like to dedicate your time to. You could be an artist, actor, lawyer, teacher, publicist, storekeeper, or politician. The world is basically your oyster. Beyond your ability to communicate clearly and effectively, you also know how to integrate everything that you want to learn or have knowledge of. You're not afraid of long studies because you are naturally curious and constantly inventive.

Hereditary Number 4

If this is your number, you have an awesome future ahead of you thanks to the skills that you've got, which are great in a working environment. Part of the reason you will be successful is that you have intrinsic motivations. The only downside to having this number as your hereditary number is that there is a chance you might be tempted towards extreme situations and positions. Because this number has serious energy to it, if this is your number, you are most likely to be a very sober individual with a reasonable outlook on life. Some people may mistake you for being dull (they may have done so, especially in childhood), but that's not the case at all. When you finally decide to master this trait you have, you will be respected by all.

You may not always be in a position of leadership, but the thing about you is that you can find solutions no matter how complex a problem is. You're able to spot things that no one else can see. This is because your mind is very organized and methodical in how it processes things. You have analytic skills that can help you work through all the information. You know what makes the world tick, and you know how to harness that information for your own benefit. You will do exceptionally well in a scientific career, especially in the social and natural sciences.

There is a lot more complexity to your character than meets the eye. You're not just about the method, but order. This is why, in situations of chaos, you seek to bring balance all the time. You're a righteous person who has a very strong moral compass, but you need to be careful about being too rigid in life because that could prevent you from experiencing greatness. You're a righteous person with a strong moral compass who is able to support society as needed. However, you need to beware of being rigid in your ways because you can be rather stubborn. On the whole, you're serious, and you have great, positive energy.

Hereditary Number 5

You're the sort of person everyone respects and accepts. Regardless of the language they speak, the country they're from, or how old they are, you tend to easily turn strangers into friends. Also, these are no ordinary friends. You inspire loyalty and everyone you meet. Your ability to seamlessly integrate with everyone does not mean that you are a master hypocrite or that you're a liar and inauthentic to yourself. You are simply truly loved and appreciated because of the positive energy that you put out. Your enthusiasm and passion for life continue to propel you forward. These are the same traits that make themselves obvious even when you crack a very simple joke or you're working on a very complex project. This is why you're a lovely person to have on your side, whether times are good or bad. You're the one who always breathes the embers of a dying flame back to life, whether it's a project or relationship.

The major themes of this number are perseverance and courage. When everyone else has thrown in the towel, you're the one who continues to fight, and you won't stop until you finally succeed. You're a dynamic person who's always going to continue pushing until you make something happen, which makes you an excellent colleague, a great worker, and a lovely friend.

Your perseverance has a very deep source. It comes from your desire to never yield to your own self. People may assume that your exuberance and continued drive mean you must have no inner demons of your own, but that's far from the case. Your drive comes from your continuous battle with the monsters under your bed.

This is why, even in the face of failure, you can find sufficient courage to carry things through. Even when you're sorely tempted to quit, you keep going. However, you do need other people by your side to make sure you're not heading straight for a ditch.

Hereditary Number 6

You are the sort of person who has learned about responsibility from a young age. In fact, it's a value that your family has, and it shapes who you are as a person. You are very particular about being ethical and moral in all that you do. You have a deep sense of justice, generosity, and honesty. You're the sort of person who people can trust because you're often dependable and can even be charitable. You have a deep, sincere love for other people, and you show your kindness very often towards them. You also have a deep sense of humanity, and this makes you very amicable because you seek nothing more than harmony between one and all.

This number bestows you with the energy of compassion and kindness, which could make you lean towards philanthropic interests. There's a huge chance that you will occupy a leadership position or eventually have a position such as this. You're a magnanimous leader, too, because you're very tolerant towards others, sometimes even more so than you are towards yourself. Because of your inherent sense of justice, you are the one who champions mighty causes, looking for truth and fairness in every situation. However, you tend to be hesitant and a little uncertain when it comes to your personal life. This is why you find it really hard to make the best decisions for yourself.

Hereditary Number 7

People with this hereditary number are often deeply interested in meditation and practice it frequently. They are naturally alert to everything that happens around them. Their inner life is really rich and intense, and this can make it very easy for them to mediate situations in real life with their intuition. They are also masters of moderation and all their affairs. These individuals have incredible skills when it comes to reflection and analysis. Their natural inclination towards meditation makes it so that there are reasonable, cautious, and discreet people.

They think that the phrase "no man is an island" is absolutely ridiculous, and they love nothing more than the life of a hermit. However, this is counterbalanced by their lust and curiosity for life, so much so that every once in a while, you may catch them coming out of their shells. These people have a very uncanny run of good luck all throughout their lives. If there's ever anyone who's always at the right place, at the right time, meeting the right people under the right circumstances, it's the one with hereditary number 7.

Hereditary Number 8

This is a number of dualities. There are times when its energy is so strong that it could be overwhelming, even though it has righteous traits. Those who have this hereditary number are very strongly determined, almost to the point of being authoritative. They command respect without uttering a single word. If you need two people who strongly oppose each other to find common ground, an 8 will make them see eye to eye. The eight are also naturals at getting people to be motivated when it comes to working, and this is why they make lovely coaches, CEOs, teachers, and heads of organizations and associations.

The strength they possess needs to be controlled, and that's why the 8s need to work on themselves to create a clear demarcation between impulsiveness and determination. The worst thing about their determination is that they can quickly become stubborn in an unproductive way.

If this is your hereditary number, you must learn to listen to others and really hear what they mean. Don't be afraid to reach out to them for advice. When you can do this, you will experience a renewal of strength with the clarity others can sometimes offer you, and being willing to ask and listen will make you an even better leader than most.

This number is also all about justice and having a strong sense of morality; the eight will make sure justice is served. They have the willpower to enforce fairness in all situations, and this is why they can't stand anything that smacks of spite or ego. They have to learn, though, that if they're not careful, they may see evil everywhere and come down so hard on it that they become the villain themselves, or at the very least, come off as obnoxious to most.

Hereditary Number 9

Those who have this number have a sense of self-respect and honor that can't be matched. When it comes to dealing with others, love, altruism, and self-esteem lead the way. They've learned how to enter or come out of all situations with their heads held high and their dignity intact. This penchant for dignity is strong in its roots. The one downside is that sometimes dignity can become pride, and it could stop them from seeing what needs to be seen or being who they need to be to advance in life.

This number has an aura of nobility about it, the sort you don't learn but naturally exude. It's rooted in empathy and devotion. The nine have a head full of generous insights that could lead them headlong into humanitarian cause after cause. As far as this number is concerned, solidarity is always the watchword, and so they're very quick to share what they have, no matter how little that may be. The furthest thing from materialistic, these people can't be swayed by offers of riches or fame or any of the shiny things the world tries to tell us are important. They are able to look at themselves and their thoughts holistically, and so they make excellent philosophers.

This number loves to travel to far-off, strange places. They love adventure, moving from pin to pin all over the map. What drives them most to move is their desire to learn about different cultures and minds, to see the differences in perspectives, and find the common threads that bind us all. They love lyricism and always welcome the opportunity to grow because, as far as they're concerned, there's no point to life if they can't be better than who they were yesterday.

Chapter 15: Numerology and Compatibility

You can use numerology to verify whether or not you and someone else are romantically compatible with each other. You don't have to just rely on sun signs, moon signs, and rising signs in astrology to find out your compatibility with someone. You can use your numbers because they're a very accurate representation of your energy and what you're about, and therefore, they can tell you how well you can blend with someone else and if your relationship has a future.

Now, to be absolutely clear, you can find love with any number, so please don't be one of those people who say, "I could never date a Scorpio" or something to that effect with numerology. All relationships require work when it comes right down to it. No one said it had to be easy, and Disney is not an accurate barometer to measure your love with. Love doesn't always have to last either, but you'll come to learn things about yourself within - and after -each relationship you're in. Love makes you grow, and it doesn't have to last forever or remain the same to do that.

Compatibility through the Lens of Numerology

When you want to work out how compatible you are with someone, using numerology, you should begin with these numbers:

- The Life Path number
- The Expression number
- The Soul Urge number

When you compare these numbers of yours with someone else's, you can quickly figure out whether or not they're a good fit—again, from the point of view of numerology. You'll know whether your ways of expressing yourselves will be a good fit or if you're likely to keep locking horns with each other.

If you're wondering if your relationship will last, there's a chance numerology can answer that question for you. However, I should mention that having to ask that question may mean you need to pause for a moment and think about what could be driving you to wonder about its longevity. Could it be that this person you're with began as a rebound that you hadn't meant to take seriously? Or are you still finding it hard to trust in love?

Another thing could be that you're both madly in love with each other, but circumstances make it, so you have no choice but to keep traveling away from each other, or you live in entirely different states. You may be wondering if things will work out for you. In this case, it's helpful to have your relationship number. You can also use numerology to learn about your partner, their needs, how you can both build a life together or amicably part ways, and so on.

Combos and Compatibility

Before we get into this, you need to know that you shouldn't be so quick to dismiss someone as being bad for you if – at first blush – it seems like you don't mesh well at all. Remember, you're talking about two people here, and the thing about people is that they're complicated. Remember, the idea is to compare each person's life path, expression, and soul urge numbers with the other's. If it seems like some numbers have been skipped, they haven't. There's no sense in looking at the 1 and 2 combinations only to look at the 2 and 1 again. With that in mind, let's get to it.

1 and 1

This is a powerful combination as long as no one feels like the other person is overpowering them. You both have very powerful ambitions, and sometimes this can cause some flooding and friction between you two. There is also a chance that you might both grow resentful of each other. However, when you give each other respect and space to be yourselves, it's possible for you to build something lovely. When it comes to clarity in communication, you're both going to find it easy to state what you want, and this means that your partnership is going to be full of honesty and clarity. The thing about this open communication is that there may be a lot of room for clashes of opinions and competition, so be on the lookout for that.

1 and 2

This is a warm relationship, but there's a chance it won't offer enough stimulation for either of you. Physical affection, support, trust, and being open and secure with emotional expression are hallmarks of this relationship. 1 takes the lead and is supported emotionally by 2. This is a lovely combination when dealing with the classic frameworks of husband and wife or employer and employee, although this doesn't mean the 1 and 2 combinations won't work in other forms of relationships. The important thing is that both parties are content to stay in their lanes. There's trouble in paradise when one decides to play a role outside of theirs.

1 and 3

These two are lovely for each other in terms of lighting a fire in their creative and imaginative endeavors and drives. This combination is full of inspiration, and there's never a dull moment for these two. In fact, there's a chance this could last a long time. The 3 is naturally open and affectionate, and this is something the 1 deeply appreciates. The 1 is a very driven person with a strong will, and this continues to inspire the 3. This is a lovely match indeed.

1 and 4

Usually, these two numbers don't mesh well with each other, at least not without a lot of love, understanding, and work. They both have very different viewpoints when it comes to life. However, this relationship has some serious gold to be mined within it because, as both parties have a very different approach to life, there are lots of lessons that can be learned that will help them stretch and grow in ways they could never have imagined if they were with someone more compatible. This doesn't mean you should go actively seeking this, but just know that if you do find yourself in this relationship, there's a lot of good even with the work. You should be aware that both numbers have a habit of not sharing their feelings, which means the emotional connection between both parties will leave a lot to be desired. The odds are this will become a source of frustration in the relationship, and, in the long term, things may not work out well. Don't just take the lessons you learned and move on.

1 and 5

1 has a strong will, while 5 has a free spirit. This seems like a match made in hell on the surface, but when both people actually put in the work to gain the other's affections, they can create a relationship that's vibrant, full of love and laughter. There's a chance that each partner will find it easy to offer the other the freedom they seek, and as a result, when they come together, it will always feel fulfilling. These two will find there's always something new to learn about each other, and this will keep the relationship going for a long time.

1 and 6

They have different ways of doing things, and yet they are huge fans of each other. There's a chance for them to build something that stands the tests of time and opposition, as long as they're each able to respect their different roles and respect each other. The 6 can be quite the nurturers, but they need to be careful about not nurturing the 1 to the point of over-mothering or "smothering" them because the 1 needs their space. Also, the 1 needs to make sure they make it clear how much they appreciate the 6. In other words, they both have to express their emotions clearly and with respect for the other person.

1 and 7

This match is an unlikely one, but it can offer loads of gifts for both parties when it does thrive. This relationship can become even richer when they choose to be understanding of each other. It's more likely than not going to be more platonic than romantic, being rooted more in the mind than the heart. The key here is to make sure they remain open and honest with each other. These two have common interests in information, history, and culture, and these pursuits can help the relationship remain interesting. If they don't have mutual interests, these two are likely to drift apart amicably.

1 and 8

"What happens when an unstoppable force meets an immovable object?" Well, this relationship is what happens. They are both dynamic and powerful numbers, and so when their worlds collide, you get fireworks. However, when it comes to the relationship, they're both domineering and assertive personalities, which may mean each person doesn't have enough room to thrive and be their best. Whether this relationship succeeds or not will come down to the willingness to compromise and offer each other enough attention, not just when it comes to work and goals but also in their personal lives. These numbers will need to learn humility and put in the work to keep their relationship alive.

1 and 9

These are at opposite ends of the numerological scale, and they can only do well together when they give each other space. They have mutual admiration for each other, but just like in the previous combination, they have to work to keep the relationship going while also not encroaching on each other's space. This relationship can be equal parts passionate and volatile.

1 and 11

This relationship will work out wonderfully well, just like with 1 and 2, except there will be double the insight and understanding here. The 11 is the visionary who gingers the 1's ambitions. However, it's important to maintain the very delicate balance of power here, particularly because of the 11's sensitivity. To thrive, these numbers have to see each other as equals.

1 and 22

As with 1 and 4, these two are going to need a lot of patience and hard work to succeed in a relationship with each other. The 1 needs to break new ground regularly, while the 22 brings twice the stability of the number 2, which could cause some frustration that ends the relationship before it's even had a chance to blossom. There are times when the 1 can drive the 22 in amazing ways, but this is the exception and not the rule.

2 and 2

This is a lovely pairing as no one could possibly understand a 2 like another 3. These people have no problem being very open with each other and offering themselves unconditional love and support. The stability and loyalty between these two are surreal. It's no Disney movie, but it is its own sort of magical. However, this pairing is not without its pitfalls because there's a chance that neither will have the chance to have the friction needed in relationships to help each other grow. In other words, it's not a match for those who value self-improvement.

2 and 3

These are very expressive partners, so this relationship will have love and passion in spades. Sometimes there may be flying tempers or colorful fireworks, but there's harmony rather than war for the most part. The 3s are easy-going and need to keep in mind that their second is very sensitive. Also, the two need to learn to express themselves in words whenever they feel their emotions or thoughts have been flippantly discarded or inadvertently disrespected by the three.

2 and 4

These could be a lovely pair. The 2 wants nothing more than loving commitment, and the four loves creating stability wherever they are; so this is a happy relationship. In fact, when these two meet and stop each other's breaths, there's a chance they'll get very serious very fast. However, it's almost like the 2 and 2 pairing in the sense that there may not be a lot of inspiration to be found here on account of the lack of friction. Perfect can become boring with time.

2 and 5

This pairing is a tricky one. The 5 wants nothing but to be free – and the 2 wants to connect. These are two different paths, and they will both feel very unfulfilled, having to deal with a lot of frustration over unmet needs. This means it's not likely that they can have a relationship that's beneficial to both of them. However, if they can find true love, there's a chance that the 5 can learn to be devoted and loyal, and the 2 can learn to let their 5 be free every now and then.

2 and 6

This relationship has potential. The 2 is emotionally sensitive; blending that with the 6's orientation toward family, this partnership can be full of understanding. However, the thing about any relationship with the two is that there's likely to be possessiveness and jealousy, and this is even more amplified with the 6. It makes sense when you consider that the 6 is very generous with their love. For this relationship to work, each side's need for personal space should be respected.

2 and 7

This combo can form a unique and lovely pairing when they're well-matched in a number of ways, and when they find these common threads they share, they can have a long-lasting relationship. These numbers lack nothing in the commitment department and are not afraid of things getting very deep to the point of having lasting love. They find a way to blend their hearts and minds beautifully well together.

2 and 8

These are among the most compatible pairs in numerology. The two bring emotional support and depth to the table, while the eight provides, which means they're both useful to each other. However, they both have to spend a fair bit of time getting to know the other person's unique traits because if they don't, they may take each other for granted, and their relationship may begin to feel like a steel cage.

2 and 9

People with these numbers are interesting together because they could either find it impossible to find their way out of the relationship with each other, or they could work toward becoming actual soul mates. They're both generous and compassionate, but the 9 exhibits these traits toward humanity as a whole, but not always toward the relationship. This could leave the two feeling very abandoned and hurt. Watching the 9 share their love with the world and not with them can be triggering for the 2, leading them to feel hurt and jealous. However, this can be fixed with affection and love within the relationship itself, leading to a romance that lasts with passion and intense affection.

2 and 11

This is a combination that could last forever. Just like with the 2 and 2, these two intuitively understand each other. The 11 is more likely to take charge in the relationship, acting as the elder or mentor, which works well for couples who find comfort in this dynamic.

2 and 22

This is a lovely combination that is similar to the 2 and 4, in that the 2 will find stability in the 22, and the 22 will find encouragement and emotional support from the 2. When these two fall in love, *they fall hard and fast.* The further along they go together, the more the 22 needs to be given space to interact with their spiritual side and not have to be the provider all the time.

3 and 3

What are you going to get with these two? Fun and chaos. The 3s are often attracted to each other right away, and they can inspire each other to lofty ideals, exciting each other at every turn. This is great if you're not looking for a long-term relationship, though, because the thing about 3s is that they're not stable, and there's hardly any commitment, at least not at first. This means that, before they know it, mundane living will get in the way, and what was once passion and fire will become boredom and exasperation. However, when these two are aware of this trait they have, they can have a love that lasts a lifetime.

3 and 4

This is a hard relationship. 3 is carefree and spontaneous, but 4 is careful and meticulous, so this will often cause issues for them both. The 3 can be quite the flirts and social butterflies, and this can make the 4 feel possessive and jealous, to the point of becoming controlling. The only way this can work for the long haul is if they make understanding each other their priority.

3 and 5

This couple is head over heels and enthusiastically into each other. They would also be awesome friends, constantly having adventures, laughs, and fun on their paths together. The thing is, they may both refuse to get into very serious conversations that need to be had, which means when problems rear their ugly heads, they're more likely to distract themselves and find ways to escape. If they both choose to work and commit to each other, there's a chance this could last a long time.

3 and 6

This is a lovely pairing that emphasizes family and social networking. They're both creative, which is a good thing. 6 is often the nurturer, making sure the relationship has all it needs for them to do well. If the 3 starts feeling a little too smothered or stifled, though, they may stray outside the bounds of their relationship and betray their partner. For this reason, 6 needs to let 3 be free. In turn, 3 needs to make sure they can give 6 the recognition and attention they need in the relationship.

3 and 7

This doesn't last a lifetime, but this pairing can defy the odds every now and then. When they find each other in love, it's an "opposites attract" situation. The 3 is caught in a flurry of social activity as usual, but the 7 desires nothing more than to enjoy their solitude. When the two can understand this about each other, and they choose to remain sensitive to their partner's opposing needs, they can do well together.

3 and 8

This is an unlikely pairing. The 3 are playful and creative, which means the materialistic and driven 8 may not get most of the time. There's, therefore, less of a chance for either one to do well in the relationship. However, there are times when they can find balance in their strengths and flaws, but that requires a lot of work, patience, and understanding.

3 and 9

These two are hard to miss in a crowd, and they always love impressing and intriguing each other. They have wisdom, passion, and creativity that keep things interesting and will make their relationship last for the long haul. However, they need to beware of financial matters and work as a team on this because finance isn't their strong suit and could be one of the major things that tear them apart.

3 and 11

This can be a successful relationship as with 3 and 2, with more depth, insight, and understanding. They're both intuitive and expressive, so as deep as their relationship can be, there's lots of fun to be had. However, 11 must take time to be on their own and recharge because they have different social needs than 3. Also, 3 needs to always remember that 11 is sensitive, even if they don't show it.

3 and 22

This one is very tough. 3 is carefree and spontaneous, but 22 is all about security and being able to see what's coming around the bend. These viewpoints can make it hard for them to coexist romantically, as they continue to feel misunderstood by each other. There can be times when the 22 funds the 3's talents and endeavors, but in the long run, this will not serve the 22 in a spiritual way.

4 and 4

This is a good match as they have the same goals and values, respect each other, understand how important order and stability are to each other and are willing to work hard for these values. They may butt heads every now and then, but their disagreements are just flashes in the pan that pass quickly. However, these partners may never be spontaneous or take risks, which means they can't have new experiences or grow.

4 and 5

These two numbers are very different temperamentally, which means they're not likely to be compatible. 5 wants to be free, but 4 wants to be stable and is looking for something for the long term. There's barely a chance these two will be able to give each other what they seek, which means a lot of unfulfillment within this relationship. The 5 will feel stifled, while the 4 will always feel anxious, never knowing if today is the day the 5 leaves for good.

4 and 6

This relationship is practical and offers the chance to have long-lasting bliss. They're practical, grounded in numbers, organized and dependable, and so this relationship will be firmly established on mutual trust, not romance and passion. They would have an even better relationship if they did their best to do something exciting every so often so that they didn't quickly get too comfortable and negligent.

4 and 7

A potentially great relationship, these numbers have traits that perfectly complement each other, yet they're different enough for things to remain interesting. There's a chance that their relationship may become more about intellectual and practical matters if they don't allow their hearts to open up to each other, so they need to fix that if they want this to last.

4 and 8

These are hard workers and great matches, who have the ability to plan for the long haul, and this brings the energy of reassurance, comfort, and stability, meaning they can both just enjoy each other with no worries. Practical issues are shouldered equally between the two, and they both feel like they're being treated equally and with respect. They just need to work on creating more of an emotional connection to make this a home run.

4 and 9

This relationship almost never happens, but it almost never lasts long when it does. The 4 is grounded and practical, which draws the 9 in because the latter tends to be quite unfocused. As the 9 remains open and relaxed, this teaches the 4 to ease up a little and not feel the need to have control over everything, going with the flow instead. If there's to be a deep connection here, that would depend on the other numbers in play with their numerology.

4 and 11

They are drawn to each other at first, but with time the 4 will find it hard to relate to the 11's spirituality, let alone share it since they're practical and very grounded. The 4 desires commitment, and the 11 can provide that. The 11 needs to feel safe, and 4 can give them that. However, 11 will eventually seek to break free, and it's not going to end well. If they both put in the work, though, they can learn a lot from each other, at least while they're still together.

4 and 22

These numbers are compatible as they have the same goals and values and therefore understand each other. However, the thing about master numbers is that at some point, they will have to be set free so they can explore their spirituality, and if the 4 doesn't give them the room to do this, the 22 will have to take it by force, or else there will be a world of resentment between these two.

5 and 5

These are twins that care about drama, adventure, and travel. They are aware of the need for them both to be free, and this means their partnership is advantageous for each other. They will never feel stifled or confined. There's a chance, though, that these numbers will completely ignore all the mundane things that, while "boring," are important to their relationship. They'd rather jump shop or distract themselves from the problem, so if this is going to be a long-term thing, they have to both commit and face the ugly as needed.

5 and 6

This is a relationship that can last, provided each party is open to making compromises. The 6 has a need for sanctuary and home, and that can clash with the 5's desire to be free. So, they both have to be very clear about what they need and how the other person can make that need happen, if at all they can. If they can make an agreement and hold up their end of the bargain, the relationship will flourish wonderfully.

5 and 7

There's so much potential with this pair. The 7 is fine with offering the 5 their freedom while they enjoy the stimulation and variety the 5 offers. In spite of them needing time apart, when they come together, sparks fly, oceans collide, and worlds are born. They just have to be willing to express their emotions as honestly as they can to keep this going.

5 and 8

This combo is a result of true admiration for one another, but there's not much to be had in terms of long-term commitment. This is due to the 8's desire for long-term commitment and structure, whereas the 5 is unwilling to have their freedom infringed upon in this manner. So, while there's a lovely dynamic between the two, it's not likely that they will make an effective team. When the love is strong enough, and they put in the work, making understanding front and center in their relationship. There's no height they can't attain together.

5 and 9

This couple is all about passion and adventure, and they can do well together when they give their "ship" enough energy and time. The only thing they need to be aware of is that their lives won't be intertwined enough to allow for a true emotional connection, so they need to be clear and open about what they want from each other.

5 and 11

This is a hard one. The 5s have to go exploring; the 11 needs to remain grounded and connected. That means they're not really suitable for each other. The 5 may think the 11 a little too intense. However, if the love they share is strong enough, it could work as long as the 11 has other connections that can feed their spiritual goals. However, this may not be enough to give depth to the relationship.

5 and 22

These have different temperaments, so they're very unlikely to go together. The 22 loves long-term commitment and stability, but the 5 isn't likely to offer that. They can mutually respect each other, but they're not likely to understand each other.

6 and 6

These twin numbers are very committed to each other, valuing creativity, health, family, and stability equally. They are intuitively in touch with each other's needs, and they can be amazing together when it comes to serving the world at large. However, they need to make sure they continue to maintain the balance in their home as well.

6 and 7

This can be tough, especially if partners aren't willing to compromise. The 6 may think the 7 is a tad too aloof for them, especially since they need some emotional certainty and control. However, if these numbers can try to be clear about what needs are going unmet with each other, and if they are both particular about making it happen, they could make it work.

6 and 8

This is a lovely combination that will do well in the long run if they both allow some compromise and put in the work. They're both very reliable and focused, which means they can have a love that lasts a lifetime. There can be trouble in paradise if they turn their docs on dissimilar interests, which is a possibility. The 8 might be more about their career and business, while the 6 may be more about the home and family, and this can be a problem if they don't take the time to understand how the other person has an equally important role and take an interest in the other's affairs.

6 and 9

This is a very fulfilling partnership for both parties. The 9 and 6 are idealistic, and they work hard too, so there's a chance they'll be able to meet each other's needs. They will have a powerful relationship when they're romantically connected, and this could last a lifetime.

6 and 11

This offers some mutual satisfaction. The 11 needs a safe base where they feel nurtured so that they can grow and explore their spirituality, and the 6 offers exactly that, which the 11 can see and appreciate. However, for this to last for long, the 6 needs to check their jealous emotions and exercise self-control so that the 11 isn't stifled in their development.

6 and 22

This is also a lovely relationship that can last a long time. They're both practical, grounded, and know how important it is to have a stable home. The ideal expression of this relationship has the 22 feeling secure enough to develop their spirituality, while the 6 understands how important their own role is as well, knowing the 22 doesn't take them for granted.

7 and 7

These are twins, so they *get* each other. This could be a deep and fulfilling relationship, and they both understand their desire to be alone and the other eccentricities they share. They are interested in each other, share their thoughts with each other, and explore their ideas and what they know. The trouble is, this number isn't the most grounded, so both of them will need to do their best to stay grounded each day.

7 and 8

This could work, but it may seem at first like these numbers have no business with each other. Where the 7 is more ephemeral and cautious in how they deal with things, the 8 is determined and a tad controlling. However, they can complement each other wonderfully and have a potentially long, rewarding relationship when they have other numbers lining up. They both have to make sure they remain emotionally open and that they're focused on more than just intellect and materialism so that they can get into the heart space and give the relationship solid ground to thrive on.

7 and 9

These numbers deeply appreciate each other and do not lack affection because their spiritual connection has remarkable depth. If they connect, there's a chance they're soul mates. If they aren't, the tension they experience being with each other will likely either gently challenge them to become better versions of themselves, keep them interested in the relationship, or have them part ways quickly. It all comes down to whether or not they will work to stay flexible and open when it comes to the other person.

7 and 11

This is like the 7 and 2, a unique blend, and if there are other commonalities with the other numbers you check them against, they can have a long life together. The 7 allows the 11 the space they need for spiritual growth, and the 11 will demonstrate how much they appreciate the 7 for partnering with them in this way. If the 7 doesn't give the 11 emotional closeness, this could become a serious problem.

7 and 22

A potentially good pairing like 4 and 7 would be ideal because they both have traits that beautifully complement each other and are different enough to keep things interesting. The 7 might become frustrated if they can't follow 22's schedule, but this is no cause for alarm because there's a chance these two will weather the storm and create a close, lasting relationship.

8 and 8

Being the same number means they understand each other. Success is equally important to this couple. This is a power couple, a prosperous one that can create the most lucrative, long-lasting business partnerships and marriages. The only issue here is that there's a risk of paying too much attention to work, to the point where the love and intimacy that *should* feed the relationship is missing. However, if they commit to keeping the flames alive, they will remain loyal to each other for a lifetime.

8 and 9

These are two strong numbers, both equally ambitious and determined, but they may have trouble connecting with each other because the 8 is more focused on power and money, while the 9 is more about humanitarian causes. The partnership may not last, or it could if they choose to see how they actually complement each other and learn from each other. It comes down to how much they want to make it work.

8 and 11

This is a pairing like the 8 and 2. 8 provides materially, and 11 offers emotional support and depth. They can be lovely together, but as time progresses, the 11 will need to pursue their spiritual goals, and this means they'll need space. If 8 can offer that, that would be great, and they could work together. However, it's not easy for these numbers to work out in a relationship because one person will definitely feel unfulfilled.

8 and 22

These two can work wonders when it comes to business and other matters. They love the security that comes with long-term plans and dealing with practical affairs, which allows them to grow in their personal lives. They can have a healthy and long-lasting marriage, and in fact, they make up a significant chunk of long-distance relationships, with them both being at ease with letting their partner have their space.

9 and 9

These two are the same, so they can last forever. They're both generous, passionate, and very happy with each other. They inspire other people in terms of relationship goals, and they bring a lot of good to the world.

9 and 11

These are a lovely pair as they're both generous and compassionate, but the thing about the 9 is that they share this love with one and all, and that could make the 11 feel like they're not being personally cared for and supported. Still, there's a chance that they both enjoy and appreciate being in the company of others and will allow each other the space to grow while having a safe space from which they can both come back and unite.

9 and 22

This is an unusual relationship that could lead to something life-long. The 22 is practical and grounded. This is not only attractive to the 9 but also useful to them. The 22s are visionaries, and their insight will continue to offer intrigue and inspiration to the 9. 9 is fine with giving 22 the space they need to grow, but they have to make sure they're there to help the spiritual master with structure and support when they need it the most.

11 and 11

The connection between these two is deep. There is unconditional support, love, and compassion, which both partners desire and offer each other. They're fine with opening up about how they feel, and they have a healing effect on each other. It's very intense in this relationship, though, so it's a good idea for them to loosen up a bit, do pleasurable activities together, and seek friendships outside of themselves so they don't become recluses.

11 and 22

These are a powerful combination, both needing safety, connection, and depth, and both need to be able to provide the same to each other. They can be themselves with each other and completely relax. These numbers are loyal and committed, so there's nothing that can shake their love for each other. Also, when it's time for one or both to go after their spiritual development, there will be a lot of understanding and no hard feelings, keeping their bond intact forever. Together, they can create great change in the world.

22 and 22

They are very compatible when it comes to their needs and desires, knowing how to support each other. Both of them are intuitive and can connect quickly and deeply. Things will move fast between them when they fall in love. They'll be fine when it's time for one or both to go after spiritual matters, and they have the potential to transform the world incredibly.

Chapter 16: Add Numerology to Your Daily Life

In numerology, the idea that numbers are valuable and meaningful is a given. Understanding the numbers that make up our birthdays and names can provide a deeper understanding of what makes us unique, similar to the way in which astrology does. Using numerology in your daily life can assist you in the following ways:

- Recognize your own personal advantages and disadvantages
- Make a list of specific objectives for yourself
- Face the challenges that come your way with confidence
- Make the most of your interpersonal interactions
- Recognize the signs and affirmations of the divine all around you on a daily basis

Although the study of numerology may appear to be extremely complex, utilizing numerology to bring insight and clarity to your existence does not have to be as complicated as it appears. This chapter will show you a few straightforward methods to use numerology to make the most of your life.

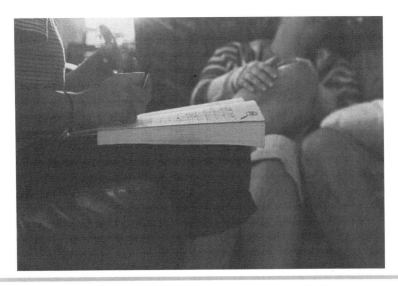

Numerology for Hiring Decisions

If you are a business owner or a manager of a company, you may have had the experience of looking for someone to hire and find yourself completely overwhelmed by the sheer number of excellent candidates for the job. The first thing you will have done, obviously, is to find out if their work experience is a match for the skill sets you require. You must have also taken a look at their qualifications, where they went to school, if they have any awards, and what their recommendations are. You may keep an eye out for professional bodies and associations or the things that they do in their free time, like volunteer work. You may have even made a few calls to their former employers to find out if they were great to work with. Now you have a shortlist that's really a long list and only one spot to fill.

Numerology can offer you a way to assess the character of the people you want to hire without needing to meet them face to face. Usually, when they apply, they'll have their date of birth on their resume and their full name, which should help you if you know enough about numerology. It's possible for someone to look very good on paper and still not be a great fit for your team. Since you know about numerology, you have an advantage when compared to other recruiters who have to sift through lots of meetings to make the right choice.

Making Good Investment Decisions

If you understand how to invest and make your money grow, that's one thing. You've handled all the technical, studied your charts, and learned all that you can about the companies that you think are worth backing with your hard-earned money. You may have tracked the performance of the CEO or chairman of a company and noticed that every time they take over a company, they tend to do extremely well. They could be all over the news on Bloomberg and CNBC as the "Person of the Year," and, for some people, that could be enough.

However, it would not be the first time someone who seemed to have integrity turned out to be nothing but a scam and fraud. They've had a long run of success, and it seems for a moment that they're doing fine until some dark and devious thing they did in the past comes to light, and that causes the stock of their company to crash. The odds are, if you had used numerology to look into them, you might have found something that would have kept you from investing your money with them. This is why, even after doing your homework with the more practical affairs, you should use numerology to suss out anything you might have missed or may not have seen in all your research. You can work with the names and birthdays of the CEOs to figure out whether or not they're worth your money.

- ## Planning Out Your Life

You can actually map your life out for the next nine years with numerology. Think of this as a forecast that helps you to figure out what's coming your way and how you can best prepare to mitigate the bad and take advantage of the good. There are many ways you can make these calculations. To make things simple, you can start by considering the date and month of each year in line with your personal numerology numbers.

The numbers indicate to you that, in certain months, you may be experiencing a lean period in finances. You can adequately prepare yourself to make sure you don't spend everything that you have. When it comes to your love life, if the predictions seem to indicate that there may be a rough period between you and your partner, you can begin to think about the things that you're dealing with or have yet to deal with and plan how best to address them going forward so that you can preserve the love you have. Numbers can be used to make life plans. Understanding how your personality is and how it works with others can help you take control of your life and make it a better one than you might have had alone. The types of relationships, financial decisions, and career paths that you choose can be based on the knowledge that numerology gives you about yourself.

• Be Clear About Your Destiny

Living life with no awareness of your destiny can be quite a scary and tumultuous experience. So, having learned such a powerful skill as understanding the energy of numbers, the first thing you should look at is what your destiny holds so that you can make sure that you're always in the right place at the right time and can take advantage of all opportunities that help you to actualize your greatness.

Since your habits form your character and your character drives your behavior, which leads to your destiny, you should understand what kind of character you have to take advantage of your strengths and mitigate the risks from your weaknesses. There's no better way to do this than by studying the numbers surrounding you. These numbers are an excellent way to learn about both your dark side and your good side so that you can see a trajectory of where you may wind up in the future, depending on which side you fuel.

• Learning How to Train Your Kids

As a parent, you naturally want the best life for your kids. You want to see them healthy and happy. As they grow older, you want them to succeed in whatever they decide to do. You send them to different classes to help them discover for themselves what they like and what they don't like. You encourage their dreams. You give them hope. However, as your life may have shown you over and over again, you know that success, happiness, and the good things in life are not necessarily a guarantee. You wish you could guide your kids right down the path that would be best for them, but how can you do that when you don't have a crystal ball? How can you be sure that you're raising them the right way and that you're not hurting them or their chances or their future?

By taking a look at the numbers in your child's life, you can learn a lot about who they really are and what would be best for them. The numbers can tell you about the negative and positive energies that they've taken on and how that will affect their character or behavior if you don't control it or help to hone it. When you have this information, you'll know what to do to help your child, and you'll be able to help them take better control of their not-so-great aspects so that they can do well for themselves in the future when you're no longer there to hold their hand.

- ## Figuring Out Viable Business Partnerships

Running a business means at some point in time, you might need a partner if you're going to take things to the next level. This partner will come in with the leverage and expertise you may not have. They could have a mouthwatering offer that makes it really difficult for you to refuse, and they may have an amazing track record as well. But the question is, does that guarantee you will find this partnership fulfilling?

You can use numerology to learn about your partner and see if they're compatible. Even though the compatibility we examined in the previous chapter is centered on love, here's the truth: the same things apply in business too. Make sure you evaluate your personal numbers and those of your potential clients, as well as the numbers attached to your business and theirs.

- ## Self-Upliftment

Numerology can be used to help you to understand your own personality and your strengths and weaknesses. Knowing your birth date can help you see how you react in different situations and find out if things are slipping through the cracks.

If you always seem a little overwhelmed under stress or feel like your impulsive traits get the better of you, studying your numerology might help you to better grasp certain hiccups in your life.

- ## Meeting New People

It is easy to spend time with only those you see as similar to yourself. If you know nothing about someone but they are a number of years or a week apart, there is a good chance that they have been through something similar to your own life, and that can be beneficial to you.

Finding out what their birth date means can help clarify why they may share certain traits with you. As you get to know them better, you can discover how the numbers in their name and birthdate relate to their personality.

- ## Understanding Your Purpose

Numerology helps us figure out why we are here on Earth, why we were created, and how we are going to live when we die. Knowing can help us make sure we're on the right path to becoming the grandest and best versions of ourselves. Every life has a purpose, and mastering our numerology can help us to find out more about that purpose. You may decipher your purpose by studying the unique attributes of your personality, the relationships in your life, and the decisions you have made throughout your life. All of these things are revealed by your numbers. Sometimes we know why we came here, and sometimes we don't. Numerology can help us figure out what the divine is trying to communicate through our name, thereby understanding how to fully express our authentic selves.

• Practical Living and Better Self-Management

As you spend more time learning what makes you unique, your life will be easier in various ways. You can manage your stress, realize why you might be impulsive, and make better decisions. The numbers are who we are; mastering their meanings and influences in *each part* of our lives will help us better manage ourselves *in all areas* of our lives.

• Improving Relationships

Your numerology information will also help you to master the relationships in your life. Learning the personality traits of others is important for happier and healthier relationships overall. You know right off the bat what your chances are with someone and whether you're willing to put in the work with them or not. Learning the numbers can also help to improve your relationships overall. You will be able to understand why certain people get on your nerves or become a source of stress in your life. Knowing what makes them tick will allow you to react in a more positive way, thereby helping everyone involved as time passes.

• Financial and Career Success

Some people excel above everyone else in every career; others seem to struggle just to make ends meet. Knowing your numerology can help you understand what makes you excel and what others do, which will help you make the best out of your career. As you start to gain more knowledge about numbers, your daily life will become easier. You get a lot of aha moments as you discover why stress might be a factor in making certain financial or career decisions or why you choose certain people as friends or associates. Knowing the numbers that matter will help you live a more fulfilling life.

- **Better Grasp of How People Think**

Numbers help us grasp why people think and react the way they do. You may find yourself in a situation where you cannot understand why an unruly child is throwing a tantrum or why an employee needs some encouragement from their boss. Knowing how the numbers affect their lives and what makes people tick will always be beneficial in daily life. You'll find yourself connecting better with others because of this, and they'll come to love you for it.

- **Finding Happiness**

To find happiness in life, we need to understand how we think and why we think the way that we do. Appreciating your personality traits and how they work with others will help you to find a more fulfilling life overall. Recognizing what makes you unique is an important part of every day, and your inherent uniqueness can be priceless. Numerology can show us why we are here on Earth, what our purpose is, why we need to make changes for the better, who our real friends are, and so much more about ourselves as individuals.

- **To Improve Your Mind and Make Better Decisions**

Figuring out what makes your mind tick, how it works, and why it works can help you be a happier and healthier person. Numerology is a factor in every aspect of life. Learning how others think and feel will help you improve your relationships, find happiness in life, and make better decisions. By recognizing the relevance of the numbers that define you, you will learn how you're perceived and present yourself so that you're less misunderstood. You will also be more aware of your cognitive biases and blind spots when the numbers show you your weaknesses. This makes you a better thinker. Numbers can show you why and how to make better decisions in life, allowing you to make the best of your time on Earth. You will be aware of what choices will give you the best overall results, and your personality traits will improve as time goes by.

- **To Improve Your Health**

Understanding what makes your body tick is a step towards bettering your life and making yourself healthier overall. Accepting how stress affects your body, how certain foods help or hinder it, and how these things affect your personality can help you make better decisions to improve the quality of your health and life.

• How to Improve Your Life

Knowing what makes us all want to work hard for our goals, be it money or success, is important. Working out why certain things or people motivate you and why others don't is equally important. Numbers, in general, and how they affect our lives on Earth, can truly help us acknowledge how we need to work on ourselves each day to improve ourselves physically, mentally, and emotionally.

Index of Terms

Life Path — Reduced number of your birth date that dictates your life.

Destiny — Reduced number of all letters in your birth name that reveal your talents and gifts.

Master Number — Number with the most powerful positive and negative traits. Often, double digits need not be reduced. 11, 22, 33 are master numbers.

Power Number — Other double-digit numbers besides 11, 22, and 33.

Karmic Debt Number — Number representing your lesson for this lifetime.

Birthday Number — Number based on your date of birth that offers insight into your character and luck.

Growth Number — Shows you the path to advancing in life.

Destiny Number — Shows your hidden skills and talents, as well as a trajectory in life.

Soul Urge Number — Reveals your inner desires and driving forces

Personality Number — Shows your kind of person and how you interact with others.

Heredity Number — Shows the familial forces that affect your life going back generations.

Part 4: Astral Projection for Beginners

The Astral Travel Guide to an Intentional Out-of-Body Experience

Introduction

So, you want to learn how to leave your body. The first time you heard about this, it was probably from that one kooky uncle of yours. He watches Gaia and insists there are reptilians and grays among us, so you had a hard time taking him seriously. Until, for whatever reason, you decided to look into this stuff, and you began to wonder how a whole lot of people could buy into the craziness. Maybe you started to notice a common thread with all the stories and decided there may be something to it after all.

Or, you may already have experience with the supernatural and paranormal and want another way to interact with the worlds beyond what we can sense. Perhaps you just saw this book, and for no particular reason, you decided it was next on your reading list. Either way, you made the right call picking this book.

There are far too many lies and myths surrounding the phenomenon of astral projection. It's tough to tell the difference between fact and fiction, especially if you've never even had a lucid dream before, let alone left your physical body. So, I've written this book to help you explore the wonderful world of the astral realm with confidence and a spirit of adventure.

Hop onto Google or another search engine, and type "astral projection." Once upon a time, you'd see a few results that could help you achieve it. Now, page one of those search results is packed full of Amazon ads. Right beneath those ads are a bunch of articles and blogs trying their hardest to convince you it's all in your head. "It's just a load of crap," they say. Or you find reviews of a show on Netflix with a premise that does more harm than good to the aspiring astral traveler. So, this book just had to be written because I felt a personal responsibility to fix that mess.

Other books tell you about the astral realm, give you one or two ways to check it out, and then leave you to your own devices. This one will take you by the hand and walk you through everything you need to know, from exit to re-entry.

Many of the best books on astral projection are sadly outdated and unnecessarily complicated, putting readers off the subject altogether. You'll find this book is a beginner-friendly and straightforward read, which will help you understand what the astral plane is and how to get there. You'll learn how to prepare your mind and body for your journeys, and the best methods to use that will give you successful projections every time.

We'll go over how to make your way through the astral plane without feeling like a total klutz and how to work through the various issues that can pop up along your journey. You'll also learn the correct way to return to your body. And we'll throw in a fantastic bonus, too. A 30-day calendar of affirmations, meditations, and mindfulness exercises that will put you on the path to successful astral projections on demand.

Section One:
Astral Projection Basics

Chapter 1: Understanding the Astral

If you're going to take a trip to a foreign country you've never been to before, then it makes sense for you to learn all you can about it. The same thing applies to the astral plane. The last thing you want is to take a trip somewhere, only to find your clothes are all wrong. Or that you're doing everything the natives find disrespectful (without meaning to, of course).

"The World in a Grain of Sand"

There is a lovely poem, "Auguries of Innocence," by William Blake, which begins with these lines:

> To see a World in a grain of sand
>
> And a Heaven in a Wild Flower
>
> Hold Infinity in the palm of your hand
>
> And Eternity in an hour

Those lines are the most beautiful and apt description of the astral plane. First things first, though. The world you know is not the only one. Now, it's easy to assume that this statement isn't true. After all, we live in times where science is king—and while that's not a bad thing, it does mean that unless you can observe a phenomenon physically, it doesn't exist. You could say that scientists are the true pioneers of the phrase, "Pics, or it didn't happen." Sure, there are those scientists who dared to explore topics considered "fringe." However, we're still a long way from the level of open-mindedness we need to make more progress in exploring consciousness.

The physical world you're in right now is but a teeny, tiny part of all of existence. Some things exist outside of waking awareness, which you cannot perceive unless you tune to the right frequency of consciousness. The trouble is, we've all been taught that there is nothing to life but the material things you can detect with your five senses.

Right from when you were a kid, your parents told you that your dreams were not real, and that your friend who cheered you up when you were down was only imaginary. Most of us heard this enough that we bought into the lie. However, some of us were fortunate enough to have had experiences that caused us to wonder, even into adulthood, "What if there's more?" Chances are you've had an experience that has led you to this book. So, you should know right now: you're not crazy. There is more to life than meets the eye.

Let's get back to William Blake's poem, so you can grasp the idea of what the astral plane is. Imagine you're holding a grain of sand and in that single grain is the Earth, all other known planets, and our universe. Now, imagine standing on the beach. Try to grasp the fact that all that sand is a universe of universes.

Think about the idea of having all of infinity, or timelessness, in the palm of your hand. In the astral plane, you could experience an entire lifetime, only to return to the physical and find that just ten minutes have gone by. I should mention that this is not always the case, though, as you can wind up in a section of the plane that closely matches physical reality and time.

The Astral Plane

You can pick up your car keys and drive to the mall, but you can't just visit the astral plane without the proper vehicle because it's outside of our 3D world.

Some believe that when you die, you leave your physical body and go to the astral plane. People think it's a spiritual waiting room, of sorts, between heaven and Earth. From this point, you can either return to Earth for another game of "Being Human," or you can ascend to higher planes of existence.

The truth is, you function on more planes of existence than just the material and the astral. Still, your waking consciousness is primarily focused here on Earth. The astral is beyond the physical; it is the world of psychic phenomena, spirits, and dreams. It connects your material world to your rich, mystical one.

Sufism, Kabbalah, and Spiritualism all acknowledge the existence of the astral realm. Likewise, the New Age Movement, Theosophy, and Eckankar have philosophies centered on it.

Helena Petrovna Blavatsky, one of the founders of the Theosophical Society, put forward the idea of Masters, also called Mahatmas. They are human, or used to be human, and have now transcended from the Earth realm to the astral.

Paul Twitchell's Eckankar is also called the Ancient Science of Soul Travel. Just as the name implies, initiates are taught various ways to commune with the astral realm and communicate with the Masters. The latter exist there to offer guidance, healing, strength, wisdom, and whatever else one may need to make it through the grueling grind of life on Earth. The students of Eckankar, called chelas, learn how to experience the Sugmad (God) by traveling along the Audible Life Current called the Eck, which flows to and from the Sugmad. The goal for the chela isn't astral travel but to finally make their way to the Sugmad.

The New Age Movement is a beast with many heads. While there are various beliefs and methodologies for getting in touch with the worlds beyond this one, they all share a common belief in the astral plane. Some schools of thought believe you can only go to the astral realm when you die, or in a dream. However, most New Agers experience this plane while alive by deliberately inducing lucid dreams or astral projections—which are also called out-of-body experiences (OBEs), soul travel, or astral travel. Other ways to get to the astral plane include meditation and near-death experiences (NDEs). The latter is something you should definitely *not* try to induce, please.

The astral dimension comprises seven key levels or planes. Each plane has its own variety of sub-planes and on and on. It may sound like you could get lost in there, but that's nothing to worry about, since one way or another, you will return to your body after every exploration. This plane of existence covers the entire material world, and yet, it does not exist spatially. Instead, it vibrates at a much higher frequency than our material world.

Think of the astral plane as the world's tallest skyscraper—but infinitely taller. Every floor is a sub-plane in the astral, with its own unique qualities, occupants, rules, physics, and energy. The floors closer to the bottom are of lower vibrations. Now, "lower" isn't necessarily bad; it just means that the energy here is denser. These planes are closest to the Earth. Chances are, when you first leave your body, this is where you will wind up. You'll find other projectors like you, as well as those who actually live in these planes.

All Your Bodies

You have at least six arms, six legs, and three heads. Before you go feeling around for them, allow me to clarify. You have three bodies:

- Physical

- Astral

- Causal

Your physical body is also called your gross body. No, not "gross" as in ugly, but as in obvious. You can see it. You already know what your physical body looks like, so I'll spare you a recap of Biology 101. It's the body you use to do everyday human things in this ordinary human world.

According to Vedanta, this body is called the **Sthula Sarira** and has three major phases: *Sambhava*, which is birth; *Jara,* meaning old age; and *Maranam*, or death. In addition, this body has five elements; *Vayu* or air, *Prithvi* or Earth, *Agni* or fire, *Apas* or water, and *Akasha* or ether. To replenish these elements, we must eat right, practice mindfulness and meditation, and consider yoga. The practice has poses that recharge each element of your body. Upon death, the elements split from one another.

Your astral body is the body that has your energy centers or chakras. In Vedanta, it is the **Suksma Sarira**. This is your energy body, the one that connects you with All That Is, or the stuff of life itself. This life is also called Prana or Qi. It keeps your physical body functioning correctly. When your mind is clouded with negative thoughts and emotions, the life force can't move freely through your body.

This body has emotional thought and vital power. When you're awake, you may have a hard time connecting to the astral body. However, when you're fast asleep and dreaming, you move about primarily in your astral body. With this body, you can feel pain or pleasure. It's intricately connected to your senses, intellect, and mind. It helps you with involuntary body functions like metabolism, breathing, digestion, and circulation. It keeps your brain, skeletal, and muscular health in check as well.

This body is usually modeled off your physical one, but there's no need for it to maintain that shape and form. I remember the first OBE I had when I realized I could see all around me at once. It was not because I had eyes all over my head, but because what we really are is consciousness. While on previous travels, I saw things as though I was looking through my regular eyes. On this occasion, I was able to see the entire room from multiple angles at the same time. That's just one of the mind-blowing phenomena you can experience during your astral explorations.

Another intriguing thing about being in your astral body is that you will realize the power of your thoughts. You will witness them come to life and notice things adapting as quickly as you change your mind about them. When you begin your practice, observe this thought power you possess and realize that this is exactly how the physical world works. The only difference is that your thoughts must move through space and time to manifest on Earth.

Your causal body possesses all the information about you and your many lives, present and past. It is the **Karana Sarira.** You can connect with your causal body from a place of deep sleep where thoughts or emotions do not bog you down. This body has all the data on your desires, hopes, fears, and perceptions. It's called the "causal" body because it affects your waking consciousness, as well as your dream states. Upon death, the causal and astral bodies leave the physical ones.

Resembling light, the astral body is already tricky enough to perceive from waking consciousness. The causal one is even more subtle than the astral one. It holds a record of all karmas from all your lives. It is thanks to the information it has that you have the character you do right now. The Creator works through the causal body to connect with us all, giving us divine revelations on how to live a joyful life—if we could only listen!

This doctrine of three bodies is held in high regard in Hindu philosophy. The physical body, which survives on food, is the frailest and the first to go. The astral body thrives on emotions, thoughts, and feelings. Therefore, it can go on for much longer. Finally, the causal body lives the longest, receiving life from the process of discovering one's self, as well as peace. Just so you know, there's no more terrific way to find yourself than to interact with the astral realm.

Mind: Cementing Your Bodies

Before you reach out for a glass of juice, you first think about doing it in your mind. You see yourself reaching out, feel the cool glass, hold it, and put it to your lips in your mind before you make an actual move physically. The same applies when it comes to your mental and causal bodies. You can't work any of your bodies without using your mind.

Sadly, a lot of people assume they cannot control their thoughts and emotions. They believe every thought they have is true. Without question, they accept those thoughts and the feelings that arise with them, even when doing that doesn't serve them. You must understand that the mind is a tool. It is a machine meant to serve you. If you're going to enjoy your astral journeys, and grow on account of them, then you need to know that your mind is a tool you use.

You are not your hands, feet, or eyes, yet you use these things like tools. You must see your mind the same way and master it. Remember I mentioned that the astral plane is very sensitive to thought? You can surely see why it pays to be in control of your mind. To be a successful astral traveler, you should train your mind to accept that soul travel is a safe and easy thing for you to do. This way, you have a greater chance of success. Your mind can achieve amazing feats because Source is quite literally the source of its power.

Most people allow their minds to run wild, sometimes to the point where they wish they could escape their own heads. If you can relate to this feeling, know that you can take back control. The first step is to realize that **you are not your mind.** The next thing you need to do is understand **the thoughts in your mind are only true IF you accept them as true.**

Who Are You?

So, you've just found out that you have at least three bodies—five if we go with Sadhguru's explanation: the physical, mental, energy, etheric (astral), and bliss bodies. On top of that, you've just learned that you're not your mind. You're not your body either. That will understandably leave you wondering about your true identity. For you to traverse the subtler worlds, you must know who you are. You are the Source itself, having a never-ending adventure here on Earth as a human being.

Like Maharaj Jagat Singh explains in *The Science of the Soul*, your soul came down into the realm of the mind and then moved further away from its real self until it forgot who it really was. It forgot that it is Alpha and Omega, undying. It chose instead to think of itself as a body. It went from being the causal body in the causal plane to identifying as the astral body in a realm full of illusion. Finally, it came down to the material world, clothed in flesh, in addition to its astral and causal coverings. For this reason, the soul's light is usually dim in this world. Many would call you a nut-job if you suggested that they are not their bodies, minds, identities, job titles, names, and so on.

Dim as the light of most souls are, the fact is you can't snuff out that light completely. Night after night, we still dream. We transcend our physical bodies to carry on other activities in nonphysical realms. It's just that some people are aware of their travels and what they do during these times, while others are not. You're reading this book, which means you would like to master your astral life. Deciding to become aware of the other aspects of yourself is a solid choice. With dedication and patience, you will enjoy all the benefits of your increased awareness in everyday life.

Chapter 2: What Is Astral Projection?

Now let's talk about astral projection—not the Israeli band that plays psychedelic trance, but the phenomenon itself. Astral projection, or astral travel, is the process of deliberately having an out-of-body experience. It is the separation of the astral body from the physical one to travel on the astral plane.

While the term was coined by the Theosophists of the 19th century, this phenomenon is as old as humans and spans various cultures. In addition, there are multiple means to achieve astral travel. For example, some use meditation, and others use relaxation and visualization techniques and hypnosis. Finally, some use hallucinogens, but that is outside the scope of this book and not recommended.

Sadhguru talks about astral projection as removing your etheric body from the physical one. Since it's such a hot topic these days, some charlatans push the idea that it's just about lying down and visualizing or imagining you're out of your body. That's not it at all. Astral projection isn't imagination. You will feel a definite sense of yourself stepping out of your physical body. You will be able to see your body on the bed or chair or wherever you left it—in the most literal sense of the word "see." There is no make-believe here.

Remember, you're none of your bodies, and you're not your mind either. As weird as that sounds, it's true. What you are, at your very core, is pure consciousness. So you see, when you astral project, you turn your awareness from the physical plane to focus on the astral one through the astral body.

When you use the proper techniques, you will be able to leave your body and go wherever you please. You can visit physical locations worldwide or locations that aren't known to us here on Earth. You can fly through the clouds, or my personal favorite, take a trip to outer space, where the colors of every star and planet burst with color and life. You can connect with other astral travelers or heal yourself or a loved one. You can receive inspiration for your next book or painting or receive instruction from your guides on issues that matter to you. You can gain clarity about what you should be doing with your life or even take a peek at what the future may have in store for you or the world as a whole.

You can do all of this and more because the astral realm is the 5th dimension of life, meaning this realm is outside the confines of time and space. Therefore, past, present, and future exist in the interminable now, so you can learn what you want.

Astral Projection versus Lucid Dreaming

Lucid dreaming and astral projection are both fantastic, yet they are not the same. Lucid dreams are subjective. They are your own experiences and allow you to play with infinite scenarios. However, astral projection is objective because the planes you visit really do exist, and much like in the physical realm, they have their own limits and laws.

Lucid dreaming happens when you wake up in your dreams. Dreams can be pretty absurd and nonsensical. You could be running around the street in your birthday suit demanding to see the Prince of Timbuktu, and you wouldn't think it strange. The reason is that when you sleep, your brain's critical faculties also take a break. This means you don't question any of the weirdness going on. Lucidity is achieved when you wake up in your dream and realize, "Hey, I'm dreaming!"

Typically, when people realize they're lucid in a dream and haven't had much practice controlling their minds, they get a little too excited. Unfortunately, this excitement causes them to slip back into thinking the dream is real or waking up completely.

Here's something super cool you should know. You can astral project *from* a lucid dream. All you have to do is intend to find your physical body, and you're now astral projecting. Whatever you do, don't get too close to your body, or you'll probably wake up. Also, you may experience a strange sense of bilocation, meaning you can feel you are two people, in two bodies (astral and physical) at once. With practice, you should find it easy to shift your awareness to the astral one, so you can get on with your travels.

Astral projection is a whole other thing. You don't dream. You enter into a state where your mind is awake and your body asleep, and then you perform the exit procedure that works best. You will experience your astral body separating itself from your sleeping form. Again, nothing about this is imagination. You will feel actual vibratory sensations, hear loud sounds, maybe voices, maybe singing. When you're astral projecting, you will know it without a doubt.

In a lucid dream, you can control everyone and everything around you. For example, you could turn the sky yellow or build an entire airplane out of marshmallows. You can make someone look like a clown or an ant. There's nothing off limits to you.

When it comes to astral projection, the only things you can manipulate like this are all things that have to do with yourself. You can change how you look, give yourself a different body or face, conjure up tools you need, and so on. However, you can't control the people and other entities you run into because they have free will like you. Like you, they are sentient beings. Just like you wouldn't appreciate someone trying to dictate your life, they don't like that either. When it comes to the environment, you may find it's not easy for you to control it by issuing commands. You'd need to generate energy by using your intention to get them to do your bidding.

Spontaneous Projections versus Deliberate Projections

Deliberate astral projection, obviously, happens when the traveler consciously decides to go visiting that plane. There's planning involved, and you know exactly what you're going to do when you come out of your body.

Now let's address spontaneous travels. I was drawn to the exploration of consciousness because I had my very first projection as a kid. It was unexpected, and it was pretty scary, but only because I was unaware of what was going on at the time. Before that experience, I would often have trouble with sleep paralysis, which is when your mind wakes up before your body does, and you can't move. The reason that happens is that when you sleep, your body shuts down all nonessential motor functions so that you don't act out your dreams. So, when your mind is up and your body hasn't noticed, you just stay there, unable to move. Had I known then what I do now, I would have begun my exploration a lot sooner!

My experience was frightening because I could see my body, and I was floating up and away from it toward the ceiling. By the time I got to the ceiling, the fear magnified by a hundred as I thought to myself, "So this is how I die. I'm not ready for judgment."

Coming from a religious background that involved a lot of guilt-tripping, you can see how scary the idea of death must have been to a teenager. With that thought, I felt a force like a giant hand shove my astral body back down, and I rejoined my physical body.

I knew it was real because everything in the room looked and sounded the same, and I was lying in the same weird position I was in—coffin style. It took about ten years for me to get the courage to research what had happened to me. It turns out, it was a spontaneous astral projection. You don't plan for them to happen. They just do, whether you want them to or not.

Have you ever felt strange, intense vibrations coursing through your body when you wake up a little, in the middle of the night, too tired to get out of bed? Or have you ever experienced the phenomenon of sleep paralysis? Then know that each of those times, you came really close to having a spontaneous astral projection.

Sometimes, during these spontaneous projections (as well as deliberate ones), you may receive help from another being or traveler with leaving your body. They may grab your hands or your feet to help you out. (Other times, no one's helping, and it's just hypnagogic hallucinations). However, because most people are unfamiliar with the astral and how the mind works with it, they become terrified. That fear causes them to misinterpret what's happening. What may have been a benevolent being helping you is misconstrued as a demon trying to yank you down to hell or something.

Scientific Proof of Astral Projection

December 1, 2011, the CIA partly declassified a sanitized copy of a document on astral projection. During the Cold War, the traveler was tasked to journey to the USSR to locate a specific facility. They found it and gave the precise coordinates of its location. The traveler also provided many valuable details about what it looked like on the outside. For example, they said there were dish antennas, helicopter pads, and other things on site. The traveler also learned that in addition to receiving the Soviet satellite's downlink, the antennas were also used to intercept downlink from US satellites.

Now for the moment of truth. The CIA went to find this facility, and they did. Even though there were different numbers of dish antennas in various dimensions from what the traveler shared, they were there all the same.

In another double-blind experiment, the CIA gave the traveler coordinates of a little island in the Indian Ocean occupied by the Soviets. The experimenters did not have this location on their map. They even thought that the traveler would encounter nothing but water—until the subject began to draw a map on a large scale, needing more and more sheets of paper. When they were done, the CIA put all the sheets together, and what they found was a precise match of the island. It was such an accurate drawing that it also detailed the topography of the island. The traveler was also able to tell the CIA exactly what was going on over there. These are just two of the experiments with astral travel documented by the CIA.

Do a quick Google search about astral projection. You'll find so many trying to discredit it, from those who say, "Well, it both is and isn't real," to those who flat out stamp it as a pseudoscience not worthy of exploring. Actual astral travelers find the confidence with which naysayers dismiss this phenomenon to be mind-boggling at worst and hilarious at best. However, the skepticism is understandable, since this is one thing that a person needs to experience themselves to accept it as valid. Without personal experience, skeptics think of astral travelers as insane. If they're polite, they'll say something like it's just the neurons in your brain doing "neuron-y stuff."

Suppose you're willing to go past page one of Google (or use a different search engine altogether) to dig into research that doesn't start out trying to disparage or disprove astral travel. In that case, you will find a lot of information that proves OBEs can be verified scientifically. Skeptics should consider that the scientific community deemed lucid dreams "unreal" until as recently as four decades ago.

To look deeper into this phenomenon, you should check out books by Robert Monroe, Robert Bruce, Hereward Carrington, Oliver Fox, Sylvan Muldoon, and Graham Nicholls. These pioneers are why modern-day astral travelers have made such great strides in their discoveries about the astral realm and the mechanics of leaving the body.

Moreover, they were unafraid to explore this "fringe" matter during times when conventional science and religion were even less accepting of taboo subjects like this than they are now. Hence, we owe them a world of gratitude.

Mind Is Key

I have already touched on this subject before, but it's so vital that it bears repeating. Your mental habits and ability to control your mind will significantly serve you when you begin astral travel. Here's why you need to keep your mind "in mind," so to speak, before you start your journey.

1. **You must mentally accept that you _can_ leave your body.** If you don't buy into this, you're simply making the process a whole lot more complicated. Ask yourself why you're fighting the idea. It could be a result of fears that you have about the phenomenon. Those fears will be addressed soon enough. Once you understand what you're getting into you will know there's no reason to be afraid. Your mind will be more receptive. You need to realize that many of the horror stories you read about astral travel resulted from the state of mind that the projectors were in. Fearful minds attract experiences to be afraid of. Remember that.

2. **You must be in the right frame of mind when you project.** For example, suppose you've had a terrible day at work. In that case, you're stressed out, anxious about something, feeling angry or hateful. You shouldn't be traveling to the astral plane in that state of mind. There's a big chance that everything you encounter in the astral world will be of a low energy vibration, which means more frightening experiences for you to contend with. When this happens, the odds are you'll never want to project again, and your mind will run with that and always shut it down no matter what.

3. **Your mind is the chief way you can control things in the astral world.** Forget about physics. Your mind is the way you move and determines your experiences. Think about flying, and you're doing it. Want to go somewhere? Think of being there, and there you are. Think of seeing someone, and there they are. So, it only makes sense that when you encounter scary-looking beings, letting your mind feast on fear will make everything worse.

In summary, your mind's job is to help you realize you can project. It's also supposed to help you relax enough to allow the phenomenon to happen and keep you in control of your reactions and impulses in the astral.

Another thing is that most first-time travelers get so excited at seeing their bodies that they're drawn right back in before they can explore. It's understandable to be excited, but you want to keep that in check and remain calm. The way to do that is to rehearse the whole trip in your mind. See it through from start to finish, refining whatever details you must. The more you imagine seeing your sleeping form, the less novel it will be when you finally do leave your body. If you don't get sucked right back in, that gives you more time to get used to your astral surroundings and execute your plan with no pressure at all.

Chapter 3: What to Expect

So, you want to go on an astral adventure. Well, it's only fitting that you should know what you're getting into and what to expect on your journey.

Vibrations

Most experienced astral projectors can tell you about the vibrations. When it's your first time experiencing them, they can feel quite disturbing. As I described before, it feels like you're being electrocuted, but there's no pain. The vibrations are simply very intense when they come. When you start to feel the vibrations, it's best to allow them to do their thing and keep your mind as calm as possible.

Some people erroneously assume that the vibrations are what cause projection. That sensation is simply a byproduct of what's going on within you on an energetic level as you stir up your astral body. During the vibratory stage of astral projection, anyone observing you would see that your physical body looks perfectly fine and isn't vibrating at all, despite what you're feeling.

Sometimes, you may get the sense that the vibration is only happening in specific parts of your body. This means that your astral body is being formed in these parts. You may feel that they're floating outside of your regular body. This is nothing to be alarmed about. This happens because those are the parts of your body that are completely relaxed and free of tension. If you carry tension in any part of your body, you may find your astral body stuck at that point when you try to leave. This is why a deep relaxation technique should be employed before you try to exit your body.

Distortion of Physics

There are some planes where the astral world seems to mimic the physics of the physical one completely, but this isn't always the case. Most of the time, you'll notice things are very odd. You could hold your cellphone, or at least the astral copy of it, and wonder why it feels as light as a piece of paper. You could walk and feel your feet are both off the floor for several seconds longer than usual.

You can walk through walls, drop through the floor, jump through the ceiling. You can make it to outer space in three seconds flat. The rules of the physical world go entirely out the window.

Mind Split

You may notice a feeling of bilocation or duality, where it's like you're in two different bodies at once. But, of course, your consciousness is limitless, so it's not such a stretch to entertain the fact that you really can be in two places (at least!) at the same time.

Your body isn't left as an empty shell when you switch your consciousness to the astral. Your consciousness is still there. So, while *Behind Her Eyes* (2021) was an excellent show, its suggestion that your body can be possessed by someone else is completely ludicrous and nothing for you to worry about.

This mind-split phenomenon has led to the assumption that such things as "astral watchers" and "sentinels" exist and require you to cast protection spells against them to stay safe. Unfortunately, many don't realize that you're always safe, and you have a silver cord that keeps you alive. It connects you to your body and can't be severed except when you die. So, there's no one watching and waiting to pounce on your "empty" body.

Get rid of the notion that your body is empty when you go exploring. You have to, because knowing this will help you get better at recalling your journeys. All you need to learn then is how to download the experiences you had in your astral form into your physical brain.

Fluctuations in Reality

As a new astral projector, you will have to contend with the fluctuations in reality when you've successfully left your body. One second, you're in your room, and the next, you're at the burger shop watching people order... cars.

A possible reason this happens is a lack of control over the mind. Most people are always thinking. You can probably relate to having steady chatter going through your head, day in and day out. You may see something or someone that causes you to think a thought in the astral realm, and that thought manifests before you, adding to the fluctuation. Your subconscious mind demonstrates its power before your very eyes. This portion of your mind is capable of creating the most intricate and impressive of worlds in a matter of seconds. If you're full of fear, then you can bet your subconscious will generate scenarios that will make you call out for your mother.

I'm Melting!

Whenever you try to take a close look at your astral body parts when you're out and about, you will notice that they melt in a matter of seconds. This is especially true when it comes to the hands. Look away, and it all feels nice and solid, but look again, and you'll notice you're getting stretchy and melting away. Likewise, your fingers can look ridiculously long, or you may have too many of them. Don't worry about any of this. If it bothers you, look away and look back, and they should be okay again. The intriguing thing is that nothing else you look at will melt away as you observe it—just you.

While we're on the subject of hands, if you ever find that your environment is too unstable, all you have to do is look at your hands. For some reason, this will send a little shock wave from the astral body to the physical. This helps keep the fluctuations in check and stops you from forgetting you're projecting.

All Here, All Now

Don't be surprised if you find yourself in a different period on Earth, whether past or future. Of course, it all exists now, but we experience linear time and not simultaneous time because we live in a world of time and space.

You can drop in on the lives of your past and future selves, as well as all other alternate selves that exist. It's a fascinating way to explore choices you may want to make for yourself in your actual life that you may never have considered if you hadn't dropped in on your other lives.

Astral Projection Stories
Leaving My Body the First Time

After being plagued by the memory of my spontaneous projection, I finally decided to look into what had happened to me. I was blown away. Then when I discovered that this was something I could deliberately induce, I just knew I had to try. I recall a long time before I had that experience, some kid at school talked about people being able to leave their bodies and travel the world. I'd thought she was full of it, but it turns out I was wrong.

When I discovered that astral projection could be deliberately induced, I had already been learning about lucid dreaming for months and making a point of keeping a dream journal, doing reality checks, and so on. So, I figured it couldn't be that hard. Intuitively, I knew I'd be able to leave on purpose this time.

I lay down and took a nap while intending to leave my body and do my best to keep my mind alert. The next thing I knew, I began to feel intense vibrations coursing through my body. The vibrations were so severe that it felt like I was being electrocuted, but in a way that felt pleasant and grew more and more enjoyable as I relaxed into it. I couldn't believe it. What was going on?

Next, I willed my astral body to leave my physical one. At first, it was a bit difficult. Imagine pulling gum out of your hair. That's how it felt, except my astral body was the gum, and my physical one just didn't seem to want to let go.

Eventually, I came out of my body and looked around the room. I didn't look at my body because I'd read that I shouldn't do that, or I'd get sucked back in. So I took a few steps toward the door, but then I had to stop because I was suddenly hit with the realization that there's no such thing as death or the finality of it as we think of it.

I realized that who we really are is so much more. We're immortal! I also realized that life really is just a game. It's real, alright, but we take it far too seriously so that we've forgotten the eternal beings we are. These realizations hit me all at once like a thought block was downloaded into my mind.

With that, I returned to my body. It was as though an intelligence had informed me telepathically that that was enough for one session. Since that experience, I've grown bolder in life, lost all fear of death, and I have pleasant psychic experiences every day. This singular experience helped me get rid of my depression and anxiety as well.

Projecting at Age Seven

Katy's favorite way to astral project is through lucid dreams. When she first decided to project, she would keep trying to get out of her body, but she failed. So, she chose to learn lucid dreaming, doing her best to recall her dreams, so she could tell what the dream signs were. Those dream signs would alert her to the fact that she was dreaming and help her achieve lucidity.

Soon, she successfully projected from a dream. As soon as she realized she was lucid, she generated a falling sensation within herself to turn the lucid dream into an astral projection. The next thing she knew, she went from being in the park to being right back in her bedroom—except she wasn't in bed. Instead, she was looking at herself in bed.

She watched as her physical body stirred, and within her, she felt odd. It was like the physical her was aware of being watched and was feeling a bit of fear. Then, intuitively, she decided to communicate to her physical self that all was well. At that moment, she felt herself both standing next to the bed *and* lying on it as well. Then, unable to contain her excitement at the sensation of being more than one person, she found herself back in her body, awake.

Launched into Outer Space

I lay still in bed, allowing the vibrations to wash over me, waiting until it all evened out nicely. Then, I rolled out of my body and immediately headed out the door, desperate to get away from my sleeping form, so I didn't get sucked right back in.

It was night when I headed out. The sky was full of stars, a lot clearer and more beautiful than in my normal waking life, where the city's lights make the night sky a tad harder to appreciate. I thought about hovering, not too high because I had a fear of heights at the time, but just high enough to look down on the rooftops in my neighborhood and journey on from there.

I gave the floor a light tap with my right foot, and the next thing I knew, I was launched up and off the floor just like a rocket! The speed was intense. The fact that the ground, then my neighborhood, then the entire Earth was rapidly receding almost sent me into a panic. To bring some calm to my mind, I held on to my wrist and pressed down hard. Then I came to a stop.

Just then, I looked around, and there was the most breathtaking view I'd ever seen in my whole life. There were all sorts of stars, planets, moons, and other debris. It looked nothing like the universe I'd seen in textbooks, on TV, and the internet. Everything was pulsing with a certain glow. The planets here had beautiful colors that I cannot describe because they have no Earthly equivalent for me to relate them to. Then, I got a thought block that made it clear I had traveled beyond the known universe.

I had a feeling of oneness with it all, a sense of peace, of being a fuller version of myself. This was incredibly humbling, in a good way. I burst into tears because I couldn't stand how beautiful it all was. The soundless sound I heard drove me to levels of ecstasy, when I worried I would soon burst and become part of the debris. Unable to keep my emotions in check, I woke up in my room to find my cheeks damp with tears and my heart filled with homesickness. The words left my mouth before their meaning hit me: "I want to go back home."

Helping From a Distance

Brandon's dad was admitted to the hospital for COVID-19. For weeks, no one was allowed to visit him. Then, things took a turn for the worst when he got bilateral pneumonia and had a stroke on top of that. Brandon's father was in a very critical condition, battling for his life.

Brandon then began to visit his father via the astral plane each night, so he wouldn't be alone through that difficult period. When Brandon realized his dad could see him, Brandon telepathically encouraged him to stay strong and hold on. He shared thoughts of love and support and let him know the entire family and all their friends were thinking about him, praying for him, hoping to be able to visit someday soon.

Eventually, Brandon's dad was allowed to have guests, and his mother and sister were the first to visit. Brandon's sister called to let him know that their father had just told her Brandon had been visiting every night the whole time. He mentioned that he had seen Brandon usually between 3 am to 5 am. His mother thought he was insane, but his sister knew Brandon had always astral projected and reminded her of this.

Brandon's dad passed on a message to him to please ask the nurse to keep it down on his next visit so he could get some sleep. So, on his next astral visit, Brandon sent a message to the nurses via telepathy, asking them to keep it down. In response, one of the nurses went over to where Brandon's dad was and shut his door so the noise wouldn't bother him.

So finally, Brandon went to visit his dad in the flesh, and his dad thanked him for helping out with the nurses, as he was able to get a good night's sleep at last.

A Peek into One of My Lives

After a session of exploring, I intended to head back to my body and record my experiences. Instead, I found myself in the body of a Roman soldier. I could tell right away that this was me in a past life, while retaining consciousness of my present life. I had a brief moment of amusement when I realized my chest was flatter than it should be, and I had all this muscle and strength.

The amusement quickly passed when I took in the scene before me. It was horrific. Bloody. I could feel myself as both my present self and the Roman soldier, who I realized was a legatus—a high-ranking Roman officer. The old me watched with a cold sort of enjoyment as my men butchered what was left of the enemy, relishing the sound of metal slicing flesh, of men begging for their lives. The present me felt very sick and disgusted with it all. I began to feel a very uncomfortable energy, almost like an electrical force field that wanted to get me out of the man's body. I gladly allowed myself to get out of there and woke up, thankfully in my own room again.

Section Two:
Getting Ready for the Astral Plane

Chapter 4: Overcome Your Mind's Limitations

Your mind can either be your best ally or your worst enemy. It's a neutral tool, simply waiting for you to program in commands for it to follow. Chances are, you have already established patterns of thought when it comes to spirituality. If those thoughts serve you, then that's great. It means you're halfway to success with leaving your body already.

Suppose those thoughts are full of superstition about nonexistent evil, or they are all misconceptions about phenomena outside the physical realm that suggest you're a powerless, helpless victim. In that case, that's not going to bode well for you. You might not even be able to leave your body to begin with. So, let's talk more about the mind and how to make it work for you, instead of against you.

Your Mind as a Barrier

Some say you need to figure out your subconscious thoughts and beliefs before finally achieving your dreams. This school of thought suggests that those beliefs remain hidden until we slave night and day through hypnosis and therapy to get them out in the open.

While it is true that the subconscious is powerful, this power needs to be channeled through your conscious mind, which you *do* have control over. For example, suppose your subconscious mind coughs up a thought about how you'll "never" be able to astral project. It's left to you to deliberately use your conscious mind to either accept that belief or replace it with a preferred one in the most nonjudgmental way that you can. Then your subconscious will begin to work with the new idea. When you feel or think something to the contrary, your job is to gently, lovingly remind yourself, your subconscious, of the new belief you have chosen. That's all there is to it.

Here's where I'm going with this: if there's even a bit of you that strongly feels you should *not* leave your body, you're going to have a hard time exiting, let alone exploring that wonderful plane. However, since you cannot go rooting about your subconscious to find the disempowering beliefs, you can try a better way to get your head in the game.

First, you must decide that you're the kind of person who always astral projects. Decide that this is who you are, that astral projection is easy, always has been, and always will be. Sure, you may be just starting out. Still, you should begin by assuming the mindset of a professional *who is always willing to learn something new and get better.* That last bit is critical because if you believe you've mastered all you need to know, you leave yourself no room for growth. You will become too proud to consider trying new methods that may work out well for you in the end.

Once you have decided you're this person, the next thing to do is *ask yourself what this version of you would think about this hang-up you have about astral travel.* When you do this, you will notice that you begin to come up with convincing reasons your fears are unfounded. You develop the courage and mind control you need in order to learn for yourself what it's like in the other realm.

Before you begin, accept that this is unfamiliar territory for you. Therefore, you will encounter the novel and the strange—and that's okay. However, if you experience any unpleasantness, don't shut it down out of fear. Instead, become curious about what you experienced, why it happened, and how you can handle it better the next time around.

If you let fear take over and make you shut down, then you have allowed your mind to become a barrier to your success. Remember, the mind is a tool given to you by the source to serve you. When you have an experience that scares you, and you shy away from it, it's the same thing as refusing to use a hammer because it dropped on your little toe that one time. Do you say to yourself, "I'm never going to touch a hammer for as long as I live?" Of course not. What you do is suck it up, pick it up, and mindfully use the tool with a firmer grip on it.

Mind as the Channel to the Astral Plane

Laws govern all planes of existence, and the astral realm is no exception. You interact with these laws with your mind. Even before you move your physical body, you first have that experience of movement in your mind.

Thankfully, you know the right way to reach for a bottle of water. Maybe as a kid, you were clumsier about it. Perhaps you'd knock the glass around a bit and send water sloshing over its sides. However, with time, working with your mind, you mastered proper motor control. Now you know how to move your hand to pick up the glass without incident. The same thing applies to using your mind to master any skill or learn something new, including the art of astral travel.

In the astral planes, the law of attraction (which states that "like attracts like") reigns supreme. You may think that sentence is a New Age scam, but that is the way life works, and you see this law manifest even faster on planes higher than this physical one. This is one more reason your mind can be a barrier to your success with soul travel. If you think you can't, then you're right. If you assume that you will succeed and that this is easy for you, you're also right.

You will find that everything is very fluid on the astral plane, very responsive to intention and thought. So, the principle of like attracting like works incredibly fast here, almost in an instant. If you have a fear that there's something sinister, terrifying, or malevolent that's out to get you, that's what will happen. However, if you calm down and use your mind to intend and realize you are safe, you are loved, and drawn only to high vibrations, then you will meet entities who resonate with what you're putting out there. You'll find them to be full of love and kindness and very willing and eager to help you. In other words, your tribe depends on your vibe.

Take charge of your mind. Understand that whatever you focus on will be magnified by *a lot.* Suppose the assumption you hold of yourself is that you're a victim, subject to the whims and caprices of whoever and whatever. In that case, you're going to create situations where you get to be the victim. You'll attract the entities who will help you embody that assumption—which is *not* what you want.

A healthy mindset to have is that you're immortal, powerful, and spiritual. You're a part of the Divine Spark itself, which means you have no end, and you cannot be hurt. You are a part of the Source, masquerading as human, having a fun adventure being an Earthling. That's it. Since you are the Source itself, you have all the energy, power, and ability you need to remain safe from whatever life throws your way.

Healthy Mindset for Astral Travel

First, treat other entities the way you'd rather be treated. Next, treat others the way they'd rather be treated. This may sound like a paradox, but it is not. The point is that you should accept the existence of all other entities as valid, understand that they are sovereign, and have their own free will. As long as they aren't forcing their will on you, you should offer them the same courtesy.

Understand that there are always limits to deal with when you're in the astral realm. There are exceptions to everything. For instance, I once found myself in a very solid zone where there was absolutely nothing I could manipulate with my mind. I couldn't walk through walls like I used to. This was new to me after many years of journeying in the astral.

Speaking of exceptions, just because you have preconceived notions about what good or evil should look like doesn't mean your first assumption about an entity is valid. Thankfully, this is a plane that engages your feelings. So, trust your intuition when you're dealing with people in the astral realm. Frankly, this is a healthy mindset to have in your waking world as well.

Fear often is a result of ignorance. By default, people fear what they don't understand. It takes a genuinely conscious person to become curious about their fears so that they can surmount them and grow even more enlightened. Having said that, I would like to address some misconceptions about astral travel so that you know you have nothing to worry about.

Clearing Up Misconceptions

Astral projection is not dangerous. You astral project every night. You just aren't aware of it, and you haven't mastered how to recall your explorations just yet. It's about as dangerous as sleeping. The difference is that you choose to become aware of what you get up to when you hit the hay.

Sleep paralysis is a natural phenomenon. There's no "demon sitting on your chest." It's a natural thing that happens to you every night, with the only difference being you caught your body doing it this time.

Your physical body is not empty and waiting to be possessed by a demon. Again, your body has its own consciousness. There's no way any being could oust you from your own body. As you project, you send out a copy of your energy body to explore the realm. You exist in multiple dimensions, always, all the time.

You will not die from astral projecting. If anyone passes on while outside the body, it's due to a preexisting medical condition or something else. You cannot die from exploring consciousness. So, don't believe the horror stories.

Every astral projector is protected all the time. You don't have to worry about someone severing your silver cord, causing you to die as you project. We all have guides and our Higher Selves who look after us. These beings are mighty and will make sure to keep you safe from all harm. Also, you would be wise just to assume you're always safe and loved. This way, you will have nothing to be protected from.

You can never get so far away from your body that you have trouble returning to it. You are connected to your Earth body by your silver cord. You may or may not see the cord, but it is there, and it only ever breaks when you die in the physical realm.

To get back to your body faster, you can simply shut your eyes and think about your body on the bed. Then, feel yourself on the bed, and you will be teleported there right away. Also, know that if your physical body experiences any disturbances, from noise to the need to pee, you will wake up right away, whether you want to or not.

Consciously Releasing Mental Blocks

If you're finding it difficult to access the astral plane, you may have mental blocks to contend with. You, like everyone else, may have assumed that all your thoughts are true, and some of those thoughts may be counterproductive to successful astral trips. The statement "I think; therefore, I am" is cute but detrimental. Instead, it should be, "I Am; therefore I Am." Everything else that seeks to define "I Am" or consciousness puts a limit on your naturally abundant, limitless nature.

The best way to reprogram your mind to give you the thoughts you would like is first to understand that **all thoughts are neutral until you give them life by assuming they are true**. Then, know that you're constantly deciding what is true for you at every given moment. Even when you're not deciding, that's simply you deciding not to decide! So, you may as well deliberately choose that your preferred, empowering thoughts are true for you.

Addicted to Thinking

Lose your addiction to thinking and thoughts. Thoughts run over and over on a loop. Little wonder most people just accept them as being their own, when really, it's just the monkey mind looking for stuff to do. So, here's how to calm the monkey in your head.

1. First, find somewhere comfortable where you can sit comfortably in an upright position. You may also lie down if you're sure you won't fall asleep. Make sure you're wearing loose, comfy clothing and that you won't be bothered or distracted for at least ten minutes, fifteen tops.

2. Next, shut your eyes and slightly part your lips.

3. Breathe in through your nose. Make it a loving, generous breath. Allow your awareness to map the path of your inhale.

4. Exhale through your slightly parted lips, following the breath with your awareness.

5. Repeat this cycle over and over until you notice your breathing and thinking slowing down. Your body will relax, deeper and deeper.

6. Place your awareness on your heart chakra, which is just in between the lungs. Just sit with your attention on that energy center. Relax with it.

7. Notice when the next thought comes into your mind. Notice the way it emerges while still keeping your awareness on the heart chakra. It doesn't matter if the idea is negative, positive, or neutral. Don't care about what it means. Just notice how it comes up and where it comes from.

8. See if you can notice the space in between your thoughts. Also, notice the space each thought emerged from.

9. With your awareness still on your heart center, observe whether you're thinking. Observe if you're the thinker of those thoughts, or simply the observer, watching as they come. Notice how you didn't bring them up, but they showed up on their own. Notice the itch the mind feels to latch onto them but be gentle and without judgment as you do so. Keep your awareness on the love flowing from your heart center as you notice the space these

thoughts come from.

This is an exercise you shouldn't rush through. Also, the more you do this, the deeper the insights you will glean. The more detached you will be from your thoughts, which is good since you're allowing the negative thoughts to fly back to wherever they came from. This is a good practice for peace in your life.

Open Your Mind

We've mastered the science of journeying into outer space. It's time to master the journey into "inner space." This is a vital thing for all of humanity to do, as the awareness of our true nature will sort out many of the problems we face today. However, the trouble is you can't master consciousness if you don't even want to keep an open mind.

The correct attitude to adopt is that of a kid learning to write their alphabets. When you were young, you could have argued that there's no reason a squiggly line should give you the "s" sound and that there's no reason it has to be written that way, either. However, you didn't do that. Instead, you learned every letter, and you learned to read and write each one. Then you learned to combine them all. Now you have access to amazing information from books because you *chose* to keep an open mind and understand what the adults were fussing about.

Keep this same energy when it comes to astral projection. Staying open means you get to learn new things, and you grow thanks to your explorations in consciousness. Staying open is how you keep your body and soul burning with passion and joy. It's how you find more and more aspects of yourself that you didn't know about. The goal of life is continuous expansion, which leads to joy, which leads to further growth. So, stay open! Get curious. Knowing what you know now, aren't you interested in learning about all of your lives?

Curiosity never killed the cat. It just made it realize it had more than nine lives—just like you do.

Chapter 5: Your Dream Journal

Keeping a journal is a potent practice that can help you see how far you've come in all areas of life. In the same vein, you should regularly record your dreams so that you can notice patterns and themes that pop up in them over time and grow in awareness. They are a treasure trove of information that can help you with the relationships, problems, and activities you engage in within your waking world.

Benefits of a Dream Journal

Stress Reduction

Journaling is a great way to review things you may have chosen to suppress instead of dealing with them. The stuff we hide can add to our stress in ways we may not be able to detect otherwise. When we sleep, a lot of what goes on in our dreams reflects our waking lives. So, writing down your dreams will help you notice what patterns show up and help you figure out what you may need to pay attention to in your physical life so you can fix it.

Increased Creativity

The more you write down your dreams, the more you'll engage your creative side, which is strongly connected to dreaming. The easier it will become for you to create new ideas and thoughts—a bonus if you work in a field that calls for right-brain thinking.

Improved Dream Recall

Let's face it. You're reading this book because you want to experience more of the other world consciously. Other waking life benefits are just extra perks. So, when you write your dreams down, your dream recall improves. This works because the process of remembering your dreams and noting them down signals to your mind that your dreams are important to you. As a result, you'll be able to remember more and more. With time, you'll find you can recall every little detail in your dreams, and this will be of immense benefit to you when you begin your astral visits.

Boost in Dream Lucidity

Recording every dream you have will cause you to notice the things that usually happen over and over in your dreams. In addition, it helps you to recognize the oddities that make dreams a distinctly different experience from waking life. Those oddities are called dream signs. The next time you see them in a dream, you will be triggered awake.

Boost in Logical Thought

Journaling also helps you to be better with left-brain, analytical thinking. For example, to realize you're in a dream, you need the rational part of you to spot the clues and dead giveaways that let you know there's something off about the world you're in. The wonderful thing is that you'll experience this boost in rational thinking in your waking life as well. For instance, you can tell when things aren't adding up. You can also think your way through any issue when everyone else is losing their minds around you. You know how to remain calm and rational when tempers are flying, so you're the one person in the room who doesn't leap to irrational conclusions and take regrettable actions.

How does this help you with astral projection? For one thing, you can convert your lucid dream into an astral projection with the correct technique. For another, you will get better at avoiding *false awakenings.*

When you travel to the astral realm's *real-time zone* (where everything closely matches your physical environment), you may mistakenly assume you are awake. Ever had a moment when you woke up, did everything you had to do for the day, and then woke up **again** to find you dreamed it all? That's an instance of false awakening.

Improved Emotional Intelligence

When you note your dreams down, you connect with your emotions better. This is because recalling and writing them will inevitably evoke feelings that you will naturally pay attention to, so you can find out why you feel the way you do.

Noting your dreams will also help you learn why it's just as important to be in charge of your mind in waking life as well as waking dreams or projections. When you choose to watch a horror flick or something sad before bed, you will notice how that colors your dreams. When you fall asleep in high spirits, you will also see that translate into your dreams. Also, you'll notice how the emotions from a dream color your morning and possibly the rest of your day. You'll be more conscious about acknowledging and sorting out your feelings. This alone will drastically improve the quality of your life.

Better Control in Dreams and Astral Projections

The more you write down your dreams, the better you'll get at manipulating everything that happens in that realm. If you're the sort of person who has to deal with poor sleep on account of constant nightmares, it should be immediately evident to you how amazing this is. Rather than give in to the fear, you can realize you're dreaming and influence the dream. For example, you could neutralize whatever is causing your fear or make it smaller than you. Or you could turn it into something hilarious, change the environment, or simply choose to end it.

Creative Problem-Solving

Any experienced lucid dreamer or astral projector can tell you many stories about how they came up with creative solutions to problems that seemed impossible to fix.

We live in a world that so desperately cleaves to logic, refusing to rock the boat, always sticking to tradition and the status quo. The beautiful thing about the astral realm is that all of those rules and conventions are tossed out the window. What this means for you is boundless, limitless creativity. You can use your dreamscape to fix a problem by intending to receive an answer in your dreams and trusting you'll understand it when you get it. As soon as you do, make sure to write the answer down.

Tips for Keeping a Dream Journal

1. **Summarize with single words.** If you wake up in the middle of the night and you're much too tired to whip out your notebook or phone to journal in your app, then consider just writing down a few words to summarize. Then, in the morning, you can fill in the rest of it. For instance, say you had a dream about being one of the Von Trapp children. You were singing and dancing on a hill with Fraulein Maria while a disapproving nun chased you all around. In that case, you could write: "Hill. Nun. Music. Von Trapp." This should be enough to jog your memory so you can fill in the details in the morning.

2. **Be generous with details.** You'll get better at noticing details the more you journal, but even if you're just starting out, do your best to note the minutiae of what you experienced or saw. Recall what time of day it was, who was with you, what you could hear, colors, sensations, and emotions. Don't be hard on yourself if you notice you're not noticing enough. Just intend that you will, and over time, that will improve. It's a worthy goal, too, because you'll be better at interpreting your dreams and won't have to rely on blogs to tell you what your dreams mean (a pointless thing to do since dreams are highly subjective).

3. **Draw your dream if it's easier.** If you're better at expressing yourself in pictures than words, then it's okay to draw your dreams. You'll capture a lot more that you might have missed had you tried to write. On the other hand, if you can express yourself in both words and pictures, that is awesome, and you should do that. You'll be even better at correctly interpreting your dreams.

4. **Not a dreamer? Here's what you should do.** First, write down how you feel when you wake up. Some people argue that they never dream. What's really going on is they *don't remember* dreaming. Everyone exists multi-dimensionally. We're not always focused on Earth all the time, so not all your nights will be dreamless. To fix this, just note down how you feel, and trust that very soon, you'll begin to get more details on your dreams. Don't beat yourself up over not knowing anything more than your emotions, or else you'll slow the process down.

5. **Contrast your waking life with your dreams.** You want to note down what your day was like and notice your final thoughts before turning in for the night. You should also pay attention to whatever you consumed mentally, whether it was a book, an article, a YouTube video, whatever. After writing your dream, the next step is to look back on what you experienced the day before the dream and see if you can find clues about why you had the dream you did. You can also use your dream to analyze how your new day goes and see if you can find any connections between the two.

6. **Be on the lookout for patterns.** Over a number of dreams, you may begin to notice a pattern unfold. For example, you may find you're constantly dreaming of a specific place, or you consistently see cats. Maybe it's someone who's always in your dreams, or the same sort of event plays out but in different locations. These patterns can lead you to issues you need to deal with in the waking world that you've been suppressing, and you can even find the solution within them as well. So, don't just write your dreams and toss your journal aside. Instead, always review it for clues. A good journal app will allow you to search for specific keywords, so you can tell if something pops up often enough for you to call it a pattern.

How to Keep a Dream Journal

You could just write the date you had your dream and its details, but ideally, noting other elements can help you learn more about yourself and your dream habits.

What kind of dream journal to use: This is primarily up to you. If you want to go old-school because you love the feel of pen and paper, then you can get a notepad. You should only use this for your dreams and their connections to your waking life. Nothing more.

If you would prefer to use your phone, that's an option as well. Switch to dark mode or any other visual mode that won't cause you to wake up fully as you type in the keywords of your dreams. This will be of immense help to you, especially if you wake up in the middle of the night to record them.

There are lots of apps you can use. You could go for the classic EverNote, Penzu, or Google's Keep. You could check out your app store and search for "dream journal," go through the reviews to find one that suits you. Some of these dream journal apps even come with alerts to help you perform reality checks throughout your day, and they also remind you to write your dreams. A good app for this is Awoken. If you'd rather record your dreams in audio format, that's an option as well. You can use the recording app on your phone or pay for one that allows you to transcribe audio to text if you'd rather read your entries.

When to write: You don't want to write your dream down as soon as you wake up. If you immediately roll out and reach for your journal, you may forget some crucial bits. So first, remain there in bed for about a minute. Next, work your way backward in the sequence of dream events until there's nothing left to remember. Then you can write out the keywords to serve as a reminder as you note down the dream in more detail.

What should be in your journal?

- The day you had the dream.
- The time you went to bed and the time you woke up.
- Whether your sleep was interrupted.
- Whether you remember your dream in full or not.
- The time of day in your dream.
- The characters you saw: animal, human, or otherwise.
- The sequence of events in the dream.
- Physical sensations, if any.
- The emotions you feel.
- Your interpretation of the dream.
- Whether you astral traveled.
- The sequence of events in your astral projection.

Where to keep your journal? Ideally, you want it as close to your bed as possible. Get a bedside table if you don't have one. If it's not uncomfortable, you can keep your journal underneath your pillow.

Your Astral Journal

If you want, you can have a separate journal for recording your astral journeys alone. However, you might find it a lot more practical to simply record your astral projections in the same journal you use for your lucid dreams. All you'd have to do is make sure that they are clearly marked, so it's easier for you to get to what you want to read.

In your astral journal, include the following details:

1. Did you deliberately leave your physical body, or did you catch your astral body as it re-entered?
2. Was your re-entry deliberate or not?
3. What time did you project?
4. What method did you use to project?
5. Did you leave your body forcefully, or was it easy for you?
6. Was your exit easier or harder than the last time?
7. Was there anything you did differently in your routine that made it easier or harder?
8. Did you give in to the urge to roll over or scratch an itch?
9. Narrate your experiences during your trip.
10. What did you eat before leaving your body, if anything?
11. How soon after eating did you attempt to leave your body?
12. Were there any peculiar energy sensations you felt that were unusual for you during the vibratory state? Describe them.
13. Did you fully recollect your astral memories, or only partially?
14. Did you have a plan, and did you execute it successfully?
15. If you didn't execute it fully, write why.

This may seem like a little too much information to write down in your journal, but the more entries you make, the more likely it is that you will see a pattern emerge. In addition, all of this information will help you to know what you're doing right and what you need to fix.

So, with each new astral trip you make, you can correct your course along the way. Soon, you will find that you've gotten a lot of the technical stuff out of the way, so you can focus on enjoying your experiences. If you decide to share your experiences, you'll be adding tremendous value to the growing body of work on this topic, which will definitely help both neophyte and veteran travelers alike.

Finally, keeping track of all these variables will show you just how far you've come on your journey. In addition, tracking your progress will give you the encouragement and enthusiasm you need to continue with your explorations, creating a positive feedback loop that will accelerate your learning process.

Chapter 6: Developing Mindfulness

If you've been paying attention, you must have already figured out this topic was coming. You need to be a master of your mind to traverse the astral world. So, what better way to learn to tame the mind than practicing mindfulness?

Mindfulness Defined

Mindfulness is a practice that requires you to be completely aware of the here and now, without trying to interpret it, or judge it, or label it. There are so many ways to practice this art of living in the moment. There's meditation with or without guided imagery and breathing methods to place your full attention on the breath. These practices have the added benefit of helping you to de-stress in body and mind. The more relaxed you are, the deeper the levels of awareness you can reach.

This is a practice that has heaps of benefits when it comes to astral projection. The ability to remain nonjudgmental in a given place and time will automatically deepen your focus regardless of what's happening. You'll pick up on details better and get whatever messages you need to help you along life's journey.

Remaining in the moment also means you'll have fewer fluctuations to deal with when you're having a lucid dream or astral projection. Since the astral realm is susceptible to your thoughts, developing mindfulness will help you be more deliberate about what you entertain in your head. You will only give energy to the ideas that give you the results you seek.

Benefits of Mindfulness

Stress reduction: this world is a high-octane one. You may not be shooting monsters or bad guys in an action movie, but chances are you're experiencing the same levels of stress anyone would in those situations. Inevitably, we have recurring negative feelings and thoughts, which further feed the pain, depression, stress, and anxiety already caused by stressful situations. Whether it's finances, health issues, or the state of the nation, these things can translate into insomnia, hypertension, and other health problems you really don't want to have to deal with.

One way to mitigate the damaging effects of these stressful times is through practicing mindfulness. When you choose to be mindful, you will find it's easier for you to accept where you are. When you no longer fight a circumstance or situation, you take away its power over your life. You put yourself in a position to see the neon exit signs clearly to escape those issues.

Improved focus and awareness: if you've always had trouble focusing, whether because of a health issue or just a lack of discipline, mindfulness will help you in spades. Your attention span will grow with practice. Soon, you'll find you're able to give your attention to single tasks for extended periods without feeling the need to look at cat videos on Facebook or something else equally distracting.

Reduction in burnout: burnout, at its core, is the exhaustion you feel when you no longer want to deal with a particularly persistent situation; have refused to accept it or to look for ways to turn it into a positive; and either can't or won't let the problematic issue go.

Practicing mindfulness puts you in touch with your emotions, allowing you to know when to persist with a problem or take a break and come back to it later without beating yourself up. With practice, you'll also find that you're able to be a part of that situation with no judgment and no push-back on your end. This allows you to find the joy in it if you want to or to energetically disconnect from it. This disconnection will set up a chain of events where you finally have the perfect solution to this persistent issue, or the problem resolves itself on its own.

Better sleep: with better control over your mind, you'll find it easier to go to bed, since you won't be bothered by stray thoughts like whether cows can swim. You can set an intention to fall asleep quickly and easily and experience precisely that. With mastery of mind, you know what it means not to give energy to your thoughts. You understand that your mind is not unlike a generator that's been running all day. You've turned it off, and it's still a bit hot, but you don't worry about it because you know it's off, and so it has no choice but to cool down.

Mindfulness and Astral Projection

Make a habit of practicing mindfulness in waking life. You'll find it's a lot easier for you to project successfully. When you're concentrating on being right here, right now, you'll see that this habit spills over to your astral projections too. You'll also find that you're constantly achieving lucidity when you dream. You'll catch yourself just as you're about to leave your body, even when you didn't plan to.

When you look at your hands in your dreams or projections, the entire world stabilizes. This happens because your attention becomes rooted in the moment. However, you don't want to spend the whole time just looking at your hands because you're afraid you'll come out of it. This is why you should take up mindfulness and make it a habit.

Without mindfulness, you'll find that your mind wanders way too much. You might assume this means you should wind up in interesting places during your astral projection, but it's not like that. Instead, you'll find yourself losing lucidity. You'll forget you're in the astral realm and go back to your uncritical way of thinking during dreams. You'll forget your experiences, so you can't even journal them when you get back. Also, you'll find yourself constantly experiencing false awakenings. I can tell you for a fact that it is pretty irritating to wake up and discover what you had assumed was waking life was the real-time zone.

When you've trained yourself to be mindful, you'll catch these false awakenings easily. For example, you may get out of bed to prepare for work and notice something out of place in your room. You'll also see how you feel a little different in your body than usual, and then it will hit you that you're projecting. The reason you'll notice is that you've made a habit of being fully here and now, so details don't escape you. Then you can choose to leave the real-time zone and go to higher levels of the astral plane.

Mindfulness Exercises

Awareness of the Present

1. Find a comfortable and quiet place where you can sit. If there are others around you, ask that you be left alone for just ten to fifteen minutes.

2. Wearing loose clothing, sit in a comfortable position. You don't have to sit in a lotus position if it hurts your knees or isn't your style. The goal is to feel as natural as you can.

3. Simply observe the moment. Don't try to silence your mind or force yourself to be calm. Just be. Notice the moment, and don't judge it.

4. When you notice yourself judging or giving the things you see around you and feel within you any meaning, just notice that and then allow the judgment to pass. Let your mind gently return to the moment, just the way it is, label-free.

5. Repeat this process of returning your mind to the present each time you notice it's back to judging, labeling, giving meaning to things. Do so lovingly. Don't judge yourself, no matter how many times you've found yourself carried away from the moment.

This exercise is a simple one, but simple doesn't mean it's easy. Don't let that scare you away. Perfection is not the goal here. Instead, you should thank yourself for noticing your mind's gone off on a tangent, to begin with, because that means you're getting better at being mindful.

Follow the Breath Meditation

1. Go somewhere peaceful and quiet. Get rid of all distractions for ten to fifteen minutes.

2. In loose and comfy clothing, sit down. You may be on the floor or in a chair, whatever works for you.

3. Keep your body relaxed and in good posture, with your spine upright. If this feels uncomfortable, adjust your body till you feel good. You may keep your hands on your thighs in whatever way feels comfortable. There should be no straining.

4. Shut your eyes and slightly part your lips.

5. Take in a deep breath through your nose. Observe its sound and the path it takes as it moves through your nostrils, filling your belly and lungs.

414

6. Hold that breath for a second or two, paying attention to the feeling within you as it waits for release.

7. Next, exhale through your slightly parted lips. You might notice that your exhale takes longer than your inhale. This is normal. Observe the breath as it flows out of your belly and lungs, through your nostrils. Notice the very point where the breath loses touch with your body.

8. If your mind wanders—and chances are it will—notice that, with no judgment, and then with love and appreciation for yourself, return your attention to your breath. Do this no matter how many times your mind wanders, never judging yourself, being kind to yourself no matter what.

9. Repeat this process until the time elapses. Do this daily.

Tips for Remaining Mindful

Observe your emotions from a relaxed, detached point of view. Whether it's joy or anger or sadness, no matter what you're feeling, pay attention to the emotion without letting it consume you. Think of it like standing on the outside, looking in on yourself. First, there's the observer, and then there's the observed. Of course, you are both, but you can mindfully switch your awareness to being the observer at any given point in time. The more you do this, the more you'll grow in mindfulness.

Use positive affirmations. When you find yourself caught in a whirlwind of negativity, you can find your center using affirmations. To be clear, it's not about the words but the meaning and feeling behind the words with which you resonate. There's no power in words on their own. So, you should always use your affirmations positively and in the present.

Incorrect: I will **not** let this situation bring me down.

Correct: I am greater than this.

Incorrect: I am going to be excellent at astral projection.

Correct: I am an excellent astral projector.

Journal your life passively. In a separate journal, practice writing about your day with no judgment. Imagine you were peeking in on your life as someone else. The more you write about your life passively, the better you'll get at noticing your emotions, as well as your thoughts.

Make a point of really listening to people. When you're listening, really be there. Don't fiddle with your phone or your hands. Don't try to anticipate where they're going with what they're saying. Make no judgments about what you hear from them either. When you listen mindfully, you also notice that you're not preparing what to say in response. You're just in the moment.

Look with no judgment. Just as you listen, you can also look at people (and objects or places) without judgment. This is not the time to think, "Oh, they're so beautiful!" or "Wow, that's an ugly piece of art." Just look with no judgment. You can make eye contact and then allow your eyes to drift around their face as well, just taking it all in.

Mind your mind. Every now and then, just check in with your mind to see what's going on in there. Don't ask the question, "What am I thinking about?" because then you're giving yourself a mental wedgie. Your mind can answer back, "Well, now I'm thinking about what I'm thinking about!" Instead, what you want to do is just peek in from a detached perspective. Just notice what's going on in there. Don't try to notice by actively looking into your mind, but simply being in the moment and allowing it to roam. Imagine, if you will, that you're a house with open windows, while the thoughts that fly in and out are birds. You're stable, ever-present, while the birds flit in and out.

Make a habit of working out. When you're exercising at a decent intensity, you're forced to bring your entire focus to the moment. At the moment, your lungs demand air. Your muscles require energy. Your willpower demands that you push one second longer, go one rep further. All of these put together force you to be entirely in the here and now.

The workout must be hard enough to force you to have to focus (but not make you want to quit) because working out means you have to breathe, and there's nothing that grounds you in the present like the breath. It's the reason breathwork is so powerful and vital when it comes to the practice of mindfulness.

Set recurring alarms. When they go off, you can take just a minute, maybe five, to just be in the moment if you weren't before. Another way you can use this to empower yourself is to create a statement about you being the kind of person you want to be. Then, when the alarm goes off, for just a few minutes, see through your eyes, live through your body, and notice everything from the state of mind that the ideal version of yourself would.

You could also imagine that you *are* in an astral projection, and you just realized it thanks to the alarm. Then, what you do next is make a decision about doing something, and then do it. For example, you could decide to get up and stretch your legs, pick up the phone and call someone, or go look outside. No matter what action you choose, you're training yourself to be mindful during your projections. You're learning to follow through on your decisions with laser precision each time you're out of your body.

Turn off your phone. It's amazing how that tiny little rectangle takes us out of the moment every so often, with its incessant demand for our attention. It's not like it's just one thing you need to focus on when using your phone, either. Chances are, you have notifications from multiple apps.

Be deliberate about disconnecting yourself. Each day dedicate time to forget about emails, the media with its barrage of bad news, your overanxious mother's constant worrisome texts. Ignore all the notifications telling you that this challenge or that challenge demands you sink hours of your time scrolling through videos that are essentially the same. Instead, take that time and focus on being in the present, whether you just observe it or really get into a creative hobby like painting, creating something, immersing yourself in family time, or whatever else. Just unplug for a bit. It's a habit worth having and one you'll soon find hard to kick. You might feel antsy and have intense FOMO when you disconnect yourself from social media at first. Still, after a bit, you will notice you feel better than you have in a long time.

Chapter 7: Astral Breathwork

I mentioned before that breath is vital when it comes to maintaining mindfulness. It's also essential for your astral travels. When you think about it, your breathing is so crucial that it isn't just your conscious mind in control. You fall asleep, and your lungs keep on trucking. Imagine being completely in charge of your breathing while having zero control over your mind. That's a scary thought. Just as the breath is essential for keeping your physical body going, it also helps with your astral one.

Breath-Work Defined

Breath-work refers to all breathing exercises designed to improve physical, mental, and spiritual health. It's about breathing intentionally. Practicing this often leads to better focus, more profound relaxation, and boundless energy when you need it.

Your job is to just breathe with breath-work, allowing whatever comes up in your mind to move on with no resistance. Conscious breathing leads to hypo-oxygenated cells, which means your blood has a lot of oxygen to work with, and your body can begin to heal at an accelerated rate. Your mind also benefits from the practice, healing what it needs to. It gets out of your way so that you can achieve more profound levels of meditation, more self-awareness, and a state of blissful surrender to the here and now.

Breathing and Stress

The next time you feel stressed, notice the way you're breathing. Typically, your breath will be shallow, ending in the upper chest. This means you're not getting as much air into your lungs as you should, and you're breathing faster than you should. Unfortunately, it's a sad truth that this is what most of us consider normal breathing.

Shallow breathing is closely connected to stress due to the sympathetic nervous system, also known as the SNS. This is the part of your autonomic nervous system in charge of your "fight, freeze, or flight" mechanism. When you're stressed, the SNS constricts your blood vessels. In turn, your heart rate goes up along with your respiration and blood pressure. Your digestive system also suffers.

Since the body and brain always influence one another, your body lets your brain know you're under stress through your shallow breathing. Your brain then sends your body information about how to act in response to the pressure, and that causes more shallow breathing and all the other harmful effects. This is why stress can seem like a rickety, never-ending roller coaster.

Your parasympathetic nervous system or PNS acts as a counterbalance to the SNS. It's your body's "rest and digest" system. What it does is help you to relax and feel calm. Just like the SNS, you can activate the PNS through your breathing. Take a moment to shut your eyes and imagine that you're somewhere that sets you at ease. You feel calm in this place. It's quiet and peaceful, and you just feel like relaxing there indefinitely. What you'll notice is that your breath is slower and deeper. That's because you feel more relaxed and are breathing with your diaphragm on account of that.

The deeper you breathe, the calmer your mind becomes, and the better you can direct it to do your bidding as it was designed to. Incorporating breath-work into your routine for mastering astral projection is an investment that will give back to you in spades.

Holotropic Breathwork

The etymology of the word "holotropic" is Greek, made up of the words *holos*, which means "whole," and *trepein*, which means "to move forward." Developed by Christina and Stanislav Grof, this breath-work technique is designed to help you feel like a whole person. With it, you can alter your state of consciousness without having to use drugs.

Also known as HB, it involves being in control of your breath, breathing faster than usual to affect your emotional, mental, and physical states of being. While this has a lot of therapeutic effects, it's usually used for spiritual purposes. You can use this breathing technique to grow awareness, which in turn will be helpful during your astral travel. When done right, you can use this to shift into higher states of consciousness. This, in turn, can trigger an awakening to the fullness of who you are or your multidimensional nature.

To practice this, you should breathe fast and evenly. As you breathe this way, you will alter your state of consciousness, and from this position, you will gain insights into who you are. Think of this as meditation on steroids. One of the tenets of HB holds that you have an inner radar that can point out to you what experiences matter the most at any point in time. Still, you can't have conscious awareness of what this experience might be until you have it.

How could this help you with astral projection? Use this before you go to bed or before projecting. You'll have all the energy you need to generate and maintain your astral body and keep up the stability you need to move around the astral plane without getting lost. Breathing this way helps increase dimethyltryptamine or DMT in your body. The rapid, even breath causes oxygenated blood to flood your brain and encourages its production in your pineal gland. This means your dreams and projections will be crisp and clear.

How to Breathe Holotropically

For your first experience, it helps to have a partner as a spotter while you do this, so you feel at ease with wherever your mind goes. Do not try this if you suffer from low or high blood pressure, cardiovascular diseases, or glaucoma. Also, be aware that strong emotions tend to arise due to this breath-work, sometimes in conjunction with suppressed, painful memories.

1. Make sure your room is cool and dark.
2. Lie down on your back on the floor, and make sure you're comfortable. You can use a mat if you want to.
3. Put on an eye mask, so you don't see any light, or you can just shut your eyes.

4. Allow all tension to melt away from your body as you take some relaxing breaths to release the tension in your muscles.

5. When you sense you're ready, breathe deeper, inhaling through your nose and allowing your belly to rise as far as it can.

6. Feel your stomach deflate as you exhale.

7. Pick up the pace with your breath while making sure your mind remains free and clear. To help maintain a clear mind, you may repeat mentally or under your breath, "Inhale, exhale." Keep this up until you sense you're in an altered state of consciousness.

Why Breathing Matters in Astral Projection

Relax better. When you breathe the right way, you relax a lot more. Being relaxed is essential because it's how you get the vibrations that allow your astral body to step out of the physical one. Breathing deep, slow, and rhythmically allows your mind to slow down, brings your blood pressure to a balanced point, and helps your chakras open up. Every cell in your body benefits from your deep breathing, and you're more in tune with the subtler energies you will be merging with shortly.

At the start, your breathing is deep. Then, the more your body relaxes, the shorter the rhythm of your breath will be, and eventually, it's almost like you're not even breathing at all. This is the stage of peak relaxation.

Slow your brain activity to access your subconscious mind. In other words, when you breathe in a calm, relaxed rhythm, you slow down your brainwave activity. Typically, in waking consciousness, our brainwaves are in the frequencies of Gamma and Beta, which are very active. When you meditate or breathe slow, the activity drops to Alpha, Theta, or even as deep as Delta. These frequencies are the best for creative thought and astral projection.

As you go deeper, your body goes to sleep while your mind opens up the subconscious for you to work with as you please. The subconscious is essential when it comes to astral projecting. This is the point where you experience hypnagogia. You see colorful patterns and sometimes snatches of images just before entering the vibrational state to separate from your body.

Boost your concentration and focus. Whatever breathing technique you use requires you to focus on your breath as you follow its flow from nostrils to the belly and back. This makes it hard for your monkey mind to hop around as it likes to, and as a result, you can deepen your relaxation. This means when you're in the astral realm, you can simply use your breath to remain calm and focused on the tasks you set out to accomplish there.

Stimulate your chakras. Your chakras must be activated before you leave your body, or you might have a hard time working with your astral body. Breath-work allows you to activate and clean out these energy centers. All you have to do is pay attention to each one in turn as you breathe. You can visualize life force or a beautiful bluish light moving into each chakra as you inhale and then see the chakra glow brighter as you exhale. For reference, you have seven major chakras:

- The root chakra, at the base of your spine or the perineum.
- The sacral chakra, just below your belly button.
- The solar plexus chakra, right in between and beneath your ribs.
- The heart chakra, in the center of your chest.
- The throat chakra, in the middle of your neck.
- The third eye chakra, in between and just above your eyebrows.
- The crown chakra, in the center of your head, on top.

Breathing Exercises

Let's get into some breathing exercises that you can do independently without a guide or a pricey facilitator. If you want to do them with a friend, you can do that. Do note some people react intensely to these exercises. So, if it starts to feel a bit much for you, please take a break and try another day.

Alternate Nostril Breathing

This is also called *Nadi Shodhana*, which is a subtle energy clearing method of breathing. It's an ancient yoga breathing method that helps you find inner peace and release anxiety and stress. It also helps to ground you and gets rid of insomnia. Your focus will sharpen. Both hemispheres of your brain will balance out and work in harmony, and you'll also clear out all the blocked chakras in your body. In addition to all of this, toxins will be eliminated from your body,

1. Sit somewhere quiet and comfortable, in the lotus pose if you prefer.

2. Place your left hand on your left knee.

3. Put your right hand up to your nose.

4. Exhale, emptying your lungs.

5. Using your right thumb, press down on your right nostril.

6. Breathe in through your left one, then press down on it with your fingers.

7. Take your thumb off the right nostril and exhale through it.

8. Inhale with your right nostril, and then exhale with the left. That's a complete cycle.

9. Repeat this for five minutes. Make sure to finish by exhaling with the left nostril.

The 4-7-8 Method

Don't have enough time? Then this method is just for you. You can use it to connect with your emotions and body and give your nervous system a much-needed break while you're at it.

1. Find a quiet, comfy place to sit.

2. Shut your eyes, and inhale through your nose for four seconds.

3. Hold your breath for seven seconds.

4. Finally, exhale through your slightly parted lips for 8 seconds, using force so that you hear a "whooshing" sound.

5. Do this cycle four times in a session.

Soft Belly Breathing

In a perfect world, we'd all be breathing from our abdomen. However, we don't. So, this is an excellent exercise to do each day. It helps you deal with nervous tension, anxious thoughts, and stress so that you can find that peaceful center within you. The key is to keep the belly soft and breathe without force. If you force it, you will feel even more anxious and wonder why it isn't working.

1. Sit on a chair or on the floor, making sure you're comfortable.

2. Shut your eyes, and take a few deep relaxing breaths, in through your nose and out through your slightly parted lips.

3. Allow your body to become very rooted to the chair or floor. Again, there's no force here, just a pleasant heaviness.

4. As you inhale, let the air move into your belly. Keep your stomach soft.

5. Exhale with no effort. The belly should remain soft.

6. It may help if you mentally repeat the words "soft" as you breathe in and "belly" as you exhale and release all tension and resistance.

7. With each breath you take in, visualize it taking care of your belly. With each exhale, allow your breath to flood you with warm relaxation, diffusing all tension in you, in thoughts, body, and emotions.

8. As emotion is held in the belly, the process of breathing softly like this will cause memories, images, and thoughts to come up. Whatever you get, welcome it all. If you notice you're engaging with these thoughts and emotions, be glad you did, and gently return your mind to your breathing.

9. Once five to ten minutes have passed, put your hands on your stomach. Notice the breath as it pushes your belly softly into your hands.

10. Bit by bit, begin to allow your awareness to flow into the space all around you.

11. End this session with an intention to remain connected to your belly and your breath as you gently come out of the meditative state.

Circular Breathing

You must do this mindfully and as gently as possible because this breathing technique can alter your consciousness. The goal is to breathe in and out with no breaks in between. You can do this quietly or make a whooshing sound on every exhale. Expect that old emotions might come up. This means you are releasing old, stale energy in your emotional body and allowing your mind to open up to deeper levels of truth.

1. Sit in a comfy position.

2. Inhale and exhale through your nose.

3. Count each inhalation and exhalation, making sure they're the same number of seconds.

4. If you like, you can include a slight pause to retain your breath between inhales and exhales. Only do this if it feels comfortable.

5. Keep this up for at least five minutes.

Visualization Breathing

There are a lot of ways you can visualize as you breathe deeply. Your visualization should fit whatever your present needs are. Here are your options:

1. See your energy centers glowing as you breathe prana or life force into them.
2. See divine light moving through your body as you breathe in and out, washing all over you.
3. See the pathway air takes as it moves through your respiratory system.
4. See tension and stress melting off your body as you breathe out.
5. Breathe in light into your chakras and breathe out darkness.
6. Inhale pain, and exhale loving-kindness (This is Ton-glen, a Buddhist practice).

Remember, your breath is life itself. Practice these exercises to make sure that you give your astral body the energy it needs to move around the astral plane.

Chapter 8: Self-Hypnosis

You're driving home from work, and you suddenly realize you're pulling into your driveway. You don't quite remember the details of the trip. Still, you've driven this route enough times that it's become second nature. So, your mind focused on other thoughts, leaving just enough consciousness for you to be aware of what you were doing and spot any potential danger along the way.

You're reading a hard-to-put-down novel, and things are really escalating with the protagonist. Your heart is racing. It feels like you're in there, in the thick of things, and not holding a book in your hands reading along. It's noisy all around you, but you don't care. All you hear and see are the voices of the characters and the world around *them.*

Self-Hypnosis Defined

What's going on in each of these instances? Self-hypnosis. This is a trance state that we slip into on a day-to-day basis. It's a natural phenomenon that happens when you have laser focus, keeping your attention trained on just one thing. It also happens when you're doing something routine, like when you brush your teeth or shower. That's why you have the most brilliant ideas while you're in the shower, by the way. Your conscious mind goes on autopilot, which allows the solutions to whatever challenges you're facing to float into your conscious awareness from the subconscious mind.

Being in a state of hypnosis allows your mind to become very open to suggestions. This is something you can take advantage of, as you can suggest things to yourself that you'd love to experience. For example, you can suggest to yourself that you will astral project tonight and that you'll find it pleasant and enjoyable. You can also tell yourself that you'll make a stop at your Aunt Edna's on your trip to see how she's doing.

Hypnosis is a state of hyper-focus. You become absorbed with the moment, or the task at hand, or whatever it is you've chosen to place your attention on. You don't have to work with a therapist to induce this state. Instead, you can put yourself in it, following the proper technique. Once you master this, it's like having a skeleton key that unlocks all the doors to everything you want in life. You'll be the master of your thoughts, in charge of your reactions and emotions.

One of the most fantastic things about hypnotizing yourself is that you can do this anywhere, anytime. It also helps that you're the one in charge, so you don't have to worry about a hypnotist giving your subconscious mind suggestions that you don't totally agree with. Instead, you get to decide what the suggestions should be, and you save yourself a ton of money by choosing to be your own therapist.

The Role of Self-Hypnosis in Astral Projection

With the right state of mind, you can accomplish anything. Never underestimate the value of focus. Having a focused mind equals having a powerful life. You'll find it easier to perform amazing feats in your career, no matter what field you're in. You'll be better at dealing with all kinds of pain, and your creativity goes through the roof as well.

With the hyper-focus of self-hypnosis, you can gain a lot more confidence when facing the unknown. The astral is a realm that constantly surprises travelers with strange, new things. Some of these things may delight you, and others may worry you if you don't get yourself together and face those situations with a healthy mix of courage and curiosity. When you're frightened in the astral, you attract more to be afraid of. You'll also find it harder to project because you don't want to experience those scary things again. Self-hypnosis can help you shed the fear and take a bold leap into the unknown.

Trying to make things happen using just the conscious mind can sometimes be a bit of an uphill climb. When it comes to changing a habit or setting yourself free from fears, it helps to work with the subconscious. This is where the belief patterns that cause those undesirable situations emerge from, making change a tedious, slow process. When you hypnotize yourself, you take your brainwaves down to Theta. In this state, you're less inhibited and very open to new ideas and thought patterns. From this state, you can mold yourself into the person you'd rather be.

The astral is an alternate state of consciousness, one which you can get into using hypnosis. With it, you can will yourself through its various levels to learn more and become a fully evolved soul.

If you find it difficult to remember your projections, self-hypnosis can rescue you. You don't recall them because your astral consciousness didn't make that connection to your physical brain for you to download them. This could happen because you've never put much stock in such things as astral travel, to begin with. Suggesting to yourself in a state of hypnosis that you always remember your trips will help you connect the physical you and astral you.

Self-Hypnosis versus Meditation

These practices are almost the same thing. Of course, you need to be in a calm, relaxed state of mind to make any headway with either. However, with self-hypnosis, you have a specific goal that you'd like to achieve so that you can live a better quality of life.

In meditation, you don't have a goal. You simply sit and allow whatever floats into your mind to do so, without labeling or controlling it, without any intention on your part. Both practices will give you a remarkable boost in your mental and physical health, giving to you in so many ways. It is worthwhile to devote equal time to both practices.

Getting into a Trance for Astral Projection

Here's a step-by-step method for getting into a deep trance state.

1. Lie down, shut your eyes, and breathe with the intent to feel relaxed and calm.

2. When you feel a pleasant wave of relaxation flow through your body, imagine you're going down a ladder in the dark. Don't see the ladder in your mind's eye. Just feel your hands and feet on the rungs as you descend.

3. On each exhale, feel your body climbing down the ladder. A step or two should do.

4. On each inhale, simply feel your hands and feet on the ladder.

5. As you go down, stir up a sensation of falling within your mind. This will change your brainwave level from Beta (alert and awake) to Alpha (asleep) and then to Theta (deeper sleep). You're in a trance once you hit the Alpha level.

6. Continue with this exercise for as long as you need. The more experience you have with deep relaxation and stilling your mind, the faster you will enter the trance state.

7. When you notice a feeling of heaviness wash over you, you can stop the falling sensation in your mind. Also, suppose you don't like the idea of a ladder. In that case, you can simply imagine you're in an elevator and simulate that falling sensation on each exhale.

What You Should Know About Getting into a Deep Trance

The depth of your trance is determined by your ability to concentrate, relax, and use your willpower. If you want to get into deeper levels from Theta and beyond, you'll need to keep your focus on the breath and falling sensation for much longer. That being said, the first trance level is more than enough for you to have a projection. You'll know you've achieved this trance level when you feel pretty heavy.

Make sure before you attempt to get into a deep trance you've had some experience with light trance. You'll know you're getting into a deep trance when:

- You feel uncomfortably cold. You're not shivering, just losing body heat.

- In your mind, you feel very weird.

- Everything feels too, too slow.

- Your thoughts have slowed down to the point where it feels like you've been drugged.

- You feel very removed from your body, as if you're floating, and everything is too far from you.

- You are completely paralyzed, unable to move.

When these signs happen *simultaneously*, then you're bordering on a deep trance. The feeling of floating is a lot milder with a light trance as your astral body begins to separate from the physical one. The same can be said for the loss of body heat and paralysis. Those happen in a light trance, but it's to a lesser degree and not as uncomfortable as a deep trance.

You don't have to worry about accidentally triggering a deep trance state, though. This can only happen when you've put in a lot of work to relax fully while staying alert. It also takes a lot of mental energy and willpower. Keep in mind that you can snap out of a trance anytime you wish, and this should mitigate whatever fears you might have. To come out of a trance, simply focus all your willpower on moving your fingers or toes. When you're able to move something, even if it's just a pinky, use that momentum to move the rest of your body. Then, get up and get out of bed. Move around a bit for some minutes. Otherwise, if you go right back to lie down, you might slip back in again.

What to Expect in a Trance

When you're in a trance, you will feel mildly paralyzed. But, right along with this, you'll notice subtle energy that seems to encompass your body. This energy might feel like a gentle tickle all over your body. Then, it will build in intensity, becoming the vibrations every projector knows. It's a feeling of buzzing with electricity all over your body, and it can be pleasant if you don't react with fear or try to fight it.

This vibration happens as your astral body expands to allow more energy in. It will use this energy to move around in the astral plane. This happens every time you go to sleep, except now, you're observing it consciously. As you vibrate, your astral body will begin to drift from your physical one, slightly out of sync with it.

Another Self-Hypnosis Method

1. Find somewhere comfortable for you to relax. If you're sitting, use a soft chair, and keep your feet and legs uncrossed. You can lie down if you prefer, but you should try sitting instead if you find that you just fall asleep each time.

2. Make sure you're wearing loose clothing for this.

3. Don't eat heavily before you attempt this.

4. Make sure there will be no distractions or interruptions for the next twenty to thirty minutes.

5. Breathe deeply, in through your nose, and out through your slightly parted lips. You want your abdomen to rise and fall with each breath so that your body gets all the oxygen it needs to foster your transition to an altered state of consciousness, thanks to DMT.

6. Now, use progressive muscle relaxation. To do this, scan your body from the soles of your feet to the crown of your head. You're looking for any tension. When you notice tension, let it melt away as you exhale. You can also tense the muscles for a second and then release them as you exhale, allowing yourself to fall deeper into relaxation.

7. As you release the tension, you can imagine it as a dark cloud that floats out of those tight spots and away, dissipating into nothing.

8. As you breathe in, imagine that your breath is a bright light, the very essence of life itself. See that light coursing through your body, removing all tension and resistance, bringing you to a state of total relaxation. Allow the light to leave you pleasantly warm. See it as a blanket that pleasantly envelopes you, keeping you safe, opening up your mind to receive the seeds you wish to plant in it.

9. Now it's time to make your suggestions. You're in a state of focused relaxation, and you can now plant the ideas you want your subconscious to work with to make you better at astral projecting. Make simple statements in the present tense and with positive wording. Keep your attitude open and trusting.

10. Next, come back to your regular waking consciousness. Don't be in a hurry, though. Count to five, as you suggest to yourself that you'll become aware of your environment. When you hit the count of five, slowly open your eyes, acknowledge that you've been transformed with gratitude, and then go about your day.

Tips for Using Suggestions

Use conviction. Don't just think or say the words without feeling their meaning. Instead, say them with confidence and a positive attitude.

Again, always use present tense. Using present continuous tense keeps your goal perpetually in the future, ever unreachable. Remember, "I *am*," not "I *will be*."

Keep it positive. "I am a successful astral projector," not "I am not a failure at astral projection." Focus on what you prefer, not the stuff you'd rather not experience.

Keep it realistic. Don't get too ambitious by saying, "I will go to the highest planes of the astral realm in just two days." Keep your goals small and specific, and you're more likely to attain them. As you smash these goals, you'll grow in confidence, and then with time, you'll be ready for the bigger stuff. Simply choosing to see the Eiffel tower, or visit a loved one, or fly over your neighborhood isn't a bad place to start.

Repeat, repeat, repeat. The more you repeat these suggestions during your trance state, the deeper they will take root, and the more successful you'll be in achieving your goals.

The Power of Trance

Entering the trance state to make suggestions to yourself can lead to transformations that will leave your jaw hanging to the floor. I cannot begin to tell you all the ways I've personally used self-hypnosis to take my life from terrible to a literal fairytale.

Am I insinuating that you can rid yourself of all the problems you have in one fell swoop? No. What I am saying is that self-hypnosis is a highly underrated tool to help you master the game of life. You can use this as a tool to create behavioral changes in yourself that will then lead you to the solutions or improved circumstances you seek.

And if that doesn't float your boat, well, you could simply focus on using this to shorten the learning curve of astral projection.

Here's a neat thing to do when you make it out of your body. Ask for your guide to show up, trusting that they will. First, express your gratitude to your guide for coming. Then, ask them to tell you anything you need to know to help you get better at astral projection. They will give you bespoke information based on your specific needs, which will beat anything you could read in any book—including mine. Who knows, they just might tell you, "All you need to do is blink three times in a trance state, and you're out in the astral realm!" Now wouldn't *that* be cool!

Chapter 9: Affirming Your Goals

Affirmations are short sentences that you state with firm conviction to achieve your goals and dreams and reach the highest heights of your potential. You repeat them often so that you can imprint them on your subconscious. Your subconscious can, in turn, take those sentences to help you change your pattern of thoughts, beliefs, habits, and paradigms so that they all line up with what you affirm.

When you "affirm" something, you declare it to be true, which automatically implies that you phrase your affirmations as very real facts grounded in the present.

Why Affirmations Work

Pick up any book on affirmations or hop on any blog post or random YouTube video, and they'll tell you that there's power in words. Well, you're not going to get that here.

Affirmations work not because there's power in the words you choose, but because of the meaning and intention you put into them. If words were powerful, we'd all be doomed. It just doesn't work like that.

So, you may wonder, how do affirmations achieve such powerful effects? How do they make things happen? The answer is, they don't— *you* do. The affirmation process is simply the conscious, focused use of your mind to craft a life that you'd prefer. That's it.

Recall that the power lies within you, and it only really shines through when you make friends with the principle of focus. The more focus you bring to the here and now, the better your results will be. So, affirmations are a focusing tool that allow you to change your world, reflecting your preferences.

Using Affirmations for Astral Projecting

Now, we're going to put together two excellent practices to give you incredible results with astral projection. First, we're going to combine astral projection with hypnosis. Done right, you should have no problems with leaving your body.

Hypnosis gives you direct access to your pleasure centers and sensory-motor cortex. You also work with your lower cerebral portions (which handle emotions) and the pleasure centers in the right hemisphere of your brain. This process naturally happens when you disengage the left brain's self-cognitive function, so it no longer screens stimulus as it should. So, when you hypnotize yourself, you can plant ideas in your head that will take root and give you your desired outcome.

Your left brain classifies all incoming information, assessing all the data streaming through your senses and giving them meaning before letting them through to the right brain. On the other hand, your right brain is noncritical. It handles information holistically and finds patterns in occurrences and all stimuli you get. It accepts what the left brain feeds it with zero questions asked. So, when you distract the left brain with boredom or put it in a trance state, it's easy for affirmations to reach your right brain. Untainted by the left brain's interpretations, the affirmations can work their magic. For example, suppose your goal is to astral project for the first time or get better at leaving your body. In that case, you will find the best results by administering suggestions to your right brain or subconscious from a trance state that you are a pro at this.

Affirmations for Astral Projection

The following are affirmations you can use to supercharge your ability to leave your body. You may reword them to feel more natural to you or use them as they are. Either way, you need to make sure you really feel the meaning of the words and uncritically accept them as accurate.

- I am more than just my physical body.
- I am consciousness in its purest form.
- I perceive things that are beyond the physical realm with ease.

- I have access to higher realms of existence.
- I am exploring these realms, one way or another, learning more about my multi-dimensional self.
- I freely receive the help and wisdom of all beings whose level of understanding of the astral realm is greater than mine.
- I freely receive guidance along my travels.
- I freely receive protection from benevolent beings with my best interests at heart.
- I am always loved and protected by my guides.
- I am light; therefore, I only attract that which is light.
- I am good; therefore, I only attract good beings and entities of high vibration.
- I am full of positive intentions; therefore, I only interact with positive beings and experiences.
- I am in control of my emotions.
- I am calm during my projections, maintaining my focus with ease.
- I am a master of leaving the physical realm to explore the astral.
- I find it so easy to leave my body.
- I find it easy to maintain my consciousness in the astral.
- I have impeccable recall and remember every detail of my astral travels.
- Regardless of how my day goes, I astral project each night.
- I am love, loving, and loved.
- I am love, and love drives out all fear.

Besides these affirmations to help you out with your astral trip, you should consider setting intentions to help you achieve very definite objectives.

Setting Intentions for Astral Projection

When you finally make it out of your body, you'll find your journey more rewarding when you know what you want to achieve before you even leave your body.

In other words, before you project, you set an intention. For example, you may decide that you'd like to speak with your guides and ask them what you need to know the most at this stage of your life to advance further. Or your goal may be to channel healing energy to a loved one who could use it or travel to a particular time and place in the past, future, or alternate present. You may intend to hear a piece of music to help you in your composition or get an idea for a movie script or vaccine. As you can probably tell, there are no limits to the intentions you can set.

What if you don't want to intend anything? Couldn't you roam freely in the astral? Well, you can, but chances are you'll find your consciousness fizzling out if you don't give it something to focus on via your intention. On the other hand, if you think you'd rather see where things take you, then you should firmly set that as an intention while in the trance state or shortly before you go (back) to bed. Still, it's best to plan whatever it is you want to accomplish in advance so that you don't wind up roaming the astral plane and forgetting you're projecting.

For instance, after working on a book for several hours and hitting a bit of a block about what else to add to it, I decided I'd call it a night and head to bed. That night, I astral projected and found myself in a library. It was the most extensive, grandest library I'd *ever* seen, physically speaking, of course. But, unfortunately, I hadn't planned to project, so I had no intentions in mind. As a result, I found myself wandering away from the library and being distracted by other stuff going on. It wasn't until I woke up that I realized, had I set a clear intention, I could have perhaps opened up some of those books with the intent to get fresh ideas for mine!

Without a clear intention, it's not unusual to immediately head from a projection to a regular dream. Sure, the dream will most definitely have a more vibrant, "real" quality to it, but then, you lose out on the chance to be a conscious traveler. So as soon as you're out of your body, get as far away from your body as possible. It's better if it's out of sight. After that, you can turn your attention back to your intention right away.

How to Set Intentions

The very process of thinking about what you're going to do when you project just before you do is often more than enough. However, you can make this intention even more solid by stating it in a trance state.

Let's assume you'd like to check out the other side of the moon tonight. You would need to get into outer space, somehow. You could decide you're going to get there with a rocket launcher, a spaceship, a flying car, or by simply flying over there. You might decide you want to create a portal for you to walk through, which will take you right to the moon's other side. You could also intend for there to be light over the entire area, so you don't find yourself in the dark or with poor astral sight, unable to see anything.

Setting your chosen intention involves repeating a simple statement in your mind that summarizes what you're going to do. Then, to further cement your intention, you can mentally rehearse all the actions you're going to take in your head. Mental rehearsals help, too. When you finally carry out your plan in the astral, you'll have done it enough times to get rid of the emotion of excitement. It's understandable why you'd feel that rush, but it can distract you or take you out of the moment.

Understand you don't have to set intentions to take care of every little detail. That would leave little room for surprise or other elements that might help you discover new ways to grow. It's like opening the map app on your phone and knowing how to get from Ohio to California. Sure, you can see the route, but you have no idea who you'll run into or what you'll experience along the way.

There's no clock on this. Don't feel like you need to hurry to see your intention through to the end. I feel the need to stress this, so you don't get mad at yourself if you keep projecting and yet haven't followed through on your intention. If it helps, you may move on to another plan. If your plan to create a portal isn't working, understand you can get where you're going through other means. It helps to have backup intentions so that your astral travel is still worth your while.

For instance, you could have a backup intention of increasing your presence and awareness to the point where everything is stable in the astral. You can see, hear, touch, taste, and smell things and focus on making them feel so real you'd be questioning whether or not you projected. Another thing to do is have conversations with the beings or entities you encounter. See what they have to say and pay attention. This way, you can gain insight into your life and some inspiration as well.

You'll find that the most rewarding astral trips are those where you set out to make something happen before you leave your body, and you actually do. Setting your intention gives you a huge advantage. You can predict that you'll run into irrational stuff, which will prepare you for any challenge you face. This foresight is a good thing, especially if you find yourself struggling to remain stable and focused in the astral—a common problem when you're just starting. So set your intentions while you're awake, and you'll do just great.

5 Ways to Set Powerful Intentions

Find the gap between your thoughts. The mind is a busy place, constantly processing emotions, thoughts, and memories like the time you stepped out of the restroom, not knowing your fly was down, and so on. However, there are pauses in between all of these activities. Sometimes the break is so short, so fleeting that you don't notice it. The way to start noticing the space between your thoughts is to make a habit of meditating. As you meditate, you surpass the ego-mind and become pure consciousness or the silence or gap between thoughts. One of the best times to set your intentions for powerful results is in this gap.

Let your desires and intentions go. When you have set your intentions, the next thing to do is to let them go. Letting them go implies that you implicitly trust that they are a done deal, and you will see their manifestation in due time. So, you want to be deliberate about letting go. It's the attitude you have when you've ordered a pizza. You don't keep checking at the window to see if it's going to get here, and you don't keep calling the pizza place to hound them about whether or not they're going to get it to you. You know it's yours, so you're relaxed and at ease.

Remain grounded in a state of divine nonchalance. If you want to turbocharge your intentions, then you want to set them from a place of power. You can't fix them when you're feeling desperate or needy or you believe you lack something. So always set them from a place of contentment and ease. Other people's opinions and your present circumstances should not affect the fact that you know your intentions are set and done. You have no idea how or when your plan will play out, but you know it's a done deal, and your higher self is on the case.

Detach yourself from the outcome. Some people worry that if they practice detachment, they will not get the results that they want. Don't bind yourself to a particular scenario. If you want security, then you must embrace uncertainty. This seems like a paradox, but that's how life works. True security lies in abandoning yourself to All That Is, trusting it knows the perfect way to give you what you need when you need it.

When you are attached to getting a specific outcome, it just means you're full of fear and feeling very insecure. Detachment is a statement of one hundred percent trust in the power that lies in your true self. Make your intentions, acknowledge that they are working out as they should, and then let go. Things will then unfold in a way to bring you to your desired end. Detachment isn't giving up. It's allowing things to play out in your favor. Don't interfere with the process.

Delegate to the universe. When you have a focused intention, you rally all the forces of the intelligent universe, Source, or All That Is, to get moving on your behalf. Your job is to trust that the very force that causes the sun to rise, keeps the planets in alignment, and grows the grass is the same one taking care of you. The difference is, where nature allows this force to do what it must, man tends to get in the way with fear, doubt, and worry. So, assign the fulfillment of your intention to the universe. Don't give in to the need to obsess or become overly vigilant. That does you no good. If you try to force a result, you won't like what comes of it. Instead, allow it to play out naturally by planting your intentions in a field fertile with pure potential. They will bloom and grow when the time is right.

Section Three:
Getting in the Astral Plane

Chapter 10: Preparing to Project

You don't just decide to run a marathon without adequate preparation. The same thing applies to learning to leave your physical body. So, in this chapter, we're going to cover everything you need to be ready for before your first projection.

Best Time to Astral Travel

There's no right or wrong time to project. It all comes down to what works for you in the end. Some people find that projecting right before bedtime is ideal. Others say it's better to leave in the early hours of the morning after you've slept for a bit so that you're still in that sleepy, drowsy state. However, you can leave your body anytime you want to.

If you fear the dark, then it might be best to practice astral projection during the day. This is ideal because your fear of the dark won't have a chance to play out in the astral realm as an unpleasant experience. You're far less likely to manifest or attract malevolent beings or thought-forms. You must deal with this fear before you practice at night. The last thing you want is to be put off astral projection forever because of one frightful experience.

There are more reasons you should project in the morning after you've had some sleep, besides having the benefit of light, especially if you're just starting. For one thing, trying to project when you're exhausted at the end of the day might cause you to be less disciplined about the procedure. In addition, you'll probably be too tired to keep your mind awake as your body shuts down for the night. Also, you may struggle to ignore the impulse to scratch an itch or rollover when you should be perfectly still.

So, it's better to project after you've had some sleep—not enough to make you wide awake and alert, but just enough to give you some energy. Say you get eight hours of sleep at night (or per day, if you work nights or something). The best time to wake up would be about three to four hours in. You need the mini recharge from those hours. Still, it also helps to be in a drowsy state with your body already relaxed, so you can slip out easier than if you tried to do it right from a wakeful state.

Setting Up Your Space

You can't afford distractions. So, eliminate as much sound and light as possible. Turn off your phone. Make sure there are no alarms that could turn it back on and pull you out of your mind-awake, body-asleep state. If you would rather leave your phone on because that's where you document your travels and dreams, then make sure that all alerts and alarms are set to silent.

Earplugs are good to have. The last thing you want is to finally reach the vibration phase of projection, only to come out of it because the neighbor decided that was a good time to play some head-banging music. Also, a sleep mask will help you a lot if light makes it hard for you to go back to bed. Keep the curtains drawn as well, if that helps.

If you share a bed with someone, you might find it very distracting when they roll over or get out of bed. Rather than get mad, consider swapping out your shared bed for twin beds, which you can keep close together but without touching. This way, your partner can roll over, get out of bed, and you won't be bothered one bit. If twin beds aren't an option, think about getting a mat. You don't have to sleep on it all night. You only move to it when you're projecting. The only other solution would be for you to move to a couch. Just make sure you're as comfortable as you can be, so you don't have to return prematurely from your trip because of a crick in your neck or something.

Sleeping Positions

You'll increase the odds of success if you lie down in a position that's unusual for you. For example, if you tend to sleep on your side or your stomach, try sleeping on your back instead so you can slow down the process of falling asleep enough to control it.

One thing you will find helpful is to start in a semi-upright position. If you have a recliner, then that's great. Otherwise, you can prop yourself up on pillows so that you're almost sitting up, but not quite. This doesn't mean you can't practice while lying down, but if you find that you often slip off into sleep before you can project, then it just might help to elevate the top half of your body somehow.

Resisting Impulses

You've spent your whole life going to bed by allowing your mind to sleep right along with your body. Judging by the fact that you're reading this, you've definitely built this habit up over years and years, which means it's going to be a particularly tricky one to break. Astral projection requires that you keep your mind awake while your body enters a state of sleep. So, let's go over what you need to do to develop the appropriate sleep habits, starting with resisting impulses.

To successfully project, you need to get to a mind-awake-body-asleep state. Typically, when you're about to drift off to sleep, your body will test your mind to see if it's awake. It will make your itch so bad you want to scratch it, or you'll feel the need to roll over, turn, or adjust your body. The only reason to give in to the latter impulse is if you weren't in a comfortable position to begin with, so you should address this before you start the process. As for the itches, there's nothing to do but resist them.

Sometimes they will hit you in multiple spots at once. They can be very persistent. Just don't scratch. If you simply observe them as a detached third party or keep your mind occupied with other things, it will pass after about ten to fifteen seconds. Interestingly, the second you raise your hand to scratch yourself, the itch disappears. It's like your body says, "Gotcha! I knew you were awake." So, don't give in to the urge.

Another thing you want to avoid is swallowing. If you swallow, it could slow down the process or cause you to have to start from scratch. To help you avoid this, elevate your head with pillows so that the urge is minimized.

Your eyes also tend to move around a lot. But, again, this is a habit from ordinary waking consciousness. When you shut your eyes, you may notice this movement. It may seem trivial, but this makes it hard for beginners to shut their bodies down. Turn both eyes towards the third eye, which is in the center of your forehead, just above the brows. Your eyes should be shut while doing this, of course. When you focus them on the third eye, it stops them from twitching, trying to see what's going on. Your body will fall asleep faster when you hold your eyes still this way.

The Thin Line between Sleep and Wakefulness

The successful astral projector knows how vital it is to maintain conscious awareness in the state between sleep and wakefulness. To execute this feat flawlessly, you need to keep your conscious mind busy with something. Whatever you do, don't keep it focused on thoughts that are too exciting, or on your problems, or what you're supposed to do tomorrow because that's a recipe for insomnia.

The best thing to do is have a mantra that you repeat over and over. It could be as simple as "Mind awake, body asleep." You repeat this in your mind, not out loud. For some people, it's hard to keep repeating a mantra because that lulls them to sleep. So, the better option is to count down from three-hundred to one. The great thing about this countdown is that it's a monotonous task, but it also keeps your mind active enough so that it doesn't fall asleep on you.

Now sometimes, you may find you've drifted off as you count. When this happens, and you catch yourself, don't sweat it. Just pick up where you left off counting, or pick any random number and resume counting from there. You don't need to be accurate. You just need to keep your mind up and busy.

Don't beat yourself up if you notice you keep drifting to sleep. This is actually a good thing if you know how to work with it. The more you practice hovering between sleep and wakefulness, the more likely you'll have successful astral trips. Also, the more you dip in and out of sleep, the closer you will get to the vibration phase (which starts with feeling a pleasant heaviness rolling up from your feet to your head).

To get better at pulling your mind out of sleep, you can use the method suggested by Robert Monroe. Lie on your back and keep one forearm up in the air. When you slip into sleep, it will drop, causing you to wake up again. If you find this uncomfortable, you can attach a weight to a piece of string and then tie the other end of the rope around a finger. Next, allow your hand to hang over the bed, holding the weight in it. When you slip into sleep, your hand will release the weight, and the force of it dropping will yank your finger, which will jolt your mind back awake. The more you practice this, the sooner you'll be able to maintain this in-between state without needing any props or unique positions to help you out.

Yoga Poses for Astral Projection

Before you astral project, you can take advantage of yoga to help you increase the odds in your favor. Ideally, these moves should be routine for you, and you should do them in a fluid movement, moving from one pose to the next. They'll help you remain alert yet relaxed, which is excellent for astral travel. You'll be more likely to stay up. The poses are easy to master, so don't worry about needing to be an acrobat or a contortionist.

Urdhva Hastasana (Upward Hand Pose): Stand with both feet hip's width apart. Move your arms right out in front of you from your side. Lift them fully over your head and stretch upwards, with your palms facing each other. Allow this stretch to work your sides, shoulders, back, and stomach. Release this pose by allowing your hands to come back down, the same way you lifted them.

Upward Hand Pose

Uttanasana (Forward Bend): You bend over at the hips as you exhale from the previous pose. Bring your chest to your knees. Keep them as close as possible without forcing them, placing your hands on the floor beside your feet or on just below your knees. Again, don't force the stretch. You'll feel this stretch in the calves, hamstrings, and lower back.

Forward Bend

Bhujangasana (Cobra Pose): From the forward bend, walk out on your hands, ensuring your body weight is evenly distributed between your hands and feet. Walk until you're in a full plank position, and then gently allow your lower abs and legs to rest on the floor. The tops of your feet should be flat on the ground if you can manage that. To make things easier, if you can't handle a plank, just lie on your stomach, keeping your arms flat and beside your belly. Then, with your elbows bent, raise your head and chest. You'll notice your shoulder blades squeezing in the middle while your chest muscles open up.

Cobra Pose

Adho Mukha Svanasana (Downward-Facing Dog): From the cobra pose, just go back into the plank position and pull your hips back. Your hands, still flat on the floor, should be extended in front of you. Done right, your body will resemble an upside-down "V." Relax into this stretch, but don't force it.

Downward Facing Dog

Virabhadrasana I (Warrior 1): From downward-facing-dog, bring one foot in between both hands, and then lift your torso. You should have one leg stretched out behind you and the other in front of you, bent. Think of it like a lunge, except your back foot lines up with the front one and also points outwards, slightly. The heel of your front foot should ideally align with the arch of the foot in the back.

Lean into this stretch, and then raise your hands so they're above you. Clasp your hands together. You'll feel this one in your legs, waist, and hips. To get out of this position, move the back leg to meet the front one.

Repeat these moves, ending with Warrior 1 on the opposite legs. You only need a few minutes to finish this routine, but you can repeat it as often as you like. It's a great way to get rid of the tension, which can keep your astral body stuck in the physical if not dealt with.

Warrior 1 Pose

More Helpful Tips for Astral Projection

Practice in the morning. At least in the beginning. Then, as you gain experience, you will be able to travel wherever you want to.

Know your plan beforehand. Are you going to visit a place, a loved one, or a guide? Or do you intend to meditate on health or wealth in the astral plane? Then when you're out, you should know precisely how you're going to do it and have backup plans as well so that each trip is fruitful.

Protect yourself. Ideally, knowing you're safe is more than enough protection. However, if you feel like you need it, you can envision yourself surrounded by golden light or white light. Think of this light like an impenetrable bubble around you, which keeps you safe from all malevolence.

Develop your energy body. You should learn about chakras and how to meditate to keep them clean, open, and energized. They feed both your astral and physical body with the energy needed to function optimally. Meditate on each one. Visualize their colors. Watch them glow brighter as they bloom within you.

Get rid of all jewelry before you project. A fascinating thing that happens when you've got jewelry on is that your entire astral body may leave the physical but can't separate at the points you've got jewelry on.

So, leave the beautiful astral cuffs behind. You can wear them when you're back.

Use the right technique for you. When you first start, some methods won't work for you. However, it doesn't mean you can't project. Just give each technique several tries until you find one that's easiest.

Don't allow yourself to be afraid. You have to remain in charge of your mind. Keep your cool, and don't let your emotions get the better of you. Remember, the astral world is influenced by thoughts and feelings, so you can't afford to let your mind feed you ideas that don't help you. Fear will take you to lower astral planes with beings that don't mean well for you. Fill your heart with love by affirming that you are love, loving, and loved. Remember, affirming means you mean *every* word. The more you accept yourself as love, the higher the realms you will visit.

Try darkening the room. I have astral projected in full daylight. In fact, my first astral projection was in full sunlight, with all the curtains up. However, if you find the light is a problem, you can darken the room and see if that helps you. ***But!*** Make sure there's a little bit of light so you can see around you, especially if you have a fear of the dark.

Read other books and consume materials on astral projection. The more you read, the more you learn. There are always lovely nuggets to be found when learning from others.

Be careful what you wish for. The astral plane affects the physical. So, while you're there, be mindful of what you wish for because you're definitely going to get it.

Master your astral body. When you first leave your body, focus on learning how to use it. Don't try to go places without understanding how it works. To do that, you may remain in your room, but pay no attention to your sleeping body on the bed, so you don't get sucked back in.

Master mental commands. If you find that you can't see properly, you could think with authority, "Improve sight, now!" Are you moving around sluggishly? Think, "Increase energy, now!" Want to go to the sun? Say, "To the sun, now!" These words aren't necessary. With time, you'll find that simply having a firm intention about what you want in the moment is enough to fulfill it.

Be precise with your commands. For instance, suppose you intend to travel back in time to Hitler's era. You need to specify whether it's when he was a baby or already doing damage in power.

You can't interact with physical people. This is because the astral and physical realms are of two different vibrations. So, don't expect to be able to interact with people. That said, every now and then, you might be able to make your presence known or felt, especially with those who are very in touch with their psychic, spiritual selves.

There is no danger to fear. If things feel a bit much, you can always come back to the physical.

Expect your guides. They will show up after some time. You'll know they're your real guides through a sense of inner knowing. The feeling will be unmistakable. So, respect them, appreciate them, and obey what they teach you.

You are free, but you must be responsible for that freedom. Don't use your abilities for evil, and don't invade other people's privacy just for your pleasure. If you're going to do that, it must be for a reason that benefits the greater good.

Chapter 11: Focusing with Music and Mantras

Music for Astral Projection

You don't need music to astral project, though you can certainly begin with it if it helps you. However, your goal should be to move on from needing music so that you can focus on your astral journey without having it be affected by the mood of the music.

Having said that, you could listen to Baroque music, like Monteverdi, Purcell, Vivaldi and so on. Music from the Baroque period is usually at about 50 to 80 beats per minute. This is the perfect pace that allows you to get into a state of deep concentration, or the Alpha brainwave frequency, conducive to leaving your body.

Hemi-Sync by the Monroe Institute is definitely worth checking out as well. It is specially designed for astral projections. That said, there are a few people that it just doesn't work for, so don't beat yourself up if you don't notice anything.

Using Shamanic Drumming for Astral Projection

We all experienced one thing when we first came into the world: rhythm. Specifically, the feeling of rhythm, not the sound. Your mother's heartbeat was the first thing you could sense, along with her steady breathing. This is where we first learned of rhythm. It's a primal thing.

When you listen to percussive music, any parts of your astral and physical body that don't have energy flowing through them immediately open up and are filled with vitality. This is further enhanced when you're drumming in a group. This also explains why you can't help but move your body to good music, even if you restrict the movement to tapping. Little wonder then that shamanic power can alter our consciousness.

To make this work for you, you need a partner, or even better, a group of friends you trust. You'll also need some drums. The African talking drum is perfect for this.

Traditionally, shamans would cross over to the other side and come back with information to help everyone around them. So feel free to ask your friends for help as you just might have some beneficial information for them. Their job is to help you with the drumming.

Next, you should make sure you're wearing loose clothing. If you would rather, you can be in your birthday suit (if you're on your own or your trusted friends don't mind, of course). The point is you should be comfortable, regardless of the temperature. Also, make sure you don't eat right before trying to project, but that you're not hungry either.

Get rid of all distractions and have your friends surround you in a circle. You're going to chant your mantra as your friends drum. Help them understand that the drumming needs to go from soft and slow to loud and frenzied as they notice you getting exhausted from going around the circle. Of course, if you prefer to work alone, that's fine too. You can find shamanic drumming music on Spotify or Deezer or check YouTube for the most liked ones to use.

Set your intentions. You should know what you're going to do once you're out of your body. Keeping your intentions in mind, you may take a moment to pay your respects to your astral guide and thank them in advance for their help with your journey.

Now it's time to dance around the circle in a clockwise motion. Move in time with the drums, feeling their impact on your heart center. Once you've made about three trips around, you'll notice your state of mind will shift. When you just can't go on, you're at what's called "the runner's wall."

Envision that this wall is the ground, and it's in the middle of the circle. With what's left of your strength, fall on that wall. Allow the momentum of your dance to take you down to the ground. Think of that momentum as astral energy empowering you, and imagine your guide riding that energy wave right along with you. Once you connect with the floor, feel your astral body break right through that wall. Feel your mind bursting wide open by that same energy. This is the point where your friends need to slow down their drumming to the same rate as your resting heartbeat.

Brainwave Entrainment Audios

Another great way to facilitate your quest is to use brainwave entrainment audio. Brainwave entrainment is also called brainwave synchronization. It is the process of generating specific brainwave frequencies in you, using a stimulus that matches the frequencies of the brain state you want to achieve.

Your brain has a habit of adjusting its main electroencephalographic frequency when there's a strong enough stimulus, which in this case would be sound. So, rather than go for regular music, you can up your chances by using music specifically created with brainwave entrainment audio. Think of it as a shortcut to getting to the astral plane. Of course, this doesn't mean you don't have to do any work focusing, but you'll surely have an easier go of leaving your body.

The following are brainwave entrainment audios worth looking at:

Binaural beats: this audio has two different signals on the left and right, which cause your brain to adjust its frequency accordingly. These signals or tones are long, continuous sounds on their own. However, when you put the headphones on, they generate a new tone, which is the beat itself. It sounds like you hear a steady, percussive beat, but you're not. It is your brain that combines both continuous sounds into a pulsing one. If you've got a tone of 505 Hertz in one ear and 495 Hertz in the other, you'll get a 10 Hertz tone, which is subsonic and is at the midpoint of the Alpha range of frequencies. Playing binaural beats with loudspeakers converts them to monaural beats, so you need headphones to use them effectively.

Monaural beats: these make use of a steadily pulsing single beat. It sounds like a pulse or click when it's in music because two tones from a single speaker come together. You don't need headphones for monaural beats, and in fact, they are a lot more effective than binaural beats. They tend to interfere with music unpleasantly, so it's best to use them on their own if that bothers you.

Isochronic beats: these are a form of monaural beats. They are single tones, but they're different from monaural beats because they have a sine wave pulse instead of a single tone with separate pulses. In English: isochronic tones are sounds that come on and off in a steady rhythm. This constant switch between "on" and "off" is what influences your brain to change its frequencies. You can play isochronic beats with your loudspeaker and still reap the full benefits.

Sound and light entrainment: this uses sound and light machines, or mind machines, if you will. The audio used with this form of entrainment includes monaural, binaural, and isochronic beats. They are a lot more powerful than audio beats independently, and they act a lot faster. You also work with glasses with diodes in them or a computer screen that shows you lights that flash in sync with the audio. Again, this is pretty powerful stuff, so don't jump right to this without checking out the other forms of entrainment. Also, use this with caution.

There are other forms of brainwave entrainment, but we're keeping our focus on what works along with music and mantras, so this is all you need to know.

Mantras

One of the most crucial requirements for mastering astral projection is raising your resting awareness level. You want to master the art of being in a state of complete rest, in body and mind, while being fully aware of what's happening, instead of drifting off to sleep on account of exhaustion or boredom. Fortunately, if you can learn any skill, you can learn this one too. A great way to speed up your learning process is by using music and mantras. The cool thing about using these tools is that they not only boost your resting level of awareness but can help with leaving your body directly from waking consciousness.

A mantra is any word or sentence that you say either mentally or aloud, over and over again. Mantras can either be meaningless or hold meaning. For astral projection, you will find it best to stick with mantras that mean something to you and keep the language positive. As always, word your mantras in the present tense, not the past or present continuous, or future tenses.

Mantras aren't an English concept. However, that doesn't mean a mantra in English is any less potent than one in Sanskrit. Remember, the true power lies not in the word itself but the meaning you ascribe to it.

So, you can boost your awareness right now with a mantra perfectly worded for your intentions.

Getting in the right frame of mind for astral projection is easy and challenging to do with mantras. You don't need to think too long and hard about them, and there are no steps for you to recall, so that's the easy part. The hard part is keeping yourself on the razor-thin edge of being awake and asleep.

When you've settled on a mantra, you must remember that you can't just repeat it mindlessly. You have to do so with full awareness, backing it up with your willpower. You can think of this as an exercise in concentration. You've got to keep your attention squarely on the meaning of your mantra. Ideally, make a habit of doing this each night, and you will reap the rewards.

To use your mantra, make sure you're in a very comfortable sleeping position so you have no reason to move or fidget. For example, if you're a bit overweight, you may snore if you lie on your back, and that sound will distract you. The best thing to do in this case is to lie on your left side for good results. Then, when you're sure that you're very comfortable and will have no reason to move, you can begin with the mantra.

Using Your Mantra

Start by chanting your chosen mantra out loud, and then as you grow more relaxed, chant it in your mind. As you repeat this mantra, dwell on its meaning. Don't be surprised if you get a successful astral projection out of it right away. This is such a powerful astral projection technique, if done right. If you're struggling to find a good mantra, you can just go with this simple one: *I am awake and aware in every realm.*

You must think about the words you're saying as you use the mantra to grow the ability of your conscious mind to maintain its awareness and grow stronger in focus. If you repeat them mindlessly, you'll be strengthening your subconscious mind—which is almost a pointless thing to do since it's already mighty.

When you've repeated your mantra enough times, you'll most likely notice you're falling asleep. You might find your words hang or slur, or you say something else. Hearing this shouldn't discourage you. It means you're aware you're falling asleep, which is good. All you need to do is resume chanting the mantra. In the process, you'll maintain that balance between sleep and wakefulness. You'll learn how to trick your body into assuming you're fast asleep when your mind is wide awake.

Don't just use your mantra when you want to astral travel. Instead, you should use it daily to increase your ability to remain aware at rest and throughout your day. Sit in a comfy chair, or a stool, or on the floor if you like, and then chant your mantra for ten to fifteen minutes.

Mantras for Astral Projection

Thanks to Samael Aun Weor's Gnostic teachings, there are so many mantras you can use to leave your body, each of them as powerful as the rest. Here's how to pronounce the vowels in these mantras:

- *A* as in "alpha."
- *E* as in "left."
- *I* and *Y* as in "thief."
- *O* as in "core."
- *U* as in "choose."

Now let's get on to the mantras.

La Ra: Samael talks about this mantra as he wrote about the Chapultepec temple in the 4th dimension in *The Greater Mysteries* (1956) book. He said all you have to do is chant the mantra in your mind while paying attention to the particularly high-pitched sound within, almost like a cricket. This is the internal sound. You need to be tired and able to hold your mind awake.

Done right, as soon as you enter the trance state, you will feel that sharp cricket sound in your head. What you need to do is lull yourself a bit deeper into sleep and then get up from your bed with your intention front and center in your mind.

Tai Re Re Re: you can lull yourself to sleep with this one. It works pretty well for those who tend to fall asleep as soon as their heads hit the pillow. Chant this in a sing-song manner, emphasizing the A in Tai. The three Resounds are to be strung together in a way that makes it melodious, like a ringing bell. Don't roll the Rs. Tai is to be chanted on a deeper, lower note than the rest of the mantra.

Fa Ra On: this is from the word "Pharaoh." Samael teaches that you must relax and then use the mantra. You can say it out loud in the beginning and then make it softer and softer. Finally, let the chanting become purely mental. As you chant this, envision the Great Pyramid of

Egypt—only if you want to. *Egypt* is yet another mantra connected to ancient Egypt if you're interested in exploring that time and place or learning from temples.

Rustic: Samael says you should lie horizontally on your bed and allow your body to relax, so there's no tension on the astral body from the physical one. Chant this in your mind and observe yourself as you fall asleep. Allow yourself to go drowsy as you chant the mantra this way: Ruuuuuuusssstiiii.

When you notice you're on that razor edge, get out of bed and leave your room. Don't overthink the process of leaving your bed, and it will be a lot easier for you to leave your physical body. Assume it requires effort, and you'll have a hard time going.

S: this mantra is easy because all you need to do is make the "S" sound in an exhausted state. When you're in the void, all you need to do is get up and out of bed. When you get out of bed, do so with the same attitude you used to roll out of bed when you knew nothing of astral projection. It's not a mind thing but is just the action of you getting up.

You now have an assortment of mantras to work with that will help you get to the astral plane.

Chapter 12: The Meditation Method

Relaxing is probably the most challenging part of astral projection for a lot of people. We all have stressors to deal with each day, at work, school, and at home. If you have mental health issues, then being able to relax might be doubly hard for you. Stress is a factor that makes it hard for us to function correctly in our day-to-day lives, so of course, it stands to reason that it would make it harder to astral project as well. Instead of resorting to harmful drugs, you should consider taking your daily "meds"—by which I mean, meditate daily.

The National Center for Complementary and Integrative Health says that meditation involves both body and mind. Historically, this practice has been used to boost physical relaxation and mental calmness, giving a balanced mind, better health, and general well-being. It's not a new practice at all. Buddhism and similar cultures are all about the process of becoming enlightened using meditation. They have practiced all kinds of meditation for hundreds of years.

Why You Should Meditate

Meditation will help you alleviate stress, which is a huge deal because when your body and mind are chronically stressed, your body's telomeres become shorter. Telomeres are responsible for keeping your body's chromosomes intact. If they fade away, your chromosomes will break down, and this will cause weakness in your bones and immune system, among other things. In June 2016, ScienceDirect published a study that shows that regular meditation reduces stress and inflammatory response to chemical *and* psychological sources of stress over the long term. This means you get to live longer and healthier.

You didn't pick up this book to learn to be healthier, though. You want to have astral projections. Meditation helps you with the process because constant practice will reveal to you the actual nature of reality. The more you meditate, the more paranormal experiences you will have, which will show you that life isn't quite what it seems and that the power is within you to be, do, and have it all. You will find your mind becoming more open and accepting of the truth about our multidimensional existence, understanding that the physical world is barely the tip of the iceberg. This is the right mindset to have towards spiritual matters like astral projection.

Astral projection requires mastery of the mind, and you'll find there's no better way to take charge of your thoughts and emotions than by practicing meditation. The more you meditate, the more fearless you become. You rid your subconscious mind of all the phobias, addictions, depression, and anxiety that stops you from leaving your body.

Here are more reasons to meditate:

1. Meditation helps you build your brain so that you're happier, less stressed, more successful, and have stellar memory. It also makes it easier for you to fall asleep (while keeping your mind alert), helps with learning, and improves your emotional and intelligence quotients.

2. It balances both hemispheres of your brain so that your brain is wholly synchronized, which leads to fantastic creativity and insight, as well as better mental health.

3. You can boost your serotonin, endorphins, and other chemicals while reducing cortisol, the stress hormone.

4. Look younger than you really are and feel that way without the need for expensive beauty products or excessive supplements.

5. Trying to lose weight? Accelerate the process with meditation. *The Journal of Obesity* (Robinson et al.) looked into the connection between weight loss and body image, working with 14,000 adults. They found that those who thought of themselves as fat were likely to put on weight in the future. Researchers from the UCLA school of medicine found that meditation improves the region of

your brain responsible for being compassionate to yourself to stop thinking of yourself as overweight. As a result, you lose fat.

6. The world's most successful people often attribute their success to meditation.

7. Your intuition improves the more you meditate, along with your mental toughness, grit, and happiness.

8. If you have insomnia, consider making meditation a practice in your life.

Preparing to Project Using Meditation

Before you start, you need to make sure you prepare yourself. You may find at the beginning that you have issues with remaining in a meditative state for extended periods since this isn't usual for you. Still, you can set things up, so your session goes relatively well anyway.

First, you have to get rid of all distractions. If you've got a pet, get someone to take care of them or put them in a different room and close the door. If you've got kids and they're at an age where getting them to quiet down is a Herculean feat, then you can practice this when it's nap time or have them go on a play date. You could also give them something to occupy their attention.

Put your phone on silent mode or turn it off completely. If you want to receive calls from certain people, you can set your phone up to ring only when they call you, so you're available in case of an emergency.

Turn the lights down low in the room to a comfortable degree, so you're not distracted by the light, and you're not worried about it being too dark. If you want to, you can use scented candles to set the mood and make your room nice and warm as well. Speaking of setting the mood, you can play some soothing meditation music. You'll find great meditation playlists on Spotify or YouTube.

Do you live in a noisy place? Then you can turn up the volume of your meditation music or use your headphones. The best kind of music is the sort without drums, something easy going that makes you feel at peace. If you're going to meditate without music, you can just use earplugs. Investing in a white noise machine is not a bad idea either. It will get rid of the noise from your neighbors, as well as traffic and electrical appliances like your fridge.

Make sure you're as comfortable as can be. For this, wear loose clothing, and keep your room at the perfect temperature, so you don't have to interrupt your trip just because it's too hot or cold. Another thing to pay attention to is how you're sitting. Make sure you won't get pins and needles over time. Finally, whatever you do, don't lie down, especially when you're just starting out. If not, you might fall asleep.

Robert Monroe's Meditation Method for Astral Projection

Robert Monroe is a legend in the field of astral travel. Here's his method for astral projection through a meditation-induced trance state.

1. **Relax.** Your body and mind need to be at ease. Use the progressive relaxation method by scanning your body from your feet, calves, thighs, torso, and arms to your neck and head. If you feel a bit of tension anywhere, breathe it out. You can scan your body several times till you feel you're ready for the next step.

2. **Get into a trance state.** Stay still, keep your eyes shut, ignore all impulses to turn and scratch any itches. Count from 300 to 1 to keep your mind alert while your body falls asleep. Remember, it's alright if you lose count. You can just start over.

3. **Induce the vibrations.** To do this, Monroe suggests you should imagine you're already vibrating. Feel the vibrations in your mind, and they will come.

4. **Own the vibrations.** Play with stopping and restarting them, so you know you're the captain of this astral ship. You can control them with simple intention and sensation.

5. **Imagine you're separating.** Remain fully aware of the thought of your astral body leaving the physical. Concentration is key. If your thoughts drift off, you will lose control and have to begin the process again.

6. **Dissociate the astral body from the physical one.** You can do this by imagining you're getting lighter and lighter, so light that you float up and out of your body with ease. If you find this hard to do, then Monroe suggests you practice a partial separation. Push your astral foot or hand through your wall or floor, and then pull it back into your regular body.

You might be wondering, where exactly is the meditation in all of this? Anytime you have to fix your awareness on something, whether it's an object, a sensation, your breath, or the mind-awake-body-asleep state, you're actually meditating. Progressive relaxation is a form of meditation. Mindfulness is another form, and the successful astral traveler knows how important it is for you to mind your mind.

Entering a Deep Meditative State

To get into deep meditation, you need to warm up properly. In other words, you must be completely relaxed. Deep breathing is essential. You should also make sure your head is in the right space, and your intention to go deep into meditation is clear and strong.

Various meditation methods will have their own unique effects on your mind, depending on how deep you allow yourself to go. Usually, you'll find yourself immersed in a sea of calmness, with your focus clear and your entire being centered on the here and now. As a result, you'll feel a sense of contentment, clarity, and complete awareness.

Before You Go Deep

First things first, slow your breath and relax your body. Your breath, body, and mind are all connected. When you breathe slower and deeper, you calm your mind, and your body unwinds. Your parasympathetic nervous system kicks in, and your stress response goes down.

Make sure you're wearing loose, comfy clothing. Sit in a chair or on a comfortable cushion and shut your eyes. Breathe in through your nose and then out through your slightly parted lips. That's one breath cycle. Repeat this twice more, or up to five times if that helps you relax better. Make your breaths deep and even. You'll notice the exhale is longer than the inhale. This is fine.

As you breathe in, feel yourself rooted to the present, fully aware of the here and now. On your exhale, allow your body to relax fully, releasing all tension in all the muscles. Pay attention to your forehead, tongue, throat, and jaw. These places tend to carry tension, so make sure to relax them consciously.

Enter a state of joy and contentment. You want to make sure this is how you feel before you meditate. This tells your mind that everything is okay, and there's no need to hop from thought to thought in restlessness.

You can recall something you're thankful for or how great it feels to meditate if you have experience with that. If you're religious, you can say a short prayer to your deity before you meditate. This will further center your focus and give you the sense of sacredness needed to make this a fruitful experience. Feel love and thankfulness that you're learning to heal your mind and grow in your mastery of this fantastic tool.

State your intention. With full awareness of the meaning of your words, state your intention, which is what you want to get out of this deep meditative state. For example, you may intend to increase your resting awareness level or gain access to unique insights that will shift your life to the next level. It helps to add a statement like this: "For the next ten minutes, I focus my full attention on my meditation. I have nothing to do and nothing to think of at this time. Mind be at peace. I will attend to all thoughts after my meditation. I will begin my focus, now."

Choose something to place your awareness on. It could be your breath, candlelight, or a spot on the wall. It doesn't matter what you choose, as long as you keep your awareness trained on it. You could focus on any of your chakras or all of them. You could simply sit with the awareness of your higher self or guide being with you. You could keep your mind focused on the memory of your vibrating body as you meditate. The choices are endless and all up to you.

Go easy on yourself when distracted—*no matter how often you lose focus.* If you beat yourself up each time you get distracted, then you've lost the essence of deep meditation, to begin with. Even if your mind strays a thousand times a minute, *go easy on yourself.* You should know it's a great thing you keep catching your mind as it wanders because it signifies that your awareness is improving. Higher awareness will do wonders for your meditation and astral projection. You have spent many years being distracted, so don't expect that's a habit you can undo with a Thanos snap.

Enjoy the process of being focused. There will be times during your meditation where your awareness is laser-sharp. Enjoy this. Enjoy the quietness in your mind. This teaches it to seek out more of it, reinforcing your new routine of daily deep meditation. The more you actively choose to enjoy the meditation, the less your mind will reach out to think mundane, filler thoughts to stuff the silence with.

Transition gently out of deep meditation. Choose a soft-sounding alarm to bring you out of your meditative state. Come back to everyday waking awareness slowly, gently. Don't be in a hurry. You'll know when the time is right to open your eyes. When you move between states gently, you'll cause the meditative state of mind to bleed into other aspects of your life.

Journal. You should take notes of your practice. Note the time and place and how you felt. If you got any insights at all as you meditated, you should write them down too. Write down how long you meditated, how you feel after meditation, and what state your mind was in during the process. The last item includes details about how often you grew distracted and the kinds of thoughts and sensations or emotions that distracted you. Note how long, on average, you were able to keep your focus.

Note that if you want to leave your body when you're in deep meditation, you can. Simply imagine your chakras opening up, and then imagine you can feel the intense but pleasant vibrations take over your entire form. Then, when you're in complete control of the vibrations, you may stand and leave in your astral form.

If you want to take meditation up a notch, you should try to meditate in the astral realm. Keep in mind you won't be there long if you just sit still. To remain in meditation in the astral plane for longer, keep up a rapid, continuous motion with your astral hands. You can rub them vigorously together, so you last longer in that state. Meditating in the astral realm will have very potent effects on your waking life. Don't be surprised when you start experiencing more synchronicity and other paranormal events in your life. It's all good stuff, as long as you don't respond with fear.

Chapter 13: The Wake-Back-to-Bed Method

The Wake-Back-to-Bed method, also called WBTB, is a very effective way to leave your body, which is why it's so popular. Initially, it was used for inducing lucidity in dreams. Still, you can use it for astral projection as well, either from a dream or from waking reality.

This technique is often used along with others. It is the foundation that lucid dreamers and astral projectors work with when experimenting with other methods or exercises for the astral plane. The point is to make sure you are very alert before you go back to bed. Since you've already had some sleep, you don't have to worry about being too tired to keep your mind focused on your intention to visit the astral realm.

Before Using This Method

You're more likely to succeed with this only if you're already familiar with becoming lucid in your dreams and remaining in control of them. Like astral projection, this is a skill that will take practice, dedication, and time. You can have a lucid dream on your first try, but you should set realistic expectations.

Record your dreams in a journal. This is one of the first and best things to do. You should keep a dream journal, which will serve as subconscious reinforcement that it matters for you to remember your dreams. Just recording them, even if you only remember one image, will boost your dream recall dramatically. Dream recall is crucial because it will give you the control and calm you need when you realize you're in a dream and when you astral project. So, make a point of writing your dreams down each time you wake up.

Reality checks. A reality check is just a test you do in your waking life to be sure you're wide awake and not just in a very vivid dream or something. You can set the alarm to go off randomly to perform these checks, and you should also do them as they occur to you. First, you will test your reality to see if the customary laws of waking life still hold. If you notice there's something off, chances are you're dreaming. The more you do them, the more you'll train your mind to ask constantly, "Am I dreaming?" There can only be one answer when you're awake— and an entirely different one in the dream state.

Every time you notice something strange, do a reality check. This is why reality checks don't work for some people. You shouldn't only check your reality when your alarm goes off. Check it when you notice something strange because dreams tend to have a lot of weird stuff going on, which can trigger you to become lucid if you've been doing your checks the right way. You should do your checks:

- When you hear, see, smell, feel, or taste something unusual.
- When you're doing nothing, just looking around the place.
- When you come face to face with one of your dream signs.
- At random intervals.
- When you look in the mirror, if you're dreaming, you'll see something weird.
- You can check every hour on the hour.
- When you look at your watch or your ring, if you have one. (Consider getting a dream totem ring to remind you to do your checks when you see it).
- Every time you see the letter "A" on the back of your hand. You have to write the letter down.
- When you drink something.

List of Reality Checks

Here are reality checks you can use that will give you outstanding results. Make sure to ask yourself, "Am I dreaming?" as you do each test.

1. Push a finger through your palm. It will go through in a dream. It doesn't hurt, so don't worry.

2. Push your hand through a wall.

3. Check your watch for the time. Look away, and then look back at it. If you're dreaming, it will give a different time or look like gibberish. Skip this if you don't do watches. You can look at your phone's clock instead.

4. Read any text around you, look away, then look back and read again. If it changes, you're dreaming.

5. Ask yourself, "Am I dreaming now?" You can ask in your head or out loud. As you ask, analyze the room you're in. Then, ask yourself how you got there. Work backward by remembering the last thing you did before asking, and the thing before, and on and on. Dreams usually don't have any continuity of events. So if you're dreaming, you'll be able to tell because there's no way you could have made it from Mexico to Paris in two minutes.

6. Ask someone else if you're dreaming. You'll get an interesting answer if you are.

7. Look at your hands. If you're dreaming, they'll look weird. If they don't look strange and you're dreaming, you'll know it anyway.

8. Check your pulse. If you don't have one, you're either a vampire or, more likely, you're dreaming.

9. Put your glasses on or take them off.

10. Look in the mirror.

11. Flip a coin and keep it floating in the air.

12. Jump with the intention to float.

13. Turn a light switch on and off. Switches don't usually work in dreams. Do other checks as well, just in case your dreams have excellent electrical wiring. If not, you might get a false positive, where you assume you're awake.

14. Lift something heavy with no effort.

15. Hold your hand out and will it to stretch to the other side of the room.

16. Stick out your tongue and pull it, so it grows ridiculously long.

17. Look at something made of glass or china and will it to break with your mind.

18. Think of a celebrity and imagine them walking through the door to meet you.

19. Pinch yourself. If you're dreaming, you won't feel any pain.

20. Imagine the floor is lava and wait to see if it changes.

21. Think of a loved one or relative who you know is eons away from you and imagine them coming out of a room in your home.

22. Put your hands together and try to make them melt into one giant fist.

Don't rush through these checks as you do them, or you risk convincing yourself you're awake when you're dreaming. The best checks are the irrefutable ones. For instance, you could never put your finger through your palm, so if you do, then you're in "La La Land." Also, meditate everyday day for ten to fifteen minutes, and make a point of doing your reality checks as soon as you wake up in the morning.

How to Use the WBTB Method

This is the WBTB method adapted to suit astral projection.

Go to bed. Before you do, set the alarm to wake you up after you've had four, maybe five hours of sleep. When it goes off, turn it off and go back to bed. What's the point of this? You want to break the sleep cycle just before you get into the REM stage of sleep. REM is short for "Rapid Eye Movement," which happens every time you dream. Usually, this sleep phase kicks in after about five hours. Still, you should experiment with various timings to find what works best for you. For most people, anywhere from three to five hours of sleep is good enough but find your sweet spot.

Stay awake for a bit. When your alarm wakes you, get out of bed and keep yourself busy for fifteen to ninty minutes. You might need to experiment to find out just how much time works for you. Most people find twenty minutes is more than sufficient. Do what you must to keep your mind active and alert, but don't get so alert that it's difficult for you to go back to sleep. Alternatively, so you don't bore yourself to sleep while waiting, you may read something about astral projection until it's time to go back to sleep.

Go back to bed. This time have a solid intention in your mind that you will recognize you're dreaming when it happens. Let yourself relax and go back to bed. This is when some dreamers choose to add a second method to increase their chances of success, like the IMP method (more on that later).

In your dream, go to your bedroom. When you realize you're dreaming, go to your room (or wherever you know you fell asleep). It doesn't matter where you are; just think about your room, and you'll be right back there. Take a good look at your body and the room as well. Examine it for details which you can check when you wake up. Some say, once you can see your body, and the room feels steady and real (about as "real" as it gets in the astral), then you're out of the body. Others say you need to experience the actual process of separation. I'm of the latter opinion, which is why I've included these extra steps. Better safe than sorry.

Alternatively, plan your exit. Once you've achieved lucidity, fill your mind with the intention to leave your body and plan how you're going to do it. Are you going to roll out or use the rope method? Are you going to allow yourself to float out of your body like a cloud? Is your intention to have your guide help with pulling you out? Also, what are you going to do when out of the body? Plan that out in your lucid dream. Having a plan in place will ensure you don't waste any time when it's time to exit. You won't feel confused or distracted by anything happening in the dream.

Begin to wake up. Again, a simple intention to do so will suffice. You will notice that the waking up process is a lot slower. This will give you all the time you need to remain on that razor edge between waking and sleeping consciousness so that it's super easy for you to exit your body using your preferred method.

Leave your body. When you feel yourself on the bed, just roll out with your astral body. You can also float out if you prefer.

The fantastic thing about the Wake-Back-to-Bed technique is you don't have to go through the process of relaxing your whole body, which is what a lot of folks struggle with. So, if you find that you're constantly falling asleep when you're trying to relax, then give WBTB a whirl.

Lucid Dream or the Astral Realm?

How can you tell the difference between the two? Anyone who has had both experiences will tell you they are two different things. Sure, they have the same element of not taking place in the physical realm and allowing you to create something with pure intention, but that's about it.

It's a feeling. One feels more dreamlike, while the other feels more "real," for lack of a better word. It's like comparing the world you see in a virtual reality game to the physical world.

Your dreams are mostly made up of reference material from your waking life; your subconscious mind generates them. It works with everything you've ever witnessed, whether you were conscious of it or not, to create that world. Your dreams are no less powerful just because they're made of subconscious material, though. You can get amazing insight that improves your psyche and will help you do better in waking life. Your dreams reflect all the troubles you go through in the day and feed you with the solution if you ask and keep your eyes open for an answer.

Astral projections are a whole other matter. You're actually leaving your body when you astral project. You enter another dimension of reality entirely, using your astral body. Here are more differences between both states:

You hear voices as you're projecting. This happens because you're between worlds. Even if you're not trying to project, as you fall asleep, you do separate from your body a bit, even if it's only a few inches. You become unaware of your physical body, more focused on your mind, until your attention moves outward when you hear the voices. It could be singing or talking. You won't always hear voices, though. Sometimes it's other sounds, thunder, or the gentle tinkling of delicate bells, or anything else, really.

Lucid dreaming only happens in your sleep state. There's nothing real about the experience. Your consciousness is still with your physical body. To leave your body, however, you cannot be asleep. Instead, your mind remains awake, which means you retain consciousness, and therefore the experience is very real.

You cannot control other beings on the astral plane. It just doesn't work. In a lucid dream, you can get others to do your bidding. After all, they are a reflection of your subconscious, so you're in charge of them. However, astral beings have autonomy. Just like you can't impose your will on others in the physical world, you can't do that in the astral. You can, however, affect some control of your interactions and conversations to a certain extent.

You can't change the environment in the astral realm. Wherever you find yourself, you can't change the setting. It is what it is. In a lucid dream, you'd be able to make night day and vice versa. In the astral, you can't because that realm exists independent to you. You'd have better luck trying to turn the Great Pyramid into the Statue of Liberty in real life than trying to change your environment in the astral plane.

You have to understand the fundamental differences between astral projection and lucid dreaming. If you confuse one for the other, you're likely losing out on the many benefits that both of them can give you. But, again, just because lucid dreaming isn't real doesn't mean it's pointless or has no benefits. You can use the power of your subconscious mind through your lucid dreams to heal yourself and others, come up with unique ideas for business or your next screenplay or painting, work out creative solutions to troubles at work or at home, and so much more.

The feeling of astral projecting is unmistakable, from being in the void to the vibrations and the sensation of the astral you separating from the physical you. If all you've done up to this point is lucid dreams, you will *know* this is a whole other ballgame when you have your first projection. You will have zero doubts in your mind that you're not dreaming because your consciousness is fully present and in control of itself, but not your environment. Also, things tend to be a lot more stable in the astral realm than in your dreams. That's another sure sign to keep in mind.

Chapter 14: Other Astral Projection Techniques

Before using any technique, you should make sure you're in a state of deep trance. Please use the relaxation techniques already mentioned in this book to achieve the trance state before attempting to exit. You can achieve trance through any of the already mentioned exercises in this book. You can also resist the urge you have to move when you wake up in the morning and keep your eyes shut. Do this right, and you might find you're in light sleep paralysis, between the waking world and the dream one.

You can use the relaxation method you're about to read in the first method below for your convenience. Subsequent methods will be written with the assumption that you have adequately relaxed your body and brought your mind into a trance state.

Robert Bruce's Seven-Step Rope Method

The rope method is a straightforward and effective way to come out of your body. It keeps the time needed to leave your body very short. But, before you do this, here's a little exercise:

- Shut your eyes and take a few relaxing breaths.
- In your mind's hands, hold an apple. Feel its shape.
- Now, hold a golf ball. Feel how hard it is. Feel the bumps all over it using your hands.

- Hold a hot potato now. Allow the heat to seep through each palm.
- Hold an ice cube. Rub it all over your hands.
- Now, hold a soccer ball. Feel what it's like in your hands.
- Feel the texture of fur.
- Use your mind's hands to rip a piece of paper to pieces. Feel the sensations with each tear.

Don't skip this exercise because it teaches you how to work with your astral hands, which is a skill that you'll need when you're leaving your body.

Relax. Sit (or lie) in a comfortable position, and then shut your eyes. Breathe in and out, deep and slow. You want to imagine that on every exhale, all the tension in your body melts away. Keep this up until you feel completely at ease. You can use a mantra to help you. Simply saying, "I am very, very relaxed" on each exhale will do. If you had tried to project before and failed to do so with full consciousness each time, you should spend at least thirty minutes relaxing even more.

Get into a trance state. This is the stage between sleep and wakefulness, with your mind very active and aware. If your mind remains active, you don't have to worry too much about totally falling asleep. Instead, you can use the counting process or a mantra.

Slip deeper into relaxation. Keeping your eyes closed, look into the darkness. You will see patterns pop up in your line of sight. Pay them no mind, and they'll go away. With time, you will notice you can't feel your body anymore. Don't panic. Sleep paralysis is a good thing.

On to the vibrations. This can be pretty hard for beginning astral travelers to achieve, but it is doable. All you need to do is imagine or feel your energy centers or chakras vibrating with energy, being filled with light to make the vibrations come. Try not to overdo this. They may start in just one body part. If this happens, putting your attention on them should make them more intense, and then you can move them around your body. As you do this, the vibrations will begin.

Control your vibrations. With your intention, play with the vibrations by increasing their frequency. For example, you can slow them down to a stop and then start them up again, or you can speed them up until they hit a very fine, high frequency. When you feel like you are in complete control of the vibrations, you can move on to the next step.

Use the rope. Imagine that there's a rope hanging right over you, just within reach. With your eyes still closed and your body still, imagine yourself reaching out for this rope and then grabbing it. Next, pull your astral self out of the physical body. The first couple of times you try this, you should only pull yourself partway out and allow your astral body to return to the physical one briefly. Do this enough times until you feel like you're in complete control of your astral body.

Separate yourself. When you've proven you're in control through the partial separation step, it's time to head out. Just pull your entire astral body out, putting one hand over the other on the rope until you've left your body. It helps if you chant in your mind or set the intention, "Light as a feather." This way, you don't take on the idea that it should be harder to pull yourself out because you erroneously assume the astral body is heavy like the physical one.

You'll know it's working when you get a feeling of vertigo in your chest and stomach. This is caused by the pressure of this method on your astral body. Continue to climb, and you will soon be out. It's essential to remain physically relaxed and mentally calm. You can practice using the rope right now before you're ready to project, so you know what to expect. Use your imagination and your memory of ropes to help you generate the natural sensation of climbing.

The IMP Method

IMP is short for "Impossible Movement Practice." The point is to attempt to do movements that are physically impossible in waking reality. The best kinds of movements are the subtle ones. However, you can be more ambitious. For example, bend your leg entirely backward from the middle of your thigh or bend your arm at the forearm (in real life, the only bending would happen at the elbow). Pick movements that wouldn't work in real life for you because of a different body part that makes it impossible.

Choose the movement you prefer, and then in your mind, repeat it over and over from the first-person point of view. Feel the chosen body part bending and moving in the most ridiculous of ways. Eventually, this sensation will go from imagined to tangible on an astral level. You will begin to feel vibrations. You can then allow the movement to transition into your astral body separating from your physical one.

The Free Fall Method

See yourself falling down swiftly. Imagine all the sensations that come with falling. Feel how fast you're falling and feel yourself tumbling over and over. If you do this right, you will feel the vibrations, and you'll get a weird sense of not knowing exactly where you are in terms of space. When you notice voices, buzzing sounds, vibrations, and your heart beating faster, just keep going with your visualization. When you notice you're close to projecting, imagine hitting the ground suddenly. This sudden collision with the ground will trigger a separation from your body.

The Yo-Yo Method

Just before you get in bed to go to sleep, pick a spot in your room that you're familiar with, whether it's your closet, door, bookshelf, or lamp. When you've chosen a location, examine it thoroughly. Notice all the details you can about what it looks like. Touch all the areas of that spot, memorize all the tactile sensations you get, and then go to bed. As soon as you're awake, move your consciousness straight to the area you studied before. Imagine it as vividly as you can for just one second, then return your awareness to the darkness behind your eyes for one second. The next second, shift your attention to the spot you've visualized and then back to the darkness after that. The yo-yo effect of moving from point to point in focus will trigger vibrations and complete separation from the physical body.

The Listening Method

Focus on the sounds inside your head when you're in the trance state. You'll notice humming, buzzing, or voices. Whatever you hear, just continue to listen, even when the intensity and volume of the sounds increase. When the sounds get really loud, use a rapid movement to separate from your body. You might find the sounds have already pulled you out into the astral plane on their own.

The Exhaustion Method

It's so easy to fall asleep when you're exhausted. The trick, then, is to find a way to keep your mind awake while your body shuts down. Considering how tired your body is, you will naturally be very relaxed, allowing you to get into sleep paralysis quickly.

Don't go to bed to use this method until you find it incredibly difficult to keep your eyes open. Next, you want to lie down somewhere uncomfortable or in an awkward position. If you're too comfy, you just might let your mind drift to sleep as well. So, if you're a belly or side sleeper, lie on your back. If you love lying on your back, try your left side.

Remain aware of all the sensations that come with falling asleep. Maintain your awareness, and don't let it fade away. Feel free to exert mental effort in this case because your body will still fall asleep no matter how much is going on in your head.

After the vibration stage with the hypnagogic sensations, get up without using your physical muscles. You will enter the astral realm.

The Forced Sleep Method

Use this one in the morning, right after you wake up. Let your eyes stay closed, and don't move. Don't concentrate on anything either. Allow yourself to sleep for ten seconds. After the ten seconds are up, aggressively separate your astral body from your physical one. This way, your brain is tricked into assuming you're actually going back to bed and will create sleep paralysis, which allows you to astral project easily.

The Rotation Method

Imagine and feel your body rotating about an axis. Do this with no tension in your body. When the rotating motion goes from only being imaginary to feeling real, or you notice your body vibrating, you should intensify the sensations you get. You might hear loud buzzing or notice your heartbeat is a little too fast. Ignore that. Just continue with the rotation, and soon you will find it easy to get out of your body.

The Body Strain Method

This method calls for strain in your entire body without using the muscles. It may sound weird, but you should give this a go. All you have to do is generate a feeling of tension inside your body. This tension isn't physical, just so you know. You will feel a slight electrical current running through you, which can intensify to become the vibrations you get before projection. You can do this once you enter sleep paralysis or right when you wake up. Strain your astral body, and notice what happens next. You should get a feeling of floating, as well as the vibrations and weird sounds.

Continue to strain until you're out.

The Brain Strain Method

Generate that same straining sensation from the previous method within your brain. Imagine the feeling of your brain being squeezed in your head. You will feel a non-physical tension, which will lead to vibrations and a feeling of vertigo. Continue to strain your brain till you attain complete separation.

The Running Method

When you have accomplished the trance state, or just after you've woken up from sleep, vividly feel yourself running very fast while keeping your physical muscles relaxed. You don't have to be able to visualize yourself running. The simple sensation of running will do. Keep going faster and faster, and you will get the vibrations. When the vibrations are very intense, imagine a solid wall just up ahead, and run towards it even quicker. When you smack the wall, you will trigger a separation from your physical body.

The Tunnel Method

Imagine a tunnel, long and dark. You're standing in it. Imagine that at the end of this tunnel is a bright light. Fly through the tunnel, feeling the sensation of flight as fully as you can. If it helps, you can generate the same feeling you do in an airplane just before take-off. Go through this tunnel with increasing speed, and soon you'll feel the vibrations and hear noises as well. Ignore both and keep your attention on the light at the end of the tunnel. Once you arrive at the white light, your astral body will separate from the physical, and you can begin your journey.

The Third Eye Method

You're going to need your third eye for this one. You can find it in between your eyes, just slightly above the eyebrows. That's the seat of your consciousness. For this projection method, you must keep your focus on this spot. Turn your physical eyes toward the third eye and keep all of your attention there. With time, you will notice the vibrations and a floating feeling. Keep your awareness there until you feel completely separate from the physical.

The Swimming Method

If you swim well, then all you need to make this work is muscle memory. When you're in a trance, imagine the sensation of swimming as vividly as you can. Remember what it feels like to be in the water and move just like that in your mind while keeping your physical muscles relaxed and motionless. You'll get the same effect as the rope technique, with the gradual increase in vibrations that lead to a complete separation.

The Eye Movement Method

This is excellent for causing the vibrations or intensifying them. When you're in the perfect state, all you have to do is move your eyes behind your lids from left to right, back and forth. The result is your focal point will be thrown off balance, and this will deepen the vibrations, leading to a projection.

The Wiggling Method

For this, just wiggle your hands or feet while keeping them relaxed and still. You're working with the astral body here. When the feelings go from imagination to actual astral sensations, that means you're on your way to leaving your body. Continue to wiggle, moving that sensation from just the hands or feet to other parts of your body. Imagine that the wiggling feeling is loosening up your astral body, prying it from the physical. Keep this up until you're out.

The Recall Method

This one works best for those who have already projected before. Imagine your previous astral projection as vividly as you can when you're in the sleep paralysis stage. Bring to mind the sights and sounds, all the sensations that came along with it. Make it as vivid as you can. Remember what it was like to leave your body. Include all the details in your recollection, like the vibrations, sounds, feelings of heaviness, and so on. As you do this, you will inevitably project.

The Room Method

Imagine you're walking around or standing in the same room you're sleeping in from the trance state. If you prefer, you could pick a different room. When I want to make sure I find myself out of body outside the house, I like to choose a location with lots of open space, like on a hill. You want to make sure you imagine you're where you are from a first-person perspective. In other words, you should be looking *through* your own eyes around the room and not looking at yourself as though you're an actor on a movie screen or something.

Feel your feet firmly connected with the floor. If you have a rug in your room, allow your toes to really sink into the material and feel it. Continue to visualize this until it feels more real than you being in bed. What this does is shift your consciousness away from your body. This is a very effective method and I can't recommend it enough.

The Backflip Method

When you wake up, try to do a backflip without moving your physical body. Unfortunately, this will cause your point of consciousness to shift so dramatically that you'll immediately be out of your body. If you have trouble with this, you should spend more time getting deeper into relaxation or trying a different method.

The Levitation Method

In sleep paralysis, or just as you awaken from a dream, immediately levitate out of your body. You must do this with a confident attitude as if you've always done this your whole life. Don't think about it, just do it. At this point, you should know that your physical body isn't supposed to move. This method will help you move to the astral plane right away, or it will at least get you closer to your exit.

The Roll Out Method

From trance or as soon as you wake up, immediately roll out of your body just the way you would in waking life if you were rolling out of bed. Remain relaxed physically while you aggressively roll your astral body out.

The Train Method

Imagine being on a high-speed train, running through its corridor to the other end. Hear the noise the train makes. This will trigger the auditory hypnagogia that accompanies astral projections. Running through the train, continue to focus on the noise and allow it to build up in intensity. At the end of the train, jump off. When you hit the ground, you will leave your body.

The Hammock Method

Imagine you're swinging in a hammock. Make the swinging sensation as natural as you can. Let the hammock swing you higher and higher and allow your astral senses to match those feelings. Eventually, you will get vibrations and hear sounds. To leave your body, simply fall off the hammock as you hit the highest point in the air.

Combining Methods

For best results, you can combine methods. Here is a list of combinations for you to try:

- The WBTB method works great with the IMP technique.
- The rope method goes very well with the third eye method.
- Use the body strain or brain strain method along with the forced sleep technique.
- Use the wiggle to lead into the rope, levitation, or backflip methods.
- The exhaustion technique works with just about any other one.
- The listening method can and should be incorporated with others for extra oomph and a successful astral projection.

Chapter 15: You're There. Now What?

Congratulations on finally making it to the astral realm. You may not have had an easy go of it, but it does get better and easier with time. When you've got the learning curve over and done with, you can now truly begin to explore all the beautiful things in store for you on this plane. You'll get to experience self-healing, transmutation, communing with spirits and other beings, getting information about the past, present, and future, as well as alternate dimensions of reality.

Before you do all of this, you need to learn three basic things:

- How to solidify your experience.
- How to extend the duration of your stay in the astral plane.
- How to navigate the space.

With a complete understanding of the basics, you will stay fully aware of the astral realm. Your sensory faculties will be extremely sharp, and your environment will be as stable for as long as you need it to be.

Solidifying Your Experience

You stand to gain a lot from thoroughly grounding your senses and self-awareness in the astral realm. Ideally, you should always solidify your experience. Do this as soon as you have separated from your body or right after attaining lucidity in your dream. Solidifying your lucidity is one way to make sure you do not lose consciousness of the fact that you're astral projecting. Sometimes, you enter the astral plane with full awareness, which leads to a steady, stable environment. Other times though, that's not the case. This will affect how long you can remain in that realm and how intense the entire journey is for you.

According to Raduga, the best way to create this solidification is through sensory amplification. This entails making the astral realm as physical as possible, allowing the quality of "realness" to fully manifest wherever you find yourself. The way to make this happen is to tune your senses to all the stimuli from the astral environment.

When you leave your body, your sense perception can be very dull. You might find your vision is too blurry or completely absent. Your sense of touch is there, but barely. This is a problem that also affects lucid dreamers the moment they realize they're dreaming. When your senses are dull, there's nothing to see or do, or you misinterpret the sensations you have, and that forces you to go back into your body. Trying to hold on to anything feels like trying to "keep a wave upon the sand." It all just disintegrates. To avoid this, you solidify your experience by amplifying your senses so that you have clarity in sight and touch.

The Other Senses in Solidification

We're not going to dwell on any other senses besides touch and sight because those two are the most important for sensory amplification. Of both senses, touch is the more universal and primitive one. As such, the first sense to work within sensory amplification is the tactile-kinesthetic one. Then, when you are grounded in the environment through touch, you'll find the other senses fix themselves (usually). It's how you can establish that you are in an actual space and not just a floating point of consciousness in the physical world.

Palpation and Peering

To solidify your environment through touch:

As soon as you leave your body, you should grab, rub, or skim the surface features of your environment. This is called *palpation.* Your vision may be useless at this point, but you'll be able to feel surfaces, objects, and other features of your surroundings. These features may or may not be familiar to you, but the more you touch them, the harder and more physical they will feel. You want to make sure you don't leave your hands on any surface or object for longer than a second, or else you will get the sense that it's all dissipating.

Rub your hands together. Doing this is a great way to make your astral body even more physical, in the same way that palpation causes the environment to become more stable. Both palpation and hand rubbing are very effective. You have to do them very deliberately, intensely, almost in a frenzy.

When it comes to vision, you might find it flooding in as soon as you begin touching things. However, palpation and hand rubbing by themselves might not work or might only restore blurry vision. This is because sight can be very slow and stubborn.

To solidify your environment through sight:

Hold up various objects about four to six inches away from your face, and glance at each one quickly. This will cause everything to become brighter and give you more visual focus. This solidification technique is called *peering.*

You can also look at your hands and get into the details you notice. Studying your hands intensely will trigger full vision in about three to ten seconds. Ensure you keep shifting your focus all around as you analyze your hands or the objects around you. If you stare too long at one spot, dissipation will occur.

Use both peering and palpation to help you solidify your experience, especially if you use the same objects or features of your surroundings. Alternating this with rubbing your hands, you will find great success.

Critical Solidification Methods

Now, it's entirely possible that even after all your attempts to bring your environment into complete focus, you still won't be able to perceive much. If this is the case, you should try the following:

1. Strain your body and/or your brain, as described in the previous chapter.
2. Spin quickly and with force. You want to spin around the head-to-toe axis like you're doing cartwheels.
3. Flail about in a very aggressive manner, exaggerating your movements, fully intending to have a clear and complete perception of your environment.
4. Dive to the floor headfirst.

The latter technique might seem a tad much, but it works pretty well. Just dive into the ground, headfirst, flying downwards. After anywhere from five to fifteen seconds, you will find yourself in a brand new environment or a dead end. Don't worry if you notice that doing this dive causes you to lose even more sensory faculties. What you're really doing is returning into the state in between sleep and wakefulness to get to a deeper level of trance before coming back into the astral plane. So don't think it weird if you find you're in a black, blank, or otherwise featureless space while you dive. We have Michael Raduga to thank for this discovery.

Whatever solidification process you use, do it deliberately, aggressively, and continuously to have a successful astral projection. Keep in mind that you're transferring all your senses from your physical body to the astral one. So, it makes sense that your astral body has its senses numb and dull at the start. So, the more force and aggression you use in your movements, peering, and palpation, the more you will embody your astral self and stabilize your environment.

Extending Your Stay in the Astral Realm

The longer you're in the astral, the higher the chances it will all dissipate. To make it last, you want to be aware long enough to at least carry out one of your plans. Fortunately, once you've got the hang of solidification, you will find it easier to extend your stay in the astral. Here's how:

1. Periodically practice peering and palpation as you go about your business in the astral realm. Don't do this the whole time you're there. Do it only every now and then, even if it doesn't seem like your experience will dissipate. If you do notice sudden dissipation, you can try the other techniques besides peering and palpation.

2. Maintain the vibrations. The pulsing, vibratory feeling you have should be kept alive. You can amplify the vibrations by straining your body or your brain. However, suppose at any point you notice that the vibratory sensation is fading. In that case, that means things are about to dissipate, and you should perform one of the critical solidification processes.

3. Examine how aware you are every so often. In other words, you want to keep checking in with yourself to make sure you're conscious you're in an astral projection and you remember

exactly why you're there. This way, you'll keep your mind from drifting back into dream consciousness.

4.Don't be spontaneous. Seriously, if you didn't plan something, then don't do it. When you do something that isn't in line with your intentions for that astral trip, you might cause your lucidity and mental acuity to go way down. Then you'll lose yourself in the experience, forgetting you're not dreaming. When anything unexpected makes its way into your environment, do the best you can to make it a part of your action plan. Suppose your goal was to visit an ancient temple to learn the secrets of wealth, but some weird, scary-looking being suddenly accosts you. You can tell it you're in a hurry, and it can either come along or play with you later. Even if the creature seems malevolent, don't be hostile to it, or you'll get the same treatment. Choose to be politely firm when you run into other beings.

Whatever you do, *never remain still.* You want to make sure you're constantly moving. Suppose it turns out part of your action plan requires that you sit still. In that case, you should compensate for this by going hard on the palpation, hand rubbing, and peering, and also amp up your vibration. Also, don't look into the distance for too long, as this can cause dissipation. Finally, if you find you've lost your place in the astral realm, don't sweat it. You can always re-enter the astral right away, no matter how often you lose it.

Astral Physics: Navigating the Space

You'll quickly find yourself falling in love with the physics of the astral plane because you don't have to deal with any of Earth's usual constraints, like gravity. Even when you encounter laws that seem to keep you in check, you can bend some of them with some effort. Still, there is some benefit to having a bit of physicality with you as you travel. For instance, it would be best to travel in a tangible form, much like your physical body. If you travel around without a form for too long, you will experience dissipation. Now, let's talk about what actions you can take in the astral.

- **You can move through solid objects.** Whatever it is, you want to fly, walk, swim, teleport, or move through it however you want. You can even move through other creatures as well. To do so successfully, you should be confident, like you've done this a million times before, and it will happen. If you're doubtful, you either won't get through, or you'll be stuck. If you get stuck, just squeeze your way out, or calm down and assume that attitude of having done this too many times already. You don't think too hard about sitting in a chair. You shouldn't overthink moving through solid objects, either.

- **You can fly.** There's nothing as thrilling as flying, defying gravity. This is one of the first things astral projectors learn and come to enjoy. However, you will need to master this. In the beginning, you may find it hard to get off the ground, and when you do, you might feel more like you're swimming through a viscous liquid rather than flying. Or you might find your problem isn't lift off, but control. You can fix this by becoming confident in your flying ability. Using your willpower, project yourself into the sky with a swift, powerful motion. Straining the body or brain is a great way to control your flight if you find you're moving too fast.

- **You can hover or float.** You're not flying in this case, just staying off the ground. To do this, just intend and imagine that you're floating off the ground, and you will immediately do so.

- **You can change your body.** Have fun adjusting your physical features. You can make yourself taller or shorter, take on a different gender, become an animal, change your hair or skin color, and so on. Begin with more minor changes, and then work your way up from there. If you have any issues at all, they're likely based on limited imagination and a lack of confidence. So be bold with this and look up images you'd like to become before you project.

- **You can modify some elements of your environment.** For instance, you could make a light bulb come on, or turn off, or change colors. Recall that you're in the astral plane and that some dimensions of this plane won't readily lend themselves to any changes you seek to create. With practice, you'll know what you can and can't change.

- **You can ditch the body.** No, not in a police procedural drama way. I mean, you don't have to travel around in a body. Remember, what you really are is consciousness, so you don't need a body to exist. However, the longer you're out of the body, the more likely you'll experience dissipation. To lose the body, you simply need to will it away. You'll notice the only senses you will use are sight and sound, and this is a blissful experience to have. You will also see you have 360-degree vision.

- **You can journey across universes in a matter of seconds.** You can think of a place, will yourself to be there, and there you are. You can point at a location, imagine the distance between it and your hand shrinking, and there you are. You can crouch down low, generate energy like a rocket, and then blast off to your chosen location in outer space in a single leap.

- **You can zoom in and out to explore worlds on your chosen scale.** You could shrink yourself till you're just a cell and interact with the world and entities on that scale. Just look at something for reference, like a grain of sand, and then will yourself zoom into it. You will find the sand grows bigger and bigger until you're at your desired level of shrinkage. You can also zoom out, using buildings or even whole planets as a reference point. So, the objects around you become smaller, and you can interact with beings on that magnitude of existence.

Translocation

When you quickly switch out one astral environment for another, this experience is called translocation. This tool is potent. You can use it to get where you need to quickly or take yourself out of undesirable situations or environments. It combines all the elements of solidification, prolonging the duration of your trip and maneuvering your astral environments. You can also use this to ramp up your awareness or lucidity to avoid dissipation, as you'll often wind up in a new environment that's even more stable than the former.

Usually, the process of translocation requires you to head back briefly to the midpoint between sleep and waking consciousness. This translates to temporarily blurry or lost vision, risking the chance that you will fully experience dissipation or experience a false awakening. It's a risk, but the more you practice, the better you'll get at it, and the less you have to worry.

You choose the environment you want to experience by using your willpower, intending yourself to be there. You can be as specific or as general as you want, in that you could choose to be on *any* mountain or on Mount Kinabalu itself. Note that the more general you are about where you want to be, the more variables you will run into in the new environment. You can also choose to keep your options open and simply will yourself to go somewhere new. Better yet, you can ask your guide to take you where they feel you should go at this stage in your life.

Translocation can move you to much more profound levels of awareness in the astral realm, as well as some exciting environments that can seem so vivid to the point that waking life looks like a cartoon. You'll also find that things are weirder, and your thought processes might be more bizarre too. The more you practice this in a session, the deeper the states you will uncover, to the point where you might forget to perform your solidification processes. With this in mind, make a point of constantly solidifying the new environment before you explore it.

The following are techniques you can use:

1. Dive headfirst, as mentioned before.
2. Spin on a head-to-toe axis.
3. Use portals. You can use any object as a portal or just use any door around you. You can will a door to appear wherever you want. You can also use a mirror, a window, or any liquid surface. With time, you can make a portal that looks just like in the movies, if you want. You can even use any cosmic object in the sky. Simply point at it and feel yourself zip-lining to it. As you approach it, it will probably look smaller than you expect, but it doesn't matter. Throw yourself into it forcefully, confidently expecting it to lead to where you want to go, and you'll be there.

Teleportation

This is translocation without any physical activity. Instead, you will yourself to a new place, using your imagination to help you. You might find this challenging; however, you simply need to close your eyes to make it work. This will help create the mini dissipation you need to successfully translocate, allowing you to refresh the scene to what you prefer. You may also do this with your eyes open, although you might find it difficult. For example, suppose you've seen special effects in a movie where a room morphs or melts into a different room. In that case, you can use this to your advantage and teleport with your eyes open, making sure to solidify as soon as you're in the new realm.

Fun Things to Do in the Astral Realm

1. Fly around your neighborhood.

2. Explore outer space.

3. Call on your guides and let them show you around.

4. Channel healing power to any body part.

5. Help heal a friend or relative from a distance by visiting them and flowing healing light to their body.

6. Meditate while in the astral realm for more powerful effects.

7. Conjure up scenarios you would like to happen in your life.

8. Request to be shown viable business ideas that would give you lots of money.

9. Visit loved ones who have passed on.

10. Intend to see your former lives or to check in on parallel ones.

11. Go to a school to rapidly accelerate your learning of any skill you're acquiring on Earth.

12. Intend to see a work of art or hear music that you can recreate on Earth.

13. Consort with the greats in your field, both living and dead, known and unknown.

14. Interact with other forms of life on micro and macro scales.

15. Rejuvenate your skin, so you look younger.

16. Get a sneak peek of possible future events that could play out in your life.

Chapter 16: Problems and Mistakes to Overcome

Distracting Sounds

When projecting, you will hear voices or noises as you come out of your body. But no matter how loud they are, no matter what they're saying, ignore them. There's nothing to them.

Distracting Sensations

Even if you feel something touching you, hands grabbing you, someone holding you, ignore it all. None of this can hurt you, but it can break your focus and make you lose your nerve. If you let this stop you, you're not going to have any success with projections.

Fixing Poor Recall

Keep your first projections short and sweet. You only need ten to twenty seconds, and then you should get back in your body. That doesn't sound exciting, but it's necessary to improve your recall of future projections. What's the point in going on an hour-long adventure you'll soon forget? Train yourself by keeping the first few projections short and then writing down that brief experience.

The Pre-Projection Rush

Just when you're about to leave the physical, you might experience a surge of energy through your chest and stomach area, almost like you're very excited. This is the point where your astral body separates from the physical. You're almost there. Whatever you do, just remain calm, and don't react to the sensation when it hits you, or you'll wake up fully.

The Mind Split Effect

Remember, you are multidimensional. Suppose you notice that you've gone through all the vibrations, and all you feel is tired and groggy. In that case, your astral body exited, but you didn't notice because your consciousness was focused through your physical body, not both bodies. You might be paralyzed at this point. That's okay. Just stay calm, and wait for your astral body to return, remaining in that trance state. You must keep your mind clear as you wait for its return. When it returns, and your mind is free and clear, you will have full recollections of everything it was up to flooding your mind.

Mistakes to Avoid When Astral Projecting

Hopping from one method to another. Some people are impatient with the process and move from one system to another. You should stick with a technique for at least two to four weeks before deciding that it doesn't work for you. I understand you might be thinking, "Well, what if I stick with the wrong system for too long? Aren't I losing precious time?" To that, I say, the astral plane is going nowhere. To mitigate the risk of sticking with a method you don't resonate with, go through all the various ones and only choose whatever your gut tells you to try. It will always be there for you to explore. Also, spending time mastering a method is not a waste because you'll get better at learning to relax properly, which is absolutely essential for successful projection.

Trying to project at night. Not if you're new. This isn't the best time, as I've already mentioned before. Start with astral projecting when you wake up, then with time, you can project at night or whenever you feel like it.

Giving up because you've got no results yet. Some folks try once, and then they go, "That's it, doesn't work, I'm done." For example, I read a blog the other day by a lady who went for an astral projection class of sorts. The instructor basically had the students do visualization techniques, leading them to believe they had astral projected! If only the students had known, they were dealing with a real-life Barney, and all they did was use their imagination, not leave their bodies. Sadly, the lady wrote it off as something she'd never try again.

You may have read articles and research that disparage this phenomenon, but the only way to know is to prove it to yourself. If you've fallen victim to scammers, don't be quick to write this off. Instead, use what you now know and give it a go. Also, don't quit just because it didn't work the first few tries. Patience is your friend. Use affirmations to help you become more dedicated and consistent with your practice.

Confusing relaxation for the "body asleep" stage. Some beginners get into the deep relaxation stage and assume that means their body is asleep. That's not the same thing. You will know when your body is genuinely sleeping because you will experience hypnagogia, or hallucinatory sounds, images, and sensations. You will also notice you have no thoughts, and your sense of time is that it's slower, almost at a standstill. You will begin to feel the vibrations as well. So, don't attempt to leave your body in the relaxation stage.

Trying to project with a mind full of fear. Yes, you're doing something brand new, but you shouldn't let that frighten you. You can't get rid of the feeling of fear, but you *can* transmute it into excitement. Both emotions show up in your body the same way. The difference is in how you've chosen to look at this novel thing. Switch up your thoughts. For example, rather than think, "What if I don't come back into my body?" you could say, "If I don't come back on time, that means more time to explore!" Your attitude is critical. Also, it helps you to learn more about astral projection. The more you know, the less you have to be afraid of.

Indulging too much mind chatter. Don't ask yourself, "Am I doing this right? Is it okay for me to leave?" while you're trying to project. Instead, stop the inner chatter and just do it. An excellent way to stop your internal monologue is to listen. You can let thoughts fly by, remaining emotionally unattached to them. You can listen to the tiny ringing sound between your ears. You can turn your attention to your third eye. Whatever you do, don't attempt to silence your mind by force because that will just cause more thoughts to flow and disrupt your process. Instead, allow them to come and go with no judgment, and gently return your awareness to the task at hand.

Scratching itches and rolling over. We've covered this one before, but it is worth repeating. Leave that itch. It isn't a mosquito biting you, I promise. Also, don't roll over. If you do, recall that you already made sure your body was in a comfy, safe position before the process.

Being startled awake by loud knocking or sounds. This is a weird one that happens. I will admit that even I have fallen for it a few times myself, especially when I project in the day and am not home alone. Sometimes, you'll hear a loud knock or sound at the door, with someone you know or love calling you. If you've gotten to the point where you can now project at night, and it's about 11 pm or even 3 am, pause and ask yourself if there's anyone you know who'd come knocking at your door at that time. You'll learn not to fall for that trick and to continue with your projection.

Being too desperate. You want this magical experience. That's understandable, but you don't want to be so desperate for it that you suffer from performance anxiety every time you want to leave your body. So, relax, and be yourself, and you'll do just fine. You can affirm gently and lovingly, "I'm making this easy and having fun with it."

Improvising with your chosen method. You shouldn't change anything about the astral projection method you're using, at least not when you're just starting out. You can experiment later on when you've got the hang of it.

Trying to make this more complicated than it is. You may read other material about fancier ways to leave your body. Still, sometimes, the simple stuff works best, which is no exception for astral projection.

Giving up at incomplete separation. Just because your body is stuck doesn't mean you've failed. Instead, get more aggressive with your effort, and assure yourself with a calm confidence that this is easy for you.

Not realizing you're in the astral. This happens when you're in the real-time zone or when you don't get the sensation of separation from your body. This is why you should do reality checks to reduce the odds of this happening.

Not having strong intentions. If you want to succeed, then you will need willpower. When you wake up from sleep, your desire to project should be powerful, and you must keep all your conscious awareness on making that happen for you to get results. It can be a bit difficult because the tug of sleep or the day's schedule can be pretty intense, but you need to will yourself to see it through. Paradoxically, you need to be able to release this focus every now and then so that you can allow your body to slip back into sleep and then exit from there. Use the affirmation, "No matter what, I am astral projecting." Repeat this to yourself before bed and when you wake up as well.

Too many consecutive attempts. Go easy with this. Practice three days a week, or four at the most. Give yourself time in between your attempts so you don't feel too much pressure, which can make it hard for you to get to the restful stage. On days when you're not projecting, keep meditating. This will increase your level of awareness and make you more sensitive to subtler energies, a skill you need to master astral projection.

Troubleshooting Projection Problems

One of my astral hands is weaker than the other, so I can't use the rope technique. Your tactile awareness needs to be improved. Find somewhere you won't be disturbed for five minutes, and then lightly brush the back of each hand with the other, then stop. Next, sit with the feeling of your hands brushing each other. Attempt to generate that feeling without the physical brushing motion. Do this for at least five minutes a day, and you'll see improvements. You could also switch to a different technique in the meantime.

I keep getting distracted by the surge of energy in my torso. This happens just as your projection reflex kicks into gear, and you'll also feel vertigo along with the energy surge in your belly and chest. This surge of energy is from your lower chakras, and they help power your astral body so you can project. Just stay calm, and don't react to it. It won't hurt you. The more you project, the less intense the surge will be. You can also go on roller coaster rides or other adventures to help you get over the sensation.

When I'm in a trance, I feel cobwebs, stinging, and itching on my face and neck. As energy moves through the major and minor chakras all over your body, you might feel them as cobwebs or itching. Typically, the sensations match various acupuncture points in the face. The feeling will reduce bit by bit as you continue to work on projecting because you'll grow better at handling the increased energy flow. To help you with this, gently brush your face and then attempt to recreate the brushing sensation without touching your face. Amplify that feeling as much as you can, and if you lose it, brush your face again. Practice this for five to ten minutes daily and do the same exercise on your neck. Also, spray your room with bug spray before your projection sessions. This way, when you get those stinging, itching sensations, you know it's definitely not a mosquito or some other bug.

I feel pressure in my head. That's actually a good thing. It means your chakras are responding to the flow of energy that happens when you're going to project. So, ignore the pressure as best as you can.

It feels like there's a very tight band wrapped around my head. That's a sign of activity in your crown chakra. If you find that this is causing you migraines and headaches, then stop. Take a break. Try again in a few days. During your break, stimulate your crown and third eye chakras gently. Sit for just five minutes and feel for each one. The crown chakra is on top of your head, while the third eye is between your eyes, slightly above both brows.

I get the feeling of choking or being strangled. If you feel pressure on your chest and throat, it's usually because your heart and throat chakras are at work. If you don't have enough oxygen, this could be due to sleep apnea, where you stop breathing in your sleep and then suddenly gasp for air when your oxygen levels are too low. Trance will help you notice whatever issues you have with breathing in sleep. You could try to position your head so that it's tilted back. This way, your airways are more open. That said, do speak with your doctor about this.

I keep getting stuck to my body at my legs/head/stomach. Avoid eating heavy protein meals before you project. Digestion takes a lot of energy, so the heavier the meal, the more the energy is funneled to the digestive process. Your astral body shuts down for an hour or longer when you've had an enormous feast, and your chakras can slow down to the point of inactivity. So cut down on huge meals, especially heavy protein, when you want to leave your body. Also, take off any jewelry you have on. Your astral body has no issues passing through objects, but for some reason, having jewelry on can interfere with your astral body's exit.

No matter what I do, I can't see properly once I'm out of my body. One of the leading causes of poor astral vision is a lack of energy flow into the astral body. The best way to deal with this problem is to draw energy from your physical body. It's a simple thing to do and has proven to be adequate time and time again. Just feel yourself drawing power from your physical body, and that energy will flow. You can visualize or imagine golden or bluish-white light flowing from your body through your silver cord to your astral double. If you can't find your silver cord, just imagine being energized by light.

- Conjure a lamp or torch in your hand.
- Move to a different room with more lighting.
- Say, "Light now!" or "Clarity now!" With a confident attitude.
- Leave a lamp on before you project.
- Imagine light suddenly flooding the room.
- Teleport to a location you know is well-lit.
- Only project during the day.

I keep encountering scary creatures or beings. First things first, stop being afraid when you project. No one can hurt you. Second, you need to be brave. The next time a creature or being makes you uncomfortable, you can imagine a blindingly bright light radiating from your heart chakra, blasting all around you. Feel it envelop you like the most comfortable blanket ever.

Another thing you can do is look at that being and feel intense love for yourself and for them too. They won't be able to stand it, and they'll leave you alone. If they are only your thought forms, they will fade into nothing. So, if you're feeling courageous, give them a big hug and really amp up the love in your heart.

Chapter 17: Exiting Strategies

A question that gets asked a lot is how do you come back from the astral plane? It's an understandable concern, which only exists because there have been many misrepresentations of astral projection in the media and myths perpetuated by the ignorant.

There's no reason to worry about your soul getting stuck somewhere or not knowing how to get back to your body. You will never return to find someone or something else has taken up residence in your body because these things do not happen. In fact, it's even harder to leave your body than it is for you to get back to it. So, to understand why you have nothing to fear, let's talk about the silver cord in detail.

After my first few conscious projections many years ago, I realized that the trouble with leaving my body wasn't staying out as long as I could. For a very long time, I struggled with trying to prolong the experience. I wasn't in the best place in my life back then, so you can understand why I'd want to just escape to the astral plane and remain there forever if I could.

What I soon learned was that this wasn't a unique struggle. It's something a lot of astral travelers have to deal with. That's why you'll find no end of material talking about how to deepen your experience or extend your stay in the astral realm. If you don't get back because of dissipation, it'll be someone knocking on your door or Mother Nature's call to take a whiz. So, you need not fear being stuck in the astral plane. One way or another, you'll return to the physical.

As I've mentioned before, if you get too excited or scared, you will find yourself back in your physical body. If you can't exit, you can just generate an intense feeling of excitement. Of course, you don't need a reason to feel excited, but if it helps you, you can think of one, so you're immediately booted back to the ordinary world. Want to stay longer? Then keep your mood even and calm, in addition to doing the solidifying exercises.

The Silver Cord

This is a literal cord that connects your body and soul together. It's this same cord that shows you the way back to your body when in the astral plane. You may or may not see it, but it's there. No one can cut it, no matter how "powerful" they are. It's no ordinary cord. It gives your body life from your higher self, allowing its consciousness to flow into your physical body, as well as your other bodies.

The cord is connected to your body at different points, depending on your present projection. Usually, they are connected to major chakra points. However, Robert Bruce describes them as connected to a convergence of strands that all lead out of the major chakras and a few minor ones.

The silver cord is eternal. The only time it gets severed is if you die— and you're not going to die from any experience in the astral plane, just to put the kibosh on that lie right away. Furthermore, it stretches endlessly, so even if you somehow journey light-years away from your body, it won't matter. It has no limits.

No one can destroy your cord—not even you. When you project, you could try and see for yourself. You can't break it or tear it, and while you'd assume all that traveling should tangle it, it doesn't wind up in knots. It is made of pure energy, which cannot be destroyed. This cord also makes sure that your body is yours and yours alone, so you don't have to worry about someone else possessing it.

Coming Back from the Astral Realm

To return, all you have to do is follow your silver cord. That's it. If you can't find it, don't panic. The mere thought of your body will return you to it. Just intend with willpower that you'd like to return to your body, and you'll be there. Remember, we've talked about the physics of this realm. Concepts like space and time don't work the same way they do on

Earth, so you don't have to worry about taking forever to find your body or teleport to it. You can trace your route back with the cord without worrying years have gone by, and your loved ones think you're in a coma at best or dead, at worst. You can speed up the process. It's all up to you.

Another worry you might have is finding your way back home, especially if the cord isn't visible to you. But, again, this realm is responsive to thought. So, it's none of your business where you are relative to your bedroom. You can be back home in the blink of an eye.

Keeping a positive state of mind before you leave your body will ensure you don't have any issues with getting back when you need to. If you leave your body while feeling like crap, that's okay. Just remember that regardless of what's happening around you at any moment in time, you can choose to radiate light and love in thought and energy. Doing that will fix things right up and help you get back home. If you'd rather be able to see your silver cord all the time, then you only need to imagine it's there, and it will show up for you.

Other Ways to Exit the Astral Realm

Have an intense emotional reaction. You can drum up the memory of something that makes you very emotional. If you're very in tune with your feelings, you can just generate the emotion without context. And that will cause you to return to your body.

Make your body tense. How is this different from straining your body? To be clear, when I say "strain your body" to solidify your environment, I mean your *astral* body. When it comes to your exit, you should strain your *physical* one. You have a connection to it, even from the astral. So the intention to strain your muscles will be communicated to the physical body through the silver cord.

High Awareness Level: Critical for Exit

When your level of awareness is too low, sometimes you can be in a projection and then slip into a state of partial lucidity. In this state, you forget you're projecting and that you're in charge, and you can get swept up in what's happening around you. This is what causes you to have very intense "dreams" (I quote the word dreams because you think you're dreaming, but you aren't) where you feel trapped and seemingly can't wake up no matter what you do.

Downloading Your Memories to Your Brain

As you prepare to exit the astral realm, you should mentally note a few keywords that summarize your experience, just like you do with a dream journal. Or, better yet, you can write out the keywords as you begin the exit process so that you can remember them when you awaken.

Suppose your physical body is awake even a little when the astral one re-enters it. In that case, you will feel energy rushing through you, bringing the physical to full awareness. It's rapid and feels almost like an adrenaline rush moving up from your lower body to your stomach and chest and then coming to an abrupt halt.

When you get these sensations, this is the best time to download the memories of your astral trip to your physical brain, so you don't forget it. What you must do is generate an intense feeling of needing to remember something, and then the keywords you shouted should come back to you.

Sit up and put your feet on the ground, and then use every effort you can to recall all keywords and all the memories. Don't give up. They're there, and you just need to pull them out. Usually, when you find even a piece, the rest of the experiences you had in the astral realm will come flooding back to you. You may find it helpful to work your way backward, meaning remember the last thing that happened, and then the thing before that, till you get to the memory of leaving your body.

The best way to make sure you always remember your trips is to time them yourself and exit deliberately rather than wait for dissipation. So, in the astral realm, solidify your world as you execute your plan. Then, when you're done, exit that world on your own terms. Don't take longer than you need. This will ensure you remember every last detail of your trip.

Remember the mind split? It comes into play here. As you return to your body, keep your awareness clear in the astral form. Do your best to ignore the intense sensations you have as you re-enter because those can cause you to break your concentration and forget your keywords. Your intention to hold your awareness in your astral form must be firm as you re-enter. Don't allow that body to succumb to the surges of energy it will feel as it gets back into your physical one. It must maintain its focus on where it's been, what it's been up to. You can shout out a trigger phrase to help you as you re-enter, like, "The Buddha laughs," if you happened to have a conversation with the Buddha on laughter or something.

Falling during Sleep

Have you ever been in bed, falling asleep, when you suddenly jerked on the bed because you felt like you were literally falling, so you wake up and "catch" yourself? This can happen a few times before you finally do sleep off. The cause of this sensation is a brief exit and re-entry of the astral body.

Suppose you notice you're very lethargic and heavy after this falling sensation. In that case, your astral body has likely left the building, so to speak. On the other hand, if you wake up fully and catch yourself, then it's back in. If the former is the case, hold a firm intention in your mind that you will immediately return to your body when you find yourself in the astral realm. Tell yourself you will yell out a trigger phrase while doing so. This will help you learn what your astral body has been up to and help you get better at downloading your memories.

Do you constantly get that falling sensation? Then next time, try to stay up a little longer than you normally would, keeping your consciousness between sleep and wakefulness. For example, you can hold up your forearms with the elbows on the bed so that when you fall asleep, your hands will slip and wake you up. This way, you have a better chance of recalling any astral experience you may have.

The One Time You Can't Return

If you attempt to re-enter your body and find you can't, chances are your physical body has entered into a deep sleep. In this stage of sleep, your astral body is temporarily locked out, and you might get the sense that your body died while you were away. If you reached out to touch your physical body, it would feel cold, almost like a corpse.

Any physical noise will cause your physical body to wake up, and then that will allow your astral body to get back in. When this happens, you get a sense of intense terror and dread when you wake up, and the memories flood your mind instantly, so you recall everything. You might find yourself dreading astral projection after this experience.

Now you know what's going on when you can't get in. You shouldn't allow yourself to feel fear. Understand this happens very often with projectors all over the world and that you're in no danger. So why not take advantage of the extra time you have? Go on even more journeys and tick off whatever other plans you might have had for the next projection.

Don't conclude that you're dead just because you can't re-enter your body. If you don't see any late relatives and friends, or religious figures, angels, or other friends from past lives, then you're probably just in a deep sleep. Don't panic.

Robert Bruce's Flicker Tape Method

This is a great one to use, especially when you want to make sure you recall everything you experienced. It's also helpful when your early tries at leaving your body don't work out or when you miss an astral exit and have no idea whether or not you were successful. You can use this method to wake up, and it's better than using a regular alarm.

Record a tapping sound using your phone or computer. For example, you want to tap your wooden desk very lightly. Use just one tap per second for five seconds. Allow ten seconds of silence and record slightly louder taps once each second for just five seconds. Allow another ten seconds to go by. The next series of taps need to be a chinking sound, light as possible. You can tap a pen against a coffee mug, or glass, for five seconds, tapping once each second. Then allow another ten seconds to pass by.

The next series of tapes should be slightly louder, still in the same format as before. You may move on to progressively sharper sounds, going as far as banging a spoon against a metal pot. You could use a xylophone or any sounds you like to keep things interesting. When you're done recording, you can set this up at your preferred volume as an alarm.

When you're out of your body, you should remain about six meters or twenty feet away from it, so you're not sucked back in. If you notice there's some pressure trying to reel you back in, resist it, and move as quickly as you can away from your body. Better yet, if there's another clock in the house, you can go to that other room and monitor it, waiting to enter your body. Then, when the alarm goes off, return to the room to re-enter your body.

Keep in mind that your physical body can be anywhere from light, medium to deep sleep. Keep your re-entry phrase firmly in your mind as you wait for the tugging sensations, which means your body is starting to wake up. As soon as you feel the tug, slide into your physical body as you yell out your phrase with intense emotion. Your intention should be to take charge of your physical body and force it to wake up, so you can write down your experience. Needless to say, your journal should be well within reach.

It is my sincere hope that with this final chapter, I've been able to thoroughly allay any fears you've had that have made you shy away from leaving your body. The door is open now. You need only walk through it, and you already know how.

Bonus: Astral Travel Daily Practice Calendar

Here's a calendar of daily practices you can use to prime yourself for a successful exit from your body. You only need fifteen minutes per day: five minutes for the affirmations, five for the meditations, and five for your mindfulness exercises.

Then, **you're going to record your dreams every time you wake up for the next 30 days.** Again, if all you remember is one image, write it down. If you don't remember dreaming, just write down how you feel, and trust that you will begin to recall your dreams in full.

Day 1

Affirmation: I am aware I exist in multiple dimensions of existence.

Meditation: sit with your eyes shut and observe your breath.

Mindfulness exercise: sit with your eyes open, and just notice your body. Look at your hands and the rest of your visible body with a detached state, like it's a vehicle. Then, ponder this question: "Who is looking through my eyes?"

Day 2

Affirmation: I am always aware of my body as it goes to sleep.

Meditation: close your eyes, lie down, and observe your breath.

Mindfulness exercise: walk from one spot to another. Shut your eyes. In your mind, recreate the sensation of walking from where you were to where you are, feeling your feet against the floor, your body pushing against the air. Open your eyes and walk back to the first spot. Close your eyes and recreate the movement again. Make sure you account for the change in location in your imagination.

Day 3

Affirmation: I am conscious as I separate from my body while it sleeps.

Meditation: sit and look at the back of your hands. Brush each one with the other. For five minutes, continue to brush your hands, but in your mind. You should feel your awareness in your hands increasing.

Mindfulness exercise: pay attention to your thoughts. Ask yourself each time you make an assumption, "But is it true? Do I want that to be true? Do I accept that as my truth?"

Day 4

Affirmation: I am far more than just my physical body.

Meditation: sit and close your eyes. Imagine a surge of white energy flooding your physical body in a straight line from your root chakra. See it moving on up through the midpoint of your belly, chest, throat, and third eye chakras, and then out the top of your head.

Mindfulness exercise: say your name out loud. Listen to your voice and notice how it sounds. Then, repeat your name again, this time as though you were addressing someone else, not yourself.

Day 5

Affirmation: I recall everything I do in the astral plane when I wake up.

Meditation: sit and close your eyes. Focus on your breath. Halfway through the time, feel yourself sitting in a different chair, facing a different wall. You should feel it in your body and mind that you're in this other position.

Mindfulness exercise: at the end of your day, recall everything that happened during your day by working your way backward, from when you hit the bed to when you brushed your teeth for bed, and on and on. Continue till the moment you woke up in the morning.

Day 6

Affirmation: I always receive value from every projection I have.

Meditation: shut your eyes and listen to the sounds around you, with no judgment and no attempt to figure out what it all means.

Mindfulness exercise: lie down. Close your eyes. From a first-person perspective, see yourself outside your home. Walk into your house, and head right to where you're lying down. Look at yourself as though you're a stranger. Notice the rising and falling of your chest as you breathe.

Day 7

Affirmation: I remain in complete control of all my astral experiences.

Meditation: sit with your eyes shut, and keep your awareness centered on your heart chakra, right in the middle of your chest.

Mindfulness exercise: close your eyes. Generate a falling sensation within yourself. Think about what it's like to go down a roller coaster or in an elevator and create that sensation—alternate between intensifying the falling feeling and slowing it down.

Day 8

Affirmation: I own my mind. I use my mind to do my will.

Meditation: sit in silence for five minutes, and contemplate the vastness of the universe, and sit with the fact that the universe is within you, not outside you.

Mindfulness exercise: every time you notice something negative cross your mind today, your job is to observe your emotions detachedly. Acknowledge they are there, and just watch them. Don't act on them. Instead, choose to do something that's the complete opposite of your usual reaction.

Day 9

Affirmation: whatever I will into being is done.

Meditation: sit in silence. Shut your eyes and allow yourself to be overwhelmed with a feeling of gratitude and completeness for no reason.

Mindfulness exercise: pay attention to your thoughts. Ask yourself each time you make an assumption, "But is it true? Do I want that to be true? Do I accept that as my truth?"

Day 10

Affirmation: I am light as a feather, steady as a rock.

Meditation: sit for five minutes, observing your breath.

Mindfulness exercise: play with feeling heavy, then feeling light. Alternate the two of them. Allow any imagery that corresponds with these sensations to come up in your mind. Notice how your body translates those sensations.

Day 11

Affirmation: the only "where" is here.

Meditation: Stand outside with bare feet. If you can stand on bare earth, even better. Shut your eyes and just breathe. Ground yourself in the moment.

Mindfulness exercise: pick a spot to sit and watch people from. In your imagination, reach out and touch the hands of people across the street from you. You can also touch objects. Practice holding them with your mind's hands. Feel their textures and shapes. Notice their heft.

Day 12

Affirmation: the only "when" is now.

Meditation: for this meditation, don't time yourself. Just sit still until you start to notice that you can't really sense how fast or slow time is, if it even exists at all. When you get this sensation, take a few deep breaths, and then come out of meditation.

Mindfulness exercise: go the whole day without looking at your watch. If you're at work and your job is time-sensitive, pick a time when you know you won't be bothered to do this. Every time you get the itch to look at what the clock says, affirm, "The only 'when' is now."

Day 13

Affirmation: nothing means anything, except what I believe it means.

Meditation: sit in silence, listening to the sounds around you. When your mind tries to ascribe it a meaning, origin, or label, let it go.

Mindfulness exercise: your exercise is to imagine a different meaning for what you hear, whether it's a song on the radio, a friend talking to you, or the news. Deliberately apply a meaning you prefer or even one you don't. Observe what happens within your mind.

Day 14

Affirmation: I am deliberate about the meanings I assign to things.

Meditation: sit with your eyes open. Look around the room at various objects and let go of all the descriptions and meanings your mind tries to assign them.

Mindfulness exercise: pick one color. Every time you see it today, in your mind's eye, give it a different color.

Day 15

Affirmation: I am in tune with my astral body.

Meditation: sit with your eyes shut and notice all the sensations you feel, within and without. When your mind tries to label it, whether it's an itch, a twinge, or subtle energy, don't dwell on your mind's definitions. Let it go.

Mindfulness exercise: for five minutes, have a friend tickle you with something light and feathery. You'll want to laugh, but ask yourself, "Do I have to?" Just sit and observe the sensation. You must do nothing. Don't try to stop them.

Start again from day 1 for the next couple of weeks.

Day 31 is when you should make your first attempt at astral projection. Do the exercises that resonate with you, and then take time to read through your dream journal. Allow yourself to sink into the memories, to immerse yourself in it as you would a novel or a movie. Then, using your preferred method of projection, leave your body.

If you're successful, make sure you only stay out for just ten to twenty seconds, solidifying the state, and then deliberately re-enter your body. That should be your only plan on the first try.

On subsequent tries, make a plan about what you want to do, have a backup plan if you can't execute for some reason, or have more time in the astral realm because your body is in a deep sleep. If you're unsure what to do with yourself, refer to chapter fifteen for ideas on what you can do in the astral plane.

If you're not successful, don't panic. Instead, do one more week of your daily astral practice, and then try again.

Conclusion

This book ends here, but it's the start of the rest of your life, for sure. Before we wrap up, I want to stress that you shouldn't quit just because you didn't leave your body the first few times. Some people get it right away, but others need more time. It's the same with any skill. Please be patient with the process and be patient with yourself too. Suppose you beat yourself up about not getting it right. In that case, you're only prolonging the process, setting yourself up for disappointment at best or permanent skepticism at worst. That would be like seeing the gates to the city of gold, locking them up with your own hands, and throwing the keys away.

Now, I know you probably looked at that bonus section and decided you're not going to wait a whole month to leave your body. I get why you'd feel that way. You want to keep the momentum going, knowing what you now know, and that is commendable! Here's the thing, though: you have to give this time. Lay the groundwork first, and that will improve the odds of your success wildly. The exercises you've been given are insanely powerful. They will give back to you in ways you couldn't possibly imagine if you invest the time and do them first.

Don't feel tempted to freestyle the exit or entry methods when you're first starting out. You have all the time in the world to follow your own hunches and experiment, but for now, you should get used to the projection process first. It's like you've never driven a car in your life, and you suddenly decide to hop into a car and make like you're starring in a *Fast and Furious* movie. Naturally, you won't like how it ends. In the same way, please follow all instructions to the letter so you don't run into any problems you could have avoided.

On that note, please keep your first few projections to no more than twenty seconds. The most successful projectors have followed this rule to the letter. You must take charge of your re-entry; otherwise, you'll just have a bunch of fantastic experiences that you don't even remember.

Respect other people's privacy and respect the beings you meet. If you run into anyone who feels off, remember to affirm that you're light and love and get on with your business. Don't be hostile or fearful, no matter what. Remember, nothing and no one can harm you in the astral plane.

Every consistent projector will tell you with no hesitation that the quality of their life has improved immensely since learning this skill. In love, family, career, health, and every other way, the effects of astral projection are very noticeable. Astral projection will help you live life with the full awareness that you are more than physical. You will know that death is simply a portal to more adventures and that you are an infinite being. This first-hand knowledge helps you lighten up and enjoy your present existence. What could be better than that?

The critical difference between astral projection and death is that you have a body to go back to in the former case. Astral projection will teach you that there is nothing to fear and will show you just how truly free you are. Imagine a world where everyone ditched the ideas they got from *Insidious* (2010) or *Behind Her Eyes* (2021) and learned to explore the truth for themselves. Imagine a world no longer crippled by the fear of death, where everyone is well aware of their limitless nature. This is why I've done my little bit in writing this book, in the hopes that we all one day will wake up to the truth of who we really are.

You see, most projectors radiate a sense of peace that just goes beyond understanding, even in the "toughest" situations in life. They have the most creative solutions to problems, and they know how to use their astral selves to manifest their desires in the physical realm because they understand the concept, "As above, so below." So, if you want something to happen in the physical world, create that scenario in the astral realm. Then, trust that your action on that plane will influence your "real" life; this is more than enough to create whatever changes you seek.

You can heal troublesome ailments and pains in your body and help others to heal as well. You can play out a problem in the astral plane and intend for the solution to make itself visible to you. You can confer with a guide, a deceased relative, or a friend if you prefer, and ask for their counsel. If you've lost something, you can find it. If you need business ideas that will yield good money, you can get them there. If you want to understand your past lives better or peek in on your alternate selves to see if there's something they're doing that you could learn from or emulate, you can too. This is the realm of infinite possibilities.

Finally, you have all of this information now, but it does absolutely no good if you just keep it in your head without putting it to work. You have to be consistent with this to see results. You must be disciplined about your daily routine. There's no other way around this. Don't be put off, though, because you're going to find the rewards are well worth it in the end. So be bold. Dare to explore this new frontier of life, and you'll find yourself richly rewarded.

Part 5: Highly Sensitive People

What You Need to Know about HSPs and Their Gifts

Introduction

Were you ever labeled as shy and introverted by teachers or parents? Or, conversely, are you the parent of a child who seems shy, at times withdrawn in big groups, and extra sensitive to different elements of their surroundings? Well, as this book will illustrate, you're definitely not alone, and the flippant usage of "shy" doesn't necessarily apply in these cases.

This guide is devoted to helping you make sense of being an HSP – a highly sensitive person – or being the parent or spouse of one. This term alludes to individuals who experience deeper responses in their central nervous system to physical, emotional, or social stimuli. It describes someone sensitive to the meaning of every word. rather than an individual who gets teary-eyed when listening to an Adele song, although that counts, too! This book is devoted to helping you understand yourself and others around you, rather than going through life feeling like some kind of emotional aberration.

Other books out there may help explain HSP as a personality trait but may leave you feeling empty-handed with how to go about experiencing the world as a result. We're here to explain what HSP is and its origins and explore different ways to cope with the condition. This isn't the kind of book that talks at you, with lots of inaccessible bits of information thrown at you. While science is important, it's not the be-all and end-all. As an HSP, or someone close to one, you're probably feeling stumped and a bit hesitant about how to move forward. You may not be sure how to deal with a world that is often callous and uncaring, particularly to the needs of those who experience such high levels of sensitivity.

Through plenty of hands-on exercises and a rundown of the methodology, you will be able to find your way out of the shadows and live a fuller, more compassionate life without fear. There is no need to go through life feeling like a wallflower - everything you need is right at your fingertips.

Everything from school to friendships to romantic relationships can be deeply discombobulating for an HSP; finding the power to cope is the crucial first step you need to take. This sort of person needs to be careful with how they share their heart, but you can't live closed off forever, fearing someone will hurt you. These are major issues that any HSP has to deal with, and this book is here to do just that. Avoid toxic relationships and stop dealing with low self-esteem. Sure, the HSP person may confront more hardship than the average Joe, but that doesn't mean there isn't a viable way out. This guide will provide all the knowledge and tools you need to feel empowered enough to conquer these demons, rather than feeling as though you need to wait for permission to simply exist.

So, set aside some time for yourself, and begin deconstructing the harmful self-image imposed upon you by society by reading the next few pages.

Chapter 1: What Is a Highly Sensitive Person?

"I didn't say anything hurtful; you are just being sensitive."

"The TV isn't that loud; you are the one who has a problem."

"This world is cruel and will chew you up; there is no place for a sensitive soul like you."

If you are a highly sensitive person, you have probably heard similar comments before when other people make you feel that being sensitive is a weakness, a character defect, or something to be ashamed of. They accuse you of being "too sensitive" every time you point out how their words and actions have hurt your feelings, or you complain about something that is making you uncomfortable – like a crowded room or loud noises. These accusations usually come from insensitive people and have a problem identifying what you are feeling. As a result, you start to believe that something is wrong with you for feeling things too deeply. However, in a cruel world like the one we live in, sensitivity has become rare, which is why many people don't seem to understand it or see that it is a source of strength rather than weakness.

Before we delve into the subject, it is important to note that there is absolutely nothing wrong with being a highly sensitive person. You will meet people in your life who will misinterpret your sensitivity as a weakness, and in turn, you will probably either try to change or hide this side of your personality. However, high sensitivity isn't a disorder but a personality trait that can be regarded as a gift and the source of your strength. Some of the most famous artists in the world were highly sensitive, like Vincent Van Gogh, Salvador Dali, Frida Kahlo, Edgar Allan Poe, William Butler Yeats, and many more. They used their gift to create beautiful works of art and poetry, and you can sense how their acute sensitivity is echoed in their work and will keep echoing till the end of time.

Being a highly sensitive person is about feeling things on a deeper level. This can make you feel various things differently from other people, but you might not be aware that it results from being a highly sensitive person.

As psychologist Dr. Elaine N. Aron labels a highly sensitive person (HSP), she believes they have a higher and deeper sensitivity in their central nervous system, also sometimes referred to as high sensory processing sensitivity – or *SPS.* An increase in SPS can increase emotional sensitivity and stronger reactions to various internal and external stimuli like loud noises, lights, and pain. Simply put, your brain processes everything more deeply than other people, so you will find yourself feeling more disturbed and overwhelmed by things that won't have the same strong impact on other people. For instance, although some people find violence disturbing, it can evoke a stronger reaction from highly sensitive people. Therefore, an HSP will most likely avoid violent, highly tense situations, bright lights, and loud noises. An HSP doesn't only feel the impact of these situations mentally or emotionally, but they also feel a physical reaction. It isn't just negative situations or emotions that evoke strong reactions from an HSP but positive situations. For example, you may find yourself deeply moved by a beautiful painting or a love song.

These deep and strong emotions are easily misinterpreted, and you could find people accusing you of being "too sensitive" and shaming you for the way you are feeling. However, being an HSP is very normal, and it is no different from any other personality trait like honesty, courage, or humility. There is no denying that being highly sensitive isn't a picnic and, like anything in life, it has its advantages and disadvantages. Highly sensitive people are considered gifted since they can be very creative and notice things that others can't. On the other hand, their minds are more sensitive, and t they are often likely to feel emotionally overwhelmed at times.

You're probably wondering: if being highly sensitive is normal, why do many people not understand it and regard it as "weird" or "abnormal"? This is because highly sensitive people are in the minority. It is a rare trait that about 15 to 20 % of people are actually highly sensitive, and because of this rarity, not much is understood about it. We also live in a world that outwardly sensitivity as a weakness – particularly in women – and shame people for feeling this way, leaving highly sensitive people feeling alone or misunderstood.

What Makes a Person Highly Sensitive?

Now that you have an idea about being an HSP, you probably wonder what makes a person highly sensitive? Sensitivity itself is a very common personality trait. However, you will find some people have higher levels of sensitivity than others, though most people usually fall somewhere in the middle. A person's level of sensitivity depends on their genes and how they are raised. Experiences also play a huge role in how sensitive you grow up to be, and, interestingly, you may find twins with the same genes yet will grow up with different levels of sensitivity.

For highly sensitive people to thrive, they need to be provided with the right environment. An HSP ideally needs to grow up in a healthy home that gives them the love and emotional support they need to nurture their gift. Additionally, an HSP's brain is different and not just how they react to certain things. As an HSP, you will find your brain functions differently when certain areas react to sensory stimuli; this is manifested in you as high emotions. For instance, empathy gives you the ability to read social cues better than most people. This means that you will be very alert during social situations and in tune with everyone around you.

An HSP is different not just in how they act but also in what they want out of their lives. You will find yourself enjoying more of a slower-paced and low-key lifestyle and experiences. While some people enjoy going to concerts or events to meet new people, an HSP will find joy in listening to a beautiful song or having their favorite coffee in the morning. This is because highly sensitive people can easily get overstimulated, so enjoying the simple things in life while taking it slow can allow them to thrive and nourish their sensitivity without feeling overwhelmed.

The lifestyle favored by an HSP may sound familiar since it resembles that of an introvert who enjoys leading a quiet life and usually avoids crowds. An HSP can easily be confused for an introvert and vice versa. Although not all introverts are highly sensitive, and not all HSPs are introverts, according to Dr. Elaine Aron, about 70% of highly sensitive people are introverts.

Many highly sensitive people are thought to have great personal relationships, appreciate beauty more than others, and are very creative. Although being an HSP has its advantages and disadvantages, it still needs to be embraced and nourished. That said, to understand more about how being an HSP is influencing your life, you need to have an idea of the traits or signs of a highly sensitive person.

Signs That You Are a Highly Sensitive Person

1. Being Misunderstood or Considered Shy

If you look back at your childhood, you may realize that many people used to say that you are shy or withdrawn. Highly sensitive people are usually inaccurately labeled and prone to misconceptions. People usually call them "anxious," "shy," "introverted," or even "dramatic," which would often make them question themselves.

2. You Are Overly Present, and You Have a Vivacious Inner World

HSPs, as children, probably have a multitude of imaginary friends and indulge in fantasies and daydreams. This comes from their habit of processing information and the world around them in great detail. As an adult, they often have weirdly vivid and realistic dreams.

3. You Feel Deeply

Highly sensitive people have stronger emotions and reactions to the world around them, so if you feel things more intensely than other people, you are more than likely an HSP. Being an empath is one thing but absorbing the emotions of others is another. Highly sensitive individuals often mistake their sensitivity for empathy. This is because they can very easily sense the mood of others as soon as they walk into a room, just like an empath would. However, HSPs are not only empathetic, but they are also very aware of the subtle details – they read people's body language, speaking tone, and facial expressions, which often leads them to experience emotions that aren't their own. This is why HSPs are constantly emotionally exhausted.

4. You Take Criticism to Heart

Harsh words can be a dagger to highly sensitive individuals. Similarly, hearing nice words can make them over the moon. Criticism can hurt HSPs deeply. They have a system that keeps them balanced. Negativity can easily disrupt it, getting in the way of their personal peace and harmony.

5. You Have a Lower Tolerance for Violence and Conflict

Highly sensitive people are more empathetic than usual, which is why they can't stand cruel behavior or violence, to the point where they often can't get through a gruesome movie or event without feeling physically and mentally upset. They are also deeply affected by disagreements in their relationships. Small arguments and tension can mentally and physically distress them beyond the norm. This is why highly sensitive people are usually conflict-avoidant to the point where they will say or do anything to keep others happy. Conflicts affect them deeply.

6. You Avoid Stress

No one wants to feel stressed, but HSPs actively avoid it by leading a slower-paced life and avoiding hectic schedules because stress can overwhelm their senses. Being under a time crunch can make them feel extremely anxious. Some HSPs may even struggle to perform up to their normal standards under time pressure. As previously mentioned, HSPs feel things more intensely, which is why their senses can be overwhelmed at times. Adult HSPs usually feel very stressed when they have many tasks to do and are under the impression that they won't be able to finish them in time. Highly sensitive people are generally easily distressed, especially when the time factor is in the picture.

7. High Sensitivity to Pain

As you know, highly sensitive individuals are easily stimulated. This makes them unable to tolerate pain as well as other people do, including physical pain like body aches, headaches, stomach aches, injuries, etc.

8. You Are Often Withdrawn

Many people associate high sensitivity with introversion, usually because HSPs are withdrawn. It may come as a surprise that many highly sensitive people are extroverts. However, this doesn't undermine the fact that they need their fair share of alone downtime. Most highly sensitive people will withdraw to a low-lit, quiet room to recover from a long day. This allows them to recover from high levels of stimulation, relax their senses, and recharge their emotional and social batteries.

9. You Are Jumpy

You don't like people sneaking up on you, even if it were just a joke. Highly sensitive people tend to be very jumpy due to their heightened startle reflex. The nervous systems of HSPs are always heightened, even when they aren't in danger.

10. You Are a Deep Thinker

Highly sensitive individuals are known for their tendency to process information deeply. This habit leaves them replaying and reflecting on various events, situations, and life experiences more than the average individual. This over-processing and deep pondering can sometimes leave them with a stream of negative thoughts – on repeat. They also like to ask existential questions and seek their answers. They want to know why things are the way they are. The "it is what it is" mantra won't suffice. HSPs usually wonder why others aren't as interested in human nature, the universe, and all their mysteries as they are.

11. You Pay Attention to Your Appearance

Most people really care about how they dress. However, highly sensitive individuals are particularly sensitive to what they should be wearing and when. Spoiler alert; it doesn't necessarily have to do anything with style and appearance. HSPs are more likely to be sensitive to certain fabrics and materials, especially restrictive or scratchy clothes or fabrics, such as wool, pantyhose, or tight jeans. While non-highly sensitive individuals are likely to dislike similar clothing articles, HSPs may obsessively organize their wardrobes to avoid these materials completely. If they somehow end up wearing a fabric they dislike, they will feel uncomfortable to the point where they cannot enjoy what they are doing.

12. You Hate Change

Highly sensitive people find comfort in planned activities and routines. This is because schedules, habits, and routines are a lot less stimulating than going with the flow and waiting to find out what comes next. New things or environments can be very unsettling. HSPs can be thrown by any type of change, even if they have a positive outlook. Surprisingly, a highly sensitive person may feel stressed out if they receive a job promotion. Dating a new person can also make them feel uncomfortable. They need a lot of time to adjust to changes compared to the average person.

Although these are signs of being highly sensitive, they can also be signs of introversion. To avoid confusion, Dr. Elaine Aron has developed certain indicators that define high sensitivity. Dr. Aron uses the acronym D.O.E.S. for these four indicators, which are:

1. Depth of processing

2. Overstimulation

3. Emotional reactivity or empathy

4. Sensing the subtle

If you are a highly sensitive person, according to Dr. Aron, then you were born with D.O.E.S. In other words, you can't acquire them from experience, trauma, or any psychological issues. Now that you have familiarized yourself with D.O.E.S., let's dig deep into understanding each indicator.

D.O.E.S

Depth of Processing

Depth of processing is the main indicator of being a highly sensitive person. The other three factors stem from this one. This indicator is not a visible trait that people notice easily, like being born with dark hair or blue ey.es. However, people can indirectly see it in how deeply you think about things and how strongly you feel and react to the world around you. Simply put, it is the depth of how you process and respond to all of the positive and negative feelings around you.

As an HSP, you will find yourself thinking and wondering about things that many people don't usually pay attention to, like pondering questions about life, death, the meaning of our existence, or any similar philosophical or spiritual topics. You will also find that making decisions doesn't come easily to you, and you like to carefully analyze every problem you encounter. You also prefer to have deep conversations rather than idle gossip or talking about the weather. Additionally, you have high levels of empathy for animals and people. HSPs, by their very nature, have a rich and vivid inner world. Not only does the mind of an HSP function differently, but so does their body which enables them to perceive various vibrations around them and respond more intensely.

There are advantages and disadvantages to feeling this way. When you are experiencing something positive like a beautiful painting or picking up on someone's happiness, this can be a beautiful feeling that enriches your life. However, when you are experiencing negative emotions or experiences, you may feel stressed or overwhelmed. Highly sensitive people experience life and process emotions very deeply, whether negative or positive, which can be challenging at times.

Overstimulation

An HSP will notice and feel things that most people miss. You also experience and process the world around you on a much deeper level. For instance, if you are in a noisy place or face a complicated situation, you will feel stressed and tired easily because you feel things intensely and process things deeply. However, people who aren't as sensitive as you will not feel the same way. For this reason, you may be the only one of your friends who feel tired or stressed after a loud concert or spending a whole night at a crowded nightclub, and therefore you may need alone and quiet time by yourself to unwind while they are still keeping the same level of energy.

That said, usually, everyone can experience high levels of arousal as a result of encountering certain stimuli. When our brains process and react to some internal and external stimuli, we can have a physiological arousal reaction, which can have a huge impact on the way we think and feel. High arousal levels can negatively impact our well-being, and we may find ourselves unable to focus or think straight. In addition to that, other people may also feel anxious and tense.

This is usually the case for people with regular sensitivity levels, so can you imagine how a highly sensitive person will feel? As mentioned a few times now, an HSP processes things deeply and strongly, so they will feel overstimulated and over-aroused faster than others. So, you may find yourself feeling irritable, tensed, or stressed when subjected to certain environments or experiences. This can prove challenging for highly sensitive people because daily situations can make them feel this way, such as a work meeting, crowded restaurants, loud noises, or even a brightly lit room.

Emotional Reactivity/Empathy

Being highly emotional is a strong indicator that you are a highly sensitive person. That said, emotional reactivity isn't specific to certain feelings or situations, negative or positive. It's something you are born with and have experienced from childhood. It's not something you pick up or develop as you grow up.

Highly sensitive people are extremely empathetic, a feeling usually related to emotional reactivity. This is because the mirror neurons in the brain are usually more active in HSP. To put it in simpler terms, we usually react in a certain way when something happens to us. For instance, we feel happy when promoted and sad when we lose someone we love. Although we will also feel happy when a friend gets promoted or sad when they lose a loved one, the emotions aren't usually on the same level. However, in both cases, highly sensitive people will experience the same level of emotions as a result of their empathy and mirror neurons. So, when an HSP looks at a picture of a happy couple, they will respond more positively than less sensitive people, and when they see a picture of a sick dog, this will trigger a more negative response. Being empathetic makes an HSP pick on other people's feelings and feel their feelings to some degree.

Sensing Subtle Stimuli

Highly sensitive people process various stimuli on a deeper level. Therefore, you will find yourself unable to sleep in a noisy room, feel uncomfortable when touching or wearing certain fabrics, and easily feel any changes in your surroundings. Being irritated by loud noise or feeling uncomfortable in certain fabrics doesn't mean you have better hearing or more developed sensory organs. You are merely someone who processes and feels things on a much deeper level, and they hit you differently and stay with you longer than most people. All your five senses, touch, taste, smell, hearing, and seeing, seem to be amplified. So, you will find yourself sensitive to certain smells, loud noises, and uncomfortable in crowded places. Additionally, highly sensitive people perceive pain and temperature differently, so you will probably experience the hot and cold weather more intensely.

Being aware of subtle stimuli can be a gift at times. For instance, you may be able to read a certain person's non-verbal cues just by paying attention to their facial expressions or their body language. The person may not even be aware of what they are giving off. For instance, if a friend of yours is pretending to be ok or happy when they aren't, you can easily detect how they are really feeling by noticing their facial expression, body language, or tone of voice. This trait can also be beneficial when it comes to knowing whether or not a person can be trusted and whether or not they can hurt you. See, we weren't lying when we said earlier that being highly sensitive is a gift.

That said, if you are overstimulated or tired, you will not notice or sense anything. As a gift, this trait makes you a really special person, a kind, good friend, and a great partner, so don't allow anyone to make you feel otherwise. People are too quick to be dismissive of what they don't understand, and since being an HSP is rare, it can confuse others and make them perceive you as weak. There is absolutely nothing wrong with you; high sensitivity is a very normal trait, although not as common as other traits. Don't listen to people who may make you feel less and try to shake your self-esteem.

High sensitivity is real and based on extensive psychological research. Again, that doesn't mean you have a psychological disorder or need therapy, as some people may try to convince you. You are a unique and gifted person with an ability that gives you strength. People say that the world chews up sensitive souls, but you know better since your gift can make you feel and see things that others miss, which gives you an advantage. You may struggle as an HSP, but you will learn more about your gift and how to cope with your strong and deep emotions in future chapters.

Chapter 2: Quiz: Are You Highly Sensitive?

"You're overreacting!"

"Why are you so dramatic?"

"You're being so fussy."

"Is there something wrong with you?"

No, nothing is wrong with being highly sensitive. Unfortunately, many people just don't understand how a highly sensitive person's brain is wired, which is why they end up making all sorts of rude, snarky, and sarcastic remarks. When others don't understand us, we tend to question ourselves.

"Maybe there is something wrong with me."

"Maybe I am being dramatic."

"I'm probably too annoying."

"Am I too much to handle?"

The voices and thoughts start to creep in.

No matter how much highly sensitive person tries to be compassionate toward themselves, they still can't help but feel affected by other people's comments. They know that it often seems like something isn't right, which can be quite hurtful. Not only are they criticized for something that they can't control, but they also often feel unsupported and overlooked for most of their life experiences.

High sensitivity, in general, is not discussed enough and, as a personality trait, is often disparaged and disregarded. Many people mistake it for a mental disorder needing treatment or an undesirable characteristic that has to be dismissed. People don't realize that high sensitivity is just as normal as introversion, extraversion, optimism, and proactivity. The belief that something is fundamentally wrong with highly sensitive individuals is extremely invalidating.

Around 30% of the world's population is highly sensitive. Although this means that HSPs don't have to feel alone, it still doesn't make up for the rest of the world's ignorance. Not only does this lack of education and awareness lead to more and more misconceptions and unkind labels, but it also makes it harder for highly sensitive individuals to understand that they're completely fine. If there are no learning opportunities about HSPs, then highly sensitive individuals may not realize that they're, in fact, just highly sensitive and not mentally ill. This means that they'll be adamant about "fixing" themselves. Highly sensitive people need to understand themselves first and learn how to love and protect themselves before communicating with them.

This chapter will help you determine whether you're a highly sensitive person. The indicators explain how and why you are likely to read deeply into subtleties, tend to over-process information, and are prone to being overly overwhelmed and stressed. There is also a quiz that will help you determine whether you are an HSP.

Quiz: Am I Highly Sensitive?

The signs that we explained should be enough to help you determine whether you're a highly sensitive individual. However, we've put together a short quiz to help you if you're still unsure. The quiz consists of 26 yes or no questions that are easy to answer. If you answer "yes" to more than 14 of the following statements, then you are very likely a highly sensitive individual. In that case, reading the following chapter about the pros and cons of being an HSP, coping techniques, maintaining relationships, dealing with toxicity, and thriving will be of great help.

• **Sensory input easily overwhelms me.**

The sensations, memories, or thoughts that certain smells, physical interactions, sounds, tastes, or sights trigger can make you feel very overwhelmed.

• **I am easily affected by other people's moods.**

Your mood is easily swayed by others. For instance, even if you're having the best day, your mood can easily shift because someone else is sad (it may even ruin your day. Similarly, someone else's happiness can be uplifting.

• **I am hyper-aware of any subtleties in the surrounding environment.**

You always notice when something seems to be off, even when it isn't visually apparent to others. You can easily sense unspoken tension or the general energy.

• **I have relatively low pain tolerance.**

You seem to sense pain more than others. Minor injuries or body aches can often feel amplified.

• **I am sensitive to caffeine and its effects.**

You tend to have a sudden adrenaline rush after drinking coffee- a few sips can give you the same effect as 5 cups of coffee. Coffee can significantly trigger your anxiety or raise your heartbeats.

• **My inner life is considered rich, deep, and complex.**

You feel like a lot is going on even when nothing much seems to be happening. You consider your brain and self to be quite deep and complex.

• I need to withdraw and self-isolate in a quiet, low-lit room when I have had a busy day to rest and recharge.

You feel very over-stimulated after social events or being around many people, in general. You need to make sure that you get your fair share of alone time afterward; otherwise, you will feel run down and out of energy.

• Pungent and strong smells, rough and scratchy fabrics, bright lights, loud sounds, sirens, and similar things often make me feel overwhelmed.

For example:

You may be particularly sensitive to certain sights (you avoid violent or horror movies, try to stay away from hospitals, etc.)

You may not tolerate certain physical interactions (you don't like hugging people for too long, or you get annoyed when someone nudges you/ rest their hand or head on your shoulders, etc.)

You may be extra sensitive to scents even when they're not that prominent to others.

Certain sounds can easily frustrate or overwhelm you (if someone's being loud or talking quickly, car horns, crying children, etc.)

Certain flavors can be too prominent or significantly stand out, even when they taste normal to others (things can be too sweet, spicy, salty, etc.)

• Loud noises make me feel extremely unsettled and uncomfortable.

Loud noises can be unreasonably irksome or unsettling. They may affect you too intensely.

• Arts and music can affect and move me deeply.

Not only do you appreciate music and art more than the average person, but they can trigger your emotions. Even if there are no lyrics, sad music can make you cry or feel burdened. You also tend to feel or sense the emotion behind paintings.

• I am conscientious.

You don't feel relaxed unless you finish your tasks diligently and thoroughly. Completing a chore simply isn't enough (not giving it your best can make you feel guilty).

- **I sometimes need to be on my own as my nervous system becomes easily stimulated.**

Your body's fight or flight response can be easily stimulated. When this happens (or when you know it's about to happen), you need to be on your own.

- **I am very easily startled.**

For instance:

Jump scares are very frequent.

You easily lose focus when something mildly inconvenient happens.

- **If I notice people feeling uncomfortable, I immediately know how I can change the environment to make it more pleasant.**

It doesn't take you long to realize when others feel uncomfortable, even if they don't communicate their emotions to you. You also know what exactly needs to be done to make that person feel more at ease. For instance, if someone is cold, you would be able to tell whether giving them a jacket, turning on the heat, or shutting the windows would make them feel the most comfortable.

- **I get very stressed and overwhelmed when I have a long to-do list and limited time.**

You find it very hard to keep your stress and anxiety at bay when you know you have plenty of things to do. You can't stop thinking about whether you will have enough time to complete them.

- **I am constantly trying to make sure I don't forget things or make mistakes.**

For some reason, you can't tolerate the thought of making a mistake. You also always worry about forgetting important details or leaving things behind. You're always very worked up, trying to ensure that nothing goes wrong.

- **I try to avoid gruesome and violent video games, TV shows, videos, and movies.**

You can't stand the sight of violence or gruesome images. You go out of your way to ensure that you don't catch a glimpse of them.

• I get very unsettled when too many things are happening at once around me.

You feel very uncomfortable when many things are happening all at once. It can make you very frustrated or zoned out.

• I hate it when someone tries to make me do several things simultaneously.

You don't like it when someone gives you several tasks to work on at the same time. You can get very overwhelmed or annoyed if you're working with people who can't seem to handle one thing at a time.

• I get shaken up easily by the minor changes in life.

It can feel like the end of the world if things don't go according to plan. You like to be informed of all plans and changes ahead of time.

• I don't like it when many things in my life are happening at the same time.

You can feel suffocated if many events suddenly start taking place in your life.

• I notice and love fine and delicate tunes, sounds, tastes, artworks, and scents.

You're especially sensitive to sounds, flavors, sights, and scents, which is why you easily notice and appreciate the good things around you.

• When I'm hungry, my mood and concentration are instantly affected. Hunger often triggers strong reactions in me.

Hunger can be a very overwhelming sensation. It can make you lose focus and become irritable.

• I can become very nervous and anxious when I am watched, have an audience, or must compete in something. I may even end up falling short of my typical standards.

You feel very anxious and stressed when someone watches you as you do something. You may be more prone to mistakes or errors than normal.

I was often labeled a "shy" or "sensitive" child.

People didn't always understand you when you were little, which is why they always thought you were shy, even if you weren't. They always said you were dramatic or overly sensitive.

• I am obsessed with arranging my life in a way that steers me clear of situations that may overwhelm or upset me. Chaotic situations and intense stimuli annoy me.

You often go out of your way to ensure that your life is clear of surprises or situations you may think are overwhelming. You avoid noisy places, the news, certain TV channels, or even people.

Highly sensitive people are often misunderstood. They are mislabeled from a very young age. Growing up, this makes them feel like outcasts. For this reason, many HSPs spend a lot of time and effort trying to "fix" their sensitivity, not realizing that it isn't an illness but is rather a blessing. Many signs can help you identify whether you're a highly sensitive individual.

Chapter 3: Pros and Cons of Being Highly Sensitive

While being a highly sensitive person is a gift, there's no denying that it has its challenges. HSPs have a strong emotional reaction to any event - positive or negative. As a highly sensitive person, you feel deeply. You also have a rich inner life and a great appreciation for movies, art, books, and everything beautiful. On the other hand, people tend to take advantage of you because of your sensitive and kind nature. They know how difficult it is for you to say no, making it easier for them to violate your boundaries until you learn how to stand up for yourself. In this chapter, we will be discussing the advantages and disadvantages that come with being a highly sensitive individual.

Pros

Let's take a look at the bright side first and discuss all the magical gifts that come with being a highly sensitive individual.

Your Thoughtfulness

It is no secret that HSPs make for the most thoughtful friends, partners, family, colleagues, and neighbors. As a highly sensitive person, you can put yourself in other people's shoes and understand where they are coming from. You can tell if something is wrong by sensing the slightest change in their mood or their tone.

Being sensitive to the subtle changes in another's behavior makes it easy for you to put them at ease. Because of this, people are often surprised and wonder how you could tell despite their efforts to hide their real emotions. Sometimes, you can detect a change in their energy before realizing it themselves.

You are naturally gifted at making other people comfortable and even putting their needs before yours. The gift of being highly aware of other people's moods makes you an extremely thoughtful person to have around. This also causes you to be mindful of your words and actions to avoid doing something that would hurt or offend other people. People know that they can be themselves around you without any worry or judgment. You like to be there for your friends and wouldn't want them to suffer alone, especially because you're quite aware of the feeling.

You're Well-Mannered and Considerate

Because you are an empath, you're well aware of other people's energies as their energies impact you as well. Moreover, you're an extremely well-mannered person who would never be intentionally rude to anyone. Highly sensitive people are highly conscientious. You are so considerate that you would put a stranger's comfort over your own in a public or extremely cramped space in an elevator or public transport. Because of your great manners, you are quick to recognize when someone is being rude to others. Seeing someone else get mistreated fires up the inner protector, making you want to rescue the underdog.

You're Incredibly Empathetic

Highly sensitive people are usually empaths. This makes them aware of other people's intentions, feelings, and moods. If someone is close to you or their suffering is intense, you may even start to feel their emotions physically. A study was carried out by Bianca Acevedo between sensitive and non-sensitive people. She showed them pictures of their loved ones feeling either happiness or sadness. The research reported increased activation in the parts of the brain related to empathy upon seeing the happy pictures of the people close to them. The activity in the empathy area of the brain was more intense when they were shown unhappy pictures of their loved ones, which reflected that they wanted to do something for them.

You Know How to Make Things Happen

As an HSP, you have the talent to make things happen. As you're so in tune with your emotions and feel everything deeply, you also have the perfect problem-solving skills- you can devise the perfect strategy to resolve a crisis by considering things from a different point of view. As an HSP, you have an intense appreciation for positive emotions such as joy, satisfaction, curiosity, pleasant desire for something, the anticipation of success, etc. This is why it is easier for you to create situations where you can get a chance to feel these emotions. Being a highly sensitive person, you love making your friends and family happy, and seeing them like that makes you feel content. You use your analytical skills and empathy to make good things happen for the people you love, and that is your superpower.

Your Attention to Detail Is Mind-Blowing

As an HSP, you are thorough and meticulous. Your attention to detail is amazing. This is the reason you outperform at your workplace as long as you are given enough space to explore your creative and analytical skills. This also means that you make fewer mistakes at work, so you don't have to go over many revisions in the projects you're involved with. Your colleagues know that you will never turn in a sloppy assignment. This is why everyone wants you in their team. Being a perfectionist, you are your own biggest critic, which means that you don't quit until you produce something you're proud of. You're a team player, you make sure to present high-quality work, and you're a genuinely good human being, making you a favorite at the workplace and among clients. Moreover, your ability to pay extra attention to details makes you a very good friend and partner because you remember the little things people tell you about themselves.

It is important to note that HSPs process information in a different way. They process the sensory information using areas of the brain associated with empathy and other, more complex areas. This is why it is easier for you to notice subtleties that other people miss. As a highly sensitive person, you're aware of the cues people unconsciously give off. For example, you're great at reading body language and other nonverbal cues, which makes it easy for you to read the room and see whether their words align with their actions and if you can trust them. This makes it easy for you to strategize your next move accordingly.

You Like to Stay In the Present

You like to savor things as you experience them. Being in the present and enjoying each moment keeps you happy and gives you a chance to unwind. You like to feel, notice, and enjoy things as you experience them. You take pleasure in checking out the details that other people tend to miss. You may even be highly attached to those subtleties because you have a special spot for things that other people tend to overlook. You feel everything deeply, and hence, you are deeply aware of the scents, sounds, and nature around you. You find inspiration from your surroundings to create your works of art. Highly sensitive people have a semantic memory; you can compare the present with the events that occurred in the past. You understand life and find meaning by comparing it to the past.

You Have the Ability to Learn Intuitively

One of your superpowers is that you can pick up things naturally. It is easy for you to learn new skills without realizing that you have learned them. You may be surprised to find how you just "know" things. Your strong intuition allows you to perceive and unconsciously learn things, which is why you come off as naturally good at things that you have never done before.

You Are Quite Creative

One of your greatest qualities is how creative you are. Your vivid imagination and a keen eye for beauty can find good in everything, and you are probably an artist, a painter, a poet, a sculptor, a musician, or some other artistic career. Your imagination knows no bounds and can do wonderful things when stimulated. Moreover, your ability to look at things meticulously makes you an even better artist as you notice things that others don't, and your ability to present them in a heart-touching way is what pulls people closer to your art. Many gifted songwriters, authors, and performers are highly sensitive individuals. This is why it is so easy for them to connect with their emotions and art to bring the most soulful content to the world. You view the world through a larger lens, your ability to add beauty to everything you touch is what makes you unique. It is quite easy for you to touch on the most difficult, tragic, or taboo topics in the most beautiful manner without offending anyone.

You Have Amazing Communication Skills

It is very easy for you to communicate deeply with other people. You have the talent to put other people's feelings into words. Your friends are often surprised at your ability to know and understand how they feel without saying a word. As an HSP, you are deeply connected with your own and your loved one's emotions. You can tune into the subliminal messages in the room, making you a communication expert. You are great at resolving issues with others and mediating fights. Your communication skills also come into play when you're at work. Your ability to exchange ideas and listen to everyone else makes you a great team player and colleague. It is also quite easy for you to learn new languages quickly among other talents.

Solitude Does Not Scare You

As an HSP, you need your alone time to process your emotions and take a break when the world around you gets to be too much. For many people, it is quite hard to alone. They are not in tune with their own thoughts and feelings, which is why the idea of being left alone with themselves is scary for them. However, it is not the same for highly sensitive people. They are deeply aware of their emotions and feelings, so much so that they start to become worried when they cannot connect with their feelings. They require solitude from time to time to understand what they are feeling. They like to get away from the noise of the world into quiet woods where they can spend some time with nature to recharge.

Moreover, nature fuels them. This is why many writers and artists find refuge in secluded forests or lakes to produce art in peace. Even being alone in a quiet room for some time makes it easy for you to catch a breath and prepare yourself to deal with stressful situations.

Cons

There are always two sides to a story, like everything else in life. Although there are many wonderful perks of being an HSP, it comes with a downside. Here are some disadvantages of being a highly sensitive person.

You're More Prone to Mental Illnesses

As a highly sensitive person, you have more chance of suffering from depression and anxiety, among many other mental disorders. This is because of your ability to feel everything to the point that it becomes difficult to process them. Your gift of empathy can turn into a curse if you do not learn to filter what you expose yourself to. Being a sensitive person means you would be more affected by things that wouldn't bother anyone else. It is extremely important to protect yourself and avoid watching violent news or films. It would also be helpful to get therapy to keep yourself afloat and to help you deal with the ups and downs in life. Your therapist can also provide you with the essential tools and skillset to protect yourself and keep yourself from getting hurt by things beyond your control.

Sensitive to Criticism

It is difficult to face criticism, even if it comes from someone who means well. As an HSP, this poses a great problem at work as it can make you shut down, and even a slight rude remark can ruin your day. It can also create problems in your relationships because you are easily hurt when your partner raises their voice at you or when you get into a fight. Even a joke or a harmless statement is seen as an insult, and you may view it as strong criticism. While you may understand where the other person is coming from, it can still be difficult to keep yourself from getting hurt. This is why it is important to create boundaries and discuss the things that hurt you with your partner to ensure that there is no room for misunderstandings.

Hectic Schedules Are Not for You

Being an HSP, you have a rich inner world. It can set you off when you don't spend time with yourself and unwind from the day. It can make you burn out and even make it hard to function normally. Your alone time is as essential as medicine for some people. Without it, it becomes hard to make sense of your surroundings. Having cramped up schedules is great for some people, but it's not the same with you. In fact, hectic schedules can be overwhelming to you and can seriously hinder your ability to perform at all. You need time to process information and do your work perfectly. Highly sensitive people find it difficult to rush through things. This is why they find it difficult to do different things simultaneously or multi-task, as it can become impossible to focus.

You Find It Difficult to Say No to People

It is very hard for you to manage other people's expectations. You can easily pick up on other people's feelings and understand what they need from you. This is why you don't like turning anyone down. This is why you often struggle with denying requests and saying no, even when your schedule is full. Many people end up taking advantage of your beautiful heart and your inability to say no. This is why you often find yourself stuck in situations you never wanted to be involved with in the first place.

It is especially hard for you to say no because you can feel your friends' disappointment. Being a highly sensitive person, you have to carefully choose where you spend your energy. If you spend all your energy fulfilling other people's demands, you will have no time left for yourself. This can easily overwhelm you and make you burn out. Knowing how to balance the things you do for others and yourself can help you maintain a healthy relationship with them and keep yourself afloat at the same time. You are not responsible for other people's happiness, and this is difficult but necessary for you to understand for your sanity.

You Tend to Avoid Conflict

Although nobody likes conflict, HSPs are considerably more stressed out by it than other personality types. You tend to overthink things, even when there's a slight change in someone's tone. You know when things seem weird in a relationship or when your partner is not communicating, and you know something is wrong. However, you also tend to misinterpret these signals as signs of conflict or anger which can cause difficulty in your relationship. Avoiding confrontation because of your fear of conflict can also cause difficulty at your workplace. You try your best to avoid conflict even when you know that you are being mistreated or there is an imbalance of responsibilities among you and your colleagues. To avoid conflict, you would rather stay quiet and suffer in silence which is bad for you in the long run.

Social Comparison Deeply Affects You

Highly sensitive people are their own biggest and worst critics. You are more aware of your shortcomings than anyone else. This is why you take it very badly when you are compared to others. You are deeply affected by the negative feelings of others and your own, which makes it very difficult for you to deal with social comparison, whether it is in your favor or vice versa. Breakups are also quite hard for you because you may feel that there is a possibility of resolving the relationship when the other person believes that nothing could be done and chooses to give up on it. It is quite difficult for you to get over someone after the breakup. This makes you more prone to obsess over people long after they have left you.

Managing Toleration

Toleration refers to what we tolerate but don't necessarily *need* in our lives. So, an HSP's toleration will include anything they find stressful and draining of their energy. *Toleration* can even be the distractions you face while working; these may stress you out, especially when focusing on a task. A foul smell or the noise outside can put you off and make it difficult to concentrate. A messy home can also make it hard for you to relax. You are also startled by surprises and more prone to anger when hungry. It is very difficult for you to function with an empty stomach. All of these factors can make daily life more troublesome for you.

Personal Failures

You are quite critical of yourself as an HSP. A small setback can make you feel overwhelmed and push you deep into self-doubt. Even an embarrassing mistake can stress you out, and it bothers you more than it would to an average person. You also don't appreciate being judged or watched while you're doing something. As a perfectionist, you want to get the job done perfectly. However, when you know that someone is watching you do it, you cannot pull it off the way you would in different circumstances.

You Find It Difficult to Make Decisions

You don't want to be stuck with the burden of making a decision. It is especially difficult for you because you always want to be hundred percent right. You easily understand the pros and cons of both sides of any situation, making it difficult for you to choose. You take a long time to make a decision, but you make sure to stick to it when you do.

You Feel Misunderstood

As a highly sensitive person, you often feel misunderstood. Other people don't feel things the way you do, which can cause them to think that you're being dramatic or exaggerating. You often hear things like "Don't take it personally" or "Why are you so sensitive?" or "Get over it!" etc. According to Dr. Aron, HSPs are mistaken as introverts when in actuality, around 30% of highly sensitive people are extroverts. HSPs are often seen as shy, but that is an innate trait and not a learned one.

Highly sensitive people are wonderfully talented human beings who have their ups and downs. They have excellent motor skills such as sculpting, drawing, sewing, etc. Although you tend to overthink, you usually think for other people and their well-being. You're not at all self-centered and are always putting your friends and family's needs above yours. However, you must put yourself first and learn to think for yourself from time to time. You are a compassionate and extremely strong individual whose good qualities outnumber the weak ones.

Chapter 4: Emotional Overwhelm: How to Cope

In previous chapters, we've discussed what it is like to be a highly sensitive person, together with the pros and cons of this personality. Although high sensitivity can be a gift, it can also be challenging. Simple tasks or activities that may come easy to less sensitive people can overstimulate HSPs. For instance, there is nothing stressful about a crowded restaurant, a fast-paced job, or a loud concert for most people. However, these activities can leave you feeling stressed and overwhelmed.

As mentioned in previous chapters, there is nothing wrong with how you are feeling. Being highly sensitive is a personality trait that occurs in people whose brain is wired differently. This can make you feel what other people are feeling and experience emotions more vividly, which can be taxing. Simply put, unlike less sensitive people, your brain processes more information, overloading your nervous system. For this reason, you feel engulfed.

Feeling emotionally overwhelmed can have a huge impact on your life and mental and physical health. However, some people may not be aware that their feelings of devastation are actually what it feels like to be emotionally overwhelmed. You may just feel stressed or worn out after certain situations, but you don't understand why. You need to understand it before learning to cope with this feeling and not letting it control your life.

What Makes an HSP Feel Overwhelmed

Understanding what makes you feel overstimulated can help you manage these feelings. Various external and internal stimuli can contribute to these feelings. It is important to note that you may not find every stimulus here overwhelming because what you may consider stressful, another HSP may find it pleasant, and vice versa.

External Stimuli

Being Overwhelmed by Your Environment

Various things in your surroundings can stress you out, for example – crowds, loud noises, bright lights, strong scents, certain fabrics, dust, smoke, and extremely hot or extremely cold weather.

Social Situations

You might find certain social situations overwhelming because being around people can drain your energy as a result of your empathetic nature. That said, not all highly sensitive people find social situations stressful. Each HSP is different. In addition to that, being an introvert or an extrovert can also play a huge role in how you handle and process social situations. An extrovert HSP can handle being around people or crowds better than an introvert HSP who will feel drained more quickly. However, this doesn't mean that an HSP doesn't like people; they just get overwhelmed at times. The brain of an HSP easily picks up on what other people are feeling, even if they are pretending to be happy when, in reality, they are sad or vice versa. This can be exhausting for an empathetic HSP when they are around many people and pick up on various social cues.

Social events like attending a party, shallow conversations, going to a concert, being surrounded by a crowd, and having to engage with them can leave an HSP extremely overwhelmed.

Internal Stimuli

Physical Pain

Some physical pains and sensations can be overstimulating for an HSP. So, you will find that thirst, hunger, pain, and exhaustion leave you more stressed than most.

Feeling Overwhelmed by Your Thoughts

As a highly sensitive person, there are probably moments when you wish you could turn your brain off. Having so many thoughts and ideas racing through your head can't be fun, and you just wish that you could mute your thoughts. This can be easy, and we'll discuss techniques to help you calm yourself later in the chapter.

HSPs' thoughts can overwhelm them when they are worried or anxious, overthinking, processing information, or learning something new.

Sometimes, this results from the fact that you can't help but care more than the average person. According to research, all of the areas in an HSP's brain that are associated with empathy are very active. This isn't just the case when it comes to family, friends, and loved ones, in general, but you also can't stop caring for strangers. You are born with the innate tendency to care and show concern for those around you. You often feel responsible for people you are not even well-acquainted with. This definitely contributes to your overthinking and therefore leaves you feeling overwhelmed.

HSPs also observe and absorb more details than other people. These details are processed by the brain and at the level of the nervous system. Processing every external and internal stimulus with this depth leaves your brain very overworked.

Feeling Emotionally Overwhelmed

As human beings, we all feel emotions, but HSPs feel their emotions more deeply and react to them more severely than non-HSPs. So certain emotions like anger, grief, joy, excitement, and sadness can leave an HSP feeling overstimulated or drained because they feel them more intensely than less sensitive people.

Think of your brain as an artist who paints your emotions into an experience. An average person's perceptions of things are often straightforward. For instance, a necklace may look pretty to one person but may be deeply sentimental to another. However, an HSP's brain is a copious artist who pains experiences with much more emotions. This means that even the most generic things in life can hit an emotional spot for an HSP. They hear music in the rain, feel the underlying spiteful tone in a conversation, or feel heightened joy when petting an animal.

All of these can trigger emotional overwhelm because they are all connected. For instance, if you feel hungry, you may feel irritated or stressed, making you feel emotionally overwhelmed.

How to Tell If You Are Feeling Overwhelmed

Certain signs can indicate an HSP is feeling overwhelmed. You may not even be aware of them, or you might think that they are the results of exhaustion or working too hard, but they can actually be the result of feeling overwhelmed by your surroundings, thoughts, or emotions.

Panic

You may be facing a small or a simple problem, and suddenly, you start feeling like it is getting bigger. You begin to feel like you are losing control, which can make you panic and feel anxious.

Unable to Focus

When an HSP is overwhelmed, they can't concentrate on anything, and their brain becomes foggy. This could become a huge problem for an HSP, especially if they are working, studying, or trying to make a big decision.

Giving Up

Have you ever felt like you just wanted to quit or give up on something you love? Maybe you consider quitting your job every day or giving up on practicing your favorite sport. If you find yourself fighting the urge to walk away from something you care about, then you are probably tired and overwhelmed.

Exhaustion

Many things can make you feel physically or mentally fatigued; feeling overwhelmed is one of the main reasons. You may find yourself drained and don't have the energy to work or even go out with your friends.

Physical Discomfort

What you are feeling inside can start showing itself in physical symptoms. If you are engulfed or stressed, you may start having headaches, stomach aches, or tension in your body. This is your body telling you that you are overwhelmed and need to slow down and relax.

Obsessive Thoughts

Having obsessive thoughts and sweating the small stuff can signify feeling overwhelmed. You start believing that you may be losing control, so you obsess and overthink when you are simply overwhelmed and just need a break.

Feeling Irritated

Another sign of being an HSP is that you feel irritated by every little thing. Maybe you need a nap or some alone time to relax, calm down and regain control of your emotions.

Feeling overwhelmed is pretty normal, and it doesn't mean you are weak or there is something wrong with you. Although HSPs feel more overwhelmed than most people, everyone sometimes feels overwhelmed for one reason or another. Your brain is like a computer; if it keeps processing more information than it can handle, it will start lagging and will eventually crash. No one has unlimited energy, and so many factors can drain a person's energy until they are burned out and overwhelmed. Now imagine a highly sensitive person who has to process more information and feel more strongly than others. This is why HSPs feel overwhelmed faster and easier.

How to Cope with Emotional Overwhelm

Now we arrive at the most important part of this chapter, coping with emotional overwhelm. High sensitivity can sometimes be challenging, especially when exterior or interior stimuli make you feel emotionally overwhelmed. However, you don't have to feel that way, constantly feeling exhausted, drained, and stressed. Learning to manage your emotions is key to a healthy life for an HSP.

Sometimes, as an HSP, it can be hard to understand how – and why – something feels emotionally overwhelming to you. This is probably because, as a kid, you may not have grown up in an environment that nourished HSPs. As a child, you were probably called too shy or too sensitive, so you never really understood what you are or why you have different needs from other people. You have probably only recently learned that you are an HSP, so you want to learn more about this trait. You may feel stressed, spacey, and just want to blank out by eating and watching TV, but you don't know what has triggered these feelings.

So, before you read the next part, we suggest that you do some self-reflection first. Get a pen and paper and write down all the situations that made you feel stressed in the last month or so. You should also write down exactly how you felt, whether you felt spacey, drained, tired, or irritated; write down your thoughts too. Also, try to write down what you were doing at the time, as this can help you identify your triggers. You can also use any of the stimuli mentioned here as a reference to help you better understand your triggers. Once you have an idea of what can overwhelm you, you can choose the best way to help you manage your feelings based on the stimuli or situation that set them off.

Turn the Stimuli Off

As mentioned before, certain stimuli can make you feel overwhelmed. The best way to remedy the situation is to simply move away from what is causing you to feel that way. You probably think that this is easier said than done, especially for people who usually feel overwhelmed at work. However, some simple things can help you manage your feelings. For instance, if the stimulus is work-related, you can either go for a walk during your lunch break or spend some quiet time alone in the bathroom.

Other things that can help you relax are listening to relaxing music, taking a hot shower, or looking at beautiful scenery or painting.

That said, you shouldn't wait until you feel overwhelmed, instead make it a habit to do things that can relax you and calm your nerves every day. Create a small quiet place in your home where you can retreat alone to recharge and relax. It can be your bedroom, garden, or any place where you can have privacy, peace, and no one to disturb you. You need to be alone for this to work. HSPs can't unwind or relax in the presence of other people because they can still drain your energy.

Be Careful with Overwhelming Emotions

The way HSPs process their emotions can make them feel extremely overwhelmed. Additionally, highly sensitive people don't only feel their feelings, but they can also sense and absorb what the people around them are feeling. You need to be able to tell the difference between your feelings and others and learn how to separate the two. This is a great way to help you avoid being overwhelmed or feeling drained when you are around people and give you peace of mind.

When it comes to your own negative feelings, you need to manage them in a healthy manner. Depending on the feeling, you can write in your diary, talk to a friend, or see a therapist. You should also avoid watching violent or scary movies, the news, and spending time with friends or family members who are always complaining about something. Take a look at your close circle, and ask yourself who makes you feel better and who makes you feel emotionally drained? Spend more time with the right people and avoid those who make you feel overstimulated. If avoiding them isn't an option - like your boss at work or a parent - you will need to set some boundaries.

You simply need to prevent negative emotions from taking over your life. Naturally, you may face situations that can cause you trauma or extreme grief, like a bad breakup or losing someone you love. As a highly sensitive person, you will grieve more intensely, and avoiding these feelings is neither realistic nor healthy. However, in this case, you will need to avoid anything that can make you feel worse or add to your stress. During this sensitive time, you will be focusing on your grief and trying to heal, so you are already overwhelmed. Therefore, you will need to avoid any extra stimuli that can mess with your healing process and cause a setback.

Adjust Your Thoughts

Being distressed can affect your thought processes, and everything will seem like doom and gloom, and the next moment everything is fine. For instance, you may wake up one day thinking that you are the smartest person on the planet, while the next day, you will feel like the dumbest person in the world. This way of thinking can make you feel more emotionally overwhelmed. It isn't healthy. Life isn't black or white and can't be lived in extremes. This mental attitude of all or nothing, either perfect or ruined, is unrealistic and will set you out for failure. There is always a middle ground, and you need to find it.

Therefore, when you face a problem, try to avoid thinking in extremes and adjust your thoughts. Look at all the options you have and all the methods you can use to solve it. Write down all of your options until you can figure out the best solution. You should also consider thinking outside the box. Another thing that can make you feel overwhelmed is the need to control a situation. The truth is, nothing in life is certain, and no matter what situation you are facing, you can never guarantee the outcome. Accepting this truth will take a huge burden off your shoulder. Only focusing on what you can actually control and what you can do will make you feel less overwhelmed when facing any complicated situation.

Accept Your Feelings

Whenever an HSP feels any strong emotions, especially negative ones, they try to find ways to help ignore and shove down these emotions. However, shoving down your emotions without acknowledging them or feeling them can have a negative effect. Learn to feel your emotions first, but do this in a healthy way. You can do this by sitting in a comfortable and quiet place and contemplating these feelings, or you can also write in your diary, cry, or even scream. Anything that can help you feel a release is a lot healthier than pretending that they don't exist or hiding from them. Acknowledging negative feelings and finding a healthy output to release them can help you manage and cope with being emotionally overwhelmed.

Distract Yourself

When you feel overwhelmed by your emotions, it can be hard to focus or think of anything else. This can make the situation worse and prolong your suffering. For this reason, it can be very beneficial to simply take your mind off things. Do something you enjoy, like reading a good book, playing with your pet, or watching your favorite TV show.

Distracting yourself can help distance you from your emotions to come back with a clear mindset, enabling you to tackle the situation from a different and fresh view. You should be aware that there is a huge difference between distraction and avoidance. Avoidance isn't a healthy coping mechanism, while distraction is a short break that will allow you to unwind and relax for the sole purpose of dealing with your problem.

Practice Mindfulness

Emotional overwhelm can make a person unfocused and unaware of their surroundings. An HSP's mind is always racing with dozens of thoughts at once; they are either overthinking about something, over-analyzing a situation, or struggling with strong emotions. Their brains never shut down. Practicing mindfulness will allow you to focus on yourself and the present moment. Being mindful will help slow down your thoughts and not be concerned with the past or worrying about the future. Focusing on the moment can help reduce negative emotions like anxiety or stress, making you feel overwhelmed.

Rest Your Body

Sometimes you may be feeling stressed because your body is tired and needs a break. Resting your body can actually reduce the emotional overload you have been feeling. Many different things can help your body relax; you can get a good night's sleep, meditate, spend time in nature, or simply take a nap. If your body makes you feel emotionally overwhelmed, resting will remedy the situation. If it is something else, sleeping or napping will make you feel refreshed so you can approach the problem with a different and fresh perspective.

You need to cope with and manage your emotional overwhelm and not try to control it. You can't control your emotions. As an HSP, you will face stimuli every day that will trigger a response from you one way or another. HSPs will always have to deal with situations that can cause them emotional distress, and they will either fight or try to get rid of these feelings altogether. However, it is better to acknowledge them and be aware of them. To respond in a healthy way to situations or stimuli that can be emotionally overwhelming, be mindful and present, so you can feel your feelings and thus react properly. So, whenever you feel overwhelmed, try to breathe slowly and be aware of your body, senses, surroundings, and the present moment.

You need to understand your emotions and what triggers them as well. Additionally, you need to constantly ask yourself how you feel so you can be aware of your emotions at all times. Last but not least, accept yourself as a highly sensitive person with all the ups and downs. Accept that sometimes you may feel things more than others, so you don't get overwhelmed every time you feel strongly about something. You are a very sensitive person, and there is absolutely nothing wrong with that.

Chapter 5: Your Well-Being Comes First

As we have read, highly sensitive people react differently to life than other people do. They possess personality traits that enable them to tune into their environment and the people around them, and they react strongly to this. If you are a highly sensitive person, these traits can take their toll on your well-being. This is why you must learn how to practice self-care. The intense feelings and deep perspective you have toward the outside world can be overwhelming for you. This chapter will discuss the problems that highly sensitive people face and how to practice self-care.

Problems That HSP Face

Highly sensitive people process things differently from others. Common situations like walking in a crowded place or being in an environment of bright lights and loud noises are overwhelming. What is exciting and fun to everyone can be a trigger for anxiety and stress. Being overly stimulated by these situations can be a challenge. You will need to learn how to maintain serenity in a climate of chaos.

As a highly sensitive person, you may worry about certain situations or feel emotional by the slightest trigger, like a sound or smell or something you saw. Your great attention to detail helps you read people's expressions, which is why you feel compassion for other people's troubles, often focusing more on their needs than your own.

The consequence of focusing on others is that you usually feel emotionally drained. This does not just have a toll on your mental well-being, but you also feel physically exhausted most of the time. This is because you receive and process things a lot more intensely. You get emotionally invested in other people's problems, concentrate too much on their well-being, and ignore your own. You may sometimes even think it is selfish if you focus on self-care because you have an irresistible urge to be there for others.

You will have to learn how to moderate your urge to help other people before yourself and be wary of being an emotional carrier for too long and to your detriment. Listen to your friend's issues and be there for them, but remember to let go of these emotions and distinguish them from your own. Part of your physical and mental exhaustion is because you hold your own emotions back, not acknowledging them. You allow the emotions of others to bury yours. Remember to take some time off away from other people so you can get your mind, body, and soul back in balance. Try to do this daily by taking an hour or two for yourself to do one of your favorite activities or practice a hobby.

Loud noises, bright sunlight, or certain smells can be very distracting and irritating for you, and it's tough to describe exactly what is bothering you in these situations. There could just be too many things going on around you that are overwhelming your senses but seem normal to everyone else. These situations can pose a challenge for you, especially when you are outdoors or with other people. If you know you will be in a potentially stressful situation, prepare yourself by keeping a few items in your bag that block loud noises or bright lights. Try to keep things that bring comfort to your senses. For example, take sunglasses and a hat with you for a bright day, noise-canceling headphones for loud noises, and a soothing smell like lavender oil or chocolate butter to help calm you down and block strong smells.

A common problem you might face is dealing with stressful situations like loud parties or social gatherings. It might be tough for you to constantly get out of these events because you may not want to upset the people around you, or you don't want to keep missing these gatherings. Remember that sometimes it is best to excuse yourself from such events and prioritize your comfort. Communicate your concerns with your friends so that they can understand how these seemingly normal situations are overwhelming for you. Try not to seclude yourself from every single outing. You should try to practice doing uncomfortable things but on your own terms. You can start in a controlled setting with small things until you feel comfortable engaging in bigger situations without getting anxious.

Sometimes, people find it difficult to understand your triggers or why you receive things so differently. You may be known as a shy person or an introvert, especially when growing up. People might have even told you that you need to toughen up or that you always make a big deal out of things.

Criticism like this can be a huge challenge, which can take its toll on your self-esteem and self-worth, which is mentally debilitating. You could be lingering on one simple mistake or odd encounter with someone for days. You may always feel like you are not allowed to express your emotions. The criticisms you've heard from people all your life can greatly influence your self-image.

You must remember that it is not your fault that people can't understand you. There will always be other people in your life who will accept you for who you are. Part of practicing self-care is surrounding yourself with good people and avoiding toxic relationships.

How to Deal with Negative Emotions

As a highly sensitive person, you probably experience a lot of emotional highs and lows because you don't process things the same way other people do; your feelings are so much deeper than others. While this allows you to experience positive emotions to their fullest extent, experiencing negative emotions can be too much for you to handle. One slightly negative thought can be magnified into an enormous concern, triggering anxiety. This is why dealing with the negatives is so important for you.

On any given day, you may be dealing with a range of emotional baggage from other people, as well as your own. This can be overwhelming when the people around you are experiencing negative emotions. You easily pick on the energy vibes in the room, which soon manifests in your emotional state. Let's say your roommate just had a tough day at work. Their frustration, exhaustion, or anger will quickly find a place in your heart and mind, and you will soon feel the same way. It is safe to say that other people's energy and emotions are often contagious to you, whether positive or negative.

Imagine how many emotions you are picking up off others throughout your day, so when you finally get some alone time, check in with your own feelings, and if you feel down, try to trace your steps for that day to find out if it's your own feeling or someone else's. Ask yourself if something upsetting happened directly to you or was it just other people's vibes. Your waiter at breakfast may have been having a rough day, your boss may have been too busy and agitated to greet you at work, or your best friend could have abruptly hung up on you when you called. These little things could accumulate and grow in your head along with their negative impact.

It is a daily struggle, and these emotions can often get the best of you. Sometimes, you won't have the energy to work, do your favorite activity, or hang out with your friends. You may feel upset, angry, or frustrated for no reason other than the emotions you've held on to during the week.

There are ways to prepare yourself for these situations when they happen. Whenever you feel a negative emotion, allow yourself to acknowledge them first. Each person has their own strategy in acknowledging those feelings. You can try sitting alone in a quiet space and thinking about all these negative emotions. Think about what happened throughout the day. Ask yourself whether these are your feelings or you just feel bad for those people.

It may help you to write your emotions down. The act of using a physical object to pour your feelings can be very therapeutic. Remember that your feelings are always worse in your head. When you get these emotions in writing, you can look back at them and see them in a different light. If you feel like crying, don't hold back. Allow yourself to feel; it's such a good way to get relief and inner cleansing. Try talking to a close friend who understands your struggles. Being in a safe space gives you permission to do everything you can to recognize your negative emotions before letting them go.

Another tip is to try doing a solo activity. You could take a nature hike to try and clear your head, mindfully practice yoga and breathing exercises, or even take a hot shower or bath to feel more relaxed. These soothing practices will help you relieve stress and renew your energy. It is a way for your body to focus on healing and letting go of your worries.

Try to distance yourself from negative situations or events that might trigger your anxiety. Avoid watching violent movies or the news, or anything packed with negative emotions. You should not subject yourself to more stress because you will soon be overwhelmed and have to start the healing process again. Similarly, try to limit your interactions with negative people. Don't think of this as a selfish act because you have your own well-being to think about. While other people think they are venting instead of complaining, it might not be the healthiest thing for you to keep surrounding yourself with them. If these people are a part of your life as a family member, it is important to set some boundaries.

Another important tip is to be careful about extreme emotions. When you experience a negative emotion, it can easily turn into a loop of negativity. Avoid the all-or-nothing perspective. Not everything will go wrong or right in any given situation. There will always be a middle ground where you can exist comfortably. For example, if you start your day on one bad event like spilling coffee on your work shirt, you may start thinking that everything will go wrong that day. You must tell yourself that it was just a little accident, which will not set the vibes for your whole day. The same thing goes for happier events or situations you think are just "perfect." Swaying both ways to the extreme emotions can make it a lot worse, even if they were good emotions, *because emotions never stay the same.*

You may be a perfectionist, and getting one thing wrong will feed your very active self-criticizing brain. But remember, there are always things you cannot control, and the trick is to accept that and allow yourself to make mistakes just like everybody else.

Setting Boundaries

While setting boundaries may seem like a cold and distant concept for most people, it is crucial to be highly sensitive. Filtering out some of the people in your life or protecting yourself from certain situations is important for your well-being. However, it may not be as easy as it sounds. In fact, you may struggle with setting boundaries with others because you'd usually feel guilty for turning people down or taking your distance.

You need to establish what you need and how comfortable you are dealing with a certain person at the moment. If you feel angry, tired, or overwhelmed, take a minute to think about the root cause of these emotions. You must listen to your body in these moments. Now, think about the situation you are facing and ask yourself whether you are ready to handle it. Permit yourself to feel your own emotions. This might seem weird, but you would usually put other people's needs and feelings first and neglect how you feel. This is why it is important to check in regularly and find out how you feel.

Since setting boundaries can be uncomfortable, try to start by making small requests. For example, you can tell your neighbor you won't be able to stay for their party or send a text to your friend telling them you will call them back later. Don't take on too many things because you are afraid you will hurt people. You must slow down and take time to practice self-care on a regular basis. This includes not taking on too many tasks at work or overburdening yourself with organizing your friend's baby shower all by yourself. You need to set boundaries for yourself as well to avoid getting overwhelmed. Taking these small steps with yourself first will help you to be more confident in setting boundaries with other people.

Practicing Self-Care

You need to practice a daily self-care routine to get rid of accumulated emotions regularly and live a better life. You have to prioritize your mental and physical well-being before being there for other people. Implementing small maintenance strategies every day is easier than waiting for a nervous breakdown, which can be tough to recover from. You can seek help from a health professional who can guide you. In the meantime, consider trying these few physical and mental habits to maintain your wellness.

1. Maintain a healthy, well-balanced diet. If you feel agitated or anxious, is it because you've had nothing to eat all day? You may be more susceptible to blood sugar fluctuations as a highly sensitive person. Try to eat smaller meals throughout the day to keep your energy stable. If your blood sugar levels are balanced, you are less likely to experience mood swings. Try to avoid overeating or eating all of your meals in one sitting at the end of the day. Make sure you have a balanced portion of protein, vegetables, healthy fat sources, and whole grains every day.

2. Try to establish an exercise routine that you enjoy. You don't have to stick to going to the gym every day if you don't like it. You have options. Nothing is cast in stone, so a hike in nature, playing a basketball game with friends, or going for a swim can break the monotony of the gym every day. This will help you continue exercising, which will physically help you feel better. Exercise promotes the release of endorphins responsible for happy emotions and can be the perfect remedy for you when you are feeling down.

3. Another important aspect of your overall wellness is making sure you get quality sleep every day. Establish a routine time to go to bed and always stick to it. If you go to bed at 10:30, it is more likely that you will be asleep by 11. It usually takes us 30 minutes to an hour to fall asleep. If you don't go to bed early because you don't feel sleepy, you may end up staying up later than usual and won't get enough sleep. Try to prepare the ambiance in your bedroom for sleep as well. Reduce screen time an hour before

going to bed to avoid stimulating your brain and limit your caffeine during the day so that you sleep better at night.

4. Try to incorporate meditation into your daily routine. You can perform 20 minutes in the morning and before going to bed to promote relaxation. There are numerous forms of meditation and physical practices that you could try, like yoga, Qigong, or Tai Chi. You can try several of these techniques to find one with which you are comfortable. These exercises are meant to maintain your overall wellness and help you to achieve inner peace and calmness.

5. You should try to set some time aside for yourself every day. Create a safe space or private room in your house where you can be alone and gather your thoughts. It could be your meditation or self-reflection room. Make sure to declutter this room and make it as open and inviting as you can. If a situation gets too overwhelming for you, just excuse yourself and take the time to decompress.

6. Another good tip is to try to avoid running errands during peak times. Go to the grocery store during weekdays instead of weekends. Try to wake up a little early to go to the gym to exercise when it's not too crowded. You will get things done faster, and you will avoid any overstimulation from crowds or loud noises.

7. Always surround yourself with beautiful things and sceneries. Take a walk in the park and appreciate nature. You should also always surround yourself with good people who respect you and understand what you are going through. The idea is to try and surround yourself with positive vibes and to be aware when negative emotions hit you so that you can know how to handle them properly.

8. Carrying around a pair of noise-cancellation headphones can be a game-changer for you. You don't need to walk around wearing it, but it will come in handy whenever you need to concentrate on a task outside or even take a temporary break from any auditory stimulants. They'll help you improve your focus at work or even enjoy reading in the park as most people do. Your high sensitivity to noise that you can't control can be very overwhelming. Having your headphones on you at all times will allow you to be in charge of your own peace.

9. Make sure that you allow yourself more than enough time to work on things. Highly sensitive individuals can't function well when their schedules are packed. If you have flexible work hours, you can push work to a later time of the day, so you don't need to rush around in the morning. You can wake up without an alarm, have a nice breakfast, take a relaxing shower, and even lounge around before you head to work. This way, you will start your day off on the right foot. If that's not practical, make sure to go to bed early so you can wake up earlier than you usually do. This way, you will still have plenty of time in the morning. Make sure not to make several appointments or put too many tasks on your to-do list for one day.

10. Highly Sensitive People are highly sensitive to caffeine. While you don't need to eliminate it completely, you need to try to limit your caffeine intake. The trick is knowing your body and learning how it affects you because each person is different. For some HSPs, even the traces of caffeine in decaf coffee can be too much to handle. If you're an avid coffee drinker, you will notice the significant difference once you limit your intake.

11. Make sure to keep the lights down low whenever you have control over the lighting. You will never imagine the role that light stimulation plays in your life once you minimize it. Keep your lights low and warm in the evening, and try to visit restaurants, cafes, and stores with gentle lighting. In addition to bright and harsh lights, local spaces can be very crowded, which would trigger your fight or flight response in no time. This brings us to our next point.

12. Being out can be overwhelming as it is, so try to keep the stimulants to a minimum. Be mindful of the restaurants, cafes, or places you visit. Pay attention to your company, as well. If some people are particularly "touchy" or use a lot of physical gestures as they communicate or even speak loudly, try to sit beside someone else.

This chapter discussed how highly sensitive people feel about themselves and how they may be their own worst critics. Remember to be kind to yourself and take the time to browse your emotions and release them appropriately. Self-care is the most important thing you can do to take care of your mental and physical well-being.

Chapter 6: Highly Sensitive People in Love

Falling in love and being extra sensory can be the perfect mix between exciting and scary. The feelings of excitement are unmatchable and magical, no matter who you are. Since highly sensitive people are easily stimulated, the feelings they experience are even more engulfing. If you're highly sensitive, learning to put in the effort to understand how your brain is wired and nurture your needs and sensitivity can help you realize that you're in possession of strength rather than a burden. It also helps you understand your expectations and your boundaries, allowing you to maintain strong relationships with others. Building a strong relationship with yourself sets the tone for all your other interactions. The relationship that you have with yourself decides the quality of the interactions that you have with others.

HSPs are naturally very considerate of their romantic partners in everything they do. If you're doing something as simple as brewing coffee in the morning or making a playlist before you set out on a car ride, the chances are that you will be thinking of your significant other in the process. Even if you don't fall in love easily, you end up taking mental notes for everything that your partner likes or cares for, and you immediately start to include them in the things you do.

Unfortunately, while being an HSP can make you naturally considerate, which is a very healthy aspect of any relationship, it also means that you're very likely to get deeply disappointed whenever this level of consideration isn't met. Highly sensitive people may also feel engulfed by the intense feelings of the relationship. They may try to create a balance between affection and their personal time and space to recharge. If this balance isn't achieved, HSPs can get very frustrated.

As you may recall from the first few chapters, highly sensitive people can read a room. They notice the subtleties in people's body language and expressions, which allows them to sense general moods and states in others. However, they often take it way too far. HSPs tend to take an interest in how other people think – not just about them but also about everything in general. When they go overboard, HSPs can forget that they don't mind readers, causing them to go too far with their assumptions.

Highly sensitive people analyze even the smallest changes in a person's manner of communication. They take it upon themselves to gather a deep understanding of everything surrounding them, to the point where it becomes exhausting. Not to mention that giving these thoughts too much power can impact their romantic, social, and even professional relationships.

When HSPs are not being overly analytical, the emotions of love can keep them present and grounded. These feelings can help them appreciate each happy moment they spend with their partners. To them, these pure and alluring moments are heavenly. Perhaps their tendency to fall in love quite deeply, give their partners their all, and their deep appreciation of their partners and the time they spend with them comes from the fact that HSPs experience a heightened intensity of situations.

Growing awareness about how you experience love can empower you to understand your skills and strength and work on yourself, to capitalize on all the good qualities you possess. Reading this chapter will help you realize that your high sensitivity can help you build strong and rich romantic relationships. This is why we are here to tell you how your high sensitivity can either harm or improve your love life.

Relationship Challenges

Your high sensitivity can undoubtedly result in challenges in keeping your love life and romantic relationships healthy. The first and biggest challenge is that you could end up being unable to set healthy boundaries. If you're a highly sensitive person, you may struggle with knowing what healthy and clear-cut boundaries are. Sometimes, it may even feel like you have no boundaries due to your deeply compassionate and giving nature. While these qualities are incredibly beautiful to have, these pure intentions can easily spiral out of control and balance, causing HSPs to lose themselves in the process. Unfortunately, we all tend to put in less effort and take things for granted when things seem to be naturally working out for us. This means that an HSP's partner may inadvertently put less work into the relationship, which, as we mentioned above, can be devastating to a highly sensitive person.

Additionally, the lack of relational boundaries can cause highly sensitive individuals to become overly consumed in their partners, thoughts, emotions, and feelings to the point where they can no longer separate them from their own. They may find it hard to maintain their friendships, talk to other people, or even know their personality. At that point, processing their feelings and needs becomes impossible as they direct their time and headspace toward their relationships and partners. Highly sensitive individuals must learn to establish healthy boundaries to maintain a healthy romantic relationship and mental well-being.

Setting boundaries may feel very difficult and unnatural at first, particularly when you want to give your partner everything and ensure that they're happy. However, boundaries are essential to your growth and success. They also help you determine how supportive and respectful your partner is. Most importantly, boundaries can help make you feel safe, and you won't feel lost whenever your partner isn't around or after a breakup. Regularly check in with yourself and re-evaluate your partner's respect for your need for personal space and other boundaries you might want to set, along with your ability to express your authentic self around them.

You also need to consider whether you're close to being a caretaker in your romantic relationships. Being a highly sensitive person brings a sense of pride, need, and relief in nurturing others to the relationship. However, being associated with a healing entity may result in unhealthy disparities and power dynamics in relationships. Caring for and nurturing your partner more than you are their significant other may cause you to put their needs above your own.

This is detrimental to your mental health and could consume all your energy and time, but it also reinforces the idea that you can do anything your partner wants. As a highly sensitive individual, this is why you must check in with your feelings. Here's food for thought: why do you always try to focus on other people's thoughts, needs, and feelings but neglect your own? Make it a daily habit to connect with all your internal and external sensations and feelings. This will help you stay in tune with your wants, needs, as well as your own emotions. As you may recall from the previous chapters, HSPs tend to adopt feelings that aren't their own.

Another challenge that highly sensitive individuals may face is hiding or diming their sensitivity. You may feel understood at times, which is perhaps why you typically feel the need to belong. This, however, may easily shift into a habit of people-pleasing. Instead of thinking about what you need, you try to adjust to what you believe is the right behavior or the perfect amount of "sensitivity." You do everything to dodge the possibility of getting rejected in your mind. After a period of continuous emotional suppression and diminishing your true self, you may end up in the heart of an identity crisis. You will struggle to determine things that are true to your authentic self and true for others. In most cases, where highly sensitive individuals turn into people-pleasers, they find themselves stuck with abusive, manipulative, or narcissistic partners.

This is why you have to be clear about your fears surrounding relationships. If you feel the need to suppress your sensitivity, know that you are afraid of something. Whether you think you are too much to handle or worried that you just won't belong, your brain may trick you into believing that you're unlovable for the person you essentially are. These unreasonable thoughts need to be shifted, which is why you need to begin by asking yourself what you are most afraid of if you allow yourself to be your authentic self. Jot these fears down on a piece of paper and release them. You can tear them to pieces or burn them to ashes – whatever brings you the most relief.

Your high sensitivity is an incredible gift. As you can probably tell, all your relationship challenges arise from positive qualities. Many people wish they were either less or more rigid. However, these are traits that come so naturally to you. Learning to use them correctly rather than allowing them to control you can help you build very healthy relationships.

HSPs and Intimacy

It's natural to be afraid of intimacy if you're a highly sensitive individual. The thought of spending your entire life with just one person is scary enough. Many HSPs struggle to balance their need to maintain their freedom with their desire for a deep connection and intimacy. Considering that HSPs make up only 30% of the population, it makes sense that they'd struggle to make connections.

If you ask anyone in the world, they'd probably tell you that maintaining a sustainable relationship requires three things: effort, love, and patience. However, that list may easily quadruple in size for a highly sensitive person. As we explained above, HSPs are often intimidated by relationships. Whether they're struggling with self-expression, can't get over previous heartbreaks, fail to have their unique needs met, or worry about being too sensitive or too much to handle, HSPs need to consider many things if they want to build long-lasting relationships.

Accounting for your sensitivity while navigating your romantic relationships can improve your ability to communicate with your partner efficiently. You will be able to explain why you react the way you do in certain situations and explain your romantic needs and expectations. Let your partner know that you pick up on the subtleties and that you may begin to overthink and analyze them. This way, your partner will let you know what's up instead of thinking that you're trying to start an argument the next time you notice that their tone is off.

Being a highly sensitive person means that you fall deeply. Your strong emotions are what drive you. This means that opening your heart to your partner is more of a commitment to you. Intimacy, profound emotions, and relationships aren't things you take lightly. This doesn't only apply to feelings of love. If you're afraid, curious, angry, upset, or excited, then the chances are that you will act on that emotion in one way or another.

Any relationship comes with conflicts and arguments. While no one likes problems, especially those with partners and significant others, it is a particularly hard situation for an HSP. You may struggle to decide between speaking up for yourself and what you believe is right or just staying silent because you don't want to anger the other person. Conflicts can also get incredibly painful. As an empath, you don't just feel your hurt, but you end up experiencing the anger and pain of both yourself and your partner. This means that you need to take some time off to deal with the overload of emotions, perhaps more than resolving your conflict.

Remember how we mentioned that HSPs need some downtime to relax and recharge? In some cases, partners may think their HSP significant other is shutting them out. This is why you need to explain to your partner that needing some alone time doesn't mean you love them any less.

Dealing with an HSP as an HSP

If there's anything that you're sure of as an HSP, it's that it isn't easy to deal with someone else who is highly sensitive as well. We mean, you are literally reading a book on how to navigate through life as an HSP. Dealing with another highly sensitive person can be a bit of a challenge, especially since it isn't easy to determine what each of you is bringing to the table.

Let's take a quick recap. As an HSP, you are an empath, you tend to adopt other people's emotions, and you are highly aware of everything going on around you. This means that you and your highly sensitive partner are quick to notice subtleties and are inclined to think deeply about them. There's a good chance that both of you have been labeled as too sensitive, dramatic, or intense, at least once.

Dealing with an HSP as an HSP is a blessing and a curse. While it can be easy, considering that you do have an idea regarding how your partner's brain is wired, there are still various challenges.

If you want this interaction to work out, you must have a serious discussion with your partner on how to deal with each other when you're both highly sensitive. This is especially true if your partner doesn't even know that they're an HSP themselves. Since you're an HSP, you likely hate small talk, prefer intimate conversations, appreciate and value intimacy. This means that your partner will too. So instead of being worried that they may reject or trivialize the issue, trust that they will be willing to listen and help you produce a solution.

A great part of being in a relationship with someone supportive is that they can be your anchor or reference point whenever you're stressed or overwhelmed. However, when your significant other is also an HSP, you need to keep in mind that they have the same heightened level of awareness and overthinking and are thus as easy to overwhelm and stress. This is why you can benefit from a plan that can help you both out. It also helps the relationship if you remind each other to take it easy when you start noticing the little subtleties. Being hyper-aware and overly empathetic can be extremely mentally and emotionally exhausting.

Keep in mind that your partner is also likely to overthink certain situations or events. Make sure to give each other the time to process emotions and thoughts. It would be nice if you let your partner know that you'd happily listen to their concerns. You should also account for the fact that you're both conflict-avoidant. It wouldn't be long before neither of you could no longer bottle up your thoughts and feelings, much less keep up your people-pleasing tendencies. It will all inevitably backfire. This is why you should try your best to work through your issues as soon as they come up and encourage your partner to do the same. You should also find out what your partner's love language is (and let them know yours) so that both of you feel understood.

Sometimes, you will understand your partner without even trying to. Other times, getting so much as a hint of what they're thinking can be a challenge. This is why it's important to directly ask your partner whenever you're feeling doubtful. Consistency, intimacy, and authenticity matter to both of you, so as long as you keep those up, the chances are that you will be able to sustain your relationship for the long term. You should make the best out of the situation and find relief knowing that someone understands how your brain works.

Help Yourself

The difficulty in being in a relationship as an HSP comes from your tendency to put other people's needs above your own. You need to learn to help yourself instead of dedicating all your time and effort to helping others. To do that, you start by getting to know yourself. Find out what your needs are and whether your partner actually meets them. Whether it's the quiet or alone time you need, more serious and intimate conversations, or even feeling more understood. If you believe you need it, attaining it will undoubtedly help your relationship.

The most important thing you need to do is learn to love, appreciate, and accept yourself the way that you are. We can make others see us the way we want them to. If you think your sensitivity is to be ignored, your partner will too. However, if you accept and love your authentic self, your partner will perceive your sensitivity as a gift. Setting boundaries and taking charge of your own life are also key.

As an HSP, it might be instinctual to jump in and help your partner if they're struggling. However, you need to accept that there are some things that you simply can't help. Be compassionate and supportive but let your significant other figure things out on their own. Sometimes, all you need to do is just focus and look after yourself.

HSPs spend much of their time thinking about how things will go and all sorts of potential outcomes. It comes as no surprise that this habit extends to their love lives, as well. They calculate everything and take each action after some careful consideration. While this makes them awesome decision-makers, it also complicates how they view life. They forget that everything isn't always the way it seems, especially when they're overanalyzing each tiny detail. All these observations and analyses often cause them to question their relationships with their partners. Everyone overthinks at some point, which is fine as it contributes to our growth. However, HSPs need to be less self-critical, give themselves space to feel through their emotions, and learn to manage their thoughts and feelings. Doing so can allow them to use their gifts to build very strong and sustainable romantic relationships.

Chapter 7: The HSP at Work

Mounting evidence suggests that highly sensitive people are quite literally built differently. At a physiological level, there are key differences between highly sensitive people and the average person in terms of serotonin and dopamine levels, and even hormonal differences, which all react to cause emotional and sensory overload. Moreover, HSP's are more observant and analytical than the average office employee. Regardless of their role or where they are in the organization's hierarchy, their approach to work and life is highly individualistic.

Over the years, we have been told that people with higher sensitivity need to "toughen up," "grow a thicker skin," and stop letting everything get to them. The current scientific evidence suggests that even if they wanted to toughen up, HSPs are not in control, either physically or emotionally. It is not like they wish they weren't so easily distracted by something or be unable to focus on work; the fact is beyond their control. While they may try to overcome these day-to-day hurdles, it may only compromise the quality of work they can do.

The workplace is an environment where we are exposed to a wide range of experiences, emotions, situations, and people. Sometimes it's good, other times it isn't that great. However, there's a difference between a work environment that is extremely taxing and simply toxic and harmful for the individual. Different people gauge these things differently. Something that is a high-stress situation for one person might not be a high-stress situation, according to someone else.

Understanding Your Environment

Value in the Workplace

One of the biggest driving forces for an employee at any position is that their work is appreciated. This involves both being rewarded for their work directly and understanding how their work is connected to the bigger picture. When an HSP can clearly see how their work contributes to the business's overall goals, they are no longer focusing on just their work but are focusing on being a team player who is helping the company achieve that goal.

This is extremely important for an HSP who is extremely sensitive to the environment around them and who is more interested in doing intrinsically valuable work. However, to get to this stage, it's also important that the HSP knows and understands whether the work that they are doing is actually beneficial.

If the company director is giving monthly seminars on the company objectives but the employees, especially the HSP employees, are not getting an annual performance evaluation on them and their work, it can be like shooting arrows in the dark. HSP's strive to make their work better, to be masters of their craft, and to in some way rationalize to themselves the effort that they put in on a daily basis.

Getting feedback at an individual level and seeing the bigger picture is crucial. If your job role deprives you of this, then it is likely that it is a toxic environment. Your task is to lay the metaphorical bricks without ever knowing the structure you contribute to. However, in some job roles, that is the nature of the job. There really isn't any larger picture that needs to be made, it is a business that requires a little bit of work from everyone, and that is how the journey goes. In both cases, looking for a different job will be the best thing to do.

Your Contribution

An HSP will excel either in an environment where they have a lot of creative freedom or where their task is so specialized that it requires someone with a very acute understanding of the position, together with the skill. In both these situations, the HSP can contribute directly, and their work will often directly impact the business. In some situations, the business owners and managers will be very open about employee involvement and want employees to play a role in decision-making and solution hunting. In other cases, the job is more of a dead end. Even though you try to voice your opinions, they will fall on deaf ears.

In some situations, you might be discouraged from saying anything at all and just keep your head down and do the work. When an HSP cannot contribute in any meaningful way, this can be a very toxic environment for them. It might be a great environment for someone who is less sensitive about the situation and enjoys being in a role where they just have to put in the hours and then leave. But for people such as HSPs who can instantly emotionally attach themselves to their work, this can be very difficult to endure.

Transparency

There are politics, favoritism, a few social problems in every work environment, all part and parcel of human nature. Your opinions will not always be accepted or implemented in a high-pressure environment. This is because not everything you say will really be something that can be incorporated into the business. This is fine, and your employers will let you know when they think something won't work.

However, even if you have the right solution in a toxic situation, it won't be implemented because it is not coming from the person they *want it to come from*. If performance meetings and overall workflow seem like more of a competition between employees rather than a group effort to improve business performance, you will be very unhappy and emotionally drained by all these little problems, to the extent that you barely have any energy. You don't want to find yourself dreading a team meeting rather than looking forward to a powerful session that will refuel you in every sense after all the hard work that you have been putting into your work.

Equality

It is not uncommon for the workload in an organization to be unequally distributed. Some days one department is under a lot of work pressure, and on other days it is a different department dealing with a higher than usual workload. Being the extremely observant people they are, HSPs tend to notice this imbalance a lot. If it is a genuine imbalance, it will come around to everyone sooner or later.

However, there is a genuinely disproportionate distribution of the workload in some scenarios. Whether that means discrimination between people of a certain religion, ethnicity, or job function, if work is unfairly distributed, it will lead to a toxic environment. If this work is distributed to the HSP where the HSP is carrying out the bulk of the work, sooner or later, something is bound to give. Unfortunately, being an HSP, these individuals will usually go along with it for a very long time, often at the cost of their health and wellness. At some point, many will have had enough and will either snap, quit, or both. Whatever the case may be, working in such an environment is not healthy in any way and working along with such people will only give you more problems in your life. The solution is to find an exit and move on as soon as possible.

Situations in the Environment

As a part of a company, you will face many different circumstances. This can be because you as a professional are transitioning through different phases of your career or might be because the business itself is going through changing times. There will be different situations that are quite difficult to deal with as an HSP in either case. Here are a few situations and what you can do about them.

How to Stay Calm and Avoid Feeling Drained during Meetings

Company meetings can be difficult for an overly sensitive person, whether it is about facing negative feedback in front of all your coworkers or hesitation to present something in front of your seniors. For some HSPs, it's about the time they have to invest in these interactions. There might be several hours where you are not directly a part of the conversation. However, you are still obliged to sit through these meetings. Moreover, when it is a meeting with clients, vendors, or other stakeholders, it can be even more challenging because you are confronted with people you have no previous interaction with. You are also under the stress of performing in front of strangers.

One of the best things you can do in such a situation is to create physical distance between yourself and the center of the stage. Whether this means distancing yourself from where all the activity is happening, or it just means sitting a couple of rows back from where the main presentation is taking place. For HSPs, their personal space is very valuable, and it is an asset they rely on to maintain comfort and control their anxiety.

To help keep your mind from wandering off to other places during the meeting, it can also help to bring some work with you. Even if you have your presentation prepared, making some final changes, some small edits are a great way to keep your mind off the stressful things and stay focused on what you need to do. Also, revising your work will help you build more momentum as you go out to present.

Taking notes and keeping track of what is going on is also a great way to keep your mind focused and stop wandering into thoughts that increase anxiety and stress. You can either take notes of what others are saying, what the boss is saying, start listing things that you want to do as soon as you get out of the work meeting, or just generally try and keep your mind busy with some kind of work.

One of the main reasons HSP individuals feel drained after meetings is that they feel like they haven't added anything to the meeting. While it is very easy for you to get overstimulated, it is just as easy to be under-stimulated.

How to Control Anxiety in Stressful Situations

As an HSP, anxiety is something that you will probably be battling within every part of life, not just at work. To handle stress and anxiety more efficiently, you need to first understand your triggers. This will give you more control over your emotions and help you find solutions.

For instance, if you get extremely stressed when you have a surprise meeting – or something that wasn't planned comes up – you need to find a way to manage that situation to give you more time for it. At work, this might mean talking to your manager, letting them know about your situation, and asking if it's ok for you to join an ad-hoc meeting 10 or 15 minutes later, so you have some time to prepare yourself for it. If you are particularly stressed by the annual shut-down, then rather than starting when everyone else starts, maybe starting a week or two earlier will help handle that time of the year more effectively.

Running away from your triggers is not going to solve the problem, and it will only make the situation worse. The longer you put something off, the less time you will have to work on it, *which you do not want.* Ideally, you want to take things on as soon as possible, which is why knowing your triggers and the overall plan for your work will help. When you already know what will happen, you can take the time to prepare yourself. Being an HSP, you will tend to stress over the smaller details that other people don't, so you will need more time to work the way you want to. Always take things head-on rather than doing it because you have to. Even if you don't want to do it, taking the first step will give you the head start you need.

Another great thing you can do to curb anxiety is practice mindfulness and have some kind of active meditation that you can do wherever and whenever you need to. This can be as simple as listening to some calming music, listening to a calming podcast, or just breathing and focusing your thoughts on your breathing technique.

When you start to get anxious, the first thing that you lose track of is your breath. Deep long breaths help mentally, and the increased flow of oxygen also has a physical impact on your body. It lowers the heart rate, increases brain activity, and curbs the stress hormones. Suppose you enjoy meditating in a different style. In that case, you can do that, as long as it is something you can do anywhere, especially at work. You don't want to have some routine that requires you to be at home, in your yoga studio to do.

Try to understand what happens when you start to stress out. For most people, this can be similar to a state of panic, and they start to imagine extreme possibilities and start to envision things that are not relevant to the situation. When you understand how your mind operates when it starts to stress out, you can identify these problems when they actually happen and tell yourself to calm down. You become more mindful of your stress, and thus, are able to better control it.

How to Handle Annoying Situations

The fact of the matter is that there is only so much you can do to avoid annoying situations. Sooner or later, you will bump into a situation where you aren't completely comfortable, and leaving that environment might not even be an option. For instance, if you have to share a workspace with someone that you just cannot tolerate because they are constantly talking to people, getting up and doing things, or just playing music while they work, you need to find a solution.

The best way to solve a situation triggering your anxiety or even anger is to voice your concerns. It can be nerve-racking to speak up for yourself as an HSP, especially if you know that it is going to be something that will most likely hurt the other person, but it is the best solution if you don't want the problem to escalate. Also, before you put your foot down to handle the situation, take a step back to evaluate the entire scenario. Sometimes, you might feel that you are being targeted, but you are actually just part of the discussion and not the main target.

If it is a coworker that you are having trouble sharing space with or just a conversation that you don't want to be a part of, let the other person know that you aren't comfortable in the current situation and you would like to end the thing right here. This way, you can clarify to the person what your boundaries are, and they will think twice before dragging you into a similar situation in the future.

Once you have managed to disconnect yourself, you can try your relaxation techniques to get your mind back to a calm state. You might want to go out for a little walk and some fresh air; you might want to go wash your face and freshen up or do anything that helps you get out of that thought cycle and brings you back to a blank page in your mind. The problem with difficult situations is that your mind is still caught up with it even when the situation is over.

Rather than moving on and doing what you need to, you are still getting stressed and angry, and that is the real issue. If this is hurting you in many areas of life and not just works, you might want to consider getting therapy. Talking to a neutral person about these problems can help you clarify the issue in your mind and shed some light on solutions that will help you.

How to Manage Small Talk

Being a highly sensitive person, it can be extremely difficult to strike up a conversation with anyone and everyone. In most cases, people who are HSP are not anti-social, and the fact is that they are very selective with who they want in their personal group.

Being a highly sensitive person, you think deeply about things, which is reflected in how you talk and discuss matters with friends. It would be unwise to think that everyone you come across in your life will be able to discuss things at your mental wavelength and will be a person that you genuinely enjoy talking with. In some cases, you will need to build up some tolerance for small talk, and you will need to be able to do this with people you meet.

This doesn't mean that you want to have a lifelong relationship with this person, but for that moment, for that interaction, being able to talk to them about things that don't necessarily interest you is to your benefit.

Chapter 8: HSP and Family: Parenting a Hypersensitive Child

Becoming a parent is a life-changing experience, with its unique challenges, highs, and lows. It can become even more stressful for you and your child if neither of you understands each other or "get" each other, and this becomes even more apparent if you are a parent to a hypersensitive child. Sometimes being sensitive to the smallest things is brushed off as a phase that the child will grow out of and isn't taken seriously. Most parents can be forgiven for thinking that their child is just being cranky or is not in the right mood that day, not realizing that they might have a hypersensitive child on their hands.

Hypersensitivity is still taken lightly, and most people are unaware of it, which is why it often goes unnoticed and unidentified. If you are a hypersensitive parent, but you don't know about it, the chances are that you won't be able to pick this up in your children either. Sometimes hypersensitive children are born in households where there is no other hypersensitive individual, and it becomes very difficult for people in the family to understand that child's unique needs. In both situations, the child's needs go unnoticed, leading to a range of other problems down the line.

As a parent, the first thing you need to realize and accept is that hypersensitivity in individuals is a real situation, they are born like that, and there is a chance that your child might be an HSP. If you find that to be the case, your child will need a different parenting style and environment, and you will need to know how to detect this in your children.

Signs of Hypersensitivity in Children

Hypersensitivity can be exhibited in children as early as 18 months old. Many psychologists and mental health professionals categorize this as a sensory processing disorder (SPD). Moreover, this can result from a system that is either over-sensitive or under-sensitive. In both cases, it impacts how a child can interact with people and their environment and plays a role in their mental development.

General Traits of Hypersensitive Children

The most common trait of hypersensitive children is their endless supply of empathy for anyone and anything. They have a nearly supernatural ability to pick up on the emotions and energy of the people around them and their environment. If they are in school and another child suddenly bursts out crying, likely, the hypersensitive child will also start crying. Similarly, they are extremely caring towards other children, love sharing, and even feel the pain of their pet animals. If a child is likely to give the family dog or the pet cat a hug, it will be the hypersensitive child.

Putting on clothing, changing clothes, or just selecting clothes can be quite a process when you have an HSP child. In fact, in most cases, it is not about the style of the clothing but rather how they feel when they wear that piece of clothing. For instance, if there is a tag in the clothing, a seam that bugs them, or if they don't like the cold sensation of a steel zipper when they put something on, they can be extremely fussy. In some cases, they might resist wearing that jacket or those socks outright just because they don't like how it feels.

If they are really young, they might not be able to communicate exactly why they don't want to wear that clothing. Even as children grow up, it can be challenging for them to really voice their concerns because they know it's not something they are comfortable with but aren't sure why. A child will probably have specific clothes they really enjoy wearing and want to wear those exact clothes every day.

Similarly, if even the slightest change happens to their clothing, they won't wear it anymore. If their clothes get wet or sand gets in their shoes – or if the laces become untied – they won't' be able to wear it at all; they need that problem to be fixed right then and there. While it is easy to tie the laces up again, it's a good idea to always have some extra clothing for your child in case something goes wrong with their clothes. Even though you might not see the tiny wet patch, because the child's senses are so highly sensitive, they will feel that change intensely, which can become unbearable for them.

You will also notice that your HSP child doesn't process things in quite the same way as you do or like other children. They have a much deeper level of understanding of everything around them. Even when they are quite young, you will notice they have a knack for language, they will use works extremely well, are proficient speakers or writers, and communicate very differently. They will reach very different conclusions because they consider a lot more elements than the average child. And this difference in their analysis impacts every part of their lives, from the way they interact with other children, the way they play, the things they like to play with, to just the way they observe the world around them. Their outlook on life is very different and very deep.

If this is not your first child, you will notice that they don't react quite the same way as your other children when you discipline them. In some cases, the disciplining methods you use might not be effective at all, or you could be dealing with extreme consequences. As they are so in-tune with their environment and physically have more sensitive senses, they might misunderstand many things happening around them. Suppose you are a little louder than usual because you are trying to call someone outside the room. In that case, your child might get scared because they feel things intensely and interpret things differently. Ideally, you need to be very gentle with these kids and use rationality and explanations rather than brute force.

Giving your child options, trying to talk them out of something, and generally trying to distract them from something will be more effective than a battle of wills. With less sensitive children, you will need to find an approach that gets their attention, as traditional disciplining methods will not get them to focus either. Instead, they will just think of it as a game or interpret it as a threat.

Another big challenge for parents is to get their highly sensitive child to rest. Even though they can be extremely heavy sleepers, getting them to slow down and fall asleep is very difficult. As they are constantly involved with the environment around them, and their minds are buzzing with ideas and thoughts, even at bedtime after a very exhausting day, they cannot calm down and just lay still in bed. Moreover, the fact that they are tired is even more stressful for them because their mind wants to keep going, but their body can't support their thoughts, which stresses them even more.

Ideally, you should have some kind of routine or exercise with them to help them take their minds off things and relax. Also, having a bedroom environment conducive to sleep, relaxing, and devoid of any distractions will help.

Even though these children love to explore and try new things, they are creatures of habit, and getting them to try something new can be close to impossible. You can get them to try anything with the right approach, but it needs to be a gradual introduction to that new thing. These are the kinds of children who have one or two specific toys that they love or activities they love being a part of, and anything else usually gets resistance. However, when you slowly bring them to the new activity or the new toy and give them the room to explore it on their own, they can end up enjoying it. This can be so extreme that once they are comfortable with the new object or activity, they forget all their previous favorites and develop a near-obsession with this new thing.

HSP children are not just emotionally and mentally more sensitive; they are also physically more sensitive than the average child. Their senses are often more acute and accurate than other children in their age group. A hypersensitive child will often hear things much more vividly; they can hear things going on in another room, and when they come home, they can smell what's cooking even before they enter the house.

Their observation is also extremely good. They can often recognize the smallest changes to a familiar space when they enter it and are very connected to their environment. If you happen to move things around in their room, not only will they notice this, but they will also be impacted by this more than the average person. They might be comfortable with the change, or it might completely ruin their mood and quite literally be something with which they can't live. This can be very difficult to deal with as a parent, but good communication can be worked through. Also, hypersensitive children tend to be more OCD about things than the average child. Things like squeaky doors, scratching sounds, the sound of a tap dripping, and other small sounds can be a big problem for these children.

Under-Stimulation

With children who have under-stimulated physiology, you will notice they constantly want to touch things, feel textures, and really experience everything by touch. Even though it can be potentially harmful to them, they can't stop themselves. Such children often have difficulty understanding the concept of physical space. They have a very different sense of what personal space is, and it is something that they will easily overlook. Similarly, you will notice that their motor skills are not the most refined, and they often suffer from "butterfingers." Since their nervous system is different, their pain threshold is also different, and they can often injure themselves.

In the same way, they cannot judge their own strength, and they are not very good at understanding how their strength feels to another person. You might notice that they hit extremely hard or play rough, whereas, in reality, they are just being normal for them. For the child they are playing with, it can be a very difficult and easily dangerous situation. Under-stimulated children need activities and things to do that give them the level of stimulation that they need. Unknowingly they can be very fidgety, constantly moving from activity to activity and to doing things that would be seen as dangerous to parents and other children. These are the kinds of children who feel completely comfortable doing things that others would classify as extreme.

Over Stimulation

In the case of overstimulated children, things are quite the opposite. They are extremely sensitive to noise, sounds, and sudden movements. They have a tendency to be lost in their own thoughts, and even if you touch them really gently during this phase, they can get shocked and be surprised. Moreover, these children don't enjoy too much physical contact, and they will try to avoid situations where they have to give hugs or even just shake hands. They might also not be comfortable being a part of a large crowd and will often look for situations to create more physical space than normal. While this is more than necessary for the average person, it is just the right amount they need to feel comfortable.

Similarly, things like swings, playground rides, cycling, or anything moving can be quite stressful for these children. They prefer to be on their own two feet and don't even enjoy activities where they have to run around too much or be too active. They are also prone to easily falling over and generally have poor balance.

How Can You Talk to Your Child about Their Emotions?

This will not be an option when your child is really young and cannot communicate their feelings or thoughts, but this is extremely important with older children. For really young children, get them into the habit of speaking and communicating. Even if it is just for the smallest of things, constantly talking to them and getting them to respond to you will instill a communication culture.

When discussing their emotions, try to understand what they are saying to you and how they are really feeling. Even if you don't feel the same way or think that they shouldn't feel a certain way, in reality, that is how they feel, and that is how they see the world around them. When talking to them about these ideas, you need to ensure you give them enough room to express themselves honestly. You don't want them to say something simply to keep you happy or to somehow fit into the cookie-cutter they think you expect of them. Secondly, try to stick to one point rather than having a broad and open-ended discussion. This will help the child to focus their thoughts on a specific subject.

You want to be as supportive as you can; this helps get the most information from them. It's not the time to change the way they think or feel. This is when you try to understand their thinking to learn how they process the world around them. Constantly giving them the confidence to speak their mind, telling them they aren't going to be judged, and that there isn't a right or a wrong answer are all good strategies.

How Can They Be Taught to Socialize Without Fear?

One of the best things you can do for your child to build their socialization skills is understanding what makes it so challenging for them. For some children, it might be the fear of speaking in front of people they don't know. It might be because they are insecure about themselves, or it might be the fear that when they are at school or in a social situation, they are away from the people they trust the most. For some children, it can just be that they feel overwhelmed with new people, and they don't know what they should say or what they should talk about.

In some cases, your child might be fine socializing with cousins and friends when there is a party at home, but they have difficulties when they are at a party at another child's house. The change in the environment can also be a limiting factor. For some children, simply knowing where they are going, who will be there, and what it is all about can be the information that gives them the freedom to socialize more freely. In this case, playing out scenarios at home and even going through a script of how they should interact with other children can be a big confidence booster and give them the tools they need to interact with others more effectively.

How Can Tantrums Be Dealt With?

The first step is to understand what the tantrum is about. Is it about using a marker to draw on walls? Is it about leaving the playground to go home? Is it about using media devices for extended periods of time? When you know the root of the problem, you can start creating a solution for that cause rather than managing the child's behavior.

Managing a child screaming, throwing things, or just being angry and passive is important, but effectively dealing with the tantrums requires you to find out the underlying cause. If the tantrum is about something your child is not allowed to play with, then keep it out of sight. If it is something like having to stop playing a video game, try to divert their attention by introducing a replacement for that source of entertainment when the time is up. When you successfully get your child to move onto something else or do what you want them to do, make sure you follow this up with a lot of praise and positive reinforcement.

HSP children can be obsessive about things; managing this at an early age is critical to helping them work through other problems later in life. This can quickly turn into an obsession with certain things, so making sure that you can handle things while they are still manageable is key. Dealing with tantrums and otherwise negative behavior is just as much about making your life easier as much as it is about helping the child live a less stressful life. When the child is crying over something, they aren't having a good time, and it is up to you to teach them how they can overcome this behavioral challenge and direct that energy into a more positive and useful channel.

Chapter 9: A Toxic Romance

Highly sensitive people are susceptible to toxic relationships. They may not realize it early on, but they start feeling bad about themselves and the person with whom they are romantically involved. While highly sensitive people do not actively choose to be in these relationships, they attract narcissistic people or manipulators who can take advantage of their vulnerability. This chapter will discuss toxic romantic relationships and how highly sensitive people can deal with toxic partners.

Relationships with Narcissistic People

Narcissistic people are those who believe that they are better than everybody else. They have this superior image about themselves and usually are psychologically unable to care about other people's feelings. They yearn for people's admiration and constantly want to feel their appreciation for feeding their low self-esteem. Their condescension is nothing but a façade that they use to hide their lack of confidence, which is why they dislike criticism and often get defensive when criticized. It takes a lot of time and effort for a narcissist to build their grandiose self-image, and this delusion shapes their dysfunctional relationships.

People describe narcissists as arrogant, self-centered, and selfish, among many other traits. They usually disregard other people's feelings and only care about how others perceive them. They work so hard to create an idealistic image of themselves so that people will admire them. Narcissists need to feel that everyone admires them, not just their romantic partners. They are also desperate to feel respect and appreciation in their professional and personal relationships with their friends and family.

Narcissistic people will resist changing their destructive behavioral patterns no matter how much harm they have caused. They will always try to shift the blame to anyone who criticizes them or disagrees with them. They tend to take criticisms very personally because they can't accept making mistakes. Many people in relationships with narcissists find it easier to comply with their demands to avoid dealing with their tantrums and indifference. To understand how you can deal with a narcissist, you will first have to learn about narcissistic personality disorder. This way, you will recognize them in your relationships and keep yourself away from them.

A narcissistic person will take advantage of your affection and admiration of them. They will never consider your emotions as they see you as a person who exists only to serve their needs. They don't feel guilty about exploiting others for their personal gain. Even if you confront them with how destructive they are, they won't recognize that they are doing anything wrong. They spent too much effort building a false image that they ended up believing.

Narcissists are not just arrogant and self-centered people. They believe they are superior and more special than others. They belittle ordinary or average people and things because they think they are too grand for them. This is why they would only deal with people or things that they feel are as special or superior as they are. They expect people to admire them for merely being around them. Narcissistic people usually oversell their skills and abilities and tell lies about themselves to make them appear better than they are. They like to be the center of attention in any group, where they will often talk about their achievements and how they always save the day.

To feed their feelings of grandeur, a narcissist creates a fantasy life fed with their delusions. They deceive people into thinking they are the best at everything. They glorify themselves through stories about how successful, talented, and intelligent they are. These stories get more intricate each time they tell them to people. This is how they hide their feelings of inadequacy and insecurity, as they are ashamed of who they truly are. Suppose anyone catches them lying or confronts them with a fact that contradicts their stories. In that case, they get defensive and may even attack the other person and accuse them of being jealous of them. They can be so manipulative that people often end up apologizing to them.

A narcissist's ultimate goal is to fill a void by receiving admiration from others. They are never satisfied with compliments as they need constant positive feedback from people. This is why they always keep people around who often feed that obsessive need. In romantic relationships, they get involved with vulnerable people who think the world of them and keep admiring them. The narcissist in this relationship only cares about getting what they want and never cares about their partner's needs. If a narcissist ever feels their partner stopped admiring them or even reduced their constant stream of praise and compliments, they act as if that person betrayed them.

Narcissistic people always expect to be everyone's priority. They believe they should always be treated better and different from everybody else. They think they should always get what they want and that people around them should work hard to please them. If those people did not comply with the narcissist's wishes, then they are expendable. Narcissists might react aggressively if their partners disagreed with them or did not want to do what they wanted. They might also give their partners the silent treatment until they feel guilty for not doing as they were told. Narcissists use all these strategies to control other people in their relationships.

A narcissist is usually threatened by people who are loved and respected by others. They feel jealous of confident and genuinely talented people. This is because they feel they will be compared to them, which frightens them because their truth might be exposed. A common defense mechanism is to demean these people, whether in their presence or behind their back. They may constantly try to belittle their achievements or dismiss them altogether. They may even try to bully or threaten them to stay out of their way so that they can become the center of attention again.

Relationships with Manipulators

Being in a relationship with a manipulative person can be devastating to any person's mental wellbeing, let alone a highly sensitive person. It can take you a long time to recognize that your partner manipulated you. A good manipulator will create scenarios that will make you doubt yourself. These tactics are so skillfully applied that you do what they want and think it is your idea. To spot a manipulator in your relationship, you will need to learn about warning signs and symptoms to get out of these toxic relationships and protect yourself from them.

Emotional manipulation entails telling people certain things or acting a certain way to make them question themselves, their relationships, achievements, and everything around them. One of the most common strategies a manipulator uses is to make you feel guilty by taking advantage of your insecurities. They may tell you that your behavior and past actions are why you feel unhappy or stressed all the time. They will make you feel that something is wrong with you to steer your focus away from them. This is also how they appear as your rescuer and the only ones who can understand and support you. A manipulator will exploit your emotions to make you feel that you need them in your life.

Inducing guilt is a common tactic to get what they want from you. This brings us to the second most common tactic used for emotional manipulation: ingratiation. This is when the manipulator makes gestures or says things that will make you think highly of them. They will do everything in their power to make you trust and admire them. In the process, they would usually use the third most common technique for manipulation, which is *deceit.* A manipulator would often lie and twist truths about themselves to appear charming and irresistible to you.

While these techniques can somewhat be easier to identify, there are other techniques that master manipulators use to control you and make you question yourself. Initially, a manipulator might use a technique called *love bombing*, which is when they would shower you with compliments and give you a ton of attention to make you feel special. This technique is used to get you hooked really quickly to that person.

Another tactic is *gaslighting*, which is commonly used to make you doubt yourself. Master gaslighters will make you question past events or things you said. Then, they dispute that you said or did whatever it was and accuse you of having a bad memory or tell you that you are crazy or too sensitive. They can be so convincing that you will end up apologizing for accusing them of lying. This technique is similar to passive-aggressive behavior. A manipulator will usually make subtle jokes about you, whether in front of other people or when you're alone. These jokes usually carry an offensive undertone, and when you call them out on it, they would usually accuse you of being too sensitive.

A manipulator can sometimes call a third person in the argument to back their story to make you question yourself even more. This technique is called *triangulation*, and they use it to make you feel more insecure. When another person agrees with your manipulator, this will make you wonder if you imagined things. Sometimes, if you confront a manipulator partner about their deceitful actions, they could deny it and try to shift the blame on you for accusing them. They would usually not permit you to speak and leave the argument without answering your questions. A common technique used in these cases is the silent treatment, where they would stop talking to you to make you feel guilty that you ever doubted them.

A manipulator would threaten you and use abusive words or actions in more violent cases. This sort of behavior has to be reported to the authorities if it ever happens to you. You should not have to bear this kind of behavior from anybody, so you need to seek help and support from trusted friends or family. A manipulator usually tries to keep you away from everyone who cares about you so that they are free to exploit you as they please.

The Warning Signs of Being Manipulated

When you are involved with an abusive partner, it can be hard to spot their behavior. You may think that they would change someday because you are holding on to the persona they created to trick you into falling for them. They also negatively influenced you and made you doubt yourself for a long time. They probably made you totally dependent on them so that you have no support or someone to turn to when you need help. This is why it is important to bear a few warning signs in mind to help you identify manipulative behavior.

First of all, you have to learn to trust yourself and rely on your gut feeling. When something doesn't feel right, try to stick to that feeling. Find out why you are unhappy or drained mentally and emotionally all the time. You may ignore these feelings and convince yourself that it is just a phase.

If you notice that your partner always acts angry when you question or disagree with them for any reason, it is a warning sign that something is not right. Pay attention to your partner's reaction and see if there is a pattern. Try to look back at your past conversations and ask yourself whether they always shift the blame to you. Master manipulators will usually make a lot of noise and accuse you of anything false, so your energy and focus shift to defending yourself. You soon forget what you were talking about initially. You may even forget the whole thing because you don't want to end up arguing again. If this is a persistent pattern, consider it a warning sign that you are being manipulated.

The second most common sign is feeling you are in the wrong all the time. A manipulative partner will constantly make you doubt yourself and your actions. You may find yourself wondering if you imagined a certain event or if you were confused about something. If you start questioning your abilities or things you did effortlessly in the past, it's time to figure out why that is.

Another warning sign is you constantly feel ashamed of your behavior. A master manipulator will always make you feel self-conscious about your actions. You may feel that you have to think about every little thing you say or do so you don't embarrass your partner in some way. A manipulator will frequently be displeased about your actions. They may tell you that they like things a certain way, and they may guilt you into canceling plans with your friends to spend time with them instead. If you feel this is a pattern, try to figure out if your partner is showing other signs of manipulative behavior.

In extreme cases, you may forget who you used to be. Being in a toxic relationship can deeply affect your self-image and self-worth. You may end up not recognizing yourself as a result of months and years of manipulation. You may find yourself that all your activities or friends, or interests are not your own but your partner's. You may have been either forced to or manipulated into these interests or lifestyle choices.

If you always feel that you need to be extremely careful around your partner, consider this a major warning sign. Your partner may not get angry often or act violently, but you may still feel uneasy or uncomfortable around them. You feel that you can't be yourself or have to calculate every action to avoid disappointing or upsetting them. If you feel afraid to speak up in your relationship because you want to avoid an argument, that is a direct result of emotional abuse from your partner.

This could be one of the most dangerous signs because it is often ignored. You may convince yourself you are mistaken or just stop talking about certain matters because you are afraid of fighting with your partner. Let's say you wanted to go out with your friends, whom your partner is not fond of. You may think long and hard before going out with them because maybe the last time you did, your partner gave you the silent treatment for a couple of days. This form of emotional abuse may not be obvious, but it is just as devastating to your mental wellbeing.

It is crucial to understand that not all forms of abuse or in the form of anger outbursts or involve a lot of screaming and obvious threats. The subtle tactics are far worse, whether to make you feel guilty or not speak to you for days without an explanation. You may frequently question yourself and your behavior to determine why your partner reacts that way. This is an important sign to watch out for. If you are constantly defending yourself or feeling you are always doing something wrong, consider your partner is manipulating you.

How Can a Highly Sensitive Person Deal with a Toxic Partner?

Highly sensitive people are the most vulnerable of all personality types to fall for manipulative or narcissistic partners. First, you must understand that they don't just treat you badly right away. They appear as the charming personality that sweeps you off your feet before shattering your self-esteem little by little. As a highly sensitive person, you are attracted to these people because you want to help them change and become better. You have something they lack, which is empathy. Narcissists and manipulators benefit from your patience and compassion, leaving you extremely emotionally, mentally, and physically drained.

To protect yourself from these abusers, the first step is not to blame yourself for their shortcomings. There is nothing wrong with your emotions or wanting to support or help them. You stayed in this relationship because you truly care for them. Remember that feeling guilty or blaming yourself is the abuser's basic strategy. Try to ask your trusted friend or close family member for their opinion. Rely on people other than your partner to get some perspective.

Ask yourself why your partner does not seem to have a proper relationship with other people. If you can identify their destructive and manipulative patterns, you must think about whether this relationship is healthy for you. Chances are you have already given your partner plenty of chances to rectify their behavior, but you can't wait around forever, hoping they will change. Try to imagine the worst-case scenario in this relationship and whether you can put up with this behavior for years to come.

The best thing you can do for yourself is to stay away from toxic people. Get out of a toxic relationship as quickly as you can. It is not worth giving them years of your life in the hopes they'll get better. You have to establish clear boundaries with these people, but at the same time, remember they will try to shatter these boundaries to stay in control of the relationship. Don't give in to their requests. They will not leave you alone and will probably keep contacting you. Don't argue with them because they will never see your point or give you the space you need. It is best to get out of these relationships immediately to protect yourself from these abusive people.

This chapter mentioned the different traits of narcissists and manipulators and how you can spot their warning signs. As a highly sensitive person, you have to prioritize your mental and emotional wellbeing. Surround yourself with people who are loving and supportive. It is best to stay away from any toxic relationships in your life to maintain your mental and emotional well-being.

Chapter 10: Toxicity in the Workplace

Like anyone else, highly sensitive people) will encounter toxic situations at work, such as bullying, manipulation by bosses and colleagues, or verbal attacks. Fortunately, there is a solution for every problem in the workplace. This chapter discusses the tips you can take when dealing with different cases.

Types of Toxicity in the Workplace

In many workplaces, highly sensitive people are often misunderstood, but the truth is that they are found almost everywhere. However, very few workplaces are designed to help HSPs do their best in terms of performance. For many HSPs, their jobs act as a source of stress which can also be overwhelming.

The main challenge is that HSPs face is that they are often viewed as weak and natural targets, particularly for controlling people and narcissists, because they give in easily on different issues. If you are a highly sensitive person, you have more than likely encountered some of the problems highlighted below at work. Toxicity in the workplace comes in different forms, and you should be aware of what they look like to protect yourself.

Bullying

Most highly sensitive employees are often forced to endure a lifetime of being teased, taunted, shamed, or bullied because of their sensitivity.

Bullying is the most prevalent challenge to HSPs since they are deficient in some people's eyes, and the bullies know that the victim will not retaliate. Commonly, sensitive individuals often find themselves being forced to do tasks that should not be part of their work. The main problem is that individuals born with high sensory processing sensitivity (HSP) are more likely to be bullied in different situations than those without this trait.

When someone IS HSP, they are often reserved, and a good number are introverts. These people will be viewed as weak in the workplace, and the managers are often bullies. The alleged bullies often lack professional interpersonal skills and have low self-esteem, where talented subordinates may threaten them. Some HSPs are highly sensitive, soft-spoken, caring, talented, and perceptive. As a result, they end up posing a threat to their managers, who will in turn resort to bullying tactics to assert their authority.

Psychological injury is growing increasingly in various workplaces, and many highly sensitive individuals often find themselves at the receiving end. HR specialists and CEOs across the globe often struggle to deal with the issue of bullying. The main issues that lead to a toxic work environment emanate from lack of awareness of, among other personalities, highly sensitive individuals, poor people management skills, and cultural prejudice. As a result, HSPs, are often victims of calculated attacks in the workplace.

Wearing Strong Perfume

If you are a highly sensitive person, you can encounter other elements that can affect you in the workplace. In most cases, these actions are not directed at you, but you will end up suffering in silence because there is nothing you can do to address the situation. For instance, if a workmate comes wearing perfume with a powerful fragrance or an overpowering scent, you may end up experiencing physical reactions or headaches.

Furthermore, lighting that is too bright can affect you if you are sensitive. The lights may flicker, and they will distract you from your work. However, it may be difficult for you to get your employer to change to different lighting that may be costly. When you realize that you are in this kind of predicament you cannot control, it is vital to look for other means of making your workspace ambient. You can achieve this by looking for alternative lighting or creating a better environment that will not impact your eyes.

There is nothing wrong with investing in ergonomic gadgets that suit your needs. If you feel that the mouse and keypad at work are not user-friendly, you can invest in your own gadgets. The good thing is that you can use these ergonomic gadgets for several years, and they significantly improve your work productivity.

Pressure from Your Boss

Your boss may give you a big task and will tell you that it must be completed that same day. The boss might also be one of those who can't plan their work schedule, and employees end up becoming the targets to douse the fire when the deadline is missed. Overworking can be chronic and stressful. Highly sensitive people are mostly hit by undue pressure from their bosses. As the HSP, you often become the target because you process information deeply and consider more details, which takes more time.

Many highly sensitive people try to do their best work slowly to get everything correct. You want to be sure that everything is perfect, and this can impact your performance if you are rushed into completing specific tasks. Working under pressure can be problematic since it will lead to rushed outcomes that may not reflect your work ethic.

Verbal Attacks

Verbal attacks are very common in the workplace, and they are mainly directed at targets perceived to be weak – often women and junior employees. People who are still new in the organization also face challenges acclimatizing to the new environment, especially if the culture is not accommodating. Some people are naturally slow and take their time to perform different tasks, and this may draw the ire of others. As a result, they become victims of verbal attacks from other individuals who believe they are authority figures.

The other issue is that some people underrate other individuals and will belittle and attack them for no apparent reason. Verbal attacks can be stressful since they are calculated to instill a sense of authority over the victims of the attackers.

How to Deal with Toxic Situations in the Workplace

If you are a highly sensitive person, you should find a way of dealing with the situation without compromising your work. There are different methods to consider in handling different situations. Some of the measures that can help you are highlighted below.

Avoid Spilling the Beans

Don't rush to spill the beans and tell your boss or manager that you are a highly sensitive person. Some people may not understand what it means, and they will mistakenly believe that it is a sign of weakness. While we need to share our personality traits with our employers, not everyone will be able to create reality from these. As a result, you may end up being misconstrued.

However, if you believe your boss and co-workers will be receptive to the concept of you being highly sensitive, you can tell them. At least your boss and other workers should talk about the issue so that you can also share your story with them. If you believe your high sensitivity risks are being misunderstood, it is good to keep it to yourself since the workplace might not be the best place to share this kind of personal information.

When dealing with your boss, you should know that you can't control their work habits and deadlines. However, you can communicate your requirements to get the task done submit the other by a specific time. No supervisor will tolerate poor results, although they may rush the deadlines. If you talk to your boss nicely, they will understand. The other thing is that you can create your work plan and send it to your boss if you feel they are not organized. However, you must state why you want to follow that route. If you convince your superior in the workplace, they will give you the green light.

Be Gentle

You should try to be gentle with yourself and do the same to your workmates. Don't view yourself as unique or special, but you need to humble yourself. Just remind yourself that your nervous system is more sensitive than other people's. If you know that you are highly sensitive, be thoughtful and conscientious when dealing with other people. Be careful of prioritizing other people's needs above your own but be careful not to t burden them with your picky requests they won't understand. However, it does not necessarily mean that you should suffer in silence.

If your sensitivity interferes with your work, you have the right to speak up. However, if it seldom affects you, you can let it go. If you want to raise an issue about someone's strong perfume, try telling your colleague gently that t you are sensitive to fragrances that give you headaches and impact your work. Any reasonable person will understand this kind of request, and they will either not use it again or tone it down. If you need to talk to your manager, you must stick to facts and request to be put in a different workspace.

Try to find a way to fit in with t the company's culture and work environment so that you can work in peace and harmony. You can use your skills to the fullest if you work in an accommodating environment. You need to understand how you can talk to your workmates to understand your concerns.

Talk to HR

You should talk to the Human Resources Manager about any issues that impact your work productivity. If your desk is too high or the lights in your office are too bright, you need to talk to your supervisor. The main purpose of HR in any organization is to address employee issues that can impact productivity. Your mental and physical health at work is important, so there is no way HR will ignore such a request from a dedicated employee.

If you fail to talk to HR to have certain issues resolved, you are likely to suffer health issues in the long term. So, speak up and communicate with HR before the situation gets out of hand. You also need to think about it from their perspective as well. Try to be authentic and raise valid points since they also want their workers to be productive and healthy. Try to minimize the discussion of your feelings at work and focus on something that will help you increase productivity, improve physical health, and reduce work distractions. However, the approach you take depends on your workplace.

Take a Break

Take time to get out of your office during a break. Go for a walk in the park to refresh your mind. You will clear your mind and reinvigorate your body if you take a walk during break time. You can also go to the workplace gym to exercise to clear your mind. You should learn to create healthy boundaries at work. During break time, try to find a serene environment to relax and focus on other things apart from your work.

It is essential to create a conflict-free zone where you can relax. You can help create a calm environment by adding things that help relieve your stress, like playing soothing music. Another aspect for consideration is setting healthy boundaries between you and your work colleagues. You can achieve this by firmly letting people know your needs and where you stand with all your co-workers.

You also need to be aware of other people's privacy. You must know your limit and never intrude on someone's sphere if you want to maintain a quality relationship in the workplace. When the pressure piles on, try to find better ways of dealing with it without passing your problems to other people.

Creating a calm environment means you should keep your close relationships conflict-free and learn how to resolve conflicts. When you encounter challenges, you should find better means to resolve them without spoiling your relationship with your loved ones. You should stay away from toxic personalities since they do not add any value to your life. Instead, focus on creating a supportive network with friends and colleagues. Aim to create networks with people willing to return your support.

Meditate and Exercise Mindfulness

Meditation and mindfulness help you create a boundary around your life experiences. When you meditate, you focus on positive things and feelings that improve your perceptions of the world around you. You need to find a cool and calm place where you can meditate. With meditation and mindfulness, you can achieve the following things.

- Create resilience against stress
- Learn to reverse stress, calm your body quickly, and return to the position of serenity
- You don't easily get distracted by emotions
- You learn to detach quickly from emotional things
- You get help easily if you stay grounded

These benefits are immense, and they make meditation worth the effort. If you are highly sensitive, meditation can help you overcome many challenges. Certain things are easy to deal with as long as you know the appropriate measures to implement.

Practice Self-Care

Self-care is good if you are a highly sensitive person. As an HSP, at some stage, you will experience challenges such as poor nutrition, sleep deprivation, and burnout if you don't have the tools to prevent them. This is where self-care comes in, which we have spoken about previously. Proper self-care will help you get enough sleep at night to improve your physical and mental health. Quality rest also helps reduce stress and other mental health-related conditions like depression and anxiety.

Remember to eat healthy meals to keep your body and mind healthy. Only you can lift your spirits, and the way to do that is to take care of yourself and focus on things that will make you happy or keep your mind stress-free. Don't try to impress other people; instead, focus on making yourself happy. This will help you learn about yourself and your strengths and weaknesses, and once you have a handle on them, you will understand how to work things out to your advantage.

Know Your Challenges

Know your unique challenges and the things that trigger them. As a highly sensitive individual, knowing the things that stress you most is critical, especially in the workplace. This will help you avoid the triggers or, at the very least, prepare for them so that they don't impact your work. When you know what stresses you, you are in a better position to avoid it and focus on positive things.

You need to pay attention to your feelings throughout the day. One way to do this is to keep a journal where you record what triggered negative emotions. Review your journal at least once a week to see any recurring feelings and take note of the triggers. It is essential to be proactive and practice resilience-building exercises in your daily life. Try to eliminate stressors and find better ways to cope with challenging situations whenever possible. If you know the stressor, take it off your mind before it affects your mind.

If you can't get it off your mind easily, try to distract yourself to not continue focusing on it. For instance, if the noise around you is stressful, try to use headphones and listen to something that does not affect you. When people play loud music in the workplace, you may need to get headphones if you don't want to hear anything. It may not be possible to ask everyone to turn the volume down on their devices. Other people thrive in noisy environments, so try to cope with the situation you may find yourself in.

Home Office

If you feel that the workplace environment continues to take a toll on your mental and physical health due to your high sensitivity, you can ask your boss if you might work remotely. If your job permits, you can ask the manager if you can work from home three days a week and visit the office for two. If you encounter resistance, you can start small and work one day at home. However, you must state valid reasons why you want to do it.

When you are granted permission to work at home, make sure you are productive. You need to prove that you can thrive when you work at home with no distractions or toxicity you often experience at work. Remember that you cannot do all types of jobs at home. If you are lucky enough to have a job that allows you to work at home, your productivity should make a difference.

You Are Not Alone

Last but not least, you should know that you are not alone in this predicament. You may feel embarrassed by the comments and reactions you receive from your workmates, but remember, it does not mean the end of the world. Some people experience similar situations and try to find better ways of dealing with them. Once you know that you are not the only person facing this challenge, you will become strong and learn to coexist with various people.

Toxicity comes in different ways to highly sensitive people. In many workplaces, it seems that little is known about HSPs, but they are found almost everywhere. Highly sensitive people are usually natural targets for narcissists or controlling individuals because of their giving nature. If you are a highly sensitive person, the chances are very high that you have encountered certain scenarios in your workplace. While this is common, the tips above can help you overcome some of these challenges.

Chapter 11: Toxicity at Home

No one is perfect all the time. Even the happiest people have a bad day, even people you get along with really well, go through difficult phases in life where you feel that this is not the person you know. Everyone experiences different seasons in life, which change how they think, feel, and behave. However, this doesn't mean that the person has changed; it is just a different side to them that even they might not have known that they had. More importantly, it is usually a passing phase. Eventually, the person returns to normal or can talk about why they changed or what affected them to temporarily change. Unfortunately, many people are not going through a phase, and they just are the negative person they seem to be. While they may not mean to be that way, maybe they even regret their actions and the behavior, but it is part of who they are as people. These are the individuals who can create a toxic environment, and if you have such a person in your home, you might be living in a toxic environment without even realizing it.

People who have a spouse, parent, or sibling with a toxic personality might think it's normal because this is all they have ever seen. They've always seen this person as the toxic individual they are, and somehow, they have also grown accustomed to it. However, when they compare this experience with any other relationship they have with a non-toxic person, the differences are easy to see and often very prominent.

Luckily, there are many things that you can do to deal with these kinds of toxic people and toxic relationships. Firstly, you need to identify the nature of the toxicity and its source.

What Is Toxic Behavior?

Toxic people come in all shapes and sizes, and they all have their own way of exuding their toxic energy. If you have ever been in a relationship or even if you feel that within your family, you don't have the room or the freedom to be yourself, the chances are that you are in a toxic environment. People who find themselves in toxic relationships often feel that they don't have room to breathe, they don't have privacy, are being used, and even they are the subject of a lot of negative treatment even when it isn't their fault.

They are stuck with a person unable to take responsibility for anything and blame everyone else for anything going wrong, even in their own personal lives. They usually are aggressive and go to any lengths to get what they want. People involved in these relationships feel manipulated and even blackmailed into doing something simply because the toxic person wants it that way. In general, people in toxic relationships will feel unhappy and even depressed, but they feel trapped and see no solution.

Of course, there are varying degrees to how bad the situation can be, stemming from various behaviors. Toxic behavior can be recognized by manipulation, force, aggression, deceit, false accusation, insecure behavior, control, lack of privacy, and other behavioral problems.

The important thing to note is that the person creating the toxic environment might not even be aware of this. They may be dealing with underlying mental challenges and how their actions result from an improper cognitive pattern. They may be suffering from depression, anxiety, hypertension, or any other range of mental problems, resulting in them being the way they are, just as with substance abuse, where individuals face a different challenge that manifests itself as substance abuse.

Types of Toxic People

These are some of the most common kinds of toxic people you can encounter, along with some of their most prominent features and behaviors.

- **The Narcissist** - This is someone who is overly in love with themselves and has little regard for anyone else. A narcissistic personality is one that constantly behaves as if they are above everyone else, and they are the center of the universe. You will often see this person talking highly about themselves and undermining everyone else around them. They are quick to point out flaws in others yet are never willing to take any criticism on their behalf.

- **The Psychopath** - This is closely linked to narcissism, but it takes this a step further as these people have no conscience, no guilt, empathy, remorse, or care for anything or anyone around them. Psychopaths can actually have a physically abnormal brain that influences and manifests the abnormality in how they behave. They will use extremely harsh and shocking means to get what they want and will not feel bad about putting people close to them through pain and suffering.

- **The Victim** - This is that person who is always talking and complaining about how bad their life is, how bad they have it, and how the entire world should take part in their pity party. After all, no one else has a bigger problem than the problems they have to face. This is a person with a defeatist mindset; they don't have the courage to get up and solve their own problems. Instead, they will always find a reason why the world is just conspiring against them and, no matter what they do, nothing will ever change, so they never even try.

- **The Compulsive Liar** - Whether it is to get out of a tricky situation or just to lie about something extremely trivial to make themselves appear better than they really are, the compulsive liar just cannot stop lying. They will lie about even the smallest things right to your face and then outright deny that they are lying. Even if you show evidence of them doing or saying something, they will just lie and live in their own fake bubble where they are perfect, and everyone else is wrong.

- **The Critic** - Whether it is about how you are dressed, where you live, or what you do for a living, the critic always has something disparaging to say to you. This trait is linked to the narcissistic personality type and can also be linked to someone with an extreme case of OCD. They need everything done a certain way, and it can become extremely stressful to live with – being criticized about every little thing you do, much like a perfectionist who isn't necessarily perfect but wants everyone to adhere to those impossible standards.

- **The Angry Type** - These people are rarely found in a good mood, and even if they are, it only takes a hot second for that to get ruined and for them to transition into anger yet again. It can be triggered by anything, but the problem is they often get angry beyond reason. Moreover, this anger can be sustained over a long period of time, and nothing seems to resolve the issue. Even if something that they didn't like is changed to how they like it, they are still angry about why that thing wasn't done right in the first place.

- **The Gaslighter** - This is also a liar, but it is infinitely more harmful in the sense that they will deny reality and try to make you believe what you think is false. They will literally lie about how things are in reality. If it is the day, they will say it is night and produce some absurd story about how you aren't able to see the reality but what they are saying is really the truth. It is a very unusual mindset linked with many other serious problems.

- **The Gossiper** - If they have anyone around who is willing to lend an ear, they will have a story about someone to talk about. It's as if all that happens in their mind is a continuous commentary about how other people around them are living their lives. While it's nice to be updated about what your friends and family are doing, when it is to the extent that you are having extended conversations about them and building entire stories without ever referring to reality, it can be a problem.

- **The Bully** - Just like the bullies in school, these fully-grown bullies also need a weakling they can push around to make themselves feel a bit better about themselves. Sometimes this can be verbal abuse and mental abuse though in some cases, it can easily move into physical abuse.

- **The Paranoid** – No matter what you do for this person, no matter what happens to this person, you cannot get them to snap out of this mindset in which they think they are a target. Unlike the victim, these people will not lay around and play dead. Rather, they will do everything they can to avoid a threat that doesn't exist.

- **The Attention Seeker** – Whether this means lying, being someone they aren't, doing things they don't want to, or even making a fool of themselves trying to impress others, the attention seeker will do everything that they can to remain the center of the universe for those around them. This can be a serious problem for them if they are not at the center of attention, and then they start to get frustrated and start to have all kinds of problems.

- **The Addict** – Whether that is substance abuse, gambling, addiction to a certain lifestyle, a workaholic, or any other kind of addiction, it is a problem for people around the addict. They need to get their fix, and they will do anything to make that happen. It's important to note that physical addiction to a chemical is only one problem; there are often other less tangible addictions that can be far worse.

How to Deal with Toxic People

Set Boundaries – The biggest problem for individuals dealing with toxic people is that they cannot differentiate their own needs from the needs of the toxic person and often fall into the trap of pandering to the toxic individual's desires rather than focusing on themselves. Especially when it is a spouse or family member, you will definitely want to take care of them and keep a positive balance at home, but in doing so, you are only feeding their toxicity. Just because they are toxic doesn't mean everything has to be done their way. You need to have a clear way of showing them when enough is enough. If they can't control themselves beyond that point, it is not your problem, and they should handle themselves rather than look for people that can carry their weight. This can often be accompanied by guilt, but you have to realize that this is for your own benefit. Not doing so will only make the situation worse for both of you.

Talk Out Your Differences – In some situations, good communication can solve the matter and prevent a serious situation from developing. For instance, if you have a control freak who won't let you live life on your own terms, you need to sit down and talk to them about what concerns them and look at the situation from a different perspective. Maybe you can manage something the other person doesn't feel insecure about, and you also get to do what you want to do.

Depending on the kind of toxicity you are dealing with, the way you tackle the situation will be different each time, but staying quiet about it and ignoring things will only make it worse. If you feel that you aren't making any progress on your own, don't be shy to get some professional help. You or your partner might often be more comfortable talking to a third person or an intermediary rather than facing you directly.

Avoid Unnecessary Problems - Nearly all kinds of toxic behaviors and toxic situations have a build-up phase, the problem phase, and the after-effects. In most cases, you can help the situation by making necessary changes at different phases. For instance, if you have someone who is constantly lying, you can help stop it from escalating into a full-blown fight by just addressing the issue and staying on topic.

Usually, the issue is one thing, but as the argument develops, many other things get dragged into the argument, and you are just arguing endlessly and aimlessly. Try not to get sidetracked and stay focused on the actual problem. If you are trying to have a discussion but don't feel like you are making any progress and could easily spill over into an argument, try to defuse the situation and handle the issue at a different time when you are both in a better state of mind. When dealing with a toxic person, you are only making things worse for each other by getting into arguments and problems that can be avoided.

It Doesn't Always Need to Be Fixed - If you are not having a problem and have a good day, you might think that this is the best time to talk to your family about the toxic problems you have been seeing and try to reach some kind of solution. In most cases, they will resist the advice, they will try and prove that you are wrong, and they are right, and it won't reach any good conclusion. Ideally, you should take the issue up with a professional.

Time - If you invest time in a relationship and it only creates problems for you, then there is no reason to continue that relationship. In fact, spending more time than necessary trying to resolve issues can aggravate the situation and worsen it. If this is a family member that you have to interact with on a daily basis, then make sure your interaction is limited to whatever is strictly necessary. Even when everything is going fine, you might end up talking about something that leads to a fight and makes a good day a bad one. If it's a friend or a partner that you can part ways with, this will be a good solution if things seem like they are beyond your control.

Don't Point Fingers - When you are dealing with a toxic person, there is a high chance that you lose your cool at times and do unnecessary things. The toxic person might be at fault, but sometimes it might be your fault too. Usually, it is a bit of both when things start to go bad, and in this situation, if you start playing the blame game, it will only worsen the situation. If you feel like things are heading to a bad destination, try to stop the conversation there, diffuse the situation and come back to it later.

Being Direct - At the same time, this doesn't mean you don't address the elephant in the room. While you don't want to blame the other person for a problem, you also don't want things to go unaddressed and left unsaid. A lot of times, the toxic person will feed off your silence. Using this is a gateway to create even more problems and worsen the situation. When you feel threatened, you need to make sure they know they are crossing the boundary. A good strategy is to leave the situation till everyone calms down and then look into the matter but playing along with their game because you fear the consequences is not an option in any circumstance.

Be Your Number One Priority - Too many times, people in relationships and families forget they need to focus on themselves to solve the problem, and not just the toxic person. When you give yourself importance, you can show this to the other person and stop playing the victim. Rather, you are an equal part of the relationship, and you need to stand up for yourself. Most people put up with toxic behavior because they don't recognize their own worth and fail to accept that it is not ok for them to be treated badly. No one will stand up for your rights, and the last thing you should expect is for the toxic person to think about your goods. They have their own problems they need to deal with, and in the process, you need to focus on yourself rather than just trying to help them get through it.

Abuse

Abuse comes in many shapes and forms. Physical abuse is definitely very dangerous, especially if it happens with a partner under the influence or in a rage. More importantly, other kinds of abuse such as gaslighting, emotional blackmailing, verbal abuse, and even sexual abuse can have just as bad, if not worse, consequences. What's more, is that the subject of the abuse also doesn't always realize the extent of the damage. Often verbal and mental abuse can have a deeply profound impact, yet it doesn't become apparent until some time passes.

In many cases, this can manifest itself later in life in the form of PTSD and various other mental illnesses. Getting out of an abusive relationship is what is in the best interest of not only the victim but also the attacker. Such a relationship will damage the attacker as well and build on the already toxic foundation that they have laid for themselves. If you are suffering any kind of abuse, your first step should be to get legal assistance and protect yourself. If you have children, this can be a very dangerous environment for them, and you need to look out for their safety.

Chapter 12: The Toxic Mind

As discussed in previous chapters, a highly sensitive person (HSP) has a heightened sensitivity to physical, social, or emotional stimuli. People often misunderstand an HSP as someone who is superficially being extra sensitive. But that is certainly not the case because, as an HSP, you are so profoundly in touch with your senses that you perceive every stimulus at a much deeper level. Obviously, this does tax you, and you may struggle to cope with everything.

Impact of Toxic Environment

If you are a highly sensitive individual, you will relate to the experience of feeling overwhelmed by simple things happening in your environment. You may know the exact feeling when stress and anxiety creep up in a toxic environment. This usually happens with you in times of conflict because you take on the emotions of people around you. Although it is a good thing to empathize, it also results in an emotional overload that gives you a sensory overwhelm. It is quite possible that because of your naturally empathic nature, you are often the target of self-centered and narcissistic people around you. These have a toxic presence and will manipulate others to gain personal benefits.

As a highly sensitive person, you usually experience severe physical or emotional pain that is sure to cause *sensory-overwhelm*. But the level of sensitivity is not the only thing contributing to this because experiences from your past also play a role in creating a shared response or emotion.

Although, you need to understand that the definition of a toxic environment is not universal and has a lot of subjectivity. Hence, it varies from one person to another. But generally, as an HSP, you try hard to avoid stressful events. For instance, this could mean even avoiding watching the news because reality is not only extremely stressful and tragic, but all of this totally overwhelms you.

One of the biggest challenges of a highly sensitive person is when someone around them blatantly tells them to "stop being overly sensitive!" What you feel is not a choice for you; it is instinctual. This enhanced sensitivity towards stimuli is your innate nature, and it is a devastating feeling for a highly sensitive person to hear such a thoughtless remark. In such instances where people question the very nature of an HSP, you must realize that it is okay to be different and stay the way you are.

Understandably, for an HSP, combatting such remarks is not always easy, and it is very natural because of their highly sensitive nature they may take it to heart. High sensitivity denotes a deeper level of self-acceptance that ought to be embraced instead of feeling ashamed or stressed about it.

Being Aware of the Toxic Matrix

As a highly sensitive person, nature has equipped you well to sense and perceive things in your environment. The only difference is that whatever experiences you go through, they come with a greater depth. Although, as an HSP having such deep, emotionally loaded experiences all the time can become hard on you. And you may have often struggled to separate yourself from that kind of harmful environment in the face of malignant toxicity.

The harmful or toxic personalities thrive in an HSP's presence because they understand that you can fully understand their feelings and pain. This interchange is beneficial only for the toxic individuals around the HSP because they can control the other person, overriding their emotions and needs and, in the process, relieve their narcissistic needs.

On the other hand, a highly sensitive person will be acutely aware of the emotional, physical, or psychological state of the toxic individuals surrounding them. And will end up suffering while trying to make the toxic individual feel better. One of the biggest drawbacks of being a highly sensitive person is that it does not work like a switch, and you cannot simply turn it off whenever you feel like it.

But this means that whenever you are in a toxic environment or face a toxic individual, you notice a dark cloud lurking around you. Highly sensitive people can often identify toxic environments and individuals after only a brief interaction, even if everything apparently seems to be calm. If you are an HSP, learn to trust the gut feeling that says something is "just not right" around here because this is not merely a bad vibe. For highly sensitive people, the gut feelings strongly signify the stressful vibes in an environment and hint towards possible distress coming their way.

What Happens in a Toxic Environment?

The real poison in a toxic environment generates from the expectation that a highly sensitive person can understand everything. Therefore, they are "obliged" to do something about it every time, all the time. This expectation by the toxic person around an HSP gets increasingly intense and exhausting. It not only sounds suffocating, but you end up feeling as if there is no way out of this situation.

Interestingly, in a toxic environment, the highly sensitive person is burdened and seen as a problem solver and caretaker of relationships and everyone in that environment. Imagining this for even a second can make anyone feel overwhelmed and exhausted. For an HSP, it could easily drain all their emotional energy.

After all of this, as an HSP, you would have to retreat or withdraw for a while to recover from all that toxic trauma and overload. However, toxic individuals will label this as abandonment or rejection. They usually perceive this attitude as selfishness, laziness, or an expression of lack of love, and consequently, they respond aggressively by rejecting or punishing the HSP. You have to practice self-compassion here and understand that there is nothing wrong with putting yourself first.

This cycle of abuse is malignant and functions as emotional cancer. The highly sensitive person usually feels extreme guilt or becomes the victim of gaslighting. If you witness subtle signs of toxicity or feel emotionally drained, this is a clear signal of a toxic environment. Instead of being extra hard on yourself, it is important to distance yourself from that environment or people.

The Unspoken Truth

Naturally, as a highly sensitive person, you know that you can read between the lines so well that you find the truth behind a lie quicker than anyone else. An HSP would be able to take note of even subtle discrepancies that others may not pick up. But unfortunately, the toxic individuals in your life will gaslight or deny everything if they are questioned. This situation creates a dilemma for you as a highly sensitive person. It is difficult to decide whether to accept the toxic reality or follow through on what they have picked up on. One of the biggest risks that a highly sensitive person may face is experiencing gaslighting, rejection, or their very nature used against them. They may usually hear comments like, "you are reading too much into things" or "you are being too sensitive." The toxic individuals will use these tactics to confuse or silence the highly sensitive person.

Depression and Self-Harm by HSP

Often, the ultimate result of living in a toxic environment is severe stress, anxiety, or depression, further complicating the situation and increasing the risk of self-harming behavior. It is like experiencing the mind of a highly sensitive person turning on themselves. While it may seem hard to believe, it is not so uncommon because after living in a toxic environment for a while, it is quite natural to experience dark thoughts that are pessimistic, negative, and debilitating in nature.

What Leads to Self-Harm?

As an HSP, you can very well relate to the fact that once you are feeling depressed, you are more likely to experience even darker and more pessimistic thought processes. This could eventually push them towards self-harm. Moreover, because a highly sensitive person tends to process everything deeply, it is easy for their minds to go over all possible consequences regarding the situation. Unfortunately, one of the consequences of this deep thought process is often self-harm, and they may experience suicidal thoughts.

More than one factor may contribute to the destructive matrix of self-harm. Since highly sensitive people are naturally empathetic, even in depression and distress, they would think for others around them. This pessimistic outlook will often lead them to conclude that people around them are in trouble because of them.

In such a depressive state, it would not occur to them that the people around them could be wrong, or the environment is totally toxic. If such a state continues, they may experience explicitly detailed suicidal ideas that are certainly a cause for alarm.

Be aware of your thought process and emotions as an HSP. If you notice any subtle signs of depression, anxiety, or pessimistic rumination, you should seek professional help right away.

Another factor that often increases the risk of depression, chronic anxiety, or pessimistic thinking in highly sensitive people is that they find it hard to blend in with the crowd and often face bullying. This may lead the HSP to hate the consequences of their sensitive personality because of feeling left out or sidelined. As an HSP, you may have often described it as "feeling weirdly different to others and a fear of missing out," which is a very sensitive situation. Such situations can easily overwhelm and push the highly sensitive person towards chronic depression, anxiety, or other drastic consequences that could usually put their lives at risk. So, you have to watch out for the subtle signs before everything turns worst.

An HSP can end up feeling exhausted or emotionally drained to such an extent that their positive energy is simply devastated. This is generally because of criticism leveled at them by others, who label them as touchy, oversensitive, or phony. Since this scenario can easily stab the heart of an HSP, it is important to stay conscious of what is happening to your emotions. You should also seek immediate professional help if you feel the slightest signs of a toxic environment taking its toll on your emotional well-being.

Other factors go into this equation, and when it comes to highly sensitive people, things get intense beyond perception. However, while it is impossible to control environmental fluctuations at all times, it is more practical to stay in touch with a professional healthcare provider who will help them manage all those pessimistic ruminations and deal with the toxicity in their environment.

Experience Examples of HSPs

As an HSP, you must be experiencing life in a different and on a much deeper level from the very start. It stems from within you, and therefore, people notice the highly sensitive aspects in their personality since their childhood. It could be as simple as contemplating whether to ask your teacher a certain question or not or trying to assess the teacher's emotions or exhaustion. One HSP that I know recalled her childhood as being one filled with frequent worrying and feeling responsible about being too empathic to ask questions in class or to wait until her teacher seemed less tensed or 1 tired. She shared that she would often ask herself, "is it really the time to pose a question?" HSPs often face peer bullying as well because of their different personalities.

Another HSP shared that they have often struggled in their relationships because they are often the center for seeking advice and help. People expect them to be nurturing and responsible for playing the role of general help in all situations. This constant state of being empathic and compassionate towards others often led to ignoring their own needs resulting in a deteriorated well-being.

It is not strange for a highly sensitive person to be drained after feeling many emotions. They often need to withdraw from the situation for a while to refresh and reconnect with their core nature. One HSP reported that as soon as she withdrew from overwhelming situations, people around her would label her as insensitive or selfish. According to her, there was always an increasing pressure to be available for everyone else, which usually came at the cost of ignoring herself.

These scenarios eventually lead a highly sensitive person towards dark thoughts, pessimism, and negative rumination. This is emotionally draining and destructive and takes a toll on their physical well-being as well. Above all, this may even lead the HSP to resent their very nature, and nothing can be more damaging for a person than feeling discomfort in their own skin.

Dealing with the Common Culprits

Everyone has an inner critic, and there is a natural tendency to think negatively, which can have a certain adaptive value. However, in the case of highly sensitive people who have been in toxic environments around toxic people for quite some time, it becomes harmful to every aspect of their mental health. Therefore, it is important to have coping strategies for times like this.

Avoid Black and White Thinking

It is common to start thinking in black and white after prolonged exposure to a toxic environment. You have to understand that life usually works within the shades of gray, and it is where beauty exists. Getting rid of this type of toxic rumination is simple because all you have to do is be aware of the thought streams using the words "never" or "always." Such thoughts often represent a distorted view of reality that is far from an accurate representation.

Dealing with Pressure and Toxicity

If you have been in a toxic environment for a long time, you will notice that it becomes more of a habit that you start succumbing to criticism now and then. Instead of letting yourself crumble under someone else's judgment of you, you can take a step back and breathe. Let a few moments pass and then evaluate whether the person passing those judgments has good reason. Instead of taking the situation at heart, try to discover the real reasons behind their behavior. Often, you will find that you have been projecting the imagined toxicity, and the situation has s nothing to do with who you are.

Get In the Habit of Practicing Self-Compassion

You must understand that you will often be your own worst critic as a highly sensitive person. It is okay to forgive your mistakes and let go of what went wrong in the past. You have to appreciate the imperfection that life brings because that is reality. Once you start practicing self-compassion, you will begin to feel much calmer and more in control of yourself. Practicing self-compassion promotes well-grounded self-worth because it stems from a stronger foundation of growth and learning.

Start Practicing Mindfulness

Meditation and mindfulness are the ultimate sanctuaries. It helps HSPs feel stronger on the inside and balance the emotional overwhelm that they are experiencing. Practicing mindfulness will help you snap out of the pessimistic and toxic rumination cycle. This is because instead of forcefully changing or blocking the negative thoughts, you are letting them pass without attaching any judgments to them. This helps you develop a deeper connection with the present moment and makes you stay in control of your mental and emotional energy.

Face Pessimism

It is important to stay focused on brighter possibilities. Often pessimistic thinking makes you believe you are out of options or nothing good can come out of anything. However, in such a situation, face this pessimistic thought process head-on and consciously steer your focus towards different possibilities (instead of zooming in on the impossible aspects). Once your mind starts thinking about different ways to overcome a challenge, you will realize that the pessimistic thought process is baseless. It may not be as easy as it sounds, but you will master the art with conscious practice.

Learning to Thrive as an HSP

With so much happening in the surrounding environment and the amount of toxicity or negativity to deal with, life may become unnecessarily challenging for a highly sensitive person. However, in such situations, recognize what you are going through- because staying in contact with your emotions will help you avoid being overwhelmed, and you will feel more in control of your situation.

Take small steps to manage stress. This may simply mean choosing to exercise regularly, sticking to a sleeping schedule, or going out with your friends. This is important because it will help you better manage your emotions and prepare or avoid the possible negative consequences, such as depression and all that it can lead to. Once you start recognizing the subtle ways of a toxic mind, you will be able to notice any signs of toxicity or pessimistic rumination within yourself as well. Above everything else, you need to show self-compassion because by directing gratitude and kindness towards yourself, you will be able to expel all the criticism that has been sabotaging you.

Chapter 13: The Highly Sensitive Skillset

By now, you must have come to realize that being a highly sensitive person has both its perks and shortcomings. However, it might feel that we've only been discussing the challenges you're likely to face in your daily life and how to deal with them positively. That is a great thing to do, but at some point, you can start getting tired of having to live your life on the hard mode every day. The truth is that you don't have to struggle with your routine just because you're an HSP. Your highly sensitive nature gives you powers far beyond your imagination, and now is the time to find and embrace these powers and be the most majestic superhuman you can be.

In this chapter, we'll be discussing all your strong points and giving you ideas of how you can use your high sensitivity to its utmost potential.

How Your High Sensitivity Gives You Superpowers

Let's start with identifying the skillset of superpowers that come with being an HSP. As a highly sensitive person, you have the following innate skills at your disposal:

1. Sharp Perception Skills

You must have realized by now that your perception skills are extraordinary compared to other people. You have a sharp eye that can discern every detail wherever you are, be it the low sounds you hear around you, the normal smells that people often take for granted, or the unique taste of ingredients thrown together to make average food or beverages. Granted, the intensity of these stimuli can vary from one HSP to another, but the fact remains that all HSPs notice these stimuli more than their peers. After all, your nervous system is much more active when compared to others, and that means your physical senses are sharper than the rest.

Physical stimuli aren't the only thing you feel more. You're naturally inclined to notice the emotional and social cues better than others. This means you can instantly recognize the emotional state of others through the faintest clues, even if you do so subconsciously. You're able to discern the relationships between other people, which gives you a unique and comprehensive insight into the overall nature of communications around you. As such, you're able to attune to the needs of those around you quickly, and being empathetic by nature, you feel the need to help them however you can.

2. Enhanced Processing Speed

Being able to see more into any specific situation gives you an unparalleled advantage, but that's not where your superpowers end. To add to your sharp perception skills, your brain can operate at a terrifying speed to process the information it receives. This means that not only do you see more into any situation, but you also automatically analyze every single detail of the said situation and can define the underlying causes and motives. To add to that, you're also inclined to analyze how you feel about analyzing the stimuli you experience, which works in your favor in two ways. Firstly, you have a natural defense against being caught up in hazardous situations, which helps you reach a more rational course of action rather than being swept up with the wind. Secondly, these analytical skills refine your intuition, making your gut feeling spot-on.

3. The Constant Search for the Optimal Option

As an HSP, your inclination for perfectionism can get the better of you. That's mainly because you're constantly searching for the best course of action. Thanks to your innate skills, you're able to catch on to social and emotional cues and analyze situations to see the gaps in communication. As such, you're able to see the bigger picture while simultaneously realizing the opportunities and risks associated with taking any course of action. While others rush into taking actions and learning lessons the hard way, you prefer to run the scenarios in your head first – only taking action once you've envisioned the various outcomes.

What's even better is that the course of action you finally decide to take doesn't only serve you. During your analytical sessions, you're inputting the emotional needs of those around you while looking for the best option to maintain harmony. You can say that all the effort you subconsciously exert is meant for the better well-being of the environment you're placed in – it's all for the greater good. You often feel responsible for maintaining the perfect atmosphere, and you save no effort in fulfilling your sense of responsibility.

4. High Social Awareness

We've touched the topic more than a few times already, but your exceptional social awareness is a great asset. Since you often feel like an outsider stuck in your mind and emotions, you know more than anyone the value of being included. This makes you appreciate the various working styles of different personalities – you're more aware of what each individual can bring to the table. This ultra-awareness motivates you to go out and beyond to maintain team morale and make everyone feel worthwhile. You quickly pick up the cues of emotional burnout and recognize customer needs as soon as you pick up the phone. You're a great asset to whatever team you join, even if they fail to see your potential at first.

5. Responding Only after Assessing All Variables

With everything going on in your mind, it's only natural you take more time to respond. Despite your quick perception, you need to be sure that the action you take is the right one, so you take your time assessing all the variables. Although this may make it seem like you're falling behind in today's hectic business world, it's actually another one of your unparalleled assets. In a world where everyone is rushing, usually ending up making wrong choices, you decide to slow down and take in all the information first. As such, you make a great diplomat whenever conflict arises – even more so since you often see the perspectives of all opposing individuals so clearly.

6. Constant Self-Reflection

Your constant self-reflection is a double-edged sword; it all depends on how you use it. If you allow it to take a negative turn, you could become imprisoned by your self-criticism, but it can also be your greatest weapon if you control your inner voice. Since you're constantly reflecting on your behavior and abilities, it can also push you into learning more and developing your current skillset. Your self-reflection makes you your biggest judge, and that pushes you into maintaining the best integrity and work ethic you can muster. All in all, your self-reflection is a crucial element in growing and becoming the best version of yourself, so be sure to embrace it.

The Highly Sensitive Person in Society

I mean it with all my heart when I say that the world could do with more HSPs. It's not uncommon for HSPs to be called out for their "sensitivity" and extreme emotional reactions. People either try to put on a smile and dismiss your worries or downright call you are annoying for feeling everything deeply. Ironically, those are the people who will come running to you once they're feeling down or they've run into a challenging obstacle since they know there's no one else who can lend them a shoulder as you will. That's because you have the following skills:

1. You Show Empathy and Compassion

Being empathetic is one of the defining traits of HSPs. You're able to feel another person's emotions at a glance, and then you feel their emotions as if they were your own. You become genuinely concerned for others and feel the need to help them however you can. Your compassion means that you get happier when others are happy and feel fulfilled when others are satisfied. Your well-being is connected to the well-being of your surroundings, so if you're happy, it most definitely means that your environment is thriving.

2. You Look For Meaningful Connections

Since you can feel much deeper emotions than most people, superficial relations just don't cut it for you. Every time you meet someone new, you try to understand them on every level until you understand them. You look for meaning in every relationship and encounter, and you can't bear to think of crossing paths with another soul without leaving a positive impact on them.

3. You Love Deeply

The harsh truth is that highly sensitive people suffer more in love than others, especially if they get in a relationship with a less sensitive person. It comes as no surprise that HSPs get bored in marriages much faster than others since they expect meaningful and intimate relationships to always be at an all-time maximum high. When you look at it from a positive and proactive lens, sensitive people are the ones who can fire up a dying relationship with all the love, vitality, and passion they bring to the table.

4. You're Extremely Aware of Your Surroundings

Your emotional and social awareness isn't limited to people or physical objects. You're more in tune with nature and the environment than others. You're the kind to have an animal as a best friend and go around befriending the puppies and kittens of the neighborhood. Environmental problems weigh on your mind, and you try your best to turn your friends vegan with you.

5. Your Sensitivity is the Best Cure for a Toxic Society

It's sad to admit that today's western society values nothing more than materialism. In a world where being called robotic is the best compliment you can get, the value of a highly sensitive person is unfairly overlooked. That's really ironic since HSPs are the only ones who can cure the toxic society we've come to live in.

The Highly Sensitive Person in the Workplace

There's a common misconception about highly sensitive people and how they can't survive in today's hectic world. It's easy to see where the notion originated from since the world today runs at a terrifying pace of hitting targets and accumulating certificates that have made most of us robotic in our routines. Most people have learned to disregard emotions to optimize their performance, which certainly sounds like a challenging place for an empathetic HSP to operate within. Ironically enough, this is exactly why today's business world needs HSPs more than ever before. As a highly sensitive person who is aware of their superpowers, you have the following innate abilities to nurture your workplace:

1. Keeping Your Teamwork Strong

You already know that tuning into other people's emotional and mental states is one of your strengths, so it's time to use it to your advantage in the workplace. By noticing the state of your fellow team members, analyzing situations, and seeing various outcomes, you can make sure everyone is on the same page. For instance, you may instantly recognize the pros and cons of a new workplace policy while your teammates struggle to understand its impact. As such, you can help your teammates by supporting them and explaining the variables of the new situation, which can help them adapt faster and more efficiently.

2. Filling the Gaps Others Have Missed

Thanks to your super observation and analytical skills, you can instantly realize the gaps in teamwork or workflows. When someone else misses something in their work, you will be the first to notice those tiny details. When your company is about to hire a newbie, you will be the first to assess if you need new hires or if it's better to revise the workflow and reallocate the budget to produce a more efficient business model. Some may call it being a perfectionist, but you know it's all about implementing the best option.

3. Exceptional Communication Skills

Most HSPs come off as shy, awkward introverts at first glance, but that's not the case for everyone. Even if you are an introvert, your self-awareness should be strong enough to keep you confident about your skills, one of which is your natural-born talent for communication. Your exceptional emotional intelligence helps you recognize and relate to various emotions, which in turn boosts your social intelligence. In other words, you can read other people like open books. As a result, you can easily communicate the missing parts with other team members and adjust your explanation to suit every individual's level of understanding.

4. Solving Problems Using Your Creativity and Intuition

You may not feel like it at times, but being in tune with your inner and external worlds makes an excellent recipe for creativity. Add to that your superhuman perception, analytical skills, and intuition, and you can technically solve any problem that comes your way. In the business world, problem-solving is one of the most sought-after skills for employees, managers, and even CEOs across all industries. There's another thing that helps you with problem-solving, and that is your ability to process a frightening amount of information seamlessly. This gives you another competitive edge to combine with your critical thinking skills, which will help you nurture the business in various ways. You may develop new business ideas, optimize the business model, spot lucrative opportunities to scale up or adopt a cost-effective structure to maximize your profits.

Prepare for Disruption

To use your potential to its best at work, you need to understand how to operate your mind, body, and emotions efficiently. In this case, it's empirical that you realize that you often need to brace yourself for your workday so that you can operate on your maximum performance. As an HSP, you need a steady routine to operate. You don't like surprises, and you get thrown off your balance when your plan is disrupted. However, that's exactly the reason why you should plan to be disrupted long before it happens so that you can reduce the lag-time as much as you can. If there's one constant in the business world, then it's the fact that it's always changing. If you can expect the unexpected and plan for disruption, you will be more likely to perform at your best despite the changes.

Know That You're Irreplaceable

There's one last thing you should know while we're discussing the workplace. If you're living at the edge of the digitally transforming world like the rest of us, you must have come across the terrifying idea that we'll soon be all replaced by robots and AI. As the technology we create becomes smarter, they'll start taking over all the clerical and robotic jobs, like administration and accounting. However, what you have is something that no robot can imitate – even most humans cannot copy your HSP skillset. Even if half of the workforce is let go in the years to come, you can be sure of one thing, and that is that you're irreplaceable.

Best Career Choices for Highly Sensitive People

With such a unique skill set, finding certain jobs more attractive than others is normal. Since an HSP always looks for a job that offers meaning rather than only money, they can be a bit picky about their professions. Luckily for you, there are quite a few professions in which you can not only survive but thrive as well. Here are a few of your top choices:

1. The Caring Professions

It stands to reason that highly sensitive people make the best caretakers. You will certainly feel fulfilled by taking care of others if you become a physician, nurse, therapist, personal coach, or social worker. That's because these professions rely heavily on a person's ability to feel others, show compassion, and fulfill their needs – all of which are skills that come naturally to you.

2. The Academic Track

You can also pursue a different track in academics. Many highly sensitive people become drained when dealing with the toxicity in their surroundings, so they prefer to save their compassion for the precious few in their lives. If you're among these people, you will be able to use your exceptional ability to process information to your advantage and become a highly respected and influential scholar in your field of choice. Alternatively, you can use your knowledge to bring up future generations by pursuing a career as a teacher or a college professor.

3. The Creative Field

You can also turn all the beauty you feel in life into art by pursuing a job in the creative industry. Producing innovative designs or creative work will come easily to you, thanks to your artistic talents. Whether you choose to be a graphic designer, writer, creative director, IT professional, photographer, filmmaker, musician, architect, or artist generally, you will be able to pursue full-time jobs or freelance land gigs as you see fit.

4. Spiritual Professions

A lot of the highly sensitive people are spiritual by nature. They value their beliefs strongly and get meaning in life from their spirituality. However, their highly sensitive nature makes them open-minded and encouraging, making them the best clergy and spiritualists.

5. Entrepreneurship

Given how challenging this track can be, recommending entrepreneurship to an HSP may feel out of place. However, once you consider the special skill set that an HSP brings to the table, it's easy to understand how they can be natural-born leaders. There's no one more driven and passionate than an HSP who is in tune with their strengths and knows what they want to do. They become a force of nature that motivates everyone around them and takes their hand to reach greater heights together.

When it comes to the skillset of a highly sensitive person, few personalities can challenge their potential. A highly sensitive person has everything it takes to be a great addition to both society and the workplace. If you learn how to unlock your potential, there's absolutely nothing that can stop you from achieving your goals.

Chapter 14: Forgiving and Nurturing Yourself

As a highly sensitive person, you are very tuned in when it comes to people around you, and you are extremely sensitive to what is said and how it is said and the behavior patterns towards you when they are with you. You are also very receptive to feedback from people about what they have heard about you and who they have heard it from. The fact that you are extremely receptive is such a positive attribute. It only becomes a problem when you start overthinking and misinterpreting signals the wrong way, which fuels your life negatively.

Sometimes people are just pulling your leg, and sometimes, they will know this weakness/strength and try to bring you down by telling you things they know will hurt you. Sometimes, you might get it wrong. It is not uncommon for highly sensitive people to spend days, weeks, even years contemplating a single thing that a person once said to them. If this happens to be a person who is very close to them (or someone they trust a lot), it can be a catastrophic event capable of changing the trajectory of their life.

There are moments in everyone's life where things happen which are beyond their control. In one way or another, anyone can end up in a situation that is quite tragic, painful, negative, and otherwise mentally harmful. For some people, it's not that difficult to overcome this hurdle and continue living an otherwise positive and successful life. Others are not so fortunate, and this one moment can ruin their life.

The fact is that we all only have a single life to live. We get different amounts of time on this planet, but at the end of it all, it's not about how much time but the quality of the time you had the privilege to live. For both the highly sensitive person and the average person, external validation is important, but the more important and more powerful validation is the one that comes from within.

Recognizing Self-Love

Self-love is not something limited to only those who can afford a luxury spa treatment every Thursday evening, and you don't have to buy yourself a million-dollar car to love yourself. Self-love can actually be very grueling and tough. Maintaining a productive routine and really working towards your goals is often challenging, but you still do it because, at the end of that process, you will reward yourself with something that you love. Letting yourself sleep in is self-harm; getting up and doing what you have to do is self-love.

However, this doesn't mean you have to live a life with every second scheduled. There is a time for play and a time for work. It is how you approach both those things that will determine whether or not you are working for your benefit or getting in your own way.

Self-love is about being comfortable in your own skin. This requires a knowledge of self, together with patience, discipline, and motivation to keep moving forward. It's not that you are suddenly the perfect version of yourself that you always wanted to be, but more about the fact that you are willing to accept who you are and where you want to go.

Sometimes, especially as an HSP, your dreams might scare you. That critical inner voice will tell you, you can never achieve that goal, that you don't deserve it, or that you don't have it in you to live the life of your dreams.

They say those who think they can and those who think they can't often are both correct.

The route you take is your decision.

Signs That You Need Self-Love

Low self-esteem is a common HSP trait. Rather than gauging your self-worth based on your own understanding, an objective evaluation of your achievements, and your overall performance, you rely on the opinion of others to validate your self-image. What's even worse is that people with low self-esteem undervalue the positive feedback they get from people and overvalue the negative. In the same way, their internal dialogue is often tilted towards the negative, perpetuating low self-esteem and driving it even further down.

Due to this low self-esteem and overall negative self-image, it becomes very difficult for individuals to talk themselves out of this situation and improve their self-worth. That internal speech that motivates us and gives us some form of motivation becomes so quiet that external validation is the only way to achieve any kind of satisfaction. After all, feeling loved, feeling important, and having some kind of positivity in life is a core requirement of any human. Hypersensitive people are more prone to this problem and consciously seek external validation more intensely than others.

All this adds up to intense stress, anxiety, and even depression, with no positive emotions. Even though they might be successful in their lives and might have the things that others desire, they are subject to a range of mental challenges because they are not mentally at peace or comfortable with themselves. Moreover, these issues of anxiety and depression exacerbate feelings of insecurity and lack of self-worth, making it a vicious spiral that they can't get out of. Also, these mental problems can lead to all kinds of other challenges that only worsen the mental and physical circumstances of the individual. For instance, hypersensitive people can have weight management problems, and depression can further worsen this situation.

As the bundle of negative energy grows larger and the HSP struggles to find a way out, this can start to aggravate the critical voice in their head. Whether that voice is going on about general daily life issues or whether it is about the larger goals and ambitions of the individual, it becomes very difficult for *even an external source* to uplift them. More importantly, they become very pessimistic and demotivated about life in general. This can lead them to detach themselves from life and withdraw from even mildly challenging things. In extreme cases, the individual might want to withdraw from the most basic aspects of life, such as eating, working, and maintaining personal hygiene.

One of the biggest signs of a person who desperately needs to work on self-compassion and self-love is that they struggle to accept compliments and praise. Even though they will genuinely have done a great job and their peers, boss, or colleagues will want to congratulate them on their achievement, the person with low self-esteem will be unable to really internalize the compliments. Instead, that internal voice will produce a story to somehow nullify the positive feedback.

If a person faces all these problems or even just one or two of these problems, it makes it extremely difficult for them to progress in life, develop self-love, and regain control over their lives. Eventually, there comes the point where even those who want to help are unable to, and the person completely loses hope. The HSP's quality of life can become permanently harmful. When these things are left untreated for too long, or they develop to a stage where these problems become out of control, things such as suicide become possible.

Start with Forgiveness

Self-compassion, a better self-image, and a better image of the person you see in the mirror start with forgiveness. Just as you would build a house on a solid foundation, working on yourself is no good if the foundation is not stable. Ideally, you should work with a professional to help you work through your negative issues. For hypersensitive people, it is not difficult to identify those key moments in life that have contributed to your poor mental capacity, but it can be difficult to manage these things on your own. With a mental health professional, you will have the guidance you need together with the tools and services to make the journey of recovery as brief as possible.

For some people coming around to forgiving themselves might be a matter of just a few days. Issues might have become problematic simply because they have never really gotten around to thinking about them or working out solutions. For others, this process might be the beginning of a lifelong battle. One that needs to be worked on every day, but the battle will get a little easier with each day that passes, and you will be one step closer to a solution.

One of the most important things to do during this process of forgiveness and change is, to begin with, an open mind. The best way forward is to stay open to the possibility that what you think might be wrong and there might be better solutions out there.

Develop Compassion

Take a break and give yourself some room. Give yourself the freedom to be wrong, make mistakes, and still be fine with yourself. Hypersensitive people tend to hold themselves up against extremely high standards in every aspect of life. When they fail to meet these expectations, they get disappointed to such a degree that it can cripple them from moving forward. As a highly sensitive person, you need to let the negative stuff out, change perspectives, and try to see all the harm as the fuel you need to grow. You need to be your own best friend and help yourself get through these times rather than be a strict disciplinarian who doesn't employ positive reinforcement. Set goals for yourself during this recovery process and motivate yourself to achieve those things. Start with physical goals. If you need to lose some weight or get in shape in any way, this is a fantastic way to push yourself in the right direction and build momentum. Our body plays a huge role in our self-image, and when you start seeing visible progress in this one area, the energy will resonate with other parts of your life.

Love Yourself

To set yourself on the path of recovery, these are some powerful techniques that you can use on your own or with the help of a professional.

Rewrite Your Negative Beliefs - We often clutter our thoughts with sweeping statements, extreme situations, and think of ideas as if they are things that have been etched in stone. Just because you didn't get the compliments that you thought you would get for the new dress you were wearing doesn't mean you are not good at dressing up, that you aren't worth the praise, that you will never look nice, and all the other things that you assume after such an incident. Rather think of it in a more positive light. Be proud that you got yourself new clothes, spent all that time getting ready, and be happy that you looked great for yourself. You can always improve, and no situation is the end of the world.

Journal – Our minds are extremely busy; even when we are sleeping, our mind is awake and creating things in the form of dreams or is busy doing its own processing, which we don't remember when we wake up. Having a journal, especially one where you note thoughts down immediately after waking, can be helpful. It is so easy to write down your notes anytime/anywhere with smartphones.

Ideally, you should be journaling your thoughts and ideas throughout your day, and at the very least, you should have a specific time when you sit down to write out everything going through your head. This doesn't have to be a book that is a blow-by-blow account of your day; it can just be about the things stressing you or things you really want to get done. In any case, writing down your thoughts forces you to restructure them in your mind, and then they get even more clarified when you transfer them to paper. This is not only to store your thoughts to reflect on later, but it also acts as a filter for your thoughts and helps you organize your thinking.

Meditate – Many people assume that meditation is linked to religion or is only practiced by people when they are praying, whereas, in reality, it is a fantastic exercise that anyone can use in any way to benefit their physical and mental health. You should choose a kind of meditation that you are comfortable doing. This can be something you do first thing in the morning or last thing at night; the important thing is that you do it. The idea is that you have one thing to focus on, this is usually your breathing, and while you are focusing on this one thing, you start to push any other ideas or thoughts away. This helps build the resilience you need to fight negative thoughts and gives you the space to refresh yourself mentally.

Use Your Advantages – Unfortunately, there will be things that you are not good at. This is something you just have to accept. If you aren't 7 ft tall, but you really want to be, chances are you are just going to stay the height that you are by the time you are in your early twenties. However, you might be extremely good with technology and have a natural talent for digital things. Rather than beating yourself up about not being able to be a basketball player, you should focus on what you can do and start working on that. When you start getting good momentum in something, you will notice that it will remove stress and worry about the weaknesses you thought you had.

Work with What You Have - hypersensitive people are extremely detail-oriented and nearly perfectionists in how they approach things in life. While this is really great for getting excellent results and can be a trait that will be useful in many fields of work, for an HSP individual, it can be a trait that restricts you from taking the first step. Just because you don't have the right tools or environment is not reason enough to not do the things you need to do to get ahead in life - especially when it comes to working on yourself and improving your life. Rely on what you have available rather than lament over not having what you wish you had. You need to make a move with the available resources, and if things go according to plan, hopefully, you will be able to upgrade to the things you really want later on.

Accept Your Body - As mentioned earlier, your self-image is significantly influenced by what you think of yourself. In this regard, your appearance - and whether it is according to the ideal version of yourself that you envision - is really important. However, just because you aren't in the best physical condition doesn't mean you should hate yourself for it. Our body, our gender, our race, the color of our hair, and several other basic physical traits are not within our control. We are born with these things, and we need to accept our bodies as they are. This doesn't mean you settle with how your body is. You can definitely make changes to improve it, but this should not be something that you beat yourself up about.

Develop Affirmations - The words we speak have a huge impact on our minds. Even how we speak these words and the emphasis we put on them can influence how we think and consequently act. Even if you feel that talking to yourself is silly and hasn't any effect on you, it will change the way you think if you do it positively and regularly. Just as businesses use consistent marketing to win you over, you can use affirmations on a daily basis to change the way you think about yourself and the way you see the world. You can easily find a list of positive affirmations online that you can say to yourself or get an audio version of these affirmations that you can simply listen to. However, being face to face with yourself in a mirror and saying them out loud is always the best choice. You can do this whenever it is convenient for you, and the more frequent it is, the better it will be.

The key thing is to get yourself to snap out of the negativity loop. When you have your thoughts cleared out, you will know what takes you back and pushes you forward through processes like journaling. You will have a better understanding of how your mind works, and you can develop other things, such as affirmations, to focus directly on the weaknesses you have found. Focus on the positive and the forward-momentum to try to develop your skills in meditation so that they can help you fight off the negative energy and resist things that tend to push you back into a negative cycle.

Chapter 15: The HSP Routine

Do you know that you can overcome certain things that overwhelm you by implementing daily routines in your life? Highly sensitive people can thrive when they follow a specific routine, even if it seems boring to other people. This chapter discusses a daily routine for HSPs. It outlines the measures you can take to create the best daily, emotionally-balancing, and non-overwhelming routine.

Why an HSP Routine?

A daily routine is a critical component of survival strategy for highly sensitive people. HSPs need to follow a schedule that will help them become productive and grounded. A routine can be monotonous and counterproductive to the ordinary worker, but this is not the case with sensitive individuals. These people usually need structure and routine in their day, so they don't experience surprises or unexpected activities. A routine that they stick to helps them to stay grounded.

A highly sensitive individual often responds more intensely to different things than the average person. In other words, an HSP will take more time to process information which means they can easily be overwhelmed by stimuli. These people are also very sensitive to touch, smell, sound, and emotions, including those of others and their own. They are vulnerable to irritation or get overwhelmed by unexpected changes around them.

To overcome the challenges they may encounter in their daily lives, HSPs should strive to live in a predictable world characterized by routines. Maintaining a routine is one of the most effective ways to help sensitive people control the world around them. A schedule helps sensitive individuals understand things they can regulate and those they cannot change. This creates an environment that is soothing and non-invasive to their highly responsive nervous systems. The following are some of the routine tips for highly sensitive people.

Make a Hot Cup of Coffee or Tea

The early morning ritual of making a hot cup of tea or coffee is probably the most important part of the day for a highly sensitive person. When you wake up every morning, prepare a cup of hot tea and sip it slowly while reading a book. Do it before you do any other work – you need to know that a hot cup of tea invigorates your nerves and mind. In other words, your favorite beverage will warm your body as you prepare to begin other routines for the day. When your body gets used to this schedule, it will be easier for you to start the day on a high note.

Walk Your Dog in the Park

Another joyous routine for your day is to take your dog for a walk; the waggy tail and bright eyes will lift your spirits and make you feel happy. Choose an appropriate time to do this in your favorite park close to home. Some people prefer to do this in the morning, and others prefer early evening. If you work from home, you can walk your pet after you have finished your work for the day or when you take a break to refresh your mind. The good thing about visiting a park is that it offers a relaxing environment. A pet is friendly and will be a great companionship when you feel low. And this activity will be great exercise for both of you.

Listen to Music

Listening to music is also a very soothing activity and can quieten a chaotic mind. When you're feeling overwhelmed by a specific task causing your perfectionist nature stress, take a break and play some music to calm your mind. Your choice of music must be mindful, don't choose something that will get you hyped- up, rather choose something that you might even dance gently to. Along with music, art is another hobby that demands focus and creativity – both of which are good for an overwhelmed HSP. It helps you to concentrate on something you enjoy doing and will take your mind off things that worry you.

While it is necessary to have something to take your mind off your emotions, try to avoid mixing activities since they can overwhelm you, which is the exact opposite of what you are trying to achieve. Make sure every task has a routine and do not mix them. However, you should not focus on leisure activities only. You can include programs that provide infotainment in your schedule. For instance, you must get time to watch your favorite film or movie on Netflix. Alternatively, you can tune in to your favorite television station.

Stretch Your Body

When you work at home or in a specific workplace, you need to remember to take time to breathe and stretch your body. Move away from your desk and stretch your muscles. Improving blood circulation and oxygen intake is good for your mental health. The flow of blood helps improve the functionality of different body organs. When your mind is overwhelmed, it can affect you in everything you do. You may find it difficult to solve even small problems.

Keep a Journal

When you feel overwhelmed by life or emotions, write down everything on your mind. The main challenge facing HSPs is that they take longer to process their experiences than other people. In some instances, the feeling of overwhelm can be a result of unprocessed experiences that have gradually built up in your subconscious. This is where journaling comes in handy since it helps you review past experiences and analyze why they overwhelmed you.

Journaling will help you stay on top of situations and clarify your thinking. Because remembering many things will be difficult for HSPs, writing everything that comes to your mind is important. You can enjoy peace when you know that your mind is free of things that trouble you. Another advantage of journaling is you can go through your journal later when you are free to get solutions to problems that may be affecting you. When you revisit previous experiences, it will be easier for you to deal with the current challenges you may be facing.

Social Interaction

As a social human being, as all humans are, scheduling intentional social time to interact with family or friends can be restorative and invigorating for highly sensitive people since it helps them connect with others. You need to have time to be around family and friends and find that person you can confide in – a person you trust to help you overcome some of the challenges you may be facing. However, other HSPs can easily get overwhelmed by endless social activities. Therefore, you should know your limit regarding the conversations you can handle before you begin to feel depleted.

If you enjoy activities like parties, dance classes, cocktails with peers, or art, enjoy them but be mindful of how much you can take before you get panicked. Becoming a socialite can cause a great toll on your mind since you may not be able to process all the stimuli at the same time. Remember that too much of anything can affect you negatively. After a big social event, you need to take time to rest.

Consider Meditation

Most HSPs have a rich inner life, and they often view themselves as deeply spiritual people. Meditation has been found to be the best tool for prayerful activities. When you meditate, you take deep breaths in a serene environment and try to focus on positive things that can make a difference in your life. Daily transcendence is vital for replenishing your inner reserves and is a state where you can enjoy the stillness and focus on constructive things.

Other important aspects that can lift your spirit involve communing with animals, plants, forest bathing, and mindful journaling. These practices are healthy and highly restorative for the nervous system. Without meditating, you could experience a feeling of disorientation or emptiness, so to avoid this, set aside about 10 minutes for meditation. Find a quiet place where you can sit and start meditating, paying attention to things that can positively influence your life.

Try to Work Alone

At work, try to work alone in a quiet place and minimize interruptions to improve productivity. When you work at home, try to create a serene home office with little or no human traffic. Do not take your work to the living room or your bedroom; this will interfere with the serenity you have created in these rooms. If you are an entrepreneur or freelancer, you can enjoy the luxury of scheduling your work the way you like and working alone. When you are busy with your tasks, make sure there are no distractions in your working space. You can also use noise-canceling headphones and put your phone away. Additionally, put a "do not disturb" sign on your office door.

If you work in the workplace with other workers, try to get a comfortable environment that can help you be as productive as possible to satisfy the inner perfectionist. If you do not have a private office or a well-designed cubicle, then use noise-canceling headphones. You also need to tell your co-workers that you are uncomfortable with noise. Try to start a conversation with your workmates and gently share your views in a non-confrontational manner. If possible, try to change your work culture and make sure it suits your needs.

Decompress after Work

As an HSP, you will need at least t 30 to 60 minutes of decompression time after school or work. Spend this time in a cool or dark place just relaxing and doing nothing, just breathing. Decompression is meant specifically to calm your nervous system after a hectic day. You can take a nap if that is what will work best for you, stretch your body, sip hot tea, or read something. Avoid activities that require a lot of concentration. Walking on the beach or in the woods can also help you decompress your nervous system. When you are out in nature, you can breathe fresh air, which is good for your mind.

Limit Screen Time

According to different studies, the average person checks their mobile phone more than 150 times every day. Some people even use their phones in bed or while doing other things. However, this habit is not recommended for a highly sensitive person since scrolling through social media and watching anything on screens is very draining. While you may feel attached to your smartphone, television, or computer, limit your time on these overwhelming gadgets. For instance, you can watch TV up to 9 pm and make sure you don't use your phone after 10 pm. Remember, blue light is disruptive, and you may not get enough rest.

HSPs need about eight hours of sleep to re-energize their bodies. However, if you can't detach from your phone, you will have a problem enjoying quality sleep. You can schedule a specific time when you do not touch any screen. This routine will make you accountable, and you can easily track your activities on social media and other aspects. If you can control your screen time, you can significantly lower your stress levels.

Schedule Exercises

Make sure you have a routine for exercises you can perform solo at times when you know you won't be interrupted. Many people hate physically demanding exercises or those that require competition, extreme environments, and social interactions. While HSPs need exercise just like anyone, solo activities are more appropriate since they do not overwhelm their minds. For instance, you can consider aspects like cycling, jogging, yoga, swimming, hiking, or lifting lightweights. Focus on anything that allows you to have contemplative and inward experience and takes your mind off the day-to-day.

While competitive sports are not ideal for HSPs, certain one-on-one intellectual activities are appropriate. For example, if you are highly sensitive, you can try sports like golf, tennis, martial arts, or tennis. Make sure you have routines of the solo practice of about 30 minutes at least four times a week. Routine exercise will help you maintain quality mental and physical health.

Track Your Energy

If you are an HSP, you need to have some time for deep work during a time that suits your schedule. However, it is vital to track your energy levels to determine a daily routine that does not drain you. Something that works for one might not be a perfect fit for you. It may not be easy to track your energy as a result of other demands like work and family, but you can take small steps. You need to use a worksheet to record your energy levels and write notes about the different energizing activities that may work for you or draining and stressful.

When you track your energy, you will get a good insight into activities that are good for your physical and mental health. As you are now aware, burnout is not good for your highly sensitive mind. You can also track your emotional energy to determine the behaviors of different people who will give out negative or positive energy. It is essential to focus on something that can transform your life. If you realize that a specific activity is affecting you, it is better to stop it to avoid further harm to your body and mind.

Focus on Positive Things about Yourself

Many HSPs unjustifiably think there is something wrong with them as a result of the way societies often treat sensitive people. However, you need to know that it is common to be sensitive, and you must view your condition as a gift. You possess rare gifts like intent listening skills, refined tastes, intellectual acumen, and an artistic eye if you are sensitive. Therefore, you need to replace negative thoughts with positive affirmations about yourself. This is the first step toward accepting the unique gifts that make you stand out from the rest.

If you can view yourself positively, you will realize that you are a special gift. You must practice speaking positive affirmations about yourself daily. You can achieve this by loving and accepting yourself. Once you accept this reality, you will be able to deal with negativity that can affect you in different things you do. If you believe that your unique gifts are valuable and they can make a difference in the world, you can overcome the challenges you often encounter. Learn how to address negative perceptions that can hamper your desire to attain specific goals in life.

Get Quality Sleep

Good sleep after a hectic day is vital to boosting your mental and physical health. If you are highly sensitive, make sure you have a long sleep time and rest on a comfortable bed. HSPs should ideally have a minimum of eight hours of sleep a night, which means they should go to bed early. If you don't get enough sleep, you are likely to burn out, leading to anxiety, depression, and an inability to function properly. If possible, you can consider afternoon naps, but make sure they will not interrupt your peaceful sleep at night. Your rest at night should not be disturbed by anything.

Another crucial element that HSPs must consider is limiting or avoiding the use of alcohol. HSPs have highly active nervous systems and lower dopamine, which means drugs and other substances that produce dopamine can be attractive. It is common that different individuals can use alcohol to calm their nervous system down, drugs for easier management of intense emotions, and combat to reduce burnout. However, HSPs may experience overwhelming and intense triggers, which could easily lead to drug and alcohol abuse. Therefore, it is critical to learn how to thrive without using alcohol or substances to cope.

Abstinence will help you make independent decisions, and you will become resilient if you overcome the temptation of using substances. When you feel overstimulated, you should make it your routine to meditate for about 10 minutes instead of grabbing a glass of wine. Another important aspect to understand regards the amount of wine you rely on to function. Caffeine is another minefield needing to be negotiated carefully. Other people process caffeine very slowly while still others process it quickly. Therefore, you should know your limits and remember caffeine overuse can cause adrenal fatigue. This condition will make you over-reliant on caffeine to function normally.

When it comes to the use of stimulants and depressants, you need to be careful. For example, you can set two cups of coffee and two cups of wine as limits whenever you drink these beverages.

Other substances like cannabis, popularly known as a central nervous system depressant, could have the opposite effect on you and make you anxious, so you should remove it from your routine. You should know that caffeine, alcohol, and cannabis can be part of a thriving and healthy lifestyle if properly used. You must use them in moderation and avoid excessive consumption.

Practice Self-Care

Another crucial routine you should never undermine or ignore is to practice self-care. This is all about taking good care of yourself and can involve yoga or practicing breathing techniques to calm you down. Taking a hot bath or, conversely, a cool shower and keeping yourself hydrated are some of the things that provide natural healing to your body. Eating healthy foods can make your body feel healthy and relaxed.

However, don't force yourself to do things that will stress you if you don't do them perfectly. There is just as much affirmation of your character as attempting something that was previously daunting and that you would shy away from because the feeling of trying and getting it right lifts your spirits and self-confidence. In other words, practicing self-care is not about goal setting but the things that can uplift your spirit.

Setting your routine as a highly sensitive person is mainly concerned with doing things that can bring you joy. Try to determine the activities that ground you and include them in your daily routine. Dedicate time for each activity, and feel free to mix things that can bring you joy. If you are highly sensitive, focus on routines that give you control over your life. This can be something you look forward to every day and know what to expect. Therefore, try to find something that works for you and remember there is no one-size-fits-all. Something that can help you reduce the overwhelming feeling might not work for the other person. Therefore, feel free to experiment with different things until you find a perfect routine that suits your personality.

Appendix: HSP Meditations

Highly sensitive people may face more challenges daily than the average person because of their sensitive nature and have to deal with panic, overwhelm, and self-criticism. This is why they can greatly benefit from a few meditation techniques to relieve stress and anxiety.

If you are a highly sensitive person, bear in mind that meditation can sometimes be an emotional experience for you. Because the only way to rid yourself of uncomfortable emotions, bad energy, or negative thoughts they have to come out, which means you may experience them all over again. That being said, mediation techniques have shown great promise in helping highly sensitive people find their inner balance become stronger and more resilient. Here are a few meditation techniques to help you manage your anxiety and stress.

Guided Imagery

This meditation technique aims to manage your stress by using the elements of visualization positive images. Imagine sitting at the beach, being surrounded by nature, or wherever your happy place might be. You listen to the audio for a meditation guide to talk you through the visualization steps in this technique. You may be asked to focus on a certain object, a place, or relaxing sounds to help you get in a relaxed mood.

By setting your intention on concentrating and seeing a calming scene or image in your head, your body will follow your mental state. If you remember an upsetting or distressful memory, your blood pressure and heart rate will rise, and your body will tense up. The whole concept is to allow your brain to focus on this peaceful setting, and in turn, your muscles will loosen up, and your body will relax. Once you reach this state of relaxation, you will be able to calm down and release any accumulated stress or anxiety that you have been carrying.

Guided imagery has numerous health benefits, especially for highly sensitive people. Many people have reported feeling calmer and stronger after practicing it daily for more than two months. Studies have shown that a half-hour guided visualization session has the same benefits as getting a massage. Some students use this technique to relieve their stress levels before an exam. It also showed some significant benefits in people about to have major surgery.

Suffering from constant stress and anxiety can be completely debilitating. One of the common side effects of anxiety is insomnia. Guided imagery has been proven to improve the quality of sleep because the session concentrates on relaxing your body, making it easier to fall asleep.

The good news is that you can do a session anywhere and at any time if you can find a quiet room or space. You don't need any special tools, but you do need to choose a quiet spot away from distracting noises. Try to be as comfortable as possible by lying down on a cozy couch, bed, or even a fitness mat. In the beginning, you could use audio recordings to guide you through the session, so you may want to use headphones as well. You can find guided image recordings online or by downloading guided imagery apps on your phone.

You can still perform this visualization technique if you don't want to use a recording. Firstly, you should lie down comfortably on your chair or bed and then close your eyes. Start by focusing on breathing in and out until you reach a steady rhythm. You will need to keep up this pace until the end of the session. Try to empty your mind of any thoughts before visualizing a peaceful image or environment.

You can choose any image you like, whether it is a luscious forest, sandy beach, or peaceful meadow. Imagine a time you spent in nature and visualize it in your mind while breathing deeply in and out. Once the image is imprinted in your head, try to imagine the sounds in that place. Visualize the crashing waves at the beach, the sounds of flying birds in the forest, or the wind passing through the mountains. Next, focus on your sense of smell by visualizing flowers, trees, or the sea. Try to incorporate all of your senses in this session. For example, imagine dipping your toes in the warm sand or crushing a bunch of tree leaves between your fingers.

Once you become familiar with your surroundings, you may visualize walking or moving in the scene. Walk to the beach and explore the scenery while trying to feel the warmth of the sun. Imagine the sounds in the forest as you are walking on the fallen leaves and twigs. You can also visualize the season if it is different from the one you are experiencing in real life. Choose your favorite setting and explore the details in your visualization scenario. You can stay in your peaceful place as long as you want until you feel completely relaxed.

If you are new to this technique, you can perform a few guided sessions first or attend some yoga classes so that your body gets into the habit of relaxation. This will help you visualize peaceful scenery a lot faster. Be sure to turn off any electronic devices or even put them away somewhere out of sight and hearing. Don't start your recording right away. Make sure your breathing is steady first, and then start the recording.

Remember that there is no right or wrong way to perform visualization techniques. Just try to let go and only focus on your breathing patterns. You can start slowing at first with a five-minute session and increase your time as and when you are more comfortable. You can look up peaceful images online and try to visualize being in those places if you have trouble visualizing on your own. It is important to track your progress after each session to determine if this technique is useful in reducing your stress levels.

Yoga Nidra

This form of yoga can be performed alone without an instructor, and it can leave you feeling rejuvenated after 45 minutes. You will be guided by a recording telling you specific steps to make you get into a relaxed state so you can perform it at home or anywhere. It is believed to provide the same benefits as taking a nap for three hours. If taking yoga classes is not your thing, you can try this deep relaxation meditation without learning complicated poses.

Yoga Nidra is about completely relaxing your body, and some people might use it in a combination of other meditative practices. While it resembles meditation and yoga in a few ways, it is also a bit different in its core concept. It entails lying down comfortably as if you are sleeping, but your mind is still wide awake. You will be able to travel from your conscious to your unconscious mind interchangeably throughout a single session.

In other words, you will reach a deeper state of relaxation than you would in a normal yoga session while still being aware of your surroundings. Unlike yoga, it involves no movement as you will just focus on reaching that deep relaxation state. Yoga Nidra is different from meditation, which involves staying conscious while allowing negative thoughts to leave your mind and allowing peaceful ones to set in. Meditation is also used to empty your mind and get in touch with your inner self while being completely aware.

Meditation helps you to access what is known as the theta state, which is the transitional phase towards the delta state. The delta state is reached when you are deeply asleep and can be incredibly healing to both body and mind. In Yoga Nidra, the goal is to reach the delta state while fully awake, so your body and mind are completely relaxed as if you are sound asleep.

The core of yoga Nidra is to access the autonomic nervous system that controls various functions like heart rate, digestive processes, and breathing rhythms, among others. This system also involves the sympathetic nervous system responsible for the fight-or-flight response.

Deep relaxation techniques can help you manage its response or calm it down and activate the parasympathetic nervous system instead. This is responsible for the rest-and-digest response. This means that your body transitions from a state of alertness and tension to a state of relaxation. When you reach a deeper state of relaxation, your body releases the hormone melatonin, which helps to enhance your immunity, improve digestion, and manage stress levels. Studies have shown that yoga Nidra is an effective technique in reducing anxiety.

You do not need any special equipment or a professional yoga instructor to practice Yoga Nidra, as you can look up videos online and practice it at home. Just make sure to lie down comfortably on your bed or couch while supporting your neck and back. It is also a good idea to place a pillow under your knees for maximum spinal support.

Start by focusing on a life objective or goal you've wanted to achieve for so long. Try to imagine you have reached that goal and how happy you are to accomplish it. Then, set your intention by figuring out what you want to achieve. Whatever your ultimate goal is, keep it in mind at the beginning of each session. Try to get in touch with your inner self and find that peaceful place within you. Part of the session is performing a body scan, which entails concentrating on different parts of your body to promote relaxation.

Like any type of meditation, you will need to maintain a regular breathing pattern. Focus on each breath and how it goes in and out of your lungs. Feel your body's muscles and tissues relaxing with each rhythm. Prepare to embrace your feelings and recognize each sensation no matter how hard your day was. Slowly let go of these emotions or try to imagine feeling a positive emotion instead.

Once you can maintain positive feelings, hold on to them. Try feeling joy and happiness throughout your body, making a mental note of how this feels in your body. Act as if you were on the outside looking in as an observer. When you are done with the session, this technique will help you remember those feelings. Remember, you can access these good feelings every day if you need to. Stay in this state for a few minutes and slowly transition back into consciousness.

While these steps may seem simple, you will still need to practice this technique several times before getting the hang of it. If you are a beginner at meditation or yoga, it might take a few tries before you easily access that deep relaxation state. Don't be discouraged because once you familiarize yourself with these steps, you will easily be able to do them as often as needed.

Make sure to prepare your environment for sleeping. Stay in a dark room or just light a few candles and keep electronic devices away. Wear loose clothes and have a blanket nearby in case you get cold during the session. You can start with only 15 minutes at first and increase the time as you see fit.

Intention Meditation

This type of meditation is simple but has been proved to be ideal for highly sensitive people. Setting your intention before meditation is required in various types of relaxation techniques, and this one is no different. Intention meditation is your guide to what you want to achieve from each session. Visualizing your goals and focusing on them will help you reach that powerful state of mind, and you will be able to actualize these objectives.

By setting your intention, you decide to bring your ultimate goals to your attention. Your body, mind, and soul are directed toward that goal. Practicing meditation involves determining what you want to feel after a session. Do you want to feel more relaxed or revitalized? Setting your intention is like having a planned meditation session. This way, you have a better chance of realizing your dreams and deepest desires.

A simple statement could be "I intend to let go of my painful memories" or "I want to allow joy and happiness in my life." You can use meditation to help you focus on work or on a certain task by saying, "I intend to be successful at this task." You can alter your intention for each session. You do not have to use the same statements every time. Try to focus on one simple statement for each session so that you can focus on one thought at a time.

Each personality type has its own way of setting intentions. Some people set their intentions for a long-term goal. Others like to take it one day at a time. There is no right or wrong in this case. Just try to decide on your own objectives and use that in your meditation. A good tip is to write your intentions down on a piece of paper. You can focus on one thought or write several statements before choosing the simplest one. Try to be as basic as you can because complicated statements will distract you from your meditation.

If you do not have a statement in mind, you can ask yourself a couple of questions to help you set your intention. For example, ask yourself what the most important thing in your life is. Do you want to feel more balanced or aim to succeed in your business? When do you feel the happiest or the most joyous? Is there someone you wish you could forgive? What blessings do you have in your life for which you are grateful? Answering these questions can help you understand how to set your intention before meditating.

Remember that you must believe in it once you have settled on your intention. Make sure you set a positive intention and try to make it a short-term one, especially if you are practicing it in the beginning. When you set shorter intentions, they are more powerful, and you will be able to focus on them better. After that, you can set intentions for long-term goals once you get the hang of it. The good idea is to keep a journal to record your intentions and track your progress. See how your objectives and intentions change over time. This will help you realize which goals you achieved and which mattered the most. It will help you focus on your lifelong journey of development and growth.

This chapter discussed how meditations are important to help you deal with intense emotions and make you feel more relaxed in your daily life. You can try some of these techniques to see which one fits you best or try different ones every once in a while to train your mind to reach a deep state of relaxation at any moment.

.

Conclusion

The thing to note is that hypersensitivity is something people of any age, race, gender, or religion can be born with. While it does directly impact how HSPs can live their life, their quality of life, and even the direction their life takes, the reason for this difference is both a physical and mental one. There is no "cure" for hypersensitivity, neither will HSPs grow out of it. Removing or suppressing this part of their nature will only lead to more problems. In many cases, this can develop into things that compromise the quality of the life that the HSOP individual can enjoy and have very physical consequences.

In different walks of life, the hypersensitivity in a person will manifest itself in different ways. It might be apparent in some cases, while in others, it will be harder to detect, but the sooner you get to grips with it, the easier it will be to manage. Whether you are the person with hypersensitivity or trying to care for a child with this condition, it is completely manageable if you are willing to put in the time and effort for it.

Also, this is not something that should be looked at as a disability. If anything, it is something that makes the person even more able. As you can see, the HSP is an individual with a very different and unique take on life, which can be a valuable asset if it is harnessed the right way.

While all areas of life represent their own challenges, one of the main challenges for a person with hypersensitivity is the battle within. Simply managing their own thoughts and behaviors can be a full-time exercise. Especially if you find yourself in a situation where your environment isn't supportive; it can be difficult to lead a life that will work in synergy with your hypersensitivity. However, one should not lose hope, and you need to keep trying out different things to see what works for you. Throughout this book, we have discussed a range of situations, possible solutions, and proven techniques you can use for yourself or a loved one. When you try these things, there will be things that don't work for you and things that will completely solve your problem. The key thing is to keep trying and figuring out how to make the most of what you have.

With the right strategy, you can fine-tune your lifestyle in ways that will help you to live happily and successfully. With the knowledge gained from this book, you can help your child or relative live a quality of life they might have never thought possible, and you can pull them out of the agony they are in with your understanding. Every person is different, and even among hypersensitive individuals, there are a lot of differences.

If you feel that you can make better progress with a professionals' help, then, by all means, seek medical attention to make your life easier. Having an expert to consult with is always a beneficial resource.

Now that you have all this knowledge, you should be able to identify and accept the different characteristics of a highly sensitive person. Whether this person is you or someone you know, this information will allow you to become more aware of what needs to be done to live a stress-free life and love everything that comes with being an HSP.

Here's another book by Silvia Hill that you might like

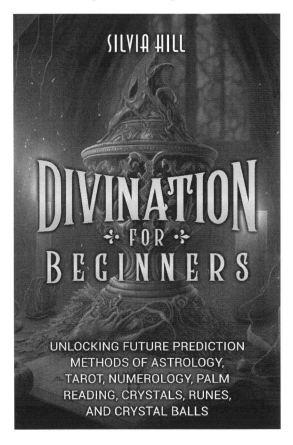

Free Bonus from Silvia Hill available for limited time

Hi Spirituality Lovers!

My name is Silvia Hill, and first off, I want to THANK YOU for reading my book.

Now you have a chance to join my exclusive spirituality email list so you can get the ebooks below for free as well as the potential to get more spirituality ebooks for free! Simply click the link below to join.

P.S. Remember that it's 100% free to join the list.

References

Kelly, A. (2018, July 2). Am I Psychic? How to Tap Into Your Own Psychic Abilities. Allure. https://www.allure.com/story/am-i-psychic-how-to-tap-into-psychic-abilities

Miller, A. (2022, June 13). Am I Psychic? How to Know if You're Psychic - A Step-by-Step Guide to Psychic Abilities. Bellingham Herald. https://www.bellinghamherald.com/health-wellness/article262457037.html

Bailey, A. (2021, December 7). 10 surprising signs that you might be psychic. Bodyandsoul.com.au. https://www.bodyandsoul.com.au/mind-body/10-surprising-signs-that-you-might-be-psychic/news-story/7220ada2fd93f329915bbaa529a78eb6

Belfast, L. (2020, June 24). How to tell if you have psychic abilities. Lovebelfast. https://lovebelfast.co.uk/how-to-tell-if-you-have-psychic-abilities/

Coughlin, S. (2017, January 20). 14 real-life psychic moments from reddit. Yahoo Life.

Cytowic, R. E., & Wood, F. B. (1982). Synesthesia. Brain and Cognition, 1(1), 36–49. https://doi.org/10.1016/0278-2626(82)90005-7

Extra-Sensory Perception (ESP), sixth sense, or intuition unlocked. (2014, November 2). WisdomTimes. https://www.wisdomtimes.com/blog/extra-sensory-perception-esp-sixth-sense-intuition-can-unlocked/

Gut feelings: What they really are & how to know if you can trust them. (2021, February 26). Mindbodygreen. https://www.mindbodygreen.com/articles/gut-feelings-what-they-really-are-when-to-trust-them

Holland, K. (2022, January 5). What is an aura? 16 FAQs about seeing auras, colors, layers, and more. Healthline. https://www.healthline.com/health/what-is-an-aura

Jackson, L. L. (2016, January 11). 4 signs you might be psychic. Oprah.com. https://www.oprah.com/inspiration/psychic-abilities

Kelly, A. (2018, July 2). Am I psychic? How to tap into your own psychic abilities. Allure. https://www.allure.com/story/am-i-psychic-how-to-tap-into-psychic-abilities

Miller, S. G. (2016, September 22). A sixth sense? It's in your genes. Live Science. https://www.livescience.com/56223-sixth-sense-genes.html

Newswire, P. R. (2021, October 8). The true story of a modern psychic - clairvoyant medium Bernadette Gold reveals how she embraced her spiritual gifts in new memoir: "the crooked path to a charmed life." Yahoo Finance.

Raypole, C. (2020, March 30). What causes déjà vu? Common theories, symptoms to watch for, and more. Healthline. https://www.healthline.com/health/mental-health/what-causes-deja-vu

Sogani, G. (2020, October 3). Psychic abilities: Do humans possess them? Wondrium Daily. https://www.wondriumdaily.com/psychic-abilities-do-humans-possess-them/

Teale, J. C., & Oâ€TMConnor, A. R. (2015). What is DÃ©jÃ vu? Frontiers for Young Minds, 3. https://doi.org/10.3389/frym.2015.00001

Theodora Blanchfield, A. (2022, May 31). What is déjà vu and why do we experience It? Verywell Mind. https://www.verywellmind.com/what-is-deja-vu-why-do-we-experience-it-5272526

WebDev, I. E. T. (1995, November 28). "psychic spying" research produces credible evidence. UC Davis. https://www.ucdavis.edu/news/psychic-spying-research-produces-credible-evidence

What IS an aura? (and how can you see yours?). (2016, June 10). Mindbodygreen. https://www.mindbodygreen.com/articles/what-is-an-aura

What is it like to have psychic abilities? (n.d.). Quora. https://www.quora.com/What-is-it-like-to-have-psychic-abilities

Childs, G. J. (2003). Rudolf Steiner: His life and work (2nd ed.). Floris Books.

How to use your intuition like A professional psychic. (2017, June 13). Mindbodygreen. https://www.mindbodygreen.com/articles/the-4-types-of-intuition-and-how-to-tap-into-each

Reader, C. (2021, February 22). How to tell if you have clairaudience: 8+ clairaudience signs, abilities, and more. Chicago Reader. https://chicagoreader.com/reader-partners/how-to-tell-if-you-have-clairaudience-8-clairaudience-signs-abilities-and-more/

Sixth Sense Abcderium. (n.d.). Sixthsensereader.org https://sixthsensereader.org/about-the-book/abcderium-index/clairaudience/

Steiner, R., & Bamford, C. (2002). What is Anthroposophy?: Three Perspectives on Self-Knowledge (M. Spiegler, Trans.). SteinerBooks.

Clairsentience: A somatic approach to intuition. (2016, June 17). Strozzi Institute | Embodied Transformation; Strozzi Institute. https://strozziinstitute.com/clairsentience-a-somatic-approach-to-intuition/

Cotroneo, H. (n.d.). The College of Psychic Studies : Workshops : Psychic and mediumship : The psychic tasting and smelling clairgustance and clairolfaction. The College of Psychic Studies. https://www.collegeofpsychicstudies.co.uk/workshops/psychic-and-mediumship/the-psychic-tasting-and-smelling-clairgustance-and-clairolfaction/

Garis, M. G. (2020, July 28). How to use each of the 4 'Clair' senses to receive information psychically. Well+Good. https://www.wellandgood.com/psychic-clair-senses/

Wahbeh, H., Yount, G., Vieten, C., Radin, D., & Delorme, A. (2019). Measuring extraordinary experiences and beliefs: A validation and reliability study. F1000Research, 8, 1741. https://doi.org/10.12688/f1000research.20409.3

Coughlin, S. (2018, August 14). 18 items that will ward off any bad vibes. Refinery29.com; Refinery29. https://www.refinery29.com/en-us/negative-energy-clearing-bad-vibes

Phillips, F. (2020, November 24). How to create a personal energy shield for protection. The Good Space. https://www.findyourgoodspace.com/blog/how-to-create-personal-energy-shield-for-protection

Aletheia. (2017, December 18). How to use a dowsing pendulum for divination - beginner's guide. LonerWolf. https://lonerwolf.com/dowsing-pendulum/

Brown, M. (2021, August 11). What is astrology? A beginners' guide to the language of the sky. InStyle. https://www.instyle.com/lifestyle/astrology/what-is-astrology

Colosimo, N. (2020, March 30). Tools for divination and developing psychic awareness. The Psychic School. https://psychicschool.com/tools-for-divination-and-developing-psychic-awareness/

Davis, F. (2021, October 13). 15 divination tools to spark your psychic abilities. Cosmic Cuts. https://cosmiccuts.com/blogs/healing-stones-blog/divination-tools

9 facts about telepathic communication. (n.d.). Operationmeditation.com. https://operationmeditation.com/discover/9-facts-about-telepathic-communication/

9 facts about telepathic communication. (n.d.). Operationmeditation.com. https://operationmeditation.com/discover/9-facts-about-telepathic-communication/

Demir, H. I. (n.d.). Quantum worlds from entanglement to telepathy. Fountainmagazine.com. https://fountainmagazine.com/2011/issue-84-november-december-2011/quantum-worlds-from-entanglement-to-telepathy

Grau, C., Ginhoux, R., Riera, A., Nguyen, T. L., Chauvat, H., Berg, M., Amengual, J. L., Pascual-Leone, A., & Ruffini, G. (2014). Conscious brain-to-brain communication in humans using non-invasive technologies. PloS One, 9(8), e105225. https://doi.org/10.1371/journal.pone.0105225

Hogan, B. (2021, August 19). Want to connect better with others? Practice telepathy to deepen your relationships. HelloGiggles. https://hellogiggles.com/what-is-telepathy/

Horowitz, J. (2016, May 31). 12 Powers You Didn't Know Professor X Has. ScreenRant. https://screenrant.com/powers-you-did-not-know-professor-x-has/

Lucia. (2019, July 1). How Zener cards work: ESP and the scientific method. The Ghost In My Machine. https://theghostinmymachine.com/2019/07/01/how-does-it-work-zener-cards-esp-and-the-scientific-method-karl-zener-j-b-rhine/

Mauro, C. (2015, July 9). Three types of telepathy. Reality Sandwich. https://realitysandwich.com/three-types-of-telepathy/

McRobbie, L. R. (2016, December 27). How one man used a deck of cards to make parapsychology a science. Atlas Obscura. https://www.atlasobscura.com/articles/how-one-man-used-a-deck-of-cards-to-make-parapsychology-a-science

Pruitt, S. (2018, October 17). The CIA recruited "mind readers" to spy on the soviets in the 1970s. HISTORY. https://www.history.com/news/cia-esp-espionage-soviet-union-cold-war

Siddhi, V. (2019). Iris publishers. Online Journal of Complementary & Alternative Medicine, 1(3), 1–4. https://irispublishers.com/ojcam/fulltext/is-telepathy-allowed-or-is-controled.ID.000515.php

Steinkamp, F. (2006). Telepathy: Or, How do I Know that this Thought is Mine? In Mind and its Place in the World (pp. 145–166). DE GRUYTER.

The biology of telepathy. (n.d.). Psychology Today. https://www.psychologytoday.com/us/blog/debunking-myths-the-mind/201804/the-biology-telepathy

What is the ganzfeld experiment? (n.d.). WebMD. https://www.webmd.com/brain/what-is-ganzfeld-experiment

Meditation for beginners - Headspace. (n.d.). Headspace.com. https://www.headspace.com/meditation/meditation-for-beginners

Shah, S., Ullman, S., & Ivanov, Z. (2022, June 17). 20 must-know meditation tips and techniques for beginners. Insider.

https://www.insider.com/guides/health/mental-health/meditation-tips-for-beginners

Meditation: A simple, fast way to reduce stress. (2022, April 29). Mayo Clinic. https://www.mayoclinic.org/tests-procedures/meditation/in-depth/meditation/art-20045858

Walton, A. G. (2015, February 9). 7 ways meditation can actually change the brain. Forbes. https://www.forbes.com/sites/alicegwalton/2015/02/09/7-ways-meditation-can-actually-change-the-brain/

Aletheia. (2015, April 3). Do you have a "low" or "high vibration"? Read these 61 signs. LonerWolf. https://lonerwolf.com/low-or-high-vibration-signs/

MacLennan, C. (2018, January 12). 10 reasons to raise your vibration. Blissful Light. https://www.blissfullight.com/en-eg/blogs/energy-healing-blog/10-reasons-to-raise-your-vibration

Rebecca Joy Stanborough, M. F. A. (2020, November 13). What is vibrational energy? Healthline. https://www.healthline.com/health/vibrational-energy

What happens when you raise your vibration? (n.d.). Abundance No Limits. https://www.abundancenolimits.com/what-happens-when-you-raise-your-vibration/

Garis, M. G. (2020, July 28). How To Use Each of the 4 'Clair' Senses To Receive Information Psychically. Well+Good. https://www.wellandgood.com/psychic-clair-senses/

Burke, J. (2020, August 30). Psychic Senses - the clairs. Creative Empowerment. https://www.creativeempowerment.com.au/post/psychic-senses-the-clairs

Kelly, A. (2018, July 2). Am I Psychic? How to Tap Into Your Own Psychic Abilities. Allure. https://www.allure.com/story/am-i-psychic-how-to-tap-into-psychic-abilities

Lombardy, J., Lou, Kayla, Wille, & Balan, A. (2021, October 19). Clairaudience: What Is It & How To Develop This Psychic Ability. A Little Spark of Joy. https://www.alittlesparkofjoy.com/clairaudience/

Estrada, J. (2020, February 25). We're All a Little Psychic—Here Are 4 Ways to Develop That Intuitive Muscle. Well+Good. https://www.wellandgood.com/how-to-develop-psychic-abilities/

23 people tell the creepiest case of 'twin telepathy' they've ever witnessed. (2021, March 1). Thought Catalog. https://thoughtcatalog.com/emily-madriga/2021/02/23-people-tell-the-creepiest-case-of-twin-telepathy-theyve-ever-witnessed/

Brunton, S. (2022, April 29). How to spiritually connect with someone far away. Spiritual Unite; Kash and Susan. https://www.spiritualunite.com/articles/how-to-spiritually-connect-with-someone-far-away/

Fierro, P. P. (2008, June 12). Twin telepathy: Separating fact from fiction. Verywell Family. https://www.verywellfamily.com/twin-telepathy-2447130

Freid, L. (n.d.). Do twins really have telepathy? Psu.edu https://sites.psu.edu/siowfa14/2014/10/07/do-twins-really-have-telepathy/

Haddington, E. L. (2016, November 7). Five simple ways to connect with someone's energy. Soul and Spirit. https://www.soulandspiritmagazine.com/five-simple-ways-connect-someones-energy/

Harrison, P. (2018, January 25). 8 couples meditation exercises for you & your partner to experience. The Daily Meditation Coaching Sessions; The Daily Meditation. https://www.thedailymeditation.com/couples-meditations

Hogan, B. (2021, August 19). Want to connect better with others? Practice telepathy to deepen your relationships. HelloGiggles. https://hellogiggles.com/what-is-telepathy/

How to sense an energetic connection. (2019, January 12). Mike Sententia - A Scientist Explores Energy. https://mikesententia.com/2019/01/how-to-sense-an-energetic-connection/

Love, F. I. (2022, July 20). 5 couples meditation exercises to try with your partner. Keep the Romance Alive. https://www.freshinlove.com/33838/5-couples-meditation-exercises-to-try-with-your-partner/

Moheban-Wachtel, R. (2020, October 15). Three Easy Mindfulness Exercises you can do with your Partner to Strengthen Your Relationship. The Relationship Suite-Marriage & Relationship Counselor in New York City - The Key to Vibrant Long Term Relationships. https://relationshipsuite.com/three-easy-mindfulness-exercises-you-can-do-with-your-partner-to-strengthen-your-relationship/

Radford, B. (2018, March 27). The riddle of twin telepathy. Livescience.com; Live Science. https://www.livescience.com/45405-twin-telepathy.html

Stone, T. R. (2021, June 22). How does it feel when you connect with someone energetically? Inspired and free. Rose Colored Glasses. https://rosecoloredglasses.com/when-you-connect-with-someone/

Tantric Meditation for Couples [3 powerful stages explained]. (2019, August 1). Unifycosmos.com. https://unifycosmos.com/tantric-meditation-couples/

Twin telepathy: Does it exist? (n.d.). Teenink.com. https://www.teenink.com/nonfiction/academic/article/539371/Twin-Telepathy-Does-It-Exist

Watson, S. (2017, May 28). 19 twin telepathy stories that'll make you scream "oh, hell no!" BuzzFeed. https://www.buzzfeed.com/shylawatson/these-twin-telepathy-stories-will-shock-you

Hogan, B. (2021, August 19). Want to connect better with others? Practice telepathy to deepen your relationships. HelloGiggles.

https://hellogiggles.com/what-is-telepathy/

Naicker, X. (2020, April 10). How to read minds in 4 easy steps (updated for 2022). Mysticmag.com; MysticMag. https://www.mysticmag.com/psychic-reading/how-to-read-minds-in-4-easy-steps/

PAIRS Foundation. (n.d.-a). PAIRS Mind-Reading exercise. Pairs.com. http://www.pairs.com/mind_reading.php

PAIRS Foundation. (n.d.-b). Shared meaning exercise for becoming a great listener. Pairs.com. http://www.pairs.com/shared_meaning_exercise.php

Scheucher, A. (2022, May 14). 13 ways to know if someone is sending you telepathic messages. Ideapod. https://ideapod.com/how-to-know-someone-is-sending-you-telepathic-messages/

Trespicio, T. (2017, November 7). Secrets of Communication from a Professional Mind Reader. MeQuilibrium. https://www.mequilibrium.com/resources/secrets-of-communication-from-a-professional-mind-reader/

Denisa. (2017, July 4). How to send telepathic message to someone you love or far away. Chi-nese.com. https://chi-nese.com/send-telepathic-message-someone/

Fey, T. (2021, November 24). How to know if your telepathic message was received. Ideapod. https://ideapod.com/how-to-know-if-your-telepathic-message-was-received/

Hogan, B. (2021, August 19). Want to connect better with others? Practice telepathy to deepen your relationships. HelloGiggles. https://hellogiggles.com/what-is-telepathy/

Annie Hanauer website. (n.d.). Anniehanauer.com. https://www.anniehanauer.com/annie-hanauer-projects/exercises-in-telepathy

Byng, A. (2022, June 20). What is Telepathy and 10 Ways You Can Practice it. Www.top10.com; Top10.com. https://www.top10.com/psychic-reading/what-is-telepathy-and-how-to-practice-it

Hogan, B. (2021, August 19). Want to connect better with others? Practice telepathy to deepen your relationships. HelloGiggles. https://hellogiggles.com/what-is-telepathy/

home. (n.d.). Home-ffm-tlv.com. from http://home-ffm-tlv.com/portfolio_page/telepathy-works/

Mauro, C. (2016, April 25). My practice: Spiritual telepathy. Spirituality & Health. https://www.spiritualityhealth.com/articles/2016/04/25/my-practice-spiritual-telepathy

StackPath. (n.d.). Mwrf.com. https://www.mwrf.com/technologies/systems/article/21158152/microwaves-rf-the-ultimate-personal-communication-method-perfected

The fourth lesson of telepathy - KSARS. (n.d.). Ksars.org.
https://ksars.org/topics/the-fourth-lesson-of-telepathy

besguerra. (2019, May 28). Transmitting feelings—and healing—through
telepathy. Lifestyle.INQ. https://lifestyle.inquirer.net/336556/transmitting-
feelings-and-healing-through-telepathy/

Kamath, V. (2017, August 1). Power of Telepathy vs Artificial/Human
Intelligence. Linkedin.Com. https://www.linkedin.com/pulse/power-telepathy-
vs-artificialhuman-intelligence-vivek-kamath

LaBay, M. L. (2021, December 20). Everything You Need to Know About Past
Life Regression Therapy. Linkedin.Com.
https://www.linkedin.com/pulse/everything-you-need-know-past-life-regression-
therapy-mary-lee-labay

Luke. (2020, July 23). Reiki Distance Healing: Learn How to Send Healing
Energy at a Distance. Thriveglobal.Com. https://thriveglobal.com/stories/reiki-
distance-healing-learn-how-to-send-healing-energy-at-a-distance/

Mental Telepathy. (n.d.). HealingCrystalsForYou.Com. https://www.healing-
crystals-for-you.com/mental-telepathy.html

BetterSleep. (2022, March 21). Chakras Explained: How to Keep Them
Aligned. Bettersleep.Com. https://www.bettersleep.com/blog/chakras-explained-
how-to-keep-chakras-in-alignment/

12 ways to recognize negative thoughts. (2019, July 15). Benevolent Health.
https://benevolenthealth.co.uk/12-ways-to-recognise-negative-thoughts/

Cuncic, A. (2012, January 31). Negative thoughts: How to stop them. Verywell
Mind. https://www.verywellmind.com/how-to-change-negative-thinking-3024843

Four ways to protect your energy. (n.d.). Kripalu.
https://kripalu.org/resources/four-ways-protect-your-energy

How do you protect yourself from someone sending you telepathic messages?
(n.d.). Quora. https://www.quora.com/How-do-you-protect-yourself-from-
someone-sending-you-telepathic-messages

Identifying negative automatic thought patterns. (n.d.). Harvard.edu.
https://sdlab.fas.harvard.edu/cognitive-reappraisal/identifying-negative-
automatic-thought-patterns

Roncero, A. (n.d.). Automatic thoughts: How to identify and fix them.
Betterup.com. https://www.betterup.com/blog/automatic-thoughts

Abraham, Karin Lee. Healing Through Numerology. 1st ed. Euclid, Ohio:
RKM Publishing Co., 1985.

Balliet, Mrs. L. Dow. Number Vibration in Questions and Answers. 2nd ed.
Albuquerque, New Mexico: Sun Publishing Co., 1983.

Eisen, William. The English Cabalah, Volume I, The Mysteries of Pi. 1st ed. Marina del Rey, Calif.: DeVorss and Company, 1980.

Guthrie, Kenneth Sylvan, comp. And trans. The Pythagorean Sourcebook and Library. Grand Rapids, Mich.: Phanes Press, 1987.

Javane, Faith, and Dusty Bunker. Numerology and the Divine Triangle.

Kline, Morris. Mathematics and the Search for Knowledge. New York: Oxford University Press, 1985. Kozminsky, Isadore. Numbers, Their Meaning, and Magic. York Beach, Maine.

Oliver, George. The Pythagorean Triangle, or The Science of Numbers. San Diego: Wizard's Bookshelf, 1984.

Wilson, Hazel. A Guide to Cosmic Numbers. Foibles Publications, 1982

Bruce, Robert. Astral Dynamics: A NEW Approach to Out-of-Body Experience. Charlotte, VA: Hampton Roads, 1999.

Crow, John L. "Taming the astral body: The Theosophical Society's ongoing problem of emotion and control", Journal of the American Academy of Religion. 2012.

Kemp, Harold. Past Lives, Dreams, and Soul Travel. Eckankar. Minneapolis, MN. 2003.

LA Berge, Stephen. Lucid Dreaming. New York: Ballantine, 1985.

Mercury, Daniel. Becoming Half Hidden: Shamanism and Initiation among the Inuit. Act Universities Stockholmiensis. Stockholm Studies in Comparative Religion. Stockholm: Almqvist & Wiksell. 1985.

Novak, Peter. The Lost Secret of Death: Our Divided Souls and the Afterlife. Charlotte, VA: Hampton Roads, 2003.

Bruce, Robert. Practical Psychic Self-Defense: Understanding and Surviving Unseen Influences. Charlotte, VA: Hampton Roads, 2002.

Rawcliffe, Donovan. Occult and Supernatural Phenomena. Dover Publications, 1988.

Bruce, Robert. Astral Dynamics: A New Approach to Out-of-Body Experiences. Hampton Roads Publishing.

Monroe, Robert. Journeys Out of the Body Doubleday. Reprinted (1989) Souvenir Press Ltd. 1971.

Muldoon, Sylvan and Carrington, Hereward. Projection of the Astral Body. Rider and Company. 1929.

Hines, Terence. Pseudoscience and the Paranormal. Prometheus Books. 2003.

Gilovich, Thomas. How We Know What Isn't So: The Fallibility of Human Reason in Everyday Life. 1993

Time-Life Books (ed). Psychic Voyages. Mysteries of the Unknown. Alexandria, VA: Time-Life Books, 1987.

Aron, E. N. (1998). The highly sensitive person: How to thrive when the world overwhelms you.

Bantam.

Granneman, J. (2019, December 13). 21 signs that you're a highly sensitive person (HSP). Highly Sensitive Refuge. https://highlysensitiverefuge.com/highly-sensitive-person-signs

Howard, S. (2019). Highly sensitive person: A complete survival guide to relieve anxiety, stop

emotional overload & eliminate negative energy for empaths & introverts. Independently

Published.

Scott, E. (n.d.). What is a highly sensitive person (HSP)? Verywell Mind. Retrieved from https://www.verywellmind.com/highly-sensitive-persons-traits-that-create-more-stress-4126393

Sólo, A. (2019, June 26). Are highly sensitive people natural-born creatives? Highly Sensitive

Refuge. https://highlysensitiverefuge.com/are-highly-sensitive-people-natural-born-creatives

Sólo, A. (2020, June 18). The difference between introverts, empaths, and highly sensitive people. IntrovertDear.Com. https://introvertdear.com/news/the-difference-between-introverts-empaths-and-highly-sensitive-people

This is what it means to be a highly sensitive person. (n.d.). Psychology Today. Retrieved from https://www.psychologytoday.com/us/blog/the-highly-sensitive-man/201912/is-what-it-means-be-highly-sensitive-person

What is a highly sensitive person? (A relatable guide). (2018, August 5). Highly Sensitive

Refuge. https://highlysensitiverefuge.com/what-is-highly-sensitive-person

Hsueh, A. (2021, October 1). 4 common ways highly sensitive people are misunderstood.

Retrieved from Highly Sensitive Refuge website: https://highlysensitiverefuge.com/4-common-ways-highly-sensitive-people-are-misunderstood

Sagansky, G. (2021, July 2). Are you a highly sensitive person? Here's how to tell. Retrieved

from Vogue website: https://www.vogue.com/article/are-you-a-highly-sensitive-person-heres-how-to-tell

Granneman, J. (2014, October 18). 14 advantages of being highly sensitive. IntrovertDear.Com. https://introvertdear.com/news/highly-sensitive-person-advantages

Marisol. (2018, February 26). The pros and cons of being a highly sensitive person. The Daily Mind. https://thedailymind.com/the-pros-and-cons-of-being-a-highly-sensitive-person

Scott, E. (n.d.). What is a highly sensitive person (HSP)? Verywell Mind. Retrieved from https://www.verywellmind.com/highly-sensitive-persons-traits-that-create-more-stress-4126393

The Daily Guru Team. (2015, October 23). The pros and cons of being highly sensitive. The Daily Guru. https://thedailyguru.com/being-highly-sensitive

Counseling Today. (2019, September 24). Finding strength in sensitivity. Counseling Today. https://ct.counseling.org/2019/09/finding-strength-in-sensitivity

Emotional regulation and HSPs. (n.d.). Psychology Today. Retrieved from https://www.psychologytoday.com/us/blog/the-highly-sensitive-person/201811/emotional-regulation-and-hsps

How to control overwhelming emotions. (2021, August 12). Steps to Recovery. https://www.stepstorecovery.com/rehab-blog/how-to-control-overwhelming-emotions

Nine ways to deal with overwhelm if you're a highly sensitive person. (n.d.). Thisgirlisonfire.Com. Retrieved from https://www.thisgirlisonfire.com/blog/nine-ways-to-deal-with-overwhelm-if-youre-a-highly-sensitive-person

Smith, A. (2017, October 23). 5 types of overwhelm you may experience as a Highly Sensitive Person (HSP). Quiet Moon Counseling. https://quietmooncounseling.com/2017/10/23/types-of-overwhelm

Sólo, A. (2019, May 27). Why highly sensitive people get overwhelmed easily (and how to fix it). Highly Sensitive Refuge. https://highlysensitiverefuge.com/overwhelmed-highly-sensitive-person

Stewart, L. (2021, February 26). How HSPs can deal with negative emotions (and actually feel better). IntrovertDear.Com. https://introvertdear.com/news/negative-emotions-highly-sensitive-person

What to do when your emotions overwhelm you. (n.d.). Psychology Today. Retrieved from https://www.psychologytoday.com/us/blog/mindful-anger/201511/what-do-when-your-emotions-overwhelm-you

Self-care practices I have discovered as A Highly Sensitive Person. (n.d.). Wellness Minneapolis. Retrieved from https://www.wellnessminneapolis.com/articles/self-care-practices-i-have-discovered-as-a-highly-sensitive-person

Stewart, L. (2021, February 26). How HSPs can deal with negative emotions (and actually feel better). IntrovertDear.Com. https://introvertdear.com/news/negative-emotions-highly-sensitive-person

Top 10 survival tips for the highly sensitive person (HSP). (n.d.). Psychology Today. Retrieved from https://www.psychologytoday.com/us/blog/prescriptions-life/201105/top-10-survival-tips-the-highly-sensitive-person-hsp

Brooks, H. (2020, June 29). 19 ways being a highly sensitive person affects your love life. Retrieved from IntrovertDear.com website: https://introvertdear.com/news/highly-sensitive-person-relationships-affects

Daniels, E. (2020, September 21). How to deal with A highly sensitive person when you're

highly sensitive too. Retrieved from Dr. Elayne Daniels website: https://www.drelaynedaniels.com/how-to-deal-with-a-highly-sensitive-person-when-youre-highly-sensitive-too

Falling in love is different when you're a highly sensitive person. (2021, July 9). Retrieved from Healthline

website: https://www.healthline.com/health/relationships/falling-in-love-highly-sensitive-person-hsp

Marci Moberg, M. S. (2019, March 30). The 3 biggest relationship challenges for highly sensitive people. Retrieved from mindbodygreen website:

https://www.mindbodygreen.com/articles/the-3-biggest-relationship-challenges-for-highly-sensitive-people-and-empaths

The HSP relationship dilemma. (n.d.). Retrieved from Psychology Today website:

https://www.psychologytoday.com/us/blog/sense-and-sensitivity/201802/the-hsp-relationship-dilemma

Turgeon, S. (2017, January 20). Here's how intimacy is different for highly sensitive people.

Retrieved from Thought Catalog website:

https://thoughtcatalog.com/sheryl-turgeon/2017/01/heres-how-intimacy-is-different-for-highly-sensitive-people

Coping with anger. (2020, June 23). Retrieved from Mental Health Foundation website: https://www.mentalhealth.org.uk/blog/coping-with-anger

Rosenberg, K. (2021, August 11). 7 annoying things people say that drive highly sensitive souls crazy. Retrieved from Curious website:

https://medium.com/curious/7-annoying-things-people-say-that-drive-highly-sensitive-souls-crazy-e440fa7587c0

Everything you need to know about raising a sensitive kid. (n.d.). Retrieved from ParentMap website: https://www.parentmap.com/article/everything-you-need-know-about-raising-sensitive-kid

How to support your highly sensitive child. (n.d.). Retrieved from PBS KIDS for Parents website: https://www.pbs.org/parents/thrive/how-to-support-your-highly-sensitive-child

Narcissistic personality disorder - HelpGuide.Org. (n.d.). Retrieved from https://www.helpguide.org/articles/mental-disorders/narcissistic-personality-disorder.htm

Sandra Silva Casabianca, K. D. (2021, September 29). 6 signs of manipulation in relationships. Psych Central. https://psychcentral.com/blog/signs-manipulation-in-relationships

Sólo, A. (2019, May 29). Do highly sensitive people attract narcissists? Highly Sensitive Refuge. https://highlysensitiverefuge.com/highly-sensitive-people-attract-narcissists

Callarman, S. (2021, June 18). Toxic work environment red flags. Retrieved from Toniamoon.com website: https://www.toniamoon.com/blog/toxic-work-environment

Kelly. (n.d.). 9 tips for coping in the workplace as a highly sensitive person. Retrieved from Highlysensitiveperson.net website: https://highlysensitiveperson.net/tips-coping-workplace-job-career-highly-sensitive-person

Sólo, A. (2019, February 15). 7 workplace problems only highly sensitive people will understand. Retrieved from Highly Sensitive Refuge website: https://highlysensitiverefuge.com/work-problems-highly-sensitive-people

Scott, E. (n.d.). How highly sensitive people can reduce stress in their lives. Retrieved from Verywell Mind website: https://www.verywellmind.com/ways-to-cope-with-stress-when-highly-sensitive-4126398

Guest Author for www. rtor.org. (2019, October 7). Ways a toxic environment can hurt to your mental health. Retrieved from Resources To Recover website: https://www.rtor.org/2019/10/07/ways-a-toxic-environment-can-be-detrimental-to-your-mental-health

Günel, S. (2021, August 6). 7 types of toxic people you should remove from your life. Retrieved from Personal Growth website: https://medium.com/personal-growth/7-types-of-toxic-people-you-should-remove-from-your-life-fb89cdd8ca39

Raypole, C. (2019, October 25). Toxic family: 25 signs and tips. Retrieved from Healthline website: https://www.healthline.com/health/toxic-family

4 ways to stop negative thinking. (n.d.). Mcleanhospital.Org. Retrieved from https://www.mcleanhospital.org/essential/4-ways-stop-negative-thinking

Dealing with negative thoughts. (2014). In Letting Go of Self-Destructive Behavio

rs (pp. 161–174). Routledge.

Elaine. (2016, February 25). Suicide and high sensitivity. Hsperson.Com. https://hsperson.com/suicide-and-high-sensitivity

Fraga, J. (2018, August 28). Being "highly sensitive" is a real trait. Here's what it feels Li. Healthline. https://www.healthline.com/health/mental-health/what-its-like-highly-sensitive-person-hsp

Howard, S. (2019). Highly sensitive person: A complete survival guide to relieve anxiety, stop emotional overload & eliminate negative energy, for empaths & introverts. Independently Published.

Latumahina, D. (2008, February 1). Being an optimist: 8 ways to overcome pessimism. Life Optimizer. https://www.lifeoptimizer.org/2008/02/01/being-optimist-ways-to-overcome-pessimism

Paist, J. (2018, October 28). The highly sensitive person in a narcissistic home —. The Center for Family Empowerment. https://www.centerforfamilyempowerment.com/blog/2018/10/28/the-highly-sensitive-person-in-a-narcissistic-home

Sagansky, G. (2021, July 2). Are you a highly sensitive person? Here's how to tell. Vogue. https://www.vogue.com/article/are-you-a-highly-sensitive-person-heres-how-to-tell

Scott, E. (n.d.-a). The toxic effects of negative self-talk. Verywell Mind. Retrieved from https://www.verywellmind.com/negative-self-talk-and-how-it-affects-us-4161304

Scott, E. (n.d.-b). What is a highly sensitive person (HSP)? Verywell Mind. Retrieved from https://www.verywellmind.com/highly-sensitive-persons-traits-that-create-more-stress-4126393

Steber, C. (2016, March 29). 7 ways to snap yourself out of toxic thoughts. Bustle. https://www.bustle.com/articles/150796-7-ways-to-snap-yourself-out-of-toxic-thoughts-feel-better-about-things

Welcome. (2020, December 23). The Kulka group. The Kulka Group. https://www.thekulkagroup.com/5-ways-to-overcome-toxic-thinking

Self-sabotaging. (N.d.). Choosingtherapy.Com. Retrieved from
https://www.choosingtherapy.com/self-sabotaging
Highly Sensitive Person. (N.d.). Choosingtherapy.Com. Retrieved from
https://www.choosingtherapy.com/highly-sensitive-person
12 reasons being a highly sensitive person is your greatest strength at work.
(n.d.). Psychology
Today. Retrieved from
https://www.psychologytoday.com/us/blog/trust-yourself/202110/12-reasons-
being-highly-sensitive-person-is-your-greatest-strength-work
Andersen, N. (2018, November 30). The 12 best things about being a highly
sensitive person. Highly Sensitive Refuge.
https://highlysensitiverefuge.com/highly-sensitive-person-best-things
Are you sensitive? Here's why it's a superpower and how to work it. (2019, July
16). Ellevate. https://www.ellevatenetwork.com/articles/10166-are-you-sensitive-
here-s-why-it-s-a-superpower-and-how-to-work-it
Bergsma, E. (2021, February 3). 10 skills created by the highly sensitive brain.
Sensitive
Evolution. https://sensitiveevolution.com/highly-sensitive-brain-10-skills
Boyer, A. (2020, October 30). Sensitive people don't need to be fixed. Society
does. Highly Sensitive Refuge.
https://highlysensitiverefuge.com/sensitive-people-dont-need-to-be-fixed-society-
does
Cook, J. (2021, July 23). 8 superpowers of highly sensitive people. Highly
Sensitive Refuge. https://highlysensitiverefuge.com/8-superpowers-of-highly-
sensitive-people
GoodTherapy.org Staff. (2015, November 12). 8 ways highly sensitive people
make the world a
better place. GoodTherapy.Org Therapy Blog.
https://www.goodtherapy.org/blog/8-ways-highly-sensitive-people-make-the-
world-a-better-place-1112157
guest. (2019, October 28). Why Highly Sensitive People are a boon to
humanity. The Financial Express.
https://www.financialexpress.com/opinion/why-highly-sensitive-people-are-a-
boon-to-humanity/1747378
Managing highly sensitive people. (n.d.). Mindtools.Com. Retrieved from
https://www.mindtools.com/pages/article/managing-highly-sensitive-people.htm
Melody. (2021, February 11). 12 reasons being an HSP in the workplace is a
strength —. Melody Wilding.

https://melodywilding.com/12-reasons-why-high-sensitivity-is-your-greatest-strength-in-the-workplace

Melody Wilding, L. (2016, November 1). Your sensitivity is A career superpower. Here's how to use it. Forbes. https://www.forbes.com/sites/melodywilding/2016/11/01/5-ways-to-turn-your-sensitivity-into-strength-at-work/?sh=3191e39b518e

Schwanke, C. (n.d.). Careers for highly sensitive people. LoveToKnow; LoveToKnow Media. Retrieved from https://jobs.lovetoknow.com/careers-highly-sensitive-people

Sólo, A. (2018, August 8). The 7 best careers for a highly sensitive person. Highly Sensitive Refuge. https://highlysensitiverefuge.com/highly-sensitive-person-careers

Survival skills for highly sensitive people. (2019, January 9). Experience Life. https://experiencelife.lifetime.life/article/survival-skills-for-highly-sensitive-people/

The 40 best jobs and careers for highly sensitive people. (2021, July 2). GenTwenty. https://gentwenty.com/best-jobs-and-careers-for-highly-sensitive-people

4 ways to boost your self-compassion. (2021, February 12). Retrieved from Harvard Health website: https://www.health.harvard.edu/mental-health/4-ways-to-boost-your-self-compassion

Walter, A.-K. (2021, March 15). Radical self-love guide for highly sensitive people and empaths. Retrieved from HiSensitives website: https://hisensitives.com/blog/radical-self-love-highly-sensitive-people-empaths

Campese, L. (2015, July 24). Why do highly sensitive people engage in routines? Retrieved from Talkspace website: https://www.talkspace.com/blog/why-do-highly-sensitive-people-engage-in-routines

Byrd, R. (2018, August 6). 11 essential daily habits for thriving as a Highly Sensitive Person —. Retrieved from Will Frolic for Food website: https://www.willfrolicforfood.com/blog/11-daily-essential-habits-for-highly-sensitive-people

Valko, L. (2021, December 22). 4 reasons why HSPs love routines (and how to create new ones). Retrieved from Highly Sensitive Refuge website: https://highlysensitiverefuge.com/4-reasons-why-hsps-love-routines-and-how-to-create-new-ones

Combiths, S. (2015, February 23). Are you a highly sensitive person? How to set up your home & routines to best fit your life. Retrieved from Apartment Therapy website:

https://www.apartmenttherapy.com/how-to-set-up-your-home-and-routines-to-help-yourself-if-youre-a-highly-sensitive-person-215636

fenneld. (2020, September 14). What is yoga Nidra? Cleveland Clinic. https://health.clevelandclinic.org/what-is-yoga-nidra

Nunez, K. (2020, September 10). Guided imagery: How to and benefits for sleep, anxiety, more.

Healthline. https://www.healthline.com/health/guided-imagery

(Owner), E. T. (2020, June 23). Meditation and HSP (highly sensitive persons). Lilac Lotus

Yoga. https://www.lilaclotusyoga.com/post/meditation-and-hsp-highly-sensitive-persons

Patel, D. (2019, March 8). How to practice intention meditation. Zenful Spirit. https://zenfulspirit.com/2019/03/08/intention-meditation

Sólo, A. (2019, May 27). Why highly sensitive people get overwhelmed easily (and how to fix it). Retrieved from Highly Sensitive Refuge website:

https://highlysensitiverefuge.com/overwhelmed-highly-sensitive-person

Top 10 survival tips for the highly sensitive person (HSP). (n.d.). Retrieved from Psychology Today website:

https://www.psychologytoday.com/us/blog/prescriptions-life/201105/top-10-survival-tips-the-highly-sensitive-person-hsp